Houghton
Mifflin
Harcourt

collections

Houghton
Mifflin
Harcourt.

collections

GRADE 9

Program Consultants:

Kylene Beers

Martha Hougen

Carol Jago

William L. McBride

Erik Palmer

Lydia Stack

bio.

About Our Program Consultants

Kylene Beers Nationally known lecturer and author on reading and literacy; 2011 recipient of the Conference on English Leadership Exemplary Leader Award; coauthor of *Notice and Note: Strategies for Close Reading;* former president of the National Council of Teachers of English. Dr. Beers is the nationally known author of *When Kids Can't Read: What Teachers Can Do* and coeditor of *Adolescent Literacy: Turning Promise into Practice,* as well as articles in the *Journal of Adolescent and Adult Literacy.* Former editor of *Voices from the Middle,* she is the 2001 recipient of NCTE's Richard W. Halley Award, given for outstanding contributions to middle-school literacy. She recently served as Senior Reading Researcher at the Comer School Development Program at Yale University as well as Senior Reading Advisor to Secondary Schools for the Reading and Writing Project at Teachers College.

Martha Hougen National consultant, presenter, researcher, and author. Areas of expertise include differentiating instruction for students with learning difficulties, including those with learning disabilities and dyslexia; and teacher and leader preparation improvement. Dr. Hougen has taught at the middle school through graduate levels. Recently her focus has been on working with teacher educators to enhance teacher and leader preparation to better meet the needs of all students. Currently she is working with the University of Florida at the Collaboration for Effective Educator Development, Accountability, and Reform Center (CEEDAR Center) to improve the achievement of students with disabilities by reforming teacher and leader licensure, evaluation, and preparation. She has led similar efforts in Texas with the Higher Education Collaborative and the College & Career Readiness Initiative Faculty Collaboratives. In addition to peer-reviewed articles, curricular documents, and presentations, Dr. Hougen has published two college textbooks: *The Fundamentals of Literacy Assessment and Instruction Pre-K–6* (2012) and *The Fundamentals of Literacy Assessment and Instruction 6–12* (2014).

Carol Jago Teacher of English with 32 years of experience at Santa Monica High School in California; author and nationally known lecturer; and former president of the National Council of Teachers of English. Currently serves as Associate Director of the California Reading and Literature Project at UCLA. With expertise in standards assessment and secondary education, Ms. Jago is the author of numerous books on education, including *With Rigor for All* and *Papers, Papers, Papers,* and is active with the California Association of Teachers of English, editing its scholarly journal *California English* since 1996. Ms. Jago also served on the planning committee for the 2009 NAEP Framework and the 2011 NAEP Writing Framework.

William L. McBride Curriculum specialist. Dr. McBride is a nationally known speaker, educator, and author who now trains teachers in instructional methodologies. He is coauthor of *What's Happening?*, an innovative, high-interest text for middle-grade readers, and author of *If They Can Argue Well, They Can Write Well*. A former reading specialist, English teacher, and social studies teacher, he holds a master's degree in reading and a doctorate in curriculum and instruction from the University of North Carolina at Chapel Hill. Dr. McBride has contributed to the development of textbook series in language arts, social studies, science, and vocabulary. He is also known for his novel *Entertaining an Elephant*, which tells the story of a veteran teacher who becomes reinspired with both his profession and his life.

Erik Palmer Veteran teacher and education consultant based in Denver, Colorado. Author of *Well Spoken: Teaching Speaking to All Students* and *Digitally Speaking: How to Improve Student Presentations*. His areas of focus include improving oral communication, promoting technology in classroom presentations, and updating instruction through the use of digital tools. He holds a bachelor's degree from Oberlin College and a master's degree in curriculum and instruction from the University of Colorado.

Lydia Stack Internationally known teacher educator and author. She is involved in a Stanford University project to support English Language Learners, *Understanding Language*. The goal of this project is to enrich academic content and language instruction for English Language Learners (ELLs) in grades K-12 by making explicit the language and literacy skills necessary to meet the Common Core State Standards (CCSS) and Next Generation Science Standards. Her teaching experience includes twenty-five years as an elementary and high school ESL teacher, and she is a past president of Teachers of English to Speakers of Other Languages (TESOL). Her awards include the TESOL James E. Alatis Award and the San Francisco STAR Teacher Award. Her publications include *On Our Way to English, Visions: Language, Literature, Content,* and *American Themes*, a literature anthology for high school students in the ACCESS program of the U.S. State Department's Office of English Language Programs.

Additional thanks to the following Program Reviewers

Rosemary Asquino
Sylvia B. Bennett
Yvonne Bradley
Leslie Brown
Haley Carroll
Caitlin Chalmers
Emily Colley-King
Stacy Collins
Denise DeBonis
Courtney Dickerson
Sarah Easley
Phyllis J. Everette
Peter J. Foy Sr.

Carol M. Gibby
Angie Gill
Mary K. Goff
Saira Haas
Lisa M. Janeway
Robert V. Kidd Jr.
Kim Lilley
John C. Lowe
Taryn Curtis MacGee
Meredith S. Maddox
Cynthia Martin
Kelli M. McDonough
Megan Pankiewicz

Linda Beck Pieplow
Molly Pieplow
Mary-Sarah Proctor
Jessica A. Stith
Peter Swartley
Pamela Thomas
Linda A. Tobias
Rachel Ukleja
Lauren Vint
Heather Lynn York
Leigh Ann Zerr

Finding Common Ground

ANCHOR TEXT	**ARGUMENT** A Quilt of a Country	Anna Quindlen		3
ANCHOR TEXT	**SHORT STORY** Once Upon a Time	Nadine Gordimer		11
	ESSAY Rituals of Memory	Kimberly M. Blaeser		21
	SPEECH The Gettysburg Address	Abraham Lincoln	▶	27
COMPARE TEXT AND MEDIA	**PHOTO ESSAY** Views of the Wall		▶	33
	POEM The Vietnam Wall	Alberto Ríos		34

COLLECTION PERFORMANCE TASKS

Present a Speech	37
Write an Analytical Essay	41

KEY LEARNING OBJECTIVES

Cite text evidence.
Support inferences about theme.
Analyze author's choices about structure.
Analyze representations in different mediums.
Determine central idea.

Analyze and evaluate author's claim.
Analyze author's purpose and rhetoric.
Delineate and evaluate an argument.
Analyze seminal U.S. documents.

Close Reader

BLOG
Making the Future Better,
Together   Eboo Patel

SHORT STORY
Night Calls   Lisa Fugard

SPEECH
Oklahoma Bombing Memorial
Address   Bill Clinton

eBook *Explore It!*

▶ **Video Links**

 Visit hmhfyi.com
for current articles and
informational texts.

The Struggle for Freedom

The March on Washington   47

COMPARE
ANCHOR
TEXTS AND
MEDIA

SPEECH
I Have a Dream   Martin Luther King Jr.   48

HISTORY WRITING
from Nobody Turn Me Around:
A People's History of the 1963
March on Washington   Charles Euchner   55

VIDEO
AMERICA The Story of Us:
March on Washington   HISTORY®   ▶   71

DIARY
from Cairo: My City, Our Revolution   Ahdaf Soueif   73

COMPARE
TEXT AND
MEDIA

MEMOIR
from Reading Lolita in Tehran   Azar Nafisi   81

GRAPHIC NOVEL
from Persepolis 2:
The Story of a Return   Marjane Satrapi   84

SHORT STORY
The Censors   Luisa Valenzuela   89

COLLECTION PERFORMANCE TASK
Write an Argument   97

KEY LEARNING OBJECTIVES

Analyze author's choices about style and structure.
Analyze author's point of view and cultural background.
Analyze how an author unfolds events.
Analyze connections between ideas and events.

Analyze impact of word choice on tone.
Determine author's point of view.
Analyze author's use of rhetoric.
Analyze accounts in different mediums.
Analyze seminal U.S. documents.

Close Reader

SPEECH
A Eulogy for Dr. Martin Luther King Jr.   Robert F. Kennedy

SHORT STORY
The Prisoner Who Wore Glasses   Bessie Head

eBook *Explore It!*

 Video Links   **Channel One News®**   **fyi** hmhfyi.com   **Visit hmhfyi.com** for current articles and informational texts.

The Bonds Between Us

ANCHOR TEXT	**SHORT STORY** When Mr. Pirzada Came to Dine	Jhumpa Lahiri		103
ANCHOR TEXT	**SCIENCE WRITING** Monkey See, Monkey Do, Monkey Connect	Frans de Waal		123
	SHORT STORY The Grasshopper and the Bell Cricket	Yasunari Kawabata		133
	INFORMATIONAL TEXT With Friends Like These...	Dorothy Rowe		141
	POEM At Dusk	Natasha Trethewey		147
MEDIA ANALYSIS	**PUBLIC SERVICE ANNOUNCEMENT** Count On Us	Corporation for National and Community Service	▶	151

COLLECTION PERFORMANCE TASKS

Write a Fictional Narrative	153
Create a Group Multimedia Presentation	157

KEY LEARNING OBJECTIVES

Cite text evidence.
Support inferences about theme.
Analyze character and theme.
Interpret figurative language.
Analyze the impact of word choice on tone.
Analyze author's point of view and cultural background.

Analyze ideas in informational text.
Analyze the purpose and development of ideas in media.
Determine technical meanings of words.
Analyze and evaluate author's claims.

Close Reader

SHORT STORY
And of Clay Are We Created   Isabel Allende

SCIENCE WRITING
from Animals in Translation   Temple Grandin and Catherine Johnson

POEM
My Ceremony For Taking   Lara Mann

POEM
The Stayer   Virgil Suárez

eBook *Explore It!*

▶ **Video Links**

 Visit hmhfyi.com for current articles and informational texts.

Image Credits: ©Carlos Sanchez Pereyra/Alamy Images

Sweet Sorrow

ESSAY
Love's Vocabulary *from*
A Natural History of Love   Diane Ackerman   163

MEDIA | **POEM AND VIDEO**
ANALYSIS | My Shakespeare   Kate Tempest ► 173

Shakespearean Drama   177

ANCHOR | **DRAMA**
TEXT | The Tragedy of Romeo and Juliet William Shakespeare ► 181

MYTH
Pyramus and Thisbe
from the Metamorphoses   Ovid   283

SHORT STORY
Duty   Pamela Rafael Berkman 289

COLLECTION PERFORMANCE TASK
Write an Analytical Essay   301

KEY Analyze character motivations. Analyze interpretations of Shakespeare.
LEARNING Analyze parallel plots. Determine word meanings.
OBJECTIVES Analyze point of view. Analyze ideas presented in an essay.
    Analyze source material.

Close Reader

DRAMA
from The Tragedy of Romeo and Juliet: William Shakespeare
   Prologue
   Act II, Scene 2

eBook *Explore It!*

▶ **Video Links**   **Visit hmhfyi.com** for current articles and informational texts.

COLLECTION 5
A Matter of Life or Death

ANCHOR TEXT | **MEMOIR**
from Night · Elie Wiesel · 307

ARGUMENT
Is Survival Selfish? · Lane Wallace · 317

SCIENCE WRITING
from Deep Survival · Laurence Gonzales · 325

SHORT STORY
The Leap · Louise Erdrich · 339

ANCHOR TEXT | **POEM**
The End and the Beginning · Wisława Szymborska · 351

COLLECTION PERFORMANCE TASKS
Write an Argument · 355
Participate in a Panel Discussion · 359

KEY LEARNING OBJECTIVES

Support inferences about theme.
Determine figurative meanings and tone.
Analyze effects of author's choices about structure.
Determine central idea of a text.

Summarize the text.
Analyze ideas and events presented in a text.
Analyze impact of word choice on tone.
Analyze author's purpose and use of rhetoric.
Delineate and evaluate an argument.

Close Reader

MEMOIR
from An Ordinary Man   Paul Rusesabagina

SPEECH
Truth at All Costs   Marie Colvin

POEM
The Survivor   Marilyn Chin

POEM
Who Understands Me But Me   Jimmy Santiago Baca

eBook *Explore It!*

▶ **Video Links**   **Visit hmhfyi.com**
for current articles and
informational texts.

COLLECTION 6

Heroes and Quests

The Epic			365
EPIC POEM *from the* Odyssey:	Homer, *translated by* Robert Fitzgerald	▶	369
Part One: The Wanderings of Odysseus			
Book 1: A Goddess Intervenes			371
Book 9: New Coasts and Poseidon's Son			372
Book 10: Circe, the Grace of the Witch			386
Book 11: The Land of the Dead			388
Book 12: The Sirens; Scylla and Charybdis			392
Part Two: The Homecoming			
Book 17: The Beggar at the Manor			401
Book 21: The Test of the Bow			403
Book 22: Death in the Great Hall			408
Book 23: The Trunk of the Olive Tree			413
TRAVEL WRITING *from* The Cruelest Journey: 600 Miles to Timbuktu	Kira Salak		421
ARGUMENT The Real Reasons We Explore Space	Michael Griffin	▶	433
POEM The Journey	Mary Oliver		441

ANCHOR TEXT

COLLECTION PERFORMANCE TASK

Research and Write an Analytical Essay	445

KEY LEARNING OBJECTIVES	Analyze character. Analyze epic poems. Analyze figurative meanings. Interpret figurative language.	Cite text evidence. Determine central idea of a text. Analyze ideas and events presented in a text. Delineate and evaluate an argument.

Close Reader

EPIC POEM
from the Odyssey:
   from The Cyclops   Homer, *translated by* Robert Fitzgerald

NONFICTION
from The Good Soldiers   David Finkel

eBook *Explore It!*

▶ **Video**
Links   **Visit hmhfyi.com**
for current articles and
informational texts.

Student Resources

Performance Task Reference Guide   R2
Writing Arguments   R2
Writing Informative Essays   R4
Writing Narratives   R6
Conducting Research   R8
Participating in a Collaborative
Discussion   R12
Debating an Issue   R14

Reading Arguments   R16
Analyzing an Argument   R16
Recognizing Persuasive Techniques   R17
Analyzing Logic and Reasoning   R17
Identifing Faulty Reasoning   R19
Evaluating Arguments   R20

Grammar   R22
Quick Reference:
Parts of Speech   R22
The Sentence and Its Parts   R24
Punctuation   R25
Capitalization   R27
Grammar Handbook:
1 Nouns   R29
2 Pronouns   R29
3 Verbs   R32
4 Modifiers   R34
5 The Sentence and Its Parts   R37
6 Phrases   R38
7 Verbals and Verbal Phrases   R39
8 Clauses   R41
9 The Structure of Sentences   R43
10 Writing Complete Sentences   R44
11 Subject-Verb Agreement   R45

Vocabulary and Spelling   R48
1 Using Context Clues   R48
2 Analyzing Word Structure   R49
3 Understanding Word Origins   R50
4 Synonyms and Antonyms   R51
5 Denotation and Connotation   R51
6 Analogies   R51
7 Homonyms and Homophones   R51
8 Words with Multiple Meanings   R52
9 Specialized Vocabulary   R52
10 Using Reference Sources   R52
11 Spelling Rules   R53
12 Commonly Confused Words   R55

**Glossary of Literary and
Informational Terms**   R57

Pronunciation Key   R76

Glossary of Academic Vocabulary   R77

Glossary of Critical Vocabulary   R78

Index of Skills   R81

Index of Titles and Authors   R92

Acknowledgments   R93

Connecting to Your World

Every time you read something, view something, write to someone, or react to what you've read or seen, you're participating in a world of ideas. You do this every day, inside the classroom and out. These skills will serve you not only at home and at school, but eventually, in your career.

The digital tools in this program will tap into the skills you already use and help you sharpen those skills for the future.

Start your exploration at my.hrw.com

fyi
hmhfyi.com
Research Explore

Close Read

WriteSmart
Produce Collaborate

eBook
Read Annotate

Channel One News®
HISTORY A&E
View Extend

myNotebook
Cite Organize

Stream to Start

Interactive Lessons
Write Communicate

Writing and
Speaking & Listening

Communication in today's world requires quite a variety of skills. To express yourself and win people over, you have to be able to write for print, for online media, and for spoken presentations. To collaborate, you have to work with people who might be sitting right next to you or at the other end of an Internet connection.

Available Only in Your eBook

Interactive Lessons

These interactive lessons will help you master the skills needed to become an expert communicator.

What Does a Strong Argument Look Like?

Read this argument and answer the questions about how the writer states and supports his position.

Tip

Pitching Perfect Pitch
by José Alvarez

Did you know that when you are listening to your favorite vocalist, you might be hearing a computer-generated pitch? Many record companies use pitch-correction software to ensure that their performers are pitch-perfect. While perfectionism is an admirable goal, there is a fine line between using technology to enhance music and using it to make performers into something they're not. Whether recording in the studio or playing a live performance, musicians should not use pitch-correction software. ●

Music production has become a digital experience. Producers use software to cut and paste pieces of music together, just like you cut and paste words together in your word-processing software. ○ When editing these different things together digitally, slight imperfections can occur where the pieces are joined. Enter the correction software. What began as a method to streamline the digital editing process has turned into an almost industry-wide standard of altering a musician"s work. "Think of it like plastic surgery," says a Grammy-winning recording engineer.

What is the writer's position, or **claim,** on the use of pitch-correction software?

- [ ] Musicians should learn to live with their imperfections.
- [x] Musicians should never use the software.
- [ ] Musicians should use the software to enhance live performances only.

Writing Arguments

Master the art of proving your point.

Interactive Lessons

1. Introduction
2. What Is a Claim?
3. Support: Reasons and Evidence
4. Building Effective Support
5. Creating a Coherent Argument
6. Persuasive Techniques
7. Formal Style
8. Concluding Your Argument

Writing Informative Texts

Shed light on complex ideas and topics.

Interactive Lessons

1. Introduction
2. Developing a Topic
3. Organizing Ideas
4. Introductions and Conclusions
5. Elaboration
6. Using Graphics and Multimedia
7. Precise Language and Vocabulary
8. Formal Style

Writing Narratives

A good storyteller can always capture an audience.

Interactive Lessons

1. Introduction
2. Narrative Context
3. Point of View and Characters
4. Narrative Structure
5. Narrative Techniques
6. The Language of Narrative

Writing as a Process

Get from the first twinkle of
an idea to a sparkling
final draft.

Interactive Lessons	1. Introduction	4. Revising and Editing
	2. Task, Purpose, and Audience	5. Trying a New Approach
	3. Planning and Drafting	

Producing and Publishing with Technology

Learn how to write for an online audience.

Interactive Lessons	1. Introduction	3. Interacting with Your Online Audience
	2. Writing for the Internet	4. Using Technology to Collaborate

Conducting Research

There's a world of information
out there. How do you find it?

Interactive Lessons	1. Introduction	5. Conducting Field Research
	2. Starting Your Research	6. Using the Internet for Research
	3. Types of Sources	7. Taking Notes
	4. Using the Library for Research	8. Refocusing Your Inquiry

Evaluating Sources
Approach all sources with a critical eye.

Interactive Lessons

1. Introduction
2. Evaluating Sources for Usefulness
3. Evaluating Sources for Reliability

Using Textual Evidence
Put your research into writing.

Interactive Lessons

1. Introduction
2. Synthesizing Information
3. Writing an Outline
4. Summarizing, Paraphrasing, and Quoting
5. Attribution

Participating in Collaborative Discussions
There's power in putting your heads together.

Interactive Lessons

1. Introduction
2. Preparing for Discussion
3. Establishing and Following Procedure
4. Speaking Constructively
5. Listening and Responding
6. Wrapping Up Your Discussion

Analyzing and Evaluating Presentations

Is there substance behind the style?

Interactive Lessons	1. Introduction	4. Tracing a Speaker's Argument
	2. Analyzing a Presentation	5. Rhetoric and Delivery
	3. Evaluating a Speaker's Reliability	6. Synthesizing Media Sources

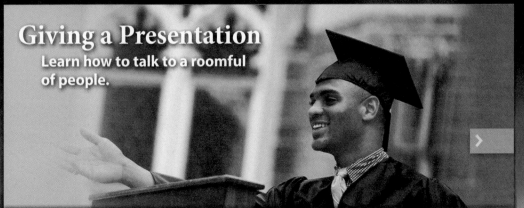

Giving a Presentation

Learn how to talk to a roomful of people.

Interactive Lessons	1. Introduction	4. Style in Presentation
	2. Knowing Your Audience	5. Delivering Your Presentation
	3. The Content of Your Presentation	6. Presenting a Recitation

Using Media in a Presentation

If a picture is worth a thousand words, just think what you can do with a video.

Interactive Lessons	1. Introduction	3. Using Presentation Software
	2. Types of Media: Audio, Video, and Images	4. Practicing Your Presentation

| eBook | myNotebook | **fyi** hmhfyi.com | my **WriteSmart** |

Supporting 21st-Century Skills

The amount of information people encounter each day keeps increasing. Whether you're working alone or collaborating with others, it takes effort to analyze the complex texts and competing ideas that bombard us in this fast-paced world. What can allow you to succeed? Staying engaged and organized. The digital tools in this program will help you to think critically and take charge of your learning.

Stream to Start

Ignite your Investigation

You learn best when you're engaged. The **Stream to Start** video at the beginning of each collection is designed to inspire interest in the topics being explored. Watch it and then let your curiosity lead your investigations.

and how do we cope?

Learn How to Do a Close Read

An effective close read is all about the details; you have to examine the language and ideas a writer includes. See how it's done by accessing the **Close Read Screencasts** in your eBook. Hear modeled conversations about anchor texts.

Who, almost dead for breath, had scarcely more
Than would make up his message.

Lady Macbeth.   Give him tending.
35 He brings great news.

[Messenger *exits.*]

The raven himself is hoarse
That croaks the fatal entrance of Duncan
Under my battlements. Come, you spirits
That tend on mortal thoughts, unsex me here,

Houghton Mifflin Harcourt

The Tragedy of Macbeth

by William Shakespeare

The raven himself is hoarse
That croaksthe fatal entrance of Duncan
Under my battlements. Come, you spirits
Thattend on mortalthoughts, unsex me here,
And fill me from the crown to the toe top-full
Of direst cruelty. Make thick my blood.
Stop up th' access and passage to remorse,
That no compunctious visitings of nature

> The raven is a symbol of death and evil.

Annotate the Texts

Practice close reading by utilizing the powerful annotation tools in your eBook. Mark up key ideas and observations using highlighters and sticky notes. Tag unfamiliar words to create a personal word list in *my*Notebook.

Find More Text Evidence on the Web

Tap into the *FYI* website for links to high-interest informational texts about collection topics. Synthesize information and connect notes and text evidence from any Web source by including it in *my*Notebook.

myNotebook

Save and Organize Your Notes

Save your annotations to *my*Notebook, where you can organize them to use as text evidence in performance tasks and other writing assignments. You can also organize the unfamiliar words you tagged by creating word lists, which will help you grow your vocabulary.

Create, Communicate, and Collaborate

Use the technology provided by the **myWriteSmart** tool to keep track of your writing assignments, create drafts, and collaborate and communicate with peers and your teacher. Use the evidence you've gathered in *my*Notebook to support your ideas.

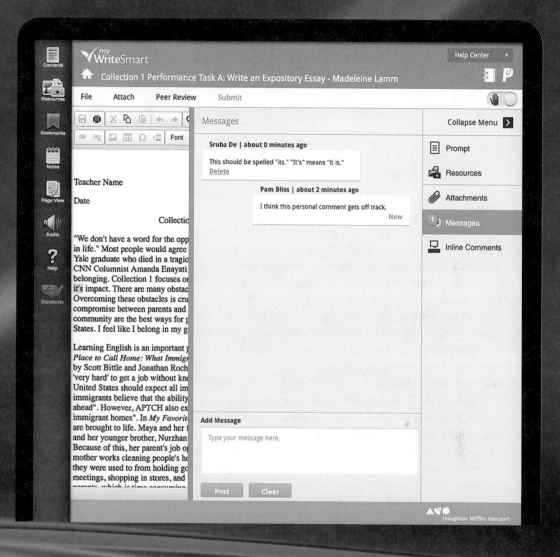

Navigating Complex Texts in the 21st Century

By Carol Jago

Reading complex literature and nonfiction doesn't need to be painful.

But to enjoy great poetry and prose you are going to have to do more than skim and scan. You will need to develop the habit of paying attention to the particular words on the page closely, systematically, even lovingly. Just because a text isn't easy doesn't mean there is something wrong with it or something wrong with you. Understanding complex text takes effort and focused attention. Do you sometimes wish writers would just say what they have to say more simply or with fewer words? I assure you that writers don't use long sentences and unfamiliar words to annoy their readers or make readers feel dumb. They employ complex syntax and rich language because they have complex ideas about complex issues that they want to communicate. Simple language and structures just aren't up to the task.

Excellent literature and nonfiction—the kind you will be reading over the course of the year—challenge readers in many ways. Sometimes the background of a story or the content of an essay is so unfamiliar that it can be difficult to understand why characters are behaving as they do or to follow the argument a writer is making. By persevering—reading like a detective and following clues in the text—you will find that your store of background knowledge grows. As a result, the next time you read about global issues, financial matters, political events, environmental news, (like the California drought), or health research, the text won't seem nearly as hard. Navigating a terrain you have been over once before never seems quite as rugged the second time through. The more you read, the better reader you become.

Good readers aren't scared off by challenging text. When the going gets rough, they know what to do. Let's take vocabulary, a common measure of text complexity, as an example. Learning new words is the business of a lifetime. Rather than shutting down when you meet a word you don't know, take a moment to think about the word. Is any part of the word familiar to you? Is there something in the context of the sentence or paragraph that can help you figure out its meaning? Is there someone or something that can provide you with a definition? When we read literature or nonfiction from a time period other than our own, the text is often full of words we don't know. Each time you meet those words in succeeding readings you will be adding to your understanding of the word and its use. Your brain is a natural word-learning machine. The more you feed it complex text, the larger vocabulary you'll have and as a result, the easier navigating the next book will be.

Have you ever been reading a long, complicated sentence and discovered that by the time you reached the end you had forgotten the beginning? Unlike the sentences we speak or dash off in a note to a friend, complex text is often full of sentences that are not only lengthy but also constructed in intricate ways. Such sentences require readers to slow down and figure out how phrases relate to one another as well as who is doing what to whom. Remember, rereading isn't cheating. It is exactly what experienced readers know to do when they meet dense text on the page. On the pages that follow you will find stories and articles that challenge you at a sentence level. Don't be intimidated. By paying careful attention to how those sentences are constructed, you will see their meanings unfold before your eyes.

That same kind of attention is required for reading the media. Every day you are bombarded with messages—online, offline, everywhere you look. These, too, are complex texts that you want to be able to see through; that is, to be able to recognize the message's source, purpose, context, intended audience, and appeals. Another way text can be complex is in terms of the density of ideas. Sometimes a writer piles on so much information that you find even if your eyes continue to move down the page, your brain has stopped taking in anything. At times like this, turning to a peer and discussing particular lines or concepts can help you pay closer attention and begin to unpack the text. Sharing questions and ideas, exploring a difficult passage together, makes it possible to tease out the meaning of even the most difficult text.

> **"Your brain is a natural word-learning machine. The more you feed it complex text, the larger a vocabulary you'll have."**

Poetry is by its nature particularly dense and for that reason poses particular challenges for casual readers. Don't ever assume that once through a poem is enough. Often, a seemingly simple poem in terms of word choice and length—for example an Emily Dickinson, Mary Oliver, or W.H. Auden poem—expresses extremely complex feelings and insights. Poets also often make reference to mythological and Biblical allusions which contemporary readers are not always familiar with. Skipping over such references robs your reading of the richness the poet intended. Look up that bird. Check out the note on the page. Ask your teacher.

You will notice a range of complexity within each collection of readings. This spectrum reflects the range of texts that surround us: some easy, some hard, some seemingly easy but hard, some seemingly hard but easy. Navigating this sea of texts should stretch you as a reader and a thinker. How could it be otherwise when your journey is in the realms of gold? Please accept this invitation to an intellectual voyage I think you will enjoy.

Finding Common Ground

" We may have different religions, different languages, different
colored skin, but we all belong to one human race. "

Finding Common Ground

The focus of this collection is the individual and society—from the individual's struggle to be a part of a society to a nation's struggle to unite for a common cause.

Stream to Start

hmhfyi.com

Channel One News®

COLLECTION
PERFORMANCE TASK Preview

At the end of this collection, you will have the opportunity to complete two tasks:

• Plan and deliver a speech about whether people can learn to live together.

• Write an essay about an individual's role in society.

ACADEMIC VOCABULARY

Study the words and their definitions in the chart below. You will use these words as you discuss and write about the texts in this collection.

Word	Definition	Related Forms
enforce (ĕn-fôrs´) *tr v.*	to compel observance of or obedience to	enforceable, enforcer, enforcement
entity (ĕn´ tĭ-tē) *n.*	a thing that exists as a unit	entities
internal (ĭn-tûr´nəl) *adj.*	inner; located within something or someone	internality, internally
presume (prĭ-zōōm´) *v.*	to take for granted as being true; to assume something is true	presumably, presumption, presumed
resolve (rĭ-zŏlv´) *v.*	to decide or become determined	resolution, resolvable

Background *Author* **Anna Quindlen** *(b. 1953) was born in Philadelphia. She is a columnist and author who has been described as having a "common touch" because so many people relate to her writings about politics and gender-specific issues. In 1992, she became the third woman to win a Pulitzer Prize for commentary. "A Quilt of a Country" was published after the World Trade Center attacks of September 11, 2001. The argument was written at a time when many people were thinking about what it means to be an American.*

A Quilt of a Country

Argument by Anna Quindlen

AS YOU READ Pay attention to how the details in the text support the idea of America as "an improbable idea." Write down any questions you generate during reading.

America is an improbable idea. A mongrel[1] nation built of ever-changing disparate[2] parts, it is held together by a notion, the notion that all men are created equal, though everyone knows that most men consider themselves better than someone. "Of all the nations in the world, the United States was built in nobody's image," the historian Daniel Boorstin wrote. That's because it was built of bits and pieces that seem **discordant,** like the crazy quilts that have been one of its great folk-art forms, velvet and calico and checks and brocades. Out of many, one. That is the ideal.

10   The reality is often quite different, a great national striving consisting frequently of failure. Many of the oft-told stories of the most **pluralistic** nation on earth are stories not of tolerance, but of bigotry. Slavery and sweatshops, the burning of crosses

discordant
(dĭ-skôr´dnt) *adj.*
conflicting or not harmonious.

pluralistic
(plŏŏr´ə-lĭs´tĭc) *adj.*
consisting of many ethnic and cultural groups.

---

[1] **mongrel:** something produced by mixing different breeds.
[2] **disparate:** distinct or not alike.

and the ostracism³ of the other. Children learn in social-studies class and in the news of the lynching of blacks, the denial of rights to women, the murders of gay men. It is difficult to know how to convince them that this amounts to "crown thy good with brotherhood," that amid all the failures is something spectacularly successful. Perhaps they understand it at this
20 moment, when enormous tragedy, as it so often does, demands a time of reflection on enormous blessings.

This is a nation founded on a conundrum,⁴ what Mario Cuomo⁵ has characterized as "community added to individualism." These two are our defining ideals; they are also in constant conflict. Historians today bemoan the ascendancy of a kind of prideful apartheid⁶ in America, saying that the clinging to ethnicity, in background and custom, has undermined the concept of unity. These historians must have forgotten the past, or have gilded it. The New York of my children is no more Balkanized,⁷ probably
30 less so, than the Philadelphia of my father, in which Jewish boys would walk several blocks out of their way to avoid the Irish divide of Chester Avenue. (I was the product of a mixed marriage, across barely bridgeable lines: an Italian girl, an Irish boy. How quaint it seems now, how incendiary then.) The Brooklyn of Francie Nolan's famous tree, the Newark of which Portnoy complained, even the uninflected WASP suburbs of Cheever's characters:⁸ they are ghettos, pure and simple. Do the Cambodians and the Mexicans in California coexist less easily today than did the Irish and Italians of Massachusetts a century ago? You know the answer.
40 What is the point of this splintered whole? What is the point of a nation in which Arab cabbies chauffeur Jewish passengers through the streets of New York—and in which Jewish cabbies chauffeur Arab passengers, too, and yet speak in theory of hatred, one for the other? What is the point of a nation in which one part seems to be always on the verge of fisticuffs with another, blacks and whites, gays and straights, left and right, Pole and Chinese and Puerto Rican and Slovenian? Other countries with such divisions have in fact divided into new nations with new names, but not this one, impossibly **interwoven** even in its hostilities.

interwoven
(ĭnˊtər-wōˊvən) *adj.* blended or laced together.

---

³ **ostracism:** exclusion or separation from society.

⁴ **conundrum:** a riddle or a puzzle.

⁵ **Mario Cuomo:** Governor of New York from 1983 until 1994.

⁶ **apartheid:** a political system of racial or ethnic separation and discrimination.

⁷ **Balkanized:** divided into small, uncooperative groups like countries on the Balkan Peninsula in the early 20ᵗʰ century.

⁸ **Francie Nolan's . . . WASP suburbs of Cheever's characters:** characters in the novels *A Tree Grows in Brooklyn* and *Portnoy's Complaint;* John Cheever's characters were generally White Anglo-Saxon Protestants, or WASPs.

"What is the point of this splintered whole?"

50   Once these disparate parts were held together by a common enemy, by the fault lines of world wars and the electrified fence of communism. With the end of the cold war[9] there was the creeping concern that without a focus for hatred and distrust, a sense of national identity would evaporate, that the left side of the hyphen— African-American, Mexican-American, Irish-American—would overwhelm the right. And slow-growing domestic traumas like economic unrest and increasing crime seemed more likely to emphasize division than community. Today the citizens of the United States have come together once more because of armed conflict and
60   enemy attack. Terrorism has led to devastation—and unity.

     Yet even in 1994, the overwhelming majority of those surveyed by the National Opinion Research Center agreed with this statement: "The U.S. is a unique country that stands for something special in the world." One of the things that it stands for is this vexing notion that a great nation can consist entirely of refugees from other nations, that people of different, even warring religions and cultures can live, if not side by side, then on either side of the country's Chester Avenues. Faced with this **diversity** there is little point in trying to isolate anything remotely resembling a national
70   character, but there are two strains of behavior that, however tenuously, abet the concept of unity.

diversity
(dĭ-vûr´sĭ-tē) *n.*
having varied
social and/or ethnic
backgrounds.

---

[9] **cold war:** diplomatic and economic hostility between the United States and the Soviet Union and their respective allies in the decades following World War II.

There is that Calvinist undercurrent[10] in the American psyche that loves the difficult, the demanding, that sees mastering the impossible, whether it be prairie or subway, as a test of character, and so glories in the struggle of this fractured coalescing. And there is a grudging fairness among the citizens of the United States that eventually leads most to admit that, no matter what the English-only advocates try to suggest, the new immigrants are not so different from our own parents or grandparents. Leonel Castillo,

80 former director of the Immigration and Naturalization Service and himself the grandson of Mexican immigrants, once told the writer Studs Terkel proudly, "The old neighborhood Ma-Pa stores are still around. They are not Italian or Jewish or Eastern European any more. Ma and Pa are now Korean, Vietnamese, Iraqi, Jordanian, Latin American. They live in the store. They work seven days a week. Their kids are doing well in school. They're making it. Sound familiar?"

Tolerance is the word used most often when this kind of coexistence succeeds, but tolerance is a vanilla-pudding word,

90 standing for little more than the allowance of letting others live unremarked and unmolested. Pride seems excessive, given the American willingness to endlessly complain about them, them being whoever is new, different, unknown, or currently under suspicion. But patriotism is partly taking pride in this unlikely ability to throw all of us together in a country that across its length and breadth is as different as a dozen countries, and still be able to call it by one name. When photographs of the faces of all those who died in the World Trade Center destruction are assembled in one place, it will be possible to trace in the skin color, the shape of

100 the eyes and the noses, the texture of the hair, a map of the world. These are the representatives of a mongrel nation that somehow, at times like this, has one spirit. Like many improbable ideas, when it actually works, it's a wonder.

COLLABORATIVE DISCUSSION Why does Anna Quindlen consider America to be "an improbable idea"? Discuss Quindlen's argument with a partner.

---

[10] **Calvinist undercurrent:** the social influence of Calvinism, a Christian religion with a strict moral code and a belief in God as absolutely sovereign.

Delineate and Evaluate an Argument

In "A Quilt of a Country," Anna Quindlen presents an **argument** about how America works as a country. An argument presents a claim, or position, on an issue and supports it with reasons and evidence. To evaluate the strength of Quindlen's argument, you must **delineate,** or describe in detail, these elements:

- Identify the **claim,** or Quindlen's position, on the issue.
- Look for the **reasons** Quindlen uses to support her claim. Reasons should be valid and logical.
- Evaluate whether the **evidence** Quindlen cites for each reason is credible, or believable, and relevant to the claim. Evidence can include facts, statistics, examples, anecdotes, or quotations.
- Look for **counterarguments,** which are statements that address opposing viewpoints. Does Quindlen anticipate opposing viewpoints and provide counterarguments to disprove them?

Analyze and Evaluate Author's Claim

To support a **claim,** authors develop and refine their ideas throughout the text. An author may use a particular sentence to develop a claim, or use an entire paragraph or larger section of the text to develop a claim with reasons and evidence.

Use a chart to help you analyze and evaluate how Anna Quindlen develops her claim in "A Quilt of a Country." First, identify the claim. Then, list specific reasons or evidence from the text. Finally, evaluate if the reason or evidence supports the claim. Read this example from a student newspaper editorial.

CLAIM	More time should be given to students to transition between classes.
Reasons/Evidence from Text	**How the Reasons/Evidence Support the Claim**
"Students have told me how rushed they are to gather materials from their lockers for their next classes."	The evidence is a quotation from the school counselor, an objective observer who hears from many students. Her statement is logical support for the claim because it would be easier to gather materials if students had more time.

Analyzing the Text

Cite Text Evidence Support your responses with evidence from the selection.

1. **Summarize** What is Anna Quindlen's claim in "A Quilt of a Country"? Summarize her claim in your own words.

2. **Interpret** In lines 7–8, what does Quindlen mean when she describes America as being "like the crazy quilts that have been one of its great folk-art forms"? How does this description support her claim?

3. **Evaluate** What opposing viewpoint does Quindlen respond to in paragraph 3? What counterargument does she offer to it? List the reasons and evidence she includes in her counterargument and evaluate if it is relevant and sufficient.

4. **Analyze** In paragraph 4, Quindlen uses **repetition** and **parallelism**— expressing related ideas using similar grammatical constructions. What sentence structure and words does she repeat? What is the effect of this repetition?

5. **Analyze** Reread Quindlen's conclusion. What specific words and phrases does she use to link the conclusion to her introduction? How do these words and phrases support her argument?

6. **Evaluate** Quindlen uses many different types of evidence throughout the argument to support her claim, for example, facts, statistics, and quotations. Identity at least three examples of evidence and evaluate how she uses each one to support her claim.

PERFORMANCE TASK

Writing Activity: Argument Using what you have learned about how to develop an argument, write and support a claim about a positive aspect of your school or community.

1. Think about something you feel is an important, positive feature of your school or community. Write a claim about it.

2. Make notes about the reasons that support your claim. Then collect evidence that supports your reasons. Consider an opposing claim and list valid counterarguments.

3. Write the draft of your argument. Work carefully to present your reasons and evidence in a logical order.

4. Revise your draft to eliminate unrelated or illogical evidence. Finally, check your work to make sure you have used the conventions of standard English.

Critical Vocabulary

Practice and Apply Answer the following questions and explain your ideas.

discordant   **pluralistic**   **interwoven**   **diversity**

1. If a piece of music is **discordant**, do you want to continue listening or not? Why?

2. Is a society made up of one cultural group a **pluralistic** society, or not? Why?

3. Is an all-school assembly an example of an **interwoven** school community? Explain.

4. What is one way that **diversity** strengthens a community? Explain your idea.

Vocabulary Strategy: Patterns of Word Changes

Words can have different meanings or be different parts of speech. Many words have several different meanings listed in the dictionary. For example, the word *equal*, as used in "A Quilt of a Country," means "having the same privileges or rights." However, it also means "being the same or identical." Knowing the different meanings of words can help you become an effective reader.

Words also change depending on the part of speech to which they belong. The Critical Vocabulary words *discordant* and *pluralistic* change spelling and meaning when the part of speech changes. Knowing how a word functions in a sentence will help you gain a complete understanding of the word's meaning.

Practice and Apply Complete the sentences with the correct word from the chart.

Noun	Verb	Adjective
discord—lack of agreement	**pluralize**—to engage in pluralism	**discordant**—conflicting
pluralism—a condition of society where many groups coexist		**pluralistic**—consisting of many ethnic and cultural groups

1. The people shouting indicated the level of _____ during the meeting.

2. Some governmental entities claim to be _____ because people of different ethnic groups work together.

3. The _____ parts of the book made it difficult to understand.

4. Even when a country tries to have _____, there can be unfairness and resentment.

Language and Style: Noun Clauses

A subordinate clause contains a subject and a verb, but it cannot stand alone in a sentence. A **noun clause** is a subordinate clause that takes the place of a noun in a sentence. It usually begins with *that, what, whatever, why, whether, how, who, whom, whoever,* or *whomever.*

A noun clause may function in a sentence as the subject, the direct object, the predicate nominative, or the object of a preposition.

Examples of Noun Clauses	
subject	**What Anna Quindlen wrote** was very thoughtful.
direct object	Many people don't appreciate **that America is made up of many diverse cultures.**
predicate nominative	My suggestion is **that we learn how to live together peacefully.**
object of a preposition	I will share my ideas with **whoever will listen.**

Writers use noun clauses to convey precise meanings and to add variety and interest to their writing. Read this sentence from the text in which Anna Quindlen strings together multiple noun clauses:

> It is difficult to know <u>how to convince them that this amounts to "crown thy good with brotherhood," that amid all the failures is something spectacularly successful.</u>

In this sentence, the first noun clause, *how to convince,* is the direct object of *know.* The second two noun clauses that begin with *that* are direct objects of *convince.* This sentence has a different structure from surrounding sentences in the paragraph. By using noun clauses to vary sentence structures, Quindlen keeps her readers engaged and interested.

Practice and Apply Look back at the argument about a positive aspect of your school or community you created in this selection's Performance Task. Revise your argument to include at least one noun clause for each of the four functions listed in the chart above. Then, discuss with a partner how the noun clauses add variety and interest to your writing.

Nadine Gordimer (1923–2014) *was born in South Africa. Her family was privileged and white in a country that practiced apartheid—an official policy of segregation of nonwhite South Africans enforced by the government. Nadine Gordimer became politically opposed to the policy. Her early works, such as* The Soft Voice of the Serpent *and* The Lying Days, *explore themes of exile and the effects of apartheid on internal life in South Africa. Before apartheid ended in 1994, some of Gordimer's writings were banned by the South African government; however, these texts were appreciated in other parts of the world. She has been awarded many literary prizes, including the Nobel Prize for Literature in 1991.*

Once Upon a Time

Short Story by Nadine Gordimer

AS YOU READ Pay attention to the relationship of the characters to the community in which they live. What steps do the parents take to ensure their family's safety?

Someone has written to ask me to contribute to an anthology of stories for children. I reply that I don't write children's stories; and he writes back that at a recent congress/book fair/seminar a certain novelist said every writer ought to write at least one story for children. I think of sending a postcard saying I don't accept that I "ought" to write anything.

And then last night I woke up—or rather was wakened without knowing what had roused me.

A voice in the echo chamber of the subconscious?

A sound.

A creaking of the kind made by the weight carried by one foot after another along a wooden floor. I listened. I felt the apertures of my ears **distend** with concentration. Again: the creaking. I was waiting for it; waiting to hear if it indicated that feet were moving from room to room, coming up the passage—to my door. I have no burglar bars, no gun under the pillow, but I have the same fears as people who do take these precautions, and my windowpanes

distend
(dĭ-stĕnd´) *v.*
to bulge or expand.

10

are thin as rime,[1] could shatter like a wineglass. A woman was murdered (how do they put it) in broad daylight in a house two blocks away, last year, and the fierce dogs who guarded an old widower and his collection of antique clocks were strangled before he was knifed by a casual laborer he had dismissed without pay.

I was staring at the door, making it out in my mind rather than seeing it, in the dark. I lay quite still—a victim already—but the arrhythmia[2] of my heart was fleeing, knocking this way and that against its body-cage. How finely tuned the senses are, just out of rest, sleep! I could never listen intently as that in the distractions of the day; I was reading every faintest sound, identifying and classifying its possible threat.

But I learned that I was to be neither threatened nor spared. There was no human weight pressing on the boards, the creaking was a buckling, an epicenter[3] of stress. I was in it. The house that surrounds me while I sleep is built on undermined ground; far beneath my bed, the floor, the house's foundations, the stopes[4] and passages of gold mines have hollowed the rock, and when some face trembles, detaches, and falls, three thousand feet below, the whole house shifts slightly, bringing uneasy strain to the balance and counterbalance of brick, cement, wood, and glass that hold it as a structure around me. The misbeats of my heart tailed off like the last muffled flourishes on one of the wooden xylophones made by the Chopi and Tsonga[5] migrant miners who might have been down there, under me in the earth at that moment. The stope where the fall was could have been disused, dripping water from its ruptured veins; or men might now be interred there in the most profound of tombs.

I couldn't find a position in which my mind would let go of my body—release me to sleep again. So I began to tell myself a story; a bedtime story.

In a house, in a suburb, in a city, there were a man and his wife who loved each other very much and were living happily ever after. They had a little boy, and they loved him very much. They had a cat and a dog that the little boy loved very much. They had a car and a caravan trailer for holidays, and a swimming pool which was fenced so that the little boy and his playmates would not fall in and drown. They had a housemaid who was absolutely trustworthy

---

[1] **rime:** a coating of frost.

[2] **arrhythmia:** an irregular heartbeat.

[3] **epicenter:** the focal point.

[4] **stopes:** step-like holes or trenches made by miners.

[5] **Chopi and Tsonga:** (chō′pē and tsôn′ga) ethnic groups that live in Mozambique.

and an itinerant[6] gardener who was highly recommended by the neighbors. For when they began to live happily ever after they were warned, by that wise old witch, the husband's mother, not to take on anyone off the street. They were inscribed in a medical benefit society, their pet dog was licensed, they were insured against fire, flood damage, and theft, and subscribed to the local Neighborhood Watch, which supplied them with a plaque for their gates lettered YOU HAVE BEEN WARNED over the silhouette of a would-be intruder. He was masked; it could not be said if he was black or white, and therefore proved the property owner was no racist.

It was not possible to insure the house, the swimming pool, or the car against riot damage. There were riots, but these were outside the city, where people of another color were quartered. These people were not allowed into the suburb except as reliable housemaids and gardeners, so there was nothing to fear, the husband told the wife. Yet she was afraid that some day such people might come up the street and tear off the plaque YOU HAVE BEEN WARNED and open the gates and stream in. . . . Nonsense, my dear, said the husband, there are police and soldiers and tear gas and guns to keep them away. But to please her—for he loved her very much and buses were being burned, cars stoned, and schoolchildren shot by the police in those quarters out of sight and hearing of the suburb—he had electronically controlled gates fitted. Anyone who pulled off the sign YOU HAVE BEEN WARNED and tried to open the gates would have to announce his **intentions** by pressing a button and speaking into a receiver relayed to the house. The little boy was fascinated by the device and used it as a walkie-talkie in cops and robbers play with his small friends.

The riots were suppressed, but there were many burglaries in the suburb and somebody's trusted housemaid was tied up and shut in a cupboard by thieves while she was in charge of her employers' house. The trusted housemaid of the man and wife and little boy was so upset by this misfortune befalling a friend left, as she herself often was, with responsibility for the possessions of the man and his wife and the little boy that she implored her employers to have burglar bars attached to the doors and windows of the house, and an alarm system installed. The wife said, She is right, let us take heed of her advice. So from every window and door in the house where they were living happily ever after they now saw the trees and sky through bars, and when the little boy's pet cat tried to climb in by the fanlight[7] to keep him company in his little bed

intention
(ĭn-tĕn´shən) *n.*
purpose or plan.

[6] **itinerant:** frequently traveling to different places.
[7] **fanlight:** an arched window, usually over a door.

at night, as it customarily had done, it set off the alarm keening[8]
through the house.

The alarm was often answered—it seemed—by other burglar
alarms, in other houses, that had been triggered by pet cats
or nibbling mice. The alarms called to one another across the
gardens in shrills and bleats and wails that everyone soon became
accustomed to, so that the din roused the inhabitants of the
suburb no more than the croak of frogs and musical grating of
cicadas'[9] legs. Under cover of the electronic harpies'[10] discourse
intruders sawed the iron bars and broke into homes, taking away
hi-fi equipment, television sets, cassette players, cameras and
radios, jewelry and clothing, and sometimes were hungry enough
to devour everything in the refrigerator or paused **audaciously**
to drink the whiskey in the cabinets or patio bars. Insurance
companies paid no compensation for single malt, a loss made
keener by the property owner's knowledge that the thieves wouldn't
even have been able to appreciate what it was they were drinking.

Then the time came when many of the people who were not
trusted housemaids and gardeners hung about the suburb because
they were unemployed. Some importuned for a job: weeding or
painting a roof; anything, *baas*,[11] madam. But the man and his wife
remembered the warning about taking on anyone off the street.
Some drank liquor and fouled the street with discarded bottles.
Some begged, waiting for the man or his wife to drive the car
out of the electronically operated gates. They sat about with their
feet in the gutters, under the jacaranda trees that made a green
tunnel of the street—for it was a beautiful suburb, spoiled only by
their presence—and sometimes they fell asleep lying right before
the gates in the midday sun. The wife could never see anyone go
hungry. She sent the trusted housemaid out with bread and tea,
but the trusted housemaid said these were loafers and *tsotsis*,[12] who
would come and tie her up and shut her in a cupboard. The husband
said, She's right. Take heed of her advice. You only encourage them
with your bread and tea. They are looking for their chance. . . . And
he brought the little boy's tricycle from the garden into the house
every night, because if the house was surely secure, once locked and
with the alarm set, someone might still be able to climb over the
wall or the electronically closed gates into the garden.

You are right, said the wife, then the wall should be higher. And
the wise old witch, the husband's mother, paid for the extra bricks

audacious
(ô-dā´shəs) *n.*
bold, rebellious.

---

[8] **keening:** wailing or crying.

[9] **cicadas:** large, loud insects.

[10] **harpies:** mythological creatures who were part woman and part bird.

[11] *baas:* (bäs) a white person in a position of authority in relation to nonwhites.

[12] *tsotsis:* (tsō´tsēs) dishonest, untrustworthy people.

as her Christmas present to her son and his wife—the little boy got a Space Man outfit and a book of fairy tales.

But every week there were more reports of **intrusion**: in broad daylight and the dead of night, in the early hours of the morning, and even in the lovely summer twilight—a certain family was at dinner while the bedrooms were being ransacked upstairs. The man and his wife, talking of the latest armed robbery in the suburb, were distracted by the sight of the little boy's pet cat effortlessly arriving over the seven-foot wall, descending first with a rapid bracing of extended forepaws down on the sheer vertical surface, and then a graceful launch, landing with swishing tail within the property. The whitewashed wall was marked with the cat's comings and goings; and on the street side of the wall there were larger red-earth smudges that could have been made by the kind of broken running shoes, seen on the feet of unemployed loiterers, that had no innocent destination.

When the man and wife and little boy took the pet dog for its walk round the neighborhood streets they no longer paused to admire this show of roses or that perfect lawn; these were hidden behind an array of different varieties of security fences, walls, and devices. The man, wife, little boy, and dog passed a remarkable choice: there was the low-cost option of pieces of broken glass embedded in cement along the top of walls, there were iron grilles ending in lance points, there were attempts at reconciling the aesthetics of prison architecture with the Spanish Villa style (spikes painted pink) and with the plastic urns of neoclassical façades (twelve-inch pikes finned like zigzags of lightning and painted pure white). Some walls had a small board affixed, giving the name and telephone number of the firm responsible for the installation of the devices. While the little boy and the pet dog raced ahead, the husband and wife found themselves comparing the possible effectiveness of each style against its appearance; and after several weeks when they paused before this barricade or that without

140

150

160

intrusion
(ĭn-trōō′ shən) *n.*
act of trespass or invasion.

needing to speak, both came out with the conclusion that only one
was worth considering. It was the ugliest but the most honest in its
suggestion of the pure concentration-camp style, no frills, all evident
efficacy. Placed the length of walls, it consisted of a continuous coil
of stiff and shining metal **serrated** into jagged blades, so that there
would be no way of climbing over it and no way through its tunnel
without getting entangled in its fangs. There would be no way out,
only a struggle getting bloodier and bloodier, a deeper and sharper
hooking and tearing of flesh. The wife shuddered to look at it. You're
right, said the husband, anyone would think twice. . . . And they
took heed of the advice on a small board fixed to the wall: Consult
DRAGON'S TEETH The People For Total Security.

Next day a gang of workmen came and stretched the razor-
bladed coils all round the walls of the house where the husband
and wife and little boy and pet dog and cat were living happily
ever after. The sunlight flashed and slashed, off the serrations, the
cornice of razor thorns encircled the home, shining. The husband
said, Never mind. It will weather. The wife said, You're wrong. They
guarantee it's rustproof. And she waited until the little boy had run
off to play before she said, I hope the cat will take heed. . . . The
husband said, Don't worry, my dear, cats always look before they
leap. And it was true that from that day on the cat slept in the little
boy's bed and kept to the garden, never risking a try at breaching
security.

One evening, the mother read the little boy to sleep with a fairy
story from the book the wise old witch had given him at Christmas.
Next day he pretended to be the Prince who braves the terrible
thicket of thorns to enter the palace and kiss the Sleeping Beauty
back to life: he dragged a ladder to the wall, the shining coiled
tunnel was just wide enough for his little body to creep in, and
with the first fixing of its razor teeth in his knees and hands and
head he screamed and struggled deeper into its tangle. The trusted
housemaid and the itinerant gardener, whose "day" it was, came
running, the first to see and to scream with him, and the itinerant
gardener tore his hands trying to get at the little boy. Then the man
and his wife burst wildly into the garden and for some reason (the
cat, probably) the alarm set up wailing against the screams while
the bleeding mass of the little boy was hacked out of the security
coil with saws, wire cutters, choppers, and they carried it—the
man, the wife, the hysterical trusted housemaid, and the weeping
gardener—into the house.

serrate
(sĕr´āt´) *adj.*
having a jagged,
saw-toothed edge.

COLLABORATIVE DISCUSSION Was the boy safer because of the
precautions his parents took to protect the family? Discuss your thoughts
with a partner using details from the story to support your ideas.

Analyze Author's Choices: Text Structure

Nadine Gordimer's "Once Upon a Time" was originally published in 1989. The late 1980s were a period of internal unrest in South Africa and this story reflects the fear and isolation that people felt as the policy of apartheid continued to be enforced. To convey her ideas, Gordimer structured her story using some of the traditional elements of fairy tales. For example, the title "Once Upon a Time" and the fact that the family is "living happily ever after" are both traditional elements of fairy tales. This **structure**, or arrangement of the parts of the story, holds together the elements of the story. The choices that Gordimer made about the structure of her story help create effects such as tension and surprise, as in a fairy tale. As you analyze the structure, look for other fairy tale elements as shown in the chart and think about how this story is similar to and different from other fairy tales you have read.

Elements of a Fairy Tale
• The main characters are opposed by an evil force.
• Animals have special abilities.
• The story is used to teach a lesson.
• Good characters have bad things happen to them.
• The setting does not seem quite real.
• Details in the story foreshadow that the problem, or conflict, will be resolved in a "happily ever after" ending.

Support Inferences About Theme

Gordimer develops the **theme,** or the underlying message, through the details and symbols she includes in the story. An author can use all the elements of a story to develop a theme, including the characters, plot, and setting. For example, to convey a theme about the rewards of working hard, an author might relate a story about a hockey team that finally wins a championship. As the story develops, the players discover each other's strengths and weaknesses and learn that working together brings success to everyone.

An author might also develop the theme through the use of a **symbol**—a person, a place, or an object that stands for something beyond itself. In the hockey team story, the author might use the symbol of a trophy to represent the team's success.

As you analyze "Once Upon a Time," make **inferences,** or logical guesses, about the theme by considering the details and symbols Gordimer includes. Pay particular attention to the characters' actions and motivations, as well as the setting— including the historical background—to help you infer the theme.

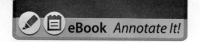
Analyzing the Text

Cite Text Evidence   Support your responses with evidence from the selection.

1. **Identify Patterns** How is the structure of this story similar to a fairy tale? What elements do they share? Cite details from the text to support your analysis.

2. **Connect** Nadine Gordimer wrote many stories about the injustices of apartheid. She was also active in bringing change to the political entities of South Africa. Even though her books were banned in South Africa for a time, she resolved to stay instead of living in exile. What do you learn about Gordimer's political point of view by reading this story? Explain your ideas using evidence from the story.

3. **Infer** Authors often leave things unstated in a story, leaving the reader with questions about the outcome. What can you infer about what Gordimer leaves unstated at the end of her story? How does it relate to her statements about the family living "happily ever after"?

4. **Evaluate** In lines 58, 136, and 194, the phrase "wise old witch" is used to describe the husband's mother. Explain how the wise old witch can be interpreted to symbolize the government of South Africa.

5. **Draw Conclusions** How does the cat symbolize and support the theme of this story? Explain.

6. **Infer** What is the theme of this story? Explain how Gordimer develops this theme through the story's elements, such as structure and symbols.

PERFORMANCE TASK

Speaking Activity: Fairy Tale Nadine Gordimer uses her writing to convey ideas about the society and country she lives in. Explore this idea by developing a modern fairy tale that you can perform with a partner.

1. Identify a community or school event that has happened or that you have observed. Then make notes about the two characters and plot of your fairy tale.

2. Think about a theme for your fairy tale. For example, you might consider the themes of fairness, justice, or equality. What important symbols can you include to convey your theme?

3. Combine your ideas to write a short fairy tale that conveys a message.

Refer back to "Once Upon a Time" to examine how Nadine Gordimer wrote a powerful political commentary using a fairy tale structure.

4. Perform your fairy tale with your partner. Use appropriate eye contact, adequate volume, and clear pronunciation as you perform. Ask your audience to evaluate if you were successful in conveying your underlying message.

Critical Vocabulary

distend **intention** **audacious** **intrusion** **serrate**

Practice and Apply Choose which of the two situations best fits the word's meaning.

1. **distend**
   a. The bicyclist will inflate the tires on her bike.
   b. The wheel rim bent when the bicyclist hit a pothole.

2. **intention**
   a. The soccer player showed his determination to shoot for the goal.
   b. The soccer player's purpose was to play better in the next game.

3. **audacious**
   a. The daring boy brought gum to the computer lab.
   b. The mischievous boy was caught by his teacher.

4. **intrusion**
   a. The newspaper talked about the girl's wrongful entrance into the clubhouse.
   b. The girl's interruption of the conversation made the club members unhappy.

5. **serrate**
   a. The edge of the paper was cut into a decorative pattern.
   b. The toothed edge of the paper looked like a set of teeth.

Vocabulary Strategy: Words from Latin

Word and Dictionary Definition	Etymology	Latin Definition
surround (line 33) "to enclose on all sides"	from the Latin *super-* + *unda*	*unda* means "wave"

Etymologies show the origin and historical development of a word. For example, the Critical Vocabulary word *distend* comes from the Latin word *distendere*, which means "to stretch." Exploring the etymology of words can help you clarify their precise meanings. It can also help you expand your vocabulary.

Practice and Apply Follow these steps for each Critical Vocabulary word:

- Look up the word in a dictionary.

- Find the etymology of each word. If you are not sure how to read the etymology, look at the front or the back of your dictionary. There will be a section that explains how the etymology is noted and what the abbreviations mean.

- Compare the Latin definition of each word with the English definition. Are they the same? How does the English definition relate to the Latin meaning?

Language and Style: Prepositional Phrases

Authors use various types of phrases to convey specific meanings and to add variety and interest to their writing. **Prepositional phrases** are phrases consisting of a preposition and an object of the preposition, usually a noun or a pronoun. Here are some common prepositions and phrases that can be created with them.

Preposition	Object of Preposition	Prepositional Phrase
from	the street	from the street
before	the rain	before the rain
during	the game	during the game
until	her test	until her test
outside	the gate	outside the gate

Read the following sentence from the story.

In a house, in a suburb, in a city, there were a man and his wife who loved each other very much and were living happily ever after.

Nadine Gordimer might have written the sentence this way:

In a suburban house, there were a man and his wife who loved each other very much and were living happily ever after.

While this sentence conveys the same meaning, it doesn't have the same interest as the original sentence. The prepositional phrases used one after another, *in a house, in a suburb, in a city,* help the author change gears from a story about something that happened to her to a story about another family. The phrases mimic the way a storyteller might use a steady beat or rhythm to start a story.

Examine another sentence from "Once Upon a Time":

One evening, the mother read the little boy to sleep <u>with a fairy tale from the book</u> the wise old witch had given him at Christmas.

Although Gordimer could have written several shorter sentences, this sentence with a series of prepositional phrases conveys the sense of a fairy tale.

Practice and Apply Review the modern fairy tale that you created about a current event for this selection's Performance Task. Working independently, revise your fairy tale to include prepositional phrases that clarify your ideas and that add variety and interest to your sentences. Compare your revisions to those of your partner.

Kimberly M. Blaeser (b. 1955), *of German and Anishinaabe ancestry, is a member of the Minnesota Chippewa tribe. Blaeser began her career as a journalist but is now a professor at the University of Wisconsin-Milwaukee. Blaeser is also a writer whose work includes poetry, personal essays, short stories, and reviews. Her first collection of poems,* Trailing You, *won the First Book Award in Poetry from the Native Writer's Circle of Americas in 1993. In her work, Blaeser often alludes to her dual heritage and to the collective nature of the human experience.*

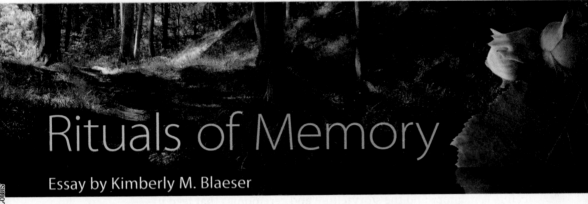

Rituals of Memory

Essay by Kimberly M. Blaeser

AS YOU READ Look for evidence about how Blaeser's mixed ancestry shapes her experiences and her ideas on memories. Write down any questions you generate during reading.

Memory begins with various wonders. For my friend Mary, it began with hair. Her hair grew tightly curled, so strong the spirals defied taming. Brushing and combing brought tears. When Mary tried to run her fingers through her hair as she saw others do, her fingers became hopelessly captured by the curls. Hair, she deduced, must grow in loops, out of our head at one point, back into it at another. Because her locks had never been cut, the loops never broken, her fingers became entangled in the loops.

Perhaps that story delights me because it stands as a wonderful
10 example of our always innocent attempts to explain the world. Or perhaps because it seems a fine metaphor for the looped relationships of family, place, and community, the **innate** patterns of ourselves that always keep us returning. No matter how long our lives, no matter how far our experience takes us from our origins, our lives remain connected, always loop back to that center of our identity, our spirit.

innate
(ĭ-nāt´) *adj.* inborn; existing at birth.

"*My memories entangle themselves oddly among the roots of several cultures.*"

I believe we belong to the circle and, for our survival, we will return in one way or another to renew those rhythms of life out of which our sense of self has emerged. Some of us have a physical place and a people we return to. We also have what Gerald Vizenor calls the "interior landscapes" of our imaginative and spiritual lives. Perhaps our strongest link to the sacred center, the pulsing core of being, is memory and the storytelling and ceremonies that feed it— our own rituals of memory.

My memories entangle themselves oddly among the roots of several cultures: Native American, perhaps **foremost** in my mind, but also a German Catholic background, the culture of rural America, the close looping of small towns in the Midwest, and what I guess could be called Minnesota wilderness culture. But these several cultures did not always exist in opposition or in isolation from one another. I remember Memorial Day celebrations when my father joined the Legionnaires[1] in their visits to all the graveyards in Mahnomen and Nay-Tah-Waush.[2] Uniformed, sometimes sweating in the early summer heat, they marched to the sites, stood at attention as taps was played, and then, as a gesture of salute to the fallen veterans, they shot over the graves. Each year, through late morning and early afternoon, we followed the men on these tours. We stood, moved to goose bumps by the lonely trumpet tune, scrambling with all the other children for spent casings when each ceremony was concluded.

The last site on their schedule was the Indian burial grounds close to the BAB landing. As a child I saw nothing unusual about a dozen American Legionnaires marching back on the little wooded

foremost
(fôr´mōst´) *adv.* most importantly.

---

[1] **Legionnaires:** members of the American Legion, a social, service-based organization of American veterans.

[2] **Mahnomen and Nay-Tah-Waush:** cities in northwestern Minnesota.

path and paying solemn respect to those Indian warriors who I would later realize were really of another nation. On this march through the tall grasses and hazelnut bushes that crowded the path, my older brother and I often fell in step. Several times I marched beside Sig Tveit and his trumpet, his arm linked through mine. We stood, all of us—those descended from settlers of Norwegian, German, or other European origins, and those descended from Anishinaabe or other Indian people. Together in a moment out of ordinary time, we paused in the little opening at the wooden grave houses, oblivious to the wood ticks, which must later be picked carefully from our clothes and our flesh, oblivious to the buzzing of mosquitoes or sand flies, oblivious as well to the more trivial tensions of contemporary politics. We stood together in a great ceremonial loop of our humanity, in our need to remember our ancestors and the lives they lived, together in our desire to **immerse** ourselves in their honor, to always carry those memories forward with us, to be ourselves somehow made holy by the ritual of those memories. We emerged quiet from those little woods, from that darker place of memory, into the too bright sunshine of a late May day in the twentieth century.

And then we arrived back at the sandy beach. The men brought out drinks from the trunks of their cars, laughter and talk sprang up, picnic foods came out, and people would disperse again—to their own families.

I don't know if the Legionnaires still march back into the woods each year. I like to believe they do. For that kind of experience has helped me keep balance when the strands of my mixed heritage seem to pull one against another. However unconscious, it was a moment of crossover, a moment when the borders of culture were **nullified** by the greater instincts of humanity to remember and to give honor.

Perhaps the Memorial Days of those early years have become one of the watermarks³ of my life because they brought to ceremonial focus the many tellings of the past that filled up the hours and days of my childhood. As children, we were never so much taught as storied. All work and play had memories attached.

"Indians," Ed Castillo says, "can hold more than one thing sacred." With school began my double life. I went to Catholic grade school, where I earned a reputation for being quiet, obedient, pious, and bright. I learned my Baltimore Catechism⁴—*"Who made you?"*

immerse
(ĭ-mûrs´) *v.* to absorb or involve deeply.

nullify
(nŭl´ə-fī´) *v.* to make of no value or consequence.

---

³ **watermarks:** marks impressed in paper that can be viewed when the paper is held up to the light.
⁴ **Baltimore Catechism:** a summary of Christian beliefs in a question-and-answer format that was taught in Catholic schools until the late 1960s.

"God made me." "Why did God make you?" "God made me because he loves me."—learned my singsong phonics—*ba be bi ba bu, ca ce ci ca cu, da de di da du*—studied my spelling—*i before e, except after c, or when it sounds like a as in neighbor and weigh.* In between school days, we gathered hazelnuts, went partridge hunting, fished, had long deer-hunting weekends, went to powwows,[5] went spearing and ice fishing, played canasta and whist, learned the daisy chain, beaded on looms, made fish house candles, sausage, and quilts. No one then questioned the necessity or value of our school education, but somehow I grew up knowing it wasn't the only—maybe not even the most important— education I would need, and sometimes we stole time from that education for the other one. My parents might keep us home from school or come and get us midday for some more lovely adventure on a lake or in the woods. I'm still thankful for those stolen moments, because now I know by heart not only the Hail Mary, the Our Father, and the National Anthem, but the misty prayers water gives off at dawn and the ancient song of the loon; I recognize not only the alphabet and the parts of the English sentence, but the silhouetted form of the shipoke and the intricate language of a beaver's teeth and tail.

My life at school and in the Catholic Church is officially recorded and documented—dates of baptism, First Communion and confirmation, quarterly grade reports, attendance records— just as my academic life is later documented at universities in Minnesota, Indiana, and Wisconsin. But for my other education, practical and spiritual, I have no grades or degrees, no certificates to commemorate the annual rituals. I have some **tangibles** of those processes—a jingle dress, fans of feathers, sometimes photos—but mostly I have stories, dreams, and memories.

tangible
(tăn´jǝ-bǝl) *n.*
something that can be touched.

COLLABORATIVE DISCUSSION With a partner, discuss Blaeser's views on how memories are formed. What does she believe influences her memories? In your discussion, cite evidence from the text.

---

[5] **powwows:** a celebration of Native American culture in which diverse nations gather for the purpose of singing, dancing, and honoring their ancestors.

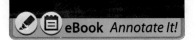
Determine Central Idea

The **central idea** of an essay is the most important point conveyed in the essay. Sometimes the central idea is stated in the first paragraph, but more often, you will need to infer the central idea that is implied by specific details. As you analyze "Rituals of Memory," keep notes using these strategies to help you understand how Blaeser develops the central idea over the course of the text:

- Identify the topic of each paragraph.
- Examine the specific details the author includes in the paragraph.
- Ask what idea or message the details convey about the topic.
- Write a sentence that states the idea or message in your own words.

Analyzing the Text

Cite Text Evidence   Support your responses with evidence from the selection.

1. **Analyze** An extended metaphor compares two unlike things at length and in a number of different ways. In the first four paragraphs, Blaeser provides an extended metaphor for rituals. To what does she compare rituals? Explain how the comparisons relate to the idea that rituals are connected and repeated.

2. **Identify Patterns** In lines 51–56, Blaeser uses repetition, or phrases that repeat the same pattern, to describe the annoyances she and the others ignored during their tribute. What is the purpose of this repetition?

3. **Connect** In line 81, Blaeser says, "With school began my double life." Explain how Blaeser has two lives. How do her two lives relate to her previous statement, "My memories entangle themselves oddly among the roots of several cultures"?

4. **Infer** What is the central idea that Blaeser develops in "Rituals of Memory"? Cite details from the text that helped you determine the central idea.

PERFORMANCE TASK

Speaking Activity: Response to Literature In her essay, Blaeser lists a few mementoes that are linked to memorable events in her life. What connections can you make between objects and memories? Share your reflections in a group discussion.

1. Collect two keepsakes or souvenirs that represent meaningful events from your life, events that you are willing to discuss. Make notes on how these objects serve as reminders and why the events are important to you.

2. Bring your notes to a group discussion along with your mementoes, if you can. If not, take a photograph or video recording of the objects to show. Share your objects, describe your events, and explain their significance.

Critical Vocabulary

innate	foremost	immerse	nullify	tangible

Practice and Apply Complete each phrase with your ideas about the Critical Vocabulary word. Share your work with a partner.

1. Weather conditions should be a **foremost** consideration when . . .

2. Her improved report card was **tangible** evidence that her extra study hours . . .

3. The sisters' bickering will **nullify** the efforts of their parents to . . .

4. Her **innate** creativity is revealed through . . .

5. 3D movies **immerse** the audience in the action by . . .

Vocabulary Strategy: Denotations and Connotations

A word may have different meanings. The literal definition of a word found in a dictionary is called the **denotation**. A **connotation** is what a word implies or suggests in addition to its literal meaning. This means that words with the same or similar denotations may have different connotations, or shades of meaning. A connotation may be positive or negative.

Kimberly Blaeser uses specific words to convey certain meanings. For example, the Critical Vocabulary word *immerse* (line 58) has a positive connotation and suggests that Blaeser's family and friends engaged themselves deeply in their tribute to their ancestors. However, notice how the connotation changes if you replace the word *immerse* with the word *involve*. The connotation of the word *involve* is also positive, but it suggests something less dedicated than *immerse*.

Practice and Apply Read each example from the text. Write an explanation of the connotation of the underlined word. Then, replace the underlined word with the word in parentheses, which has a similar denotation. Explain how the connotation of the new word changes the meaning of the sentence.

1. Line 9: "Perhaps the story <u>delights</u> me because it stands as a wonderful example of our always innocent attempts to explain the world." (intrigues)

2. Line 25: "My memories entangle themselves <u>oddly</u> among the roots of several cultures . . . ." (ridiculously)

3. Line 38: "We stood, moved to goose bumps by the lonely trumpet tune, <u>scrambling</u> with all the other children for spent casings when each ceremony was concluded." (pushing)

4. Line 91: "No one then <u>questioned</u> the necessity or value of our school education . . . ." (challenged)

Background *President **Abraham Lincoln** (1809–1865) is considered an American hero for preserving the Union and emancipating the slaves. He was a skillful politician, leader, and orator. One of his most famous speeches was delivered at the dedication of the National Cemetery at Gettysburg, Pennsylvania, in 1863, site of one of the most deadly battles of the Civil War. The victory for the Union forces marked a turning point in the Civil War, but losses on both sides at Gettysburg were staggering: 28,000 Confederate soldiers and 23,000 Union soldiers were killed or wounded. Lincoln was assassinated by John Wilkes Booth in 1865. Lincoln's dedication to the ideals of freedom and equality continue to inspire people around the world.*

The Gettysburg Address

Speech by Abraham Lincoln

AS YOU READ Pay attention to how Lincoln's speech emphasizes the importance of ending the Civil War and reuniting the country.

Four score and seven[1] years ago our fathers brought forth on this continent, a new nation, **conceived** in liberty, and dedicated to the proposition that all men are created equal.

Now we are engaged in a great civil war, testing whether that nation, or any nation so conceived and so dedicated, can long endure. We are met on a great battle field of that war. We have come to dedicate a portion of that field, as a final resting place for those who here gave their lives that that nation might live. It is altogether fitting and proper that we should do this.

But, in a larger sense, we cannot dedicate—we cannot consecrate[2]—we cannot hallow[3]—this ground. The brave men, living and dead, who struggled here have consecrated it, far above our poor power to add or **detract**. The world will little note, nor long remember what we say here, but it can never forget what they did here. It is for us, the living, rather, to be dedicated here to the

conceive
(kən-sēv´) *v.*
to form or develop in the mind; devise.

detract
(dĭ-trăkt´) *v.*
to take away from.

---

[1] **four score and seven:** eighty-seven.
[2] **consecrate:** to dedicate as sacred.
[3] **hallow:** define as holy.

unfinished work which they who fought here have thus far so nobly advanced. It is rather for us to be here dedicated to the great task remaining before us—that from these honored dead we take increased devotion to that cause for which they gave the last full
20 measure of devotion—that we here highly **resolve** that these dead shall not have died in vain—that this nation, under God, shall have a new birth of freedom—and that government of the people, by the people, for the people, shall not **perish** from the earth.

resolve
(rĭ-zŏlv´) *v.*
to decide or become determined.

perish
(pĕr´ĭsh) *v.*
to die or come to an end.

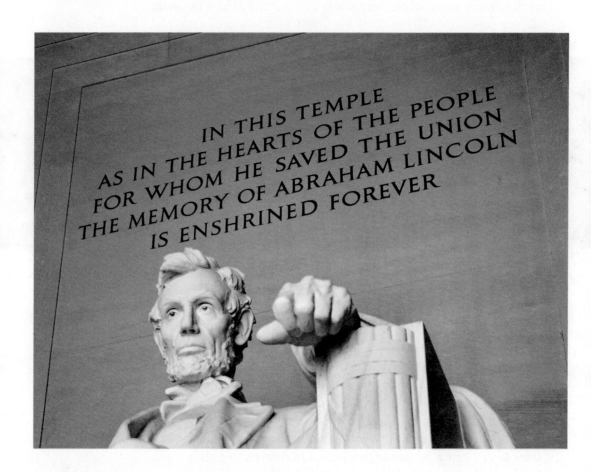

COLLABORATIVE DISCUSSION With a partner, discuss Lincoln's beliefs about the importance of reuniting the country. Cite specific evidence from the speech to support your ideas.

Analyze Seminal U.S. Documents

Speeches, essays, and other texts that have great historical and literary significance are called **seminal documents.** In the United States, the Gettysburg Address is a seminal document, as are George Washington's Farewell Address, Franklin D. Roosevelt's Four Freedoms Speech, and Martin Luther King Jr.'s "Letter from Birmingham Jail." As you analyze the speech, look for these characteristics that can help you recognize and analyze seminal documents:

Strong themes such as freedom, equality, strength, democracy

Concepts such as fairness, justice, respect, honor

Seminal Documents

Engaging ideas presented in an original way

Themes and concepts that encourage the audience to take action

Analyze Author's Purpose and Rhetoric

An author may write a speech for one or more reasons. These reasons are called the **author's purpose.** An author's purpose might be to inform or explain, to persuade, to express thoughts or feelings, or to entertain.

To help advance a purpose, an author will often use **rhetoric,** or the art of using specific words and language structures to make the message memorable. In the Gettysburg Address, Lincoln makes effective use of two rhetorical devices:

- **Repetition** is the use of the same word or words more than once. Repetition is used to emphasize key ideas.
- **Parallelism** is a form of repetition in which a grammatical pattern is repeated. Parallelism is used to create rhythm and evoke emotions.

Look at this example from President Ronald Reagan's Remarks at Moscow State University. Notice how he repeats the word *freedom* and uses parallelism to emphasize a key idea:

"The key is freedom—freedom of thought, freedom of information, freedom of communication."

As you analyze the Gettysburg Address, notice the repeated words and parallel clauses and phrases, such as *we are engaged, we are met, we have come.* Think about how Lincoln uses both repetition and parallelism to advance his purpose.

Analyzing the Text

Cite Text Evidence Support your responses with evidence from the selection.

1. **Analyze** Why did Lincoln write and deliver the Gettysburg Address? What were his two main purposes? Explain using evidence from the speech.

2. **Infer** What is "the unfinished work" of those who died (line 16)?

3. **Infer** What does Lincoln mean when he refers to "a new birth of freedom" (line 22)? Explain your response with evidence from the text.

4. **Identify Patterns** The word *dedicate* is repeated several times in the speech. What does *dedicate* mean? What idea does Lincoln emphasize with the repetition of this word?

5. **Identify Patterns** Identify two examples of parallelism in the speech. How does Lincoln use parallel structure to persuade the audience to accept his message?

6. **Draw Conclusions** Seminal U.S. documents often refer to themes and ideals that are important to the audience they address. What is the **theme,** or underlying message, of the Gettysburg Address? Are those themes still important today? Explain the underlying message and the American ideals that the speech upholds.

PERFORMANCE TASK

Speaking Activity: Informative Presentation The Gettysburg Address is one of the most famous speeches in U. S. history. Work in a small group to prepare an oral presentation of the speech. Follow these steps:

1. Reread the speech silently to yourself, making notes about pacing and emphasis. Pay particular attention to the effects of punctuation on your presentation.

2. In a small group, have a volunteer read the speech aloud. Discuss any questions about the meaning of the speech and the best way to present it. Summarize in writing points of agreement and disagreement, acknowledging that different people may want to emphasize different words or phrases in the speech.

3. Practice your speech with a partner. After each partner has delivered the speech, discuss what was effective in the performance. Use your summary to help guide your constructive criticism.

4. Use the feedback from your partner to deliver the speech to your class.

Critical Vocabulary

conceive   detract   resolve   perish

Practice and Apply Choose which Critical Vocabulary word is most closely associated with the underlined word or phrase in each sentence.

1. Additional details in a speech sometimes <u>take away from</u> the whole message.

2. A special election can be used to <u>decide</u> a tie in the vote for the student body president.

3. It takes a creative person <u>to form an idea</u> in his or her mind about an important issue and then convey that message to an audience.

4. Sometimes organizations such as clubs <u>come to an end</u> when the members are no longer interested.

Vocabulary Strategy: Multiple-Meaning Words

Words that have more than one definition are considered **multiple-meaning words.** To determine a word's appropriate meaning within a text, you need to look for context clues in the words, sentences, and paragraphs that surround it. Look at the word *fitting* in this sentence from the Gettysburg Address:

> **It is altogether <u>fitting</u> and proper that we should do this. (lines 8–9)**

The word *fitting* can mean "the act of trying on clothes" or "a small part for a machine." However, the word *proper* is a context clue that the tells you the correct meaning of *fitting* in this sentence is "appropriate."

Practice and Apply Find these multiple-meaning words in the speech: *engaged* (line 4), *testing* (line 4), *poor* (line 13), *measure* (line 20). Working with a partner, use context clues to determine each word's meaning as it is used in the speech.

1. Determine how the word functions in the sentence. Is it a noun, an adjective, a verb, or an adverb?

2. If the sentence does not provide enough information, read the paragraph in which the word appears and consider the larger context of the speech.

3. Write down your definition and the clues you used to determine the correct meaning of each word.

Language and Style: Parallel Structure

One grammatical feature that makes Abraham Lincoln's rhetoric so effective is his use of **parallel structure**, or the repetition of grammatical forms within a sentence. The repetition can occur at the word, phrase, or clause level. Lincoln uses parallel structure to express and connect ideas that are related or equal in importance and to create rhythm and evoke emotions. Consider these examples from the Gettysburg Address:

Type of Structure	Example from the Gettysburg Address
parallel words	living and dead (line 12)

Type of Structure	Example from the Gettysburg Address
parallel phrases	of the people, by the people, for the people (lines 22–23)

Type of Structure	Example from the Gettysburg Address
parallel clauses	we cannot dedicate—we cannot consecrate— we cannot hallow (lines 10–11)

Practice and Apply With a partner, look back at the Gettysburg Address and identify additional examples of parallel structure. Then imagine you were at Gettysburg on the day President Lincoln delivered his speech. Write a brief letter to Lincoln explaining how you were affected by his remarks. Use at least two examples of parallel structure in your letter. Exchange letters with a partner and discuss how effectively you each used parallel structure to communicate your message to Lincoln.

Background *The Vietnam Veterans Memorial was dedicated in 1982 to commemorate the 2.7 million military men and women who served in the conflict. There are approximately 58, 272 names inscribed on the wall in chronological order from the first death, injury, or missing-in-action date to the last. The polished black granite V-shaped wall was designed by Maya Lin and was intended to be a place of reflection and harmony without any political message.*

MEDIA

Views of the Wall
Photo Essay

The Vietnam Wall
Poem by Alberto Ríos

AS YOU VIEW AND READ Consider how both the photographs and the poem express the reactions of visitors to the Vietnam Veterans Memorial. Write down any questions you generate.

Views of the Wall
Photo Essay

The Vietnam Wall

Poem by Alberto Ríos

I
Have seen it
And I like it: The magic,
The way like cutting onions
5   It brings water out of nowhere.
Invisible from one side, a scar
Into the skin of the ground
From the other, a black winding
Appendix line.
10   A dig.
            An archaeologist can explain.
The walk is slow at first
Easy, a little black marble wall
Of a dollhouse,
15 A smoothness, a shine
The boys in the street want to give.
One name. And then more
Names, long lines, lines of names until
They are the shape of the U.N. building[1]
20 Taller than I am: I have walked
Into a grave.
And everything I expect has been taken away, like that, quick:
            The names are not alphabetized.
            They are in the order of dying.
25   An alphabet of—somewhere—screaming.
I start to walk out. I almost leave
But stop to look up names of friends,
My own name. There is somebody
Severiano Ríos.
30 Little kids do not make the same noise
Here, junior high school boys don't run
Or hold each other in headlocks.
No rules, something just persists
Like pinching on St. Patrick's Day
35 Every year for no green.
            No one knows why.

---

[1] **U. N. Building:** headquarters of the United Nations in New York City.

Flowers are forced
Into the cracks
Between sections.
40 Men have cried
At this wall.
I have
Seen them.

COLLABORATIVE DISCUSSION In a small group, discuss how the photographs and the poem depict visitors' reactions to the Vietnam Veterans Memorial. What details are emphasized in each? Use details from the photo essay and the poem to support your discussion.

Analyze Representations in Different Mediums

A subject, such as the Vietnam Veterans Memorial, can be represented in different **artistic mediums,** such as poems, stories, paintings, or photographs. Each artistic medium can emphasize certain aspects of the subject. For example, an author might emphasize an emotion evoked by the subject and give a personal, internal reaction. A visual artist, on the other hand, may show intricate, physical details of the subject that a writer might not be able to express. Rather than using words to describe people's emotions, an artist shows them using visual images. Analyzing how different mediums express the same or similar ideas can help you become a more critical reader and viewer.

Analyzing Text and Media

Cite Text Evidence Support your responses with evidence from the selections.

1. **Draw Conclusions** What is the central idea of both the photo essay and the poem? How is the subject matter related to the central idea that the photographs and the poem convey?

2. **Analyze** A **simile** makes a comparison between two unlike things, using the words *like* or *as*. Explain the simile Ríos uses in lines 3–4. Are the photographs in the photo essay able to show this kind comparison? Explain.

3. **Compare** What are the similarities and differences between presenting ideas in photographs versus a poem? What does each emphasize or leave out?

PERFORMANCE TASK

Media Activity: Reflection Choose between two mediums (Activity A or B) to express ideas about the value of war memorials.

A. Think about the ideas expressed in the poem and the photo essay. Draw a picture or paint a scene to express similar ideas. Then write a short description of the difference between what a painting or drawing can express as compared to photographs or a poem.

B. Work with a partner to produce a short video interviewing classmates and teachers about the memorial. Include a final scene in which you and your partner discuss the advantages and disadvantages of using film to capture emotions about the memorial.

Present a Speech

Recall the quotation from Kofi Annan that opened this collection: "We may have different religions, different languages, different colored skin, but we all belong to one human race." Do you think individuals can live together as "one human race"? Using evidence from the collection texts, you will present your ideas on this topic in a speech.

An effective speech

- has a clear, logical thesis statement supported by reasons and evidence
- includes an introduction, a logically structured body including connecting and transitional words, and a conclusion
- demonstrates appropriate and clear use of language
- uses suitable expression, volume, and pronunciation
- engages listeners through gestures and eye contact

PLAN

Analyze the Text Choose three texts from this collection, including "A Quilt of a Country," and identify what each author suggests about whether individuals can live together as members of "one human race." Look for examples of the difficulties that arise because of people's differences. Find examples of and details about whether these differences can be overcome. Use the annotation tools in your eBook to help you. Save each piece of evidence to *my*Notebook in a file titled *Collection 1 Performance Task A*.

ACADEMIC VOCABULARY

As you share your ideas about how individuals live together, be sure to use these words.

enforce
entity
internal
presume
resolve

myNotebook

"A Quilt of a Country"

"Many of the oft-told stories of the most pluralistic nation on earth are stories not of tolerance, but of bigotry."

With this sentence, Quindlen suggests that people from different cultures living together often have problems with intolerance.

Write a Thesis Statement Based on these texts and your own experience, write a thesis statement presenting your position on whether individuals can live as "one human race." For example, you might state that people can live together as one human race when they are united by a common purpose. Remember that you will need to provide sufficient evidence to support your thesis statement. Review the details you gathered in *my*Notebook to find evidence that supports your thesis statement.

Get Organized Organize your notes in an outline.

- Write your thesis statement about whether individuals can live as "one human race" in the introduction section of your outline.

- In the body section, list reasons and evidence that support your thesis statement.

- Summarize your main points in the concluding section.

PRODUCE

Write Your Speech Use your notes to write a clearly organized speech. Keep in mind the purpose of your speech and your audience. Remember to include

- quotations and examples from the texts and your own experience to support your thesis statement

- connecting and transitional words or phrases to link your ideas

- language choices appropriate for an oral presentation

- a variety of grammatical structures that will help keep your audience interested in your speech

Plan Your Presentation When you deliver your speech to an audience, use appropriate expression, volume, and gestures. Mark places in the text where you might want to

- adjust your volume to emphasize a word or phrase

- pause to give the audience time to consider an important idea

- use gestures to convey meaning or emotion

- make eye contact to engage your listeners

Interactive Lessons
To help you plan your speech, complete the following lesson:
- Writing Arguments: Support: Reasons and Evidence

Write your rough draft in *my*WriteSmart. Focus on getting your ideas down rather than perfecting your choice of language.

Interactive Lessons
To help you plan your presentation, complete the following lesson:
- Giving a Presentation: Knowing Your Audience

Have your partner or a group of peers review your draft in *my*WriteSmart. Ask your reviewers to note places where you should add emphasis or gestures when you deliver your speech.

Review Your Draft Use the following chart to revise your draft.

Questions	Tips	Revision Techniques
Does the introduction include a clear thesis statement?	**Highlight** the thesis statement.	**Clarify** your thesis statement so it clearly expresses your thoughts on the issue.
Does evidence from the text support the thesis?	**Underline** at least three examples of text evidence that support the thesis.	**Add** evidence from the text that supports your thesis.
Do connecting and transitional words or phrases link ideas throughout the speech?	**Highlight** connecting and transitional words or phrases that link ideas.	**Add** connecting and transitional words or phrases that link ideas.
Is the language used appropriate for the purpose and task?	**Underline** examples of formal language that is appropriate for a speech to your classmates.	**Revise** as needed, adapting language choices so that they are appropriate.
Does the conclusion summarize the main points?	**Highlight** the summary of your main points.	**Add** a summary of your main points to your conclusion.

Language and Style: Understand Cohesion

Look for places where you can use connecting and transitional words or phrases to increase cohesion. Read the following example from "The Gettysburg Address."

> **"** We have come to dedicate a portion of that field, as a final resting place. . . . But, in a larger sense, we cannot dedicate . . . this ground. **"**

Note how Lincoln uses the transition word *but* to suggest a contrast with his first statement. Using a transition in this way adds cohesion to Lincoln's speech.

Practice Your Delivery Before presenting to the class, practice with a partner.

Interactive Lessons
To help you deliver your presentation, complete the following lesson:
• Giving a Presentation: Delivering Your Presentation

- Mark your text to show where you will adjust your volume or use a gesture to emphasize a point.
- Use correct pronunciation so your audience understands you.
- Maintain appropriate eye contact to engage your audience.
- Allow your partner to give you feedback, and then make any changes to your speech before presenting to the whole class.

PERFORMANCE TASK A RUBRIC
SPEECH

	Ideas and Evidence	Organization	Language
4	• The introduction immediately engages the audience; the thesis statement clearly states the speaker's position. • Valid reasons and relevant evidence from the texts and from the speaker's experience strongly support the speaker's thesis statement. • The concluding section effectively summarizes the main points.	• The reasons and evidence are organized consistently and logically throughout the speech. • Varied connecting and transitional words and phrases link ideas and add cohesion.	• The speech reflects a formal style and an objective, or controlled, tone. • Sentence beginnings, lengths, and structures vary and have a rhythmic flow. • Grammar, usage, and mechanics are correct.
3	• The introduction could do more to capture the audience's attention; the speaker's thesis statement states a position. • Most reasons and evidence from the texts and from the speaker's experience support the speaker's thesis statement, but they could be more substantial. • The concluding section restates the main points.	• The organization of reasons and evidence is confusing in a few places. • Some connecting and transitional words and phrases are needed to link ideas and add cohesion.	• The style is informal in a few places, and the tone is defensive at times. • Sentence beginnings, lengths, and structures vary somewhat. • Some grammatical and usage errors are repeated in the speech.
2	• The introduction is ordinary; the speaker's thesis statement identifies an issue, but the position is not clearly stated. • The reasons and evidence from the texts and from the speaker's experience are not always logical or relevant. • The concluding section includes an incomplete summary of the main points.	• The organization of reasons and evidence is logical in some places, but it often doesn't follow a pattern. • Many more connecting and transitional words and phrases are needed to link ideas and add cohesion.	• The style becomes informal in many places, and the tone is often dismissive of other viewpoints. • Sentence structures barely vary, and some fragments or run-on sentences are evident. • Grammar and usage are incorrect in many places, but the speaker's ideas are still clear.
1	• The introduction is confusing. • Significant supporting reasons and evidence from the texts and from the speaker's experience are missing. • The concluding section is missing.	• A logical organization is not used; reasons and evidence are presented randomly. • Connecting and transitional words and phrases are not used, making the speech difficult to understand.	• The style is inappropriate, and the tone is disrespectful. • Repetitive sentence structure, fragments, and run-on sentences make the speech monotonous and hard to follow. • Many grammatical and usage errors change the meaning of the speaker's ideas.

Write an Analytical Essay

The texts in this collection focus on the tension between individuals and society. Look back at the anchor text "Once Upon a Time" and at the other texts you have read in this collection. You will discuss the ideas they present about an individual's role in society in an analytical essay.

An effective analytical essay

- clearly and accurately analyzes the texts
- provides quotations or examples to support main points
- has an introduction, a logically structured body including transitions, and a conclusion
- follows the conventions of written English

Mentor Text In this excerpt from "Rituals of Memory," note how the author uses a description of her friend Mary to illustrate her ideas about memory.

> " Memory begins with various wonders. For my friend Mary, it began with hair. Her hair grew tightly curled, so strong the spirals defied taming. Brushing and combing brought tears. When Mary tried to run her fingers through her hair as she saw others do, her fingers became hopelessly captured by the curls. "

myNotebook

Use the annotation tools in your eBook to locate evidence that supports your thesis statement. Save each piece of evidence to your notebook.

PLAN

Analyze the Text Choose three texts from this collection, including "Once Upon a Time," and analyze the ideas they convey about the individual's role in society.

- Take notes on the relationship between the individual and society presented in each text. Is the relationship agreeable, combative, or something else?
- What is the most important idea expressed in each text? Think about what this idea suggests about an individual's role in society.

Develop a Thesis Statement Once you have analyzed your chosen texts, you will need to develop a thesis statement. A thesis statement states your point of view on a subject. In this case, your thesis will express your ideas about the way an individual's role in society is presented in the texts you have read.

ACADEMIC VOCABULARY

As you share your ideas about the role of individuals in society, be sure to use these words.

> enforce
> entity
> internal
> presume
> resolve

Gather Evidence You will need to support your thesis by citing text evidence, including quotations and examples from the text. For literary texts, you might focus your analysis on the conflict the main character faces or on the theme of the work. For informational texts, analyze the writer's claim and the evidence that supports the claim.

Organize Your Essay Your essay should include an introduction, a body, and a conclusion.

- Your introduction should include your thesis statement and the titles and authors of the works you are discussing.

- The body of your essay should present evidence in support of your thesis. Each paragraph in the body of your essay should focus on a main point that supports your thesis.

- The conclusion summarizes the main points in your essay and includes an original insight.

Interactive Lessons
To help you plan your essay, complete the following lesson:
- Writing Informative Texts: Organizing Ideas

PRODUCE

Write a Draft Use your outline to write an analytical essay explaining how the authors express ideas about the individual and society. Remember to

- provide a clear and cohesive introduction, body, and conclusion

- support your main points with evidence from the text

- explain how the evidence supports your ideas

- use language that is appropriate for your audience

- connect related ideas within a paragraph by combining clauses

- include transitions to link the major sections of the text

As you draft your analytical essay, remember that this kind of writing requires formal language and a respectful tone. Essays that analyze texts are expected to be appropriate for an academic context.

my WriteSmart

Write your rough draft in *my*WriteSmart. Focus on getting your ideas down rather than perfecting your choice of language.

Interactive Lessons
To help you cite text evidence in your essay, complete the following lesson:
- Using Textual Evidence: Summarizing, Paraphrasing, and Quoting

Language and Style: Combine Ideas

Look for places where you can combine ideas to make connections between or join ideas. Read the following passage from Anna Quindlen's "A Quilt of a Country."

> " Today the citizens of the United States have come together once more because of armed conflict and enemy attack. "

In this example, Quindlen joins two ideas to explain the cause that leads the citizens of the United States to come together.

Review Your Draft Have your partner or group of peers review your draft. Use the following chart to revise your draft.

Questions	Tips	Revision Techniques
Does the introduction include a clear thesis statement?	**Underline** the thesis statement.	**Add** or **clarify** the thesis statement.
Are there quotations and examples to support the main points?	**Underline** quotations and **highlight** examples that support the main points.	**Add** quotations and examples to support the main points.
Are ideas combined effectively in the essay?	**Underline** sentences in which ideas are combined.	**Combine** two sentences to link ideas.
Do transitions link the major ideas in the text?	**Highlight** transitions used between paragraphs and key points.	**Add** transitional words or phrases or direct references between key points, if needed.
Is appropriate language and a respectful tone used throughout the essay?	**Highlight** instances of formal language and a respectful tone.	**Delete** instances where the language is informal and the tone is not respectful.
Does the conclusion summarize the main points of the essay?	**Highlight** the summary of the key points.	**Add** one or more sentences that summarize the key points of the essay.

Have your partner or a group of peers review your draft in *my*WriteSmart. Ask your reviewers to note any main points that are not adequately supported with text evidence.

Interactive Lessons
To help you revise your essay, complete the following lesson:
• Writing Informative Texts: Formal Style

Create a Finished Copy Once you have revised your draft, choose a way to share your analytical essay with your audience.

- Submit your essay to the school newspaper or literary magazine.
- If your class has a Web page, find out if you can post it there.
- Hold a meetup in the school library. You and your fellow students can exchange papers and discuss your views on the topic.

PERFORMANCE TASK B RUBRIC
ANALYTICAL ESSAY

	Ideas and Evidence	Organization	Language
4	• An eloquent introduction includes the titles and authors of the works; the thesis statement presents a unique idea about the texts. • Specific, relevant evidence from the texts supports the key points. • A satisfying concluding section synthesizes the ideas, summarizes the analysis, and offers a unique insight into the texts.	• Key points and supporting details are organized effectively and logically throughout the analysis. • Varied transitions successfully show the relationships between ideas.	• The analysis has an appropriately formal style and a knowledgeable, objective tone. • Language is precise and captures the writer's thoughts with originality. • Ideas are combined in a variety of ways. • Grammar and usage are correct.
3	• The introduction identifies the titles and authors of the works but could be more engaging; the thesis statement presents a clear idea about the texts. • One or two key points need more support. • The concluding section synthesizes most of the ideas and summarizes most of the analysis, but it doesn't provide an original insight.	• The organization of key points and supporting details is confusing in a few places. • A few more transitions are needed to clarify the relationships between ideas.	• The style becomes informal in a few places, and the tone does not always communicate confidence. • Most language is precise. • Many ideas are linked by combining sentences. • Some grammatical and usage errors are repeated in the analysis.
2	• The introduction identifies the titles and the authors of the works; the thesis statement only hints at the main idea of the analysis. • Details support some key points but are often too general. • The concluding section gives an incomplete summary of the analysis and restates the thesis statement.	• Most key points are organized logically, but many supporting details are out of place. • More transitions are needed throughout the analysis to connect ideas.	• The style is informal in many places, and the tone reflects a superficial understanding of the works. • Language is repetitive or vague at times. • Few sentences combine ideas. • Grammar and usage are incorrect in many places, but the writer's ideas are still clear.
1	• The appropriate elements of an introduction are missing. • Details and evidence are irrelevant or missing. • The analysis lacks a concluding section.	• A logical organization is not used; ideas are presented randomly. • Transitions are not used, making the analysis difficult to understand.	• The style and tone are inappropriate for the analysis. • Language is inaccurate, repetitive, and vague. • Ideas are not combined. • Many grammatical and usage errors change the meaning of the writer's ideas.

The Struggle for Freedom

❝If there is no struggle, there is no progress.❞

—Frederick Douglass

The Struggle for Freedom

From the American civil rights movement to the Middle East and Latin America, this collection explores the universal desire for freedom.

Stream to Start

hmhfyi.com

Channel One News®

ACADEMIC VOCABULARY

Study the words and their definitions in the chart below. You will use these words as you discuss and write about the texts in this collection.

Word	Definition	Related Forms
decline (dĭ-klīn´) v.	to fall apart or deteriorate slowly	declinable, decliner
enable (ĕ-nā´bəl) tr.v.	to give the means or opportunity	enabler
impose (ĭm-pōz´) v.	to bring about by force	imposer, imposition
integrate (ĭn´tĭ-grāt´) v.	to pull together into a whole; unify	integration, disintegrate
reveal (rĭ-vēl´) tr.v.	to show or make known	revealable, revealment

The March on Washington

I Have a Dream
Speech by Martin Luther King Jr.

from Nobody Turn Me Around: A History of the 1963 March on Washington
History Writing by Charles Euchner

MEDIA

AMERICA The Story of Us: March on Washington
Video by HISTORY®

Background *On August 28, 1963, thousands of Americans marched on Washington, D.C., to urge Congress to pass a civil rights bill. Martin Luther King Jr. delivered his "I Have a Dream" speech on the steps of the Lincoln Memorial before more than 250,000 people. After you read and analyze the speech, you will read an excerpt from a history text which describes the historic speech in detail and includes first-hand accounts from people who were on the National Mall that day. Then you will watch a short video about the march and compare the two accounts.*

Martin Luther King Jr. *(1929–1968) became a catalyst for social change in the 1950s and 1960s. Preaching a philosophy of nonviolence, he galvanized people of all races to participate in boycotts, marches, and demonstrations against racial injustice. His moral leadership stirred the conscience of the nation and helped bring about the passage of the Civil Rights Act of 1964. In that same year, he was awarded the Nobel Peace Prize. King continued his work for justice and equality until he was assassinated in 1968.*

I Have a Dream
Speech by Martin Luther King Jr.

AS YOU READ Note ways in which Dr. King uses words and phrases to inspire his audience. Write down any questions you have.

▤ myNotebook

As you read, mark up the text. Save your work to **myNotebook**.
- Highlight details.
- Add notes and questions.
- Add new words to **myWordList**.

I am happy to join with you today in what will go down in history as the greatest demonstration for freedom in the history of our nation.

Five score[1] years ago, a great American, in whose symbolic shadow we stand today, signed the Emancipation Proclamation.[2] This momentous decree came as a great beacon light of hope to millions of Negro slaves who had been seared in the flames of withering injustice. It came as a joyous daybreak to end the long night of their captivity.

10 But one hundred years later, the Negro still is not free; one hundred years later, the life of the Negro is still sadly crippled by the manacles of segregation and the chains of discrimination; one hundred years later, the Negro lives on a lonely island of poverty in the midst of a vast ocean of material prosperity; one hundred years later, the Negro is still languishing in the corners of American society and finds himself in exile in his own land.

So we've come here today to dramatize a shameful condition. In a sense we've come to our nation's capital to cash a check. When the architects of our republic wrote the magnificent words of the 20 Constitution and the Declaration of Independence, they were signing a promissory note[3] to which every American was to fall heir. This note was the promise that all men, yes, black men as well as white men, would be guaranteed the unalienable rights of life, liberty, and the pursuit of happiness.

It is obvious today that America has **defaulted** on this promissory note insofar as her citizens of color are concerned. Instead of honoring this sacred obligation, America has given the Negro people a bad check, a check which has come back marked "insufficient funds." But we refuse to believe that the bank of justice 30 is bankrupt. We refuse to believe that there are insufficient funds in the great vaults of opportunity of this nation. And so we've come to

default
(dĭ-fôlt´) *v.*
to fail to keep a promise to repay a loan.

---

[1] **five score:** 100; *score* means "twenty." (This phrasing recalls the beginning of Abraham Lincoln's Gettysburg Address: "Four score and seven years ago . . .")

[2] **Emancipation Proclamation:** a document signed by President Lincoln in 1863, during the Civil War, declaring that all slaves in states still at war with the Union were free.

[3] **promissory note:** a written promise to repay a loan.

cash this check, a check that will give us upon demand the riches of
freedom and the security of justice.

We have also come to this hallowed spot to remind America of
the fierce urgency of now. This is no time to engage in the luxury
of cooling off or to take the tranquilizing drug of gradualism. Now
is the time to make real the promises of democracy; now is the
time to rise from the dark and **desolate** valley of segregation to the
sunlit path of racial justice; now is the time to lift our nation from
the quicksands of racial injustice to the solid rock of brotherhood;
now is the time to make justice a reality for all of God's children.
It would be fatal for the nation to overlook the urgency of the
moment. This sweltering summer of the Negro's legitimate
discontent will not pass until there is an invigorating autumn of
freedom and equality.

Nineteen sixty-three is not an end, but a beginning. And those
who hope that the Negro needed to blow off steam and will now be
content will have a rude awakening if the nation returns to business
as usual. There will be neither rest nor tranquility in America until
the Negro is granted his citizenship rights. The whirlwinds of revolt
will continue to shake the foundations of our nation until the bright
day of justice emerges.

But there is something that I must say to my people, who stand
on the worn threshold which leads into the palace of justice. In
the process of gaining our rightful place, we must not be guilty of
wrongful deeds. Let us not seek to satisfy our thirst for freedom by
drinking from the cup of bitterness and hatred. We must forever
conduct our struggle on the high plain of dignity and discipline.
We must not allow our creative protests to **degenerate** into physical
violence. Again and again we must rise to the majestic heights
of meeting physical force with soul force. The marvelous new
militancy, which has engulfed the Negro community, must not lead
us to a distrust of all white people. For many of our white brothers,
as evidenced by their presence here today, have come to realize that
their destiny is tied up with our destiny. And they have come to
realize that their freedom is **inextricably** bound to our freedom. We
cannot walk alone. And as we walk, we must make the pledge that
we shall always march ahead. We cannot turn back.

There are those who are asking the devotees of civil rights,
"When will you be satisfied?" We can never be satisfied as long
as the Negro is the victim of the unspeakable horrors of police
brutality; we can never be satisfied as long as our bodies, heavy
with the fatigue of travel, cannot gain lodging in the motels of
the highways and the hotels of the cities; we cannot be satisfied
as long as the Negro's basic mobility is from a smaller ghetto to
a larger one; we can never be satisfied as long as our children are

desolate
(dĕs´ə-lĭt) *adj.*
unhappy; lonely.

degenerate
(dĭ-jĕn´ər-āt) *v.*
to decline morally.

inextricably
(ĭn-ĕk´strĭ-kə-blē)
adv. in a way
impossible to
untangle.

stripped of their selfhood and robbed of their dignity by signs stating For Whites Only; we cannot be satisfied as long as the Negro in Mississippi cannot vote and a Negro in New York believes he has nothing for which to vote. No! No, we are not satisfied, and we will not be satisfied until "justice rolls down like waters and righteousness like a mighty stream."

I am not unmindful that some of you have come here out of great trials and tribulations. Some of you have come fresh from narrow jail cells. Some of you have come from areas where your quest for freedom left you battered by the storms of persecution and staggered by the winds of police brutality. You have been the veterans of creative suffering. Continue to work with the faith that unearned suffering is **redemptive**. Go back to Mississippi. Go back to Alabama. Go back to South Carolina. Go back to Georgia. Go back to Louisiana. Go back to the slums and ghettos of our Northern cities, knowing that somehow this situation can and will be changed. Let us not wallow in the valley of despair.

redemptive
(rǐ-děmp′tǐv) *adj.* causing freedom or salvation.

I say to you today, my friends, even though we face the difficulties of today and tomorrow, I still have a dream. It is a dream deeply rooted in the American dream. I have a dream that one day this nation will rise up and live out the true meaning of its creed, "We hold these truths to be self-evident; that all men are created equal." I have a dream that one day on the red hills of Georgia, sons of former slaves and the sons of former slave owners will be able to sit down together at the table of brotherhood. I have a dream that one day even the state of Mississippi, a state sweltering with the heat of injustice, sweltering with the heat of oppression, will be transformed into an oasis of freedom and justice. I have a dream that my four little children will one day live in a nation where they will not be judged by the color of their skin, but by the content of their character.

I have a dream today!

I have a dream that one day down in Alabama—with its vicious racists, with its Governor having his lips dripping with the words of interposition and nullification[4]—one day right there in Alabama, little black boys and black girls will be able to join hands with little white boys and white girls as sisters and brothers.

I have a dream today!

I have a dream that one day every valley shall be exalted, and every hill and mountain shall be made low. The rough places will be plain and the crooked places will be made straight, "and

---

[4] **Governor . . . nullification:** Rejecting a federal order to desegregate the University of Alabama, Governor George Wallace claimed that the principle of nullification (a state's alleged right to refuse a federal law) allowed him to resist federal "interposition," or interference, in state affairs.

the glory of the Lord shall be revealed, and all flesh shall see it together."

120   This is our hope. This is the faith that I go back to the South with. With this faith we will be able to hew out of the mountain of despair a stone of hope. With this faith we will be able to transform the jangling discords of our nation into a beautiful symphony of brotherhood. With this faith we will be able to work together, to pray together, to struggle together, to go to jail together, to stand up for freedom together, knowing that we will be free one day. And this will be the day. This will be the day when all of God's children will be able to sing with new meaning, "My country 'tis of thee, sweet land of liberty, of thee I sing. Land where my fathers died,
130 land of the pilgrims' pride, from every mountainside, let freedom ring." And if America is to be a great nation, this must become true.

     So let freedom ring from the prodigious hilltops of New Hampshire; let freedom ring from the mighty mountains of New York; let freedom ring from the heightening Alleghenies of Pennsylvania; let freedom ring from the snowcapped Rockies of Colorado; let freedom ring from the curvaceous slopes of California. But not only that. Let freedom ring from Stone Mountain of Georgia; let freedom ring from Lookout Mountain of Tennessee; let freedom ring from every hill and molehill of
140 Mississippi. "From every mountainside, let freedom ring."

     And when this happens, and when we allow freedom to ring, when we let it ring from every village and every hamlet, from every state and every city, we will be able to speed up that day when all of God's children—black men and white men, Jews and Gentiles, Protestants and Catholics—will be able to join hands and sing in the words of the old Negro spiritual, "Free at last. Free at last. Thank God Almighty, we are free at last."

COLLABORATIVE DISCUSSION Which parts of the speech did you find the most inspiring? With a partner, discuss how King uses words and phrases to support his argument. Cite specific textual evidence from the speech in your discussion.

Analyze Author's Use of Rhetoric

To establish a point of view or purpose, authors and speakers like Martin Luther King Jr. use **rhetorical devices** to shape the structure of sentences and paragraphs within a work. Rhetorical devices can evoke an emotional response in an audience and make the message memorable. Here are some examples.

Repetition	Parallelism	Extended Metaphor
Uses the same word or words more than once for emphasis	Uses similar grammatical constructions to express ideas that are related or equal in importance. It often creates a rhythm.	Makes a comparison between two unlike things that continues at some length
"Let there be justice for all. Let there be peace for all. Let there be work, bread, water, and salt for all."	"We cannot, we must not, refuse to protect the right of every American to vote in every election. . . . And we ought not, and we cannot, and we must not wait another eight months before we get a bill."	"'A house divided against itself cannot stand.' I believe this government cannot endure permanently half slave and half free. I do not expect the Union to be dissolved; I do not expect the house to fall; but I do expect it will cease to be divided. It will become all one thing, or all the other.
—from "Glory and Hope" by Nelson Mandela	—from "We Shall Overcome" by Lyndon Baines Johnson	— from "A House Divided" by Abraham Lincoln

Analyze Seminal U.S. Documents

A **seminal U. S. document** is a document or speech from which a change in our nation's laws, society, or ideas about itself grew. Reading and analyzing important speeches like "I Have a Dream" is one of the best ways to understand our history and our national experience. To understand a speech's importance, you need to know something about its background, or **historical context.** Asking questions will help you understand its context better. To answer some of these questions, you may need to research information about the speaker and the events and attitudes of the day.

- Who is the speaker?
- Who was the audience?
- When and where was the speech presented?
- What was the purpose of the speech?
- How did the speech contribute to our national experience?

Analyzing the Text

Cite Text Evidence   Support your responses with evidence from the selection.

1. **Infer** The central point of an **argument** is the **claim,** or proposition. What is King's claim in this speech? What evidence does he cite to support his claim?

2. **Analyze** How does King structure, or organize, his speech? Explain how each section integrates his ideas and advances his argument.

3. **Interpret** An **allusion** is an indirect reference to something that the audience is expected to know. In his speech, King makes more than one allusion to the Declaration of Independence. Identify the allusions and explain how they advance King's argument.

4. **Interpret** King uses an extended metaphor to compare a familiar object—a bad check—to an abstract idea. How does King develop the metaphor? What does he believe was promised to African Americans? How has America given African Americans a "bad check?"

5. **Analyze** Find examples of parallelism in lines 36–41. What effect does the parallel structure create? What point is King emphasizing?

6. **Analyze** Identify two examples of repetition in the speech. Explain why these words or phrases are important and how they advance King's argument.

7. **Evaluate** Why do you think King's "I Have a Dream" speech is remembered as one of the most significant speeches in American history? Explain what makes the speech memorable and how it contributes to the ideal of an American society.

PERFORMANCE TASK

Writing Activity: Analysis In Collection 1, you read another seminal United States speech, Abraham Lincoln's Gettysburg Address. Compare the ideas in Lincoln's speech to "I Have a Dream." Write a one- to two-page analytical essay in which you compare how Lincoln and King address the theme of freedom.

1. Identify each speaker's purpose.

2. Evaluate how the idea of freedom is articulated in each speech.

3. Give examples of how each speaker uses rhetorical devices to achieve his purpose.

4. Use the conventions of standard English.

Critical Vocabulary

default   desolate   degenerate   inextricably   redemptive

Practice and Apply Answer the following questions in complete sentences, incorporating the Critical Vocabulary words and their meanings.

1. Look back at line 25. Why does King say that America has **defaulted,** and what makes this word choice especially effective?

2. Look back at line 38. In what ways is segregation **desolate**? How might referring to segregation as **desolate** help persuade listeners?

3. Look back at line 59. How is physical violence a good example of how protests might **degenerate**? How does this reflect King's views?

4. Look back at line 66. How is the freedom of white people **inextricably** bound to that of black people?

5. Look back at line 89. How and why does King use the word **redemptive** to link the concepts of freedom and religious faith?

Language and Style: Repetition and Parallelism

One grammatical feature that makes King's rhetoric so effective is his use of **repetition** and **parallelism**—expressing related ideas using similar grammatical constructions. By creating a pattern through repeated phrases and structures, King both creates a strong rhythm in his speech and links his ideas in listeners' minds. Here are some examples from "I Have a Dream":

Repetition

> We can never be satisfied as long as the Negro is the victim of the unspeakable horrors of police brutality; we can never be satisfied as long as our bodies, heavy with the fatigue of travel, cannot gain lodging in the motels of the highways and the hotels of the cities; . . .

Parallelism

> ". . . we will be able to work together, to pray together, to struggle together, to go to jail together, to stand up for freedom together . . ."

Practice and Apply Look back at the essay you wrote for this selection's Performance Task. Find two places where you can revise your wording to make it parallel. Then, locate two places where you can use repetition for effect. Finally, write two sentences explaining how repetition and parallel structure helped you communicate your ideas to readers.

Background *This excerpt from* Nobody Turn Me Around: A People's History of the 1963 March on Washington *provides a detailed account of one of the most iconic days in American history.*

from **Nobody Turn Me Around: A People's History of the 1963 March on Washington**
History Writing by Charles Euchner

AS YOU READ Note how the author structures the text to help you visualize the event. Write down any questions you generate.

Always, he begins slowly, like thunder rolling from a distance before a great storm.

Martin Luther King speaks deliberately, like a 45 rpm record being played at 33⅓ rpm speed.[1] His long, thick, baritone words stretch out to establish a new mood. In a low drawl, he emphasizes syllables to create his own **cadence,** to bring his audience into the flow of emotions.

"I am *happy* to *join* with you to*day*," he says, sounding mournful, "in what will go *down* in *his*tory as the *great*est
10 *demon*stration for *free*dom in the *his*tory of our *nat*ion."

Martin Luther King invokes Abraham Lincoln and tells the long, hard story of the subjection of American blacks.

"Five score years ago, a great American, in whose symbolic shadow we stand today, signed the Emancipation Proclamation. This momentous decree came as a great beacon light of hope to millions of Negro slaves who had been seared in the flames of withering injustice. It came as a joyous daybreak to end the long night of their captivity."

King's Southern accent, softened by time spent in his family's
20 bourgeois circles[2] and tempered by years in the North, put a special emphasis on his words: "in the *his-tor-eh* of our *ow-a* nation" . . . "a *gret* American" . . . "symbolic *shadda*" . . . "*gret beckon* light."

Long night of captivity. King's brooding voice tells two **parallel** stories of exile and return. For hundreds of years, Jews were held in captivity, as slaves, in Egypt—like blacks in America. They struggled to maintain their own identity—like blacks in America. They endured because of their faith in God—like blacks in

cadence
(kād´ns) *n.* lyrical rhythm.

parallel
(păr´ə-lĕl´) *adj.* related; corresponding.

---

[1] **45 rpm record . . . 33 ½ speed:** a recorded disc, designed to spin on a turntable at 45 revolutions per minute, playing at a slower speed (33 ½ rpm), which produces a deeper, drawn-out sound.

[2] **bourgeois circles (bŏŏr-zhwa´):** middle-class group of friends.

America. And then one day, they freed themselves from bondage—
like blacks will, one day, as well.

His voice is steady, but King wants to find his pacing. If he
moves slowly, he will not falter, and he will find a way to bring the
crowd with him.

Right away, King uses anaphora, the repetition of key words
and phrases at the beginning of successive statements. Repetition
brings the listener back to a familiar place, then connects to a
new thought or image. Repetition keeps the audience involved.
Repetition makes it easy to remember the words and to get into a
rhythm, as they become familiar. Repetition invites the call and
response in black churches across the South. *Yeah! Uh-huh! Amen!*
That's right!

After recalling the story of Lincoln freeing the slaves, with the
simple stroke of a pen in the middle of a bloody war, King laments
the inferior position of blacks a century later. Each mournful
repetition deepens the pain, raises the dramatic tension. Each
repetition condemns the oppressor. The oration becomes poetry:

> But one hundred years later, the Negro still is not free.
> One hundred years later, the life of the Negro is still
>   sadly crippled by the manacles of segregation and
>   the chains of discrimination.
> One hundred years later, the Negro lives on a lonely
>   island of poverty in the midst of a vast ocean of
>   material prosperity.
> One hundred years later, the Negro is still languished
>   in the corners of American society and finds
>   himself in exile in his own country.

King looks down at his text, shakes his head as he speaks. He
rocks back and forth on the balls of his feet as he finds his rhythm.

Every **invocation** of "one hundred years" emphasizes the
horrors of the black's position in American life. *Not free. Crippled.*
Manacles. Chains. Lonely island of poverty. Languished in the
corners. Exile in his own country.

And then King introduces Clarence Jones's[3] metaphor of the
bad check, so simple and so basic. A bad check represents bad faith,
failed promises, broken contracts.

> In a sense we have come to our nation's capital to cash
>   a check. When the architects of our republic wrote
>   the magnificent words of the Constitution and the

invocation
(ĭn'və-kā'shən) *n.* a
formal appeal, often
used in prayer.

---

[3] **Clarence Jones:** (b. 1931) King's attorney and advisor, who helped prepare many
speeches.

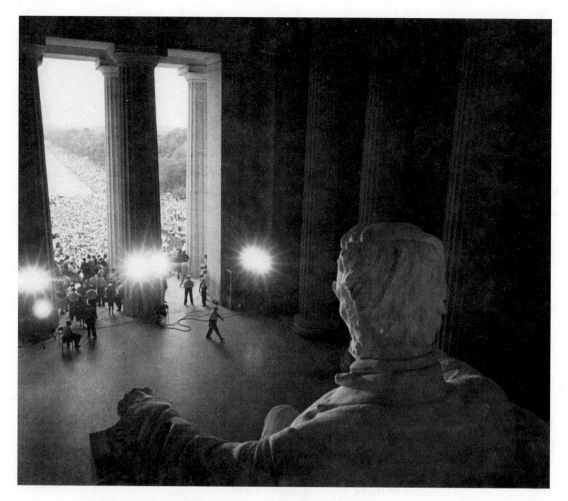

Declaration of Independence, they were signing a
promissory note to which every American was to
fall heir. This note was a promise that all men—
yes, black men as well as white men—would be
guaranteed the unalienable rights of life, liberty, and
the pursuit of happiness.

It is obvious today that America has defaulted on this
promissory note insofar as her citizens of color
are concerned. Instead of honoring this sacred
obligation, America has given the Negro people a
bad check, a check which has come back marked
"insufficient funds."

The first burst of applauses rises up from the crowd.

"But we *refuse* to believe that the bank of justice is bankrupt.
We *refuse* to believe that there are insufficient funds in the great
vaults of opportunity of this nation."

Laughter from the crowd. Shouts: "Uh huh!" "Yeah!" "Sure enough!"

"So we have come to cash this check—a check that will give us upon demand the riches of freedom and the security of justice."

A second, greater burst of applause.

Now King honors his country, calling attention to the **civic** power of Lincoln's monument. He rejects calls to "go slow" and "cool off."

"We have also come to this hallowed spot to remind America of *the fierce urgency of now*. This is no time to engage in the luxury of cooling off or to take the tranquilizing drug of gradualism."

The crowd ripples with recognition, then knowing laughter. A thin black man sitting close to the stage hears the tranquilizer reference, looks down for a moment, thoughtfully, then looks up and explodes in laughter. King's line releases some toxin from the body.

For this one moment, the stubbornness of racism lifts and the people revel in a moment of integrated community.

> Now is the time to make real the promises of
> democracy.
> Now is the time to rise from the dark and desolate
> valley of segregation to the sunlit path of racial
> justice.
> Now is the time to lift our nation from the quicksands
> of racial injustice to the solid rock of brotherhood.
> Now is the time to make justice a reality for all of
> God's children.

Each invocation pulls the audience into the future. And people in the crowd respond. *You got it! Yes it is! Yeah! Amen! Now is the time! Now! That's right!*

Across the Mall, people have quieted down. King's voice echoes, his baritone voice triumphing over the tinny sounds of the loudspeakers. Whispers can be heard in spots. A soft breeze, occasionally rippling over the crowd, is louder than the sounds of the masses below.

King now warns the Washington establishment—and the vast middle class, what one politician would call the "forgotten middle class" and the "silent majority"—that gradual improvements will not satisfy blacks anymore. Conflict could turn into a bloodbath unless the American people redeem the promise of freedom.

> It would be fatal for the nation to overlook
> the urgency of the moment.

This sweltering summer of the Negro's legitimate
discontent will not pass until there is an
invigorating autumn of freedom and equality.
Nineteen sixty-three is not an end, but a beginning.
130   Those who hope that the Negro needed to blow off
steam and will now be content will have a rude
awakening if the nation returns to business as usual.
There will be neither rest nor tranquility in America
until the Negro is granted his citizenship rights.
The whirlwinds of revolt will continue to shake the
foundations of our nation until the bright day of
justice emerges.

Subtly, King conjures images of apocalypse. The "whirlwinds
of revolt" echo the countless moments where the Bible talks about
140 staggering catastrophe, when evil brings forth flood, famine,
drought, a plague of locusts, and the chaos of the Tower of Babel.[4]
As Jeremiah (4:20) teaches: "Disaster on disaster is proclaimed / For
the whole land is devastated."

> **For this one moment, the stubbornness of racism lifts and the people revel in a moment of integrated community.**

King warns his people to maintain their own dignity, to avoid
the temptation to embrace bitterness or violence. He speaks to the
followers of Malcolm X, who offers a simpler, purer, solution—
fighting back, by any means necessary.[5]

---

[4] **Tower of Babel:** according to the bible, a tall structure built when people all
spoke the same language. God disrupted the work by so confusing the language
of the workers they could no longer work together.

[5] **Malcolm X...necessary:** (1925–1965) African American activist who believed
that people should demand and protect their human rights in any way they can.

"But there is something that I must say to my people who stand on the warm threshold which leads into the palace of justice. In the process of gaining our rightful place, we must not be guilty of wrongful deeds.

"Let us not seek to satisfy our thirst for freedom by drinking from the cup of bitterness and hatred."

O Lord! Amen! Yes! Sure enough!

"We must forever conduct our struggle on the high plane of dignity and discipline. We must not allow our creative protest to degenerate into physical violence. Again and again, we must rise to the majestic heights of meeting physical force with soul force.

"The marvelous new militancy which has engulfed the Negro community must not lead us to a distrust of all white people, for many of our white brothers, as evidenced by their presence here today, have come to realize"—his voice rises—"that their destiny is tied up with our destiny."

Marvelous militancy. All summer, critics of the civil rights movement have wondered why blacks cannot be more patient. The president, congressmen, newspaper publishers, TV commentators, professors, mayors, unions, corporate CEOs, churches, social organizations—everyone seemed to be saying to go slow. But the time for patience is over. Militancy—*marvelous militancy,* borne of great patience and suffering, expressed with love, and applied with the tools of nonviolence—is now the movement's watchword.

Cheers rise up, louder and more sustained than before. People smile.

"They have come to realize that their freedom is inextricably bound to our freedom. We cannot walk alone.

"As we walk, we must make the pledge that we shall always march ahead. We cannot turn back. There are those who are asking the devotees of civil rights, 'When will you be satisfied?'"

Not everyone could hear King's words. The sound system, the best available, still crackled and blanked out. Far from the Lincoln Memorial, people followed the words on transistor radios—and by watching the movement of bodies ahead. "Down near the front there were people jumping up, waving hands and flags and signs," Elsa Rael said. "We were a little out of it, so we had to make our own joy—so we were singing. We got small bursts of words from King and shut up."

We can never be satisfied as long as the Negro is the victim of the unspeakable horrors of police brutality.

190 We can never be satisfied, as long as our bodies, heavy
with the fatigue of travel, cannot gain lodging in the
motels of the highways and the hotels of the cities.
We cannot be satisfied as long as the Negro's basic
mobility is from a smaller ghetto to a larger one.
We can never be satisfied as long as our children
are stripped of their selfhood and robbed of their
dignity by signs stating "For Whites Only."
We cannot be satisfied as long as a Negro in
Mississippi cannot vote and a Negro in New York
200 believes he has nothing for which to vote.
No, no, we are not satisfied, and we will not be
satisfied until justice rolls down like waters and
righteousness like a mighty stream.

With each line, King increases the stakes for his movement. He
begins with police brutality, the search for night lodging and food,
and life in the ghetto. He moves on to children's dignity and the
right to vote. He ends with the prophet Amos's great image of the
Kingdom of Heaven on earth.

Each round gets cheers. First scattered clapping and cheers and
210 calls. *Yes!* Then more. *That's right!* Finally, huge applause. *My Lord!*

Every good preacher—every good leader—connects with the
real circumstances of his audience's lives. *I know your pain. I have
shared in your pain. I have been beaten and jailed and **reviled**. I have
not forgotten how you have suffered. I know, so you can trust me.*
King has spent a decade learning about the problems of the people
assembled before him. He has worked, intimately, with people at
the highest and lowest levels of society.

revile
(rĭ-vīl´) *v.* to
condemn or insult.

I am not unmindful that some of you have come here
out of great trials and tribulations.
220 Some of you have come fresh from narrow jail cells.
Some of you have come from areas where your quest
for freedom left you battered by the storms of
persecution and staggered by the winds of police
brutality.
You have been the veterans of creative suffering.
Continue to work with the faith that unearned
suffering is redemptive.

That brief phrase—*unearned suffering is redemptive*—strikes
Harold Bragg "like an electric shock."
230 Harold and his wife, Lynn, traveled all night from Kent, Ohio,
in their VW Beetle. Harold sits on a stool, holding an umbrella over

Lynn's head to block the sun. For the first part of King's speech,
they listen to King "like it was a lesson from a great master."

Now the idea of suffering for redemption surges through Harold's
body. He remembers his father telling him about his grandfather—
one of the few black landowners in Alabama—sitting on a horse,
getting shot by a white farmer who was jealous that a colored man
could command such an **expanse**. His father, five years old when this
happened back in 1917, saw his father fall dead off the horse.

240   The lesson his father and mother passed on when he told their
children that story was: "You return hatred with love."

King's whole speech has told of the hard, violent, brutal, unfair,
unjust life of blacks in America. The wrong people have suffered.
So many people have been teargassed, beaten, kicked, burned,
bombed, shot.

expanse
(ĭk-spăns´) *n.* a large
area.

But that suffering—like Christ's suffering on the cross—can bring a better day. That suffering can change people's hearts. That suffering can clear poison from the system.

Then change can come.

250 *Unearned suffering is redemptive.* Believe it, and you will fight on—with Martin. Disbelieve it, and you will be gripped by despair—or the combative, uncompromising, separatist jingoism of Malcolm.[6]

For now, the crowd stands with King. Even the separatists stand with King, now.

For that redemption to happen—to change the world—people need to return to their homes to fight and suffer, still more, for the cause of justice. So:

> Go back to Mississippi,
> go back to Alabama,
260 > go back to South Carolina,
> go back to Georgia,
> go back to Louisiana,
> go back to the slums and ghettos of our northern
>   cities,
> knowing that somehow this situation can and will be
>   changed. Let us not wallow in the valley of despair,
> I say to you today, my friends.

Just feet from King, Mahalia Jackson[7] calls out. Mahalia is an old family friend of the Kings. She has been a guest in the Kings' 270 house. She was with King in Detroit about a month ago when King talked about a dream.

"Tell them about the dream, Martin!" she shouts. "*Please* . . . tell them about the dream!"

King does not hear her, but he doesn't need to hear her. He already knows he's going to talk about the dream. He shouted out his dream last night, in his hotel room, after everyone else went to bed.

Clarence Jones, sitting about fifteen feet away, sees King grab the podium, lean back, and turn over his prepared text. "These 280 people don't know it," Jones says, "but they are about to go to *church.*"

> So even though we face the difficulties of today and
>   tomorrow, I still have a dream.
> It is a dream deeply rooted in the American Dream . . . .

---

[6] **separatist jingoism of Malcolm:** Malcolm X's belief that African Americans should develop and support their own social institutions and communities.

[7] **Mahalia Jackson:** (1911–1972) a leading African American singer of gospel music who became very active in the civil-rights movement.

I have a dream that one day this nation will rise up
and live out the true meaning of its creed: "We
hold these truths to be self-evident: that all men are
created equal."
I have a dream that one day on the red hills of Georgia
290   the sons of former slaves and the sons of former
slave owners will be able to sit down together at the
table of brotherhood.
I have a dream that one day even the state of
Mississippi, a state sweltering with the heat of
injustice, sweltering with the heat of oppression, will
be transformed into an oasis of freedom and justice.

Richard Pritchard, a skinny white preacher from Wisconsin
who returned to the United States from Africa just last night, sits
by the reflecting pool. When his wife told him about the march, he
300 jumped into a car at his family's home in New Jersey. All day he's
been jet-lagged and weary from his early morning drive.

But now, lightning shoots through his body as he hears about
the dream. He remembers—*feels*—his own dream, which called
him to the ministry decades before.

Pritchard became a minister because he believed God saved
him as a small child, when he spent three years in the hospital

"Talk about the dream transforms time and space."

with tuberculosis. And then, as a young priest, he saw racism in God's own flock. White priests wouldn't take assignments in black churches—and so he decided to become the pastor of a black parish in Kansas City. Later, at a different church, members of his own parish made racist statements. Didn't they understand that God loved blacks as much as whites?

"My dream was to make Christ more realistic," he says. "I used to talk about it—*my dream*. When I was a kid I used to hear how the English talked about the Welsh as savages in the hills, and that's what they were saying about blacks. I could feel how blacks would feel. In Christ there is no Jew or Greek, slave or free, male or female. We are all free in Christ."

So skinny you can see his bones, the Reverend Pritchard dangles his feet in the water. He is being baptized anew. King's dream is his dream. The image almost removes him from the throng, and at the same time connects him even more with the throng.

"It's funny, it hit me with such force."

> I have a dream that my four little children will one
>> day live in a nation where they will not be judged
>> by the color of their skin but by the content of their
>> character.
> I have a dream today.
> I have a dream that one day, down in Alabama, with
>> its vicious racists, with its governor having his
>> lips dripping with the words of interposition and
>> nullification; one day right there in Alabama, little
>> black boys and black girls will be able to join hands
>> with little white boys and white girls as sisters and
>> brothers.
> I have a dream today.
> I have a dream that one day every valley shall be
>> exalted, every hill and mountain shall be made
>> low, the rough places will be made plain, and the
>> crooked places, will be made straight, and the glory
>> of the Lord shall be revealed, and all flesh shall see
>> it together.

Talk about the dream transforms time and space. What might come to pass, later, seems at hand, *now*. With faith, ideals can be more real than the pain or poverty of the here and now.

Sitting on a patch of grass far from the Lincoln Memorial, sipping cold drinks from thermoses, Ruth bat Mordecai and some

kids from a New York-based American Jewish Congress youth
group listen to Martin Luther King's dream.

As King gives voice to his dream, Ruth watches some black
boys nearby. The boys laugh as King's voice climbs the ladder,
higher and higher. They laugh so freely that their bodies shake.
Ruth knows the crowd includes cynics, and she resents having her
experience of King's dream ruined by *these ones*. How can you
openly mock *Dr. King*—at an event like *this*? And nobody seems to
care!

"Suddenly," she recalls, "we understand. The black boys are
laughing not in mockery but in joy—at the utter preposterousness
of what Dr. King promises, and at its unutterable beauty."

Across the Mall, people call out the lines to each other.

"I have a dream," one says,

"That *one* day, little black boys and black girls . . ." says another.
"I have a *dream!*" someone else says.

"*Dowwwn* in Alabama . . ." comes the response.

Strangers shout out: "I have a *dream!*"

Tears fill Harold Bragg's eyes. "It's like being before the pearly
gates, as though we had reached the Promised Land," he says, "even
though King was laying out what was *to come.*"

With this dream, King brings his audience into a separate
world, a distant, far-off place, but still so familiar. What is unreal is
also very real.

Then King moves to sustain his people for the hard journey
ahead. He reminds the crowd that they need faith—stronger than
any troubles of the moment—to realize the dream.

> This is our hope. This is the faith that I go back to the
>   South with.
> With this faith we will be able to hew out of the
>   mountain of despair a stone of hope.
> With this faith we will be able to transform the
>   jangling discords of our nation into a beautiful
>   symphony of brotherhood.
> With this faith we will be able to work together, to pray
>   together, to struggle together, to go to jail together,
>   to stand up for freedom together, knowing that we
>   will be free one day.

King connects simple statements, repeated again and
again—"One hundred years later," "Now is the time," "We cannot
be satisfied," "Go back," "I have a dream," "With this faith"—to
America's true national anthem.

"This will be the day," he says, "when all of God's children will be able to sing with a new meaning, 'My country, 'tis of thee, sweet land of *liberty,* of *thee* I sing. Land where my *fathers* died, land of the *pilgrim's* pride, from *every* mountainside, *let freedom ring.*' And if America is to be a great nation this *must* become true."

If . . .

Then, full of the passion of the words of that simple anthem, King imagines freedom ringing—a dreamlike image—and **exhorts** the crowd to make this vision happen. He sings out lines full of
400 sounds and sights—postcards from the American Dream.

> So let freedom ring from the prodigious hilltops of
>   New Hampshire.
> Let freedom ring from the mighty mountains of New
>   York.
> Let freedom ring from the heightening Alleghenies of
>   Pennsylvania!
> Let freedom ring from the snowcapped Rockies of
>   Colorado!
> Let freedom ring from the curvaceous slopes of
410   California!

All of these are Northern places, and their images are ones of pure beauty. But that's not enough, King now **invokes** the sites of repression across the South.

> But not only that.
> Let freedom ring from Stone Mountain of Georgia!
> Let freedom ring from Lookout Mountain of
>   Tennessee!
> Let freedom ring from every hill and molehill of
>   Mississippi!
420 From every mountainside,
> let freedom ring!

Those lines come from one of King's old friends, a preacher from Chicago named Archibald Carey. In a speech at the 1952 Republican Convention, Carey sang "My Country, 'Tis of Thee" and cried "Let freedom ring!" and issued some of those same postcards.

Finally, dizzy from the view of a nation teeming with freedom, King offers the moment of deliverance.

He sways now. He lifts his whole body with the speech. The
430 people in the crowd follow their King. They sway, they smile, and they laugh with anticipation of every new image.

exhort
(ĭg-zôrt´) *v.* to strongly urge or encourage.

invoke
(ĭn-vōk´) *v.* to refer or call attention to.

And when this happens,
when we allow freedom to ring,
when we let it *ring* from every village and every
    hamlet,
from *every* state and *every* city,
we will be able to speed up that day when all of God's
    children,
black men and *white* men,
Jews and *Gentiles*,
Protestants and *Catholics*—

Martin Luther King turns to his right and raises his right arm high, his elbow bent slightly, blessing the congregation at this great mass.

"—will be able to join hands and sing in the *words* of the old Negro spiritual, "Free at *last*! Free at *last*! Thank God *Almighty*, we are *free at last*!"

COLLABORATIVE DISCUSSION With a partner, discuss how the writer structures his account of the March on Washington. Cite specific details and examples from the text.

Analyze Ideas and Events

To show connections between ideas, authors structure a text so that each sentence and paragraph supports and develops a central idea. In recounting a historical event, authors usually provide readers with details and support for the central idea such as:

- a factual account of the event
- background information
- quotations and anecdotes, or personal stories, from eyewitnesses

Charles Euchner's approach is unusual because he goes beyond what we usually see in a history text to offer his own detailed analysis of the text of Martin Luther King Jr.'s "I Have a Dream" speech. For example, in lines 62–64, Euchner analyzes King's extended metaphor of the bad check.

> **And then King introduces Clarence Jones's metaphor of the bad check, so simple and so basic. A bad check represents bad faith, failed promises, broken contracts.**

Euchner then goes on to quote from King's speech and includes details of how the audience responds to the metaphor. This structure of support enables Euchner's readers to visualize the actual effect of the speech as it was delivered. This type of idea development throughout the history text shapes and refines the central idea. Think about the other kinds of support Euchner uses in his account. How do the details he includes relate to his analysis of the speech?

Analyzing the Text

Cite Text Evidence   Support your responses with evidence from the selection.

1. **Analyze** Briefly describe the text structure Euchner uses in his account. How does he organize the text so that each idea is connected and developed? Cite specific examples to support your response.

2. **Analyze** Notice that Euchner uses present-tense verbs in his account. In what verb tense is historical text usually written? What effect does using present-tense verbs create? Cite specific examples to support your response.

3. **Infer** Describe the eyewitness accounts and anecdotes Euchner includes. Why do you think he chose these witnesses? What inference about the crowd can you make based on the witnesses he includes?

4. **Evaluate** Euchner provides background information on historic events and biblical allusions included in "I Have a Dream." Identify one example and explain how it helped you better understand the speech.

Critical Vocabulary

cadence	parallel	invocation	civic
revile	expanse	exhort	invoke

Practice and Apply Explain which Critical Vocabulary word is most closely associated with the underlined word.

1. Which word goes with town? Why?

2. Which word goes with convince? Why?

3. Which word goes with similar? Why?

4. Which word goes with distance? Why?

5. Which word goes with dislike? Why

6. Which word goes with point out? Why?

7. Which word goes with prayer? Why?

8. Which word goes with music? Why?

Vocabulary Strategy: Words from Greek and Latin

Studying the **etymology** of words means that you look at the historical development of words and determine their basic elements. Many words in the English language come from Greek and Latin roots. Knowing the meaning of **roots,** or basic word elements, can help you determine the meaning of unfamiliar words. For example, the Critical Vocabulary word *civic* contains the Latin root *civ-* that means "citizen." Another example is contained in the word *parallel*. This word contains the Greek root *par(a)* that means "beside, near." Knowing the meanings of *civ-* and *par(a)* can help you determine the meanings of other words with the same roots.

Practice and Apply Look up these words from the selection in a dictionary. Write the meaning of the Latin or Greek root word, and then write a sentence using another word with that same root.

Word	Root	Word	Root
audience (line 6)	*audi-*	**liberty** (line 72)	*lib-*
symbolic (line 13)	*sym-*	**bankrupt** (line 81)	*rupt-*
capital (line 65)	*cap-*	**politician** (line 120)	*poli-*

MEDIA

AMERICA The Story of Us:
March on Washington

Video by HISTORY®

AS YOU VIEW Identify similarities and differences between the history text and the video. Write down any questions you generate as you watch the video.

COLLABORATIVE DISCUSSION With a partner, discuss the similarities and differences in the history text and the video, supporting your ideas with evidence from both.

Analyze Accounts in Different Mediums

Factual information about historic events can be presented in a variety of ways, including written histories and short documentary videos. Each **medium** has particular strengths and weaknesses, and imposes different structures. For example, a short documentary video is under time limitations that require the producer to carefully consider what aspects of the event to include. On the other hand, a video includes images and audio that a written text cannot. To get the most complete picture of a historic event, choose a variety of media sources, and think about the kinds of information that are included, omitted, and emphasized in each account. You might ask yourself these questions about each medium:

- Who is narrating the account?
- What background information is included in the account?
- What details are emphasized in the account?
- What details are missing from the account?

Analyzing Text and Media

Support your responses with evidence from the selections.

1. **Compare** Describe how the video presents the March on Washington. How does it differ from the history text's account? Cite specific examples from the video and the text.

2. **Analyze** The history text includes eyewitness accounts of the day, while the video uses interviews with people commenting on the significance of the day. How does each type of account affect your understanding of the day?

3. **Evaluate** What ideas are emphasized in both the text and the video? Explain how the video and text together give you a more complete understanding of the March on Washington.

PERFORMANCE TASK

Writing Activity: Account Imagine that you were in the audience for King's speech, and write a one-page first-person account of your experience.

- Gather information and impressions about the event from both the history text and the video.

- Consider how you would respond in that situation, and write a one-page letter or diary entry.

- Be sure to include specific details that convey the atmosphere in the Mall.

- Use the conventions of standard written English.

Background *In 2010, the call for democratic reforms reverberated throughout the Middle East and North Africa in a movement known as the Arab Spring. In Egypt, the unrest forced Hosni Mubarak's long-ruling regime out of power. This excerpt from* **Ahdaf Soueif's** *personal account of the revolution describes the third day of mass protests in Cairo. Soueif (b. 1950) was born in Egypt and resides in both Cairo and London. Her novel* The Map of Love *was a finalist for the Booker Prize for Fiction, and she contributes to the* Guardian *and other English and Arabic news organizations.*

from Cairo: My City, Our Revolution

Diary by Ahdaf Soueif

AS YOU READ Pay attention to details that reveal the author's feelings about Cairo and the revolution.

Friday 28 January, 5.00 p.m.

The river is a still, steely grey, a dull pewter. Small scattered fires burn and fizz in the water. We've pushed out from the shore below the Ramses Hilton and are heading into mid-stream. My two nieces, Salma and Mariam, are on either side of me in the small motor boat. As we get further from the shore our coughing and choking subsides. We can draw breath, even though the breath burns. And we can open our eyes—

To see an **opaque** dusk, heavy with tear gas. Up ahead, Qasr el-Nil Bridge is a mass of people, all in motion, but all in place.
10 We look back at where we were just minutes ago, on 6 October Bridge,[1] and see a Central Security Forces personnel carrier on fire, backing off, four young men chasing it, leaping at it, beating at its windscreen. The vehicle is reversing wildly, careering backwards east towards Downtown. Behind us, a ball of fire lands in the river;

opaque
(ō-pāk´) *adj.*
clouded, difficult to see through.

---

[1] **Qasr el–Nil Bridge . . . 6 October Bridge:** two bridges, about two miles apart, that cross the Nile River in central Cairo.

a bright new pool of flame in the water. The sky too is grey—so
different from the airy twilight you normally get on the river at this
time of day. The Opera House looms dark on our right and we can
barely make out the slender height of the Cairo Tower. We don't
know it yet, but the lights of Cairo will not come on tonight.

20   A great shout goes up from Qasr el-Nil. I look at Salma and
Mariam. 'Yes, let's,' they say. I tell the boatman we've changed our
minds: we don't want to cross the river to Giza[2] and go home, we
want to be dropped off under Qasr el-Nil Bridge.

        And that is why we—myself and two beautiful young women—
appeared suddenly in the Qasr el-Nil underpass among the Central
Security vehicles racing to get out of town and all the men leaning
over the parapet[3] above us with stones in their hands stopped in
mid-throw and yelled 'Run! Run!' and held off with the stones so
they wouldn't hit us as we skittered through the screeching vehicles
30   to a spot where we could scramble up the bank and join the people
at the mouth of the bridge. . . .

_____

[2] **Giza:** city southwest of Cairo and site of the great pyramids.
[3] **parapet:** a low protective wall along the edge of a raised structure.

So we ran through the underpass, scrambled up the bank and found ourselves within, inside, and part of the masses. When we'd seen the crowd from a distance it had seemed like one bulk, solid. Close up like this it was people, individual persons with spaces between them—spaces into which you could fit. We stood on the traffic island in the middle of the road. Behind us was Qasr el-Nil Bridge, in front of us was Tahrir,[4] and we were doing what we Egyptians do best, and what the regime ruling us had tried so hard
40 to destroy: we had come together, as individuals, millions of us, in a great cooperative effort. And this time our project was to save and to **reclaim** our country. We stood on the island in the middle of the road and that was the moment I became part of the revolution. . . .

reclaim
(rĭ-klām´) v. to retake possession; reform.

For twenty years I have shied away from writing about Cairo. It hurt too much. But the city was there, close to me, looking over my shoulder, holding up the **prism** through which I understood the world, inserting herself into everything I wrote. It hurt. And now, miraculously, it doesn't. Because my city is mine again.

prism
(prĭz´əm) n. a transparent, light-refracting object which figuratively refers to an individual's viewpoint.

'Masr' is Egypt, and 'Masr' is also what Egyptians call Cairo.
50 On Tuesday 1 February, I watched a man surveying the scene in Tahrir with a big smile: the sun was shining and people were everywhere, old and young, rich and poor, they talked and walked and sang and played and joked and chanted. Then he said it out loud: 'Ya Masr, it's been a long time. We have missed you.' . . .

On the traffic island at the Qasr el-Nil entrance to Tahrir you turned 360 degrees and everywhere there were people. I could not tell how many thousands I could see. Close up, people were handing out tissues soaked in vinegar for your nose, Pepsi to bathe your eyes, water to drink. I stumbled and a hand under my elbow
60 steadied me. The way ahead of us was invisible behind the smoke. From time to time there would be a burst of flame. The great hotels: the Semiramis Intercontinental, Shepheard's, the Ramses Hilton, had all darkened their lower floors and locked their doors. On the upper-floor balconies stick figures were watching us. At the other end of the Midan,[5] from the roof of the American University, the snipers were watching us, too. Silently. Everywhere there was a continuous thud of guns and from time to time a loud, **intermittent** rattling sound. We stood. That was our job, the people at the back: we stood and we chanted our declaration of peace: 'Selmeyya!
70 Selmeyya!' while our comrades at the front, unarmed, fought with the security forces. From time to time a great cry would go up and

intermittent
(ĭn´tər-mĭt´nt) adj. occurring at erratic or irregular intervals.

---

[4] **Tahrir (te-rər´):** Arabic word for "liberation." Tahrir Square is a large, open area in downtown Cairo.
[5] **Midan (mīdān):** Arabic word for "Square."

we would surge forward: our friends had won us another couple of metres and we followed them and held our ground. We sang the national anthem. Eight months ago some young protestors from the 6 April Group had been arrested in Alexandria for singing the national anthem; it was 'instigatory'[6] the prosecution said. We sang it. On 28 January, standing at that **momentous** crossroads, the Nile behind us, the Arab League building to our left, the old Ministry of Foreign Affairs to our right, seeing nothing up ahead except the gas and smoke and fire that stood between us and our capital, we stood our ground and sang and chanted and placed our lives, with all trust and confidence, in each other's hands.
Some of us died.

momentous
(mō-měn′təs) *adj.*
very important;
fateful.

COLLABORATIVE DISCUSSION Why does Soueif change her mind about going home? With a partner, discuss how she feels about her decision to become part of the revolution. Cite specific textual evidence from the diary to support your ideas.

---

[6] **instigatory:** action that encourages people to rebel.

Analyze Ideas and Events

A **diary** is a form of **autobiographical narrative** that includes a daily record of an author's thoughts, experiences, or feelings. Diaries typically recount events in **chronological order;** however, authors often explore relationships between present and past events. For example, Ahdaf Soueif highlights the significance of the protesters singing the Egyptian national anthem by telling readers about protesters who had previously been arrested for doing so. In her diary, Soueif also alludes to events that occur after the entry date of January 28.

When you analyze how an author describes events in a diary, look closely at the order of events and the connections between them. If the author includes information about past and future events, consider how this connects to the current events, helps provide context, and contributes to the overall meaning. Think about why the author chooses to include certain events in a particular order and how this affects your understanding of the text.

Analyze Impact of Word Choice on Tone

Tone is an author's attitude toward his or her subject. To create a tone, authors choose words with specific **connotations,** or the attitudes or feelings associated with a word. The connotation of a word or phrase may be positive or negative. For example, the phrase *president's administration* has positive associations, while *president's regime* has negative ones. By noticing an author's choice of words, you can detect and analyze his or her tone.

In "Cairo: My City, Our Revolution," Ahdaf Soueif shifts or changes her tone to reflect the events she is describing. As you analyze the text, think about how specific words impact the tone of particular sentences or whole sections of the text. Use a chart to help you analyze specific words and details.

Word Choice	Tone
"The Opera House looms dark on our right"	*Looms* has a negative connotation and creates a threatening tone in the sentence.

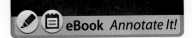

Analyzing the Text

Cite Text Evidence   Support your responses with evidence from the selection.

1. **Analyze** Soueif first describes Cairo as viewed from the river at a distance, rather than from within the protest. How does this help the reader visualize the scene?

2. **Cite Evidence** Describe the tone of the first two paragraphs. How does Soueif's word choice in the first two paragraphs affect the tone? Give specific examples to support your analysis.

3. **Infer** At the end of the second paragraph Soueif tells readers that "the lights of Cairo will not come on tonight," referring to a government-imposed curfew and shutdown of Internet and phone communications. How does this glimpse into the future contribute to Soueif's description of the present?

4. **Cite Evidence** Once Soueif and her nieces join the protest, there is a distinct shift in the tone. Describe this change, citing specific examples of language that contribute to the tone.

5. **Interpret** Personification is a type of figurative language in which human qualities are given to nonliving things. In lines 45–47, how does Soueif **personify** the city of Cairo?

6. **Infer** In lines 49–54, Soueif provides a description of the scene in Tahrir on February 1. How does this scene help the reader understand how the events are unfolding?

7. **Analyze** Notice how Soueif ends this diary entry with the simple sentence, "Some of us died." How does this sentence contrast with the events she describes in lines 55–58? How does it change the tone of the text?

PERFORMANCE TASK

Research Activity: Informative Oral Report In her diary, Ahdaf Soueif provides her own personal account of the Egyptian revolution of 2011. Explore the topic in greater depth through two brief tasks:

1. Conduct research about a specific event in the revolution. Gather information from multiple sources and remember to cite them following standard format.

2. Write a brief report of your findings and share it with the class. Be sure to include well-chosen, relevant, and sufficient facts in your report.

Critical Vocabulary

| opaque | reclaim | prism | intermittent | momentous |

Practice and Apply Use the Critical Vocabulary words to answer each question. Then, with a partner, take turns supporting your answers.

1. Which word is an antonym, or a word opposite in meaning, to the word **insignificant**?

2. Which word most closely relates to the word **irregular**?

3. Which word is an antonym to the word **transparent**?

4. Which word most closely relates to the word **reflection**?

5. Which word most closely relates to the word **restore**?

Vocabulary Strategy: Reference Sources

When you read an informational text, looking up words or terms in print and digital **reference sources** such as dictionaries, glossaries or thesauruses can help you better understand the central ideas of the text.

Read this sentence from Ahdaf Soueif's diary.

And this time our project was to save and to <u>reclaim</u> our country.

In this sentence, you can determine the general meaning of the Critical Vocabulary word *reclaim* by using the context clue "to save." However, if you also look up the word *reclaim* in a dictionary, you gain a further understanding that the people were working to reclaim, or bring back, their country from the ruling regime that had restricted their freedoms.

Practice and Apply The underlined words in these sentences are also used in "Cairo: My City, Our Revolution." Use context clues in each sentence to write a definition for the underlined word. Then look up the words in a dictionary, glossary, or thesaurus. Confirm or revise your definitions with additional information from the reference sources.

1. The protester avoided contact and <u>shied</u> away from the angry crowd.

2. The car went <u>careering</u> toward the barrier at full speed to break it down.

3. The people sent the government a message when they wrote their <u>declaration</u> of freedom.

4. The tall fences could not hold back the crowd as they slowly pushed and <u>surged</u> down the street.

Language and Style: Noun Phrases

A **noun phrase** includes a noun and its **modifiers,** or the words that affect the noun's meaning. In "Cairo: My City, Our Revolution," Ahdaf Soueif uses noun phrases to add vivid descriptions of the protests.

Read the following sentence from the diary:

> And we can open our eyes—
> To see <u>an opaque dusk, heavy with tear gas.</u>

By splitting the sentence between the first and second paragraphs, the author emphasizes the underlined noun phrase. The author could have provided the information in this sentence much more simply:

> The tear gas limits our visibility.

Instead, she uses the noun phrase to allow readers to see and feel what the air feels like. Later in the paragraph, the author uses another descriptive noun phrase to contrast this image from the usual appearance and feel of the sky:

> The sky too is grey—so different from the <u>airy twilight</u> you normally get at this time of day.

When you revise your own writing to add descriptive noun phrases, think about the specific meaning you want to convey to your audience. Ask yourself what details need more variety and interest. It may help to jot down ideas in a graphic organizer.

Practice and Apply Look back at the report you created for this selection's Performance Task. Revise the report to add more descriptive noun phrases. Remember to use the conventions of standard English grammar and usage. When you have finished revising, exchange reports with a partner and discuss how you strengthened your writing.

Background *The Iranian Revolution in the late 1970's resulted in the overthrow of the pro-western Shah of Iran. Iranians established a theocracy, or religious government, based on the rule of Islam. The new government passed laws that segregate men and women and that force women to adhere to an Islamic dress code. Iranian women are required to wear veils that cover their hair and neck and coats that cover their arms and legs. The "morality police" ensure that people comply with the laws. People who do not comply may be taken to the morality police headquarters (called* the Committee *in Persepolis 2) to be questioned, beaten, or jailed.*

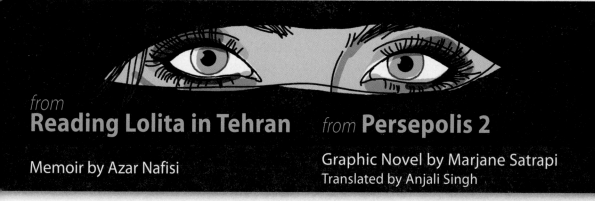

from
Reading Lolita in Tehran

Memoir by Azar Nafisi

from **Persepolis 2**

Graphic Novel by Marjane Satrapi
Translated by Anjali Singh

Azar Nafisi (b. 1947), *an Iranian, taught English literature in Tehran from 1979 until 1995. The laws passed after the revolution made Nafisi's job difficult. University faculty scrutinized novels that Nafisi taught, and Nafisi was chastised for not wearing a veil. In 1995, Nafisi left the university and began teaching a small group of women in her home, where they were free to discuss books, like* Lolita, *that were considered unacceptable by Iranian authorities. In 1997, she left Iran for the United States, where she now teaches.*

Marjane Satrapi (b. 1969) *was born in Iran. After the revolution, Satrapi's parents sent her to Europe to attend school. Later, she studied illustration and learned to create comics.* Persepolis 1 *tells the story of her childhood in Iran, and* Persepolis 2 *tells the story of her adolescence in Europe and Iran and of her struggle to fit in. Both books were made into the animated movie ,* Persepolis, *which won many awards. Satrapi has written other graphic novels, including* Chicken with Plums. *She lives in Paris with her husband.*

AS YOU READ Identify points of comparison between the memoir and the graphic novel. Write down any questions you generate as you read.

from Reading Lolita in Tehran
Memoir by Azar Nafisi

How can I create this other world outside the room? I have no choice but to appeal once again to your imagination. Let's imagine one of the girls, say Sanaz, leaving my house and let us follow her from there to her final destination. She says her good-byes and puts on her black robe and scarf over her orange shirt and jeans, coiling her scarf around her neck to cover her huge gold earrings. She directs wayward strands of hair under the scarf, puts her notes into her large bag, straps it on over her shoulder and walks out into the hall. She pauses a moment on top of the stairs to put on thin lacy black gloves to hide her nail polish.

We follow Sanaz down the stairs, out the door and into the street. You might notice that her gait[1] and her gestures have changed. It is in her best interest not to be seen, not be heard or noticed. She doesn't walk upright, but bends her head towards the ground and doesn't look at passersby. She walks quickly and with a sense of determination. The streets of Tehran and other Iranian cities are patrolled by militia, who ride in white Toyota patrols, four gun-carrying men and women, sometimes followed by a minibus. They are called the Blood of God. They patrol the streets to make sure that women like Sanaz wear their veils properly, do not wear makeup, do not walk in public with men who are not their fathers, brothers or husbands. She will pass slogans on the walls, quotations from Khomeini[2] and a group called the Party of God: MEN WHO WEAR TIES ARE U.S. LACKEYS.[3] VEILING IS A WOMAN'S PROTECTION. Beside the slogan is a charcoal drawing of a woman: her face is featureless and framed by a dark chador.[4] MY SISTER, GUARD YOUR VEIL. MY BROTHER, GUARD YOUR EYES.

If she gets on a bus, the seating is **segregated**. She must enter through the rear door and sit in the back seats, **allocated** to women. Yet in taxis, which accept as many as five passengers, men and women are squeezed together like sardines, as the saying goes, and the same goes with minibuses, where so many of my students complain of being harassed by bearded and God-fearing men.

You might well ask, What is Sanaz thinking as she walks the streets of Tehran? How much does this experience affect her? Most

segregate
(sĕg´rĭ-gāt´) *v.* to cause people to be separated based on gender, race, or other factors.

allocate
(ăl´ə-kāt´) *v.* to assign or designate for.

---

[1] **gait:** manner of walking.

[2] **Khomeini (kō-mā´ nē):** Ruhollah Khomeini (1902–1989), religious and political leader of Iran after the 1979 revolution.

[3] **U.S. lackeys:** people who serve United States policies. The Iranian government is hostile to the U.S. because it supported the former Shah of Iran.

[4] **chador:** a long scarf that covers a Muslim woman's hair, neck, and shoulders.

probably, she tries to distance her mind as much as possible from her surroundings. Perhaps she is thinking of her brother, or of her distant boyfriend and the time when she will meet him in Turkey.

40 Does she compare her own situation with her mother's when she was the same age? Is she angry that women of her mother's generation could walk the streets freely, enjoy the company of the opposite sex, join the police force, become pilots, live under laws that were among the most progressive in the world regarding women? Does she feel humiliated by the new laws, by the fact that after the revolution, the age of marriage was lowered from eighteen to nine, that stoning became once more the punishment for adultery and prostitution?

In the course of nearly two decades, the streets have been
50 turned into a war zone, where young women who disobey the rules are hurled into patrol cars, taken to jail, flogged, fined, forced to wash the toilets and humiliated, and as soon as they leave, they go back and do the same thing. Is she aware, Sanaz, of her own power? Does she realize how dangerous she can be when her every stray gesture is a disturbance to public safety? Does she think how vulnerable the Revolutionary Guards are who for over eighteen years have patrolled the streets of Tehran and have had to endure young women like herself, and those of other generations, walking, talking, showing a strand of hair just to remind them that they have
60 not **converted**?

We have reached Sanaz's house, where we will leave her on her doorstep, perhaps to confront her brother on the other side and to think in her heart of her boyfriend.

These girls, my girls, had both a real history and a fabricated one. Although they came from very different backgrounds, the regime that ruled them had tried to make their personal identities and histories **irrelevant**. They were never free of the regime's definition of them as Muslim women.

convert
(kən-vûrt′) *v.* to change one's system of beliefs.

irrelevant
(ĭ-rĕl′ə-vənt) *adj.* insignificant, unimportant.

from **Persepolis 2: The Story of a Return**

Graphic Novel by Marjane Satrapi

WE CONFRONTED THE REGIME AS BEST WE COULD.

IN 1990, THE ERA OF GRAND REVOLUTIONARY IDEAS AND DEMONSTRATIONS WAS OVER. BETWEEN 1980 AND 1983, THE GOVERNMENT HAD IMPRISONED AND EXECUTED SO MANY HIGH-SCHOOL AND COLLEGE STUDENTS THAT WE NO LONGER DARED TO TALK POLITICS.

OUR STRUGGLE WAS MORE DISCREET.

IT HINGED ON THE LITTLE DETAILS. TO OUR LEADERS, THE SMALLEST THING COULD BE A SUBJECT OF SUBVERSION.

SHOWING YOUR WRIST.

A LOUD LAUGH.

HAVING A WALKMAN.

IN SHORT . . . EVERYTHING WAS A PRETEXT TO ARREST US.

I EVEN REMEMBER SPENDING AN ENTIRE DAY AT THE COMMITTEE BECAUSE OF A PAIR OF RED SOCKS.

THE REGIME HAD UNDERSTOOD THAT ONE PERSON LEAVING HER HOUSE WHILE ASKING HERSELF:

ARE MY TROUSERS LONG ENOUGH?

IS MY VEIL IN PLACE?

CAN MY MAKE-UP BE SEEN?

ARE THEY GOING TO WHIP ME?

NO LONGER ASKS HERSELF:

WHERE IS MY FREEDOM OF THOUGHT?

WHERE IS MY FREEDOM OF SPEECH?

MY LIFE, IS IT LIVABLE?

WHAT'S GOING ON IN THE POLITICAL PRISONS?

IT'S ONLY NATURAL! WHEN WE'RE AFRAID, WE LOSE ALL SENSE OF ANALYSIS AND REFLECTION. OUR FEAR PARALYZES US. BESIDES, FEAR HAS ALWAYS BEEN THE DRIVING FORCE BEHIND ALL DICTATORS' REPRESSION.

SHOWING YOUR HAIR OR PUTTING ON MAKEUP LOGICALLY BECAME ACTS OF REBELLION.

COLLABORATIVE DISCUSSION With a partner, discuss common elements in the memoir and graphic novel. How is the way the authors communicate with readers similar and different in the texts? Support your ideas with evidence from both.

Determine Author's Point of View

Point of view refers to how an author thinks or feels about a subject. In a memoir, an author uses rhetoric, choosing words carefully to advance a point of view. Graphic novelists, however, use both graphics and rhetoric to advance their points of view.

- Azar Nafisi wrote *Reading Lolita in Tehran* after she left Iran to live abroad. Her **perspective** as a woman and a scholar living under an oppressive regime is reflected in the rhetoric she uses. In the excerpt, Nafisi reproduces slogans that scream in uppercase letters: MY SISTER, GUARD YOUR VEIL. MY BROTHER, GUARD YOUR EYES. She constructs phrases such as, "flogged, fined, forced to wash toilets and humiliated," and "when her every stray gesture is a disturbance to public safety" to communicate her point of view.

- Unlike the memoir, *Persepolis 2* tells Marjane Satrapi's story through words and stark black and white images. In this excerpt, the author's perspective as a young woman out of place in a rigid and uncompromising society is reflected in the way the main character's face is drawn. It is also shown in the juxtaposition of panels next to each other. Careful readers must study details in the drawings, as well as read captions and thought bubbles, to understand the author's point of view.

Analyze Accounts in Different Mediums

A personal story can be told using different **mediums,** or ways of communicating. Mediums may include memoirs, graphic novels, plays, or films. Each format allows the author to emphasize details that help to tell his or her story. The challenge for the author is determining which medium tells the story in the most compelling way. The challenge for readers or viewers is to determine which details are emphasized and how those details convey the author's message.

Read this sentence from *Reading Lolita in Tehran*:

> They patrol the streets to make sure that women like Sanaz wear their veils properly, do not wear makeup, do not walk in public with men who are not their fathers, brothers or husbands.

Notice how this memoir is a personal account written from memory or first-hand knowledge. The writer uses concrete details and sensory words to help the reader visualize events and people.

In contrast, the middle panel in the second row of *Persepolis 2* provides visuals for the reader to understand a similar situation. Graphic novels show action through images and use words sparingly, through speech bubbles and captions. Readers must pay attention to the visual details in the drawings and to the sequence of the panels to understand the author's message.

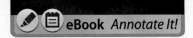

Analyzing Text and Media

Cite Text Evidence Support your responses with evidence from the selections.

1. **Interpret** Identify details the author of *Reading Lolita in Tehran* uses to describe Sanaz. Why might the author have included these details?

2. **Critique** How is the rhetoric that both authors use effective in conveying their points of view? Explain with evidence from the texts.

3. **Infer** The author of *Reading Lolita in Tehran* wonders aloud if Sanaz is aware of her own power. What power is the author referring to? Does the main character in *Persepolis* feel that she has a similar power? Explain.

4. **Analyze** Look at the second and third panels in *Persepolis 2*. How does the author use both words and graphics to make a point about how the people's struggle had changed?

5. **Infer** The narrator of *Persepolis 2* says that she spent an entire day at the Committee because of a pair of red socks. What might red socks have **symbolized,** or represented, to the Committee?

6. **Interpret** In *Persepolis 2*, the narrator's facial expression remains the same in each of the panels. How would you describe the narrator's facial expression? How does this consistency help reveal the author's point of view?

7. **Synthesize** What ideas are emphasized in both the text and the graphic novel? Explain how the graphic novel and text together enable readers to have a more complete understanding of the problems women face in Iran.

PERFORMANCE TASK

Media Activity: Graphic Novel Imagine that Nafisi had written her memoir in the form of a graphic novel. How would she have integrated graphics and rhetoric?

- Using a computer or poster board and a pencil, create a series of graphic novel panels that follow Sanaz as she leaves the author's home.

- Add captions and speech and thought bubbles, including details from the memoir that you think advance the story.

- In a small group, compare your graphic representations of Nafisi's memoir. Discuss whether you were able to convey the same ideas and point of view through graphics as Nafisi was able to convey in her memoir. Was your use of rhetoric in your graphic representation as effective as Nafisi's in her memoir?

Critical Vocabulary

segregate	allocate	irrelevant	convert

Practice and Apply Use your understanding of the vocabulary words to answer the questions.

1. Are your friends' opinions ever **irrelevant**? Explain.

2. If you were in charge of **allocating** money to each of the clubs or sports teams in school, how would you do it?

3. Why might you **segregate** children according to age?

4. Is someone who believes fiercely in something likely to **convert**? Explain.

Vocabulary Strategy: Denotations and Connotations

A word's **denotation** is its strict dictionary definition. But many words have slight nuances or differences in meaning. These nuances, or **connotations,** have associated meanings and emotions.

Nafisi explains that in Iran, the buses are segregated. The Critical Vocabulary word *segregate* has a similar denotation to the word *separate*. They both mean "to set apart." But the word *segregate* has an altogether different connotation. To segregate suggests separating people or things forcefully, often in an unfair way.

Practice and Apply For each Critical Vocabulary word below, write the word's denotation. Then write the connotation of the word as it appears in the story.

Vocabulary Word	Denotation	Connotation
allocate		
irrelevant		
convert		

Language and Style: Rhetorical Questions

Authors strive to make effective choices for meaning or style. In her memoir *Reading Lolita in Tehran*, Azar Nafisi makes repeated use of rhetorical questions to engage the audience and to make a point. **Rhetorical questions** are questions that do not require or expect an answer. Depending on the context, they are often posed for dramatic effect.

Read the following sentence from the memoir.

Does she realize how dangerous she can be when her every stray gesture is a disturbance to public safety?

Nafisi could instead have written the sentence this way:

She is dangerous because her every stray gesture is a disturbance to public safety.

By using a rhetorical question instead of a statement, Nafisi invites the reader to think carefully about the scene described and to agree with her viewpoint. The question does not expect an answer. Instead, it makes a dramatic statement about the way the Iranian regime views women.

Here are some other examples of rhetorical questions in the excerpt from *Reading Lolita in Tehran*.

Rhetorical Question	Meaning
"How can I create this other world outside the room?"	Nafisi uses the rhetorical question as an opener to explain why she creates an imaginary scene involving Sanaz.
"Does she compare her own situation with her mother's when she was the same age?"	The question engages readers and invites them to consider any background knowledge they have about Iran's history.
"Is she aware, Sanaz, of her own power?"	Nafisi uses the rhetorical question to provide dramatic effect and to give the questions that follow meaning.

Practice and Apply Think of an injustice that you have observed or read about. Write a brief paragraph describing and reflecting on the injustice. Use rhetorical questions, as Nafisi does, to convey meaning and for dramatic effect. Remember to check your work for standard English grammar and usage.

Background *Born in Argentina,* **Luisa Valenzuela** *(b. 1938) published her first story at the age of seventeen. After graduating from the University of Buenos Aires, she moved to Paris and traveled abroad for several years. She returned home in 1974 to find political turmoil and oppression: a fascist dictatorship, a system of government in which a leader suppresses opposition through violent means, now ruled Argentina. Despite threats of censorship and physical harm, she began using her writing to document the horrors of life under a dictator.*

The Censors

Short Story by Luisa Valenzuela   Translated by David Unger

AS YOU READ Pay attention to the clues that reveal how Juan's feelings about his work change during the story.

Poor Juan! One day they caught him with his guard down before he could even realize that what he had taken as a stroke of luck was really one of fate's dirty tricks. These things happen the minute you're careless and you let down your guard, as one often does. Juancito let happiness—a feeling you can't trust—get the better of him when he received from a confidential source Mariana's new address in Paris and he knew that she hadn't forgotten him. Without thinking twice, he sat down at his table and wrote her a letter. *The* letter that keeps his mind off his job during the day and won't let him sleep at night (what had he scrawled, what had he put on that sheet of paper he sent to Mariana?).

Juan knows there won't be a problem with the letter's contents, that it's irreproachable, harmless. But what about the rest? He knows that they examine, sniff, feel, and read between the lines of each and every letter, and check its tiniest comma and most accidental stain. He knows that all letters pass from hand to hand and go through all sorts of tests in the huge censorship offices and that, in the end, very few continue on their way. Usually it

takes months, even years, if there aren't any snags; all this time
the freedom, maybe even the life, of both sender and receiver is in
jeopardy. And that's why Juan's so down in the dumps: thinking
that something might happen to Mariana because of his letters.
Of all people, Mariana, who must finally feel safe there where she
always dreamed she'd live. But he knows that the *Censor's Secret
Command* operates all over the world and cashes in on the discount
in air rates; there's nothing to stop them from going as far as that
hidden Paris neighborhood, kidnapping Mariana, and returning to
their cozy homes, certain of having fulfilled their noble mission.

Well, you've got to beat them to the punch, do what everyone
tries to do: sabotage the machinery, throw sand in its gears, get to
the bottom of the problem so as to stop it.

This was Juan's sound plan when he, like many others, applied
for a censor's job—not because he had a calling or needed a job:
no, he applied simply to intercept his own letter, a consoling but
unoriginal idea. He was hired immediately, for each day more and
more censors are needed and no one would bother to check on his
references.

Ulterior motives couldn't be overlooked by the *Censorship
Division*, but they needn't be too strict with those who applied.
They knew how hard it would be for those poor guys to find the
letter they wanted and even if they did, what's a letter or two when
the new censor would snap up so many others? That's how Juan
managed to join the *Post Office's Censorship Division*, with a certain
goal in mind.

The building had a festive air on the outside which contrasted
with its inner **staidness**. Little by little, Juan was absorbed by his
job and he felt at peace since he was doing everything he could to
get his letter for Mariana. He didn't even worry when, in his first
month, he was sent to *Section K* where envelopes are very carefully
screened for explosives.

It's true that on the third day, a fellow worker had his right
hand blown off by a letter, but the division chief claimed it was
sheer **negligence** on the victim's part. Juan and the other employees
were allowed to go back to their work, albeit feeling less secure.
After work, one of them tried to organize a strike to demand higher
wages for unhealthy work, but Juan didn't join in; after thinking it
over, he reported him to his superiors and thus got promoted.

You don't form a habit by doing something once, he told
himself as he left his boss's office. And when he was transferred to
Section J, where letters are carefully checked for poison dust, he felt
he had climbed a rung in the ladder.

By working hard, he quickly reached *Section E* where the job
was more interesting, for he could now read and analyze the letters'

staidness
(stād´nĭs) *n.* the
quality of being
steady, calm, and
serious.

negligence
(nĕg´lĭ-jəns) *n.*
carelessness or
failure to take normal
precautions.

> **Soon his work became so absorbing to him that his noble mission blurred in his mind.**

contents. Here he could even hope to get hold of his letter which, judging by the time that had elapsed, had gone through the other sections and was probably floating around in this one.

Soon his work became so absorbing that his noble mission blurred in his mind. Day after day he crossed out whole paragraphs in red ink, pitilessly chucking many letters into the censored basket.
70 These were horrible days when he was shocked by the subtle and conniving ways employed by people to pass on **subversive** messages; his instincts were so sharp that he found behind a simple 'the weather's unsettled' or 'prices continue to soar' the wavering hand of someone secretly scheming to overthrow the Government.

His zeal brought him swift promotion. We don't know if this made him happy. Very few letters reached him in *Section B*—only a handful passed the other hurdles—so he read them over and over again, passed them under a magnifying glass, searched for microprint with an electronic microscope, and tuned his sense
80 of smell so that he was beat by the time he made it home. He'd barely manage to warm up his soup, eat some fruit, and fall into bed, satisfied with having done his duty. Only his darling mother worried, but she couldn't get him back on the right road. She'd say, though it wasn't always true: Lola called, she's at the bar with the girls, they miss you, they're waiting for you. Or else she'd leave a bottle of red wine on the table. But Juan wouldn't overdo it: any distraction could make him lose his edge and the perfect censor

subversive
(səb-vûr´sĭv) *adj.*
intended to undermine or overthrow those in power.

had to be alert, keen, attentive, and sharp to nab cheats. He had a truly patriotic task, both self-denying and uplifting.

90   His basket for censored letters became the best fed as well as the most cunning basket in the whole *Censorship Division*. He was about to congratulate himself for having finally discovered his true mission, when his letter to Mariana reached his hands. Naturally, he censored it without regret. And just as naturally, he couldn't stop them from executing him the following morning, another victim of his devotion to his work.

COLLABORATIVE DISCUSSION Were you surprised by Juan's change of heart? With a partner, discuss what hints the author provided to make the story's ending plausible. Cite specific evidence from the text to support your ideas.

Analyze Point of View: Cultural Background

Luisa Valenzuela's cultural experience as an Argentine writer is reflected in both the content and style of this short story. Valenzuela wrote it upon returning to her native country in 1974 after spending several years abroad. The mood in Buenos Aires, the capital, was one of fear and oppression. Valenzuela once wrote, "Upon returning to my city after a long absence… it wasn't mine any longer. Buenos Aires belonged then to violence and state terrorism." Argentina was rapidly falling under the control of a fascist dictatorship. Working under the threat of censorship, suppression, and violence, Valenzuela believed it was her responsibility as a writer to witness and record the atrocities of the day. Her works, including this short story, explore such difficult topics as censorship, extreme violence, and political repression.

Analyze Author's Choices

To communicate their experiences and ideas, writers make specific stylistic and structural choices. You can analyze Valenzuela's choices in this short story by looking at these elements.

Pacing	Foreshadowing	Irony
Pacing is the way in which an author manipulates time. Authors may use techniques to slow the action, thereby creating a mood of tension or mystery. For example, Valenzuela builds tension by devoting the first part of the story to Juan's fear that his letter to Mariana will be found. Conversely, authors may accelerate a story's pace by presenting a series of plot events in rapid succession.	**Foreshadowing** is a writer's use of clues to hint at events that will occur later in the story. Foreshadowing creates suspense, mystery, and surprise, and makes readers eager to find out what will happen next. In this story, the description of a fellow worker's gruesome injury is an example of foreshadowing.	Irony takes place when something happens that is the opposite of what readers would expect. One type is **verbal irony,** when what is said is the opposite of what is meant. The narrator's description of the Censorship Bureau as having "a festive air" is an example of verbal irony. Another type is **situational irony,** in which a character or the reader expects one thing to happen but something else happens instead. Juan's increasing dedication to his job as a censor is an example of situational irony.

Analyzing the Text

Cite Text Evidence Support your responses with evidence from the selection.

1. **Infer** The narrator uses many **idioms,** commonly-used expressions that mean something other than the literal meaning of their words. For example, when Juan is "caught . . . with his guard down," the author means that he wasn't being cautious, not that he physically protected himself most of the time. What tone, or attitude toward the character and the audience, do the idioms create?

2. **Analyze** In his career as a censor, Juan moves from *Section K* to *Section B.* Describe the pacing or progression of his advancement. Besides the Section letters, what devices and word choices does the author use to speed up or slow down the pace of the story?

3. **Cite Evidence** How does the author foreshadow, or hint at, the changes that will occur in Juan's personality and his life? Provide examples of foreshadowing from the text, and explain their connection to the story's outcome.

4. **Compare** Compare Juan's work goal or motivation near the beginning of the story with his goal or motivation near the end. How does the author communicate the way this change occurs?

5. **Infer** The narrator calls Juan's basket of letters "the best fed as well as the most cunning basket in the whole *Censorship Division.*" What does this statement reveal about the way Juan performs his job?

6. **Interpret** Why does Juan censor his own letter "without regret"? How is his final action as a censor an example of irony? How does this ending illustrate Valenzuela's point of view about the political situation in Argentina?

PERFORMANCE TASK

Writing Activity: Letter Juan's letter to Mariana is central to this story's plot. Explore that letter through two brief writing tasks. In both pieces of writing, include evidence from the text and use the conventions of standard English.

1. In the character of Juan, write the one-page letter you imagine he wrote to Mariana at the beginning of the story. Then annotate a copy of the letter to identify evidence of anti-government ideas that a censor might find.

2. Write a one-page report in the character of Juan as a *Censorship Division* employee explaining why the letter shows that Juan is a traitor to his country.

Critical Vocabulary

staidness   **negligence**   **subversive**

Practice and Apply Create a semantic map like the one that follows for each Critical Vocabulary word. Use a dictionary or thesaurus as needed. This example is for a word appearing in line 30 of the story.

Vocabulary Strategy: Suffixes That Form Nouns

The Critical Vocabulary words *staidness* and *negligence* are formed by adding a noun suffix to an adjective, or describing word. Something that is *staid* shows *staidness*; someone who is *negligent* reveals his *negligence*. Noticing word patterns will help you more quickly develop an accurate definition for any unfamiliar words you encounter in your reading. Here are some common noun suffixes you will see in English words:

Suffixes	Meanings	Examples
–ance, –ence	act or condition of	radiance, excellence
–cy	state or condition of	sufficiency, redundancy
–dom	state, rank, or condition	officialdom, martyrdom
–hood	state or condition of	likelihood, childhood

Practice and Apply For each row of the chart, identify an additional example that uses a suffix shown. With each word you choose, follow these steps:

1. Identify the base—that is, the main word part without the suffix. Note the part of speech (adjective, verb, noun) and meaning of each base word.

2. Write a definition for each word you chose that incorporates the base word meaning and the suffix meaning.

3. Finally, use each word you chose in a sample sentence.

Language and Style: Colons and Semicolons

An author's use of punctuation not only can help readers understand the message but also can help create meaning and tone. In "The Censors," Luisa Valenzuela uses colons and semicolons to great effect.

Read the following sentence from the story.

And that's why Juan's so down in the dumps: thinking that something might happen to Mariana because of his letter.

The author could instead have written the sentence this way:

Juan's down in the dumps from thinking that something might happen to Mariana because of his letter.

By setting up the sentence as she does, the author involves readers in making meaning. The two-part sentence provides readers with a question (What's bothering Juan?) followed by its answer (Thinking that he's endangered Mariana). Readers naturally pause at the colon to prepare for what comes after it. Here are some other common uses of colons:

Uses of Colons	
Purpose	Example
illustrate or provide an example of what was just stated	Argentina has seen much political turmoil: since World War II the nation has endured numerous military coups and dictatorships.
introduce a quotation	Valenzuela is no stranger to censorship: "I wrote . . . thinking that I should write in illegible handwriting so that no one could read over my shoulder."
introduce a list	Valenzuela has lived in many places: Paris, New York, Barcelona, and Buenos Aires.

Now read this sentence from "The Censors":

Usually it takes months, even years, if there aren't any snags; all this time the freedom, maybe even the life, of both sender and receiver is in jeopardy.

Valenzuela could have chosen to create two separate sentences; her use of the semicolon shows that the second idea results from the first.

Practice and Apply Look back at the letter and report you created in response to this selection's Performance Task. Revise each to add at least one colon and one semicolon. Then discuss with a partner how each punctuation mark you added improves your meaning or tone.

Write an Argument

Some people argue that freedom is never given; it must be demanded. Choose three texts from this collection, including the anchor text, "I Have a Dream," and identify how each writer addresses the struggle for freedom in his or her society. Then, write an argument in which you cite evidence from all three texts to support your claim.

An effective argument should

- make a claim and develop the claim with valid reasons and relevant evidence from the texts

- anticipate opposing claims and counter them with well-supported reasons and relevant evidence

- establish clear, logical relationships among claims, counterclaims, reasons, and evidence

- include an introduction, a logically structured body linked with transitions, and a conclusion

- follow the conventions of standard written English

PLAN

Analyze the Texts Reread "I Have a Dream" and take notes about how Martin Luther King Jr. addresses the struggle for freedom in American society. Does he believe that freedom is universal or that it must be demanded by the people? Pay attention to specific details as you gather evidence from the text. Then review your two other texts, looking at how the authors address the struggle for freedom.

Gather Evidence Use the annotation tools in your eBook to find evidence about how the authors of your chosen texts address the struggle for freedom. Save each piece of evidence to *my*Notebook, in a folder titled *Collection 2 Performance Task*.

ACADEMIC VOCABULARY

As you share your ideas about freedom, be sure to use these words.

decline
enable
impose
integrate
reveal

myNotebook

"Cairo: My City, Our Revolution"

"... we had come together, as individuals, millions of us, in a great cooperative effort. And this time our project was to save and to reclaim our country. We stood on the island in the middle of the road and that was the moment I became part of the revolution...."

This passage shows how Soueif thinks it is the job of the Egyptian people to demand freedom from the ruling regime.

Mentor Text See how this example from "I Have a Dream" anticipates an opposing claim and counters it.

> " And those who hope that the Negro needed to blow off steam and will now be content will have a rude awakening if the nation returns to business as usual. There will be neither rest nor tranquility in America until the Negro is granted his citizenship rights. "

Get Organized Organize your notes in an outline.

- Decide what organizational pattern you will use. Will you present your claim along with all the reasons to support it, and then write about potential opposing claims? Or, will you present one reason to support your claim followed by an opposing claim, and then continue with the next reason and opposing claim?

- Use your organizational pattern to sort the textual evidence you have gathered into a logical order. Will you discuss evidence from each text one by one in different sections of your essay, or will you present evidence from multiple texts in the same section?

- Choose an engaging quotation or detail to introduce your essay.

- Use a closing statement that supports your argument.

PRODUCE

Draft Your Essay Write a draft of your essay, following your outline.

- Introduce your claim. Present your argument in an interesting way that will grab the attention of your readers.

- Present your reasons, evidence, and opposing claims in logically ordered paragraphs.

- Explain how the evidence from the texts supports your ideas about the struggle for freedom in a society.

- Use transitions to clarify the relationships between claims and reasons, between reasons and evidence, and between claims and counterclaims.

- Write a conclusion that follows from and supports your argument.

Interactive Lessons
To help you plan your essay, complete the following lessons:
- Support: Reasons and Evidence
- Building Effective Support

Write your rough draft in *my*WriteSmart. Focus on getting your ideas down rather than perfecting your choice of language.

Interactive Lessons
To help you draft your essay, complete the following lesson:
- Creating a Coherent Argument

Improve Your Draft Have your partner or a group of peers use the questions in the chart to review your draft.

Questions	Tips	Revision Techniques
Does the introduction grab the audience's attention and include a clear claim?	**Underline** the attention-grabbing text. Highlight the claim.	**Revise** the introduction to make it attention-grabbing. Add a claim.
Do valid reasons support the claim? Is each reason supported by evidence?	**Underline** each reason. Highlight each piece of evidence.	**Add** reasons or revise existing ones to make them more valid. Add relevant evidence.
Are opposing claims acknowledged and countered with reasons and evidence?	**Highlight** opposing claims. Underline reasons and evidence that counter them.	**Add** opposing claims. Include reasons and evidence that counter them.
Do transitions clarify relationships between ideas?	**Underline** each transition.	**Add** words, phrases, or clauses to connect related ideas.
Does the conclusion follow logically from and support the argument?	**Highlight** the text that supports the argument.	**Add** or revise text to make clear how the conclusion supports the argument.

Have your partner or a group of peers review your draft in *my*WriteSmart. Ask your reviewers to note any reasons that do not support your claim.

Interactive Lessons
To help you revise your essay, complete the following lesson:
• What Is a Claim?

Language and Style: Paraphrase or Summarize

To make texts more cohesive, writers often include paraphrases or summaries to refer to an idea provided earlier. Read this passage from "Nobody Turn Me Around: A People's History of the 1963 March on Washington."

> ❝ After recalling the story of Lincoln freeing the slaves, with the simple stroke of a pen in the middle of a bloody war, King laments the inferior position of blacks a century later. ❞

Euchner summarizes Lincoln's signing of the Emancipation Proclamation, which was discussed earlier, rather than explaining it in detail. This makes the text cohesive. Look for places in your essay where you can paraphrase or summarize ideas explained earlier.

Exchange Essays When your final draft is completed, exchange essays with a partner. Read your partner's essay and point out aspects of the essay that are strong and areas that could be improved.

PERFORMANCE TASK RUBRIC
ARGUMENT

	Ideas and Evidence	Organization	Language
4	• The introduction is memorable and persuasive; the claim clearly states a position on a substantive topic. • Valid reasons and relevant evidence from the texts convincingly support the writer's claim. • Opposing claims are anticipated and effectively addressed with counterclaims. • The concluding section effectively summarizes the claim.	• Reasons and textual evidence are organized consistently and logically. • Varied transitions connect reasons and evidence to the writer's claim. • Paraphrases or summaries make the argument more cohesive.	• The writing reflects a formal style and an objective, or controlled, tone. • Sentence beginnings, lengths, and structures vary and have a rhythmic flow. • Spelling, capitalization, and punctuation are correct. If handwritten, the argument is legible. • Grammar and usage are correct.
3	• The introduction could do more to capture the reader's attention; the claim states a position on an issue. • Most reasons and evidence from the texts support the writer's claim, but they could be more convincing. • Opposing claims are anticipated, but the counterclaims need to be developed more. • The concluding section restates the claim.	• The organization of reasons and textual evidence is confusing in a few places. • A few more transitions are needed to connect reasons and evidence to the claim. • Some paraphrases or summaries make the argument cohesive in some places.	• The style is informal in a few places, and the tone is defensive at times. • Sentence beginnings, lengths, and structures vary somewhat. • Several spelling and capitalization mistakes occur, and punctuation is inconsistent. If handwritten, the argument is mostly legible. • Some grammatical and usage errors are repeated in the argument.
2	• The introduction is ordinary; the claim identifies an issue, but the writer's position is not clearly stated. • The reasons and evidence from the texts are not always logical or relevant. • Opposing claims are anticipated but not addressed logically. • The concluding section includes an incomplete summary of the claim.	• The organization of reasons and textual evidence is logical in some places, but it often doesn't follow a pattern. • Many more transitions are needed to connect reasons and evidence to the writer's position. • Paraphrases or summaries are needed to make the argument more cohesive.	• The style becomes informal in many places, and the tone is often dismissive of other viewpoints. • Sentence structures barely vary, and some fragments or run-on sentences are present. • Spelling, capitalization, and punctuation are often incorrect but do not make reading the argument difficult. If handwritten, the argument may be partially illegible. • Grammar and usage are incorrect in many places, but the writer's ideas are still clear.
1	• The introduction is missing. • Significant supporting reasons and evidence from the texts are missing. • Opposing claims are neither anticipated nor addressed. • The concluding section is missing.	• An organizational strategy is not used; reasons and textual evidence are presented randomly. • Transitions are not used, making the argument difficult to understand. • Paraphrases or summaries are not used.	• The style is inappropriate, and the tone is disrespectful. • Repetitive sentence structure, fragments, and run-on sentences make the writing monotonous and hard to follow. • Spelling and capitalization are often incorrect, and punctuation is missing. If handwritten, the argument may be partially or mostly illegible. • Many grammatical and usage errors change the meaning of the writer's ideas.

Image Credits: © Carlos Sanchez Pereyra/Alamy Images

The Bonds Between Us

"The welfare of each of us is dependent fundamentally upon the welfare of all of us."

—Theodore Roosevelt

The Bonds Between Us

In this collection, you will explore what links us to family, friends, pets, and community.

Stream to Start

hmhfyi.com

Channel One News®

COLLECTION
PERFORMANCE TASK Preview

At the end of this collection, you will have the opportunity to complete two tasks:

• Use narrative techniques in a fictional narrative about interpersonal connections.

• Develop a group multimedia presentation that explores the bonds that people form.

ACADEMIC VOCABULARY

Study the words and their definitions in the chart below. You will use these words as you discuss and write about the texts in this collection.

Word	Definition	Related Forms
capacity (kə-păs´ĭ-tē) *n.*	the ability to contain, hold, produce, or understand something	capacities, incapacitate
confer (kən-fûr´) *v.*	to grant or give to	conferral, conferrable
emerge (ĭ-mûrj´) *v.*	to come forth , out of, or away from	emergence, emergent
generate (jĕn´ə-rāt´) *v.*	to produce or cause something to happen or exist	generative, degenerate
trace (trās) *v.*	to discover or determine the origins or developmental stages of something	traceability, traceable, retrace

Background *In 2000,* **Jhumpa Lahiri** *(b. 1967) was awarded the Pulitzer Prize for her debut work of fiction, the short-story collection* The Interpreter of Maladies. *This story from the collection is set in 1971, the year in which civil war erupted in Pakistan. At the time, Pakistan had two distinct parts, West Pakistan and East Pakistan. India invaded the region in support of the eastern Pakistani people. The Pakistani army surrendered in the city of Dhaka (Dacca), and East Pakistan became a new nation, Bangladesh.*

When Mr. Pirzada Came to Dine

Short Story by Jhumpa Lahiri

AS YOU READ Pay attention to details that reveal the conflicts faced by the characters during the story. Note any questions as you read.

As you read, save new words to *my***WordList**.

In the autumn of 1971 a man used to come to our house, bearing confections in his pocket and hopes of ascertaining the life or death of his family. His name was Mr. Pirzada, and he came from Dacca, now the capital of Bangladesh, but then a part of Pakistan. That year Pakistan was engaged in civil war. The eastern frontier, where Dacca was located, was fighting for **autonomy** from the ruling regime in the west. In March, Dacca had been invaded, torched, and shelled by the Pakistani army. . . . By the end of the summer, three hundred thousand people were said to have died. In
10 Dacca Mr. Pirzada had a three-story home, a lectureship in botany[1] at the university, a wife of twenty years, and seven daughters between the ages of six and sixteen whose names all began with the letter A. "Their mother's idea," he explained one day, producing from his wallet a black-and-white picture of seven girls at a picnic, their braids tied with ribbons, sitting cross-legged in a row, eating

autonomy
(ô-tŏn′ə-mē) *n.*
independent
self-governance.

---

[1] **botany (bŏt′n-ē):** the science or study of plants.

chicken curry off of banana leaves. "How am I to distinguish? Ayesha, Amira, Amina, Aziza, you see the difficulty."

Each week Mr. Pirzada wrote letters to his wife, and sent comic books to each of his seven daughters, but the postal system, along with most everything else in Dacca, had collapsed, and he had not heard a word of them in over six months. Mr. Pirzada, meanwhile, was in America for the year, for he had been awarded a grant from the government of Pakistan to study the foliage of New England. In spring and summer he had gathered data in Vermont and Maine, and in autumn he moved to a university north of Boston, where we lived, to write a short book about his discoveries. The grant was a great honor, but when converted into dollars it was not generous. As a result, Mr. Pirzada lived in a room in a graduate dormitory, and did not own a proper stove or a television set. And so he came to our house to eat dinner and watch the evening news.

At first I knew nothing of the reason for his visits. I was ten years old, and was not surprised that my parents, who were from India, and had a number of Indian acquaintances at the university, should ask Mr. Pirzada to share our meals. It was a small campus, with narrow brick walkways and white pillared buildings, located on the fringes of what seemed to be an even smaller town. The supermarket did not carry mustard oil, doctors did not make house calls, neighbors never dropped by without an invitation, and of these things, every so often, my parents complained. In search of **compatriots**, they used to trail their fingers, at the start of each new semester, through the columns of the university directory, circling surnames familiar to their part of the world. It was in this manner that they discovered Mr. Pirzada, and phoned him, and invited him to our home.

I have no memory of his first visit, or of his second or his third, but by the end of September I had grown so accustomed to Mr. Pirzada's presence in our living room that one evening as I was dropping ice cubes into the water pitcher, I asked my mother to hand me a fourth glass from a cupboard still out of my reach. She was busy at the stove, presiding over a skillet of fried spinach with radishes, and could not hear me because of the drone of the exhaust fan and the fierce scrapes of her spatula. I turned to my father, who was leaning against the refrigerator, eating spiced cashews from a cupped fist.

"What is it, Lilia?"

"A glass for the Indian man."

"Mr. Pirzada won't be coming today. More importantly, Mr. Pirzada is no longer considered Indian," my father announced,

compatriot
(kəm-pā′trē-ət) *n.*
a fellow citizen or person from same country.

brushing salt from the cashews out of his trim black beard. "Not
60 since Partition.[2] Our country was divided. 1947."

When I said I thought that was the date of India's independence
from Britain, my father said, "That too. One moment we were free
and then we were sliced up," he explained, drawing an X with his
finger on the countertop, "like a pie. Hindus here, Muslims there.
Dacca no longer belongs to us." He told me that during Partition
Hindus and Muslims had set fire to each other's homes. For many,
the idea of eating in the other's company was still unthinkable.

It made no sense to me. Mr. Pirzada and my parents spoke the
same language, laughed at the same jokes, looked more or less the
70 same. They ate pickled mangoes with their meals, ate rice every
night for supper with their hands. Like my parents, Mr. Pirzada
took off his shoes before entering a room, chewed fennel seeds after
meals as a digestive, drank no alcohol, for dessert dipped austere
biscuits[3] into successive cups of tea. Nevertheless my father insisted
that I understand the difference, and he led me to a map of the
world taped to the wall over his desk. He seemed concerned that
Mr. Pirzada might take offense if I accidentally referred to him as
an Indian, though I could not really imagine Mr. Pirzada being
offended by much of anything. "Mr. Pirzada is Bengali, but he is
80 a Muslim," my father informed me. "Therefore he lives in East
Pakistan, not India." His finger trailed across the Atlantic, through
Europe, the Mediterranean, the Middle East, and finally to the
sprawling orange diamond that my mother once told me resembled
a woman wearing a sari[4] with her left arm extended. Various
cities had been circled with lines drawn between them to indicate
my parents' travels, and the place of their birth, Calcutta, was
signified by a small silver star. I had been there only once and had
no memory of the trip. "As you see, Lilia, it is a different country,
a different color," my father said. Pakistan was yellow, not orange.
90 I noticed that there were two distinct parts to it, one much larger
than the other, separated by an expanse of Indian territory; it was
as if California and Connecticut **constituted** a nation apart from
the U.S.

My father rapped his knuckles on top of my head. "You are,
of course, aware of the current situation? Aware of East Pakistan's
fight for sovereignty?"[5] I nodded, unaware of the situation.

constitute
(kŏn′stĭ-tōōt′) *v.*
to form or comprise.

---

[2] **Partition:** the division in 1947 of the Indian subcontinent into two
independent countries, India and Pakistan, after British withdrawal.

[3] **biscuits:** a British term for cookies or crackers.

[4] **sari (sä′rē):** a garment worn mostly by women of Pakistan and India, consisting
of a length of fabric with one end wrapped around the waist to form a skirt and
the other end draped over the shoulder or covering the head.

[5] **sovereignty:** complete independence and self-governance.

We returned to the kitchen, where my mother was draining a pot of boiled rice into a colander. My father opened up the can on the counter and eyed me sharply over the frames of his glasses as he ate some more cashews. "What exactly do they teach you at school? Do you study history? Geography?"

"Lilia has plenty to learn at school," my mother said. "We live here now, she was born here." She seemed genuinely proud of the fact, as if it were a reflection of my character. In her estimation, I knew, I was assured a safe life, an easy life, a fine education, every opportunity. I would never have to eat rationed food, or obey curfews, or watch riots from my rooftop, or hide neighbors in water tanks to prevent them from being shot, as she and my father had. "Imagine having to place her in a decent school. Imagine her having to read during power failures by the light of kerosene lamps. Imagine the pressures, the tutors, the constant exams." She ran a hand through her hair, bobbed to a suitable length for her part-time job as a bank teller. "How can you possibly expect her to know about Partition? Put those nuts away."

"But what does she learn about the world?" My father rattled the cashew can in his hand. "What is she learning?"

We learned American history, of course, and American geography. That year, and every year, it seemed, we began by studying the Revolutionary War. We were taken in school buses on field trips to visit Plymouth Rock,[6] and to walk the Freedom Trail, and to climb to the top of the Bunker Hill Monument.[7] We made dioramas out of colored construction paper depicting George Washington crossing the choppy waters of the Delaware River, and we made puppets of King George wearing white tights and a black bow in his hair. During tests we were given blank maps of the thirteen colonies, and asked to fill in names, dates, capitals. I could do it with my eyes closed.

The next evening Mr. Pirzada arrived, as usual, at six o'clock. Though they were no longer strangers, upon first greeting each other, he and my father maintained the habit of shaking hands.

"Come in, sir. Lilia, Mr. Pirzada's coat, please."

He stepped into the foyer, **impeccably** suited and scarved, with a silk tie knotted at his collar. Each evening he appeared in ensembles of plums, olives, and chocolate browns. He was a compact man, and though his feet were perpetually splayed, and his

impeccably
(ĭm-pĕk´ə-blē) *adv.*
perfectly.

---

[6] **Plymouth Rock:** a boulder in Plymouth, Massachusetts, said to be the site where the Pilgrims disembarked from the *Mayflower*.

[7] **Freedom Trail . . . Bunker Hill Monument:** historic sites in Boston, which commemorate critical events in the American struggle for independence from Great Britain.

belly slightly wide, he nevertheless maintained an efficient posture, as if balancing in either hand two suitcases of equal weight. His ears were insulated by tufts of graying hair that seemed to block out the unpleasant traffic of life. He had thickly lashed eyes shaded with a trace of camphor,[8] a generous mustache that turned up playfully at the ends, and a mole shaped like a flattened raisin in the very center of his left cheek. On his head he wore a black fez[9] made from the wool of Persian lambs, secured by bobby pins, without which I was never to see him. Though my father always offered to fetch him in our car, Mr. Pirzada preferred to walk from his dormitory to our neighborhood, a distance of about twenty minutes on foot, studying trees and shrubs on his way, and when he entered our house his knuckles were pink with the effects of the crisp autumn air.

"Another refugee, I am afraid, on Indian territory."

"They are estimating nine million at the last count," my father said.

Mr. Pirzada handed me his coat, for it was my job to hang it on the rack at the bottom of the stairs. It was made of finely checkered gray-and-blue wool, with a striped lining and horn buttons, and carried in its weave the faint smell of limes. There were no recognizable tags inside, only a hand-stitched label with the phrase "Z. Sayeed, Suitors" embroidered on it in cursive with glossy black thread. On certain days a birch or maple leaf was tucked into a pocket. He unlaced his shoes and lined them against the baseboard; a golden paste clung to the toes and heels, the result of walking through our damp, unraked lawn. Relieved of his trappings, he grazed my throat with his short, restless fingers, the way a person feels for solidity behind a wall before driving in a nail. Then he followed my father to the living room, where the television was tuned to the local news. As soon as they were seated my mother appeared from the kitchen with a plate of mincemeat kebabs with coriander chutney. Mr. Pirzada popped one into his mouth.

"One can only hope," he said, reaching for another, "that Dacca's refugees are as heartily fed. Which reminds me." He reached into his suit pocket and gave me a small plastic egg filled with cinnamon hearts. "For the lady of the house," he said with an almost **imperceptible** splay-footed bow.

"Really, Mr. Pirzada," my mother protested. "Night after night. You spoil her."

"I only spoil children who are incapable of spoiling."

imperceptible
(ĭm′pər-sĕp′tə-bəl)
adj. unnoticeable.

---

[8] **camphor (kăm′fər):** a fragrant compound from an Asian evergreen tree, used in skin-care products.

[9] **fez (fĕz):** a man's felt hat in the shape of a flat-topped cone, worn mainly in the eastern Mediterranean region.

It was an awkward moment for me, one which I awaited in part with dread, in part with delight. I was charmed by the presence of Mr. Pirzada's rotund elegance, and flattered by the faint theatricality of his attentions, yet unsettled by the superb ease of his gestures, which made me feel, for an instant, like a stranger in my own home. It had become our ritual, and for several weeks, before we grew more comfortable with one another, it was the only time he spoke to me directly. I had no response, offered no comment, betrayed no visible reaction to the steady stream of honey-filled lozenges, the raspberry truffles, the slender rolls of sour pastilles. I could not even thank him, for once, when I did, for an especially spectacular peppermint lollipop wrapped in a spray of purple cellophane, he had demanded, "What is this thank-you? The lady at the bank thanks me, the cashier at the shop thanks me, the librarian thanks me when I return an overdue book, the overseas operator thanks me as she tries to connect me to Dacca and fails. If I am buried in this country I will be thanked, no doubt, at my funeral."

It was inappropriate, in my opinion, to consume the candy Mr. Pirzada gave me in a casual manner. I coveted each evening's treasure as I would a jewel, or a coin from a buried kingdom, and I would place it in a small keepsake box made of carved sandalwood beside my bed, in which, long ago in India, my father's mother used to store the ground areca nuts[10] she ate after her morning bath. It was my only memento of a grandmother I had never known, and until Mr. Pirzada came to our lives I could find nothing to put inside it. Every so often before brushing my teeth and laying out my clothes for school the next day, I opened the lid of the box and ate one of his treats.

That night, like every night, we did not eat at the dining table, because it did not provide an unobstructed view of the television set. Instead we huddled around the coffee table, without conversing, our plates perched on the edges of our knees. From the kitchen my mother brought forth the **succession** of dishes: lentils with fried onions, green beans with coconut, fish cooked with raisins in a yogurt sauce. I followed with the water glasses, and the plate of lemon wedges, and the chili peppers, purchased on monthly trips to Chinatown and stored by the pound in the freezer, which they liked to snap open and crush into their food.

Before eating Mr. Pirzada always did a curious thing. He took out a plain silver watch without a band, which he kept in his breast pocket, held it briefly to one of his tufted ears, and wound it with three swift flicks of his thumb and forefinger. Unlike the watch on

succession
(sək-sĕsh´ən) *n.*
sequence; ordered
arrangement.

---

[10] **areca (ə-rē´kə) nuts:** seeds of the betel palm, chewed as a stimulant.

his wrist, the pocket watch, he had explained to me, was set to the local time in Dacca, eleven hours ahead. For the duration of the meal the watch rested on his folded napkin on the coffee table. He never seemed to consult it.

Now that I had learned Mr. Pirzada was not an Indian, I began to study him with extra care, to try to figure out what made him different. I decided that the pocket watch was one of those things. When I saw it that night, as he wound it and arranged it on the coffee table, an uneasiness possessed me; life, I realized, was being lived in Dacca first. I imagined Mr. Pirzada's daughters rising from sleep, tying ribbons in their hair, anticipating breakfast, preparing for school. Our meals, our actions, were only a shadow of what had already happened there, a lagging ghost of where Mr. Pirzada really belonged.

At six-thirty, which was when the national news began, my father raised the volume and adjusted the antennas. Usually I occupied myself with a book, but that night my father insisted that I pay attention. On the screen I saw tanks rolling through dusty streets, and fallen buildings, and forests of unfamiliar trees into which East Pakistani refugees had fled, seeking safety over

the Indian border. I saw boats with fan-shaped sails floating on
240   wide coffee-colored rivers, a barricaded university, newspaper
offices burnt to the ground. I turned to look at Mr. Pirzada; the
images flashed in miniature across his eyes. As he watched he had
an immovable expression on his face, composed but alert, as if
someone were giving him directions to an unknown destination.

During the commercial my mother went to the kitchen to get
more rice, and my father and Mr. Pirzada deplored the policies
of a general named Yahyah Khan. They discussed intrigues I did
not know, a catastrophe I could not comprehend. "See, children
your age, what they do to survive," my father said as he served me
250   another piece of fish. But I could no longer eat. I could only steal
glances at Mr. Pirzada, sitting beside me in his olive green jacket,
calmly creating a well in his rice to make room for a second helping
of lentils. He was not my notion of a man burdened by such grave
concerns. I wondered if the reason he was always so smartly dressed
was in preparation to endure with dignity whatever news **assailed**
him, perhaps even to attend a funeral at a moment's notice. I
wondered, too, what would happen if suddenly his seven daughters
were to appear on television, smiling and waving and blowing
kisses to Mr. Pirzada from a balcony. I imagined how relieved he
260   would be. But this never happened.

That night when I placed the plastic egg filled with cinnamon
hearts in the box beside my bed, I did not feel the ceremonious
satisfaction I normally did. I tried not to think about Mr. Pirzada,
in his lime-scented overcoat, connected to the unruly, sweltering
world we had viewed a few hours ago in our bright, carpeted living
room. And yet for several moments that was all I could think about.
My stomach tightened as I worried whether his wife and seven
daughters were now members of the drifting, clamoring crowd that
had flashed at intervals on the screen. In an effort to banish the
270   image I looked around my room, at the yellow canopied bed with
matching flounced curtains, at framed class pictures mounted on
white and violet papered walls, at the penciled inscriptions by the
closet door where my father had recorded my height on each of my
birthdays. But the more I tried to distract myself, the more I began
to convince myself that Mr. Pirzada's family was in all likelihood
dead. Eventually I took a square of white chocolate out of the box,
and unwrapped it, and then I did something I had never done
before. I put the chocolate in my mouth, letting it soften until the
last possible moment, and then as I chewed it slowly, I prayed that
280   Mr. Pirzada's family was safe and sound. I had never prayed for
anything before, had never been taught or told to, but I decided,
given the circumstances, that it was something I should do. That
night when I went to the bathroom I only pretended to brush my

assail
(ə-sāl´) v.
attack, disturb.

teeth, for I feared that I would somehow rinse the prayer out as well. I wet the brush and rearranged the tube of paste to prevent my parents from asking any questions, and fell asleep with sugar on my tongue.

No one at school talked about the war followed so faithfully in my living room. We continued to study the American Revolution, and learned about the injustices of taxation without representation, and memorized passages from the Declaration of Independence. During recess the boys would divide in two groups, chasing each other wildly around the swings and seesaws, Redcoats against the colonies. In the classroom our teacher, Mrs. Kenyon, pointed frequently to a map that emerged like a movie screen from the top of the chalkboard, charting the route of the *Mayflower*, or showing us the location of the Liberty Bell. Each week two members of the class gave a report on a particular aspect of the Revolution, and so one day I was sent to the school library with my friend Dora to learn about the surrender at Yorktown. Mrs. Kenyon handed us a slip of paper with the names of three books to look up in the card catalogue. We found them right away, and sat down at a low round table to read and take notes. But I could not concentrate. I returned to the blond-wood shelves, to a section I had noticed labeled "Asia." I saw books about China, India, Indonesia, Korea. Eventually I found a book titled *Pakistan: A Land and Its People*. I sat on a footstool and opened the book. The laminated jacket crackled in my grip. I began turning the pages, filled with photos of rivers and rice fields and men in military uniforms. There was a chapter about Dacca, and I began to read about its rainfall, and its jute[11] production. I was studying a population chart when Dora appeared in the aisle.

"What are you doing back here? Mrs. Kenyon's in the library. She came to check up on us."

I slammed the book shut, too loudly. Mrs. Kenyon emerged, the aroma of her perfume filling up the tiny aisle, and lifted the book by the tip of its spine as if it were a hair clinging to my sweater. She glanced at the cover, then at me.

"Is this book a part of your report, Lilia?"

"No, Mrs. Kenyon."

"Then I see no reason to consult it," she said, replacing it in the slim gap on the shelf. "Do you?"

As weeks passed it grew more and more rare to see any footage from Dacca on the news. The report came after the first

---

[11] **jute:** the fiber from an Asian plant, used for sacking and cording.

set of commercials, sometimes the second. The press had been censored, removed, restricted, rerouted. Some days, many days, only a death toll was announced, prefaced by a **reiteration** of the general situation. . . . More villages set ablaze. In spite of it all, night after night, my parents and Mr. Pirzada enjoyed long, leisurely meals. After the television was shut off, and the dishes washed and dried, they joked, and told stories, and dipped biscuits in their tea. When they tired of discussing political matters they discussed, instead, the progress of Mr. Pirzada's book about the deciduous trees[12] of New England, and my father's nomination for tenure, and the peculiar eating habits of my mother's American coworkers at the bank. Eventually I was sent upstairs to do my homework, but through the carpet I heard them as they drank more tea, and listened to cassettes of Kishore Kumar, and played Scrabble on the coffee table, laughing and arguing long into the night about the spellings of English words. I wanted to join them, wanted, above all, to console Mr. Pirzada somehow. But apart from eating a piece of candy for the sake of his family and praying for their safety, there was nothing I could do. They played Scrabble until the eleven o'clock news, and then, sometime around midnight, Mr. Pirzada walked back to his dormitory. For this reason I never saw him leave, but each night as I drifted off to sleep I would hear them, anticipating the birth of a nation on the other side of the world.

One day in October Mr. Pirzada asked upon arrival, "What are these large orange vegetables on people's doorsteps? A type of squash?"

"Pumpkins," my mother replied. "Lilia, remind me to pick one up at the supermarket."

"And the purpose? It indicates what?"

"You make a jack-o'-lantern," I said, grinning ferociously. "Like this. To scare people away."

"I see," Mr. Pirzada said, grinning back. "Very useful."

The next day my mother bought a ten-pound pumpkin, fat and round, and placed it on the dining table. Before supper, while my father and Mr. Pirzada were watching the local news, she told me to decorate it with markers, but I wanted to carve it properly like others I had noticed in the neighborhood.

"Yes, let's carve it," Mr. Pirzada agreed, and rose from the sofa. "Hang the news tonight." Asking no questions, he walked into the kitchen, opened a drawer, and returned, bearing a long serrated knife. He glanced at me for approval. "Shall I?"

reiteration
(rē-ĭt´ə-rā´shən) n.
restatement or
repetition.

---

[12]**deciduous (də-sĭj´ōōəs) trees:** trees that shed or lose leaves at the end of the growing season.

I nodded. For the first time we all gathered around the dining table, my mother, my father, Mr. Pirzada, and I. While the television aired unattended we covered the tabletop with newspapers. Mr. Pirzada draped his jacket over the chair behind him, removed a pair of opal cuff links, and rolled up the starched sleeves of his shirt.

"First go around the top, like this," I instructed, demonstrating with my index finger.

He made an initial incision and drew the knife around. When he had come full circle he lifted the cap by the stem; it loosened effortlessly, and Mr. Pirzada leaned over the pumpkin for a moment to inspect and inhale its contents. My mother gave him a long metal spoon with which he gutted the interior until the last bits of string and seeds were gone. My father, meanwhile, separated the seeds from the pulp and set them out to dry on a cookie sheet, so that we could roast them later on. I drew two triangles against the ridged surface for the eyes, which Mr. Pirzada dutifully carved, and crescents for eyebrows, and another triangle for the nose. The mouth was all that remained, and the teeth posed a challenge. I hesitated.

"Smile or frown?" I asked.

"You choose," Mr Pirzada said.

As a compromise I drew a kind of grimace, straight across, neither mournful nor friendly. Mr. Pirzada began carving, without the least bit of intimidation, as if he had been carving jack-o'-lanterns his whole life. He had nearly finished when the national news began. The reporter mentioned Dacca, and we all turned to listen: An Indian official announced that unless the world helped to relieve the burden of East Pakistani refugees, India would have to go to war against Pakistan. The reporter's face dripped with sweat as he relayed the information. He did not wear a tie or jacket, dressed instead as if he himself were about to take part in the battle. He shielded his scorched face as he hollered things to the cameraman. The knife slipped from Mr. Pirzada's hand and made a gash dipping toward the base of the pumpkin.

"Please forgive me." He raised a hand to one side of his face, as if someone had slapped him there. "I am—it is terrible. I will buy another. We will try again."

"Not at all, not at all," my father said. He took the knife from Mr. Pirzada, and carved around the gash, evening it out, dispensing altogether with the teeth I had drawn. What resulted was a disproportionately large hole the size of a lemon, so that our jack-o'-lantern wore an expression of placid astonishment, the eyebrows no longer fierce, floating in frozen surprise above a vacant, geometric gaze.

For Halloween I was a witch. Dora, my trick-or-treating partner, was a witch too. We wore black capes fashioned from dyed pillowcases and conical hats with wide cardboard brims. We shaded our faces green with a broken eye shadow that belonged to Dora's mother, and my mother gave us two burlap sacks that had once contained basmati rice, for collecting candy. That year our parents decided that we were old enough to roam the neighborhood unattended. Our plan was to walk from my house to Dora's, from where I was to call to say I had arrived safely, and then

420 Dora's mother would drive me home. My father equipped us with flashlights, and I had to wear my watch and synchronize it with his. We were to return no later than nine o'clock.

When Mr. Pirzada arrived that evening he presented me with a box of chocolate-covered mints.

"In here," I told him, and opened up the burlap sack. "Trick or treat!"

"I understand that you don't really need my contribution this evening," he said, depositing the box. He gazed at my green face, and the hat secured by a string under my chin. Gingerly he lifted

430 the hem of the cape, under which I was wearing a sweater and zipped fleece jacket. "Will you be warm enough?"

I nodded, causing the hat to tip to one side.

He set it right. "Perhaps it is best to stand still."

The bottom of our staircase was lined with baskets of miniature candy, and when Mr. Pirzada removed his shoes he did not place them there as he normally did, but inside the closet instead. He began to unbutton his coat, and I waited to take it from him, but Dora called me from the bathroom to say that she needed my help drawing a mole on her chin. When we were finally ready my mother took a picture of us in front of the fireplace, and then I opened the front door to leave. Mr. Pirzada and my father, who had not gone into the living room yet, hovered in the foyer. Outside it was already dark. The air smelled of wet leaves, and our carved jack-o'-lantern flickered impressively against the shrubbery by the door. In the distance came the sounds of scampering feet, and the howls of the older boys who wore no costume at all other than a rubber mask, and the rustling apparel of the youngest children, some so young that they were carried from door to door in the arms of their parents.

"Don't go into any of the houses you don't know," my father warned.

Mr. Pirzada knit his brows together. "Is there any danger?"

"No, no," my mother assured him. "All the children will be out. It's a tradition."

"Perhaps I should accompany them?" Mr. Pirzada suggested. He looked suddenly tired and small, standing there in his splayed, stockinged feet, and his eyes contained a panic I had never seen before. In spite of the cold I began to sweat inside my pillowcase.

"Really, Mr. Pirzada," my mother said, "Lilia will be perfectly safe with her friend."

"But if it rains? If they lose their way?"

"Don't worry," I said. It was the first time I had uttered those words to Mr. Pirzada, two simple words I had tried but failed to tell him for weeks, had said only in my prayers. It shamed me now that I had said them for my own sake.

He placed one of his stocky fingers on my cheek, then pressed it to the back of his own hand, leaving a faint green smear. "If the lady insists," he **conceded**, and offered a small bow.

We left, stumbling slightly in our black pointy thrift-store shoes, and when we turned at the end of the driveway to wave good-bye, Mr. Pirzada was standing in the frame of the doorway, a short figure between my parents, waving back.

"Why did that man want to come with us?" Dora asked.

"His daughters are missing." As soon as I said it, I wished I had not. I felt that my saying it made it true, that Mr. Pirzada's daughters really were missing, and that he would never see them again.

concede
(kən-sēd´) v.
to surrender or acknowledge defeat.

"You mean they were kidnapped?" Dora continued. "From a park or something?"

"I didn't mean they were missing. I meant, he misses them. They live in a different country, and he hasn't seen them in a while, that's all."

We went from house to house, walking along pathways and pressing doorbells. Some people had switched off all their lights for effect, or strung rubber bats in their windows. At the McIntyres' a coffin was placed in front of the door, and Mr. McIntyre rose from it in silence, his face covered with chalk, and deposited a fistful of candy corns into our sacks. Several people told me that they had never seen an Indian witch before. Others performed the transaction without comment. As we paved our way with the parallel beams of our flashlights we saw eggs cracked in the middle of the road, and cars covered with shaving cream, and toilet paper garlanding the branches of trees. By the time we reached Dora's house our hands were chapped from carrying our bulging burlap bags, and our feet were sore and swollen. Her mother gave us bandages for our blisters and served us warm cider and caramel popcorn. She reminded me to call my parents to tell them I had arrived safely and when I did I could hear the television in the background. My mother did not seem particularly relieved to hear from me. When I replaced the phone on the receiver it occurred to me that the television wasn't on at Dora's house at all. Her father was lying on the couch, reading a magazine, with a glass of wine on the coffee table, and there was saxophone music playing on the stereo.

After Dora and I had sorted through our plunder, and counted and sampled and traded until we were satisfied, her mother drove me back to my house. I thanked her for the ride, and she waited in the driveway until I made it to the door. In the glare of her headlights I saw that our pumpkin had been shattered, its thick shell strewn in chunks across the grass. I felt the sting of tears in my eyes, and a sudden pain in my throat, as if it had been stuffed with the sharp tiny pebbles that crunched with each step under my aching feet. I opened the door, expecting the three of them to be standing in the foyer, waiting to receive me, and to grieve for our ruined pumpkin, but there was no one. In the living room Mr. Pirzada, my father, and mother were sitting side by side on the sofa. The television was turned off, and Mr. Pirzada had his head in his hands.

What they heard that evening, and for many evenings after that, was that India and Pakistan were drawing closer and closer to war. Troops from both sides lined the border, and Dacca was insisting on nothing short of independence. The war was soon to

"Just as I have no memory of his first visit, I have no memory of his last."

be waged on East Pakistani soil. The United States was siding with West Pakistan, the Soviet Union with India and what was soon to be Bangladesh. War was declared officially on December 4, and twelve days later, the Pakistani army, weakened by having to fight three thousand miles from their source of supplies, surrendered in Dacca. All of these facts I know only now, for they are available to me in any history book, in any library. But then it remained, for the most part, a remote mystery with haphazard clues. What

530 I remember during those twelve days of the war was that my father no longer asked me to watch the news with them, and that Mr. Pirzada stopped bringing me candy, and that my mother refused to serve anything other than boiled eggs with rice for dinner. I remember some nights helping my mother spread a sheet and blankets on the couch so that Mr. Pirzada could sleep there, and high-pitched voices hollering in the middle of the night when my parents called our relatives in Calcutta to learn more details about the situation. Most of all I remember the three of them operating during that time as if they were a single person, sharing a

540 single meal, a single body, a single silence, and a single fear.

In January, Mr. Pirzada flew back to his three-story home in Dacca, to discover what was left of it. We did not see much of him in those final weeks of the year; he was busy finishing his manuscript, and we went to Philadelphia to spend Christmas with friends of my parents. Just as I have no memory of his first visit, I have no memory of his last. My father drove him to the airport one afternoon while I was at school. For a long time we did not hear from him. Our evenings went on as usual, with dinners in front of the news. The only difference was that Mr. Pirzada and his extra watch were not there to accompany us. According to reports Dacca was repairing itself slowly, with a newly formed parliamentary government. The new leader, Sheikh Mujib Rahman, recently released from prison, asked countries for building materials to replace more than one million houses that had been destroyed in the war. Countless refugees returned from India, greeted, we learned, by unemployment and the threat of famine. Every now and then I studied the map above my father's desk and pictured Mr. Pirzada on that small patch of yellow, perspiring heavily, I imagined, in one of his suits, searching for his family. Of course, the map was outdated by then.

Finally, several months later, we received a card from Mr. Pirzada **commemorating** the Muslim New Year, along with a short letter. He was reunited, he wrote, with his wife and children. All were well, having survived the events of the past year at an estate belonging to his wife's grandparents in the mountains of Shillong. His seven daughters were a bit taller, he wrote, but otherwise they were the same, and he still could not keep their names in order. At the end of the letter he thanked us for our hospitality, adding that although he now understood the meaning of the words "thank you" they still were not adequate to express his gratitude. To celebrate the good news my mother prepared a special dinner that evening, and when we sat down to eat at the coffee table we toasted our water glasses, but I did not feel like celebrating. Though I had not seen him for months, it was only then that I felt Mr. Pirzada's absence. It was only then, raising my water glass in his name, that I knew what it meant to miss someone who was so many miles and hours away, just as he had missed his wife and daughters for so many months. He had no reason to return to us, and my parents predicted, correctly, that we would never see him again. Since January, each night before bed, I had continued to eat, for the sake of Mr. Pirzada's family, a piece of candy I had saved from Halloween. That night there was no need to. Eventually, I threw them away.

commemorate
(kə-mĕm′ə-rāt′) *v.*
to celebrate or honor.

COLLABORATIVE DISCUSSION What conflicts does Mr. Pirzada experience in the story? What conflicts does Lilia face? Who is changed more at the end of the story? Cite textual evidence from the story to support your ideas.

Support Inferences About Theme

A **theme,** or central idea, is an underlying message about life or human nature that emerges from specific details in a story. Authors do not usually state the theme directly; instead, they convey themes with descriptive details, by repeating specific words and images, and through the words and actions of the story's characters. As a reader, you must look for important details and make **inferences,** or logical guesses, about the theme.

In "When Mr. Pirzada Came to Dine," look for clues about theme in the interactions between Mr. Pirzada and Lilia, the 10-year-old narrator of the story. What does Lilia focus on when she describes Mr. Pirzada, his family, and his life in eastern Pakistan? What does Lilia share about her own life? Focus on these key details to make inferences about the theme of the story.

Analyze Character and Theme

An author develops **characters** by describing what they do and say, how they interact with other characters, and how they change during the story. Details about the characters often develop the story's themes. The chart provides examples of how to use text evidence to analyze characters and make inferences about theme.

Text Evidence	Examples	Inferences and Questions
Descriptive details about a character's appearance	"He stepped into the foyer, impeccably suited and scarved, with a silk tie knotted at his collar. . . . On his head he wore a black fez made from the wool of Persian lambs, secured by bobby pins. . . ."	This description of Mr. Pirzada shows that he cares about his appearance. What can you infer from his choice of a suit and tie paired with the fez of his homeland?
Character's words and actions	"He reached into his suit pocket and gave me a small plastic egg filled with cinnamon hearts. 'For the lady of the house,' he said . . ."	Mr. Pirzada presents Lilia with gifts throughout the story. What is the meaning behind this special attention?
Character's thoughts and observations	"I began to study him with extra care, to try to figure out what made him different. I decided that the pocket watch was one of those things."	Lilia thinks about Mr. Pirzada's pocket watch. What does she realize about him as she watches him care for his watch?

Analyzing the Text

Cite Text Evidence Support your responses with evidence from the selection.

1. **Infer** Describe the gifts that Mr. Pirzada gives Lilia and how Lilia cares for these gifts. Why might she feel she should not eat the candy "in a casual manner"?

2. **Interpret** How is Mr. Pirzada's pocket watch different from the watch he wears on his wrist? What does the pocket watch help Lilia understand about Mr. Pirzada and his situation?

3. **Infer** How does Mr. Pirzada react to the idea of Lilia going out trick-or-treating? What does Lilia mean when she tries to explain it to her friend by saying, "His daughters are missing"?

4. **Analyze** Throughout the story, Lilia listens as her parents and Mr. Pirzada discuss the war between India and Pakistan. Why does she become more interested in the war? What deeper change does this interest represent in Lilia?

5. **Interpret** A **symbol** is something that stands for or represents both itself and something else. The objects associated with characters in a story are often symbols that provide clues about who they are and what they are experiencing. What are at least three objects associated with Mr. Pirzada, and what do they symbolize?

6. **Cite Evidence** What theme about growing up does the story convey? Think about Lilia's experiences and the way she changes during the story.

7. **Draw Conclusions** At the end of the story, why does Lilia feel she can finally throw away her remaining candies from Mr. Pirzada?

PERFORMANCE TASK

Writing Activity: Letters "When Mr. Pirzada Came to Dine" is told from the point of view of 10-year-old Lilia. What might we learn if we could know Mr. Pirzada's point of view? Write two letters from Mr. Pirzada to his family in Dacca. Be sure to base the details in your letters on insights we gain through Lilia's observations in the story.

- In the first letter, have Mr. Pirzada describe Lilia and her family. Have him explain why he enjoys giving Lilia candy and what she does with it.

- In the second letter, have him describe Halloween. Include details about the pumpkin carving and Lilia's trick-or-treating.

Critical Vocabulary

autonomy	compatriot	constitute	impeccably	imperceptible
succession	assail	reiteration	concede	commemorate

Practice and Apply With a partner, describe what is similar and different about the words in each pair.

1. autonomy/freedom
2. compatriot/friend
3. constitute/assemble
4. impeccably/neatly
5. imperceptible/slight

6. succession/parade
7. assail/trouble
8. reiteration/emphasis
9. concede/quit
10. commemorate/remember

Vocabulary Strategy: Patterns of Word Changes

Suffixes change a word's meaning and part of speech. For example, the Critical Vocabulary word *succession* is formed by adding the noun suffix *-ion* to a verb, or action word. The verb *succeed*, which means "to follow," becomes the noun *succession*, which means "a series or sequence." Identifying patterns of word changes will help you define unfamiliar words you encounter in your reading. Here are some common English suffixes:

Suffix	Part of Speech	Meaning	Examples
-tion, -ion	noun	act or condition of	revolution, explosion
-ify, -fy	verb	make or become	terrify, specify
-able, -ible	adjective	ability	understandable, approachable

Practice and Apply For each row of the chart, identify another example that uses one of the suffixes shown. With each word you choose, follow these steps:

1. Identify the base, the main word part without the suffix. Note the part of speech (noun, verb, adjective) and meaning of each base word.

2. Write a definition for each word.

3. Use each word in a sample sentence.

Language and Style: Adverbial Clauses

A **subordinate clause** has a subject and verb but cannot stand alone as a sentence. It is introduced by a subordinating conjunction, such as *how, when, where, why, because,* or *whether.*

An **adverbial clause** is a subordinate clause that functions as an adverb—that is, it modifies a verb, an adjective, or an adverb in a sentence. Authors use adverbial clauses to convey specific meaning and to add variety to their writing.

In the following example from "When Mr. Pirzada Came to Dine," an adverbial clause beginning with the subordinating conjunction *when* modifies the verb *said*:

> <u>When I said I thought that was the date of India's independence from Britain,</u> my father said, "That too."

The adverbial clause makes the connection between the two ideas—what Lilia said and what her father said—clear to readers. Remove the adverbial clause, and the writing becomes choppier and slightly less clear:

> I said I thought that was the date of India's independence from Britain. My father said, "That too."

Now read this sentence:

> He seemed concerned <u>that Mr. Pirzada might take offense if I accidentally referred to him as an Indian,</u> though I could not really imagine Mr. Pirzada being offended by much of anything.

This sentence contains two adverbial clauses. The clause *that Mr. Pirzada might take offense* modifies the verb *concerned*, and the clause *if I accidentally referred to him as an Indian* modifies the verb *take*. These clauses pack a great deal of detail into one complex sentence. Without them, it would not be clear exactly why Lilia's father is concerned:

> He seemed concerned, though I could not really imagine Mr. Pirzada being offended by much of anything.

Practice and Apply Review the letters you created in response to this selection's Performance Task. In both letters, find two places where you can incorporate adverbial clauses into your writing. Have a partner review your work.

Frans B.M. de Waal (b. 1948) *was born in the Netherlands. Trained in biology , de Waal analyzes the behaviors and social interactions of primates, an order of mammals that includes monkeys, chimpanzees, gorillas, lemurs, and* homo sapiens, *or humans. He is the director of The Living Links Center at the Yerkes National Primate Research Center in Lawrenceville, Georgia, and the author of numerous books including* Chimpanzee Politics.

Monkey See, Monkey Do, Monkey Connect

Science Writing by Frans de Waal

AS YOU READ Trace and consider the examples de Waal provides about human and primate behavior. Write down any questions.

What intrigues me most about laughter is how it spreads. It's almost impossible not to laugh when everybody else is. There have been laughing epidemics, in which no one could stop and some even died in a prolonged fit. There are laughing churches and laugh therapies based on the healing power of laughter. The must-have toy of 1996—Tickle Me Elmo—laughed hysterically after being squeezed three times in a row. All of this because we love to laugh and can't resist joining laughing around us. This is why comedy shows on television have laugh tracks and why theater

10 audiences are sometimes sprinkled with "laugh plants": people paid to produce raucous laughing at any joke that comes along.

The infectiousness of laughter even works across species. Below my office window at the Yerkes Primate Center, I often hear my chimps laugh during rough-and-tumble games, and I cannot suppress a chuckle myself. It's such a happy sound. Tickling and wrestling are the typical laugh triggers for apes, and probably the original ones for humans. The fact that tickling oneself is notoriously ineffective attests to its social significance. And when

young apes put on their play face, their friends join in with the
20 same expression as rapidly and easily as humans do with laughter.

Shared laughter is just one example of our primate sensitivity
to others. Instead of being Robinson Crusoes sitting on separate
islands,[1] we're all interconnected, both bodily and emotionally.
This may be an odd thing to say in the West, with its tradition of
individual freedom and liberty, but *Homo sapiens*[2] is remarkably
easily swayed in one emotional direction or another by its fellows.

This is precisely where **empathy** and sympathy start—not in
the higher regions of imagination, or the ability to consciously
reconstruct how we would feel if we were in someone else's
30 situation. It began much more simply, with the **synchronization**
of bodies: running when others run, laughing when others laugh,
crying when others cry, or yawning when others yawn. Most of us
have reached the incredibly advanced stage at which we yawn even
at the mere mention of yawning—as you may be doing right now!—
but this is only after lots of face-to-face experience.

Yawn **contagion**, too, works across species. Virtually all animals
show the peculiar "paroxystic respiratory cycle characterized by a
standard cascade of movements over a five- to ten-second period,"
which is the way the yawn has been defined. I once attended
40 a lecture on involuntary pandiculation (the medical term for
stretching and yawning) with slides of horses, lions, and monkeys—
and soon the entire audience was pandiculating. Since it so easily
triggers a chain reaction, the yawn reflex opens a window onto
mood transmission, an essential part of empathy. This makes it all
the more intriguing that chimpanzees yawn when they see others
do so.

Yawn contagion reflects the power of unconscious synchrony,
which is as deeply ingrained in us as in many other animals.
Synchrony may be expressed in the copying of small body
50 movements, such as a yawn, but also occurs on a larger scale,
involving travel or movement. It is not hard to see its survival value.
You're in a flock of birds and one bird suddenly takes off. You have
no time to figure out what's going on: You take off at the same
instant. Otherwise, you may be lunch.

Or your entire group becomes sleepy and settles down, so you
too become sleepy. Mood contagion serves to coordinate activities,
which is crucial for any traveling species (as most primates are). If
my companions are feeding, I'd better do the same, because once
they move off, my chance to forage will be gone. The individual
60 who doesn't stay in tune with what everyone else is doing will lose

empathy
(ĕm´pə-thē) *n.* the
ability to understand
and identify with
another's feelings.

synchronization
(sĭng´krə-nĭ-zā´shən)
n. coordinated,
simultaneous action.

contagion
(kən-tā´jən) *n.* the
spreading from one
to another.

---

[1] **Robinson Crusoes . . . islands:** Crusoe, the title character of Daniel Defoe's
1719 novel, was stranded alone on a tropical island.

[2] *Homo sapiens* (hō´mō sā´pē-ənz): the species of primates that includes humans.

out like the traveler who doesn't go to the restroom when the bus has stopped.

The herd instinct produces weird phenomena. At one zoo, an entire baboon troop gathered on top of their rock, all staring in exactly the same direction. For an entire week they forgot to eat, mate, and groom. They just kept staring at something in the distance that no one could identify. Local newspapers were carrying pictures of the monkey rock, speculating that perhaps the animals had been frightened by a UFO. But even though this explanation had the unique advantage of combining an account of primate behavior with proof of UFOs, the truth is that no one knew the cause except that the baboons clearly were all of the same mind.

Finding himself in front of the cameras next to his pal President George W. Bush, former British prime minister Tony Blair—known to walk normally at home—would suddenly metamorphose into a distinctly un-English cowboy. He'd swagger with arms hanging loose and chest puffed out. Bush, of course, strutted like this all the time and once explained how, back home in Texas, this is known as "walking." Identification is the hook that draws us in and makes us adopt the situation, emotions, and behavior of those we're close to. They become role models: We empathize with them and emulate[3] them. Thus children often walk like the same-sex parent or mimic their tone of voice when they pick up the phone.

How does one chimp imitate another? Does he identify with the other and absorb its body movements? Or could it be that he doesn't need the other and instead focuses on the problem faced by the other? This can be tested by having a chimpanzee show another how to open a puzzle box with goodies inside. Maybe all that the watching ape needs to understand is how the thing works. He may notice that the door slides to the side or that something needs to be lifted up. The first kind of imitation involves reenactment of observed manipulations; the second merely requires technical know-how.

Thanks to ingenious studies in which chimps were presented with a so-called ghost box, we know which of these two explanations is correct. A ghost box derives its name from the fact that it magically opens and closes by itself so that no actor is needed. If technical know-how were all that mattered, such a box should suffice. But in fact, letting chimps watch a ghost box until they're bored to death—with its various parts moving and producing rewards hundreds of times—doesn't teach them anything.

---

[3] **emulate:** to imitate or behave like.

To learn from others, apes need to see actual fellow apes: Imitation requires identification with a body of flesh and blood. We're beginning to realize how much human and animal cognition runs via the body. Instead of our brain being like a little computer that orders the body around, the body-brain relation is a two-way street. The body produces internal sensations and communicates with other bodies, out of which we construct social connections and an appreciation of the surrounding reality. Bodies insert themselves into everything we perceive or think. Did you know, for example, that physical condition colors perception? The same hill is assessed as steeper, just from looking at it, by a tired person than by a well-rested one. An outdoor target is judged as farther away than it really is by a person burdened with a heavy backpack than by one without it.

Or ask a pianist to pick out his own performance from among others he's listening to. Even if this is a new piece that the pianist has performed only once, in silence (on an electronic piano and without headphones on), he will be able to recognize his own play. While listening, he probably re-creates in his head the sort of bodily sensations that accompany an actual performance. He feels the closest match listening to himself, thus recognizing himself through his body as much as through his ears.

The field of "embodied" **cognition** is still very much in its infancy but has profound **implications** for how we look at human relations. We involuntarily enter the bodies of those around us so that their movements and emotions echo within us as if they're our own. This is what allows us, or other primates, to re-create what we have seen others do. Body mapping is mostly hidden and unconscious, but sometimes it "slips out," such as when parents make chewing mouth movements while spoon-feeding their baby. They can't help but act the way they feel their baby ought to. Similarly, parents watching a singing performance of their child often get completely into it, mouthing every word. I myself still remember as a boy standing on the sidelines of soccer games and involuntarily making kicking or jumping moves each time someone I was cheering for got the ball.

The same can be seen in animals, as illustrated in an old black-and-white photograph from Wolfgang Köhler's classic tool-use studies on chimpanzees. One ape, Grande, stands on boxes that she has stacked up to reach bananas hung from the ceiling, while Sultan watches intently. Even though Sultan sits at a distance, he raises his arm in precise synchrony with Grande's grasping movement. Another example comes from a chimpanzee filmed while using a heavy rock as a hammer to crack nuts. The actor is being observed by a younger ape, who swings his own (empty) hand

cognition
(kŏg-nĭsh´ən) *n.* the process or pattern of gaining knowledge.

implication
(ĭm´plĭ-kā´shən) *n.* consequence or effect.

down in sync every time the first one strikes the nut. Body mapping
provides a great shortcut to imitation.

150   When I see synchrony and mimicry—whether it concerns
yawning, laughing, dancing, or aping—I see social connection
and bonding. I see an old herd instinct that has been taken up
a notch. It goes beyond the tendency of a mass of individuals
galloping in the same direction, crossing the river at the same
time. The new level requires that one pay better attention to what
others do and absorb how they do it. For example, I knew an old
monkey matriarch with a curious drinking style. Instead of the
typical slurping with her lips from the surface, she'd dip her entire
underarm in the water, then lick the hair on her arm. Her children
started doing the same, and then her grandchildren. The entire
160 family was easy to recognize.

    There is also the case of a male chimpanzee who had injured
his fingers in a fight and hobbled around leaning on a bent wrist
instead of his knuckles. Soon all of the young chimpanzees in
the colony were walking the same way in single file behind the
unlucky male. Like chameleons changing their color to match the
environment, primates automatically copy their surroundings.

When I was a boy, my friends in the south of the Netherlands always ridiculed me when I came home from vacations in the north, where I played with boys from Amsterdam. They told me that I talked funny. Unconsciously, I'd return speaking a poor imitation of the harsh northern accent.

The way our bodies—including voice, mood, posture, and so on—are influenced by surrounding bodies is one of the mysteries of human existence, but one that provides the glue that holds entire societies together. It's also one of the most underestimated phenomena, especially in disciplines that view humans as rational decisionmakers. Instead of each individual independently weighing the pros and cons of his or her own actions, we occupy nodes within a tight network that connects all of us in both body and mind.

COLLABORATIVE DISCUSSION What is de Waals's claim about how humans are connected? With a partner, discuss the examples he provides in support of his ideas.

Analyze and Evaluate Author's Claims

A **claim** is the author's position on a topic or issue. The science article "Monkey See, Monkey Do, Monkey Connect" is an informational text that states a specific claim about the behavior of human beings. Although Frans de Waal is an expert on the topic, it is not enough for him to simply state his claim and expect readers to accept what he is saying. He must **support** his claim throughout the essay with **reasons,** or declarations made to justify an action, decision, or belief, and **evidence** such as facts, details, and examples.

To evaluate de Waal's support for his claim, it is important to delineate, or outline, the reasons and evidence he provides. This will help you evaluate whether he has presented valid reasons and enough support for his claim.

Determine Technical Meanings

"Monkey See, Monkey Do, Monkey Connect" contains **technical vocabulary** that may be unfamiliar to you. When you encounter an unfamiliar word, you can use context clues to determine its meaning. The context of a word is made up of the punctuation marks, words, sentences, and paragraphs that surround the word. The chart below shows how a reader might use context clues to define the technical terms *empathy* and *synchronization*.

Technical Words	Context	Meaning of Words
empathy synchronization	"This is precisely where **empathy** and sympathy start—not in the higher regions of imagination, or the ability to consciously reconstruct how we would feel if we were in someone else's situation. It began much more simply, with the **synchronization** of bodies: running when others run, laughing when others laugh, crying when others cry, or yawning when others yawn."	• The word *sympathy* and the phrase "how we would feel if we were in someone else's situation" explains the meaning of *empathy*. • The image of bodies "running when others run, laughing when others laugh, crying when others cry, or yawning when others yawn" helps readers visualize *synchronization*.

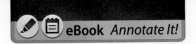
Analyzing the Text

Cite Text Evidence   Support your responses with evidence from the selection.

1. **Analyze** An author carefully chooses words and phrases to establish **tone**, or a particular attitude toward his or her subject. For example, some articles use formal language to convey a serious tone while others have a more conversational style. What tone does de Waal establish in the opening paragraphs of his essay? What words and phrases create this tone?

2. **Cite Evidence** What is the primary claim that emerges in this essay? Provide evidence from the text to support your idea.

3. **Interpret** In what ways are the laughing humans described in the first paragraph like the playful chimps de Waal observes? How does this information support his claim?

4. **Identify** In lines 25-26, what does de Waal say developed because ". . . *Homo sapiens* is remarkably easily swayed in one emotional direction or another by its fellows"? Cite evidence from the text in your explanation.

5. **Infer** What is the "herd instinct"? According to de Waal, what is the positive side of people watching and imitating one another? What might be a potential downside to this part of human nature?

6. **Interpret** Explain the significance of the "ghost box." Trace what researchers learned from the ghost box experiment, and how might it relate to the ways in which people learn.

7. **Draw Conclusions** What, according to de Waal, is the "glue that holds entire societies together"? What are the strongest pieces of evidence in the text to support this claim?

PERFORMANCE TASK

Speaking Activity: Argument The author of "Monkey See, Monkey Do, Monkey Connect" presents one view of the ways in which humans relate to one another. Do you agree with his view, or do you believe that people are, or should be, "Robinson Crusoes sitting on separate islands"?

- Form teams of two to three students each, with half arguing the points of the article and half taking the position that humans are, or should be, more "rational decisionmakers."
- Each team should gather evidence to support its position.

- Follow the rules for debating found in the Handbook at the end of this book. Be sure to use appropriate eye contact, adequate volume, and clear pronunciation. Afterward, write a brief evaluation of which side presented a stronger case.

Critical Vocabulary

empathy   **chronization**   **contagion**   **cognition**   **implication**

Practice and Apply Explain which Critical Vocabulary word listed above is most closely associated with the familiar word shown below.

1. Which vocabulary word is associated with *thinking*?

2. Which vocabulary word is associated with *suggestion*?

3. Which vocabulary word is associated with *sympathy*?

4. Which vocabulary word is associated with *disease*?

5. Which vocabulary word is associated with *coordination*?

Vocabulary Strategy: Words from Greek

A **root** is a word part that contains the core meaning of a word. Many English words contain roots that come from Greek. The Critical Vocabulary word *synchronization* contains the prefix *syn-*, meaning "with or together," combined with the Greek root *chrono*, meaning "time." *Chrono* is the basis of many other words in our everyday vocabulary.

The Greek Root *Chrono*		
chronic	anachronistic	chronometer
chronicle	synchronicity	chronograph

Understanding the meaning of the root *chrono* and using the context clues in the sentences below can help you determine the meaning of the words in the chart.

1. My sister has a *chronic* cough that keeps her awake every night.

2. The book will *chronicle* the history of our town.

3. A computer is *anachronistic* on the set of a play about colonial life.

4. It was *synchronicity* that we bumped into each other without planning to meet.

5. The *chronometer* accurately calculated when it would arrive.

6. We timed ourselves with a *chronograph*.

Practice and Apply The Critical Vocabulary word *empathy* also contains a Greek root, *pathos*. Work with a partner to define the Greek root *pathos*. Then, write about how the meaning of this root, combined with the word's other parts, relates to the meaning of the word *empathy*. Work together to create a chart of other words containing the root *pathos*. Write sentences with the words you identify.

Language and Style: Colons

Authors use colons to add clarity to their writing. They also use colons for emphasis in order to draw attention to key ideas. In an essay, colons are commonly used to introduce a list, quotation, or independent clause.

Read this sentence from the essay.

> **This is why comedy shows on television have laugh tracks and why theater audiences are sometimes sprinkled with "laugh plants": people paid to produce raucous laughing at any joke that comes along.**

Notice how de Waal uses the colon to lead into a definition of the term "laugh plants."

In this section of the essay, the colon has a different purpose. It introduces a list.

> **It began much more simply, with the synchronization of bodies: running when others run, laughing when others laugh, crying when others cry, or yawning when others yawn.**

Now read the same sentence without the colon. Consider how the sentence loses clarity without the colon to introduce the list.

> **It began much more simply, with the synchronization of bodies running when others run, laughing when others laugh, crying when others cry, or yawning when others yawn.**

You can also use a colon to introduce a long quotation or a related independent clause.

> **They become role models: We empathize with them and emulate them.**

When an independent clause follows a colon, the clause usually begins with a capital letter.

Practice and Apply Write two paragraphs summarizing key points in the article, "Monkey See, Monkey Do, Monkey Connect." Use colons in at least three places. At least one should introduce a list and one should introduce a quotation or independent clause.

Yasunari Kawabata (1899–1972) *was born in Osaka, Japan, and became an orphan when he was quite young. This experience may have led to the themes of loneliness and death in much of his writing. He published his first story "Izu Dancer" in 1926, and he became a major author in Japan after his novel* Snow Country *was published in 1948. In 1968, he was awarded the Nobel Prize in Literature "for his narrative mastery, which with great sensibility expresses the essences of the Japanese mind."*

The Grasshopper and the Bell Cricket

Short Story by Yasunari Kawabata   Translated by Lane Dunlop and J. Martin Holman

AS YOU READ Consider the details that show the narrator's feelings throughout the story.

Walking along the tile-roofed wall of the university, I turned aside and approached the upper school. Behind the white board fence of the school playground, from a dusky clump of bushes under the black cherry trees, an insect's voice could be heard. Walking more slowly and listening to that voice, and feeling reluctant to part with it, I turned right so as not to leave the playground behind. When I turned to the left, the fence gave way to an embankment[1] planted with orange trees. At the corner, I exclaimed with surprise. My eyes gleaming at what they saw up

10 ahead, I hurried forward with short steps.

At the base of the embankment was a bobbing cluster of beautiful varicolored lanterns, such as one might see at a festival in a remote country village. Without going any farther, I knew that it was a group of children on an insect chase among the bushes of the embankment. There were about twenty lanterns. Not only were

---

[1] **embankment:** a man-made elevated area of land used to prevent flooding or to raise a roadway.

there crimson, pink, indigo, green, purple, and yellow lanterns, but one lantern glowed with five colors at once. There were even some little red store-bought lanterns. But most of the lanterns were beautiful square ones that the children had made themselves with love and care. The bobbing lanterns, the coming together of children on this lonely slope—surely it was a scene from a fairy tale?

One of the neighborhood children had heard an insect sing on this slope one night. Buying a red lantern, he had come back the next night to find the insect. The night after that, there was another child. This new child could not buy a lantern. Cutting out the back and front of a small carton and papering it, he placed a candle on the bottom and fastened a string to the top. The number of children grew to five, and then to seven. They learned how to color the paper that they stretched over the windows of the cutout cartons, and to draw pictures on it. Then these wise child-artists, cutting out round, three-cornered, and **lozenge** leaf shapes in the cartons, coloring each little window a different color, with circles and diamonds, red and green, made a single and whole decorative pattern. The child with the red lantern discarded it as a tasteless object that could be bought at a store. The child who had made his own lantern threw it away because the design was too simple. The pattern of light that one had had in hand the night before was unsatisfying the morning after. Each day, with cardboard, paper, brush, scissors, penknife, and glue, the children made new lanterns out of their hearts and minds. Look at my lantern! Be the most unusually beautiful! And each night, they had gone out on their insect hunts. These were the twenty children and their beautiful lanterns that I now saw before me.

Wide-eyed, I **loitered** near them. Not only did the square lanterns have old-fashioned patterns and flower shapes, but the names of the children who had made them were cut in squared letters of the syllabary.[2] Different from the painted-over red lanterns, others (made of thick cutout cardboard) had their designs drawn onto the paper windows, so that the candle's light seemed to **emanate** from the form and color of the design itself. The lanterns brought out the shadows of the bushes like dark light. The children crouched eagerly on the slope wherever they heard an insect's voice.

"Does anyone want a grasshopper?" A boy, who had been peering into a bush about thirty feet away from the other children, suddenly straightened up and shouted.

"Yes! Give it to me!" Six or seven children came running up. Crowding behind the boy who had found the grasshopper, they peered into the bush. Brushing away their outstretched hands and

lozenge
(lŏz´ĭnj) *n.* a diamond-shaped object.

loiter
(loi´tər) *v.* to stand or wait idly.

emanate
(ĕm´ə-nāt´) *v.* to emit or radiate from.

---

[2] **syllabary:** A set of written characters for a language, with each character representing a syllable.

spreading out his arms, the boy stood as if guarding the bush where
60 the insect was. Waving the lantern in his right hand, he called again
to the other children.

"Does anyone want a grasshopper? A grasshopper!"

"I do! I do!" Four or five more children came running up.
It seemed you could not catch a more precious insect than a
grasshopper. The boy called out a third time.

"Doesn't anyone want a grasshopper?"

Two or three more children came over.

"Yes. I want it."

It was a girl, who just now had come up behind the boy who'd
70 discovered the insect. Lightly turning his body, the boy gracefully
bent forward. Shifting the lantern to his left hand, he reached his
right hand into the bush.

"It's a grasshopper."

"Yes. I'd like to have it."

The boy quickly stood up. As if to say "Here!" he thrust out his
fist that held the insect at the girl. She, slipping her left wrist under
the string of her lantern, enclosed the boy's fist with both hands.
The boy quietly opened his fist. The insect was transferred to
between the girl's thumb and index finger.

80 "Oh! It's not a grasshopper. It's a bell cricket." The girl's eyes
shone as she looked at the small brown insect.

"It's a bell cricket! It's a bell cricket!" The children echoed in an
envious chorus.

"It's a bell cricket. It's a bell cricket."

Glancing with her bright intelligent eyes at the boy who had
given her the cricket, the girl opened the little insect cage hanging
at her side and released the cricket in it.

"It's a bell cricket."

"Oh, it's a bell cricket," the boy who'd captured it muttered.
90 Holding up the insect cage close to his eyes, he looked inside it. By
the light of his beautiful many-colored lantern, also held up at eye
level, he glanced at the girl's face.

Oh, I thought. I felt slightly jealous of the boy, and **sheepish**.
How silly of me not to have understood his actions until now! Then
I caught my breath in surprise. Look! It was something on the girl's
breast that neither the boy who had given her the cricket, nor she
who had accepted it, nor the children who were looking at them
noticed.

In the faint greenish light that fell on the girl's breast, wasn't the
100 name "Fujio" clearly **discernible**? The boy's lantern, which he held
up alongside the girl's insect cage, inscribed his name, cut out in the
green papered aperture, onto her white cotton kimono. The girl's
lantern, which dangled loosely from her wrist, did not project its

sheepish
(shē′pĭsh) *adj.*
showing
embarrassment.

discernible
(dĭ-sûr′nə-bəl) *adj.*
recognizable or
noticeable.

pattern so clearly, but still one could make out, in a trembling patch of red on the boy's waist, the name "Kiyoko." This chance interplay of red and green—if it was chance or play—neither Fujio nor Kiyoko knew about.

Even if they remembered forever that Fujio had given her the cricket and that Kiyoko had accepted it, not even in dreams would Fujio ever know that his name had been written in green on Kiyoko's breast or that Kiyoko's name had been inscribed in red on his waist, nor would Kiyoko ever know that Fujio's name had been inscribed in green on her breast or that her own name had been written in red on Fujio's waist.

Fujio! Even when you have become a young man, laugh with pleasure at a girl's delight when, told that it's a grasshopper, she is given a bell cricket; laugh with affection at a girl's chagrin when, told that it's a bell cricket, she is given a grasshopper.

Even if you have the wit to look by yourself in a bush away from the other children, there are not many bell crickets in the world. Probably you will find a girl like a grasshopper whom you think is a bell cricket.

And finally, to your clouded, wounded heart, even a true bell cricket will seem like a grasshopper. Should that day come, when it seems to you that the world is only full of grasshoppers, I will think it a pity that you have no way to remember tonight's play of light, when your name was written in green by your beautiful lantern on a girl's breast.

COLLABORATIVE DISCUSSION How does the narrator react to the scene on the hill? What does he feel as he watches? With a partner, discuss what details the author provides to show varied emotions. Cite textual evidence to support your ideas.

Analyze Point of View: Cultural Background

Point of view involves the perspective from which a story is told. An author's cultural background and experience are part of this perspective, and are often reflected in works of literature. You may need some additional information about the author's cultural background in order to understand what the author is trying to express. "The Grasshopper and the Bell Cricket" was written in the early twentieth century by a Japanese author. Knowing some facts about Japanese culture will help you understand the author's point of view and, as a result, enrich your analysis of this story.

- Traditionally nature is quite important in Japanese culture. The roots of this reverence for nature come from the Shinto religion, which honors all aspects of the natural world: water, rocks, trees, sun, birds, insects.
- Instead of hoping to tame or conquer nature, Japanese aim to live in harmony with it. Japanese culture shows both respect and gratitude for nature.
- In Japan, as in other cultures, crickets are symbols of good luck. The bell cricket is an insect appreciated for its song, not its beauty.

Analyze Impact of Word Choice: Tone

Tone is the writer's attitude toward the subject and characters in a literary work. Authors create tone through the word choices they make. One way to classify tone is as **formal** or **informal**. The chart shows some examples of elements authors use to create a specific tone. You can use this information to help you analyze Kawabata's word choice and evaluate the tone that is created in this short story.

Colloquialisms	Abbreviations and Contractions	Sentence Structure
Colloquialisms are words or phrases used in informal conversation. Consider for example these phrases: *bunch of kids* and *group of children*. The first one is more colloquial and creates a more informal tone.	The use of **abbreviations** and **contractions** tends to make writing more informal. In this story, Kawabata uses some contractions in dialogue, but mostly avoids them.	In addition to word choice, **sentence structure** can contribute to tone. Longer, more complex sentences tend to create a more formal tone, while simpler sentences often create a more informal tone.

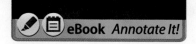

Analyzing the Text

Cite Text Evidence   Support your responses with evidence from the selection.

1. **Interpret** Examine the first two paragraphs of the story. What is the tone of these paragraphs? Cite words and phrases that contribute to the tone.

2. **Cite Evidence** Remember that nature is important in Japanese culture. What point of view about nature emerges in this selection? Cite details from the story to support your answer.

3. **Analyze** In lines 80–92, what point of view does the narrator express about people? Why is it important to understand the role of bell crickets in Japanese culture in order to understand the narrator's point of view? Explain using details from the story.

4. **Infer** Determine the **theme**, or underlying message, that the narrator expresses in lines 119–122 when he writes, "Even if you have the wit to look by yourself in a bush away from the other children, there are not many bell crickets in the world. Probably you will find a girl like a grasshopper whom you think is a bell cricket".

5. **Draw Conclusions** Think about the narrator's perspective as an older person. What point of view about life is the narrator trying to express in the advice given to Fujio in lines 115–118?

6. **Compare** Is the tone of this story the same at the beginning and at the end? Explain.

PERFORMANCE TASK

Writing Activity: Journal Entry or Letter Think about how specific words can create either an informal or formal tone. In both responses, use key details from the text and standard English.

1. In the character of the girl who receives the bell cricket, use informal language to describe the insect hunts and what happened on this night, as you would in a journal entry.

2. Look at the last three paragraphs. In the character of the narrator, write a personal letter to Fujio. Use a formal tone as you give him your advice.

Critical Vocabulary

lozenge   loiter   emanate   sheepish   discernible

Practice and Apply Answer the questions to show your understanding of the Critical Vocabulary words. Use a dictionary or thesaurus as needed.

1. Which would you be more likely to do if you are feeling **sheepish:** blush and grin or scowl and shout? Why?

2. If a container **emanates** light, can you see the light or not? Why?

3. Which would be more **discernible,** something written in crayon or in invisible ink? Why?

4. If I **loiter,** do I run away or do I hang around? Why?

5. Which item has a **lozenge** shape: kite or egg? Why?

Vocabulary Strategy: Context Clues

When you read, you can use **context clues** to understand unfamiliar words. **Context** is how a word relates to the overall meaning of a sentence, paragraph, or piece of writing.

Here are some types of context clues you may find in texts:

Synonyms or Definition	Contrast	Examples
The text may provide a definition or synonym.	The text may give an antonym, or contrasting information.	The text may list examples of the word.

Look at this example from the story.

> Then these wise child-artists, cutting out round, three-cornered, and *lozenge* leaf shapes in the cartons . . .

You read that *lozenge* is part of a list of shapes, an example of a shape. You also know from contrasting information that a *lozenge* is not round or three-cornered.

Practice and Apply Locate these words in the story: *discarded* (line 35), *crouched* (line 52), *inscribed* (line 101). Then, use context clues to write definitions for each word. Check your definitions in a dictionary.

Language and Style: Using Verb Phrases

Verb phrases are a combination of one or more helping verbs and a main verb. In "The Grasshopper and the Bell Cricket," Yasunari Kawabata uses many verb phrases to express shifts in time.

Read this sentence from the story.

> At the base of the embankment was a bobbing cluster of beautiful varicolored lanterns such as one **might see** at a festival in a remote country village.

By using the verb phrase *might see,* the author creates a possibility for a comparison—lanterns on the embankment and lanterns at a festival.

Now, read this sentence from the story.

> But most of the lanterns were beautiful square ones which the children **had made** themselves with love and care.

Here the author uses the verb phrase *had made* to show that the children's action of making the lanterns took place in the past prior to the narrator seeing them.

Note that words might come between the parts of the verb phrase. In this example from the story, *does* and *want* create the verb phrase, and the phrase is interrupted by the subject, a common occurrence in a question.

> **Does** anyone **want** a grasshopper?

The table shows some common helping verbs. You can use these helping verbs in their different forms in verb phrases.

Common Helping Verbs in Verb Phrases		
be	can	am
do	have	may
might	shall	should
will	would	could

Practice and Apply With a partner, review your journal entries or letters you created in response to this selection's Performance Task. Note the use of verb phrases in your works. Help each other revise verb phrases to make your writing more effective in showing shifts in time, or work together to create sentences that contain verb phrases. Remember to consider the tense of the verbs when you are revising.

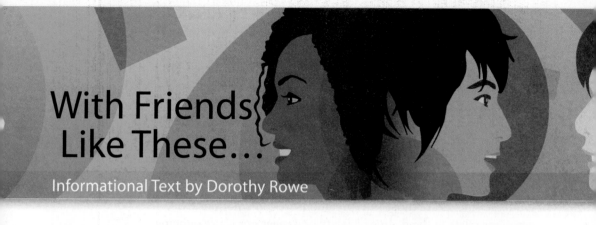

With Friends Like These...

Informational Text by Dorothy Rowe

AS YOU READ Pay attention to the author's ideas about what makes friendship possible between two people. Write down any questions.

We value friends, but the path of friendship, like love, rarely runs smooth. We may feel jealous of a friend's achievements when we want to feel happy for her. We might find it hard to give friends objective advice, unrelated to the person we want them to be. We can be reluctant to allow each other to change, sometimes falling out in a way that is painful for all involved. And yet, friendships are vitally important; central to our enjoyment of life.

More fundamentally, friendships are essential to our sense of who we are. Neuroscientists have shown that our brain does not reveal to us the world as it is, but rather as possible interpretations of what is going on around us, drawn from our past experience. Since no two people ever have exactly the same experience, no two people ever see anything in exactly the same way.

Most of our brain's constructions are unconscious. Early in our life our stream of conscious and unconscious constructions create, like a real stream, a kind of whirlpool that quickly becomes our most precious possession, that is, our sense of being a person, what we call "I," "me," "myself." Like a whirlpool, our sense of being a person cannot exist separately from the stream that created it.

Because we cannot see reality directly, all our ideas are guesses about what is going on. Thus our sense of being a person is made up of these guesses. All the time we are creating ideas about who we are, what is happening now, what has happened in our world, and what our future will be. When these ideas are shown by events to be reasonably accurate, that is, our ideas are **validated,** we feel secure in ourselves, but when they are proved wrong, we feel that we are falling apart.

Friends are central to this all-important sense of validation. When a friend confirms to us that the world is as we see it, we feel

validate
(văl´ĭ-dāt´) *v.* to establish the value, truth, or legitimacy of.

With Friends Like These... **141**

30 safer, reassured. On the other hand, when we say, "I'm shattered," or "I'm losing my grip," we might not be using clichés to describe a bad day but talking about something quite terrifying that we are experiencing: our sense of who we are is being challenged. So terrifying is this experience that we develop many different tactics aimed at warding off invalidation and defending ourselves against being annihilated as a person.

Emotional support

We are constantly **assessing** how safe our sense of being a person is. Our assessments are those interpretations we call emotions. All our emotions relate to the degree of safety or danger our sense of being
40 a person is experiencing. So important are these interpretations to our survival that we do not need to put them into words, although of course we can. Our positive emotions are interpretations to do with safety, while the multitude of negative emotions define the particular kind of danger and its degree. Joy is: "Everything is the way I want it to be"; jealousy is: "How dare that person have something that is rightly mine."

assess (ə-sĕs´) v. to evaluate.

We can be invalidated by events such as the bankruptcy of the firm that employs us, but most frequently we are invalidated by other people.
50 A friend told me how her husband had used her password and pin to drain her bank account and fund his secret gambling habit. Losing her savings was a terrible blow, but far worse was her loss of trust in the person she saw as her best friend.

When she described herself as falling apart, I assured her that what was falling apart were some of her ideas. All she had to do was to endure a period of uncertainty until she could construct ideas that better reflected her situation.

Friendship can be rewarding but, like all relationships, it can also be risky. Other people can let us down, insult or humiliate
60 us, leading us to feel diminished and in danger. Yet we need other people to tell us when we have got our guesses right, and, when we get things wrong, to help us make more accurate assessments. Live completely on your own and your guesses will get further and further away from reality.

The degree of risk we perceive from our friends relates directly to the degree of self-confidence we feel. When confident of ourselves, we feel that we can deal with being invalidated; when lacking self-confidence, we often see danger where no danger need exist. Take jealousy, for example. Feeling self-confident, we can
70 rejoice in our friend's success at a new job; feeling inferior, we see danger and try to defend ourselves with: "It's not fair." We can fail

to see that our friendship should be more important to us than our injured pride.

Our levels of confidence also relate to how ready we are to accept change, and how able we are to allow our friends to change. To feel secure in ourselves, we need to be able to predict events reasonably accurately. We think we know our friends well, and so can predict what they will do. We create a mental image of our friends, and we want to keep them within the bounds of that image.
80 Our need to do this can override our ability to see our friends in the way they see themselves. We do not want them to change because then we would have to change our image of them. Change creates uncertainty, and uncertainty can be frightening.

Falling out

However, an inability to allow change can lead to the end of a friendship. Falling out with a friend shows us that our image of them, from which we **derive** our predictions about that friend, is wrong; and if that is the case, our sense of being a person is threatened.

derive
(dĭ-rīv´) *v.* to obtain or extract from.

If we lose a friend, we have to change how we see ourselves and
90 our life. Each of us lives in our own individual world of meaning. We need to find friends whose individual world is somewhat similar to our own so that we are able to communicate with one another.

The people who can validate us best are those we can see as equals, and with whom there can be mutual affection, trust, loyalty and acceptance. Such people give us the kind of validation that builds a lasting self-confidence despite the difficulties we encounter.

These are our true friends.

COLLABORATIVE DISCUSSION Why do certain people become friends while others do not? With a partner, discuss the factors that allow two people to become friends, and the factors that prevent it in other cases. Cite specific textual evidence to support your ideas.

Analyze Ideas

An informational text presents a series of facts and ideas on a particular topic. The author's challenge is to present his or her ideas in a way that will make sense to readers. An effective informational text

- introduces each idea clearly and in a way that engages readers' interest
- presents ideas in a logical order
- develops ideas with examples and supporting facts
- shows readers the connections between ideas

"With Friends Like These . . ." presents facts and ideas about the important role of friendship in human life. To analyze this text, identify the central idea that the author introduces in each paragraph or section. Think about how the author develops and supports each idea, and how it relates to the ideas presented before and after. Trace the order in which ideas are presented, and consider why the author chose that order. Finally, ask yourself what the author does to engage readers and make them interested in her topic.

Analyzing the Text

Cite Text Evidence   Support your responses with evidence from the selection.

1. **Infer** Reread the first paragraph. What **tone**, or attitude, is created by the author's use of the first-person pronouns *we* and *our*? Why do you think she chose to introduce her topic to readers in this way?

2. **Connect** In lines 9–27, the author develops her ideas with information from the fields of neuroscience and psychology. How does she connect this information back to the idea that "friendships are essential to our sense of who we are"?

3. **Analyze** In lines 74–83, the author discusses people's capacity to accept change. Why does she introduce these ideas immediately before the section "Falling out"?

PERFORMANCE TASK

Speaking Activity: Response to Literature Reread lines 94–99 at the end of the selection. Then confer with a partner on the ideas about friendship expressed in these lines.

- Analyze the passage closely by making a list of the specific aspects of true friendship it mentions.
- Discuss each aspect and decide whether you agree that it is essential for a lasting friendship.

- Generate a brief presentation based on your discussion. Include the conclusions you reached and your reasons for them. As you present, use appropriate eye contact, adequate volume, and clear pronunciation.

Critical Vocabulary

validate   assess   derive

Practice and Apply Working with a partner, develop a brief scene that depicts the meaning of each Critical Vocabulary word but does not include the word. Swap your scenes with another pair. Pairs will then analyze each other's scenes and identify the Critical Vocabulary word that is being conveyed in each one.

- an experience that makes a character feel **validated**
- a character **assessing** a situation or another character
- a character who **derives** an idea from something he or she observes

Vocabulary Strategy: Patterns of Word Changes

You have probably noticed that many words can change form to become new words with related meanings. When you learn the common **patterns of word changes,** you can recognize different forms of familiar words and figure out what they mean. Knowing the patterns will also help you spell different forms of a word correctly.

The Critical Vocabulary word *validate* is a verb. By adding affixes, you can change the part of speech and meaning of the word. Adding the suffix *-ion* creates the noun *validation*, which means "the act of establishing the truth or legitimacy of something." Removing *-ate* creates the adjective *valid*, which means "true or legitimate." Adding the prefix *in-* creates the verb *invalidate*, which means "establish that something is not true or legitimate."

This chart shows more words from the selection and their various forms. Note the patterns of spelling changes that occur between verb, noun, and adjective forms.

Verb	Noun	Adjective
relate	relation, relationship	relative
describe	description	descriptive
defend	defense	defensive, indefensible
perceive	perception	perceptive

Practice and Apply For each verb in the chart, identify one new verb that has the same ending (*-ate, -ibe, -end, -ceive*). Then, follow these steps:

1. Create a chart with your words in the first column. Complete the chart with noun and adjective forms of each word.

2. Use a dictionary to check your spelling of the new words.

3. Choose one word from each row of your chart and use it in a sentence.

Language and Style:
Adjective and Adverb Phrases

A **prepositional phrase** is a phrase that consists of a preposition, its object, and any modifiers of the object. Prepositional phrases that modify nouns or pronouns are called **adjective phrases**. Prepositional phrases that modify verbs, adjectives, or adverbs are called **adverb phrases**.

"With Friends Like These . . ." opens with these sentences:

> We value friends, but the path <u>of friendship</u>, like love, rarely runs smooth. We may feel jealous <u>of a friend's achievements</u> when we want to feel happy <u>for her</u>.

The prepositional phrase *of friendship* functions as an adjective modifying *path*. The phrases *of a friend's achievements* and *for her* act as adverbs modifying *jealous* and *happy*. Notice how removing the adverb phrases makes the second sentence much less specific:

> We may feel jealous when we want to feel happy.

This chart shows sentences from the selection that use prepositional phrases as either adjectives or adverbs. Read each sentence carefully and note the relationship between the phrase and the word it modifies. There may be other words between the phrase and the word it modifies.

Adjective Phrase	Adverb Phrase
Each of us lives in our own individual world *of meaning*. (modifies the noun *world*)	More fundamentally, friendships are essential *to our sense of who we are.* (modifies the adjective *essential*)

Practice and Apply Write a summary of the author's ideas about how friendships validate our sense of who we are. Then, revise your paragraph to include at least one of each kind of phrase shown in the chart—a prepositional phrase that functions as an adjective and a prepositional phrase that functions as an adverb.

At Dusk

Poem by Natasha Trethewey

Natasha Trethewey (b. 1966) *was named United States Poet Laureate in 2012. She views her responsibility in this role as being someone who has "really got to do the work of bringing poetry to the widest audience possible." A native of Gulfport, Mississippi, Trethewey has published several collections of poetry and is a professor of English and creative writing at Emory University. Her first collection,* Domestic Work (2000), *earned her the Cave Canem Poetry Prize, awarded each year to the best first book by an African American poet. Trethewey has since won many other honors, including the Pulitzer Prize for poetry in 2007 for her book* Native Guard.

AS YOU READ Think about the decision faced by the cat in the poem, and the advantages and disadvantages of each possible course of action. Write down any questions you generate as you read the poem.

At Dusk

At first I think she is calling a child,
my neighbor, leaning through her doorway
at dusk, street lamps just starting to hum
the backdrop of evening. Then I hear
5   the high-pitched wheedling we send out
to animals who know only sound, not
the meanings of our words—*here here*—
nor how they sometimes fall short.
In another yard, beyond my neighbor's
10 sight, the cat lifts her ears, turns first
toward the voice, then back
to the constellation of fireflies flickering
near her head. It's as if she can't decide
whether to leap over the low hedge,
15 the neat row of flowers, and bound
onto the porch, into the steady circle
of light, or stay where she is: luminous
possibility—all that would keep her
away from home—flitting before her.
20 I listen as my neighbor's voice trails off.
She's given up calling for now, left me
to imagine her inside the house waiting,
perhaps in a chair in front of the TV,
or walking around, doing small tasks;
25 left me to wonder that I too might lift
my voice, sure of someone out there,
send it over the lines stitching here
to there, certain the sounds I make
are enough to call someone home.

COLLABORATIVE DISCUSSION Confer with a partner to discuss how the cat's situation is similar to one that a person might face. Generate a list of advantages and disadvantages to returning home versus exploring new possibilities.

Interpret Imagery

A poem captures a moment and often tells a story using compact language. Poets use **imagery,** or descriptive words and phrases that re-create sensory experiences for the reader. They also choose words and phrases carefully to convey a certain **tone**—the attitude an author takes toward a subject; and **mood**—the feeling or atmosphere an author creates for the reader. A poem's tone might be formal or informal, serious or sarcastic. The mood might be dark and brooding,or light and energetic.

Analyzing the word choices Natasha Trethewey makes throughout "At Dusk" will help you see the overall impact that her choices have on the poem's tone, mood, and meaning. This chart can help guide your interpretation of the poem's imagery.

Lines from Poem	Interpretation
"street lamps just starting to hum / the backdrop of evening"	This image establishes the scene. • What does the poet want readers to see and hear? • What mood is created by the darkening sky?
"the cat lifts her ears, turns first / toward the voice, then back / to the constellation of fireflies flickering / near her head. It's as if she can't decide/ whether to leap over the low hedge, / . . .or stay where she is"	The speaker imagines what the cat might be thinking or feeling. • Why might the cat have trouble deciding what to do? • What do you learn about the speaker by the thoughts and feelings she assigns to the cat?
"She's given up calling for now, left me / to imagine her inside the house waiting, / perhaps in a chair in front of the TV"	The speaker watches the neighbor's reaction. • What feeling does the image of someone giving up and settling in front of the TV convey?
"certain the sounds I make / are enough to call someone home"	The poem ends with the speaker's thoughts about what he or she has observed. • What is the mood of the last line of the poem? • Whom might the speaker want to call home?

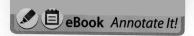
Analyzing the Text

Cite Text Evidence Support your responses with evidence from the selection.

1. **Interpret** The speaker talks about the cat not hearing meanings of our words "nor how they sometimes fall short" (line 8). What might this mean?

2. **Interpret** What might keep the cat from returning home? What might the image of a "constellation of fireflies flickering" represent to the speaker?

3. **Infer** Judging from the speaker's observations, is he or she alone or with people? Support your inference with details from the poem.

4. **Analyze** What connection does the speaker have to the neighbor at this moment? How does the speaker feel when the neighbor gives up on calling the cat?

5. **Analyze** What is the tone of this poem? What words and phrases convey the tone?

6. **Draw Conclusions** Explain the significance of the title "At Dusk."

PERFORMANCE TASK

Speaking Activity: Poetry Reading The language of poetry is meant to be heard as well as read. Get together with a partner or small group to read "At Dusk" aloud.

- Sit across from one another; or, if you are in a small group, sit in a circle facing one another.
- Take turns reading the poem aloud. Practice reading with feeling, emphasizing key words and phrases.

- After your reading, discuss what words and phrase stand out to you when you hear them read aloud.
- Write a brief summary of what you learned by reading the poem aloud.

Background *A public service announcement (PSA) is a message usually produced for television or radio about a topic or issue of interest to the public. The purpose of a PSA is to raise public awareness and encourage the audience to take action. Media and news organizations distribute public service announcements at no charge. This particular announcement is for the* Corporation for National and Community Service, *a federal agency that provides support to volunteer organizations and to individual volunteers around the country.*

MEDIA ANALYSIS

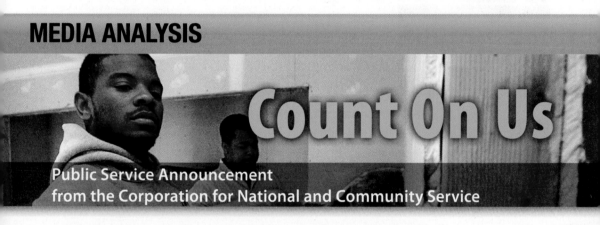

Public Service Announcement
from the Corporation for National and Community Service

AS YOU VIEW Pay attention to how the visuals, music, and text work together to send a message. Write down any questions you generate during viewing.

COLLABORATIVE DISCUSSION In a small group, discuss how this public service announcement compares to others you have seen or heard. What are some common topics or issues that PSAs try to bring to public attention? What kinds of visuals are used to convey ideas?

Analyze Purpose and Development of Ideas

A **public service announcement** (PSA) is a type of advertisement. Advertisements are structured to achieve a purpose. A television commercial, for example, is usually created to encourage people to buy something. A PSA's purpose is to encourage the audience to take action, such as by donating goods and services to victims of a natural disaster. PSAs have these common elements:

clear and concise message	message or central idea is clear even without the audio
logical presentation	visuals, text, and music are arranged logically to support each other in conveying the central idea
emotional hook	visuals and music evoke, or bring forth, particular emotions to engage the audience
critical information	important information is included, such as the name of the organization or important statistics
call to action	viewers understand what the announcement wants them to do

Analyzing the Media

Cite Text Evidence Support your responses with evidence from the selection.

1. **Draw Conclusions** How is this public service announcement structured to "hook" the viewer emotionally?

2. **Analyze** Is this PSA organized logically? Do the visuals, text, and music work together to send a coherent message? Cite specific scenes to support your answer.

3. **Identify** Explain the central idea and purpose of this announcement. What "call to action" does it express to viewers?

PERFORMANCE TASK

Media Activity: Informative Announcement Create a public service announcement in which you send a message and call for action.

- Create a PSA to raise awareness of a school issue. Generate a list of possible issues.
- Use video, audio, or a poster format to produce your PSA.
- Remember to give your audience specific details and organize your visuals so that the message and call to action is clear.
- Share your PSA with your class.

Write a Fictional Narrative

The texts in this collection focus on our connections to family, friends, pets, and community. Look back at "When Mr. Pirzada Came to Dine" and the other fiction and poetry in this collection. How do these texts use narrative techniques to explore interpersonal connections? Write a narrative that shows how we connect with others.

An effective fictional narrative

- begins by introducing a setting, a narrator, and a main character
- has an engaging plot with a central conflict
- provides a clear sequence of events
- uses a variety of narrative techniques
- includes sensory language and descriptive details
- ends with a logical and satisfying resolution to the conflict

PLAN

myNotebook

Identify Narrative Techniques Reread your chosen texts, taking notes on narrative techniques. Ask yourself:

- What point of view does each author use to tell the story? Identify the narrator as first person or third person.

- How does the author reveal characters' personalities? Find examples of dialogue or descriptive details.

- How does the author allow important ideas to emerge through the text without stating them directly? For example, what details does the author use to reveal a character's feelings?

- How does the author control pacing? Look for passages with descriptive detail that makes readers slow down. Contrast them with passages in which events take place very quickly.

- How does the author convey themes through the story?

Use the notebook in your eBook to record examples of narrative techniques in the selections, such as dialogue, pacing, description, and plot lines.

ACADEMIC VOCABULARY

As you discuss narrative techniques with your group, try to use these words.

> capacity
> confer
> emerge
> generate
> trace

Mentor Text See how this example from "When Mr. Pirzada Came to Dine" reveals that Mr. Pirzada is upset about the news without saying so directly.

> " An Indian official announced that unless the world helped to relieve the burden of East Pakistani refugees, India would have to go to war against Pakistan. . . . The knife slipped from Mr. Pirzada's hand and made a gash dipping toward the base of the pumpkin. "

Have a Group Discussion Discuss your analysis of narrative techniques in a group with two other classmates. Each classmate will present his or her reflections on one text.

- Take turns presenting your analyses.
- Take notes on the points your classmates raise and questions you might ask. Answer questions from your classmates respectfully.
- After all three texts have been presented, evaluate the narrative techniques used in each text. Which techniques were effective?
- Decide which narrative techniques to use in your own story.

Brainstorm Use a web diagram or other graphic organizer to generate ideas for your narrative. Think about things that connect people to one another, such as interests, goals, ethnicity, nationality, neighborhood, or school. Building on one of these connections, write down ideas for characters, setting, plot, conflict, and theme.

Get Organized Create an outline or use a story map to clarify the structure of your narrative. Refer to your notes and the texts to help you. Ask yourself:

- How can the beginning of my story engage readers?
- What is the story's plot? What is the central conflict?
- What is the sequence of events? How do they lead to a climax—a turning point or moment of greatest intensity?
- How does the story end? Is the conflict resolved? How?
- Which point of view will you use in your narrative? Take notes on other narrative techniques you plan to use.
- What will readers want to know about your characters and setting? Describe your characters' appearance, personality, and other unique characteristics. Give details about the setting.
- What details convey a theme about personal connections?

Interactive Lessons
To help you plan your narrative, complete the following lesson:
- Narrative Techniques

PRODUCE

Draft Your Narrative Write a draft of your narrative, following your notes, outline, and graphic organizers.

- Begin by introducing the setting, the main character(s), and an experience or conflict that will be central to the plot.
- Describe a sequence of events surrounding the conflict.
- Use descriptive details, sensory language, and narrative techniques such as dialogue.
- Provide a satisfying ending that resolves the central conflict.

Write your rough draft in *my*WriteSmart. Focus on getting your ideas down, rather than perfecting your choice of language.

Interactive Lessons
To help you draft your narrative, complete the following lesson:
- Narrative Structures

Language and Style: Add Details

Adverbs, adverb phrases, and prepositional phrases can add detail to descriptions by telling about the time, place, manner, or cause of an action. Read the following passage from "When Mr. Pirzada Came to Dine."

> ❝ I nodded. For the first time we all gathered around the dining table, my mother, my father, Mr. Pirzada, and I. While the television aired unattended we covered the tabletop with newspapers. ❞

Note that details about the characters' actions are revealed through the phrases "for the first time" and "while the television aired unattended." Look for places in your own narrative where you can improve your descriptions by adding details like these.

REVISE

Review Your Draft Have your partner or group of peers review your draft. Use the following chart to revise your draft.

Have your partner or a group of peers review your draft in *my*WriteSmart. Ask your reviewers to note any places where the plot could be better developed.

Questions	Tips	Revision Techniques
Does the beginning of the story introduce the setting, the main characters, and the conflict?	**Underline** details that reveal the setting. **Highlight** the names of the main characters. **Note** the main conflict in the story.	**Add** information about the setting, characters, and conflict, if needed.
Is the narrative told from a consistent point of view?	**Note** any instances where the point of view changes.	**Change** any pronouns to make the point of view consistent.
Is the sequence of events clear?	**Number** the sequence of events as they appear in the narrative.	**Reorder** events in chronological order, if needed.
Are narrative techniques such as dialogue, pacing, and description included?	**Note** at least one example of each narrative technique in your story.	**Elaborate** by adding more narrative techniques as needed.
Does the conclusion include a logical and satisfying resolution to the main conflict?	**Underline** details that reveal the resolution to the conflict.	**Add** details that tell how the conflict is resolved.

PRESENT

Create a Finished Copy Choose a way to share your fictional narrative. You might post it to a class blog or read it out loud to a group of classmates. Be prepared to answer questions or respond to comments from the people you share it with.

PERFORMANCE TASK A RUBRIC
FICTIONAL NARRATIVE

	Ideas and Evidence	Organization	Language
4	• The story begins memorably; the exposition clearly introduces the setting and a main character and establishes the conflict in a unique way. • The writer uses precise description and realistic dialogue to develop characters and events. • The plot is thoroughly developed; the story reveals a significant theme. • The story ends by resolving the conflict and tying up loose ends.	• The sequence of events is effective, clear, and logical. • The pace and organization keep the reader curious about the next plot event.	• The point of view is effective and consistent throughout the story. • Vivid sensory details reveal the setting and characters. • Sentence beginnings, lengths, and structures vary and have a rhythmic flow. • Spelling, capitalization, and punctuation are correct. If handwritten, the narrative is legible. • Grammar and usage are correct.
3	• The exposition introduces the setting, a main character, and a conflict, but it could be more engaging. • The writer often uses description and dialogue to develop characters and events. • The plot is adequately developed; the story suggests a theme. • The story resolves the conflict, but more details are needed to bring the plot to a satisfying conclusion.	• The sequence of events is mostly clear and logical. • The pace could move along more quickly to hold the reader's interest.	• The point of view is mostly consistent. • A few more sensory details are needed to describe the setting and characters. • Sentence beginnings, lengths, and structures mostly vary. • Several spelling, capitalization, and punctuation mistakes occur. If handwritten, the narrative is mostly legible. • Some grammatical and usage errors are repeated in the story.
2	• The story opening is uneventful; the exposition identifies a setting and a main character but only hints at a conflict. • The writer occasionally uses description and dialogue to develop characters and events. • The plot development is uneven in a few places; a theme is only hinted at. • The story resolves some parts of the conflict.	• The sequence of events is confusing in a few places. • The pace often lags.	• The point of view shifts in a few places. • The sensory details are ordinary or not used regularly enough. • Sentence structures vary somewhat. • Spelling, capitalization, and punctuation are often incorrect but do not make comprehending the story difficult. If handwritten, the narrative may be partially illegible. • Grammar and usage are incorrect in many places, but the writer's ideas are still clear.
1	• The exposition is missing critical information about the setting and main character and does not set up a conflict. • The writer does not use description and dialogue to develop characters and events. • The plot is barely developed and lacks a theme. • The story lacks a clear resolution.	• There is no clear sequence of events, making it easy for the reader to lose interest in the plot. • The pace is ineffective.	• The story lacks a clear point of view. • Sensory details are rarely or never used to describe the setting and characters. • A repetitive sentence structure makes the writing monotonous. • Spelling, capitalization, and punctuation are incorrect throughout. If handwritten, the narrative may be partially or mostly illegible. • Many grammatical and usage errors change the meaning of the writer's ideas.

Create a Group Multimedia Presentation

This collection focuses on the connections we form with others. Look back at the anchor text "Monkey See, Monkey Do, Monkey Connect" and at the other texts in the collection. Then collaborate on a multimedia presentation about the way people form bonds with others.

An effective multimedia presentation	Participants in an effective collaboration
• uses technology to share information through text, graphics, images, and sound • integrates information from a variety of sources and media • presents information and evidence from the texts clearly, concisely, and logically • uses language and structures appropriate for a presentation	• prepare in advance by reading and analyzing the chosen texts • work with group members to decide on the goals and deadlines of the project and to assign individual roles • encourage participation from all group members • allow for different perspectives and seek to achieve consensus

PLAN

Analyze the Texts Reread "Monkey See, Monkey Do, Monkey Connect" and two other texts from the collection. Use the annotation tools in your eBook to find examples, details, and quotations about how bonds are formed. Save each idea to *my*Notebook, in a folder called *Collection 3 Performance Task B*.

ACADEMIC VOCABULARY

As you share ideas for your multimedia presentation, try to use these words.

> *capacity*
> *confer*
> *emerge*
> *generate*
> *trace*

myNotebook

"Monkey See, Monkey Do, Monkey Connect"

"Thus children often walk like the same-sex parent or mimic their tone of voice when they pick up the phone."

This sentence provides two examples of how mimicking behavior can act as a form of bonding between humans.

Get Organized
Join a small group to prepare for the presentation.

- Select an effective leader and a reliable recorder.
- Determine rules for discussions, including how participants will take turns, make decisions, and resolve disagreements.
- Remind all participants to contribute relevant information, listen attentively, ask pertinent questions, and clarify ideas.

Assign Parts of the Presentation
Select an element of the presentation for each group member to produce.

- Discuss the texts, and generate ideas for the main points of the presentation. The recorder should write down final decisions.
- Find out what types of software and technology are available to you. Your school may have an authoring program that will allow you to combine word processing with different types of media.
- Decide which type of media (video, audio, slide show, and so on) you will use to present each main point.
- Assign a group member to write and produce a specific part of the presentation. For example, each group member might focus on a unique way that human beings form bonds or on a particular chosen text.

Interactive Lessons

To help you plan your presentation, complete the following lessons:
- Participating in Collaborative Discussions: Establishing and Following Procedure
- Using Media in a Presentation: Types of Media: Audio, Video, and Images

PRODUCE

Write and Produce Your Part
Use your notes and the available technology to create your part of the presentation.

- Write down a clear statement of the main point you will convey.
- Use the type of media your group selected to illustrate your main idea. Try to use the technology to its full capacity. For example, don't use a video clip to show a still image; instead, use it to show a scene with action and movement.
- Trace your main points back to evidence from the texts.

Storyboard the Parts
Join your group and combine individual parts of the presentation to form a logically ordered, cohesive whole.

- Have each group member share his or her part.
- Determine a logical order in which you will present the parts.
- Create a storyboard to show exactly what your audience will see and hear in each part of the presentation. Remember that a storyboard is a series of sketches that presents scenes in sequential order.

Produce a rough draft of your presentation using the authoring software of your choice. Then upload your draft to *my*WriteSmart for a peer and teacher review.

Interactive Lessons

To help you draft your presentation, complete the following lesson:
- Using Media in a Presentation: Using Presentation Software

Have your group of peers review your draft in *my*WriteSmart. Ask your reviewers to note any main points that are not adequately supported with evidence.

Practice Your Presentation

Your group should now have a rough version of your final presentation. Following your storyboard, practice delivering the presentation. As you observe how it unfolds, keep these questions in mind:

- Does the opening to each part of the presentation grab the audience's attention? If not, consider starting with an intriguing question or an interesting video clip.

- Are the transitions between ideas and between types of media smooth? If not, can pieces of the presentation be rearranged or reworked?

- Are there any problems with the technology that need to be solved? For example, will the audience have trouble seeing or hearing anything? Is it possible to start audio and video clips at exactly the right time?

Interactive Lessons

To help you revise your presentation, complete the following lesson:
- Using Media in a Presentation: Practicing Your Presentation

Make Sense of Things

Now that you've practiced, it's time to revise your presentation. Refer to the chart on the following page for the characteristics of a well-planned multimedia presentation. With your group, make any adjustments necessary to ensure that

- your presentation begins in a way that engages the audience

- your audience will easily understand your main points and the evidence you present for each point

- the presentation integrates a variety of media in an effective way

- each part of the presentation takes full advantage of the type of technology used

- the presentation ends with a satisfying conclusion

- the entire presentation demonstrates an appropriate use of standard English

Share Your Presentation

Discuss with your group how to deliver your presentation to the rest of your classmates. The way you present will depend on the types of technology used. You may be able to have small groups explore your project independently, or you may need to present to the whole class. In either situation, allow your audience to comment, ask questions, and provide feedback.

- Find out what aspects of your presentation were strong.

- Ask how your presentation could be improved.

PERFORMANCE TASK B RUBRIC
MULTIMEDIA PRESENTATION

	Ideas and Evidence	Organization	Language
4	• The presentation begins memorably and engages the audience's attention. • Information and supporting evidence are presented clearly, concisely, and logically. • The presentation uses digital media strategically to enhance the audience's understanding and to add interest.	• The topic is clearly introduced at the start of the presentation. • The presentation maintains a consistent focus on the topic. • The presentation ends with a satisfying and thought-provoking conclusion.	• The presentation maintains a consistent and appropriately formal tone through the use of standard English. • The presentation uses specialized and technical vocabulary as appropriate, clearly defining these terms for the audience. • Narration flows smoothly with the use of transitions and varied sentence structures.
3	• The presentation starts in a way that engages the audience. • Information and supporting evidence are presented clearly and logically, although some unnecessary information is included. • The presentation uses digital media in a way that helps the audience understand the topic.	• The topic is introduced at the start of the presentation. • The presentation stays focused on the topic, with a few minor lapses. • The presentation ends with an appropriate conclusion.	• The presentation mostly maintains a formal tone through the use of standard English. • The presentation uses some specialized and technical vocabulary and defines these terms for the audience. • Narration mostly flows smoothly with the use of transitions and varied sentence structures.
2	• The presentation has a somewhat bland opening that may not engage the audience. • Most information and supporting evidence are presented clearly, but there is some unnecessary information and some gaps in logic. • The use of digital media does not work to enhance the audience's understanding.	• The topic is hinted at but not made clear at the start of the presentation. • The presentation strays from the topic in several places. • The presentation ends with a brief concluding statement but leaves some ideas unresolved.	• The presentation has an inconsistent tone, sometimes using nonstandard or very informal English. • The presentation uses few specialized or technical vocabulary words and fails to define these terms for the audience. • Narration needs more transitions to clarify links between ideas and uses monotonous sentence structures.
1	• The presentation opens in a way that does not engage the audience. • Information is not presented clearly and logically, and supporting evidence is lacking. • The presentation uses digital media ineffectively, causing confusion for the audience.	• No clear topic is introduced at the start of the presentation. • The presentation lacks focus throughout. • The presentation ends abruptly.	• The presentation has an overly informal tone, using nonstandard English and/or slang. • The presentation uses vague language and no specialized terms. • Narration lacks transitions to clarify links between ideas and uses choppy simple sentences.

Sweet Sorrow

"Love is the great intangible."

—Diane Ackerman

Sweet Sorrow

This collection explores the nature of love and the conflicts surrounding it.

Stream to Start

hmhfyi.com

Channel One News®

COLLECTION

PERFORMANCE TASK Preview

At the end of this collection, you will have the opportunity to complete a task:

• Write an analytical essay exploring an aspect of love.

ACADEMIC VOCABULARY

Study the words and their definitions in the chart below. You will use these words as you discuss and write about the texts in this collection.

Word	Definition	Related Forms
attribute (ăt´rə-byōot´) *n.*	a characteristic, quality, or trait	attributable, attributed
commit (kə-mĭt´) *v.*	to carry out, engage in, or perform	commitment, recommit
expose (ĭk-spōz´) *v.*	to make visible or reveal	exposure, exposition
initiate (ĭ-nĭsh´ē-āt´) *v.*	to start or cause to begin	initiative, initiator
underlie (ŭn´dər-lī´) *v.*	to be the cause or support of	underlying, underlay

Diane Ackerman (b. 1948), *author of* A Natural History of the Senses, An Alchemy of Mind, *and* The Zookeeper's Wife, *weaves her love of science and natural history into her poetry, fiction, and nonfiction. Her memoir,* One Hundred Names for Love, *chronicles her husband's struggle to reclaim language after a stroke. In describing that time, Ackerman said, "I've always transcended best by pretending that I'm Margaret Mead viewing a scene for the first time or an alien from another planet regarding the spectacle of life on Earth and discovering how spectacular, unexpected, and beautiful it is."*

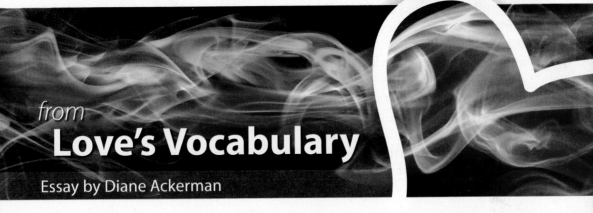

from
Love's Vocabulary

Essay by Diane Ackerman

AS YOU READ Pay attention to the many creative descriptions of love throughout the essay. Write down any questions you generate during reading.

▤ myNotebook

As you read, save new words to *my*WordList.

Love is the great **intangible**. In our nightmares, we can create beasts out of pure emotion. Hate stalks the streets with dripping fangs, fear flies down narrow alleyways on leather wings, and jealousy spins sticky webs across the sky. In daydreams, we can maneuver with poise, foiling an opponent, scoring high on fields of glory while crowds cheer, cutting fast to the heart of an adventure. But what dream state is love? Frantic and serene, vigilant and calm, wrung-out and fortified, explosive and sedate—love commands a vast army of moods. Hoping for victory, limping from the latest

10 skirmish, lovers enter the arena once again. Sitting still, we are as daring as gladiators.

When I set a glass prism on a windowsill and allow the sun to flood through it, a spectrum of colors dances on the floor. What we call "white" is a rainbow of colored rays packed into a small space. The prism sets them free. Love is the white light of emotion. It includes many feelings which, out of laziness and confusion, we crowd into one simple word. Art is the prism that sets them free,

intangible
(ĭn-tăn´jə-bəl) *n.*
something that is difficult to grasp or explain.

then follows the gyrations[1] of one or a few. When art separates this thick tangle of feelings, love bares its bones. But it cannot be measured or mapped. Everyone admits that love is wonderful and necessary, yet no one can agree on what it is. I once heard a sportscaster say of a basketball player, "He does all the intangibles. Just watch him do his dance." As lofty as the idea of love can be, no image is too profane to help explain it. Years ago, I fell in love with someone who was both a sport and a pastime. At the end, he made fade-away jump shots in my life. But, for a while, love did all the intangibles. It lets us do our finest dance.

Love. What a small word we use for an idea so immense and powerful it has altered the flow of history, calmed monsters, kindled works of art, cheered the forlorn, turned tough guys to mush, consoled the enslaved, driven strong women mad, glorified the humble, fueled national scandals, bankrupted robber barons, and made mincemeat of kings. How can love's spaciousness be conveyed in the narrow confines of one syllable? If we search for the source of the word, we find a history vague and confusing, stretching back to the Sanskrit *lubhyati* ("he desires"). I'm sure the etymology rambles back much farther than that, to a one-syllable word heavy as a heartbeat. Love is an ancient delirium, a desire older than civilization, with taproots[2] stretching deep into dark and mysterious days.

We use the word *love* in such a sloppy way that it can mean almost nothing or absolutely everything. It is the first conjugation[3] students of Latin learn. It is a universally understood motive for crime. "Ah, he was in love," we sigh, "well, that explains it." In fact, in some European and South American countries, even murder is forgivable if it was "a crime of passion." Love, like truth, is the unassailable defense. Whoever first said "love makes the world go round" (it was an anonymous Frenchman) probably was not thinking about celestial mechanics, but the way love seeps into the machinery of life to keep generation after generation in motion. We think of love as a positive force that somehow ennobles the one feeling it. When a friend confesses that he's in love, we congratulate him.

In folk stories, unsuspecting lads and lasses ingest a love potion and quickly lose their hearts. As with all intoxicants, love comes in many **guises** and strengths. It has a mixed bouquet, and may include some piquant ingredients.[4] One's taste in love will have a

guise
(gīz) *n.* form or outward appearance; outfit.

---

[1] **gyrations:** spiral or circular movements.

[2] **taproots:** the main roots of a tree or plant from which other roots grow.

[3] **conjugation:** in grammar, the various forms of a verb.

[4] **piquant (pē´kənt) ingredients:** components that make something pleasantly spicy.

"We use the word love in such a sloppy way that it can mean almost nothing or absolutely everything."

lot to do with one's culture, upbringing, generation, religion, era, gender, and so on. Ironically, although we sometimes think of it
60 as the ultimate Oneness, love isn't monotone or uniform. Like a batik[5] created from many emotional colors, it is a fabric whose pattern and brightness may vary. What is my goddaughter to think when she hears her mother say: "I love Ben & Jerry's Cherry Garcia ice cream"; "I really loved my high school boyfriend"; "Don't you just love this sweater?" "I'd love to go to the lake for a week this summer"; "Mommy loves you." Since all we have is one word, we talk about love in **increments** or unwieldy ratios. "How much do you love me?" a child asks. Because the parent can't answer *I* (verb that means unconditional parental love) *you,* she may fling her
70 arms wide, as if welcoming the sun and sky, stretching her body to its limit, spreading her fingers to encompass all of Creation, and say: "This much!" Or: "Think of the biggest thing you can imagine. Now double it. I love you a hundred times that much!"

When Elizabeth Barrett Browning wrote her famous sonnet "How do I love thee?" she didn't "count the ways" because she had an arithmetical turn of mind, but because English poets have always had to search hard for personal signals of their love. As a society, we are embarrassed by love. We treat it as if it were an obscenity. We reluctantly admit to it. Even saying the word makes
80 us stumble and blush. Why should we be ashamed of an emotion so beautiful and natural? In teaching writing students, I've sometimes given them the assignment of writing a love poem. "Be precise, be

increment
(ĭn′krə-mənt) *n.* an addition or increase by a standard measure of growth.

---

[5] **batik (bə-tēk′):** colorful design created by applying different dyes and wax to fabric.

individual, and be descriptive. But don't use any clichés," I caution them, "or any curse words." Part of the reason for this assignment is that it helps them understand how inhibited we are about love. Love is the most important thing in our lives, a passion for which we would fight or die, and yet we're reluctant to linger over its name. Without a **supple** vocabulary, we can't even talk or think about it directly. On the other hand, we have many sharp verbs for the ways in which human beings can hurt one another, dozens of verbs for the subtle **gradations** of hate. But there are pitifully few synonyms for love. Our vocabulary of love and lovemaking is so paltry that a poet has to choose among clichés, profanities, or euphemisms. Fortunately, this has led to some richly imagined works of art. It has inspired poets to create their own private vocabularies. Mrs. Browning sent her husband a poetic abacus[6] of love, which in a roundabout way expressed the sum of her feelings. Other lovers have tried to calibrate their love in equally ingenious ways. In "The Flea," John Donne watches a flea suck blood from his arm and his beloved's, and rejoices that their blood marries in the flea's stomach.

Yes, lovers are most often reduced to comparatives and quantities. "Do you love me more than her?" we ask. "Will you love me less if I don't do what you say?" We are afraid to face love head-on. We think of it as a sort of traffic accident of the heart. It is an emotion that scares us more than cruelty, more than violence, more than hatred. We allow ourselves to be foiled by the vagueness of the word. After all, love requires the utmost vulnerability. We equip someone with freshly sharpened knives; strip naked; then invite him to stand close. What could be scarier?

If you took a woman from ancient Egypt and put her in an automobile factory in Detroit, she would be understandably disoriented. Everything would be new, especially her ability to stroke the wall and make light flood the room, touch the wall elsewhere and fill the room with summer's warm breezes or winter's blast. She'd be astonished by telephones, computers, fashions, language, and customs. But if she saw a man and woman stealing a kiss in a quiet corner, she would smile. People everywhere and everywhen understand the phenomenon of love, just as they understand the appeal of music, finding it deeply meaningful even if they cannot explain exactly what that meaning is, or why they respond viscerally to one composer and not another. Our Egyptian woman, who prefers the birdlike twittering of a sistrum,[7] and a twentieth-century man, who prefers the clashing jaws of heavy

supple
(sŭp´əl) *adj.* flexible or easily adaptable.

gradation
(grā-dā´shən) *n.* a slight, successive change in color, degree or tone.

---

[6] **abacus:** a device for performing calculations by manipulating beads strung on wires in a rectangular frame.

[7] **sistrum:** an ancient percussion instrument that sounds like a metal rattle.

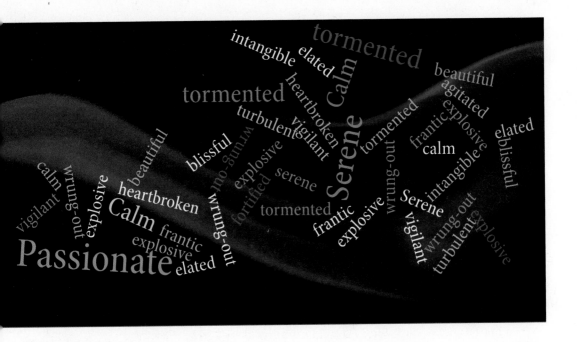

metal, share a passion for music that both would understand. So it is with love. Values, customs, and protocols may vary from ancient days to the present, but not the majesty of love. People are unique in the way they walk, dress, and gesture, yet we're able to look at two people—one wearing a business suit, the other a sarong[8]—

130 and recognize that both of them are clothed. Love also has many fashions, some bizarre and (to our taste) shocking, others more familiar, but all are part of a phantasmagoria[9] we know. In the Serengeti[10] of the heart, time and nation are irrelevant. On that plain, all fires are the same fire.

Remember the feeling of an elevator falling in your chest when you said good-bye to a loved one? Parting is more than sweet sorrow, it pulls you apart when you are glued together. It feels like hunger pains, and we use the same word, *pang*. Perhaps this is why Cupid is depicted with a quiver of arrows, because at times love feels like

140 being pierced in the chest. It is a wholesome violence. Common as child birth, love seems rare nonetheless, always catches one by surprise, and cannot be taught. Each child rediscovers it, each couple redefines it, each parent reinvents it. People search for love as if it were a city lost beneath the desert dunes, where pleasure is the law, the streets are lined with brocade cushions, and the sun never sets.

---

[8] **sarong:** a traditional Southeast Asian women's garment made from a long piece of fabric that is wrapped around the body.

[9] **phantasmagoria (făn-tăz′mə-gôr′ē-ə):** a dreamlike sequence of surreal images or events.

[10] **Serengeti:** a vast plain in Tanzania known for its migratory animals.

If it's so obvious and popular, then what is love? I began researching this book because I had many questions, not because I knew at the outset what answers I might find. Like most people, I believed what I had been told: that the idea of love was invented by the Greeks, and romantic love began in the Middle Ages. I know now how misguided such hearsay is. We can find romantic love in the earliest writings of our kind. Much of the vocabulary of love, and the imagery lovers use, has not changed for thousands of years. Why do the same images come to mind when people describe their romantic feelings? Custom, culture, and tastes vary, but not love itself, not the essence of the emotion.

COLLABORATIVE DISCUSSION Does the author answer the question "What is love?" With a partner, discuss how love is described in the essay. Select the description you think is best and support your choice with evidence from the text.

Analyze Ideas

In her essay, Diane Ackerman explores the concept of love in all of its mystery and complexity. Calling love "the great intangible" that no one can adequately define, she unfolds a series of ideas about love, from across time and place, and she supports each idea by providing facts, details, and examples. Throughout the essay, Ackerman makes connections to her central point about the language we use to describe love.

In analyzing the ideas presented in the essay, consider these questions:

- What is the significance of the order in which Ackerman introduces her ideas or makes her points?
- How does the author introduce, develop, and support each idea?
- How does the author make connections between her many ideas on love? Does she repeat any of these ideas?

Determine Word Meanings

Nonfiction writers often use literary techniques and elements such as figures of speech and allusions to convey ideas and to set a tone. Analyze Ackerman's use of literary techniques in this essay by looking at the elements in the chart.

Figurative Language	Connotation	Tone
Authors use **figurative language**—such as similes, metaphors, and personification—to help readers make connections to their own experiences. **Personification,** for example, attributes human qualities or abilities to an object, animal, or idea. In the first paragraph, how does the author personify the emotions of hate, fear, and jealousy? What does this personification imply about the power of emotions?	To influence how readers respond to their ideas, authors choose words and phrases that have **connotations,** or shades of associated meaning. For example, consider the underlying message the author conveys by using words and phrases such as "fields of glory," "love commands," "victory," and "daring as gladiators." What is the cumulative effect of employing so many figurative words?	**Tone** is the writer's attitude toward the subject or toward the reader of a work. To analyze tone, consider the writer's word choices. Are the connotations mostly positive or mostly negative? What kind of images do figures of speech present? How does Ackerman's use of an invented word ("People everywhere and *everywhen* …") convey her tone?

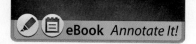
Analyzing the Text

Cite Text Evidence Support your responses with evidence from the selection.

1. **Infer** Ackerman begins by stating that "Love is the great intangible." What does she mean by this statement? What details and examples in the first two paragraphs help to support this idea?

2. **Evaluate** In lines 28–33, what human qualities does Ackerman attribute to love? Describe the tone she creates by this use of personification.

3. **Cite Evidence** In lines 60–62, how does Ackerman use figurative language to support her idea that love "isn't monotone or uniform"? What additional evidence does she provide to support this point?

4. **Analyze** Why does Ackerman include references to Elizabeth Barrett Browning's poem "How Do I Love Thee?" and John Donne's poem "The Flea"? What point is she trying to make by citing these literary works?

5. **Infer** In line 105, Ackerman calls love "a sort of traffic accident of the heart." What idea about love is she conveying?

6. **Interpret** In lines 126–127, Ackerman writes, "Values, customs, and protocols may vary from ancient days to the present, but not the majesty of love." What does she mean by this statement? What example does she use to develop this idea?

7. **Evaluate** What is Ackerman's tone throughout the essay? Cite specific words and phrases she uses to create the tone.

PERFORMANCE TASK

Speaking Activity: Informative Presentation With a group, prepare a presentation on Ackerman's view that, as a nation, "we are embarrassed by love."

1. As the basis of your presentation, ask yourself these questions:

   - Why does Ackerman say we are embarrassed by love or inhibited about it? What evidence does she cite?
   - Does Ackerman herself find love embarrassing? Cite examples from the text.

2. Give a presentation based on your findings. Be sure to include specific examples from the text. Use appropriate eye contact and adequate volume to emphasize important ideas. As you speak, remember to use the conventions of standard English and to pronounce every word clearly and correctly.

Critical Vocabulary

intangible   **guise**   **increment**   **supple**   **gradation**

Practice and Apply Create a semantic map like the one shown for the remaining Critical Vocabulary words. Use a dictionary or thesaurus as needed.

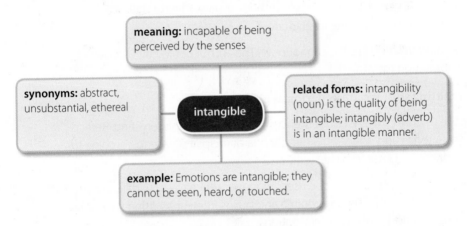

meaning: incapable of being perceived by the senses

synonyms: abstract, unsubstantial, ethereal

intangible

related forms: intangibility (noun) is the quality of being intangible; intangibly (adverb) is in an intangible manner.

example: Emotions are intangible; they cannot be seen, heard, or touched.

Vocabulary Strategy: Synonyms

When you encounter an unfamiliar word in an essay, you can often determine its meaning by substituting a **synonym**—a word with a similar meaning—for the unfamiliar word. For example, in the first line of the essay, Ackerman uses the Critical Vocabulary word *intangible*. The context clue "dream state" later in the paragraph indicates something unsubstantial. The synonym *unsubstantial* makes sense in the sentence.

Practice and Apply Work with a partner to locate these words in the essay: *immense* (line 28), *ennobles* (line 51), *monotone* (line 60), *inhibited* (line 85). Follow these steps:

1. Look for a synonym in the sentence or paragraph where the unfamiliar word occurs.

2. Use context clues to determine meaning and think of a synonym that fits.

3. Substitute your synonym for the unfamiliar word to see if it makes sense.

4. Consult a dictionary or a thesaurus to confirm the meaning.

Language and Style: Participial Phrases

A **participle** is a verb form that functions as an adjective. Like adjectives, they modify nouns and pronouns. Most participles are present-participle forms, ending in *–ing*, or past-participle forms, ending in *–ed* or *–en*. A **participial phrase** is a group of words that consists of either the present or past participle form of a verb and its modifiers. For example, the participial phrase in this sentence from "Love's Vocabulary" consists of a present participle (sitting) and an adverb (still):

> <u>Sitting still</u>, we are as daring as gladiators.

The phrase *sitting still* modifies the pronoun *we*. The author could have conveyed the same information this way:

> We are sitting still. We are as daring as gladiators.

However, the rhythm of these two sentences is choppy and uninteresting. Reread Ackerman's sentence and notice how her use of a participial phrase to combine the ideas adds variety and interest to her writing.

Several participial phrases may be used in one sentence to show different actions. Ackerman creates a sense of drama and builds interest by using participial phrases in combination to show several actions:

> <u>Hoping for victory</u>, <u>limping from the latest skirmish</u>, lovers enter the arena once again.

Here, two participial phrases, separated by commas, modify the noun *lovers*. Ackerman could have written simply, "Lovers enter the arena once again." However, she includes participial phrases to tell us more about the lovers. She adds meaning by describing the lovers' states of mind and by presenting a dramatic visual image.

Participial phrases may be placed at the beginning, the middle, or the end of a sentence. When using participial phrases in your own writing, it is important to place them carefully and to use punctuation correctly for clarity.

- A participial phrase should be placed close to the word it modifies, to avoid confusing the reader.
- A participial phrase that begins a sentence is followed by a comma.
- A participial phrase that is at the end of a sentence is preceded by a comma.
- A participial phrase that occurs in the middle of a sentence is set off by two commas, unless it is essential to the meaning of the sentence. If the sentence would not make sense without the phrase, omit the commas.

Practice and Apply Look back at the summary of the discussion about love and embarrassment you created in this selection's Performance Task. In your same group, revise the summary to add at least three participial phrases. Then discuss how the participial phrases improve the meaning or tone of the summary.

Background **Kate Tempest** *is a London-born poet, playwright, and rapper. She began performing at age 16 and has performed all over the world, winning acclaim and awards at music festivals and poetry slams. Her first collection of poetry,* Everything Speaks in its Own Way, *was published in 2012 and includes a CD and a DVD along with the text. The Royal Shakespeare Company commissioned Kate to write and perform "My Shakespeare" for the World Shakespeare Festival in 2012. Thousands of artists from around the world participated in this festival throughout Britain as well as online.*

MEDIA ANALYSIS

My Shakespeare

Poem by Kate Tempest

AS YOU VIEW AND READ Think about what Kate Tempest's delivery—her voice and gestures—add to the poem. Write down any questions you generate during both viewing and reading.

My Shakespeare

Performance by Kate Tempest

He's in every lover who ever stood alone beneath a window,
In every jealous whispered word,
in every ghost that will not rest.
He's in every father with a favorite,
5   Every eye that stops to linger
On what someone else has got, and feels the tightening in their
     chest.

He's in every young man growing boastful,
Every worn out elder, drunk all day;
muttering false prophecies and squandering their lot.
10 He's there—in every mix-up that spirals far out of control—and
     never seems to end,
even when its beginnings are forgot.

He's in every girl who ever used her wits. Who ever did her best.
In every vain admirer,
Every passionate, ambitious social climber,
15 And in every misheard word that ever led to tempers fraying,
Every pawn that moves exactly as the player wants it to,
And still remains convinced that it's not playing.

He's in every star crossed lover, in every thought that ever set your
teeth on edge, in every breathless hero, stepping closer to the ledge,
20 his is the method in our madness, as pure as the driven snow—his is
the hair standing on end, he saw that all that glittered was not gold.
He knew we hadn't slept a wink, and that our hearts were upon our
sleeves, and that the beast with two backs had us all upon our knees
as we fought fire with fire, he knew that too much of a good thing,
25 can leave you up in arms, the pen is mightier than the sword, still
his words seem to sing our names as they strike, and his is the milk
of human kindness, warm enough to break the ice—his, the green
eyed monster, in a pickle, still, discretion is the better part of valor,
his letters with their arms around each others shoulders, swagger
30 towards the ends of their sentences, pleased with what they've done,
his words are the setting for our stories—he has become a poet who
poetics have embedded themselves deep within the fabric of our
language, he's in our mouths, his words have tangled round our own
and given rise to expressions so effective in expressing how we feel,
35 we can't imagine how we'd feel without them.

See—he's less the tights and garters—more the sons demanding
    answers from the absence of their fathers.
The hot darkness of your last embrace.
He's in the laughter of the night before, the tightened jaw of the
    morning after,
He's in us. Part and parcel of our Royals and our rascals.
40 He's more than something taught in classrooms, in language that's
    hard to understand,
he's more than a feeling of inadequacy when we sit for our exams,
He's in every wise woman, every pitiful villain,
Every great king, every sore loser, every fake tear.
His legacy exists in the life that lives in everything he's written,
45 And me, I see him everywhere, he's my Shakespeare.

COLLABORATIVE DISCUSSION With a partner, discuss the overall effect
of the video. Cite words and phrases in the video that depart from the
text of the poem and consider whether these variations affect your
response.

Analyze Source Material: Interpretations of Shakespeare

Kate Tempest's passionate performance of her poem demonstrates the great appeal Shakespeare has for today's youth. Shakespeare's work has been translated into more than 80 languages; it has been adapted, televised, filmed, recorded, and digitized. Shakespeare's significant presence on the Internet attests to the fact that his work has inspired—and is still inspiring—the work of countless artists.

Authors often draw on historical, literary, and cultural sources for themes or topics, using their own imagination to transform the source material into their own original works of art. Just as Shakespeare drew inspiration from earlier sources, Kate Tempest attributes her inspiration for "My Shakespeare" to the works of Shakespeare himself. In the first three stanzas, she makes allusions to the characters, themes, and scenarios exposed in Shakespeare's well-known plays. The fourth stanza comprises phrases coined by Shakespeare that are still in use today. In the last stanza, Tempest gets at the heart of Shakespeare's continued relevance.

Analyzing Text and Video

Cite Text Evidence   Support your responses with evidence from the selection.

1. **Infer** "He's in every lover . . . beneath a window" is an allusion to Romeo that is recognizable even to readers who have not read *Romeo and Juliet*. What does the repetition of the words "in every" throughout the poem signal to readers? What message does Tempest convey through these words?

2. **Cite Evidence** Explain the statement that Shakespeare is "in our mouths, his words have tangled round our own." What evidence does the author provide to support this idea?

3. **Analyze** In the last stanza, Tempest acknowledges the negative ideas that today's young people might have about Shakespeare. How do the text and the video work together to refute these ideas?

PERFORMANCE TASK

Media Activity: Reflection   Can Kate Tempest's Shakespeare be *your* Shakespeare?

- Create a blog that features Kate Tempest's performance of "My Shakespeare."
- Write an introduction or make your own video to introduce Kate Tempest's performance.

- Explain how you responded to the poem, citing specific examples from the text and the video.
- Use conventions of standard written English.

Shakespearean Drama

*Shakespeare's 38 plays may be more popular today than they were in Elizabethan times. While Shakespeare's comedies and histories remain crowd-pleasing classics, his tragedies are perhaps his most powerful works. One of the most famous, **The Tragedy of Romeo and Juliet,** relates the tale of two love-struck teens caught between the tension of their feuding families.*

Characteristics of Shakespearean Tragedy

A **tragedy** is a drama that results in a catastrophe—most often death—for the main characters. Shakespearean tragedies, however, offer us more than just despair; they provide comic moments that counter the underlying tension of the serious plot. Before you begin *The Tragedy of Romeo and Juliet*, familiarize yourself with some of the character types and dramatic conventions of Shakespearean tragedy.

Characters	Dramatic Conventions
Tragic Hero • the protagonist, or central character • usually fails or dies because of a character flaw or a cruel twist of fate	**Soliloquy** • a speech given by a character alone • exposes a character's thoughts and feelings to the audience
Antagonist • the adversary or hostile force opposing the protagonist • can be a character, a group of characters, or a nonhuman entity	**Aside** • a character's remark that others on stage do not hear • reveals the character's private thoughts
Foil • a character whose personality and attitude contrast sharply with those of another character • emphasizes another character's attributes and traits, such as a timid, introverted character making a talkative one seem even chattier	**Dramatic Irony** • when the audience knows more than the characters • helps build suspense
	Comic Relief • a humorous scene or speech intended to relieve tension • heightens the seriousness of the main action by contrast

The Language of Shakespeare

Blank Verse Shakespeare wrote his plays primarily in blank verse, unrhymed lines of **iambic pentameter**, a meter that contains five unstressed syllables (˘), each followed by a stressed syllable (´). Read the following lines aloud, making sure to emphasize each stressed syllable:

> Here's much to do with hate but more with love.

While this pattern forms the general rule, variations in the rhythm prevent the play from sounding monotonous. As you read, pay close attention to places where characters speak in rhyming poetry instead of unrhymed verse.

Allusion and Word Play An **allusion** is a reference to a literary or historical person or event that the audience is expected to know. Shakespeare's audience was familiar with Greek and Roman mythology and the Bible, so his plays include many references to these works.

Shakespeare also includes many **puns,** humor resulting from words with similar sounds and different meanings. For example, a depressed Romeo utters a pun using the word *light* when he offers to carry a torch: "Being but heavy, I will bear the light."

Elizabethan Words to Know

'a: he.

an, and: if.

anon: soon; right away.

aught: anything.

coz: short for cousin; used to refer to relatives or close friends.

ere: before.

e'er: ever.

god-den: good evening.

God gi' go-den: God give you a good evening.

hence: from here.

hie: hurry.

hither: here.

marry: a short form of "by the Virgin Mary" and so a mild exclamation.

morrow: morning.

naught: nothing.

o'er: over.

prithee: pray thee, or please.

sirrah: a term used to address a servant.

soft: be still; quiet; wait a minute.

thither: there.

whence: where.

wherefore: why.

wot: know.

yond, yonder: over there.

Reading Shakespearean Drama

Use the following tips to help you better understand *Romeo and Juliet*:

Reading Drama

- Study the opening cast of characters to see who's in the play.
- Read the stage directions to find out where a scene takes place as well as who's on stage and what they're doing. Stage directions in *Romeo and Juliet* are minimal, so you'll sometimes have to infer what's happening from the dialogue.
- Visualize the setting and the action by noting key details in the stage directions.

Reading Shakespearean Tragedy

- Keep track of the relationships between characters—are they friends, relatives, or enemies? Also, consider a character's dramatic function—tragic hero, antagonist, foil, or comic relief—which will help you interpret his or her words and actions.
- Note important character traits revealed through dialogue, soliloquies, and asides, as well as the through the action. Do the characters exhibit any flaws or weaknesses?
- Look for cause-and-effect relationships between events, especially those events that lead to the tragic outcome. You can keep track of them by using a graphic like this flowchart.

Cause
To cheer up Romeo, Benvolio and some other Montagues lead him to a party that the Capulets are giving.

Effect
At the party, Romeo sees Juliet for the first time, and he falls madly in love with her.

Reading Shakespeare's Language

- Use the marginal notes to figure out word meanings and unusual sentence structures. Record difficult lines and then rephrase them in modern speech.
- Paraphrase passages to help clarify their meaning and to summarize events, ideas, and themes. Use your own words without including your own opinions.
- Just as when you read poetry, don't automatically stop reading when you come to the end of a line. Look carefully at each line's punctuation and consider the meaning of the complete sentence or phrase.

Elizabethan Theater

A Wide Audience

Though acting companies toured throughout England, London was the center of the Elizabethan stage. One reason that London's theaters did so well was that they attracted an avid audience of rich and poor alike. In fact, Elizabethan theaters were among the few forms of entertainment available to working-class people, and one of the only places where people of all classes could mix. Shakespeare appealed to English audience members of all classes because he always included variety in his plays. He presented poetic speeches, exciting action scenes, fast-paced humor, and wise observations about human nature. His characters performed acts of bravery and kindness and committed heinous crimes. As a result, his work was respected by the educated and powerful people of the day, and the common people loved him too.

The Globe

In 1599, Shakespeare and other shareholders of The Lord Chamberlain's Men built the Globe Theater, a three-story wooden structure with an open courtyard at its center where the actors performed on an elevated platform. The theater held 3,000 people, with most of them standing near the courtyard stage in an area known as the pit. The pit audience paid the lowest admission fee—usually just one penny. Theatergoers willing and able to pay more sat in the covered inner balconies that surrounded the courtyard.

The audiences became emotionally involved in the performances and openly displayed their pleasure or disapproval. They cheered, booed and hissed, and even threw rotten vegetables. They roared their approval at battle scenes and swordfights, the cheers competing with such dramatic sound effects as trumpet blares, drum rolls, and thunder claps.

Staging

Elizabethan theater relied heavily on an audience's imagination. Most theaters had no curtains, no lighting, and very little scenery. Instead, props, sound effects, and certain lines of dialogue defined the setting of a scene. While the staging was simple, the scenes were hardly dull. Flashing swords, brightly colored banners, and elegant costumes contributed to the spectacle.

The costumes also helped audience members imagine that women appeared in the female roles, which were actually performed by young men. In Shakespeare's time, women could not belong to theater companies in England—Elizabethan society considered it highly improper for a woman to appear on stage. As a result, boys underwent a rigorous initiation into the dramatic techniques, dance routines, and vocal qualities necessary to perform the female parts.

The Tragedy of Romeo and Juliet

Drama by William Shakespeare

William Shakespeare *has long been considered the greatest writer in the English language—and perhaps the greatest playwright of all time. Four hundred years after their premier performances, his plays remain more popular than ever, and they have been produced more often and in more countries than those of any other author. However, despite Shakespeare's renown we have relatively few details about his life and career as an actor, poet, and playwright.*

Shakespeare came from Stratford-upon-Avon, a small village about 90 miles northwest of London, and was probably born in 1564. Though no records exist, we assume that he attended the local grammar school. In 1582 he married Anne Hathaway, daughter of a farmer. The couple's first child arrived in 1583, and twins, a boy and a girl, followed two years later.

We know nothing about the next seven years of Shakespeare's life, but he likely left his family behind and joined a traveling theater troupe. His trail resurfaces in London, where he had become a successful poet and playwright. He wrote for and acted with The Lord Chamberlain's Men, a popular theater troupe. By 1597, the year that The Tragedy of Romeo and Juliet *was published, he had become a shareholder of the theater company. As his popularity grew, Shakespeare also became part owner of London's Globe Theater. In 1603 King James I became a patron of the Globe Theater, and the theater troupe became known as The King's Men.*

In 1609 Shakespeare published his sonnets, a series of poems that received wide popular acclaim. Shakespeare then began to take advantage of his wealth and fame, spending more time in Stratford-upon-Avon and retiring there permanently around 1612. He would write no more plays after that year. No records confirm the cause or date of his death; a monument marking his gravesite indicates that he passed away on April 23, 1616. Although we have little data documenting his life, more pages have been written about Shakespeare than about any author in the history of Western civilization.

THE TIME: The 14th century

THE PLACE: Verona (və-rō´nə) and Mantua (măn´choo-ə) in northern Italy

CAST

The Montagues

Lord Montague (mŏn´tə-gyoo´)
Lady Montague
Romeo, son of Montague
Benvolio (bĕn-vō´lē-ō), nephew of Montague and friend of Romeo
Balthasar (băl´thə-sär´), servant to Romeo
Abram, servant to Montague

The Capulets

Lord Capulet (kăp´yoo-lĕt´)
Lady Capulet
Juliet, daughter of Capulet
Tybalt (tĭb´əlt), nephew of Lady Capulet
Nurse to Juliet
Peter, servant to Juliet's nurse
Sampson, servant to Capulet
Gregory, servant to Capulet
An Old Man of the Capulet family

Others

Prince Escalus (ĕs´kə-ləs), ruler of Verona
Mercutio (mĕr-kyoo´shē-ō), kinsman of the prince and friend of Romeo
Friar Laurence, a Franciscan priest
Friar John, another Franciscan priest
Count Paris, a young nobleman, kinsman of the prince
Apothecary (ə-pŏth´ĭ-kĕr´ē)
Page to Paris
Chief Watchman
Three Musicians
An Officer
Chorus
Citizens of Verona, **Gentlemen** and **Gentlewomen** of both houses, **Maskers, Torchbearers, Pages, Guards, Watchmen, Servants,** and **Attendants**

AS YOU READ Look for clues that reveal the personalities of Romeo and Juliet. Write down any questions you generate during reading.

Prologue

[*Enter* Chorus.]

Chorus. Two households, both alike in dignity,
In fair Verona, where we lay our scene,
From ancient grudge break to new mutiny,
Where civil blood makes civil hands unclean.
5 From forth the fatal loins of these two foes,
A pair of star-crossed lovers take their life,
Whose misadventured piteous overthrows
Doth with their death bury their parents' strife.
The fearful passage of their death-marked love,
10 And the continuance of their parents' rage,
Which, but their children's end, naught could remove,
Is now the two hours' traffic of our stage,
The which if you with patient ears attend,
What here shall miss, our toil shall strive to mend.

[*Exit.*]

ACT I

Scene 1 *A public square in Verona.*

[*Enter* Sampson *and* Gregory, *servants of the house of Capulet, armed with swords and bucklers (shields).*]

Sampson. Gregory, on my word, we'll not carry coals.

Gregory. No, for then we should be colliers.

Sampson. I mean, an we be in choler, we'll draw.

Gregory. Ay, while you live, draw your neck out of collar.

5 **Sampson.** I strike quickly, being moved.

Gregory. But thou art not quickly moved to strike.

Sampson. A dog of that house of Montague moves me.

Gregory. To move is to stir, and to be valiant is to stand. Therefore, if thou art moved, thou runnest away.

10 **Sampson.** A dog of that house shall move me to stand. I will take the wall of any man or maid of Montague's.

Gregory. That shows thee a weak slave, for the weakest goes to the wall.

3–4 ancient . . . unclean: A new outbreak of fighting (**mutiny**) between families has caused the citizens of Verona to have one another's blood on their hands.

6 star-crossed: doomed. The position of the stars when the lovers were born was not favorable. In Shakespeare's day, people took astrology very seriously.

7 misadventured: unlucky.

11 but: except for; **naught:** nothing.

14 what . . . mend: The play will fill in the details not mentioned in the prologue.

1–2 we'll not carry coals: we won't stand to be insulted; **colliers:** those involved in the dirty work of hauling coal, who were often the butt of jokes.

3–4 in choler: angry; **collar:** a hangman's noose.

11 take the wall: walk. People of higher rank had the privilege of walking closer to the wall, to avoid any water or garbage in the street.

Sampson. 'Tis true; and therefore women, being the weaker
vessels, are ever thrust to the wall. Therefore push I will
Montague's men from the wall and thrust his maids to the wall.

Gregory. The quarrel is between our masters and us their men.

Sampson. 'Tis all one. I will show myself a tyrant. When I have
fought with the men, I will be cruel with the maids: I will cut
off their heads.

Gregory. The heads of the maids?

Sampson. Ay, the heads of the maids, or their maidenheads.
Take it in what sense thou wilt.

Gregory. They must take it in sense that feel it.

Sampson. Me they shall feel while I am able to stand;
and 'tis known I am a pretty piece of flesh.

Gregory. 'Tis well thou art not fish; if thou hadst, thou hadst
been poor-John. Draw thy tool! Here comes two of the house
of Montagues.

[*Enter* Abram *and* Balthasar, *servants to the Montagues.*]

Sampson. My naked weapon is out. Quarrel! I will back thee.

Gregory. How? turn thy back and run?

Sampson. Fear me not.

Gregory. No, marry. I fear thee!

Sampson. Let us take the law of our sides; let them begin.

Gregory. I will frown as I pass by, and let them take it as they list.

Sampson. Nay, as they dare. I will bite my thumb at them;
which is disgrace to them, if they bear it.

Abram. Do you bite your thumb at us, sir?

Sampson. I do bite my thumb, sir.

Abram. Do you bite your thumb at us, sir?

Sampson [*aside to* Gregory]. Is the law of our side if I say ay?

Gregory [*aside to* Sampson]. No.

Sampson. No, sir, I do not bite my thumb at you, sir; but I bite
my thumb, sir.

Gregory. Do you quarrel, sir?

Abram. Quarrel, sir? No, sir.

Sampson. But if you do, sir, I am for you. I serve as good a man
as you.

14–24 Sampson's tough talk includes boasts about his ability to overpower women.

28 poor-John: a salted fish, considered fit only for poor people to eat.

33 marry: a short form of "by the Virgin Mary" and so a mild exclamation.

34–44 Gregory and Sampson decide to pick a fight by insulting the Montague servants with a rude gesture (bite my thumb).

Abram. No better.

50 **Sampson.** Well, sir.

[*Enter* Benvolio, *nephew of Montague and first cousin of Romeo.*]

Gregory [*aside to* Sampson]. Say "better." Here comes one of my master's kinsmen.

Sampson. Yes, better, sir.

Abram. You lie.

55 **Sampson.** Draw, if you be men. Gregory, remember thy swashing blow.

[*They fight.*]

Benvolio. Part, fools!　　　　　　　　[*beats down their swords*]
Put up your swords. You know not what you do.

[*Enter* Tybalt, *hot-headed nephew of Lady Capulet and first cousin of Juliet.*]

Tybalt. What, art thou drawn among these heartless hinds?
60 Turn thee, Benvolio! look upon thy death.

> 59 **heartless hinds:** cowardly servants.

Benvolio. I do but keep the peace. Put up thy sword,
Or manage it to part these men with me.

Tybalt. What, drawn, and talk of peace? I hate the word
As I hate hell, all Montagues, and thee.
65 Have at thee, coward!

> 63 **drawn:** with your sword out.

> 65 **Have at thee:** Defend yourself.

[*They fight.*]

[*Enter several of both houses, who join the fray; then enter* Citizens *and* Peace Officers, *with clubs.*]

Officer. Clubs, bills, and partisans! Strike! beat them down!

> 66 **bills, and partisans:** spears.

Citizens. Down with the Capulets! Down with the Montagues!

[*Enter old* Capulet *and* Lady Capulet.]

Capulet. What noise is this? Give me my long sword, ho!

Lady Capulet. A crutch, a crutch! Why call you for a sword?

> 69 **A crutch . . . sword:** You need a crutch more than a sword.

70 **Capulet.** My sword, I say! Old Montague is come
And flourishes his blade in spite of me.

[*Enter old* Montague *and* Lady Montague.]

Montague. Thou villain Capulet!—Hold me not, let me go.

Lady Montague. Thou shalt not stir one foot to seek a foe.

[*Enter* Prince Escalus, *with attendants. At first no one hears him.*]

Prince. Rebellious subjects, enemies to peace,
75 Profaners of this neighbor-stained steel—
Will they not hear? What, ho! you men, you beasts,
That quench the fire of your pernicious rage
With purple fountains issuing from your veins!
On pain of torture, from those bloody hands
80 Throw your mistempered weapons to the ground
And hear the sentence of your moved prince.
Three civil brawls, bred of an airy word
By thee, old Capulet, and Montague,
Have thrice disturbed the quiet of our streets
85 And made Verona's ancient citizens
Cast by their grave beseeming ornaments
To wield old partisans, in hands as old,
Cankered with peace, to part your cankered hate.
If ever you disturb our streets again,
90 Your lives shall pay the forfeit of the peace.
For this time all the rest depart away.
You, Capulet, shall go along with me;
And, Montague, come you this afternoon,
To know our farther pleasure in this case,
95 To old Freetown, our common judgment place.
Once more, on pain of death, all men depart.

[*Exeunt all but* Montague, Lady Montague, *and* Benvolio.]

Montague. Who set this ancient quarrel new abroach?
Speak, nephew, were you by when it began?

Benvolio. Here were the servants of your adversary
100 And yours, close fighting ere I did approach.
I drew to part them. In the instant came
The fiery Tybalt, with his sword prepared;
Which, as he breathed defiance to my ears,
He swung about his head and cut the winds,
105 Who, nothing hurt withal, hissed him in scorn.
While we were interchanging thrusts and blows,
Came more and more, and fought on part and part,
Till the Prince came, who parted either part.

Lady Montague. O, where is Romeo? Saw you him today?
110 Right glad I am he was not at this fray.

Benvolio. Madam, an hour before the worshiped sun
Peered forth the golden window of the East,
A troubled mind drave me to walk abroad,
Where, underneath the grove of sycamore
115 That westward rooteth from the city's side,
So early walking did I see your son.

74–81 The prince is furious about the street fighting caused by the feud. He orders the men to drop their weapons and pay attention.

77 pernicious: destructive.

82–90 Three . . . peace: The prince holds Capulet and Montague responsible for three recent street fights, each probably started by an offhand remark or insult (**airy word**). He warns that they will be put to death if any more fights occur.

Exeunt: the plural form of *exit,* indicating that more than one person is leaving the stage.

97 Who . . . abroach: Who reopened this old argument?

99 adversary: enemy.

100 ere: before.

107 on part and part: some on one side, some on the other.

110 fray: fight.

113 drave: drove.

115 rooteth: grows.

Towards him I made, but he was ware of me
And stole into the covert of the wood.
I—measuring his affections by my own,
120 Which then most sought where most might not be found,
Being one too many by my weary self—
Pursued my humor, not pursuing his,
And gladly shunned who gladly fled from me.

Montague. Many a morning hath he there been seen,
125 With tears augmenting the fresh morning's dew,
Adding to clouds more clouds with his deep sighs;
But all so soon as the all-cheering sun
Should in the farthest East begin to draw
The shady curtains from Aurora's bed,
130 Away from light steals home my heavy son
And private in his chamber pens himself,
Shuts up his windows, locks fair daylight out,
And makes himself an artificial night.
Black and portentous must this humor prove
135 Unless good counsel may the cause remove.

Benvolio. My noble uncle, do you know the cause?

Montague. I neither know it nor can learn of him.

Benvolio. Have you importuned him by any means?

Montague. Both by myself and many other friends;
140 But he, his own affections' counselor,
Is to himself—I will not say how true—
But to himself so secret and so close,
So far from sounding and discovery,
As is the bud bit with an envious worm
145 Ere he can spread his sweet leaves to the air
Or dedicate his beauty to the sun.
Could we but learn from whence his sorrows grow,
We would as willingly give cure as know.

[*Enter* Romeo *lost in thought.*]

Benvolio. See, where he comes. So please you step aside,
150 I'll know his grievance, or be much denied.

Montague. I would thou wert so happy by thy stay
To hear true shrift. Come, madam, let's away.

[*Exeunt* Montague *and* Lady.]

Benvolio. Good morrow, cousin.

Romeo.   Is the day so young?

Benvolio. But new struck nine.

117–123 made: moved; **covert:** covering. Romeo saw Benvolio coming and hid in the woods. Benvolio himself was seeking solitude and did not go after him.

124–135 Romeo has been seen wandering through the woods at night, crying. At dawn he returns home and locks himself in his room. Montague feels that his son needs guidance.

129 Aurora's bed: Aurora was the goddess of the dawn.

134 portentous: indicating evil to come; threatening.

138 importuned: asked in an urgent way.

140 his own affections' counselor: Romeo keeps to himself.

143–148 so far from … know: Finding out what Romeo is thinking is almost impossible. Montague compares his son to a young bud destroyed by the bite of a worm before it has a chance to open its leaves. Montague wants to find out what is bothering Romeo so he can help him.

152 shrift: confession.

153 cousin: any relative or close friend. The informal version is *coz.*

Romeo.   Ay me! sad hours seem long.
155 Was that my father that went hence so fast?

Benvolio. It was. What sadness lengthens Romeo's hours?

Romeo. Not having that which having makes them short.

Benvolio. In love?

Romeo. Out—

160 **Benvolio.** Of love?

Romeo. Out of her favor where I am in love.

Benvolio. Alas that love, so gentle in his view,
Should be so tyrannous and rough in proof!

Romeo. Alas that love, whose view is muffled still,
165 Should without eyes see pathways to his will!
Where shall we dine?—O me! What fray was here?—
Yet tell me not, for I have heard it all.

162–165 love:
references to Cupid, the
god of love, typically
pictured as a blind boy
with wings and a bow
and arrow. Anyone hit
by one of his arrows falls
in love instantly.

Here's much to do with hate, but more with love.
Why then, O brawling love! O loving hate!
170 O anything, of nothing first create!
O heavy lightness! serious vanity!
Misshapen chaos of well-seeming forms!
Feather of lead, bright smoke, cold fire, sick health!
Still-waking sleep, that is not what it is!
175 This love feel I, that feel no love in this.
Dost thou not laugh?

Benvolio.　　　　　No, coz, I rather weep.

Romeo. Good heart, at what?

Benvolio.　　　　　　At thy good heart's oppression.

Romeo. Why, such is love's transgression.
Griefs of mine own lie heavy in my breast,
180 Which thou wilt propagate, to have it prest
With more of thine. This love that thou hast shown
Doth add more grief to too much of mine own.
Love is a smoke raised with the fume of sighs;
Being purged, a fire sparkling in lovers' eyes;
185 Being vexed, a sea nourished with lovers' tears.
What is it else? A madness most discreet,
A choking gall, and a preserving sweet.
Farewell, my coz.

Benvolio.　　　Soft! I will go along.
An if you leave me so, you do me wrong.

190 **Romeo.** Tut! I have lost myself; I am not here:
This is not Romeo, he's some other where.

Benvolio. Tell me in sadness, who is that you love?

Romeo. What, shall I groan and tell thee?

Benvolio.　　　　　　　　Groan? Why, no;
But sadly tell me who.

195 **Romeo.** Bid a sick man in sadness make his will.
Ah, word ill urged to one that is so ill!
In sadness, cousin, I do love a woman.

Benvolio. I aimed so near when I supposed you loved.

Romeo. A right good markman! And she's fair I love.

200 **Benvolio.** A right fair mark, fair coz, is soonest hit.

Romeo. Well, in that hit you miss. She'll not be hit
With Cupid's arrow. She hath Dian's wit,
And, in strong proof of chastity well armed,

168–176 Romeo, confused and upset, tries to describe his feelings about love. He uses phrases like "loving hate" and other contradictory expressions.

176–182 Benvolio expresses his sympathy for Romeo. Romeo replies that this is one more problem caused by love. He now feels worse than before because he must carry the weight of Benvolio's sympathy along with his own grief.

184 purged: cleansed (of the smoke).

185 vexed: troubled.

187 gall: something causing bitterness or hate.

188 Soft: Wait a minute.

192 sadness: seriousness.

201–204 She'll . . . unharmed: The girl isn't interested in falling in love. She is like Diana, the goddess of chastity.

From Love's weak childish bow she lives unharmed.
205 She will not stay the siege of loving terms,
Nor bide the encounter of assailing eyes,
Nor ope her lap to saint-seducing gold.
O, she is rich in beauty; only poor
That, when she dies, with beauty dies her store.

205–207 **She will not ... gold:** She is not swayed by Romeo's love or his wealth.

210 **Benvolio.** Then she hath sworn that she will still live chaste?

Romeo. She hath, and in that sparing makes huge waste;
For beauty, starved with her severity,
Cuts beauty off from all posterity.
She is too fair, too wise, wisely too fair,
215 To merit bliss by making me despair.
She hath forsworn to love, and in that vow
Do I live dead that live to tell it now.

212–213 **For beauty ... posterity:** She wastes her beauty, which will not be passed on to future generations.

215–216 **To merit ... despair:** The girl will reach heaven (**bliss**) by being so virtuous, which causes Romeo to feel despair; **forsworn to:** sworn not to.

Benvolio. Be ruled by me: forget to think of her.

Romeo. O, teach me how I should forget to think!

220 **Benvolio.** By giving liberty unto thine eyes:
Examine other beauties.

221–222 **'Tis ... more:** That would only make me appreciate my own love's beauty more.

Romeo.   'Tis the way
To call hers (exquisite) in question more.
These happy masks that kiss fair ladies' brows,
Being black, puts us in mind they hide the fair.
225 He that is strucken blind cannot forget
The precious treasure of his eyesight lost.
Show me a mistress that is passing fair,
What doth her beauty serve but as a note
Where I may read who passed that passing fair?
230 Farewell. Thou canst not teach me to forget.

223 Masks were worn by Elizabethan women to protect their faces from the sun.

227–229 **Show me ... fair:** A woman who is exceedingly (**passing**) beautiful will only remind me of my love, who is even prettier.

Benvolio. I'll pay that doctrine, or else die in debt.

231 **I'll pay ... debt:** I'll convince you you're wrong, or die trying.

[*Exeunt.*]

Scene 2 *A street near the Capulet house.*

[*Enter* Capulet *with* Paris, *a kinsman of the Prince, and* Servant.]

Capulet. But Montague is bound as well as I,
In penalty alike; and 'tis not hard, I think,
For men so old as we to keep the peace.

1 **bound:** obligated.

Paris. Of honorable reckoning are you both,
5 And pity 'tis you lived at odds so long.
But now, my lord, what say you to my suit?

4 **reckoning:** reputation.

Capulet. But saying o'er what I have said before:
My child is yet a stranger in the world,

6 **what say ... suit:** Paris is asking for Capulet's response to his proposal to marry Juliet.

She hath not seen the change of fourteen years;

10 Let two more summers wither in their pride
Ere we may think her ripe to be a bride.

Paris. Younger than she are happy mothers made.

Capulet. And too soon marred are those so early made.
The earth hath swallowed all my hopes but she;

15 She is the hopeful lady of my earth.
But woo her, gentle Paris, get her heart;
My will to her consent is but a part.
An she agree, within her scope of choice
Lies my consent and fair according voice.

20 This night I hold an old accustomed feast,
Whereto I have invited many a guest,
Such as I love, and you among the store,
One more, most welcome, makes my number more.
At my poor house look to behold this night

25 Earth-treading stars that make dark heaven light.
Such comfort as do lusty young men feel
When well-appareled April on the heel
Of limping Winter treads, even such delight
Among fresh female buds shall you this night

30 Inherit at my house. Hear all, all see,
And like her most whose merit most shall be;
Which, on more view of many, mine, being one,
May stand in number, though in reck'ning none.
Come, go with me.   [*to* Servant, *giving him a paper*]

Go, sirrah, trudge about

35 Through fair Verona; find those persons out
Whose names are written there, and to them say,
My house and welcome on their pleasure stay.

[*Exeunt* Capulet *and* Paris.]

Servant. Find them out whose names are written here! It is
written that the shoemaker should meddle with his yard and the

40 tailor with his last, the fisher with his pencil and the painter
with his nets; but I am sent to find those persons whose names
are here writ, and can never find what names the writing person
hath here writ. I must to the learned. In good time!

[*Enter* Benvolio *and* Romeo.]

Benvolio. Tut, man, one fire burns out another's burning;

45 One pain is lessened by another's anguish;
Turn giddy, and be holp by backward turning;
One desperate grief cures with another's languish.

Take thou some new infection to thy eye,
And the rank poison of the old will die.

50 **Romeo.** Your plantain leaf is excellent for that.

Benvolio. For what, I pray thee?

Romeo.   For your broken shin.

Benvolio. Why, Romeo, art thou mad?

Romeo. Not mad, but bound more than a madman is;
Shut up in prison, kept without my food,
55 Whipped and tormented and—God-den, good fellow.

55 God-den: good evening. Romeo interrupts his lament to talk to the servant.

Servant. God gi' go-den. I pray, sir, can you read?

Romeo. Ay, mine own fortune in my misery.

Servant. Perhaps you have learned it without book. But
I pray, can you read anything you see?

56 God gi' go-den: God give you a good evening.

60 **Romeo.** Ay, if I know the letters and the language.

Servant. Ye say honestly. Rest you merry!

[*Romeo's joking goes over the clown's head. He concludes that
Romeo cannot read and prepares to seek someone who can.*]

Romeo. Stay, fellow; I can read.   [*He reads.*]
"Signior Martino and his wife and daughters;
County Anselmo and his beauteous sisters;
65 The lady widow of Vitruvio;
Signior Placentio and his lovely nieces;
Mercutio and his brother Valentine;
Mine uncle Capulet, his wife, and daughters;
My fair niece Rosaline and Livia;
70 Signior Valentio and his cousin Tybalt;
Lucio and the lively Helena."
[*gives back the paper*]
A fair assembly. Whither should they come?

69 Rosaline: This is the woman that Romeo is in love with. Mercutio, a friend of both Romeo and the Capulets, is also invited to the party.

Servant. Up.

Romeo. Whither?

72 whither: where.

75 **Servant.** To supper, to our house.

Romeo. Whose house?

Servant. My master's.

Romeo. Indeed I should have asked you that before.

Servant. Now I'll tell you without asking. My master is the great
80 rich Capulet; and if you be not of the house of Montagues, I
pray come and crush a cup of wine. Rest you merry!

81 crush a cup of wine: slang for "drink some wine."

[*Exit.*]

Benvolio. At this same ancient feast of Capulet's
Sups the fair Rosaline whom thou so lovest,
With all the admired beauties of Verona.
85   Go thither, and with unattainted eye
Compare her face with some that I shall show,
And I will make thee think thy swan a crow.

Romeo. When the devout religion of mine eye
Maintains such falsehood, then turn tears to fires;
90   And these, who, often drowned, could never die,
Transparent heretics, be burnt for liars!
One fairer than my love? The all-seeing sun
Ne'er saw her match since first the world begun.

Benvolio. Tut! you saw her fair, none else being by,
95   Herself poised with herself in either eye;
But in that crystal scales let there be weighed
Your lady's love against some other maid
That I will show you shining at this feast,
And she shall scant show well that now shows best.

100 **Romeo.** I'll go along, no such sight to be shown,
But to rejoice in splendor of mine own.

[*Exeunt.*]

Scene 3 *Capulet's house.*

[*Enter* Lady Capulet *and* Nurse.]

Lady Capulet. Nurse, where's my daughter? Call her forth to
me.

Nurse. Now, by my maidenhead at twelve year old,
I bade her come. What, lamb! what, ladybird!
God forbid! Where's this girl? What, Juliet!

[*Enter* Juliet.]

5 **Juliet.** How now? Who calls?

Nurse. Your mother.

Juliet. Madam, I am here. What is your will?

Lady Capulet. This is the matter—Nurse, give leave awhile,
We must talk in secret. Nurse, come back again;
10 I have remembered me, thou's hear our counsel.
Thou knowest my daughter's of a pretty age.

Nurse. Faith, I can tell her age unto an hour.

Lady Capulet. She's not fourteen.

85 unattainted:
unbiased; unprejudiced.

88–91 When . . . liars:
If the love I have for
Rosaline, which is like
a religion, changes
because of such a lie
(that others may be
more beautiful), let my
tears be turned to fire
and my eyes be burned.

94–99 Tut . . . best:
You've seen Rosaline
alone; now compare
her with some other
women.

100–101 Romeo agrees
to go to the party, but
only to see Rosaline.

**8–11 give leave . . .
counsel:** Lady Capulet
seems nervous, not sure
whether she wants the
nurse to stay or leave;
of a pretty age: of an
attractive age, ready for
marriage.

Nurse. I'll lay fourteen of my teeth—
And yet, to my teen be it spoken, I have but four—
15 She's not fourteen. How long is it now
To Lammastide?

Lady Capulet. A fortnight and odd days.

Nurse. Even or odd, of all days in the year,
Come Lammas Eve at night shall she be fourteen.
Susan and she (God rest all Christian souls!)
20 Were of an age. Well, Susan is with God;
She was too good for me. But, as I said,
On Lammas Eve at night shall she be fourteen;
That shall she, marry; I remember it well.
'Tis since the earthquake now eleven years;
25 And she was weaned (I never shall forget it),
Of all the days of the year, upon that day.
For I had then laid wormwood to my dug,
Sitting in the sun under the dovehouse wall.
My lord and you were then at Mantua—
30 Nay, I do bear a brain—But, as I said,
When it did taste the wormwood on the nipple
Of my dug and felt it bitter, pretty fool,
To see it tetchy and fall out with the dug!
Shake, quoth the dovehouse! 'Twas no need, I trow,
35 To bid me trudge.
And since that time it is eleven years,
For then she could stand alone; nay, by the rood,
She could have run and waddled all about;
For even the day before, she broke her brow;
40 And then my husband (God be with his soul!
'A was a merry man) took up the child.
"Yea," quoth he, "dost thou fall upon thy face?
Thou wilt fall backward when thou has more wit,
Wilt thou not, Jule?" And, by my holidam,
45 The pretty wretch left crying, and said "Ay."
To see now how a jest shall come about!
I warrant, an I should live a thousand years,
I never should forget it. "Wilt thou not, Jule?" quoth he,
And, pretty fool, it stinted, and said "Ay."

50 **Lady Capulet.** Enough of this. I pray thee hold thy peace.

Nurse. Yes, madam. Yet I cannot choose but laugh
To think it should leave crying and say "Ay."
And yet, I warrant, it had upon its brow
A bump as big as a young cock'rel's stone;
55 A perilous knock; and it cried bitterly.

14 teen: sorrow.

16 Lammastide: August 1, a religious feast day. It is two weeks (**a fortnight**) away.

17–49 The nurse babbles about Juliet's childhood. Her own daughter, Susan, was the same age as Juliet, and died in infancy, leaving the nurse available to become a wet nurse to (that is, breastfeed) Juliet. An earthquake happened on the day she stopped breastfeeding Juliet (**she was weaned**).

27 laid wormwood to my dug: applied a plant with a bitter taste to her breast to discourage the child from breastfeeding.

33 tetchy: cranky.

34–35 Shake ... trudge: When the dove house shook, I knew enough to leave.

37 by the rood: by the cross of Christ (a mild oath).

39 broke her brow: cut her forehead.

42–49 "Yea," ... "Ay": The nurse's husband made a crude joke, asking the baby whether she'd fall the other way (on her back) when she was older. Although Juliet didn't understand the question, she stopped crying (**stinted**) and answered "Yes." The nurse finds the story so funny that she can't stop retelling it.

"Yea," quoth my husband, "fallst upon thy face?
Thou wilt fall backward when thou comest to age,
Wilt thou not, Jule?" It stinted, and said "Ay."

Juliet. And stint thou too, I pray thee, nurse, say I.

60 **Nurse.** Peace, I have done. God mark thee to his grace!
Thou wast the prettiest babe that e'er I nursed.
An I might live to see thee married once,
I have my wish.

Lady Capulet. Marry, that "marry" is the very theme
65 I came to talk of. Tell me, daughter Juliet,
How stands your disposition to be married?

Juliet. It is an honor that I dream not of.

Nurse. An honor? Were not I thine only nurse,
I would say thou hadst sucked wisdom from thy teat.

70 **Lady Capulet.** Well, think of marriage now. Younger than you,
Here in Verona, ladies of esteem,
Are made already mothers. By my count,
I was your mother much upon these years
That you are now a maid. Thus then in brief:
75 The valiant Paris seeks you for his love.

Nurse. A man, young lady! lady, such a man
As all the world—why he's a man of wax.

Lady Capulet. Verona's summer hath not such a flower.

64 Marry . . . "marry":
two different usages of
the same word—the first
meaning "by the Virgin
Mary" and the second
meaning "to wed."

73–74 I was . . . maid:
I was your mother at
about your age, yet you
are still unmarried.

77 a man of wax: a man
so perfect he could be a
wax statue, of the type
sculptors once used as
models for their works.

Nurse. Nay, he's a flower, in faith—a very flower.

80 **Lady Capulet.** What say you? Can you love the gentleman?
This night you shall behold him at our feast.
Read o'er the volume of young Paris' face,
And find delight writ there with beauty's pen;
Examine every several lineament,
85 And see how one another lends content;
And what obscured in this fair volume lies
Find written in the margent of his eyes.
This precious book of love, this unbound lover,
To beautify him only lacks a cover.
90 The fish lives in the sea, and 'tis much pride
For fair without the fair within to hide.
That book in many's eyes doth share the glory,
That in gold clasps locks in the golden story;
So shall you share all that he doth possess,
95 By having him making yourself no less.

Nurse. No less? Nay, bigger! Women grow by men.

Lady Capulet. Speak briefly, can you like of Paris' love?

Juliet. I'll look to like, if looking liking move;
But no more deep will I endart mine eye
100 Than your consent gives strength to make it fly.

[*Enter a* Servingman.]

Servingman. Madam, the guests are come, supper served up, you
called, my young lady asked for, the nurse cursed in the pantry,
and everything in extremity. I must hence to wait. I beseech you
follow straight.

105 **Lady Capulet.** We follow thee. [*Exit* Servingman.] Juliet, the
County stays.

Nurse. Go, girl, seek happy nights to happy days.

[*Exeunt.*]

Scene 4 *A street near the Capulet house.*

[*Enter* Romeo, Mercutio, Benvolio, *with five or six other* Maskers;
Torchbearers.]

Romeo. What, shall this speech be spoke for our excuse?
Or shall we on without apology?

Benvolio. The date is out of such prolixity.
We'll have no Cupid hoodwinked with a scarf,
5 Bearing a Tartar's painted bow of lath,
Scaring the ladies like a crowkeeper;
Nor no without-book prologue, faintly spoke

82–89 Read . . . cover:
Lady Capulet uses an extended metaphor that compares Paris to a book that Juliet should read.

84 every several lineament: each separate feature (of Paris' face).

87 margent . . . eyes: She compares Paris' eyes to the margin of a page, where notes are written to explain the content.

88–91 This . . . hide: This beautiful book (Paris) needs only a cover (wife) to become even better. He may be hiding even more wonderful qualities inside.

96 Women get bigger (pregnant) when they marry.

98–100 I'll look . . . fly: I'll look at him with the intention of liking him, if simply looking can make me like him; **endart:** look deeply, as if penetrating with a dart.

103–104 extremity: great confusion; **straight:** immediately.

105 the County stays: Count Paris is waiting for you.

1–10 What, shall this . . . be gone: Romeo asks whether they should send a messenger announcing their arrival at the party. Benvolio says that they'll dance one dance (**measure them a measure**) and then leave.

After the prompter, for our entrance;
But let them measure us by what they will,
10 We'll measure them a measure, and be gone.

Romeo. Give me a torch. I am not for this ambling;
Being but heavy, I will bear the light.

Mercutio. Nay, gentle Romeo, we must have you dance.

Romeo. Not I, believe me. You have dancing shoes
15 With nimble soles; I have a soul of lead
So stakes me to the ground I cannot move.

Mercutio. You are a lover. Borrow Cupid's wings
And soar with them above a common bound.

Romeo. I am too sore enpierced with his shaft
20 To soar with his light feathers, and so bound
I cannot bound a pitch above dull woe.
Under love's heavy burden do I sink.

Mercutio. And, to sink in it, should you burden love—
Too great oppression for a tender thing.

25 **Romeo.** Is love a tender thing? It is too rough,
Too rude, too boist'rous, and it pricks like thorn.

Mercutio. If love be rough with you, be rough with love.
Prick love for pricking, and you beat love down.
Give me a case to put my visage in.
30 A visor for a visor! What care I
What curious eye doth quote deformities?
Here are the beetle brows shall blush for me.

Benvolio. Come, knock and enter, and no sooner in
But every man betake him to his legs.

35 **Romeo.** A torch for me! Let wantons light of heart
Tickle the senseless rushes with their heels;
For I am proverbed with a grandsire phrase,
I'll be a candle-holder and look on;
The game was ne'er so fair, and I am done.

40 **Mercutio.** Tut, dun's the mouse, the constable's own word!
If thou art Dun, we'll draw thee from the mire
Of, save your reverence, love, wherein thou stickst
Up to the ears. Come, we burn daylight, ho!

Romeo. Nay, that's not so.

Mercutio.   I mean, sir, in delay
45 We waste our lights in vain, like lamps by day.

12 heavy: sad. Romeo makes a joke based on the meanings of *heavy* and *light*.

14–32 Romeo continues to talk about his sadness, while Mercutio jokingly makes fun of him to try to cheer him up.

29–32 Give . . . for me: Give me a mask for an ugly face. I don't care if people notice my appearance. Here, look at my bushy eyebrows.

34 betake . . . legs: dance.

35–38 Let . . . look on: Let playful people tickle the grass (**rushes**) on the floor with their dancing. I'll follow the old saying (**grandsire phrase**) and just be a spectator.

40–43 Tut . . . daylight: Mercutio jokes, using various meanings of the word *dun*, which sounds like Romeo's last word, *done*. He concludes by saying they should not waste time (**burn daylight**).

Take our good meaning, for our judgment sits
Five times in that ere once in our five wits.

Romeo. And we mean well in going to this masque;
But 'tis no wit to go.

Mercutio.   Why, may one ask?

50 **Romeo.** I dreamt a dream tonight.

Mercutio.   And so did I.

Romeo. Well, what was yours?

Mercutio.   That dreamers often lie.

Romeo. In bed asleep, while they do dream things true.

Mercutio. O, then I see Queen Mab hath been with you.
She is the fairies' midwife, and she comes
55 In shape no bigger than an agate stone
On the forefinger of an alderman,

53–95 Mercutio talks of Mab, queen of the fairies, a folktale character well-known to Shakespeare's audience. His language includes vivid descriptions, puns, and satires of people; and ultimately he gets caught up in his own wild imaginings.

55 agate stone: jewel for a ring.

Drawn with a team of little atomies
Athwart men's noses as they lie asleep;
Her wagon spokes made of long spinners' legs,
60 The cover, of the wings of grasshoppers;
Her traces, of the smallest spider's web;
Her collars, of the moonshine's wat'ry beams;
Her whip, of cricket's bone; the lash, of film;
Her wagoner, a small grey-coated gnat,
65 Not half so big as a round little worm
Pricked from the lazy finger of a maid;
Her chariot is an empty hazelnut,
Made by the joiner squirrel or old grub,
Time out o' mind the fairies' coachmakers.
70 And in this state she gallops night by night
Through lovers' brains, and then they dream of love;
O'er courtiers' knees, that dream on curtsies straight;
O'er lawyers' fingers, who straight dream on fees;
O'er ladies' lips, who straight on kisses dream,
75 Which oft the angry Mab with blisters plagues,
Because their breaths with sweetmeats tainted are.
Sometime she gallops o'er a courtier's nose,
And then dreams he of smelling out a suit,
And sometime comes she with a tithe-pig's tail
80 Tickling a parson's nose as 'a lies asleep,
Then dreams he of another benefice.
Sometime she driveth o'er a soldier's neck,
And then dreams he of cutting foreign throats,
Of breaches, ambuscadoes, Spanish blades,
85 Of healths five fathom deep; and then anon
Drums in his ear, at which he starts and wakes,
And being thus frighted, swears a prayer or two
And sleeps again. This is that very Mab
That plaits the manes of horses in the night
90 And bakes the elflocks in foul sluttish hairs,
Which once untangled much misfortune bodes.
This is the hag, when maids lie on their backs,
That presses them and learns them first to bear,
Making them women of good carriage.
95 This is she—

Romeo.   Peace, peace, Mercutio, peace!
Thou talkst of nothing.

Mercutio.   True, I talk of dreams;
Which are the children of an idle brain,
Begot of nothing but vain fantasy;
Which is as thin of substance as the air,

100 And more inconstant than the wind, who woos
Even now the frozen bosom of the North
And, being angered, puffs away from thence,
Turning his face to the dew-dropping South.

Benvolio. This wind you talk of blows us from ourselves.
105 Supper is done, and we shall come too late.

Romeo. I fear, too early; for my mind misgives
Some consequence, yet hanging in the stars,
Shall bitterly begin his fearful date
With this night's revels and expire the term
110 Of a despised life, closed in my breast,
By some vile forfeit of untimely death.
But he that hath the steerage of my course
Direct my sail! On, lusty gentlemen!

Benvolio. Strike, drum.

[*Exeunt.*]

Scene 5 *A hall in Capulet's house; the scene of the party.*

[Servingmen *come forth with napkins.*]

First Servingman. Where's Potpan, that he helps not to take
away? He shift a trencher! he scrape a trencher!

Second Servingman. When good manners shall lie all in one or
two men's hands, and they unwashed too, 'tis a foul thing.

5 **First Servingman.** Away with the joint-stools, remove the court-
cupboard, look to the plate. Good thou, save me a piece of
marchpane and, as thou lovest me, let the porter let in Susan
Grindstone and Nell. Anthony, and Potpan!

Second Servingman. Ay, boy, ready.

10 **First Servingman.** You are looked for and called for, asked for
and sought for, in the great chamber.

Third Servingman. We cannot be here and there too. Cheerly,
boys! Be brisk awhile, and the longer liver take all.

[*Exeunt.*]

[Maskers *appear with* Capulet, Lady Capulet, Juliet, *all the*
Guests, *and* Servants.]

Capulet. Welcome, gentlemen! Ladies that have their toes
15 Unplagued with corns will have a bout with you.
Ah ha, my mistresses! which of you all
Will now deny to dance? She that makes dainty,
She I'll swear hath corns. Am I come near ye now?
Welcome, gentlemen! I have seen the day

106–111 Romeo, still depressed, fears that some terrible event caused by the stars will begin at the party. Remember the phrase "star-crossed lovers" from the prologue.

1–13 These opening lines are a comic conversation among three servants as they work.

2 trencher: wooden plate.

6–7 plate: silverware and silver plates; **marchpane:** marzipan, a sweet made from almond paste.

14–27 Capulet welcomes his guests and invites them all to dance. He alternates talking with his guests and telling the servants what to do.

17–18 She that . . . corns: Any woman too shy to dance will be assumed to have corns, ugly and painful growths on the toes.

20 That I have worn a visor and could tell
    A whispering tale in a fair lady's ear,
    Such as would please. 'Tis gone, 'tis gone, 'tis gone!
    You are welcome, gentlemen! Come, musicians, play.
    A hall, a hall! give room! and foot it, girls.

    [*Music plays and they dance.*]

25 More light, you knaves! and turn the tables up,
    And quench the fire, the room is grown too hot.
    Ah, sirrah, this unlooked-for sport comes well.
    Nay, sit, nay, sit, good cousin Capulet,
    For you and I are past our dancing days.
30 How long is't now since last yourself and I
    Were in a mask?

    Second Capulet. By'r Lady, thirty years.

    Capulet. What, man? 'Tis not so much, 'tis not so much!
    'Tis since the nuptial of Lucentio,
    Come Pentecost as quickly as it will,
35 Some five-and-twenty years, and then we masked.

    Second Capulet. 'Tis more, 'tis more! His son is elder, sir;
    His son is thirty.

    Capulet.   Will you tell me that?
    His son was but a ward two years ago.

    Romeo [*to a* Servingman]. What lady's that, which doth enrich
        the hand
40 Of yonder knight?

    Servant. I know not, sir.

    Romeo. O, she doth teach the torches to burn bright!
    It seems she hangs upon the cheek of night
    Like a rich jewel in an Ethiop's ear—
45 Beauty too rich for use, for earth too dear!
    So shows a snowy dove trooping with crows
    As yonder lady o'er her fellows shows.
    The measure done, I'll watch her place of stand
    And, touching hers, make blessed my rude hand.
50 Did my heart love till now? Forswear it, sight!
    For I ne'er saw true beauty till this night.

    Tybalt. This, by his voice, should be a Montague.
    Fetch me my rapier, boy. What, dares the slave
    Come hither, covered with an antic face,
55 To fleer and scorn at our solemnity?
    Now, by the stock and honor of my kin,
    To strike him dead I hold it not a sin.

20 **visor:** mask.

28–38 Capulet and his relative watch the dancing as they talk of days gone by.

33 **nuptial:** marriage.

44–45 **Ethiop's ear:** the ear of an Ethiopian (African); **for earth too dear:** too precious for this world.

52–57 Tybalt recognizes Romeo's voice and tells his servant to get his sword (**rapier**). He thinks Romeo has come to make fun of (**fleer**) their party.

Capulet. Why, how now, kinsman? Wherefore storm you so?

Tybalt. Uncle, this is a Montague, our foe;
60   A villain, that is hither come in spite
To scorn at our solemnity this night.

Capulet. Young Romeo is it?

Tybalt.   'Tis he, that villain Romeo.

Capulet. Content thee, gentle coz, let him alone.
'A bears him like a portly gentleman,   **64 portly:** dignified.
65   And, to say truth, Verona brags of him
To be a virtuous and well-governed youth.
I would not for the wealth of all this town   **68 do him**
Here in my house do him disparagement.   **disparagement:** speak
Therefore be patient, take no note of him.   critically or insultingly
70   It is my will; the which if thou respect,   to him.
Show a fair presence and put off these frowns,
An ill-beseeming semblance for a feast.   **72 semblance:** outward
                                                         appearance.

Tybalt. It fits when such a villain is a guest.
I'll not endure him.

Capulet.   He shall be endured.
75 What, goodman boy? I say he shall. Go to!
Am I the master here, or you? Go to!
You'll not endure him? God shall mend my soul!
You'll make a mutiny among my guests!
You will set cock-a-hoop! You'll be the man.

80 **Tybalt.** Why, uncle, 'tis a shame.

Capulet.   Go to, go to!
You are a saucy boy. Is't so, indeed?
This trick may chance to scathe you. I know what.
You must contrary me! Marry, 'tis time.—
Well said, my hearts!—You are a princox—go!
85 Be quiet, or—More light, more light!—For shame!
I'll make you quiet; what!—Cheerly, my hearts!

Tybalt. Patience perforce with willful choler meeting
Makes my flesh tremble in their different greeting.
I will withdraw; but this intrusion shall,
90 Now seeming sweet, convert to bitter gall.

[*Exit.*]

Romeo. If I profane with my unworthiest hand
This holy shrine, the gentle fine is this:
My lips, two blushing pilgrims, ready stand
To smooth that rough touch with a tender kiss.

95 **Juliet.** Good pilgrim, you do wrong your hand too much,
Which mannerly devotion shows in this;
For saints have hands that pilgrims' hands do touch,
And palm to palm is holy palmers' kiss.

Romeo. Have not saints lips, and holy palmers too?

100 **Juliet.** Ay, pilgrim, lips that they must use in prayer.

Romeo. O, then, dear saint, let lips do what hands do!
They pray; grant thou, lest faith turn to despair.

Juliet. Saints do not move, though grant for prayers' sake.

Romeo. Then move not while my prayer's effect I take.
105 Thus from my lips, by thine my sin is purged.

[*kisses her*]

Juliet. Then have my lips the sin that they have took.

Romeo. Sin from my lips? O trespass sweetly urged!
Give me my sin again.

75 goodman boy: a term used to address an inferior; **Go to:** Stop, that's enough!

79 set cock-a-hoop: cause everything to be upset.

82–83 scathe: harm; **I know . . . contrary me:** I know what I'm doing! Don't you dare challenge my authority.

84–86 Capulet intersperses his angry speech to Tybalt with comments to his guests and servants.

87–90 Patience . . . gall: Tybalt says he will restrain himself, but his suppressed anger (**choler**) makes his body shake.

91–108 Romeo and Juliet are in the middle of the dance floor, with eyes only for each other. They touch the palms of their hands. Their conversation revolves around Romeo's comparison of his lips to pilgrims who have traveled to a holy shrine. Juliet goes along with the comparison.

105 purged: washed away.

[*kisses her*]

Juliet.   You kiss by the book.

Nurse. Madam, your mother craves a word with you.

110 **Romeo.** What is her mother?

Nurse.   Marry, bachelor,
Her mother is the lady of the house.
And a good lady, and a wise and virtuous.
I nursed her daughter that you talked withal.
I tell you, he that can lay hold of her
115 Shall have the chinks.

Romeo.   Is she a Capulet?
O dear account! my life is my foe's debt.

Benvolio. Away, be gone, the sport is at the best.

Romeo. Ay, so I fear; the more is my unrest.

Capulet. Nay, gentlemen, prepare not to be gone;
120 We have a trifling foolish banquet towards.

[*They whisper in his ear.*]
Is it e'en so? Why then, I thank you all.
I thank you, honest gentlemen. Good night.
More torches here! [*Exeunt* Maskers.] Come on then, let's to bed.
Ah, sirrah, by my fay, it waxes late;
125 I'll to my rest.

[*Exeunt all but* Juliet *and* Nurse.]

Juliet. Come hither, nurse. What is yond gentleman?

Nurse. The son and heir of old Tiberio.

Juliet. What's he that now is going out of door?

Nurse. Marry, that, I think, be young Petruchio.

130 **Juliet.** What's he that follows there, that would not dance?

Nurse. I know not.

Juliet. Go ask his name.—If he be married,
My grave is like to be my wedding bed.

Nurse. His name is Romeo, and a Montague,
135 The only son of your great enemy.

Juliet. My only love, sprung from my only hate!
Too early seen unknown, and known too late!
Prodigious birth of love it is to me
That I must love a loathed enemy.

140 **Nurse.** What's this? what's this?

108 kiss by the book: Juliet could mean "You kiss like someone who has practiced." Or she could be teasing Romeo, meaning "You kiss coldly, as though you had learned how by reading a book."

109 At the nurse's message, Juliet walks to her mother.

115 shall have the chinks: shall become rich.

116 my life . . . debt: my life belongs to my enemy.

120 towards: coming up.

137–138 Too early . . . too late: I fell in love with him before I learned who he is; **prodigious:** abnormal; unlucky.

Juliet.   A rhyme I learnt even now
Of one I danced withal.

[*One calls within, "Juliet."*]

Nurse.   Anon, anon!
Come, let's away; the strangers all are gone.

[*Exeunt.*]

COLLABORATIVE DISCUSSION With a partner, discuss your first
impressions of Romeo and Juliet. What are they like? What actions or
lines of dialogue reveal their personalities?

Analyzing the Text

Cite Text Evidence   Support your responses with evidence from the selection.

1. **Interpret** An important **theme,** or message, in *Romeo and Juliet* is the struggle against fate, or forces that determine how a person's life will turn out. Explain how Act I's Prologue establishes the fate of the main characters and introduces the struggles they will face.

2. **Infer** In Scene 1, Tybalt says, "What, drawn, and talk of peace? I hate the word / As I hate hell, all Montagues, and thee. / Have at thee, coward!" (lines 63–65). What can you infer about Tybalt's personality and his role in the play, based on these words?

3. **Analyze** A **foil** is a character who highlights, through sharp contrast, the qualities of another character. Which two sets of characters in Act I are foils for each other? What do you learn about the characters by seeing them in contrast to one another?

4. **Identify** *Romeo and Juliet* is a play that deals with serious and tragic events, yet Shakespeare does weave jokes and comical situations into Act I. One example is the conversation among the servants at the beginning of Scene 5. Identify other examples of humor in the first act.

5. **Interpret** Foreshadowing is the use of hints or clues to suggest events that will happen later in the story. Explain the **foreshadowing** in these lines from Act I:

   - Scene 4, lines 106–111
   - Scene 5, line 133

6. **Predict** Which events in Act I seem key to setting up the conflicts that will move the action of the rest of the play forward? Explain your response.

PERFORMANCE TASK

Speaking Activity: Discussion In *Romeo and Juliet*, characters are motivated by passion and strong emotions.

- Notice that throughout Act I, Shakespeare contrasts themes of love and hate through characters' words and actions.
- Work with a partner to identify passages that express love or hate. Read the passages aloud with your partner. Read with feeling to express the emotions that underlie the words.

- Discuss what dramatic effect Shakespeare creates by pairing these two emotions in the first act of the play.
- Write a summary that outlines the main points of your discussion.

AS YOU READ Look for words and phrases that reveal the developing relationship between Romeo and Juliet and the intensity of their feelings for each other. Write down any questions you generate during reading.

Prologue

[*Enter* Chorus.]

Chorus. Now old desire doth in his deathbed lie,
And young affection gapes to be his heir.
That fair for which love groaned for and would die,
With tender Juliet matched, is now not fair.
5 Now Romeo is beloved, and loves again,
Alike bewitched by the charm of looks;
But to his foe supposed he must complain,
And she steal love's sweet bait from fearful hooks.
Being held a foe, he may not have access
10 To breathe such vows as lovers use to swear,
And she as much in love, her means much less
To meet her new beloved anywhere;
But passion lends them power, time means, to meet,
Temp'ring extremities with extreme sweet.

[*Exit.*]

1–4 Now . . . fair: Romeo's love for Rosaline (**old desire**) is now dead. His new love for Juliet (**young affection**) replaces the old.

7 but . . . complain: Juliet, a Capulet, is Romeo's supposed enemy, yet she is the one to whom he must plead (**complain**) his love.

14 Temp'ring . . . sweet: moderating great difficulties with extreme delights.

ACT II

Scene 1 *A lane by the wall of Capulet's orchard.*

[*Enter* Romeo *alone.*]

Romeo. Can I go forward when my heart is here?
Turn back, dull earth, and find thy center out.

[*climbs the wall and leaps down within it*]

[*Enter* Benvolio *with* Mercutio.]

Benvolio. Romeo! my cousin Romeo! Romeo!

Mercutio.   He is wise,
And, on my life, hath stol'n him home to bed.

5 **Benvolio.** He ran this way, and leapt this orchard wall.
Call, good Mercutio.

Mercutio.   Nay, I'll conjure too.
Romeo! humors! madman! passion! lover!
Appear thou in the likeness of a sigh;
Speak but one rhyme, and I am satisfied!
10 Cry but "Ay me!" pronounce but "love" and "dove";
Speak to my gossip Venus one fair word,
One nickname for her purblind son and heir,
Young Adam Cupid, he that shot so trim

1–2 Can . . . out: How can I leave when Juliet is still here? My body (**dull earth**) has to find its heart (**center**).

6 conjure: use magic to call him.

8–21 Appear . . . us: Mercutio jokes about Romeo's lovesickness.

When King Cophetua loved the beggar maid!
15 He heareth not, he stirreth not, he moveth not;
The ape is dead, and I must conjure him.
I conjure thee by Rosaline's bright eyes,
By her high forehead and her scarlet lip,
By her fine foot, straight leg, and quivering thigh,
20 And the demesnes that there adjacent lie,
That in thy likeness thou appear to us!

Benvolio. An if he hear thee, thou wilt anger him.

Mercutio. This cannot anger him. 'Twould anger him
To raise a spirit in his mistress' circle
25 Of some strange nature, letting it there stand
Till she had laid it and conjured it down.
That were some spite; my invocation
Is fair and honest and in his mistress' name
I conjure only but to raise up him.

30 **Benvolio.** Come, he hath hid himself among these trees
To be consorted with the humorous night.
Blind is his love, and best befits the dark.

Mercutio. If love be blind, love cannot hit the mark.
Now will he sit under a medlar tree
35 And wish his mistress were that kind of fruit
As maids call medlars when they laugh alone.
Oh, Romeo, that she were, O, that she were
An open et cetera, thou a pop'rin pear!
Romeo, good night. I'll to my truckle bed;
40 This field-bed is too cold for me to sleep.
Come, shall we go?

Benvolio.   Go then, for 'tis in vain
To seek him here that means not to be found.

[*Exeunt.*]

Scene 2 *Capulet's orchard.*

[*Enter* Romeo.]

Romeo. He jests at scars that never felt a wound.

[*Enter* Juliet *above at a window.*]

But soft! What light through yonder window breaks?
It is the East, and Juliet is the sun!
Arise, fair sun, and kill the envious moon,
5 Who is already sick and pale with grief
That thou her maid art far more fair than she.
Be not her maid, since she is envious;

20 demesnes: areas; **adjacent:** next to.

23–29 'Twould . . . raise up him: It would anger him if I called a stranger to join his beloved (**mistress**), but I'm only calling Romeo to join her.

31 To be . . . night: to keep company with the night, which is as gloomy as Romeo is.

34 medlar: a fruit that looks like a small brown apple.

39 truckle bed: trundle bed, a small bed that fits in beneath a bigger one.

1 He jests . . . wound: Romeo has overheard Mercutio and comments that Mercutio makes fun of love because he has never been wounded by it.

Her vestal livery is but sick and green,
And none but fools do wear it; cast it off.

10 It is my lady; O, it is my love!
O that she knew she were!
She speaks, yet she says nothing. What of that?
Her eye discourses; I will answer it.
I am too bold; 'tis not to me she speaks.

15 Two of the fairest stars in all the heaven,
Having some business, do entreat her eyes
To twinkle in their spheres till they return.
What if her eyes were there, they in her head?
The brightness of her cheek would shame those stars

20 As daylight doth a lamp; her eyes in heaven
Would through the airy region stream so bright
That birds would sing and think it were not night.
See how she leans her cheek upon her hand!
O that I were a glove upon that hand,

25 That I might touch that cheek!

Juliet.   Ay me!

Romeo.   She speaks.
O, speak again, bright angel! for thou art
As glorious to this night, being o'er my head,

13–14 Her eye . . . speaks: Romeo shifts back and forth between wanting to speak to Juliet and being afraid.

15–22 Two of . . . not night: Romeo compares Juliet's eyes to stars in the sky.

25 Juliet begins to speak, not knowing that Romeo is nearby.

26–32 thou art . . . of the air: He compares Juliet to an angel (**winged messenger of heaven**) who stands on (**bestrides**) the clouds.

As is a winged messenger of heaven
Unto the white-upturned wond'ring eyes
30 Of mortals that fall back to gaze on him
When he bestrides the lazy-pacing clouds
And sails upon the bosom of the air.

Juliet. O Romeo, Romeo! wherefore art thou Romeo?
Deny thy father and refuse thy name!
35 Or, if thou wilt not, be but sworn my love,
And I'll no longer be a Capulet.

Romeo [*aside*]. Shall I hear more, or shall I speak at this?

Juliet. 'Tis but thy name that is my enemy.
Thou art thyself, though not a Montague.
40 What's Montague? It is nor hand, nor foot,
Nor arm, nor face, nor any other part
Belonging to a man. O, be some other name!
What's in a name? That which we call a rose
By any other name would smell as sweet.
45 So Romeo would, were he not Romeo called,
Retain that dear perfection which he owes
Without that title. Romeo, doff thy name;
And for that name, which is no part of thee,
Take all myself.

Romeo.   I take thee at thy word.
50 Call me but love, and I'll be new baptized;
Henceforth I never will be Romeo.

Juliet. What man art thou that, thus bescreened in night,
So stumblest on my counsel?

Romeo.   By a name
I know not how to tell thee who I am.
55 My name, dear saint, is hateful to myself,
Because it is an enemy to thee.
Had I it written, I would tear the word.

Juliet. My ears have yet not drunk a hundred words
Of that tongue's utterance, yet I know the sound.
60 Art thou not Romeo, and a Montague?

Romeo. Neither, fair saint, if either thee dislike.

Juliet. How camest thou hither, tell me, and wherefore?
The orchard walls are high and hard to climb,
And the place death, considering who thou art,
65 If any of my kinsmen find thee here.

Romeo. With love's light wings did I o'erperch these walls;
For stony limits cannot hold love out,

And what love can do, that dares love attempt.
Therefore thy kinsmen are no let to me.

70   **Juliet.** If they do see thee, they will murder thee.

Romeo. Alack, there lies more peril in thine eye
Than twenty of their swords! Look thou but sweet,
And I am proof against their enmity.

Juliet. I would not for the world they saw thee here.

75   **Romeo.** I have night's cloak to hide me from their sight;
And but thou love me, let them find me here.
My life were better ended by their hate
Than death prorogued, wanting of thy love.

Juliet. By whose direction foundst thou out this place?

80   **Romeo.** By love, that first did prompt me to enquire.
He lent me counsel, and I lent him eyes.
I am no pilot, yet, wert thou as far
As that vast shore washed with the farthest sea,
I would adventure for such merchandise.

85   **Juliet.** Thou knowest the mask of night is on my face;
Else would a maiden blush bepaint my cheek
For that which thou hast heard me speak tonight.
Fain would I dwell on form—fain, fain deny
What I have spoke; but farewell compliment!
90   Dost thou love me? I know thou wilt say "Ay";
And I will take thy word. Yet, if thou swearst,
Thou mayst prove false. At lovers' perjuries,
They say Jove laughs. O gentle Romeo,
If thou dost love, pronounce it faithfully.
95   Or if thou thinkst I am too quickly won,
I'll frown, and be perverse, and say thee nay,
So thou wilt woo; but else, not for the world.
In truth, fair Montague, I am too fond,
And therefore thou mayst think my 'havior light;
100   But trust me, gentleman, I'll prove more true
Than those that have more cunning to be strange.
I should have been more strange, I must confess,
But that thou overheardst, ere I was ware,
My true love's passion. Therefore pardon me,
105   And not impute this yielding to light love,
Which the dark night hath so discovered.

Romeo. Lady, by yonder blessed moon I swear,
That tips with silver all these fruit-tree tops—

72–73 Look . . . enmity:
Smile on me, and I will
be defended against
my enemies' hatred
(**enmity**).

**78 than death . . .
love:** than my death
postponed (**prorogued**)
if you don't love me.

**85–89 Thou . . .
compliment:** Had
I known you were
listening, I would have
gladly (**fain**) behaved
more properly, but now
it's too late for good
manners (**farewell
compliment**).

92–93 At . . . laughs:
Jove, the king of the
gods, laughs at lovers
who lie to each other.

**95–101 Or if . . .
strange:** You might think
I've fallen in love too
easily and that I'm too
outspoken. But I'll be
truer to you than those
who play games to hide
their real feelings (**be
strange**).

Juliet. O, swear not by the moon, the inconstant moon,
110 That monthly changes in her circled orb,
Lest that thy love prove likewise variable.

Romeo. What shall I swear by?

Juliet. Do not swear at all;
Or if thou wilt, swear by thy gracious self,
Which is the god of my idolatry,
115 And I'll believe thee.

Romeo. If my heart's dear love—

Juliet. Well, do not swear. Although I joy in thee,
I have no joy of this contract tonight.
It is too rash, too unadvised, too sudden;
Too like the lightning, which doth cease to be
120 Ere one can say "It lightens." Sweet, good night!
This bud of love, by summer's ripening breath,
May prove a beauteous flow'r when next we meet.
Good night, good night! As sweet repose and rest
Come to thy heart as that within my breast!

125 **Romeo.** O, wilt thou leave me so unsatisfied?

Juliet. What satisfaction canst thou have tonight?

Romeo. The exchange of thy love's faithful vow for mine.

Juliet. I gave thee mine before thou didst request it;
And yet I would it were to give again.

130 **Romeo.** Wouldst thou withdraw it? For what purpose, love?

Juliet. But to be frank and give it thee again.
And yet I wish but for the thing I have.
My bounty is as boundless as the sea,
My love as deep; the more I give to thee,
135 The more I have, for both are infinite.
I hear some noise within. Dear love, adieu!

[Nurse *calls within.*]

Anon, good nurse! Sweet Montague, be true.
Stay but a little, I will come again.

[*Exit.*]

Romeo. O blessed, blessed night! I am afeard,
140 Being in night, all this is but a dream,
Too flattering-sweet to be substantial.

[*Re-enter* Juliet, *above.*]

Juliet. Three words, dear Romeo, and good night indeed.
If that thy bent of love be honorable,

117 I have ... contract:
I am concerned about
this declaration of love
(**contract**).

Thy purpose marriage, send me word tomorrow,
By one that I'll procure to come to thee,
Where and what time thou wilt perform the rite;
And all my fortunes at thy foot I'll lay
And follow thee my lord throughout the world.

Nurse [*within*]. Madam!

Juliet. I come, anon.—But if thou meanst not well,
I do beseech thee—

Nurse [*within*].   Madam!

Juliet.   By-and-by I come.—
To cease thy suit and leave me to my grief.
Tomorrow will I send.

Romeo.   So thrive my soul—

Juliet. A thousand times good night! [*Exit.*]

Romeo. A thousand times the worse, to want thy light!
Love goes toward love as schoolboys from their books;
But love from love, towards school with heavy looks.

[*Enter* Juliet *again, above.*]

Juliet. Hist! Romeo, hist! O for a falc'ner's voice
To lure this tassel-gentle back again!
Bondage is hoarse and may not speak aloud;
Else would I tear the cave where Echo lies,
And make her airy tongue more hoarse than mine
With repetition of my Romeo's name.
Romeo!

Romeo. It is my soul that calls upon my name.
How silver-sweet sound lovers' tongues by night,
Like softest music to attending ears!

Juliet. Romeo!

Romeo.   My sweet?

Juliet.   What o'clock tomorrow
Shall I send to thee?

Romeo.   By the hour of nine.

Juliet. I will not fail. 'Tis twenty years till then.
I have forgot why I did call thee back.

Romeo. Let me stand here till thou remember it.

Juliet. I shall forget, to have thee still stand there,
Rememb'ring how I love thy company.

150–151 But if . . . thee: Juliet is still worried that Romeo is not serious.

156–157 Love . . . looks: The simile means that lovers meet as eagerly as schoolboys leave their books; lovers separate with the sadness of boys going to school.

158–163 Hist . . . name: I wish I could speak your name as loudly as a falconer calls his falcon (**tassel-gentle**), but because of my parents I must whisper. **Echo** was a nymph in Greek mythology whose unreturned love for Narcissus caused her to waste away till only her voice was left.

Romeo. And I'll still stay, to have thee still forget,
Forgetting any other home but this.

Juliet. 'Tis almost morning. I would have thee gone—
And yet no farther than a wanton's bird,
That lets it hop a little from her hand,
Like a poor prisoner in his twisted gyves,
And with a silk thread plucks it back again,
So loving-jealous of his liberty.

Romeo. I would I were thy bird.

Juliet.   Sweet, so would I.
Yet I should kill thee with much cherishing.
Good night, good night! Parting is such sweet sorrow,
That I shall say good night till it be morrow.

[Exit.]

Romeo. Sleep dwell upon thine eyes, peace in thy breast!
Would I were sleep and peace, so sweet to rest!
Hence will I to my ghostly father's cell,
His help to crave and my dear hap to tell.

[Exit.]

Scene 3 *Friar Laurence's cell in the monastery.*

[Enter Friar Laurence alone, with a basket.]

Friar Laurence. The grey-eyed morn smiles on the frowning
   night,
Chequ'ring the Eastern clouds with streaks of light;
And flecked darkness like a drunkard reels
From forth day's path and Titan's fiery wheels.
Now, ere the sun advance his burning eye
The day to cheer and night's dank dew to dry,
I must upfill this osier cage of ours
With baleful weeds and precious-juiced flowers.
The earth that's nature's mother is her tomb,
What is her burying grave, that is her womb;
And from her womb children of divers kind
We sucking on her natural bosom find;
Many for many virtues excellent,
None but for some, and yet all different.
O, mickle is the powerful grace that lies
In plants, herbs, stones, and their true qualities;
For naught so vile that on the earth doth live
But to the earth some special good doth give;
Nor aught so good but, strained from that fair use,
Revolts from true birth, stumbling on abuse.

Line numbers: 175, 180, 185, 190; Scene 3 lines 5, 10, 15, 20

177–182 I would . . . liberty: I know you must go, but I want you close to me like a pet bird that a thoughtless child (**wanton**) keeps on a string.

189–190 ghostly father: spiritual adviser or priest; **dear hap:** good fortune.

4 Titan is the god whose chariot pulls the sun into the sky each morning.

7 osier cage: willow basket.

9–12 The earth . . . find: The same earth that acts as a tomb is also the womb, or birthplace, of various useful plants that people can harvest.

15–18 mickle: great. The friar says that nothing from the earth is so evil that it doesn't do some good.

Virtue itself turns vice, being misapplied,
And vice sometime's by action dignified.
Within the infant rind of this small flower
Poison hath residence, and medicine power;
25 For this, being smelt, with that part cheers each part;
Being tasted, slays all senses with the heart.
Two such opposed kings encamp them still
In man as well as herbs—grace and rude will;
And where the worser is predominant,
30 Full soon the canker death eats up that plant.

[*Enter* Romeo.]

Romeo. Good morrow, father.

Friar Laurence.   Benedicite!
What early tongue so sweet saluteth me?
Young son, it argues a distempered head
So soon to bid good morrow to thy bed.
35 Care keeps his watch in every old man's eye,
And where care lodges sleep will never lie;
But where unbruised youth with unstuffed brain
Doth couch his limbs, there golden sleep doth reign.
Therefore thy earliness doth me assure
40 Thou art uproused with some distemp'rature;

28 grace and rude will: good and evil. Both exist in people as well as in plants.

31 Benedicite (bĕ´nĕ-dī´sĭ-tē´): God bless you.

33–42 it argues . . . tonight: Only a disturbed (**distempered**) mind could make you get up so early. Old people may have trouble sleeping, but it is not normal for someone as young as you. Or were you up all night?

Or if not so, then here I hit it right—
Our Romeo hath not been in bed tonight.

Romeo. That last is true, the sweeter rest was mine.

Friar Laurence. God pardon sin! Wast thou with Rosaline?

45 **Romeo.** With Rosaline, my ghostly father? No.
I have forgot that name, and that name's woe.

Friar Laurence. That's my good son! But where hast thou been
      then?

Romeo. I'll tell thee ere thou ask it me again.
I have been feasting with mine enemy,
50 Where on a sudden one hath wounded me
That's by me wounded. Both our remedies
Within thy help and holy physic lies.
I bear no hatred, blessed man, for, lo,
My intercession likewise steads my foe.

55 **Friar Laurence.** Be plain, good son, and homely in thy drift.
Riddling confession finds but riddling shrift.

Romeo. Then plainly know my heart's dear love is set
On the fair daughter of rich Capulet;
As mine on hers, so hers is set on mine,
60 And all combined, save what thou must combine
By holy marriage. When, and where, and how
We met, we wooed, and made exchange of vow,
I'll tell thee as we pass; but this I pray,
That thou consent to marry us today.

65 **Friar Laurence.** Holy Saint Francis! What a change is here!
Is Rosaline, that thou didst love so dear,
So soon forsaken? Young men's love then lies
Not truly in their hearts, but in their eyes.
Jesu Maria! What a deal of brine
70 Hath washed thy sallow cheeks for Rosaline!
How much salt water thrown away in waste,
To season love, that of it doth not taste!
The sun not yet thy sighs from heaven clears,
Thy old groans ring yet in mine ancient ears.
75 Lo, here upon thy cheek the stain doth sit
Of an old tear that is not washed off yet.
If e'er thou wast thyself, and these woes thine,
Thou and these woes were all for Rosaline.
And art thou changed? Pronounce this sentence then:
80 Women may fall when there's no strength in men.

Romeo. Thou chidst me oft for loving Rosaline.

49–56 Romeo tries to explain the situation, asking for help both for himself and his "foe" (Juliet). The friar does not understand Romeo's convoluted language and asks him to speak clearly so that he can help.

69 brine: salt water—that is, the tears that Romeo has been shedding for Rosaline.

80 Women . . . men: If men are so weak, women may be forgiven for sinning.

81–82 chidst: scolded. The friar replies that he scolded Romeo for being lovesick, not for loving.

Friar Laurence. For doting, not for loving, pupil mine.

Romeo. And badest me bury love.

Friar Laurence.   Not in a grave
To lay one in, another ought to have.

85 **Romeo.** I pray thee chide not. She whom I love now
Doth grace for grace and love for love allow.
The other did not so.

Friar Laurence.   O, she knew well
Thy love did read by rote, that could not spell.
But come, young waverer, come go with me.
90 In one respect I'll thy assistant be;
For this alliance may so happy prove
To turn your households' rancor to pure love.

Romeo. O, let us hence! I stand on sudden haste.

Friar Laurence. Wisely, and slow. They stumble that run fast.

[*Exeunt.*]

Scene 4 *A street.*

[*Enter* Benvolio *and* Mercutio.]

Mercutio. Where the devil should this Romeo be?
Came he not home tonight?

Benvolio. Not to his father's. I spoke with his man.

Mercutio. Why, that same pale hard-hearted wench, that
      Rosaline,
5 Torments him so that he will sure run mad.

Benvolio. Tybalt, the kinsman to old Capulet,
Hath sent a letter to his father's house.

Mercutio. A challenge, on my life.

Benvolio. Romeo will answer it.

10 **Mercutio.** Any man that can write may answer a letter.

Benvolio. Nay, he will answer the letter's master, how he dares,
being dared.

Mercutio. Alas, poor Romeo, he is already dead! stabbed with a
white wench's black eye; shot through the ear with a love song;
15 the very pin of his heart cleft with the blind bow-boy's butt-shaft;
and is he a man to encounter Tybalt?

Benvolio. Why, what is Tybalt?

85–88 She whom . . . spell: Romeo says that the woman he loves feels the same way about him. That wasn't true of Rosaline. The friar replies that Rosaline knew that he didn't know what real love is.

91–92 For this . . . prove: this marriage may work out so well; **rancor:** bitter hate.

3 man: servant.

6–12 Tybalt . . . dared: Tybalt, still angry with Romeo, has sent a letter challenging Romeo to a duel. Benvolio says that Romeo will accept Tybalt's challenge and fight him.

15 blind bow-boy's butt-shaft: Cupid's dull practice arrow. Mercutio suggests that Romeo fell in love with very little work on Cupid's part.

Mercutio. More than Prince of Cats, I can tell you. O, he's the courageous captain of compliments. He fights as you sing
20 pricksong—keeps time, distance, and proportion; rests me his minim rest, one, two, and the third in your bosom! the very butcher of a silk button, a duelist, a duelist! a gentleman of the very first house, of the first and second cause. Ah, the immortal *passado!* the *punto reverso!* the *hay!*

25 **Benvolio.** The what?

Mercutio. The pox of such antic, lisping, affecting fantasticoes— these new tuners of accent! "By Jesu, a very good blade! a very tall man! a very good whore!" Why, is not this a lamentable thing, grandsire, that we should be thus afflicted with these strange flies,
30 these fashion-mongers, these perdona-mi's, who stand so much on the new form that they cannot sit at ease on the old bench? O, their bones, their bones!

[*Enter* Romeo, *no longer moody.*]

Benvolio. Here comes Romeo! here comes Romeo!

Mercutio. Without his roe, like a dried herring. O, flesh, flesh,
35 how art thou fishified! Now is he for the numbers that Petrarch flowed in. Laura, to his lady, was but a kitchen wench (marry, she had a better love to berhyme her), Dido a dowdy, Cleopatra a gypsy, Helen and Hero hildings and harlots, Thisbe a grey eye or so, but not to the purpose. Signior Romeo, *bon jour!* There's
40 a French salutation to your French slop. You gave us the counterfeit fairly last night.

Romeo. Good morrow to you both. What counterfeit did I give you?

Mercutio. The slip, sir, the slip. Can you not conceive?

45 **Romeo.** Pardon, good Mercutio. My business was great, and in such a case as mine a man may strain courtesy.

Mercutio. That's as much as to say, such a case as yours constrains a man to bow in the hams.

Romeo. Meaning, to curtsy.

50 **Mercutio.** Thou hast most kindly hit it.

Romeo. A most courteous exposition.

Mercutio. Nay, I am the very pink of courtesy.

Romeo. Pink for flower.

Mercutio. Right.

55 **Romeo.** Why, then is my pump well-flowered.

18–24 More than . . . hay: Prince of Cats refers to a cat in a fable, named Tybalt. Mercutio makes fun of Tybalt's new style of dueling, comparing it to singing (**pricksong**). *Passado, punto reverso,* and *hay* were terms used in the new dueling style.

26–32 The pox . . . their bones: Mercutio continues to make fun of people who embrace new styles and new manners of speaking.

34–39 without his roe: only part of himself (Mercutio makes fun of Romeo's name and his lovesickness; **numbers:** verses. Petrarch wrote sonnets to his love, Laura. According to Mercutio, Romeo's feelings for Rosaline are so intense that great loves in literature could never measure up.

39–44 bon jour: "Good day" in French; **There's . . . last night:** Here's a greeting to match your fancy French trousers (**slop**). You did a good job of getting away from us last night. (A piece of counterfeit money was called a **slip.**)

55 pump: shoe; **well-flowered:** Shoes with flowerlike designs.

Mercutio. Well said! Follow me this jest now till thou hast worn out thy pump, that, when the single sole of it is worn, the jest may remain, after the wearing, solely singular.

Romeo. Oh, single-soled jest, solely singular for the singleness!

60 **Mercutio.** Come between us, good Benvolio! My wits faint.

Romeo. Switch and spurs, switch and spurs! or I'll cry a match.

Mercutio. Nay, if our wits run the wild-goose chase, I am done; for thou hast more of the wild goose in one of thy wits than, I am sure, I have in my whole five. Was I with you there for the
65 goose?

Romeo. Thou wast never with me for anything when thou wast not there for the goose.

Mercutio. I will bite thee by the ear for that jest.

Romeo. Nay, good goose, bite not!

70 **Mercutio.** Thy wit is a very bitter sweeting; it is a most sharp sauce.

Romeo. And is it not, then, well served in to a sweet goose?

61 Switch . . . match: Keep going, or I'll claim victory.

64–65 Was . . . goose: Have I proved that you are a foolish person?

Mercutio. O, here's a wit of cheveril, that stretches from an inch narrow to an ell broad!

75 **Romeo.** I stretch it out for that word "broad," which, added to the goose, proves thee far and wide a broad goose.

Mercutio. Why, is not this better now than groaning for love? Now art thou sociable, now art thou Romeo; now art thou what thou art, by art as well as by nature. For this driveling love is like

80 a great natural that runs lolling up and down to hide his bauble in a hole.

Benvolio. Stop there, stop there!

Mercutio. Thou desirest me to stop in my tale against the hair.

Benvolio. Thou wouldst else have made thy tale large.

85 **Mercutio.** O, thou art deceived! I would have made it short; for I was come to the whole depth of my tale, and meant indeed to occupy the argument no longer.

[*Enter* Nurse *and* Peter, *her servant. He is carrying a large fan.*]

Romeo. Here's goodly gear!

Mercutio. A sail, a sail!

90 **Benvolio.** Two, two! a shirt and a smock.

Nurse. Peter!

Peter. Anon.

Nurse. My fan, Peter.

Mercutio. Good Peter, to hide her face; for her fan's the fairer of
95 the two.

Nurse. God ye good morrow, gentlemen.

Mercutio. God ye good-den, fair gentlewoman.

Nurse. Is it good-den?

Mercutio. 'Tis no less, I tell ye, for the bawdy hand of the dial is
100 now upon the prick of noon.

Nurse. Out upon you! What a man are you!

Romeo. One, gentlewoman, that God hath made himself to mar.

Nurse. By my troth, it is well said. "For himself to mar," quoth'a? Gentlemen, can any of you tell me where I may find the young
105 Romeo?

Romeo. I can tell you; but young Romeo will be older when you have found him than he was when you sought him. I am the youngest of that name, for fault of a worse.

73 **cheveril:** kidskin, which is flexible. Mercutio means that a little wit stretches a long way.

80–81 **great natural:** an idiot, like a jester or clown who carries a fool's stick (**bauble**).

88–89 **goodly gear:** something fine to joke about; **a sail:** Mercutio likens the nurse in all her petticoats to a huge ship coming toward them.

93 Fans were usually carried only by fine ladies. The nurse is trying to pretend that she is more than a servant.

Nurse. You say well.

110 **Mercutio.** Yea, is the worst well? Very well took, i' faith! wisely, wisely.

Nurse. If you be he, sir, I desire some confidence with you.

Benvolio. She will endite him to some supper.

Mercutio. A bawd, a bawd, a bawd! So ho!

115 **Romeo.** What hast thou found?

Mercutio. No hare, sir; unless a hare, sir, in a lenten pie, that is something stale and hoar ere it be spent.

[*sings*]

    "An old hare hoar,
    And an old hare hoar,
120   Is very good meat in Lent.
    But a hare that is hoar,
    Is too much for a score
    When it hoars ere it be spent."
Romeo, will you come to your father's? We'll to dinner thither.

125 **Romeo.** I will follow you.

Mercutio. Farewell, ancient lady. Farewell, [*sings*] lady, lady, lady.

[*Exeunt* Mercutio *and* Benvolio.]

Nurse. Marry, farewell! I pray you, sir, what saucy merchant was this that was so full of his ropery?

Romeo. A gentleman, nurse, that loves to hear himself talk and
130 will speak more in a minute than he will stand to in a month.

Nurse. An 'a speak anything against me, I'll take him down, an 'a were lustier than he is, and twenty such Jacks; and if I cannot, I'll find those that shall. Scurvy knave! I am none of his flirt-gills; I am none of his skainsmates. [*turning to* Peter] And thou must
135 stand by too, and suffer every knave to use me at his pleasure?

Peter. I saw no man use you at his pleasure. If I had, my weapon should quickly have been out, I warrant you. I dare draw as soon as another man, if I see occasion in a good quarrel, and the law on my side.

140 **Nurse.** Now, afore God, I am so vexed that every part about me quivers. Scurvy knave! Pray you, sir, a word; and as I told you, my young lady bade me enquire you out. What she bid me say, I will keep to myself; but first let me tell ye, if ye should lead her into a fool's paradise, as they say, it were a very gross kind of
145 behavior, as they say; for the gentlewoman is young; and

112–113 confidence: The nurse means *conference*; she uses big words without understanding their meaning; **endite:** Benvolio makes fun of the nurse by using this word rather than *invite*.

114–124 Mercutio calls the nurse a **bawd,** or woman who runs a house of prostitution. His song uses the insulting puns **hare,** a rabbit or prostitute, and **hoar,** old.

128 ropery: roguery, or jokes.

133–134 The nurse is angry that Mercutio treated her like one of his loose women (**flirt-gills**) or his gangsterlike friends (**skainsmates**).

142–147 The nurse warns Romeo that he'd better mean what he said about marrying Juliet.

therefore, if you should deal double with her, truly it were an ill thing to be offered to any gentlewoman, and very weak dealing.

Romeo. Nurse, commend me to thy lady and mistress. I protest unto thee—

148 **commend me:** give my respectful greetings.

150 **Nurse.** Good heart, and i' faith I will tell her as much. Lord, Lord! she will be a joyful woman.

Romeo. What wilt thou tell her, nurse? Thou dost not mark me.

Nurse. I will tell her, sir, that you do protest, which, as I take it, is a gentlemanlike offer.

155–159 Romeo tells the nurse to have Juliet come to Friar Laurence's cell this afternoon, using the excuse that she is going to confess her sins (**shrift**). There she will receive forgiveness for her sins (**be shrived**) and be married.

155 **Romeo.** Bid her devise
Some means to come to shrift this afternoon;
And there she shall at Friar Laurence' cell
Be shrived and married. Here is for thy pains.

Nurse. No, truly, sir; not a penny.

160 **Romeo.** Go to! I say you shall.

Nurse. This afternoon, sir? Well, she shall be there.

Romeo. And stay, good nurse, behind the abbey wall.
Within this hour my man shall be with thee
And bring thee cords made like a tackled stair,
165 Which to the high topgallant of my joy
Must be my convoy in the secret night.
Farewell. Be trusty, and I'll quit thy pains.
Farewell. Commend me to thy mistress.

164–165 **tackled stair:** rope ladder; **topgallant:** highest point.

167 **quit thy pains:** reward you.

Nurse. Now God in heaven bless thee! Hark you, sir.

170 **Romeo.** What sayst thou, my dear nurse?

Nurse. Is your man secret? Did you ne'er hear say,
Two may keep counsel, putting one away?

Romeo. I warrant thee my man's as true as steel.

174–177 The nurse begins to babble about Paris' proposal but says that Juliet would rather look at a toad than at Paris.

Nurse. Well, sir, my mistress is the sweetest lady. Lord, Lord!
175 when 'twas a little prating thing—O, there is a nobleman in town, one Paris, that would fain lay knife aboard; but she, good soul, had as lief see a toad, a very toad, as see him. I anger her sometimes, and tell her that Paris is the properer man; but I'll warrant you, when I say so, she looks as pale as any clout in the
180 versal world. Doth not rosemary and Romeo begin both with a letter?

179–186 **clout:** old cloth; **the versal world:** the entire world; **Doth not . . . hear it:** The nurse tries to recall a clever saying that Juliet made up about Romeo and rosemary, the herb, but cannot remember it. She is sure that the two words couldn't begin with *R* because this letter sounds like a snarling dog; **sententious:** The nurse means *sentences.*

Romeo. Ay, nurse, what of that? Both with an R.

Nurse. Ah, mocker! that's the dog's name. R is for the—No; I know it begins with some other letter; and she hath the prettiest

185 sententious of it, of you and rosemary, that it would do you good
to hear it.

Romeo. Commend me to thy lady.

Nurse. Ay, a thousand times. [*Exit* Romeo.] Peter!

Peter. Anon.

190 **Nurse.** Peter, take my fan, and go before, and apace.

[*Exeunt.*]

Scene 5 *Capulet's orchard.*

[*Enter* Juliet.]

Juliet. The clock struck nine when I did send the nurse;
In half an hour she promised to return.
Perchance she cannot meet him. That's not so.
O, she is lame! Love's heralds should be thoughts,
5 Which ten times faster glide than the sun's beams
Driving back shadows over lowering hills.
Therefore do nimble-pinioned doves draw Love,
And therefore hath the wind-swift Cupid wings.
Now is the sun upon the highmost hill
10 Of this day's journey, and from nine till twelve
Is three long hours; yet she is not come.
Had she affections and warm youthful blood,
She would be as swift in motion as a ball;
My words would bandy her to my sweet love,
15 And his to me.
But old folks, many feign as they were dead—
Unwieldy, slow, heavy, and pale as lead.
[*Enter* Nurse *and* Peter.] O God, she comes! O honey nurse,
    what news?
Hast thou met with him? Send thy man away.

20 **Nurse.** Peter, stay at the gate.

[*Exit* Peter.]

Juliet. Now, good sweet nurse—O Lord, why lookst thou sad?
Though news be sad, yet tell them merrily;
If good, thou shamest the music of sweet news
By playing it to me with so sour a face.

25 **Nurse.** I am aweary, give me leave awhile.
Fie, how my bones ache! What a jaunce have I had!

Juliet. I would thou hadst my bones, and I thy news.
Nay, come, I pray thee speak. Good, good nurse, speak.

190 apace: quickly.

4–6 Love's . . . hills: Love's messengers should be thoughts, which travel ten times faster than sunbeams.

7 nimble-pinioned . . . Love: Swift-winged doves pull the chariot of Venus, goddess of love.

14 bandy: toss.

16 feign as: act as if.

21–22 The nurse teases Juliet by putting on a sad face as if the news were bad.

25–26 give me . . . I had: Leave me alone for a while. I ache all over because of the running back and forth I've been doing.

Nurse. Jesu, what haste! Can you not stay awhile?
30 Do you not see that I am out of breath?

Juliet. How art thou out of breath when thou hast breath
To say to me that thou art out of breath?
The excuse that thou dost make in this delay
Is longer than the tale thou dost excuse.
35 Is thy news good or bad? Answer to that.
Say either, and I'll stay the circumstance.
Let me be satisfied, is't good or bad?

36 I'll … circumstance: I'll wait for the details.

Nurse. Well, you have made a simple choice; you know not how
to choose a man. Romeo? No, not he. Though his face be better
40 than any man's, yet his leg excels all men's; and for a hand and a
foot, and a body, though they be not to be talked on, yet they are
past compare. He is not the flower of courtesy, but, I'll warrant
him, as gentle as a lamb. Go thy ways, wench; serve God. What,
have you dined at home?

38 simple: foolish.

45 **Juliet.** No, no. But all this did I know before.
What say he of our marriage? What of that?

Nurse. Lord, how my head aches! What a head have I!
It beats as it would fall in twenty pieces.
My back o' t'other side—ah, my back, my back!
50 Beshrew your heart for sending me about
To catch my death with jauncing up and down!

50–51 Beshrew … down: Curse you for making me endanger my health by running around.

Juliet. I' faith, I am sorry that thou art not well.
Sweet, sweet, sweet nurse, tell me, what says my love?

Nurse. Your love says, like an honest gentleman, and a
courteous,
55 and a kind, and a handsome, and, I warrant, a virtuous—Where
is your mother?

Juliet. Where is my mother? Why, she is within.
Where should she be? How oddly thou repliest!
"Your love says, like an honest gentleman,
60 'Where is your mother?'"

Nurse.   O God's Lady dear!
Are you so hot? Marry come up, I trow.
Is this the poultice for my aching bones?
Hence forward do your messages yourself.

61–62 Marry … bones: Control yourself! Is this the treatment I get for my pain?

Juliet. Here's such a coil! Come, what says Romeo?

64 coil: fuss.

65 **Nurse.** Have you got leave to go to shrift today?

Juliet. I have.

Nurse. Then hie you hence to Friar Laurence' cell;
There stays a husband to make you a wife.
Now comes the wanton blood up in your cheeks:
70 They'll be in scarlet straight at any news.
Hie you to church; I must another way,
To fetch a ladder, by the which your love
Must climb a bird's nest soon when it is dark.
I am the drudge, and toil in your delight;
75 But you shall bear the burden soon at night.
Go; I'll to dinner; hie you to the cell.

71–73 The nurse will get the ladder that Romeo will use to climb to Juliet's room after they are married.

Juliet. Hie to high fortune! Honest nurse, farewell.

[*Exeunt.*]

Scene 6 *Friar Laurence's cell.*

[*Enter* Friar Laurence *and* Romeo.]

Friar Laurence. So smile the heavens upon this holy act
That after-hours with sorrow chide us not!

1–2 So smile . . . us not: May heaven so bless this act that we won't regret it in the future (**after-hours**).

Romeo. Amen, amen! But come what sorrow can,
It cannot countervail the exchange of joy
5 That one short minute gives me in her sight.

4 **countervail:** outweigh.

Do thou but close our hands with holy words,
Then love-devouring death do what he dare—
It is enough I may but call her mine.

Friar Laurence. These violent delights have violent ends
10   And in their triumph die, like fire and powder,
Which, as they kiss, consume. The sweetest honey
Is loathsome in his own deliciousness
And in the taste confounds the appetite.
Therefore love moderately: long love doth so;
15   Too swift arrives as tardy as too slow.

[*Enter* Juliet.]

Here comes the lady. O, so light a foot
Will ne'er wear out the everlasting flint.
A lover may bestride the gossamer
That idles in the wanton summer air,
20   And yet not fall; so light is vanity.

Juliet. Good even to my ghostly confessor.

Friar Laurence. Romeo shall thank thee, daughter, for us both.

Juliet. As much to him, else is his thanks too much.

Romeo. Ah, Juliet, if the measure of thy joy
25   Be heaped like mine, and that thy skill be more
To blazon it, then sweeten with thy breath
This neighbor air, and let rich music's tongue
Unfold the imagined happiness that both
Receive in either by this dear encounter.

30   **Juliet.** Conceit, more rich in matter than in words,
Brags of his substance, not of ornament.
They are but beggars that can count their worth;
But my true love is grown to such excess
I cannot sum up sum of half my wealth.

35   **Friar Laurence.** Come, come with me, and we will make short work;
For, by your leaves, you shall not stay alone
Till Holy Church incorporate two in one.

[*Exeunt.*]

9–15 These . . . slow: The friar compares Romeo's passion to gunpowder and the fire that ignites it—both are destroyed—then to honey, whose sweetness can destroy the appetite. He reminds Romeo to practice moderation in love.

23 as much to him: I give the same greeting to Romeo that he offers to me.

24–29 if the measure . . . encounter: If you are as happy as I am and have more skill to proclaim it, then sweeten the air by singing of our happiness to the world.

30–31 Conceit . . . ornament: True understanding (**conceit**) needs no words.

COLLABORATIVE DISCUSSION Romeo and Juliet fall in love and make life-changing decisions in a matter of days. Meet with a partner to discuss how this speed and intensity creates tension for the audience and affects the characters' actions.

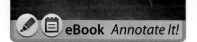

Analyzing the Text

Cite Text Evidence Support your responses with evidence from the selection.

1. **Interpret** In literature, a **motif** is a repeated image, idea, or theme. Explain the light/dark or day/night motif in Romeo's speech at the beginning of Act II, Scene 2. What does he mean when he refers to Juliet as "the sun"? Where else in Act II does this motif appear?

2. **Analyze** In Act II, Scene 2, Juliet says, "What's in a name? That which we call a rose / By any other name would smell as sweet" (lines 43–44). What does she mean? How does this comparison relate to one of the conflicts in her life?

3. **Infer** After declaring their love for one another, why do Romeo and Juliet want to commit themselves right away to marriage? Support your inference with evidence from the text.

4. **Cite Evidence** In Scene 3, why is Friar Laurence suspicious of Romeo's declaration of love for Juliet? What is his motivation for agreeing to marry Romeo and Juliet, despite his reservations?

5. **Analyze** Explain Juliet's relationship with her nurse. What is the Nurse's primary motivation in helping Juliet to be with Romeo?

6. **Predict** In Scene 6, Friar Laurence urges Romeo to be cautious. Given what you know about Romeo, and about the fates guiding the "star-crossed lovers," do you think Romeo will take his advice? Explain.

PERFORMANCE TASK

Speaking Activity: Debate Both Friar Laurence and Mercutio have personal attributes that put them at odds with Romeo's passion. Analyze their differences and hold a debate in which each character presents his point of view.

- Working with two other students, discuss the characteristics and motivations of Friar Laurence, Mercutio, and Romeo. What differences do these three demonstrate in Act II?

- With each person in your group taking the point of view of one of these characters, debate Romeo's plan to marry Juliet.
- Work together to write a summary of your debate.

AS YOU READ Notice how events begin to shift in a more ominous or dangerous direction in this act. Write down any questions you generate during reading.

ACT III

Scene 1 *A public place.*

[*Enter* Mercutio, Benvolio, Page, *and* Servants.]

Benvolio. I pray thee, good Mercutio, let's retire.
The day is hot, the Capulets abroad,
And if we meet, we shall not scape a brawl,
For now, these hot days, is the mad blood stirring.

> **3–4 we shall . . . stirring:** We shall not avoid a fight, since the heat makes people ill-tempered.

5   **Mercutio.** Thou art like one of those fellows that, when he enters the confines of a tavern, claps me his sword upon the table and says "God send me no need of thee!" and by the operation of the second cup draws him on the drawer, when indeed there is no need.

> **7–8 by the . . . drawer:** feeling the effects of a second drink, is ready to fight (**draw on**) the waiter who's pouring the drinks (**drawer**).

10   **Benvolio.** Am I like such a fellow?

Mercutio. Come, come, thou art as hot a Jack in thy mood as any in Italy; and as soon moved to be moody, and as soon moody to be moved.

> **12–13 as soon moved . . . to be moved:** as likely to get angry and start a fight.

Benvolio. And what to?

15   **Mercutio.** Nay an there were two such, we should have none shortly, for one would kill the other. Thou! why, thou wilt quarrel with a man that hath a hair more or a hair less in his beard than thou hast. Thou wilt quarrel with a man for cracking nuts, having no other reason but because thou hast hazel eyes.
20   What eye but such an eye would spy out such a quarrel? Thy head is as full of quarrels as an egg is full of meat; and yet thy head hath been beaten as addle as an egg for quarreling. Thou hast quarreled with a man for coughing in the street, because he hath wakened thy dog that hath lain asleep in the sun. Didst
25   thou not fall out with a tailor for wearing his new doublet before Easter? with another for tying his new shoes with old riband? And yet thou wilt tutor me from quarreling!

> **15–27** Mercutio teases his friend by insisting that Benvolio is quick to pick a fight, though everyone knows that Benvolio is gentle and peace loving.

> **25 doublet:** jacket.
> **26 riband:** ribbon or laces.

Benvolio. An I were so apt to quarrel as thou art, any man should buy the fee simple of my life for an hour and a quarter.

> **28–29 An I . . . quarter:** If I picked fights as quickly as you do, anybody could own me for the smallest amount of money.

30   **Mercutio.** The fee simple? O simple!

[*Enter* Tybalt *and others.*]

Benvolio. By my head, here come the Capulets.

Mercutio. By my heel, I care not.

Tybalt. Follow me close, for I will speak to them. Gentlemen, good den. A word with one of you.

35 **Mercutio.** And but one word with one of us? Couple it with something; make it a word and a blow.

Tybalt. You shall find me apt enough to that, sir, an you will give me occasion.

Mercutio. Could you not take some occasion without giving?

40 **Tybalt.** Mercutio, thou consortest with Romeo.

Mercutio. Consort? What, dost thou make us minstrels? An thou make minstrels of us, look to hear nothing but discords. Here's my fiddlestick; here's that shall make you dance. Zounds, consort!

45 **Benvolio.** We talk here in the public haunt of men.
Either withdraw unto some private place
And reason coldly of your grievances,
Or else depart. Here all eyes gaze on us.

Mercutio. Men's eyes were made to look, and let them gaze.
50 I will not budge for no man's pleasure, I.

[*Enter* Romeo.]

Tybalt. Well, peace be with you, sir. Here comes my man.

Mercutio. But I'll be hanged, sir, if he wear your livery.
Marry, go before to field, he'll be your follower!
Your worship in that sense may call him man.

55 **Tybalt.** Romeo, the love I bear thee can afford
No better term than this: thou art a villain.

Romeo. Tybalt, the reason that I have to love thee
Doth much excuse the appertaining rage
To such a greeting. Villain am I none.
60 Therefore farewell. I see thou knowst me not.

Tybalt. Boy, this shall not excuse the injuries
That thou hast done me; therefore turn and draw.

Romeo. I do protest I never injured thee,
But love thee better than thou canst devise
65 Till thou shalt know the reason of my love;
And so, good Capulet, which name I tender
As dearly as mine own, be satisfied.

Mercutio. O calm, dishonorable, vile submission!
Alla stoccata carries it away.

40–44 consortest: friends with; Mercutio pretends to misunderstand him, assuming that Tybalt is insulting him by calling Romeo and him a **consort,** a group of traveling musicians. He then refers to his sword as his **fiddlestick,** the bow for a fiddle.

51–54 Mercutio again pretends to misunderstand Tybalt. By **my man,** Tybalt means "the man I'm looking for." Mercutio takes it to mean "my servant." (**Livery** is a servant's uniform.)

57–59 I forgive your anger because I have reason to love you.

61 Boy: an insulting term of address.

66 tender: cherish.

68–70 Mercutio assumes that Romeo is afraid to fight. *Alla stoccata* is a move used in sword fighting.

[*draws*]

70 Tybalt, you ratcatcher, will you walk?

Tybalt. What wouldst thou have with me?

Mercutio. Good King of Cats, nothing but one of your nine lives.
That I mean to make bold withal, and, as you shall use me
hereafter, dry-beat the rest of the eight. Will you pluck your
75 sword out of his pilcher by the ears? Make haste, lest mine be
about your ears ere it be out.

Tybalt. I am for you.

[*draws*]

Romeo. Gentle Mercutio, put thy rapier up.

Mercutio. Come, sir, your *passado!*

[*They fight.*]

80 **Romeo.** Draw, Benvolio; beat down their weapons.
Gentlemen, for shame! forbear this outrage!
Tybalt, Mercutio, the Prince expressly hath

**72–74 nothing but...
eight:** I intend to take
one of your nine lives (as
a cat supposedly has)
and give a beating to the
other eight.

79 *passado:* a sword-
fighting maneuver.

80–84 Romeo wants
Benvolio to help him
stop the fight. They
are able to hold back
Mercutio.

Forbid this bandying in Verona streets.
Hold, Tybalt! Good Mercutio!

[Tybalt, *under* Romeo's *arm, thrusts* Mercutio *in, and flies with his* Men.]

Mercutio.   I am hurt.
85 A plague o' both your houses! I am sped.
Is he gone and hath nothing?

Benvolio.   What, art thou hurt?

Mercutio. Ay, ay, a scratch, a scratch. Marry, 'tis enough.
Where is my page? Go, villain, fetch a surgeon.

[*Exit* Page.]

Romeo. Courage, man. The hurt cannot be much.

90 **Mercutio.** No, 'tis not so deep as a well, nor so wide as a church
door; but 'tis enough, 'twill serve. Ask for me tomorrow, and you
shall find me a grave man. I am peppered, I warrant, for this
world. A plague o' both your houses! Zounds, a dog, a rat, a
mouse, a cat, to scratch a man to death! A braggart, a rogue, a
95 villain, that fights by the book of arithmetic! Why the devil
came you between us? I was hurt under your arm.

Romeo. I thought all for the best.

Mercutio. Help me into some house, Benvolio,
Or I shall faint. A plague o' both your houses!
100 They have made worms' meat of me. I have it,
And soundly too. Your houses!

[*Exit, supported by* Benvolio.]

Romeo. This gentleman, the Prince's near ally,
My very friend, hath got this mortal hurt
In my behalf—my reputation stained
105 With Tybalt's slander—Tybalt, that an hour
Hath been my kinsman, O sweet Juliet,
Thy beauty hath made me effeminate
And in my temper softened valor's steel!

[*Reenter* Benvolio.]

Benvolio. O Romeo, Romeo, brave Mercutio's dead!
110 That gallant spirit hath aspired the clouds,
Which too untimely here did scorn the earth.

Romeo. This day's black fate on mo days doth depend;
This but begins the woe others must end.

[*Reenter* Tybalt.]

83 bandying: fighting.

85 A plague ... sped: I curse both the Montagues and the Capulets. I am destroyed.

102–108 This gentleman ... valor's steel: My friend has died protecting my reputation against a man who has been my relative for only an hour. My love for Juliet has made me less manly and brave.

110 aspired: soared to.

112–113 This day's ... must end: This awful day will be followed by more of the same.

Benvolio. Here comes the furious Tybalt back again.

115 **Romeo.** Alive in triumph, and Mercutio slain?
Away to heaven respective lenity,
And fire-eyed fury be my conduct now!
Now, Tybalt, take the "villain" back again
That late thou gavest me, for Mercutio's soul
120 Is but a little way above our heads,
Staying for thine to keep him company.
Either thou or I, or both, must go with him.

Tybalt. Thou, wretched boy, that didst consort him here,
Shalt with him hence.

Romeo.   This shall determine that.

[*They fight.* Tybalt *falls.*]

125 **Benvolio.** Romeo, away, be gone!
The citizens are up, and Tybalt slain.
Stand not amazed. The Prince will doom thee death
If thou art taken. Hence, be gone, away!

Romeo. O, I am fortune's fool!

Benvolio.   Why dost thou stay?

[*Exit* Romeo.]

[*Enter* Citizens.]

130 **Citizen.** Which way ran he that killed Mercutio?
Tybalt, that murderer, which way ran he?

Benvolio. There lies that Tybalt.

Citizen.   Up, sir, go with me.
I charge thee in the Prince's name obey.

[*Enter* Prince *with his* Attendants, Montague, Capulet, *their* Wives, *and others.*]

Prince. Where are the vile beginners of this fray?

135 **Benvolio.** O noble Prince, I can discover all
The unlucky manage of this fatal brawl.
There lies the man, slain by young Romeo,
That slew thy kinsman, brave Mercutio.

Lady Capulet. Tybalt, my cousin! O my brother's child!
140 O Prince! O cousin! O husband! O, the blood is spilled
Of my dear kinsman! Prince, as thou art true,
For blood of ours shed blood of Montague.
O cousin, cousin!

Prince. Benvolio, who began this bloody fray?

116 respective lenity: considerate mildness.

124 The sword fight probably goes on for several minutes, till Romeo runs his sword through Tybalt.

129 I am fortune's fool: Fate has made a fool of me.

135–136 Benvolio says he can tell (**discover**) what happened.

141–142 as thou ... Montague: If your word is good, you will sentence Romeo to death for killing a Capulet.

145 **Benvolio.** Tybalt, here slain, whom Romeo's hand did slay.
Romeo, that spoke him fair, bid him bethink
How nice the quarrel was, and urged withal
Your high displeasure. All this—uttered
With gentle breath, calm look, knees humbly bowed—
150 Could not take truce with the unruly spleen
Of Tybalt deaf to peace, but that he tilts
With piercing steel at bold Mercutio's breast;
Who, all as hot, turns deadly point to point,
And, with a martial scorn, with one hand beats
155 Cold death aside and with the other sends
It back to Tybalt, whose dexterity
Retorts it. Romeo he cries aloud,
"Hold, friends! friends, part!" and swifter than his tongue,
His agile arm beats down their fatal points,
160 And 'twixt them rushes; underneath whose arm
An envious thrust from Tybalt hit the life
Of stout Mercutio, and then Tybalt fled,
But by-and-by comes back to Romeo,
Who had but newly entertained revenge,
165 And to't they go like lightning; for, ere I
Could draw to part them, was stout Tybalt slain;
And, as he fell, did Romeo turn and fly.
This is the truth, or let Benvolio die.

Lady Capulet. He is a kinsman to the Montague;
170 Affection makes him false, he speaks not true.
Some twenty of them fought in this black strife,
And all those twenty could but kill one life.
I beg for justice, which thou, Prince, must give.
Romeo slew Tybalt; Romeo must not live.

175 **Prince.** Romeo slew him; he slew Mercutio.
Who now the price of his dear blood doth owe?

Montague. Not Romeo, Prince; he was Mercutio's friend;
His fault concludes but what the law should end,
The life of Tybalt.

Prince. And for that offense
180 Immediately we do exile him hence.
I have an interest in your hate's proceeding,
My blood for your rude brawls doth lie a-bleeding;
But I'll amerce you with so strong a fine
That you shall all repent the loss of mine.
185 I will be deaf to pleading and excuses;
Nor tears nor prayers shall purchase out abuses.
Therefore use none. Let Romeo hence in haste,

146–147 Romeo, that . . . was: Romeo talked calmly (**fair**) and told Tybalt to think how trivial (**nice**) the argument was.

150–151 could . . . peace: could not quiet the anger of Tybalt, who would not listen to pleas for peace.

156–157 whose dexterity retorts it: whose skill returns it.

159–160 his agile . . . rushes: He rushed between them and pushed down their swords.

164 entertained: thought of.

178–179 Romeo is guilty only of avenging Mercutio's death, which the law would have done anyway.

179–190 The prince banishes Romeo from Verona. He angrily points out that one of his own relatives is dead because of the feud and declares that Romeo will be put to death unless he flees immediately.

Else, when he is found, that hour is his last.
Bear hence this body, and attend our will.
190 Mercy but murders, pardoning those that kill.

[*Exeunt.*]

Scene 2 *Capulet's orchard.*

[*Enter* Juliet *alone.*]

Juliet. Gallop apace, you fiery-footed steeds,
Toward Phoebus' lodging! Such a wagoner
As Phaëton would whip you to the West,
And bring in cloudy night immediately.
5 Spread thy close curtain, love-performing night,
That runaways' eyes may wink, and Romeo
Leap to these arms, untalked of and unseen.
Lovers can see to do their amorous rites
By their own beauties; or, if love be blind,
10 It best agrees with night. Come, civil night,
Thou sober-suited matron, all in black,
And learn me how to lose a winning match,
Played for a pair of stainless maidenhoods.
Hood my unmanned blood bating in my cheeks
15 With thy black mantle; till strange love, grown bold,
Think true love acted simple modesty.
Come, night; come, Romeo, come; thou day in night;
For thou wilt lie upon the wings of night
Whiter than new snow on a raven's back.
20 Come, gentle night; come, loving, black-browed night;
Give me my Romeo; and, when he shall die,
Take him and cut him out in little stars,
And he will make the face of heaven so fine
That all the world will be in love with night
25 And pay no worship to the garish sun.
O, I have bought the mansion of a love,
But not possessed it; and though I am sold,
Not yet enjoyed. So tedious is this day
As is the night before some festival
30 To an impatient child that hath new robes
And may not wear them. Oh, here comes my nurse,

[*Enter* Nurse, *wringing her hands, with the ladder of cords in her lap.*]

And she brings news; and every tongue that speaks
But Romeo's name speaks heavenly eloquence.
Now, nurse, what news? What hast thou there? the cords
35 That Romeo bid thee fetch?

2–3 Phoebus: Apollo, the god of the sun; **Phaëton:** a mortal who lost control of the sun's chariot when he drove it too fast.

14–16 Hood . . . modesty: Juliet asks that the darkness hide her blushing cheeks on her wedding night.

26–27 I have . . . possessed it: Juliet protests that she has gone through the wedding ceremony (**bought the mansion**) but is still waiting to enjoy the rewards of marriage.

34 the cords: the rope ladder.

Nurse. Ay, ay, the cords.

Juliet. Ay me! what news? Why dost thou wring thy hands?

Nurse. Ah, well-a-day! he's dead, he's dead, he's dead!
We are undone, lady, we are undone!
Alack the day! he's gone, he's killed, he's dead!

40 **Juliet.** Can heaven be so envious?

Nurse. Romeo can,
Though heaven cannot. O Romeo, Romeo!
Who ever would have thought it? Romeo!

Juliet. What devil art thou that dost torment me thus?
This torture should be roared in dismal hell.
45 Hath Romeo slain himself? Say thou but "I,"
And that bare vowel "I" shall poison more
Than the death-darting eye of a cockatrice.
I am not I, if there be such an "I,"
Or those eyes shut, that make thee answer "I."
50 If he be slain, say "I," or if not, "no."
Brief sounds determine of my weal or woe.

Nurse. I saw the wound, I saw it with mine eyes,
(God save the mark!) here on his manly breast.
A piteous corse, a bloody piteous corse;
55 Pale, pale as ashes, all bedaubed in blood,
All in gore blood. I swounded at the sight.

Juliet. O, break, my heart! poor bankrout, break at once!
To prison, eyes; ne'er look on liberty!
Vile earth, to earth resign; end motion here,
60 And thou and Romeo press one heavy bier!

Nurse. O Tybalt, Tybalt, the best friend I had!
O courteous Tybalt! honest gentleman!
That ever I should live to see thee dead!

Juliet. What storm is this that blows so contrary?
65 Is Romeo slaughtered, and is Tybalt dead?
My dear-loved cousin, and my dearer lord?
Then, dreadful trumpet, sound the general doom!
For who is living, if those two are gone?

Nurse. Tybalt is gone, and Romeo banished;
70 Romeo that killed him, he is banished.

Juliet. O God! Did Romeo's hand shed Tybalt's blood?

Nurse. It did! it did! alas the day, it did!

37–42 well-a-day: an expression used when someone has bad news. The nurse wails and moans without clearly explaining what has happened, leading Juliet to assume that Romeo is dead.

45–50 Juliet's "I" means "aye," or "yes." A **cockatrice** is a mythological beast whose glance kills its victims.

51 my weal or woe: my happiness or sorrow.

53–56 God...mark: an expression meant to scare off evil powers, similar to "Knock on wood"; **corse:** corpse; **swounded:** fainted.

57–60 Juliet say her heart is broken and bankrupt (**bankrout**). She wants to be buried with Romeo, sharing his burial platform (**bier**).

Juliet. O serpent heart, hid with a flow'ring face!
Did ever dragon keep so fair a cave?
75 Beautiful tyrant! fiend angelical!
Dove-feathered raven! wolvish-ravening lamb!
Despised substance of divinest show!
Just opposite to what thou justly seemst,
A damned saint, an honorable villain!
80 O nature, what hadst thou to do in hell
When thou didst bower the spirit of a fiend
In mortal paradise of such sweet flesh?
Was ever book containing such vile matter
So fairly bound? O, that deceit should dwell
85 In such a gorgeous palace!

81 bower ... fiend: give
a home to the spirit of a
demon.

Nurse.   There's no trust,
No faith, no honesty in men; all perjured,
All forsworn, all naught, all dissemblers.
Ah, where's my man? Give me some aqua vitae.
These griefs, these woes, these sorrows make me old.
90 Shame come to Romeo!

87 all ... dissemblers:
All are liars and
pretenders.

88 aqua vitae: brandy.

Juliet.   Blistered be thy tongue
For such a wish! He was not born to shame.
Upon his brow shame is ashamed to sit;
For 'tis a throne where honor may be crowned
Sole monarch of the universal earth.
95 O, what a beast was I to chide at him!

Nurse. Will you speak well of him that killed your cousin?

Juliet. Shall I speak ill of him that is my husband?
Ah, poor my lord, what tongue shall smooth thy name
When I, thy three-hours' wife, have mangled it?
100 But wherefore, villain, didst thou kill my cousin?
That villain cousin would have killed my husband.
Back, foolish tears, back to your native spring!
Your tributary drops belong to woe,
Which you, mistaking, offer up to joy.
105 My husband lives, that Tybalt would have slain;
And Tybalt's dead, that would have slain my husband.
All this is comfort; wherefore weep I then?
Some word there was, worser than Tybalt's death,
That murdered me. I would forget it fain;
110 But O, it presses to my memory
Like damned guilty deeds to sinners' minds!
"Tybalt is dead, and Romeo—banished."
That "banished," that one word "banished,"
Hath slain ten thousand Tybalts. Tybalt's death

102–106 Juliet is
uncertain whether her
tears should be of joy or
of sorrow.

115 Was woe enough, if it had ended there;
Or, if sour woe delights in fellowship
And needly will be ranked with other griefs,
Why followed not, when she said "Tybalt's dead,"
Thy father, or thy mother, nay, or both,
120 Which modern lamentation might have moved?
But with a rearward following Tybalt's death,
"Romeo is banished"—to speak that word
Is father, mother, Tybalt, Romeo, Juliet,
All slain, all dead. "Romeo is banished"—
125 There is no end, no limit, measure, bound,
In that word's death; no words can that woe sound.
Where is my father and my mother, nurse?

Nurse. Weeping and wailing over Tybalt's corse.
Will you go to them? I will bring you thither.

130 **Juliet.** Wash they his wounds with tears? Mine shall be spent,
When theirs are dry, for Romeo's banishment.
Take up those cords. Poor ropes, you are beguiled,
Both you and I, for Romeo is exiled.
He made you for a highway to my bed;
135 But I, a maid, die maiden-widowed.
Come, cords; come, nurse. I'll to my wedding bed;
And death, not Romeo, take my maidenhead!

114–127 If the news of Tybalt's death had been followed by the news of her parents' deaths, Juliet would have felt grief. To follow the story of Tybalt's death with the news of Romeo's banishment creates a sorrow so deep it cannot be expressed in words.

132 beguiled: cheated.

**135–137 I...
maidenhead:** I will die a widow without ever really having been a wife. Death, not Romeo, will be my husband.

The Tragedy of Romeo and Juliet: Act III, Scene 2   **237**

Nurse. Hie to your chamber. I'll find Romeo
To comfort you. I wot well where he is.
140 Hark ye, your Romeo will be here at night.
I'll to him; he is hid at Laurence' cell.

Juliet. O, find him! give this ring to my true knight
And bid him come to take his last farewell.

[*Exeunt.*]

Scene 3 *Friar Laurence's cell.*

[*Enter* Friar Laurence.]

Friar Laurence. Romeo, come forth; come forth, thou fearful man.
Affliction is enamored of thy parts,
And thou art wedded to calamity.

[*Enter* Romeo.]

Romeo. Father, what news? What is the Prince's doom?
5 What sorrow craves acquaintance at my hand
That I yet know not?

Friar Laurence.   Too familiar
Is my dear son with such sour company.
I bring thee tidings of the Prince's doom.

Romeo. What less than doomsday is the Prince's doom?

10 **Friar Laurence.** A gentler judgment vanished from his lips—
Not body's death, but body's banishment.

Romeo. Ha, banishment? Be merciful, say "death";
For exile hath more terror in his look,
Much more than death. Do not say "banishment."

15 **Friar Laurence.** Hence from Verona art thou banished.
Be patient, for the world is broad and wide.

Romeo. There is no world without Verona walls,
But purgatory, torture, hell itself.
Hence banished is banish'd from the world,
20 And world's exile is death. Then "banishment,"
Is death misterm'd. Calling death "banishment,"
Thou cuttst my head off with a golden axe
And smilest upon the stroke that murders me.

Friar Laurence. O deadly sin! O rude unthankfulness!
25 Thy fault our law calls death; but the kind Prince,
Taking thy part, hath rushed aside the law,
And turned that black word death to banishment.
This is dear mercy, and thou seest it not.

139 wot: know.

2 affliction...parts:
Trouble loves you.

4 doom: sentence.

9 doomsday: death.

10 vanished: came.

**17–23 There is...
murders me:** Being
exiled outside Verona's
walls is as bad as being
dead. And yet you smile
at my misfortune.

Romeo. 'Tis torture, and not mercy. Heaven is here,
30 Where Juliet lives; and every cat and dog
And little mouse, every unworthy thing,
Live here in heaven and may look on her;
But Romeo may not. More validity,
More honorable state, more courtship lives
35 In carrion flies than Romeo. They may seize
On the white wonder of dear Juliet's hand
And steal immortal blessing from her lips,
Who, even in pure and vestal modesty,
Still blush, as thinking their own kisses sin;
40 But Romeo may not—he is banished.
This may flies do, when I from this must fly;
They are free men, but I am banished.
And sayst thou yet that exile is not death?
Hadst thou no poison mixed, no sharp-ground knife,
45 No sudden mean of death, though ne'er so mean,
But "banished" to kill me—"banished"?
O friar, the damned use that word in hell;
Howling attends it! How hast thou the heart,
Being a divine, a ghostly confessor,
50 A sin-absolver, and my friend professed,
To mangle me with that word "banished"?

Friar Laurence. Thou fond mad man, hear me a little speak.

Romeo. O, thou wilt speak again of banishment.

Friar Laurence. I'll give thee armor to keep off that word;
55 Adversity's sweet milk, philosophy,
To comfort thee, though thou art banished.

Romeo. Yet "banished"? Hang up philosophy!
Unless philosophy can make a Juliet,
Displant a town, reverse a prince's doom,
60 It helps not, it prevails not. Talk no more.

Friar Laurence. O, then I see that madmen have no ears.

Romeo. How should they, when that wise men have no eyes?

Friar Laurence. Let me dispute with thee of thy estate.

Romeo. Thou canst not speak of that thou dost not feel.
65 Wert thou as young as I, Juliet thy love,
An hour but married, Tybalt murdered,
Doting like me, and like me banished,
Then mightst thou speak, then mightst thou tear thy hair,
And fall upon the ground, as I do now,
70 Taking the measure of an unmade grave.

33–35 More validity . . . than Romeo: Even flies that live off the dead (**carrion**) will be able to get closer to Juliet than Romeo will.

44–46 Hadst . . . to kill me: Couldn't you have killed me with poison or a knife instead of with that awful word *banished*?

52 fond: foolish.

54–56 The friar offers philosophical comfort and counseling (**adversity's sweet milk**) as a way to overcome hardship.

63 dispute: discuss; **estate:** situation.

[Nurse *knocks within.*]

Friar Laurence. Arise; one knocks. Good Romeo, hide thyself.

Romeo. Not I; unless the breath of heartsick groans
Mist-like infold me from the search of eyes.

72–73 Romeo will hide only if his sighs create a mist and shield him from sight.

[*knock*]

Friar Laurence. Hark, how they knock! Who's there? Romeo, arise;
75   Thou wilt be taken.—Stay awhile!—Stand up;

[*knock*]

Run to my study.—By-and-by!—God's will,
What simpleness is this.—I come, I come!

[*knock*]

Who knocks so hard? Whence come you? What's your will?

Nurse [*within*]. Let me come in, and you shall know my errand.
80   I come from Lady Juliet.

Friar Laurence.   Welcome then.

[*Enter* Nurse.]

Nurse. O holy friar, O, tell me, holy friar,
Where is my lady's lord, where's Romeo?

Friar Laurence. There on the ground, with his own tears made drunk.

Nurse. O, he is even in my mistress' case,
85   Just in her case! O woeful sympathy!
Piteous predicament! Even so lies she,
Blubb'ring and weeping, weeping and blubbering.
Stand up, stand up! Stand, an you be a man.
For Juliet's sake, for her sake, rise and stand!
90   Why should you fall into so deep an O?

84–85 he is even ... her case: He is acting the same way that Juliet is.

90 into so deep an O: into such deep grief.

Romeo [*rises*]. Nurse—

Nurse. Ah sir! ah sir! Well, death's the end of all.

Romeo. Spakest thou of Juliet? How is it with her?
Doth not she think me an old murderer,
95   Now I have stained the childhood of our joy
With blood removed but little from her own?
Where is she? and how doth she? and what says
My concealed lady to our canceled love?

96 blood ... from her own: the blood of a close relative of hers.

98 concealed lady: secret bride.

Nurse. O, she says nothing, sir, but weeps and weeps;
100   And now falls on her bed, and then starts up,
And Tybalt calls; and then on Romeo cries,
And then down falls again.

Romeo. As if that name,
Shot from the deadly level of a gun,
Did murder her; as that name's cursed hand
105 Murdered her kinsman. O tell me, friar, tell me,
In what vile part of this anatomy
Doth my name lodge? Tell me, that I may sack
The hateful mansion.

[*draws his dagger*]

Friar Laurence. Hold thy desperate hand.
Art thou a man? Thy form cries out thou art;
110 Thy tears are womanish, thy wild acts denote
The unreasonable fury of a beast.
Unseemly woman in a seeming man!
Or ill-beseeming beast in seeming both!
Thou hast amazed me. By my holy order,
115 I thought thy disposition better tempered.
Hast thou slain Tybalt? Wilt thou slay thyself?
And slay thy lady too that lives in thee,
By doing damned hate upon thyself?
Why railst thou on thy birth, the heaven, and earth?
120 Since birth and heaven and earth, all three do meet
In thee at once; which thou at once wouldst lose.
Fie, fie, thou shamest thy shape, thy love, thy wit,
Which, like a usurer, aboundst in all,
And usest none in that true use indeed
125 Which should bedeck thy shape, thy love, thy wit.
Thy noble shape is but a form of wax,
Digressing from the valor of a man;
Thy dear love sworn but hollow perjury,
Killing that love which thou hast vowed to cherish;
130 Thy wit, that ornament to shape and love,
Misshapen in the conduct of them both,
Like powder in a skilless soldier's flask,
Is set afire by thine own ignorance,
And thou dismembered with thine own defense.
135 What, rouse thee, man! Thy Juliet is alive,
For whose dear sake thou wast but lately dead.
There art thou happy. Tybalt would kill thee,
But thou slewest Tybalt. There art thou happy.
The law, that threatened death, becomes thy friend
140 And turns it to exile. There art thou happy.
A pack of blessings light upon thy back;
Happiness courts thee in her best array;
But, like a misbehaved and sullen wench,
Thou poutst upon thy fortune and thy love.

102 that name: the name Romeo.

106–108 in what vile part . . . mansion: Romeo asks where in his body (**anatomy**) his name can be found so that he can cut the name out.

108–125 Hold thy . . . bedeck thy shape, thy love, thy wit: You're not acting like a man. Would you send your soul to hell by committing suicide (**doing damned hate upon thyself**)? Why do you curse your birth, heaven, and earth? You are refusing to make good use of your advantages, just as a miser refuses to spend his money.

126–134 The friar explains how by acting as he is, Romeo is misusing his shape (his outer form or body), his love, and his wit (his mind or intellect).

145 Take heed, take heed, for such die miserable.
Go get thee to thy love, as was decreed,
Ascend her chamber, hence and comfort her.
But look thou stay not till the watch be set,
For then thou canst not pass to Mantua,
150 Where thou shalt live till we can find a time
To blaze your marriage, reconcile your friends,
Beg pardon of the Prince, and call thee back
With twenty hundred thousand times more joy
Than thou wentst forth in lamentation.
155 Go before, nurse. Commend me to thy lady,
And bid her hasten all the house to bed,
Which heavy sorrow makes them apt unto.
Romeo is coming.

Nurse. O Lord, I could have stayed here all the night
160 To hear good counsel. O, what learning is!
My lord, I'll tell my lady you will come.

Romeo. Do so, and bid my sweet prepare to chide.

[Nurse *offers to go and turns again.*]

Nurse. Here is a ring she bid me give you, sir.
Hie you, make haste, for it grows very late.

[*Exit.*]

165 **Romeo.** How well my comfort is revived by this!

Friar Laurence. Go hence; good night; and here stands all your
state:
Either be gone before the watch be set,
Or by the break of day disguised from hence.
Sojourn in Mantua. I'll find out your man,
170 And he shall signify from time to time
Every good hap to you that chances here.
Give me thy hand. 'Tis late. Farewell; good night.

Romeo. But that a joy past joy calls out on me,
It were a grief so brief to part with thee.
175 Farewell.

[*Exeunt.*]

Scene 4 *Capulet's house.*

[*Enter* Capulet, Lady Capulet, *and* Paris.]

Capulet. Things have fall'n out, sir, so unluckily
That we have had no time to move our daughter.
Look you, she loved her kinsman Tybalt dearly,
And so did I. Well, we were born to die.

**148–149 look...
Mantua:** Leave before
the guards take their
places at the city gates;
otherwise you will not
be able to escape.

151 blaze...friends:
announce your marriage
and get the families
(**friends**) to stop
feuding.

162 bid...chide: Tell
Juliet to get ready to
scold me for the way I've
behaved.

**166–171 and here...
here:** Either leave before
the night watchmen go
on duty, or get out at
dawn in a disguise. Stay
awhile in Mantua. I'll find
your servant and send
messages to you about
what good things are
happening here.

**1–2 Things have...our
daughter:** Such terrible
things have happened
that we haven't had time
to persuade (**move**)
Juliet to think about
your marriage proposal.

5 'Tis very late; she'll not come down tonight.
   I promise you, but for your company,
   I would have been abed an hour ago.

   Paris. These times of woe afford no time to woo.
   Madam, good night. Commend me to your daughter.

8 Sad times are not good times for talking of marriage.

10 **Lady Capulet.** I will, and know her mind early tomorrow;
   Tonight she's mewed up to her heaviness.

11 Tonight she is locked up with her sorrow.

   [Paris *offers to go and* Capulet *calls him again.*]

   Capulet. Sir Paris, I will make a desperate tender
   Of my child's love. I think she will be ruled
   In all respects by me; nay more, I doubt it not.

12 **desperate tender:** bold offer.

15 Wife, go you to her ere you go to bed;
   Acquaint her here of my son Paris' love
   And bid her (mark you me?) on Wednesday next—
   But, soft! what day is this?

   Paris.   Monday, my lord.

   Capulet. Monday! ha, ha! Well, Wednesday is too soon.
20 A Thursday let it be—a Thursday, tell her,
   She shall be married to this noble earl.

Will you be ready? Do you like this haste?
We'll keep no great ado—a friend or two;
For hark you, Tybalt being slain so late,
25 It may be thought we held him carelessly,
Being our kinsman, if we revel much.
Therefore we'll have some half a dozen friends,
And there an end. But what say you to Thursday?

Paris. My lord, I would that Thursday were tomorrow.

30 **Capulet.** Well, get you gone. A Thursday be it then.
Go you to Juliet ere you go to bed;
Prepare her, wife, against this wedding day.
Farewell, my lord.—Light to my chamber, ho!
Afore me, it is so very very late
35 That we may call it early by-and-by.
Good night.

[*Exeunt.*]

Scene 5 *Capulet's orchard.*

[*Enter* Romeo *and* Juliet *above, at the window.*]

Juliet. Wilt thou be gone? It is not yet near day.
It was the nightingale, and not the lark,
That pierced the fearful hollow of thine ear.
Nightly she sings on yond pomegranate tree.
5 Believe me, love, it was the nightingale.

Romeo. It was the lark, the herald of the morn;
No nightingale. Look, love, what envious streaks
Do lace the severing clouds in yonder East.
Night's candles are burnt out, and jocund day
10 Stands tiptoe on the misty mountain tops.
I must be gone and live, or stay and die.

Juliet. Yond light is not daylight; I know it, I.
It is some meteor that the sun exhales
To be to thee this night a torchbearer
15 And light thee on thy way to Mantua.
Therefore stay yet; thou needst not to be gone.

Romeo. Let me be ta'en, let me be put to death.
I am content, so thou wilt have it so.
I'll say yon grey is not the morning's eye,
20 'Tis but the pale reflex of Cynthia's brow;
Nor that is not the lark whose notes do beat
The vaulty heaven so high above our heads.
I have more care to stay than will to go.

23 **no great ado:** no big festivity.

34–35 **it is ... by-and-by:** It's so late at night that soon we'll be calling it early in the morning.

2 **It was ... lark:** The nightingale sings at night; the lark sings in the morning.

9 **Night's candles:** stars.

12–25 Juliet continues to pretend it is night to keep Romeo from leaving. Romeo says he'll stay if Juliet wishes it, even if it means death.

20 **Cynthia's brow:** Cynthia is another name for Diana, the Roman goddess of the moon. She was often pictured with a crescent moon on her forehead.

Come, death, and welcome! Juliet wills it so.
25 How is't, my soul? Let's talk; it is not day.

Juliet. It is, it is! Hie hence, be gone, away!
It is the lark that sings so out of tune,
Straining harsh discords and unpleasing sharps.
Some say the lark makes sweet division;
30 This doth not so, for she divideth us.
Some say the lark and loathed toad changed eyes;
O, now I would they had changed voices too,
Since arm from arm that voice doth us affray,
Hunting thee hence with hunt's-up to the day!
35 O, now be gone! More light and light it grows.

Romeo. More light and light—more dark and dark our woes!

[*Enter* Nurse, *hastily.*]

Nurse. Madam!

Juliet. Nurse?

Nurse. Your lady mother is coming to your chamber.
40 The day is broke; be wary, look about.

[*Exit.*]

Juliet. Then, window, let day in, and let life out.

Romeo. Farewell, farewell! One kiss, and I'll descend.

[*He starts down the ladder.*]

26 Romeo's mention of death frightens Juliet, and she urges him to leave quickly.

29 division: melody.

31–34 I wish the lark had the voice of the hated (**loathed**) toad, since its voice is frightening us apart and acting as a morning song for hunters (**hunt's-up**).

Juliet. Art thou gone so, my lord, my love, my friend?
I must hear from thee every day in the hour,
45 For in a minute there are many days.
O, by this count I shall be much in years
Ere I again behold my Romeo!

46 **much in years:** very old.

Romeo. Farewell!
I will omit no opportunity
50 That may convey my greetings, love, to thee.

Juliet. O, thinkst thou we shall ever meet again?

Romeo. I doubt it not; and all these woes shall serve
For sweet discourses in our time to come.

Juliet. O God, I have an ill-divining soul!
55 Methinks I see thee, now thou art below,
As one dead in the bottom of a tomb.
Either my eyesight fails, or thou lookst pale.

54–56 **I have . . . tomb:** Juliet sees an evil vision of the future.

Romeo. And trust me, love, in my eye so do you.
Dry sorrow drinks our blood. Adieu! adieu!

[*Exit.*]

60 **Juliet.** O Fortune, Fortune! all men call thee fickle.
If thou art fickle, what dost thou with him
That is renowned for faith? Be fickle, Fortune,
For then I hope thou wilt not keep him long
But send him back.

59 **Dry . . . blood:** People believed that sorrow drained the blood from the heart, causing a sad person to look pale.

60–62 **fickle:** changeable in loyalty or affection. Juliet asks fickle Fortune why it has anything to do with Romeo, who is the opposite of fickle.

Lady Capulet [*within*]. Ho, daughter! are you up?

65 **Juliet.** Who is't that calls? It is my lady mother.
Is she not down so late, or up so early?
What unaccustomed cause procures her hither?

67 **What . . . hither:** What unusual reason brings her here?

[*Enter* Lady Capulet.]

Lady Capulet. Why, how now, Juliet?

Juliet.   Madam, I am not well.

Lady Capulet. Evermore weeping for your cousin's death?
70 What, wilt thou wash him from his grave with tears?
An if thou couldst, thou couldst not make him live.
Therefore have done. Some grief shows much of love;
But much of grief shows still some want of wit.

72–73 **have . . . wit:** Stop crying (**have done**). A little grief is evidence of love, while too much grief shows a lack of good sense (**want of wit**).

Juliet. Yet let me weep for such a feeling loss.

75 **Lady Capulet.** So shall you feel the loss, but not the friend
Which you weep for.

Juliet.   Feeling so the loss,
I cannot choose but ever weep the friend.

Lady Capulet. Well, girl, thou weepst not so much for his death
As that the villain lives which slaughtered him.

80 **Juliet.** What villain, madam?

Lady Capulet.   That same villain Romeo.

Juliet [*aside*]. Villain and he be many miles asunder.—
God pardon him! I do, with all my heart;
And yet no man like he doth grieve my heart.

Lady Capulet. That is because the traitor murderer lives.

85 **Juliet.** Ay, madam, from the reach of these my hands.
Would none but I might venge my cousin's death!

Lady Capulet. We will have vengeance for it, fear thou not.
Then weep no more. I'll send to one in Mantua,
Where that same banished runagate doth live,
90 Shall give him such an unaccustomed dram
That he shall soon keep Tybalt company;
And then I hope thou wilt be satisfied.

Juliet. Indeed I never shall be satisfied
With Romeo till I behold him—dead—
95 Is my poor heart so for a kinsman vexed.
Madam, if you could find out but a man
To bear a poison, I would temper it;
That Romeo should, upon receipt thereof,
Soon sleep in quiet. O, how my heart abhors
100 To hear him named and cannot come to him,
To wreak the love I bore my cousin Tybalt
Upon his body that hath slaughtered him!

Lady Capulet. Find thou the means, and I'll find such a man.
But now I'll tell thee joyful tidings, girl.

105 **Juliet.** And joy comes well in such a needy time.
What are they, I beseech your ladyship?

Lady Capulet. Well, well, thou hast a careful father, child;
One who, to put thee from thy heaviness,
Hath sorted out a sudden day of joy
110 That thou expects not nor I looked not for.

Juliet. Madam, in happy time! What day is that?

Lady Capulet. Marry, my child, early next Thursday morn
The gallant, young, and noble gentleman,
The County Paris, at Saint Peter's Church,
115 Shall happily make thee there a joyful bride.

81–102 In these lines Juliet's words have double meanings. To avoid lying to her mother, she chooses her words carefully. They can mean what her mother wants to hear—or what Juliet really has on her mind.

89 runagate: runaway.

90 unaccustomed dram: poison.

93–102 Dead could refer either to Romeo or to Juliet's heart. Juliet says that if her mother could find someone to carry a poison to Romeo, she would mix (**temper**) it herself.

Juliet. Now by Saint Peter's Church, and Peter too,
He shall not make me there a joyful bride!
I wonder at this haste, that I must wed
Ere he that should be husband comes to woo.
120 I pray you tell my lord and father, madam,
I will not marry yet; and when I do, I swear
It shall be Romeo, whom you know I hate,
Rather than Paris. These are news indeed!

Lady Capulet. Here comes your father. Tell him so yourself,
125 And see how he will take it at your hands.

[*Enter* Capulet *and* Nurse.]

Capulet. When the sun sets the air doth drizzle dew,
But for the sunset of my brother's son
It rains downright.
How now? a conduit, girl? What, still in tears?
130 Evermore show'ring? In one little body
Thou counterfeitst a bark, a sea, a wind:
For still thy eyes, which I may call the sea,
Do ebb and flow with tears; the bark thy body is,
Sailing in this salt flood; the winds, thy sighs,
135 Who, raging with thy tears and they with them,
Without a sudden calm will overset
Thy tempest-tossed body. How now, wife?
Have you delivered to her our decree?

127 the sunset . . . son: the death of Tybalt.

129–137 conduit: fountain. Capulet compares Juliet to a boat (**bark**), an ocean, and the wind because of her excessive crying.

Lady Capulet. Ay, sir; but she will none, she gives you thanks.
140 I would the fool were married to her grave!

Capulet. Soft! take me with you, take me with you, wife.
How? Will she none? Doth she not give us thanks?
Is she not proud? Doth she not count her blest,
Unworthy as she is, that we have wrought
145 So worthy a gentleman to be her bridegroom?

141 take me with you: let me understand you.

146–148 Not proud . . . meant love: I'm not pleased, but I am grateful for your intentions.

Juliet. Not proud you have, but thankful that you have.
Proud can I never be of what I hate,
But thankful even for hate that is meant love.

Capulet. How, how, how, how, choplogic? What is this?
150 "Proud"—and "I thank you"—and "I thank you not"—
And yet "not proud"? Mistress minion you,
Thank me no thankings, nor proud me no prouds,
But fettle your fine joints 'gainst Thursday next
To go with Paris to Saint Peter's Church,
155 Or I will drag thee on a hurdle thither.
Out, you green-sickness carrion! out, you baggage!
You tallow-face!

149–157 Capulet calls Juliet a person who argues over fine points (**choplogic**) and a spoiled child (**minion**). He tells her to prepare herself (**fettle your fine joints**) for the wedding or he'll haul her there in a cart for criminals (**hurdle**). He calls her a piece of dead flesh (**green-sickness carrion**) and a coward (**tallow-face**).

Lady Capulet. Fie, fie; what, are you mad?

Juliet. Good father, I beseech you on my knees,

[*She kneels down.*]

Hear me with patience but to speak a word.

160 **Capulet.** Hang thee, young baggage! disobedient wretch!
I tell thee what—get thee to church a Thursday
Or never after look me in the face.
Speak not, reply not, do not answer me!
My fingers itch. Wife, we scarce thought us blest
165 That God had lent us but this only child;
But now I see this one is one too much,
And that we have a curse in having her.
Out on her, hilding!

Nurse.   God in heaven bless her!
You are to blame, my lord, to rate her so.

170 **Capulet.** And why, my Lady Wisdom? Hold your tongue,
Good Prudence. Smatter with your gossips, go!

Nurse. I speak no treason.

Capulet.   O, God-i-god-en!

Nurse. May not one speak?

Capulet.   Peace, you mumbling fool!
Utter your gravity o'er a gossip's bowl,
175 For here we need it not.

Lady Capulet.   You are too hot.

Capulet. God's bread! it makes me mad. Day, night, late, early,
At home, abroad, alone, in company,
Waking or sleeping, still my care hath been
To have her matched; and having now provided
180 A gentleman of princely parentage,
Of fair demesnes, youthful, and nobly trained,
Stuffed, as they say, with honorable parts,
Proportioned as one's thought would wish a man—
And then to have a wretched puling fool,
185 A whining mammet, in her fortunes tender,
To answer "I'll not wed, I cannot love;
I am too young, I pray you pardon me"!
But, an you will not wed, I'll pardon you.
Graze where you will, you shall not house with me.
190 Look to't, think on't; I do not use to jest.
Thursday is near; lay hand on heart, advise:
An you be mine, I'll give you to my friend;

164 My fingers itch: I feel like hitting you.

168 hilding: a good-for-nothing person.

171 smatter: chatter.

174 Utter . . . bowl: Save your words of wisdom for a gathering of gossips.

179 matched: married.

184 puling: crying.
185 mammet: doll.

189–195 Capulet swears that he'll kick Juliet out and cut her off financially if she refuses to marry.

An you be not, hang, beg, starve, die in the streets,
For, by my soul, I'll ne'er acknowledge thee,
195 Nor what is mine shall never do thee good.
Trust to't. Bethink you. I'll not be forsworn.

[*Exit.*]

Juliet. Is there no pity sitting in the clouds
That sees into the bottom of my grief?
O sweet my mother, cast me not away!
200 Delay this marriage for a month, a week;
Or if you do not, make the bridal bed
In that dim monument where Tybalt lies.

Lady Capulet. Talk not to me, for I'll not speak a word.
Do as thou wilt, for I have done with thee.

[*Exit.*]

205 **Juliet.** O God!—O nurse, how shall this be prevented?
My husband is on earth, my faith in heaven.
How shall that faith return again to earth
Unless that husband send it me from heaven
By leaving earth? Comfort me, counsel me.
210 Alack, alack, that heaven should practice stratagems
Upon so soft a subject as myself!
What sayst thou? Hast thou not a word of joy?
Some comfort, nurse.

196 I'll not be forsworn: I will not break my promise to Paris.

207–211 Juliet is worried about the sin of being married to two men. She asks how heaven can play such tricks (**practice stratagems**) on her.

Nurse. Faith, here it is.
Romeo is banish'd; and all the world to nothing
215 That he dares ne'er come back to challenge you;
Or if he do, it needs must be by stealth.
Then, since the case so stands as now it doth,
I think it best you married with the County.
O, he's a lovely gentleman!
220 Romeo's a dishclout to him. An eagle, madam,
Hath not so green, so quick, so fair an eye
As Paris hath. Beshrew my very heart,
I think you are happy in this second match,
For it excels your first; or if it did not,
225 Your first is dead—or 'twere as good he were
As living here and you no use of him.

Juliet. Speakst thou this from thy heart?

Nurse. And from my soul too; else beshrew them both.

Juliet. Amen!

230 **Nurse.** What?

Juliet. Well, thou hast comforted me marvelous much.
Go in; and tell my lady I am gone,
Having displeased my father, to Laurence' cell,
To make confession and to be absolved.

235 **Nurse.** Marry, I will; and this is wisely done.

[*Exit.*]

Juliet. Ancient damnation! O most wicked fiend!
Is it more sin to wish me thus forsworn,
Or to dispraise my lord with that same tongue
Which she hath praised him with above compare
240 So many thousand times? Go, counselor!
Thou and my bosom henceforth shall be twain.
I'll to the friar to know his remedy.
If all else fail, myself have power to die.

[*Exit.*]

222 beshrew: curse.

223–225 This new marriage will be better than the first, which is as good as over.

229 Amen: I agree—that is, curse your heart and soul.

236–238 Ancient damnation: old devil; **dispraise:** criticize.

241 Thou ... twain: I'll no longer tell you my secrets.

COLLABORATIVE DISCUSSION Discuss with a partner the chain of events that begins to turn the story of Romeo and Juliet into a tragedy. Do you believe the main characters are making mistakes that will lead them down a tragic path? Cite textual evidence to support your ideas.

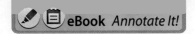

Analyzing the Text

Cite Text Evidence Support your responses with evidence from the selection.

1. **Interpret** What is the meaning of Mercutio's repeated curse, "A plague o' both your houses!" (Scene 1, lines 85, 93)? What might this curse foreshadow?

2. **Evaluate** What is Romeo's motivation for killing Tybalt? Is his action justified or a mistake? Explain your response.

3. **Cite Evidence** In what ways do Romeo and Juliet need the help of Friar Laurence and the Nurse in order to save their love and move forward? Support your response with evidence from the text.

4. **Analyze** In Scene 5, Lord Capulet becomes enraged when Juliet says she will not marry Paris. In what way are his words and actions in this scene like those of Romeo and Juliet? What are the likely consequences of his actions?

5. **Interpret** Explore how Shakespeare continues to use the light/dark or day/night motif in Scene 5, lines 1–35. Why does Juliet want the darkness to continue?

6. **Analyze** How and why does Juliet's relationship with her nurse change? Do you believe Juliet is justified in her feelings toward the nurse? Explain, citing details from the text.

PERFORMANCE TASK

Writing Activity: Journal Entries Use two brief writing tasks to explore the parallel feelings of despair Romeo and Juliet feel in Act III.

1. Write a one-page journal entry from the point of view of Juliet when she learns of the death of Tybalt.

2. Write a one-page journal entry from the point of view of Romeo when he is at the Friar's cell awaiting exile.

Base both pieces of writing on evidence from the text.

AS YOU READ Note the details of the plan Juliet and Friar Laurence initiate in this act. Pay attention to the reactions of other characters as the plan unfolds. Write down any questions you generate during reading.

ACT IV

Scene 1 *Friar Laurence's cell.*

[*Enter* Friar Laurence *and* Paris.]

Friar Laurence. On Thursday, sir? The time is very short.

Paris. My father Capulet will have it so,
And I am nothing slow to slack his haste.

Friar Laurence. You say you do not know the lady's mind.
5   Uneven is the course; I like it not.

Paris. Immoderately she weeps for Tybalt's death,
And therefore have I little talked of love;
For Venus smiles not in a house of tears.
Now, sir, her father counts it dangerous
10   That she do give her sorrow so much sway,
And in his wisdom hastes our marriage
To stop the inundation of her tears,
Which, too much minded by herself alone,
May be put from her by society.
15   Now do you know the reason of this haste.

Friar Laurence [*aside*]. I would I knew not why it should be
   slowed.—
Look, sir, here comes the lady toward my cell.

[*Enter* Juliet.]

Paris. Happily met, my lady and my wife!

Juliet. That may be, sir, when I may be a wife.

20   **Paris.** That may be must be, love, on Thursday next.

Juliet. What must be shall be.

Friar Laurence.   That's a certain text.

Paris. Come you to make confession to this father?

Juliet. To answer that, I should confess to you.

Paris. Do not deny to him that you love me.

25   **Juliet.** I will confess to you that I love him.

Paris. So will ye, I am sure, that you love me.

Juliet. If I do so, it will be of more price,
Being spoke behind your back, than to your face.

2–3 My...haste: Capulet is eager to have the wedding on Thursday and so am I.

4–5 You...course: You don't know how Juliet feels about this. It's a very uncertain (**uneven**) plan.

13–14 Which... society: which, thought about too much by her in privacy, may be put from her mind if she is forced to be with others.

Paris. Poor soul, thy face is much abused with tears.

30 **Juliet.** The tears have got small victory by that,
For it was bad enough before their spite.

Paris. Thou wrongst it more than tears with that report.

Juliet. That is no slander, sir, which is a truth;
And what I spake, I spake it to my face.

35 **Paris.** Thy face is mine, and thou hast slandered it.

Juliet. It may be so, for it is not mine own.
Are you at leisure, holy father, now,
Or shall I come to you at evening mass?

Friar Laurence. My leisure serves me, pensive daughter, now.
40 My lord, we must entreat the time alone.

Paris. God shield I should disturb devotion!
Juliet, on Thursday early will I rouse ye.
Till then, adieu, and keep this holy kiss.

[*Exit.*]

Juliet. O, shut the door! and when thou hast done so,
45 Come weep with me—past hope, past cure, past help!

Friar Laurence. Ah, Juliet, I already know thy grief;
It strains me past the compass of my wits.
I hear thou must, and nothing may prorogue it,
On Thursday next be married to this County.

50 **Juliet.** Tell me not, friar, that thou hearst of this,
Unless thou tell me how I may prevent it.
If in thy wisdom thou canst give no help,
Do thou but call my resolution wise
And with this knife I'll help it presently.
55 God joined my heart and Romeo's, thou our hands;
And ere this hand, by thee to Romeo's sealed,
Shall be the label to another deed,
Or my true heart with treacherous revolt
Turn to another, this shall slay them both.
60 Therefore, out of thy long-experienced time,
Give me some present counsel; or, behold,
'Twixt my extremes and me this bloody knife
Shall play the umpire, arbitrating that
Which the commission of thy years and art
65 Could to no issue of true honor bring.
Be not so long to speak. I long to die
If what thou speakst speak not of remedy.

Friar Laurence. Hold, daughter, I do spy a kind of hope,
Which craves as desperate an execution

**30–31 The tears . . .
spite:** The tears haven't
ruined my face; it wasn't
all that beautiful before
they did their damage.

35 Paris says he owns
Juliet's face (since she
will soon marry him).
Insulting her face, he
says, insults him, its
owner.

47–48 compass: limit;
prorogue: postpone.

52–53 If in . . . wise: If
you can't find a way to
help me, at least agree
that my plan is wise.

**56–67 And ere this
hand . . . of remedy:**
Before I sign another
wedding agreement
(**deed**), I will use this
knife to kill myself. If
you, with your years
of experience (**long-
experienced time**),
can't help me, I'll end my
sufferings (**extremes**)
and solve the problem
myself.

70　As that is desperate which we would prevent.
　　If, rather than to marry County Paris,
　　Thou hast the strength of will to slay thyself,
　　Then is it likely thou wilt undertake
　　A thing like death to chide away this shame,
75　That copest with death himself to scape from it;
　　And, if thou darest, I'll give thee remedy.

**71–76 If, rather than
... remedy:** If you are
desperate enough to kill
yourself, then you'll be
daring enough to try the
deathlike solution that I
propose.

　　Juliet. O, bid me leap, rather than marry Paris,
　　From off the battlements of yonder tower,
　　Or walk in thievish ways, or bid me lurk
80　Where serpents are; chain me with roaring bears,
　　Or shut me nightly in a charnel house,
　　O'ercovered quite with dead men's rattling bones,
　　With reeky shanks and yellow chapless skulls;
　　Or bid me go into a new-made grave
85　And hide me with a dead man in his shroud—
　　Things that, to hear them told, have made me tremble—
　　And I will do it without fear or doubt,
　　To live an unstained wife to my sweet love.

77–88 Juliet lists the
things she would do
rather than marry
Paris. **charnel house:** a
storehouse for bones;
reeky shanks: stinking
bones; **chapless:**
without jaws.

　　Friar Laurence. Hold, then. Go home, be merry, give consent
90　To marry Paris. Wednesday is tomorrow.
　　Tomorrow night look that thou lie alone:
　　Let not the nurse lie with thee in thy chamber.
　　Take thou this vial, being then in bed,
　　And this distilled liquor drink thou off;

93 vial: small bottle.

95　When presently through all thy veins shall run
　　A cold and drowsy humor; for no pulse
　　Shall keep his native progress, but surcease;
　　No warmth, no breath, shall testify thou livest;
　　The roses in thy lips and cheeks shall fade
100　To paly ashes, thy eyes' windows fall
　　Like death when he shuts up the day of life;
　　Each part, deprived of supple government,
　　Shall, stiff and stark and cold, appear like death;
　　And in this borrowed likeness of shrunk death
105　Thou shalt continue two-and-forty hours,
　　And then awake as from a pleasant sleep.
　　Now, when the bridegroom in the morning comes
　　To rouse thee from thy bed, there art thou dead.
　　Then, as the manner of our country is,
110　In thy best robes uncovered on the bier
　　Thou shalt be borne to that same ancient vault
　　Where all the kindred of the Capulets lie.
　　In the meantime, against thou shalt awake,
　　Shall Romeo by my letters know our drift;

96–106 humor: liquid;
**no pulse ... pleasant
sleep:** Your pulse will
stop (**surcease**), and you
will turn cold, pale, and
stiff, as if you were dead;
this condition will last
for 42 hours.

**111–112 same ancient
vault ... lie:** same
ancient tomb where all
members of the Capulet
family are buried.

114 drift: plan.

115 And hither shall he come; and he and I
Will watch thy waking, and that very night
Shall Romeo bear thee hence to Mantua.
And this shall free thee from this present shame,
If no inconstant toy nor womanish fear
120 Abate thy valor in the acting it.

119–120 **inconstant toy:** foolish whim; **abate thy valor:** weaken your courage.

Juliet. Give me, give me! O, tell me not of fear!

Friar Laurence. Hold! Get you gone, be strong and prosperous
In this resolve. I'll send a friar with speed
To Mantua, with my letters to thy lord.

125 **Juliet.** Love give me strength! and strength shall help afford.
Farewell, dear father.

[*Exeunt.*]

Scene 2 *Capulet's house.*

[*Enter* Capulet, Lady Capulet, Nurse, *and* Servingmen.]

Capulet. So many guests invite as here are writ.

[*Exit a* Servingman.]

Sirrah, go hire me twenty cunning cooks.

Servingman. You shall have none ill, sir; for I'll try if they can
lick their fingers.

5 **Capulet.** How canst thou try them so?

Servingman. Marry, sir, 'tis an ill cook that cannot lick his own
fingers. Therefore he that cannot lick his fingers goes not with
me.

1–8 Capulet is having a cheerful conversation with his servants about the wedding preparations. One servant assures him that he will test (**try**) the cooks he hires by making them taste their own food (**lick their fingers**).

Capulet. Go, begone.

[*Exit* Servingman.]

10 We shall be much unfurnished for this time.
What, is my daughter gone to Friar Laurence?

10 unfurnished: unprepared.

Nurse. Ay, forsooth.

Capulet. Well, he may chance to do some good on her.
A peevish self-willed harlotry it is.

14 A silly, stubborn girl she is.

[*Enter* Juliet.]

15 **Nurse.** See where she comes from shrift with merry look.

Capulet. How now, my headstrong? Where have you been
gadding?

Juliet. Where I have learnt me to repent the sin
Of disobedient opposition
To you and your behests, and am enjoined

19 behests: orders; **enjoined:** commanded.

20 By holy Laurence to fall prostrate here
To beg your pardon. Pardon, I beseech you!
Henceforward I am ever ruled by you.

Capulet. Send for the County. Go tell him of this.
I'll have this knot knit up tomorrow morning.

24 I'll have this wedding scheduled for tomorrow morning.

25 **Juliet.** I met the youthful lord at Laurence' cell
And gave him what becomed love I might,
Not stepping o'er the bounds of modesty.

Capulet. Why, I am glad on't. This is well. Stand up.
This is as't should be. Let me see the County.
30 Ay, marry, go, I say, and fetch him hither.
Now, afore God, this reverend holy friar,
All our whole city is much bound to him.

Juliet. Nurse, will you go with me into my closet
To help me sort such needful ornaments
35 As you think fit to furnish me tomorrow?

Lady Capulet. No, not till Thursday. There is time enough.

36–39 Lady Capulet urges her husband to wait until Thursday as originally planned. She needs time to get food (**provision**) ready for the wedding party.

Capulet. Go, nurse, go with her. We'll to church tomorrow.

[*Exeunt* Juliet *and* Nurse.]

Lady Capulet. We shall be short in our provision.
'Tis now near night.

Capulet.   Tush, I will stir about,

39–46 Capulet is so set on Wednesday that he promises to make the arrangements himself.

40 And all things shall be well, I warrant thee, wife.
Go thou to Juliet, help to deck up her.
I'll not to bed tonight; let me alone.
I'll play the housewife for this once. What, ho!
They are all forth; well, I will walk myself
45 To County Paris, to prepare him up
Against tomorrow. My heart is wondrous light,
Since this same wayward girl is so reclaimed.

[*Exeunt.*]

Scene 3 *Juliet's bedroom.*

[*Enter* Juliet *and* Nurse.]

Juliet. Ay, those attires are best; but, gentle nurse,
I pray thee leave me to myself tonight;
For I have need of many orisons
To move the heavens to smile upon my state,
5 Which, well thou knowest, is cross and full of sin.

3 orisons: prayers.

[*Enter* Lady Capulet.]

Lady Capulet. What, are you busy, ho? Need you my help?

Juliet. No madam; we have culled such necessaries
As are behooveful for our state tomorrow.
So please you, let me now be left alone,
10 And let the nurse this night sit up with you;
For I am sure you have your hands full all
In this so sudden business.

Lady Capulet.   Good night.
Get thee to bed and rest, for thou hast need.

[*Exeunt* Lady Capulet *and* Nurse.]

Juliet. Farewell! God knows when we shall meet again.
15 I have a faint cold fear thrills through my veins
That almost freezes up the heat of life.
I'll call them back again to comfort me.
Nurse!—What should she do here?
My dismal scene I needs must act alone.
20 Come, vial.
What if this mixture do not work at all?
Shall I be married then tomorrow morning?
No, no! This shall forbid it. Lie thou there.

[*lays down a dagger*]

What if it be a poison which the friar
25 Subtly hath ministered to have me dead,
Lest in this marriage he should be dishonored
Because he married me before to Romeo?
I fear it is; and yet methinks it should not,
For he hath still been tried a holy man.

30　How if, when I am laid into the tomb,
　　I wake before the time that Romeo
　　Come to redeem me? There's a fearful point!
　　Shall I not then be stifled in the vault,
　　To whose foul mouth no healthsome air breathes in,
35　And there die strangled ere my Romeo comes?
　　Or, if I live, is it not very like
　　The horrible conceit of death and night,
　　Together with the terror of the place—
　　As in a vault, an ancient receptacle
40　Where for this many hundred years the bones
　　Of all my buried ancestors are packed;
　　Where bloody Tybalt, yet but green in earth,
　　Lies fest'ring in his shroud; where, as they say,
　　At some hours in the night spirits resort—
45　Alack, alack, is it not like that I,
　　So early waking—what with loathsome smells,
　　And shrieks like mandrakes torn out of the earth,
　　That living mortals, hearing them, run mad—
　　O, if I wake, shall I not be distraught,
50　Environed with all these hideous fears,
　　And madly play with my forefathers' joints,
　　And pluck the mangled Tybalt from his shroud,
　　And, in this rage, with some great kinsman's bone
　　As with a club dash out my desp'rate brains?
55　O, look! methinks I see my cousin's ghost
　　Seeking out Romeo, that did spit his body
　　Upon a rapier's point. Stay, Tybalt, stay!
　　Romeo, I come! this do I drink to thee.

[*She drinks and falls upon her bed within the curtains.*]

Scene 4 *Capulet's house.*

[*Enter* Lady Capulet *and* Nurse.]

Lady Capulet. Hold, take these keys and fetch more spices, nurse.

Nurse. They call for dates and quinces in the pastry.

[*Enter* Capulet.]

Capulet. Come, stir, stir, stir! The second cock hath crowed,
　　The curfew bell hath rung, 'tis three o'clock.
5　Look to the baked meats, good Angelica;
　　Spare not for cost.

Nurse.　　　　　　Go, you cot-quean, go,
　　Get you to bed! Faith, you'll be sick tomorrow
　　For this night's watching.

36–43 Juliet fears the vision (**conceit**) she might have on waking in the family tomb and seeing the rotting body of Tybalt.

45–54 She fears that the smells together with the sounds of ghosts screaming might make her lose her mind and commit bizarre acts. Mandrake root was thought to look like the human form and to scream when pulled from the ground.

57 stay: stop.

2 pastry: the room where baking is done.

5 Angelica: In his happy mood, Capulet calls the nurse by her name.

6 cot-quean: a "cottage quean," or housewife. This is a joke about Capulet doing women's work (arranging the party).

Capulet. No, not a whit. What, I have watched ere now
10 All night for lesser cause, and ne'er been sick.

Lady Capulet. Ay, you have been a mouse-hunt in your time;
But I will watch you from such watching now.

[*Exeunt* Lady Capulet *and* Nurse.]

Capulet. A jealous hood, a jealous hood!

[*Enter three or four* Servants, *with spits and logs and baskets.*]

Now, fellow,
What is there?

15 **First Servant.** Things for the cook, sir; but I know not what.

Capulet. Make haste, make haste. [*Exit* Servant.] Sirrah, fetch
drier logs.
Call Peter; he will show thee where they are.

Second Servant. I have a head, sir, that will find out logs
And never trouble Peter for the matter.

20 **Capulet.** Mass, and well said, merry whoreson, ha!
Thou shalt be loggerhead. [*Exit* Servant.] Good faith, 'tis day.
The County will be here with music straight,
For so he said he would. [*music within*] I hear him near.
Nurse! Wife! What, ho! What, nurse, I say!

[*Reenter* Nurse.]

25 Go waken Juliet; go and trim her up.
I'll go and chat with Paris. Hie, make haste,
Make haste! The bridegroom he is come already:
Make haste, I say.

[*Exeunt.*]

Scene 5 *Juliet's bedroom.*

[*Enter* Nurse.]

Nurse. Mistress! what, mistress! Juliet! Fast, I warrant her, she.
Why, lamb! why, lady! Fie, you slugabed!
Why, love, I say! madam! sweetheart! Why, bride!
What, not a word? You take your pennyworths now,
5 Sleep for a week; for the next night, I warrant,
The County Paris hath set up his rest
That you shall rest but little. God forgive me,
Marry and amen, how sound is she asleep!
I needs must wake her. Madam, madam, madam!
10 Aye, let the County take you in your bed,
He'll fright you up, i' faith. Will it not be?

[*opens the curtains*]

11–13 Lord and Lady Capulet joke about his being a woman chaser (**mouse-hunt**) as a young man. He makes fun of her jealousy (**jealous hood**).

20–23 The joking between Capulet and his servants includes the mild oath **Mass,** short for "by the Mass," and **loggerhead,** a word for a stupid person as well as a pun, since the servant is searching for drier logs. **straight:** right away.

1–11 The nurse chatters as she bustles around the room. She calls Juliet a **slugabed,** or sleepyhead, who is trying to get her **pennyworths,** or small portions, of rest now, since after the wedding Paris won't let her get much sleep.

What, dressed and in your clothes and down again?
I must needs wake you. Lady! lady! lady!
Alas, alas! Help, help! my lady's dead!
15 O well-a-day that ever I was born!
Some aqua vitae, ho! My lord! my lady!

[*Enter* Lady Capulet.]

Lady Capulet. What noise is here?

Nurse.   O lamentable day!

17 lamentable: filled with grief.

Lady Capulet. What is the matter?

Nurse.   Look, look! O heavy day!

Lady Capulet. O me, O me! My child, my only life!
20 Revive, look up, or I will die with thee!
Help! help! Call help.

[*Enter* Capulet.]

Capulet. For shame, bring Juliet forth; her lord is come.

Nurse. She's dead, deceased; she's dead! Alack the day!

Lady Capulet. Alack the day, she's dead, she's dead, she's dead!

25 **Capulet.** Ha! let me see her. Out alas! she's cold,
Her blood is settled, and her joints are stiff;
Life and these lips have long been separated.
Death lies on her like an untimely frost
Upon the sweetest flower of all the field.

30 **Nurse.** O lamentable day!

Lady Capulet.   O woeful time!

Capulet. Death, that hath ta'en her hence to make me wail,
Ties up my tongue and will not let me speak.

[*Enter* Friar Laurence *and* Paris, *with* Musicians.]

Friar Laurence. Come, is the bride ready to go to church?

Capulet. Ready to go, but never to return.
35 O son, the night before thy wedding day
Hath death lain with thy wife. See, there she lies,
Flower as she was, deflowered by him.
Death is my son-in-law, Death is my heir;
My daughter he hath wedded. I will die
40 And leave him all. Life, living, all is Death's.

40 Life . . . Death's: My life, my possessions, and everything else of mine belongs to Death.

Paris. Have I thought long to see this morning's face,
And doth it give me such a sight as this?

Lady Capulet. Accursed, unhappy, wretched, hateful day!
Most miserable hour that e'er time saw

45 In lasting labor of his pilgrimage!
But one, poor one, one poor and loving child,
But one thing to rejoice and solace in,
And cruel Death hath catched it from my sight!

Nurse. O woe! O woeful, woeful, woeful day!
50 Most lamentable day, most woeful day
That ever, ever I did yet behold!
O day! O day! O day! O hateful day!
Never was seen so black a day as this.
O woeful day! O woeful day!

55 **Paris.** Beguiled, divorced, wronged, spited, slain!
Most detestable Death, by thee beguiled,
By cruel, cruel thee quite overthrown!
O love! O life! not life, but love in death!

Capulet. Despised, distressed, hated, martyred, killed!
60 Uncomfortable time, why camest thou now
To murder, murder our solemnity?
O child! O child! my soul, and not my child!
Dead art thou, dead! alack, my child is dead,
And with my child my joys are buried!

65 **Friar Laurence.** Peace, ho, for shame! Confusion's cure lives not
In these confusions. Heaven and yourself
Had part in this fair maid! now heaven hath all,
And all the better is it for the maid.
Your part in her you could not keep from death,
70 But heaven keeps his part in eternal life.
The most you sought was her promotion,
For 'twas your heaven she should be advanced;
And weep ye now, seeing she is advanced
Above the clouds, as high as heaven itself?
75 O, in this love, you love your child so ill
That you run mad, seeing that she is well.
She's not well married that lives married long,
But she's best married that dies married young.
Dry up your tears and stick your rosemary
80 On this fair corse, and, as the custom is,
In all her best array bear her to church;
For though fond nature bids us all lament,
Yet nature's tears are reason's merriment.

Capulet. All things that we ordained festival
85 Turn from their office to black funeral—
Our instruments to melancholy bells,
Our wedding cheer to a sad burial feast;

46–48 But one ... my sight: I had only one child to make me happy, and Death has taken (**catched**) her from me.

55 Beguiled: tricked

60–61 why ... solemnity: Why did Death have to come to murder our celebration?

65–78 The friar says that the cure for disaster (**confusion**) cannot be found in cries of grief. Juliet's family and heaven once shared her; now heaven has all of her. All the family ever wanted was the best for her; now she's in heaven—what could be better than that? It is best to die young, when the soul is still pure, without sin.

79–80 stick ... corse: Put rosemary, an herb, on her corpse.

82–83 though ... merriment: Though it's natural to cry, common sense tells us we should rejoice for the dead.

84 ordained festival: intended for the wedding.

Our solemn hymns to sullen dirges change;
Our bridal flowers serve for a buried corse;
90 And all things change them to the contrary.

Friar Laurence. Sir, go you in; and, madam, go with him;
And go, Sir Paris. Every one prepare
To follow this fair corse unto her grave.
The heavens do lower upon you for some ill;
95 Move them no more by crossing their high will.

[*Exeunt* Capulet, Lady Capulet, Paris, *and* Friar.]

First Musician. Faith, we may put up our pipes, and be gone.

Nurse. Honest good fellows, ah, put up, put up,
For well you know this is a pitiful case.

[*Exit.*]

Second Musician. Aye, by my troth, the case may be amended.

[*Enter* Peter.]

100 **Peter.** Musicians, oh, musicians, "Heart's ease, heart's ease." Oh,
an you will have me live, play "Heart's ease."

First Musician. Why "Heart's ease"?

Peter. Oh, musicians, because my heart itself plays "My heart is
full of woe." Oh, play me some merry dump, to comfort me.

105 **First Musician.** Not a dump we, 'tis no time to play now.

Peter. You will not, then?

First Musician. No.

Peter. I will then give it you soundly.

First Musician. What will you give us?

88 **sullen dirges:** sad, mournful tunes.

94–95 **The heavens . . . will:** The fates (**heavens**) frown on you for some wrong you have done. Don't tempt them by refusing to accept their will (Juliet's death).

110   **Peter.** No money, on my faith, but the gleek. I will give you the minstrel.

First Musician. Then will I give you the serving creature.

Peter. Then will I lay the serving creature's dagger on your pate. I will carry no crotchets. I'll re you, I'll fa you, do you note me?

113 pate: top of the head.

115   **First Musician.** An you re us and fa us, you note us.

Second Musician. Pray you put up your dagger, and put out your wit.

Peter. Then have at you with my wit! I will drybeat you with an iron wit, and put up my iron dagger. Answer me like men:

120   "When griping grief the heart doth wound
      And doleful dumps the mind oppress,
      Then music with her " "He ask—"
Why "silver sound"? Why "music with her silver sound"?—What say you, Simon Catling?

125   **First Musician.** Marry, sir, because silver hath a sweet sound.

Peter. Pretty! What say you, Hugh Rebeck?

Second Musician. I say "silver sound" because musicians sound for silver.

Peter. Pretty too! What say you, James Soundpost?

130   **Third Musician.** Faith, I know not what to say.

Peter. Oh, I cry you mercy, you are the singer. I will say for you. It is "music with her silver sound" because musicians have no gold for sounding.
      "Then music with her silver sound
135   With speedy help doth lend redress."

  [Exit.]

First Musician. What a pestilent knave is this same!

136 pestilent: bothersome; irritating.

Second Musician. Hang him, Jack! Come, we'll in here. Tarry for the mourners, and stay dinner.

  [Exeunt.]

COLLABORATIVE DISCUSSION With a partner, discuss the measures taken by Juliet and Friar Laurence to fool Juliet's family. Do you agree with their plan and think there were no other options, or do you think the plan was selfish or unwise? Support your ideas with details from the play.

Analyzing the Text

Cite Text Evidence Support your responses with evidence from the selection.

1. **Analyze** Review Juliet's dialogue with Paris in Scene 1. If Juliet had never met Romeo, might she have fallen in love with Paris? Explain your response.

2. **Identify** Shakespeare often employs a literary technique known as dramatic irony. **Dramatic irony** exists when the reader or viewer knows something that one or more of the characters do not. For example, when Paris asks Juliet to confess to Friar Laurence that she loves him, she carefully avoids denying it. We know that Juliet loves Romeo, not Paris. Identify two other examples of dramatic irony in Act IV. Explain how these ironic moments contribute to the building tension in the play.

3. **Analyze** In Scene 2, how does Shakespeare increase the pace of the plot even further? What effect is this likely to have on the audience?

4. **Interpret** What fears does Juliet have before going through with Friar Laurence's plan? What do her fears reveal about her state of mind?

5. **Compare** Juliet drinks the sleeping potion, despite her fears. What does this reveal about her character? Has she changed from the beginning of the play, before she met Romeo? Explain your response.

6. **Analyze** Shakespeare includes a humorous exchange between Peter and the musicians at the end of Act IV, right after Juliet's family discovers her body. What is the impact of this choice on the audience? What message is conveyed by having a humorous scene immediately follow a tragic one?

PERFORMANCE TASK

Speaking and Writing Activity: Dramatic Reading With a small group, prepare a dramatic reading of Scene 4 and Scene 5 (lines 1–21).

1. Assign roles to each member of the group.

2. Read over your role and memorize your lines. Notice the excitement expressed by the characters in Scene 4 and the grief they express in Scene 5.

3. Make notes on how you will convey the emotion of the words on the page in your reading. Think about when you might change your tone, adjust your voice, or read more quickly or slowly.

4. Give your dramatic reading. Try to capture the emotion of the words on the page as Shakespeare wrote them.

AS YOU READ Notice the unexpected events, misunderstandings, and examples of poor timing that finally bring the play to its tragic end. Write down any questions you generate during reading.

ACT V

Scene 1 *A street in Mantua.*

[*Enter* Romeo.]

Romeo. If I may trust the flattering truth of sleep,
My dreams presage some joyful news at hand.
My bosom's lord sits lightly in his throne,
And all this day an unaccustomed spirit
5   Lifts me above the ground with cheerful thoughts.
I dreamt my lady came and found me dead
(Strange dream that gives a dead man leave to think!)
And breathed such life with kisses in my lips
That I revived and was an emperor.
10   Ah me! how sweet is love itself possessed,
When but love's shadows are so rich in joy!

[*Enter Romeo's servant,* Balthasar, *booted.*]

News from Verona! How now, Balthasar?
Dost thou not bring me letters from the friar?
How doth my lady? Is my father well?
15   How fares my Juliet? That I ask again,
For nothing can be ill if she be well.

Balthasar. Then she is well, and nothing can be ill.
Her body sleeps in Capels' monument,
And her immortal part with angels lives.
20   I saw her laid low in her kindred's vault
And presently took post to tell it you.
O, pardon me for bringing these ill news,
Since you did leave it for my office, sir.

Romeo. Is it e'en so? Then I defy you, stars!
25   Thou knowst my lodging. Get me ink and paper
And hire posthorses. I will hence tonight.

Balthasar. I do beseech you, sir, have patience.
Your looks are pale and wild and do import
Some misadventure.

Romeo.   Tush, thou art deceived.
30   Leave me and do the thing I bid thee do.
Hast thou no letters to me from the friar?

Balthasar. No, my good lord.

17–19 Balthasar replies that Juliet is well, since although her body lies in the Capulets' (**Capels'**) burial vault, her soul (**her immortal part**) is with the angels.

21 presently took post: immediately rode (to Mantua).

23 you did . . . office: you gave me the duty of reporting important news to you.

24 I . . . stars: Romeo angrily challenges fate, which has caused him so much grief.

28–29 import some misadventure: suggest that something bad will happen.

Romeo.   No matter. Get thee gone
And hire those horses. I'll be with thee straight.

[*Exit* Balthasar.]

Well, Juliet, I will lie with thee tonight.
35 Let's see for means. O mischief, thou art swift
To enter in the thoughts of desperate men!
I do remember an apothecary,
And hereabouts he dwells, which late I noted
In tattered weeds, with overwhelming brows,
40 Culling of simples. Meager were his looks,
Sharp misery had worn him to the bones;
And in his needy shop a tortoise hung,
An alligator stuffed, and other skins
Of ill-shaped fishes; and about his shelves
45 A beggarly account of empty boxes,
Green earthen pots, bladders, and musty seeds,
Remnants of packthread, and old cakes of roses
Were thinly scattered, to make up a show.
Noting this penury, to myself I said,
50 "An if a man did need a poison now
Whose sale is present death in Mantua,
Here lives a caitiff wretch would sell it him."
O, this same thought did but forerun my need,
And this same needy man must sell it me.
55 As I remember, this should be the house.
Being holiday, the beggar's shop is shut.
What, ho! apothecary!

[*Enter* Apothecary.]

Apothecary.   Who calls so loud?

Romeo. Come hither, man. I see that thou art poor.
Hold, there is forty ducats. Let me have
60 A dram of poison, such soon-speeding gear
As will disperse itself through all the veins
That the life-weary taker may fall dead,
And that the trunk may be discharged of breath
As violently as hasty powder fired
65 Doth hurry from the fatal cannon's womb.

Apothecary. Such mortal drugs I have; but Mantua's law
Is death to any he that utters them.

Romeo. Art thou so bare and full of wretchedness
And fearest to die? Famine is in thy cheeks,
70 Need and oppression starveth in thine eyes,
Contempt and beggary hangs upon thy back:

**35–40 Let's . . .
means:** Let me find a
way (to join Juliet in
death); **apothecary:**
pharmacist; **tattered
weeds:** ragged clothes;
culling of simples:
selecting herbs.

47 cakes of roses: rose
petals pressed together
to create a perfume.

49 penury: poverty.

**50–52 "An if a man . . .
sell it him":** Though it is
a crime to sell poison in
Mantua, the apothecary
is such a miserable
(**caitiff**) wretch that he
would probably do it for
the money.

59 ducats: gold coins.

60–65 Romeo wants
fast-acting (**soon-
speeding**) poison that
will work as quickly as
gunpowder exploding in
a cannon.

67 any . . . them: any
person who dispenses or
sells them.

The world is not thy friend, nor the world's law;
The world affords no law to make thee rich;
Then be not poor, but break it and take this.

75 **Apothecary.** My poverty but not my will consents.

Romeo. I pay thy poverty and not thy will.

Apothecary. Put this in any liquid thing you will
And drink it off, and if you had the strength
Of twenty men, it would dispatch you straight.

80 **Romeo.** There is thy gold—worse poison to men's souls,
Doing more murder in this loathsome world,
Than these poor compounds that thou mayst not sell.
I sell thee poison; thou hast sold me none.
Farewell. Buy food and get thyself in flesh.
85 Come, cordial and not poison, go with me
To Juliet's grave; for there must I use thee.

[*Exeunt.*]

Scene 2 *Friar Laurence's cell in Verona.*

[*Enter* Friar John.]

Friar John. Holy Franciscan friar, brother, ho!

[*Enter* Friar Laurence.]

Friar Laurence. This same should be the voice of Friar John.
Welcome from Mantua. What says Romeo?
Or, if his mind be writ, give me his letter.

5 **Friar John.** Going to find a barefoot brother out,
One of our order to associate me,
Here in this city visiting the sick,
And finding him, the searchers of the town,
Suspecting that we both were in a house
10 Where the infectious pestilence did reign,
Sealed up the doors, and would not let us forth,
So that my speed to Mantua there was stayed.

Friar Laurence. Who bare my letter, then, to Romeo?

Friar John. I could not send it—here it is again—
15 Nor get a messenger to bring it thee,
So fearful were they of infection.

Friar Laurence. Unhappy fortune! By my brotherhood,
The letter was not nice, but full of charge,
Of dear import, and the neglecting it
20 May do much danger. Friar John, go hence,

72–74 Romeo urges the apothecary to improve his situation by breaking the law and selling him the poison.

75 I'm doing this for the money, not because I think it's right.

79 dispatch you straight: kill you instantly.

85 Romeo refers to the poison as a **cordial,** a drink believed to be good for the heart.

5–12 Friar John asked another friar (**barefoot brother**) to go with him to Mantua. The health officials of the town, believing that the friars had come into contact with a deadly plague (**infectious pestilence**), locked them up to keep them from infecting others.

13 bare: carried (bore).

18–20 The letter wasn't trivial (**nice**) but contained a message of great importance (**dear import**). The fact that it wasn't sent (**neglecting it**) may cause great harm.

Get me an iron crow and bring it straight
Unto my cell.

Friar John.   Brother, I'll go and bring it thee.

[*Exit.*]

Friar Laurence. Now must I to the monument alone.
Within this three hours will fair Juliet wake.
25 She will beshrew me much that Romeo
Hath had no notice of these accidents;
But I will write again to Mantua,
And keep her at my cell till Romeo come—
Poor living corse, closed in a dead man's tomb!

[*Exit.*]

Scene 3 *The cemetery that contains the Capulets' tomb.*

[*Enter* Paris *and his* Page *with flowers and a torch.*]

Paris. Give me thy torch, boy. Hence, and stand aloof.
Yet put it out, for I would not be seen.
Under yond yew tree lay thee all along,
Holding thine ear close to the hollow ground.
5 So shall no foot upon the churchyard tread
(Being loose, unfirm, with digging up of graves)
But thou shalt hear it. Whistle then to me,
As signal that thou hearst something approach.
Give me those flowers. Do as I bid thee, go.

10 **Page** [*aside*]. I am almost afraid to stand alone
Here in the churchyard; yet I will adventure.

[*withdraws*]

21 **iron crow:** crowbar.

25–26 **She . . .
accidents:** She will be
furious with me when
she learns that Romeo
doesn't know what has
happened.

1 **aloof:** some distance
away.

Paris. Sweet flower, with flowers thy bridal bed I strew

[*He strews the tomb with flowers.*]

(O woe! thy canopy is dust and stones)
Which with sweet water nightly I will dew;

15 Or, wanting that, with tears distilled by moans.
The obsequies that I for thee will keep
Nightly shall be to strew thy grave and weep.

[*The* Page *whistles.*]

The boy gives warning something doth approach.
What cursed foot wanders this way tonight

20 To cross my obsequies and true love's rite?
What, with a torch? Muffle me, night, awhile.

[*withdraws*]

[*Enter* Romeo *and* Balthasar *with a torch, a mattock, and a crow of iron.*]

Romeo. Give me that mattock and the wrenching iron.
Hold, take this letter. Early in the morning
See thou deliver it to my lord and father.

25 Give me the light. Upon thy life I charge thee,
Whate'er thou hearest or seest, stand all aloof
And do not interrupt me in my course.
Why I descend into this bed of death
Is partly to behold my lady's face,

30 But chiefly to take thence from her dead finger
A precious ring—a ring that I must use
In dear employment. Therefore hence, be gone.
But if thou, jealous, dost return to pry
In what I farther shall intend to do,

35 By heaven, I will tear thee joint by joint
And strew this hungry churchyard with thy limbs.
The time and my intents are savage-wild,
More fierce and more inexorable far
Than empty tigers or the roaring sea.

40 **Balthasar.** I will be gone, sir, and not trouble you.

Romeo. So shalt thou show me friendship. Take thou that.
Live, and be prosperous; and farewell, good fellow.

Balthasar [*aside*]. For all this same, I'll hide me hereabout.
His looks I fear, and his intents I doubt.

[*withdraws*]

45 **Romeo.** Thou detestable maw, thou womb of death,
Gorged with the dearest morsel of the earth,

12–17 Paris promises to decorate Juliet's grave with flowers and sprinkle it with either perfume (**sweet water**) or his tears. He will perform these honoring rites (**obsequies**) every night.

20 cross: interfere with.

21 muffle: hide.

mattock . . . iron: an ax and a crowbar.

32 in dear employment: for an important purpose.

33 jealous: curious.

37–39 Romeo's intention is more unstoppable (**inexorable**) than hungry (**empty**) tigers or the waves of an ocean.

45–48 Romeo addresses the tomb as though it were devouring people. He calls it a hateful stomach (**detestable maw**) that is filled (**gorged**) with Juliet, the **dearest morsel of the earth**.

Thus I enforce thy rotten jaws to open,
And in despite I'll cram thee with more food.

[Romeo *opens the tomb.*]

Paris. This is that banish'd haughty Montague
50 That murdered my love's cousin—with which grief
It is supposed the fair creature died—
And here is come to do some villainous shame
To the dead bodies. I will apprehend him.
Stop thy unhallowed toil, vile Montague!
55 Can vengeance be pursued further than death?
Condemned villain, I do apprehend thee.
Obey, and go with me; for thou must die.

Romeo. I must indeed; and therefore came I hither.
Good gentle youth, tempt not a desp'rate man.
60 Fly hence and leave me. Think upon these gone;
Let them affright thee. I beseech thee, youth,
Put not another sin upon my head
By urging me to fury. O, be gone!
By heaven, I love thee better than myself.
65 For I come hither armed against myself.
Stay not, be gone. Live, and hereafter say
A madman's mercy bid thee run away.

Paris. I do defy thy conjuration
And apprehend thee for a felon here.

70 **Romeo.** Wilt thou provoke me? Then have at thee, boy!

[*They fight.*]

Page. O Lord, they fight! I will go call the watch.

[*Exit.*]

Paris. O, I am slain! [*falls*] If thou be merciful,
Open the tomb, lay me with Juliet.

[*dies*]

Romeo. In faith, I will. Let me peruse this face.
75 Mercutio's kinsman, noble County Paris!
What said my man when my betossed soul
Did not attend him as we rode? I think
He told me Paris should have married Juliet.
Said he not so? or did I dream it so?
80 Or am I mad, hearing him talk of Juliet,
To think it was so? O, give me thy hand,
One writ with me in sour misfortune's book!
I'll bury thee in a triumphant grave.
A grave? O, no, a lantern, slaughtered youth,

49–53 Recognizing Romeo, Paris speaks these first few lines to himself. He is angry with Romeo, believing that Romeo's killing Tybalt caused Juliet to die of grief.

68 I reject your appeal.

82 Romeo notes that, like himself, Paris has been a victim of bad luck.

84–87 Romeo will bury Paris with Juliet, whose beauty fills the tomb with light. Paris' corpse (**Death**) is being buried (**interred**) by a dead man in that Romeo expects to be dead soon.

85 For here lies Juliet, and her beauty makes
This vault a feasting presence full of light.
Death, lie thou there, by a dead man interred.

[*lays* Paris *in the tomb*]

How oft when men are at the point of death
Have they been merry! which their keepers call
90 A lightning before death. O, how may I
Call this a lightning? O my love! my wife!
Death, that hath sucked the honey of thy breath,
Hath had no power yet upon thy beauty.
Thou art not conquered. Beauty's ensign yet

94 ensign: sign.

95 Is crimson in thy lips and in thy cheeks,
And death's pale flag is not advanced there.
Tybalt, liest thou there in thy bloody sheet?
O, what more favor can I do to thee
Than with that hand that cut thy youth in twain

98–100 O, what . . . enemy: I can best repay you (Tybalt) by killing your enemy (myself) with the same hand that cut your youth in two (**twain**).

100 To sunder his that was thine enemy?
Forgive me, cousin! Ah, dear Juliet,
Why art thou yet so fair? Shall I believe
That unsubstantial Death is amorous,
And that the lean abhorred monster keeps

102–105 Romeo can't get over how beautiful Juliet still looks. He asks whether Death is loving (**amorous**) and whether it has taken Juliet as its lover (**paramour**).

105 Thee here in dark to be his paramour?
For fear of that I still will stay with thee
And never from this palace of dim night
Depart again. Here, here will I remain
With worms that are thy chambermaids. O, here
110 Will I set up my everlasting rest
And shake the yoke of inauspicious stars
From this world-wearied flesh. Eyes, look your last!

111–112 shake . . . flesh: rid myself of the burden of an unhappy fate (**inauspicious stars**).

Arms, take your last embrace! and, lips, O you
The doors of breath, seal with a righteous kiss
115 A dateless bargain to engrossing death!
Come, bitter conduct; come, unsavory guide!
Thou desperate pilot, now at once run on
The dashing rocks thy seasick weary bark!
Here's to my love! [*drinks*] O true apothecary!

115 dateless: eternal; never-ending. Romeo means that what he is about to do can never be undone.

120 Thy drugs are quick. Thus with a kiss I die.

[*falls*]

[*Enter* Friar Laurence, *with lantern, crow, and spade.*]

Friar Laurence. Saint Francis be my speed! how oft tonight
Have my old feet stumbled at graves! Who's there?

Balthasar. Here's one, a friend, and one that knows you well.

117–118 Romeo compares himself to the pilot of a ship (**bark**) who is going to crash on the rocks because he is so weary and sick.

Friar Laurence. Bliss be upon you! Tell me, good my friend,

125 What torch is yond that vainly lends his light
To grubs and eyeless skulls? As I discern,
It burneth in the Capels' monument.

Balthasar. It doth so, holy sir; and there's my master,
One that you love.

Friar Laurence.   Who is it?

Balthasar.   Romeo.

130 **Friar Laurence.** How long hath he been there?

Balthasar.   Full half an hour.

Friar Laurence. Go with me to the vault.

Balthasar.   I dare not, sir.
My master knows not but I am gone hence,
And fearfully did menace me with death
If I did stay to look on his intents.

132–134 **My master ... intents:** My master told me to go away and threatened me with death if I watched what he did.

135 **Friar Laurence.** Stay then; I'll go alone. Fear comes upon me.
O, much I fear some ill unthrifty thing.

136 **unthrifty:** unlucky.

Balthasar. As I did sleep under this yew tree here,
I dreamt my master and another fought,
And that my master slew him.

Friar Laurence.   Romeo!

[*stoops and looks on the blood and weapons*]

140 Alack, alack, what blood is this which stains
The stony entrance of this sepulcher?
What mean these masterless and gory swords
To lie discolored by this place of peace?

140–143 **Alack ... place of peace?** Why are these bloody swords lying here at the tomb (**sepulcher**), a place that should be peaceful? (The swords are also **masterless,** or without their owners.)

[*enters the tomb*]

Romeo! O, pale! Who else? What, Paris too?
145 And steeped in blood? Ah, what an unkind hour
Is guilty of this lamentable chance!
The lady stirs.

[Juliet *rises.*]

Juliet. O comfortable friar! where is my lord?
I do remember well where I should be,
150 And there I am. Where is my Romeo?

148 **comfortable:** comforting.

Friar Laurence. I hear some noise. Lady, come from that nest
Of death, contagion, and unnatural sleep.
A greater power than we can contradict
Hath thwarted our intents. Come, come away.

153–154 **A greater ... intents:** A greater force than we can fight (**contradict**) has ruined our plans (**thwarted our intents**).

155   Thy husband in thy bosom there lies dead;
     And Paris too. Come, I'll dispose of thee
     Among a sisterhood of holy nuns.
     Stay not to question, for the watch is coming.
     Come, go, good Juliet. I dare no longer stay.

156–157 I'll dispose . . . nuns: I'll find a place for you in a convent of nuns.

160   **Juliet.** Go, get thee hence, for I will not away.

     [*Exit* Friar Laurence.]

     What's here? A cup, closed in my true love's hand?
     Poison, I see, hath been his timeless end.
     O churl! drunk all, and left no friendly drop
     To help me after? I will kiss thy lips.
165   Haply some poison yet doth hang on them
     To make me die with a restorative.

162 timeless: happening before its proper time.

163 churl: miser.

165 Haply: perhaps.

     [*kisses him*]

     Thy lips are warm!

     Chief Watchman [*within*]. Lead, boy. Which way?

     Juliet. Yea, noise? Then I'll be brief. O happy dagger!

     [*snatches Romeo's dagger*]

170   This is thy sheath; there rust, and let me die.

     [*She stabs herself and falls.*]

     [*Enter* Watchmen *with the* Page *of Paris.*]

     Page. This is the place. There, where the torch doth burn.

     Chief Watchman. The ground is bloody. Search about the
       churchyard.
     Go, some of you; whoe'er you find attach.

173 attach: arrest.

[*Exeunt some of the* Watch.]

Pitiful sight! here lies the County slain;
175 And Juliet bleeding, warm, and newly dead,
Who here hath lain this two days buried.
Go, tell the Prince; run to the Capulets;
Raise up the Montagues; some others search.

[*Exeunt others of the* Watch.]

We see the ground whereon these woes do lie,
180 But the true ground of all these piteous woes
We cannot without circumstance descry.

[*Reenter some of the* Watch, *with* Balthasar.]

Second Watchman. Here's Romeo's man. We found him in the
churchyard.

Chief Watchman. Hold him in safety till the Prince come hither.

[*Reenter* Friar Laurence *and another* Watchman.]

Third Watchman. Here is a friar that trembles, sighs, and weeps.
185 We took this mattock and this spade from him
As he was coming from this churchyard side.

Chief Watchman. A great suspicion! Stay the friar too.

[*Enter the* Prince *and* Attendants.]

Prince. What misadventure is so early up,
That calls our person from our morning rest?

[*Enter* Capulet, Lady Capulet, *and others.*]

190 **Capulet.** What should it be, that they so shriek abroad?

Lady Capulet. The people in the street cry "Romeo,"
Some "Juliet," and some "Paris"; and all run,
With open outcry, toward our monument.

Prince. What fear is this which startles in our ears?

195 **Chief Watchman.** Sovereign, here lies the County Paris slain;
And Romeo dead, and Juliet, dead before,
Warm and new killed.

Prince. Search, seek, and know how this foul murder comes.

Chief Watchman. Here is a friar, and slaughtered Romeo's man,
200 With instruments upon them fit to open
These dead men's tombs.

Capulet. O heavens! O wife, look how our daughter bleeds!
This dagger hath mista'en, for, lo, his house
Is empty on the back of Montague,
205 And it missheathed in my daughter's bosom!

178 Raise up: awaken.

**179–181 We see...
descry:** We see the earth
(**ground**) these bodies
lie on. But the real cause
(**true ground**) of these
deaths is yet for us to
discover (**descry**).

182–187 The guards
arrest Balthasar and Friar
Laurence as suspicious
characters.

194 startles: causes
alarm.

**203–205 This dagger
... in my daughter's
bosom:** This dagger
has missed its target. It
should rest in the sheath
(**house**) that Romeo
wears. Instead it is in
Juliet's chest.

Lady Capulet. O me! this sight of death is as a bell
That warns my old age to a sepulcher.

[*Enter* Montague *and others.*]

Prince. Come, Montague; for thou art early up
To see thy son and heir now early down.

210 **Montague.** Alas, my liege, my wife is dead tonight!
Grief of my son's exile hath stopped her breath.
What further woe conspires against mine age?

Prince. Look, and thou shalt see.

Montague. O thou untaught! what manners is in this,
215 To press before thy father to a grave?

Prince. Seal up the mouth of outrage for a while,
Till we can clear these ambiguities
And know their spring, their head, their true descent;
And then will I be general of your woes
220 And lead you even to death. Meantime forbear,
And let mischance be slave to patience.
Bring forth the parties of suspicion.

Friar Laurence. I am the greatest, able to do least,
Yet most suspected, as the time and place
225 Doth make against me, of this direful murder;
And here I stand, both to impeach and purge
Myself condemned and myself excused.

Prince. Then say at once what thou dost know in this.

Friar Laurence. I will be brief, for my short date of breath
230 Is not so long as is a tedious tale.
Romeo, there dead, was husband to that Juliet;
And she, there dead, that Romeo's faithful wife.
I married them; and their stol'n marriage day
Was Tybalt's doomsday, whose untimely death
235 Banish'd the new-made bridegroom from this city;
For whom, and not for Tybalt, Juliet pined.
You, to remove that siege of grief from her,
Betrothed and would have married her perforce
To County Paris. Then comes she to me
240 And with wild looks bid me devise some mean
To rid her from this second marriage,
Or in my cell there would she kill herself.
Then gave I her (so tutored by my art)
A sleeping potion; which so took effect
245 As I intended, for it wrought on her
The form of death. Meantime I writ to Romeo

210 **liege:** lord.

214–215 **what manners . . . grave:** What kind of behavior is this, for a son to die before his father?

216–221 **Seal . . . patience:** Stop your emotional outbursts until we can find out the source (**spring**) of these confusing events (**ambiguities**). Wait (**forbear**) and be patient, and let's find out what happened.

223–227 Friar Laurence confesses that he is most responsible for these events. He will both accuse (**impeach**) himself and clear (**purge**) himself of guilt.

236 It was Romeo's banishment, not Tybalt's death, that made Juliet so sad.

That he should hither come as this dire night
To help to take her from her borrowed grave,
Being the time the potion's force should cease.
250　But he which bore my letter, Friar John,
Was stayed by accident, and yesternight
Returned my letter back. Then all alone
At the prefixed hour of her waking
Came I to take her from her kindred's vault;
255　Meaning to keep her closely at my cell
Till I conveniently could send to Romeo.
But when I came, some minute ere the time
Of her awaking, here untimely lay
The noble Paris and true Romeo dead.
260　She wakes; and I entreated her come forth
And bear this work of heaven with patience;
But then a noise did scare me from the tomb,
And she, too desperate, would not go with me,
But, as it seems, did violence on herself.
265　All this I know, and to the marriage
Her nurse is privy; and if aught in this
Miscarried by my fault, let my old life
Be sacrificed, some hour before his time,
Unto the rigor of severest law.

270　**Prince.** We still have known thee for a holy man.
Where's Romeo's man? What can he say in this?

Balthasar. I brought my master news of Juliet's death;
And then in post he came from Mantua
To this same place, to this same monument.
275　This letter he early bid me give his father,
And threatened me with death, going in the vault,
If I departed not and left him there.

Prince. Give me the letter. I will look on it.
Where is the County's page that raised the watch?
280　Sirrah, what made your master in this place?

Page. He came with flowers to strew his lady's grave;
And bid me stand aloof, and so I did.
Anon comes one with light to ope the tomb;
And by-and-by my master drew on him;
285　And then I ran away to call the watch.

Prince. This letter doth make good the friar's words,
Their course of love, the tidings of her death;
And here he writes that he did buy a poison
Of a poor 'pothecary, and therewithal

248 borrowed:
temporary.

254 kindred's: family's.

265–269 and to
. . . law: Her nurse can
bear witness to this
secret marriage. If I am
responsible for any of
this, let the law punish
me with death.

273 in post: at full
speed.

279–280 The Prince
asks for Paris' servant,
who notified the guards
(**raised the watch**).
Then he asks the servant
why Paris was at the
cemetery.

283–285 Anon . . . call
the watch: Soon (**anon**)
someone with a light
came and opened the
tomb. Paris drew his
sword, and I ran to call
the guards.

290 Came to this vault to die and lie with Juliet.
Where be these enemies? Capulet, Montague,
See what a scourge is laid upon your hate,
That heaven finds means to kill your joys with love!
And I, for winking at your discords too,
295 Have lost a brace of kinsmen. All are punished.

Capulet. O brother Montague, give me thy hand.
This is my daughter's jointure, for no more
Can I demand.

Montague.   But I can give thee more;
For I will raise her statue in pure gold,
300 That whiles Verona by that name is known,
There shall no figure at such rate be set
As that of true and faithful Juliet.

Capulet. As rich shall Romeo's by his lady's lie—
Poor sacrifices of our enmity!

305 **Prince.** A glooming peace this morning with it brings.
The sun for sorrow will not show his head.
Go hence, to have more talk of these sad things;
Some shall be pardoned, and some punished;
For never was a story of more woe
310 Than this of Juliet and her Romeo.

[*Exeunt.*]

**292–295 See what
. . . punished:** Look at
the punishment your
hatred has brought on
you. Heaven has killed
your children (**joys**) with
love. For shutting my
eyes to your arguments
(**discords**), I have lost
two relatives. We have all
been punished.

297–298 jointure:
dowry, the payment
a bride's father
traditionally made to
the groom. Capulet
means that no one
could demand more of
a bride's father than he
has already paid.

301 at such rate be set:
be valued so highly.

303–304 Capulet
promises to do for
Romeo what Montague
will do for Juliet. Their
children have become
sacrifices to their hatred
(**enmity**).

COLLABORATIVE DISCUSSION Working in a small group, review the
events that lead to the tragic ending. Then discuss what makes *The
Tragedy of Romeo and Juliet* still popular with today's audiences.

Analyze Character: Motivations

Characters in a literary work, like real people, have **motivations,** or reasons, for their actions. A character can be motivated by a variety of factors: by a goal, by loyalty to a group or cause, or by an emotion such as love, anger, or jealousy. A **complex character** is one who is driven by multiple, and sometimes conflicting, motivations at the same time.

In *Romeo and Juliet*, the character of Tybalt is an example of a character who is not particularly complex. What is Tybalt's single motivation before he meets his demise? The characters of Romeo and Juliet, on the other hand, are complex characters tormented throughout the play by conflicting motivations. Their struggles form the basis of the action in the play—and time after time prevent them from being able to live happily ever after. Think about the following factors:

- **Family obligation** In what ways do their families create conflict in their lives?
- **Love and passion** How does their love motivate them to meet new challenges?
- **Fear** How does fear shape their actions and prevent them from living and loving each other freely?
- **Misunderstanding** What twists and turns in the plot, as well as miscommunication, create conflict and drive them to make bad choices?
- **Despair** What actions by Romeo and Juliet are driven by extreme feelings of hopelessness?

Analyze Author's Choices: Parallel Plots

Romeo and Juliet is not a simple love story. It is a complex drama featuring **parallel plots**—separate story lines happening at the same time and linked by common characters and themes. The chart can help you identify and understand parallel plots in the play.

Plot	Purpose
The feud between the Capulets and the Montagues	How does this plot contribute to the drama of the play?
Romeo's unrequited love for Rosaline	What do we learn about Romeo through this experience?
Juliet's marriage proposal from Paris	What do we learn about Juliet and her relationship with her family?

Shakespeare also carefully structures his drama in a meaningful way. Recall that Acts I and II are comedic, featuring jokes and young love, while Act III leads to the final tragedy. What is the effect of this contrast?

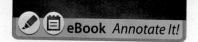
Analyzing the Text

Cite Text Evidence Support your responses with evidence from the selection.

1. **Interpret** What dream does Romeo describe at the beginning of Act V, Scene 1? What part of his dream foreshadows events to come?

2. **Analyze** What plan does Romeo immediately formulate when he learns of Juliet's death? What does his response to her death expose about his character?

3. **Infer** In Scene 2, why is Friar Laurence in a panic when he finds out that his letter was not delivered to Romeo? Why is this a key turning point in the plot?

4. **Analyze** Reread Friar Laurence's speech in Scene 3, lines 223–269. What various and possibly conflicting motivations does he have for making these remarks?

5. **Interpret** Whom does Prince Escalus blame for the tragic events? Support your answer with details from his words in the last scene of the play.

6. **Connect** Recall Juliet's response when her mother suggests the idea of marrying Paris (Act I, Scene 3, lines 98–100). What does this reveal about Juliet's character before she meets Romeo? How does this contrast with Romeo's character in the parallel plot involving Rosaline? By Act V, how has Juliet changed?

7. **Analyze** Fate, or forces over which people have no control, is an important theme in this tragedy. Many events are blamed upon fate, starting with Shakespeare's description of Romeo and Juliet as "star-crossed lovers" in the Prologue. However, many events can also be blamed on the actions of characters. Do you believe fate or free will caused this tragic ending? Explain.

8. **Analyze** In a tragedy, a hero or heroine's character flaw is usually the cause of his or her downfall. Do you believe Romeo or Juliet had a character flaw that led to his or her death? Support your idea with evidence from the play.

PERFORMANCE TASK

Writing Activity: Eulogy Use your knowledge of Romeo and Juliet to write a eulogy, a tribute to someone who has died, for both of them.

1. With a partner, brainstorm important details about their lives and their relationship. Think about their motivations, how they fell in love, the challenges they faced, and how they changed each other.

2. With your partner, craft your eulogy, highlighting key details about the characters of the two young people. Be sure your ideas are grounded in details from the play.

In both pieces of writing, include evidence from the text and use the conventions of standard English.

Vocabulary Strategy: Puns

Shakespeare was a master of clever word play, including the use of puns. A **pun** is a joke built upon multiple meanings of a word or upon two words that sound similar but have different meanings. Near the end of Act IV, Peter challenges the musicians to help him develop a pun based on a verse.

Peter. "When griping grief the heart doth wound
   And doleful dumps the mind oppress,
   Then music with her silver sound—"

Why "silver sound"? Why "music with her silver sound"?—What say you, Simon Catling?

First Musician. Marry, sir, because silver hath a sweet sound.

Peter. Pretty! What say you, Hugh Rebeck?

Second Musician. I say "silver sound" because musicians sound for silver.

Peter. Pretty too! What say you, James Soundpost?

Third Musician. Faith, I know not what to say.

Peter. Oh, I cry you mercy, you are the singer. I will say for you. It is "music with her silver sound" because musicians have no gold for sounding.

Notice the multiple meanings for the phrase *silver sound*. The first musician uses *sound* as a noun. The adjective *silver* has a pleasant connotation, making the phrase mean "a sweet or beautiful sound." The second musician and Peter use *sound* as a verb. They use the word *silver* as a reference to money and to a metal that has a lesser value than gold. To the second musician and Peter, the phrase *silver sound* means "to make music for money, silver money, though, not gold."

Practice and Apply With a partner, locate and explain these puns from the play. Then brainstorm a few multiple-meaning words and words that sound similar but have different meanings that you could use in original puns. Write a brief dialogue like the one between Peter and the musicians that uses your puns.

1. "You have dancing shoes / With nimble soles; I have a soul of lead / So stakes me to the ground I cannot move." (Act I, Scene 4, lines 14–16)

2. "Ask for me tomorrow, and you shall find me a grave man." (Act III, Scene 1, lines 91–92)

Language and Style: Parallel Structure

Parallel structure is the repetition of words, phrases, or grammatical structures in order to add emphasis or to improve the sound and rhythm of a piece of writing. Shakespeare regularly makes use of parallel structure to create cadence, or a balanced, rhythmic flow of words. Here is an example from Act II, Scene 1, lines 8–11:

> Appear thou in the likeness of a sigh;
> Speak but one rhyme, and I am satisfied!
> Cry but "Ay me!" pronounce but "love" and "dove";
> Speak to my gossip Venus one fair word . . .

Shakespeare repeats the phrasing of a verb followed by *but*: "Speak but . . . Cry but . . . pronounce but. . . ." The parallel grammatical structures give equal weight to each phrase. Any one of these three tiny gestures from Rosaline, Mercutio jokes, would cause lovesick Romeo to rejoice. Read the passage aloud and you will hear the cadence that the parallel structures lend to the verse.

This example from Act I, Scene 5, lines 10–11 contains a series of four past-tense verbs, each followed by the word *for*:

> You are looked for and called for, asked for and sought for, in the great chamber.

In this case, the speaker (a servant) sounds rather ridiculous, as if he is trying to use flowery language to deliver a simple message.

In the next example, from Act IV Scene 1, lines 102–103, Shakespeare repeats three parallel adjectives:

> Each part, deprived of supple government,
> Shall, stiff and stark and cold, appear like death;

Friar Laurence uses these grim adjectives to describe what Juliet's body will be like once she drinks the potion. The repetition gives his speech a somber rhythm, like a funeral march.

Practice and Apply Revise the eulogy you wrote in this selection's Performance Task to include at least two examples of parallel structures. Share your revised work with a partner and discuss how the parallel structures increase the power and clarity of your language.

Publius Ovidius Naso (Ovid) (43 BC–AD 17) *is considered one of the greatest Roman poets. His family expected him to become a government official. However, his overriding interest in writing poetry initiated a change in career. His first published work,* Amores (The Loves), *a series of short poems about a love affair, was a success. After becoming popular through his early poems about love and intrigue, he started an ambitious narrative poem called* Metamorphoses. *This work retells important myths from ancient Greece and Rome , including "Pyramus and Thisbe."*

Pyramus and Thisbe

Myth Retold by Ovid   Translated by Allen Mandelbaum

AS YOU READ Pay attention to the similarities between the plot of this myth and other stories you have read or movies that you have seen. Write down any questions you generate during reading.

The house of Pyramus[1] and that of Thisbe[2]
stood side by side within the mighty city
ringed by the tall brick walls Semíramis
had built[3]—so we are told. If you searched all
5 the East, you'd find no girl with greater charm
than Thisbe; and no boy in Babylon
was handsomer than Pyramus. They owed
their first encounters to their living close
beside each other—but with time, love grows.
10 Theirs did—indeed they wanted to be wed,
but marriage was forbidden by their parents:
yet there's one thing that parents can't prevent:

---

[1] **Pyramus** (pĭr´ə-məs).
[2] **Thisbe** (thĭz´be).
[3] **the mighty city . . . had built:** the walled city of Babylon (băb´ə-lən), the ruins of which are south of Baghdad, Iraq. In Greek mythology, it was founded by Semíramis (sə-mĭr´ə-məs), a powerful Assyrian queen.

the flame of love that burned in both of them.
They had no confidant—and so used signs:
15   with these each lover read the other's mind:
when covered, fire acquires still more force.

The wall their houses shared had one thin crack,
which formed when they were built and then was left;
in all these years, no one had seen that cleft;
20   but lovers will discover every thing:
you were the first to find it, and you made
that cleft a passageway which speech could take.
For there the least of whispers was kept safe:
it crossed that cleft with words of tenderness.
25   And Pyramus and Thisbe often stood,
he on this side and she on that; and when
each heard the other sigh, the lovers said:
"O jealous wall, why do you block our path?
Oh wouldn't it be better if you let
30   our bodies join each other fully or,
if that is asking for too much, just stretched
your fissure wide enough to let us kiss!
And we are not ungrateful: we admit
our words reach loving ears." And having talked
35   in vain, the lovers still remained apart.
Just so, one night, they wished each other well,
and each delivered kisses to the wall—
although those kisses could not reach their goal.
But on the morning after, when firstlight
40   had banished night's bright star-fires from the sky
and sun had left the brine-soaked[4] meadows dry,
again they took their places at the cleft.
Then, in low whispers—after their laments—
those two devised this plan: they'd circumvent
45   their guardians' watchful eyes[5] and, cloaked by night,
in silence, slip out from their homes and reach
a site outside the city. Lest each lose
the other as they wandered separately
across the open fields, they were to meet
50   at Ninus' tomb[6] and hide beneath a tree
in darkness; for beside that tomb there stood

---

[4] **brine-soaked:** dew-covered.

[5] **they'd circumvent ... eyes:** They would sneak past their parents.

[6] **Ninus' (nī´nəs) tomb:** According to Greek legend, King Ninus was Semíramis'
husband. When he died, she marked his burial place with a tall monument
outside the walls of Babylon.

a tall mulberry[7] close to a cool spring,
a tree well weighted down with snow-white berries.
Delighted with their plan—impatiently—
55 they waited for the close of day. At last
the sun plunged down into the waves, and night
emerged from those same waves.

                   Now Thisbe takes
great care, that none detect her as she makes
her way out from the house amid the dark;
60 her face is veiled; she finds the tomb; she sits
beneath the tree they'd chosen for their tryst.
Love made her bold. But now a lioness
just done with killing oxen—blood dripped down
her jaws, her mouth was frothing—comes to slake
65 her thirst at a cool spring close to the tree.
By moonlight, Thisbe sees the savage beast;
with trembling feet, the girl is quick to seek
a shadowed cave; but even as she flees,
her shawl slips from her shoulders. Thirst appeased,
70 the lioness is heading for the woods
when she, by chance, spies the abandoned shawl
upon the ground and, with her bloodstained jaws,
tears it to tatters.

               Pyramus had left
a little later than his Thisbe had,
75 and he could see what surely were the tracks
of a wild beast left clearly on deep dust.
His face grew ashen. And when he had found
the bloodstained shawl, he cried: "Now this same night
will see two lovers lose their lives: she was
80 the one more worthy of long life: it's I
who bear the guilt for this. O my poor girl,
it's I who led you to your death; I said
you were to reach this fearful place by night;
I let you be the first who would arrive.
85 O all you lions with your lairs beneath
this cliff, come now, and with your fierce jaws feast
upon my wretched guts! But cowards talk
as I do—longing for their death but not
prepared to act." At this he gathered up
90 the bloody tatters of his Thisbe's shawl

---

[7] **mulberry:** a type of tree that produces small, sweet berries, which are usually
deep red or purple in color.

and set them underneath the shady tree
where he and she had planned to meet. He wept
and cried out as he held that dear shawl fast:
"Now drink from my blood, too!" And then he drew
95 his dagger from his belt and thrust it hard
into his guts. And as he died, he wrenched
the dagger from his gushing wound. He fell,
supine, along the ground. The blood leaped high;
it spouted like a broken leaden pipe
100 that, through a slender hole where it is worn,
sends out a long and hissing stream as jets
of water cleave the air. And that tree's fruits,
snow-white before, are bloodstained now; the roots
are also drenched with Pyramus' dark blood,
105 and from those roots the hanging berries draw
a darker, purple color.

               Now the girl
again seeks out the tree: though trembling still,
she would not fail his tryst;[8] with eyes and soul
she looks for Pyramus; she wants to tell
110 her lover how she had escaped such perils.
She finds the place—the tree's familiar shape;
but seeing all the berries' color changed,
she is not sure. And as she hesitates,
she sights the writhing body on the ground—
115 the bloody limbs—and, paler than boxwood,[9]
retreats; she trembles—even as the sea
when light wind stirs its surface. She is quick
to recognize her lover; with loud blows
she beats her arms—though they do not deserve
120 such punishment. She tears her hair, enfolds
her love's dear form; she fills his wounds with tears
that mingle with his blood; and while she plants
her kisses on his cold face, she laments:
"What struck you, Pyramus? Why have I lost
125 my love? It is your Thisbe—I—who call
your name! Respond! Lift up your fallen head!"
He heard her name; and lifting up his eyes
weighed down by death, he saw her face—and then
he closed his eyes again.

---

[8] **fail his tryst:** neglect to meet him.
[9] **boxwood:** a white or light yellow type of wood.

                              She recognized
130 her own shawl and his dagger's ivory sheath.
     She cried: "Dear boy, you died by your own hand:
     your love has killed you. But I, too, command
     the force to face at least this task: I can
     claim love, and it will give me strength enough
135 to strike myself. I'll follow you in death;
     and men will say that I—unfortunate—
     was both the cause and comrade of your fate.
     Nothing but death could sever you from me;
     but now death has no power to prevent
140 my joining you. I call upon his parents
     and mine; I plead for him and me—do not
     deny to us—united by true love,
     who share this fatal moment—one same tomb.
     And may you, mulberry, whose boughs now shade
145 one wretched body and will soon shade two,
     forever bear these darkly colored fruits
     as signs of our sad end, that men remember
     the death we met together." With these words,
     she placed the dagger's point beneath her breast,
150 then leaned against the blade still warm with her
     dear lover's blood. The gods and parents heard
     her prayer, and they were stirred. Her wish was granted.

COLLABORATIVE DISCUSSION With a partner, discuss the underlying
story of this myth. How is it similar to other stories you have read or
movies you have seen? Cite details from the myth as you compare it with
other stories.

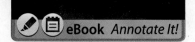
Analyze Source Material

Authors often gain inspiration from the works of other writers. For example, in his retelling of "Pyramus and Thisbe," Ovid was influenced by an ancient myth, passed down orally and in writing for generations. Ovid transformed the story of the unlucky Pyramus and Thisbe into a narrative poem by approaching the themes and topic from a fresh perspective, adjusting the character development, and strengthening the structure of the earlier myth. In the same manner, Shakespeare was influenced by and drew upon the works of Ovid as he wrote *The Tragedy of Romeo and Juliet*. Consider these points as you analyze how an author draws upon and transforms ideas from a specific text.

- What elements does the writer borrow from the source text?
- Do the texts share a topic or theme—that is, an enduring message?
- How does the writer transform elements from the original text?

Analyzing the Text

Cite Text Evidence Support your responses with evidence from the selection.

1. **Connect** In the Prologue to *Romeo and Juliet*, the play is summarized in this manner, "A pair of star-crossed lovers take their life, / Whose misadventured piteous overthrows / Doth with their death bury their parents' strife." What changes did Shakespeare make to the central ideas of "Pyramus and Thisbe"?

2. **Compare** Reread lines 107–152 in the poem. How does this scene compare to Act V, Scene 3, lines 74–120, of *Romeo and Juliet*?

3. **Connect** What common **theme,** or message, can be attributed to both "Pyramus and Thisbe" and *Romeo and Juliet*? Is this theme still relevant to audiences today? Cite evidence from both sources.

PERFORMANCE TASK

Writing Activity: Essay Write a comparison of "Pyramus and Thisbe" and *Romeo and Juliet*.

- Consider the fact that *Romeo and Juliet* is a play, while "Pyramus and Thisbe" is a narrative poem.
- Compare and contrast the play and the narrative poem in terms of plot, conflict, and characters.

- In your essay, consider how the genre of each text affects these elements.
- Review your essay with a partner and revise for standard English grammar and usage.

Duty

Short Story by Pamela Rafael Berkman

AS YOU READ Notice who is telling the story and think about what you already know about the play *The Tragedy of Romeo and Juliet*. Write down any questions you generate during reading.

We heard the running in the streets, we heard the name "Romeo!" called out, but not "Juliet." We had no reason to think Juliet. We knew nothing of what had happened, we thought our daughter already dead. But then we found ourselves summoned, not by servants but by armed men, come from the prince. We were sent for, my husband and I, to come to the opening of our tomb, the tomb of our family, the great yawning maw[1] of death. It had been newly fed.

When we came we found the stone rolled away, like that which
10 covered Our Savior's grave.[2] Now I stand over the bodies of my girl and my enemy's boy, here in the dusty crypt. They are coiled like pale snakes, young serpents of death, he contorted more awfully, by cause of the poison. She stabbed herself instead, made a dagger's sheath of her breasts. And her earlier death was a pretense, to get her to this place and away from us.

The chamber is lined with gloomy stones, the skeletons are faded, gray, common in the sickly light of day that feebly shines—if "shine" is the word could be used for it—through the opening. My nephew Tybalt is over there, a few feet off, green and stinking on his
20 bier,[3] dead three days ago. Crumpled beside him is that fool Paris, who no less than Romeo died for love of my daughter. And I stand and look across the children, across all these pallets of the dead, adorned with jewels, flowers still fresh around Juliet, kept so in

---

[1] **yawning maw:** jaws opened wide.

[2] **the stone . . . Our Savior's grave:** three women who visited the burial site of Jesus discovered that the stone sealing the tomb had been moved and that his body was gone.

[3] **bier (bîr):** a platform that holds a body or a coffin before it is buried.

the cool of this underground place. I stare across them at Romeo's father, Montague.

'Tis not only ourselves, the **bereaved** parents, my husband and I and *his* father and mother, about the tomb now. The county Paris's page, the wretched boy Romeo's attendant Balthasar, the old friar, the prince, Nurse—all are clustered here. And outside the entrance,
30   so short a time ago closed off by the great stone, there gather peasants, working men, merchants, beggars in rags, courtesans, and prostitutes, all the city. The day will not be bright, we feel that even now, the dawn so gray and stale, not fresh and cool as a dawn should be. No breezy wind and yet no heat. A still, dead dawn.

My daughter is pale. When she was alive I wondered if she was **afflicted** with the greensickness, that odd anemic draining of the blood from the face that makes girls her age often so white, with no roses in their skins. I was not so afflicted myself, though many of my sisters and cousins were so. I was, I fear, not sympathetic to
40   their weakness, flushed and strong as I always was, their faces white as tallow.[4]

Now I know she could not have been ill in that kind. I had not seen pale until I saw this face before me; in life she was a red rose compared with this creature drained of blood, all the blood of her body warm on these disgusting stones, running in rivulets[5] between them, dyeing the mortar, the source of the river the sharp little dagger still in her left breast. *He* does not bleed, though he is twisted about horribly, his face an ugly contortion of death, one side of his mouth high in a kind of crooked smile, his fingers held
50   up, bent backward and stiff before his eyes, as though he wished to obscure those orbs[6] from our sight but could not succeed before the last convulsion seized him.

Mistress Montague—I do beg pardon, *Lady* Montague—is about to faint. Not I. I do not **succumb** to the female weakness of fear of blood, or of the dead. But she cries out to her husband, who stands, it seems, amazed, without comprehension or action. Clouds pass over the faint sun outside, and the light is for a moment yet more gray.

And it is very strange, to be watching so closely the clouds
60   and the light outside the tomb at this moment, and I am sure if I were more foolish I would wonder if I were heartless. Perhaps I do wonder yet. How strange, to watch myself watch the clouds and the light, to feel so very much abroad from here where I am, so removed that I watch myself *watching myself* watch the clouds and the light

---

bereaved
(bĭ-rēvd´) *adj.* having suffered the loss of a loved one; grieving.

afflict
(ə-flĭkt´) *v.* to cause pain to; to trouble.

succumb
(sə-kŭm´) *v.* to surrender or fall victim to.

---

[4] **tallow:** hard fat derived from animals, used to make candles and soap.

[5] **rivulets:** small streams.

[6] **orbs:** globes or spheres; here it is referring to Romeo's eyes.

this morning, while my own girl, my own little poppet,[7] my bean, as she once was within me, lies here curled at my feet, curled around *him,* for *that,* that boy. Oh, she was too young to know there is little more useless than a boy! I did not so succumb to such foolishness, I did *not;* when my turn came, I held my head high, I gathered my

---

[7] **poppet:** a cute, darling child.

strength, I performed the duty required of me, the duty that was
best for all, for me, even now. I know this.

How was the stone at the door of the tomb rolled away? I
suppose that boy wrenched it aside with the strength of his doomed
love. Boys. No boy ever did any such thing for me, despite my
beauty. I am still beautiful. I am twenty-seven. I was only a year
older than she is—was—now when my old husband, Capulet, and
I conceived her. The boy's father, Montague, is yet only thirty. He
may have another son, if he has none already. He is not old. Not
gray and cantankerous,[8] like my husband. Who smells of decay.
Like this tomb.

She has no age now, I suppose, my daughter. My bean.

We have been waiting for the prince to speak first. He carries in
his hand a letter, the red seal of which he breaks, and then begins.

"Here he writes that he did buy poison of a poor apothecary,
and therewithal came to this vault to die and lie with Juliet."

We know it all. We heard it shouted among the crowd in the
streets as we came, despite the rhythmic metal steps of our escorts.
"Romeo is dead!" "Juliet did love him!" "They lie now in each
other's arms in the tomb in the churchyard!" "She was not truly
dead yesterday! Did you hear?" "They were married and none
knew!" How do such things creep so quickly, like the plague, into
the common knowledge of the city?

Yet the prince would have none but himself give the story
authority. He would officiate at it. He further reads the note, the
confession of the mortal sin of suicide, left by that boy to his father
confessor, Friar Lawrence. The friar nods sagely, as though he
knows something, as though he can build for us from this fleshy,
deadly crypt some sense and order. But he cannot. Who could build
such things, with three boys and a girl slimy with death arranged
about us? Order? Cause? Effect? He **deludes** himself with his own
importance.

The friar speaks. "Romeo, there, was husband to that Juliet, and
she, there dead, that Romeo's faithful wife. I married them."

Why? How dare he marry children against what he knew would
be the wishes of their parents! He's to blame, *I* know, however
history may hold it, however gently the prince looks on him now.

"How came your master here?" His Grace requests of poor
Paris's page. "To duel with Romeo Montague and die, before this
pair then took their own lives?"

The servant stutters, a simpleton, addressed by so great a
personage, then manages, "He came with flowers to strew his lady's
grave, and bid me stand aloof, and so I did."

delude
(dĭ-lood´) *v.* to
deceive or instill a
false belief in.

---

[8] **cantankerous:** grouchy.

Oh, Paris. Milksop.[9] Even as she rejected him in death, he was slave to my daughter's beauty, which was not fine or perfect but simply youthful. Paris, you tadpole, you eunuch.[10]

Nurse is babbling, telling all, hysterical. "You were too hot!" she screams at my husband, as I did when Juliet refused to marry the county Paris, only the day before yesterday—though I was enraged with my daughter, no less than my husband was. How was I to know the fool had already surrendered the prize to this callow boy, this stepped-upon worm at my feet? Yet my lord threatened to turn her from the house, and that I would have no woman suffer. Now with Nurse and all the company, I turn accusing upon my husband, old Lord Capulet. His nose so long, his hair so thin and falling about his ears. He had no time to dress, his doublet is on over his nightshirt, his legs are scrawny and goatlike, though his stomach bulges. Tears quiver over the end of his nose. Regret. Can it be that my hot-blooded lord and master feels regret? I have no mercy on him. There, do you see? I say with my accusing eyes. 'Twas his doing, all his and his men's fancies and prides.

But Nurse turns on me. She nursed me, too, when she was a girl and I but three weeks old, and yet she turns on me. "God in heaven bless her!" she cries, spittle on her purple face, waving her arms above my blood-drained daughter. Her own daughter dead, she poured all herself into mine. What a creature. "You were to blame, my lady, to rate her so!" Well.

She turns to the prince. "I tried, Your Grace, to defend her from the second marriage, unholy as it was." Liar. "And my lady told her, 'Talk not to me, for I'll not speak a word. Do as thou wilt, for I have done with thee.' Oh, how could a mother?"

I see the **repulsed** stares turn toward me. Simperers. It is unexpected in a mother? But yet not in a father? I did what must be done. What else was I to do? 'Twas her father's word was law, not mine.

Yet Nurse babbles on. "Cold, cold mother. My lamb, she was a faithful wife!" she screams, and throws herself upon her. The prince's men drag her away as she screams, and there is an awkward moment as they push her through the narrow opening, out into the street and the crowd. We hear her screams continue, though they fade, and are finally drowned by the steps, the clinks, of her guardians.

Friar Lawrence, now, must have his say. He whirls upon me and my husband. "You!"

repulsed
(rĭ-pŭlsd´) *adj.*
disgusted.

---

[9] **Milksop:** a weak, cowardly man.
[10] **eunuch:** a person who lacks "masculinity"; one who has been castrated.

"Are you content, bloodthirsty woman? *Are* you a woman? Unnatural creature!"

"Good Father?" I answer. I am calm. I answer with dignity.

"You betrothed and would have married her perforce to county Paris! Then she comes to me." He gulps air and turns to the little group about us, his hand outstretched to point me out. "And you called for the death of Romeo when he killed your hot-blooded kinsman! Are you content, bloodthirsty woman? *Are* you a woman? Unnatural creature!"

A man, a *eunuch*, to judge a mother! How dare he! When in old Sparta a prisoner of war was to be executed, was it not to their women that he was handed? Was it not their women who tore him to bits? "Unnatural creature," indeed!

And cold, am I? "Do as thou wilt, for I have done with thee." So I did say. And had her father not already spoken? I was merciful, quick, as I hear are the mothers in that far-off savage land of legend, Tchin, where they must by law break their daughter's feet, to keep them small as a child's forever. Best for young Juliet to close her eyes and get it done with, the thing accomplished, go to the wedding as though one were a guest, get to the church, only go, no need to think, allow yourself to be dressed by your maids beforehand as though only for a feast, as I did when I was married to this old man. It is like saying one's rosary; simply making the mouth and body move, no need to hold the thoughts in your mind as you do what you do. The things you need do are most often simple enough. So I would have told her on her wedding morning, had I been given the chance. I knew that in the end such a course would be easiest for her.

I did not know, of course, about *his* son. Montague's. I confess I see why my daughter had a preference. Paris is—was—milk toast, certainly. Here he lies now, dead at our feet, not even a good hand with a rapier. He is smaller and paler than, and defeated by, that son of the handsome, broad-chested Montague, Montague who is so close to me now that if I put out my hand I could lay it upon his round arm. He meets my eyes across the bodies of the dead children. All here do look on me now, but he does not appear to hear the friar's insults. He thinks, perhaps, on something else. His own white nightshirt only partially covers his shoulders, hard and firm as they are, and sharp and yet youthful. His jewels are about his neck, his dressing gown shimmering red and green and gold— he was perhaps on his way to bed, not freshly roused out of it. Yet he breaks his look from mine to whisper to the stained red stones we tread upon, where lies his son. He whispers, "What manners is in this, to press before thy father to a grave?" Any might take him for a loving family man, not one who is less in his own bed than a courtesan's, which is what he is. He who left his son to wander the city unchecked and encounter my daughter.

I make no sound. I am the highest-ranking woman in Verona, the highest-ranking personage after the prince and my husband, and though the friar may rant, none other dare do me any open disrespect. My neck is straight. My eyes are level.

Juliet, child, wretched fool! Paris would have been grateful to her for being beautiful, would have petted and worshiped her. I said I would she were wedded to her grave when she refused him, and so she is. Why under heaven would she believe she might marry where she would, an unsuitable boy? Who told her such a thing? Not I. I was far too mindful a mother. How could she? Well, she has found her deserved punishment. May she revel in it. She has paid for her one night with her love, a thing I never had, a thing I was denied, denied *myself,* and what harm would it have done me? None might ever have known.

I stare at Montague. He feels it, brings his eyes back to mine. My heart softens, only a moment, as I see the anguish. Only a moment.

"Do you remember?" I say. That is all, but he knows what I mean. All those about us think I am merely cruelly taunting him, reminding him of when his son yet lived, and sharpen their sneers at me. My husband reaches across bodies to him, they grip each other's right arms, they kiss, they embrace. They vow statues of these children raised in pure gold, peace evermore. None consult *me*. None ask if I want peace evermore. I watch Montague's white shirt falling over the soft, curling dark hair of his chest.

He knows that I ask if he remembers the night fourteen years ago of my father's Christmas revels. The night I pushed him away, pushed away his warm kisses in the cold, silent garden, his hands hot on me. The night long ago when I knew nothing. I thought my worth was in my worth to my family. Soiled, I had no price.

Him I loved. Him I did not marry.

COLLABORATIVE DISCUSSION What did you notice about the narrator of the story? With a partner, discuss how *The Tragedy of Romeo and Juliet* influenced Berkman's "Duty." Cite specific textual evidence to support your ideas.

Analyze Source Material:
Interpretations of Shakespeare

The brilliant works of William Shakespeare have inspired writers and other artists for hundreds of years. In his play *The Tragedy of Romeo and Juliet*, Shakespeare explores the ideas of youthful love, family rivalry, a woman's duty to her family, and the role of fate in one's life. It is one of Shakespeare's best-known and most-beloved plays, especially among young people. In "Duty," contemporary author Pamela Rafael Berkman transforms Shakespeare's familiar tale of "star-crossed lovers" by exploring the story from an unexpected angle.

When authors interpret the work of other artists, they often choose to highlight a particular aspect of the original work. For example, they may borrow the setting or plot of the original work and use it to introduce new characters and situations. Or they may focus on a theme or character from the original and use that as a springboard to initiate a new story. Such new interpretations may deepen the reader's understanding and appreciation of the original work.

Author's Choices: Point of View

An author's choice of **point of view,** or the perspective from which a story is told, has an enormous impact on how readers experience and interpret the story's events. In "Duty," Berkman retells the last scene from *The Tragedy of Romeo and Juliet* through Lady Capulet's eyes. The chart shows how a shift in perspective can affect a reader's interpretation of a story.

Readers understand the narrator's thoughts and feelings.

Readers witness only those events that the narrator does.

Events and characters are filtered through the narrator's opinions and biases.

How point of view affects a story

The narrator's experiences may reveal themes.

By presenting events from Lady Capulet's powerful, first-person point of view, the author invites readers to develop new opinions about Shakespeare's story of young love. As you analyze "Duty," keep these questions in mind:

- How does the point of view expose readers to additional facts about Lady Capulet?
- What is surprising about Lady Capulet's perspective on events and on other characters in the story?
- Does retelling the story from Lady Capulet's point of view affect your interpretation of the source material, *Romeo and Juliet*?

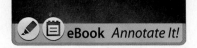

Analyzing the Text

Cite Text Evidence Support your responses with evidence from the selection.

1. **Infer** "Duty" is told from Lady Capulet's point of view. What is her opinion of Juliet and Romeo?

2. **Identify** Identify several specific details from Shakespeare's play that Berkman incorporates in her story. How does she transform each one?

3. **Identify** What surprising facts do readers learn about the characters from the play when Lady Capulet tells the story? What hints about the surprise ending does Berkman provide throughout the story?

4. **Analyze** How does the author reveal the narrator's views on duty? Describe the importance of these views to the story.

5. **Analyze** In what ways does the narrator's point of view influence the reader's opinions of the characters of Romeo and Juliet?

6. **Interpret** Lady Capulet observes that Juliet "was too young to know that there is little more useless than a boy." What themes about love and duty are revealed through her point of view?

7. **Analyze** How does the author's use of first-person point of view affect the **mood,** or emotional atmosphere, of the story? In what way is this mood surprising?

8. **Compare** Whose story is more tragic, Juliet's or Lady Capulet's? Explain.

PERFORMANCE TASK

Writing Activity: Journal Entries Use characters from *Romeo and Juliet*, as presented in "Duty," to explore how point of view can be used to transform source material.

1. In the character of Lady Capulet, create a journal entry in which she delivers her opinions on the responsibilities of children to their parents and their families.

2. In the character of Juliet's nurse, create another journal entry in which the nurse delivers her opinion on how Lady Capulet raised her daughter, Juliet.

In both pieces of writing, include evidence from the text and use the conventions of standard English.

Critical Vocabulary

bereaved　　　**afflict**　　　**succumb**　　　**delude**　　　**repulse**

Practice and Apply Choose which of the two sentences best fits the meaning of each Critical Vocabulary word. Then write a sentence to explain your answer.

bereaved:
1. A boy sobs over the death of his favorite dog.
2. A boy demands a new dog when his old dog dies.

afflict:
1. A girl quickly brushes an insect off of her arm.
2. A girl scratches at the bug bites covering her arms and legs.

succumb:
1. The boy stared at the bowl of candy, then licked his lips.
2. The boy stared at the bowl of candy, then grabbed a handful.

delude:
1. A student thinks he made the best science project in the school's history.
2. A student thinks he could have worked harder on his science project.

repulse:
1. A shopkeeper refuses to wait on a poorly dressed customer.
2. A shopkeeper hangs a sign on the door that reads CLOSED.

Vocabulary Strategy: Context Clues

The meaning of unfamiliar words can often be determined based on **context,** or how words are used within a text. Ask yourself the following questions:

- What is the overall meaning of the sentence, paragraph, or text?
- How does the unfamiliar word function in the sentence?
- Does my guess match the word's dictionary meaning?

For example, the word *bereaved* in this story is used as an adjective to modify *parents*, and the "bereaved parents" are in a tomb. Later in the paragraph, the narrator describes a day that is a "still, dead dawn." The mood evoked is one of intense sadness. Therefore, you may guess that *bereaved* means "saddened." To verify if a guess is correct, check a dictionary.

Practice and Apply Determine the meanings of these four words from the story: *crypt* (line 11), *pallets* (line 22), *contortion* (line 48), *apothecary* (line 84).

1. Identify the function of the word in the sentence: Is it a noun, a verb, or an adjective?

2. Infer the word's meaning based on the context.

3. Look up the word in a dictionary to check your inference.

Language and Style:
Independent and Dependent Clauses

A **clause** is a group of words with a subject and a verb. There are two types of clauses: **independent clauses** can stand alone as a sentence; **dependent clauses** cannot. Instead, dependent clauses act as modifiers by adding meaning to independent clauses. Dependent clauses often begin with these words: *as if, as, since, than, that, though, until, whenever, where, while, who,* and *why.* These words are conjunctions that clarify the connection between clauses.

Read the following sentence from the story.

> **When we came** we found the stone rolled away, <u>like that which covered Our Savior's grave.</u>

This sentence contains one independent clause and two dependent clauses. Notice how the independent clause *we found the stone rolled away* forms a complete thought and can stand alone as a sentence. The two dependent clauses, which are underlined, provide additional information about the independent clause, but they cannot stand alone.

The two types of clauses function together effectively to convey the author's meaning. Without the clauses, the author's ideas might be presented this way:

> We came. We found the stone rolled away. It resembled Our Savior's grave.

These simple sentences are choppy and less interesting to read. Here are more examples of effective independent and dependent clauses from "Duty." The dependent clauses are underlined.

> Crumpled beside him is that fool Paris, <u>who no less than Romeo died for love of my daughter.</u>

> I was not so afflicted myself, <u>though many of my cousins and sisters were so.</u>

Practice and Apply Return to the journal entries you created for this selection's Performance Task. Revise each entry to include two sentences that are independent clauses and two sentences that contain dependent clauses. Share your work with a partner and discuss how the clauses help show connections between ideas and events and add variety to your writing.

Write an Analytical Essay

This collection explores the many facets of love—joy, pain, passion, and conflict, to name just a few. Look back at the anchor text, *Romeo and Juliet*, and at the other texts in the collection. Consider the attributes or characteristics of love that are represented in each text. Synthesize your ideas by writing an analytical essay.

An effective analytical essay

- includes a clear thesis statement
- develops a comparison using examples from the texts
- organizes central ideas in a logically structured body
- uses transitions to create cohesion between sections of the essay
- has a concluding section that relates back to the introduction and leaves the reader with a thought-provoking statement about love

PLAN

Analyze the Texts Review *Romeo and Juliet* to identify several aspects of love that Shakespeare explores in the play. Then look for connections between the play and other texts.

- What aspect of love is explored in both Shakespeare's play and two other texts? Choose three texts, including *Romeo and Juliet*, that explore the same characteristic of love.
- Examine all three texts and take notes on how the portrayal of love is similar and different in each. In your notes, list details, examples, and quotations that support your conclusions.

ACADEMIC VOCABULARY

As you share your ideas about how love is portrayed, be sure to use these words.

> attribute
> commit
> expose
> initiate
> underlie

Gather Evidence Use the annotation tools in your eBook to find evidence from your chosen texts. Save each piece of evidence to *my*Notebook, in a folder titled *Collection 4 Performance Task*.

myNotebook

"Love's Vocabulary"

"Frantic and serene, vigilant and calm, wrung-out and fortified, explosive and sedate—love commands a vast army of moods."

With this sentence, Ackerman reveals the contrasting emotions that love brings out in people.

Get Organized Organize your details and evidence in an outline.

- Write a clear thesis statement about how a particular aspect of love is depicted in *Romeo and Juliet* and in other texts.

- Decide which organizational pattern you will use for your essay. You might present all your ideas about *Romeo and Juliet* first, then write about the second text, and finally write about the third text. Or, you could discuss the similar ideas in all three texts, followed by a discussion of their differences.

- Use your organizational pattern to sort the evidence you have gathered from the selections into a logical order.

- Search for an interesting quotation or detail to complement your thesis statement.

- Write down some ideas for your concluding section.

Interactive Lessons
To help you plan your essay, complete the following lesson:
- Organizing Ideas

PRODUCE

Draft Your Essay Use your outline to write a draft of your essay.

- Introduce your thesis statement, the underlying idea on which your essay will be based. Be explicit and clear so readers will immediately understand your point of view on the topic.

- Present your details, quotations, and examples from the texts in logically ordered paragraphs. Each paragraph should have a central idea related to your thesis with evidence to support it.

- Use transitions to link sections of the text and to clarify the relationships among your ideas. Some transitions that are commonly used to compare and contrast ideas are *similarly, however, even though, on the one hand,* and *in the same way*.

- Write a concluding section that follows logically from the body of the essay. Leave your readers with an interesting statement about love that will give them something to think about.

✓ my WriteSmart

Write your rough draft in *my*WriteSmart. Focus on getting your ideas down, rather than perfecting your choice of language.

Interactive Lessons
To help you draft your essay, complete these lessons:
- Introductions and Conclusions
- Elaboration

Language and Style: Precise Language

Look for places in your essay where you can use precise language to describe something specifically rather than vaguely. Read this passage from Diane Ackerman's essay, "Love's Vocabulary."

> " Love is the white light of emotion. It includes many feelings which, out of laziness and confusion, we crowd into one simple word. "

Note how Ackerman uses the metaphor "the white light of emotion" and the vivid verb "crowd." Her language choices make the sentences more precise and interesting.

Improve Your Draft

Have your partner or group of peers use the questions in the chart to review your draft.

Questions	Tips	Revision Techniques
Does the thesis statement introduce readers to the subject and points of comparison?	**Underline** the subject. **Highlight** each point of comparison.	**Elaborate** on your thesis statement by identifying the aspect of love explored in each text.
Are key ideas presented logically and supported by textual evidence?	**Highlight** each key idea. **Underline** each piece of evidence that supports it.	**Add** evidence for any key idea that is not fully supported.
Are appropriate and varied transitions used to connect and contrast ideas?	**Underline** each transitional word or phrase.	**Add** transitions where needed to clarify the relationships between ideas.
Is a formal style maintained throughout the analysis?	**Highlight** slang and informal language.	**Reword** text to replace informal language with formal language.
Does the concluding section give the audience something to think about?	**Highlight** the concluding insight offered to readers.	**Add** a final thought-provoking statement about love.

Have your partner or a group of peers review your draft in *my*WriteSmart. Ask your reviewers to note any reasons that do not support the thesis statement or that lack sufficient evidence.

Interactive Lessons

To help you revise your essay, complete these lessons:

- Precise Language and Vocabulary
- Formal Style

Exchange Essays

Exchange essays in a small group. Read your group members' essays. Use the following questions to provide feedback to your group members.

- Which aspects of the essay are particularly strong? Did any sections of the essay leave you feeling confused? How could they be clarified?
- Do you agree with your group members' analyses? Was there sufficient textual evidence to support views?

PERFORMANCE TASK RUBRIC
ANALYTICAL ESSAY

	Ideas and Evidence	Organization	Language
4	• The introduction is appealing; the thesis statement clearly identifies the subjects and sets up points for comparison and contrast. • Concrete, relevant details and examples from the texts skillfully support each key point. • The concluding section summarizes the points of comparison and contrast and leaves the reader with a thought-provoking idea.	• Key points and supporting textual evidence are organized logically, effectively, and consistently throughout the essay. • Transitions are well crafted and successfully connect related ideas.	• The writing reflects a formal style and an objective, knowledgeable tone. • Language is vivid and precise. • Sentence beginnings, lengths, and structures vary and have a rhythmic flow. • Spelling, capitalization, and punctuation are correct. If handwritten, the analysis is legible. • Grammar and usage are correct.
3	• The introduction could be more engaging; the thesis statement identifies the subjects and sets up one or two points for comparison and contrast. • One or two key points need more textual support. • The concluding section synthesizes most of the ideas and summarizes most points of comparison and contrast but offers no new insight.	• The organization of key points and supporting textual evidence is confusing in a few places. • A few more transitions are needed to connect ideas.	• The style is inconsistent in a few places, and the tone is subjective at times. • Vague language is used in a few places. • Sentence beginnings, lengths, and structures vary somewhat. • Some spelling, capitalization, and punctuation mistakes occur. If handwritten, the analysis is mostly legible. • Some grammatical and usage errors are repeated in the essay.
2	• The thesis statement identifies the subjects and only hints at the points of comparison and contrast. • Evidence from the texts supports some key points but is often too general. • The concluding section gives an incomplete summary of the points of comparison and contrast and restates the thesis.	• Some key points are organized logically, but many supporting details from the texts are out of place. • More transitions are needed throughout the essay to connect ideas.	• The style is too informal; the tone conveys subjectivity and a lack of understanding of the topic. • Vague, general language is used in many places. • Sentence structures barely vary, and some fragments or run-on sentences are present. • Spelling, capitalization, and punctuation are often incorrect but do not make comprehending the essay difficult. If handwritten, the analysis may be partially illegible. • Grammar and usage are incorrect in many places, but the writer's ideas are still clear.
1	• The appropriate elements of an introduction are missing. • Evidence from the texts is irrelevant or missing. • An identifiable concluding section is missing.	• A logical organization is not used; ideas are presented randomly. • Transitions are not used, making the essay difficult to understand.	• The style and tone are inappropriate for the essay. • Language is too vague or general to convey the information. • Repetitive sentence structure, fragments, and run-on sentences make the writing monotonous and difficult to follow. • Spelling, capitalization, and punctuation are incorrect throughout. If handwritten, the analysis may be partially or mostly illegible. • Many grammatical and usage errors change the meaning of the writer's ideas.

Image Credits: ©The Asahi Shimbun/Getty Images

A Matter of Life or Death

❝To endure what is unendurable is true endurance.**❞**

—Japanese proverb

A Matter of Life or Death

This collection provides a wide-ranging look at how humans endure in the face of adversity.

Stream to Start

Channel One News®

COLLECTION

PERFORMANCE TASK Preview

At the end of this collection, you will have the opportunity to complete two tasks:

- Write an argument about the personal qualities necessary for survival.
- Participate in a panel discussion about how people adapt in order to survive.

ACADEMIC VOCABULARY

Study the words and their definitions in the chart below. You will use these words as you discuss and write about the texts in this collection.

Word	Definition	Related Forms
dimension (dǐ-měn´shən) *n.*	a feature, scale, or measurement of something	dimensional, dimensionality
external (ǐk-stûr´nəl) *adj.*	related to, part of, or from the outside	externalize, externally
statistic (stə-tǐs´tǐk) *n.*	a piece of numerical data	statistical, statistician
sustain (sə-stān´) *v.*	to support or cause to continue	sustainable, unsustainable
utilize (yōot´l-īz´) *v.*	to make use of	utility, utilization

Elie Wiesel (b. 1928) *is a teacher, writer, and Nobel Peace Prize winner. Born in Romania, Wiesel, along with his family, was among millions of European Jews deported to concentration camps during the Holocaust. In 1944, the Nazis sent the family to Auschwitz, where Wiesel's mother and sister perished. Months later, when Wiesel and his father were moved to Buchenwald concentration camp, his father also died. Buchenwald was eventually liberated, and Wiesel went on to write about his experience. His many works include* Dawn *and* The Accident, *both sequels to* Night.

from

Night

Memoir by Elie Wiesel

AS YOU READ Pay attention to how the descriptions of life in the concentration camp compare to what you already know about the topic. Write down any questions you generate during reading.

myNotebook

As you read, save new words to *my*WordList.

The SS[1] offered us a beautiful present for the new year. We had just returned from work. As soon as we passed the camp's entrance, we sensed something out of the ordinary in the air. The roll call was shorter than usual. The evening soup was distributed at great speed, swallowed as quickly. We were anxious.

I was no longer in the same block as my father. They had transferred me to another Kommando,[2] the construction one, where twelve hours a day I hauled heavy slabs of stone. The head of my new block was a German Jew, small with piercing eyes. That

10 evening he announced to us that henceforth no one was allowed to leave the block after the evening soup. A terrible word began to circulate soon thereafter: selection.

---

[1] **SS:** abbreviation of *Schutzstaffel*, German for "defense force"; an armed unit of the Nazi Party that controlled concentration camps.

[2] **Kommando (kə-măn´dō):** German for "command," a small-group organization for laborers in the camps.

We knew what it meant. An SS would examine us. Whenever he found someone extremely frail—a "Muselman" was what we called those inmates—he would write down his number: good for the crematorium.

After the soup, we gathered between the bunks. The veterans told us: "You're lucky to have been brought here so late. Today, this is paradise compared to what the camp was two years ago. Back
20   then, Buna[3] was a veritable hell. No water, no blankets, less soup and bread. At night, we slept almost naked and the temperature was thirty below. We were collecting corpses by the hundreds every day. Work was very hard. Today, this is a little paradise. The Kapos[4] back then had orders to kill a certain number of prisoners every day. And every week, selection. A merciless selection . . . Yes, you are lucky."

"Enough! Be quiet!" I begged them. "Tell your stories tomorrow, or some other day."

They burst out laughing. They were not veterans for nothing.
30   "Are you scared? We too were scared. And, at that time, for good reason."

The old men stayed in their corner, silent, motionless, hunted-down creatures. Some were praying.

One more hour. Then we would know the verdict: death or **reprieve.**

And my father? I first thought of him now. How would he pass selection? He had aged so much. . . .

Our *Blockälteste*[5] had not been outside a concentration camp since 1933. He had already been through all the slaughterhouses, all
40   the factories of death. Around nine o'clock, he came to stand in our midst:

"*Achtung!*"[6]

There was instant silence.

"Listen carefully to what I am about to tell you." For the first time, his voice quivered. "In a few moments, selection will take place. You will have to undress completely. Then you will go, one by one, before the SS doctors. I hope you will all pass. But you must try to increase your chances. Before you go into the next room, try to move your limbs, give yourself some color. Don't walk slowly, run!
50   Run as if you had the devil at your heels! Don't look at the SS. Run, straight in front of you!"

He paused and then added:

reprieve
(rĭ-prēv´) *n.* The cancellation or postponement of punishment.

---

[3] **Buna (boo'nə):** a section of the concentration camp at Auschwitz.

[4] **Kapos (kä´pōs):** prisoners who performed certain duties for the guards.

[5] **Blockälteste (blŏk´ĕl´təs-tə):** a rank of Kapos; a prisoner designated by the Nazis to be the leader or representative of a block, or group of barracks.

[6] **Achtung! (ăk´tōong):** German command for "Attention!"

"And most important, don't be afraid!"

That was a piece of advice we would have loved to be able to follow.

I undressed, leaving my clothes on my cot. Tonight, there was no danger that they would be stolen.

Tibi and Yossi, who had changed Kommandos at the same time I did, came to urge me:

60 "Let's stay together. It will make us stronger."

Yossi was mumbling something. He probably was praying. I had never suspected that Yossi was religious. In fact, I had always believed the opposite. Tibi was silent and very pale. All the block inmates stood naked between the rows of bunks. This must be how one stands for the Last Judgment.

"They are coming!"

Three SS officers surrounded the notorious Dr. Mengele,[7] the very same who had received us in Birkenau. The *Blockälteste* attempted a smile. He asked us:

70 "Ready?"

Yes, we were ready. So were the SS doctors. Dr. Mengele was holding a list: our numbers. He nodded to the *Blockälteste*: we can begin! As if this were a game.

---

[7] **Dr. Mengele (měn-gə´lə):** Josef Mengele (1911–1979), Nazi physician at Auschwitz known for conducting cruel experiments on prisoners.

The first to go were the "notables" of the block, the *Stubenälteste*,[8] the Kapos, the foremen, all of whom were in perfect physical condition, of course! Then came the ordinary prisoners' turns. Dr. Mengele looked them over from head to toe. From time to time, he noted a number. I had but one thought: not to have my number taken down and not to show my left arm.

80   In front of me, there were only Tibi and Yossi. They passed. I had time to notice that Mengele had not written down their numbers. Someone pushed me. It was my turn. I ran without looking back. My head was spinning: you are too skinny . . . you are too weak . . . you are too skinny, you are good for the ovens . . . The race seemed endless; I felt as though I had been running for years . . . You are too skinny, you are too weak . . . At last I arrived. Exhausted. When I had caught my breath, I asked Yossi and Tibi:

    "Did they write me down?"

    "No," said Yossi. Smiling, he added, "Anyway, they couldn't
90 have. You were running too fast . . ."

    I began to laugh. I was happy. I felt like kissing him. At that moment, the others did not matter! They had not written me down.

    Those whose numbers had been noted were standing apart, abandoned by the whole world. Some were silently weeping.

    THE SS OFFICERS left. The *Blockälteste* appeared, his face reflecting our collective weariness.

    "It all went well. Don't worry. Nothing will happen to anyone. Not to anyone . . ."

    He was still trying to smile. A poor **emaciated** Jew questioned
100 him anxiously, his voice trembling:

    "But . . . sir. They *did* write me down!"

    At that, the *Blockälteste* vented his anger: What! Someone refused to take his word?

    "What is it now? Perhaps you think I'm lying? I'm telling you, once and for all: nothing will happen to you! Nothing! You just like to wallow in your despair, you fools!"

    The bell rang, signaling that the selection had ended in the entire camp.

    With all my strength I began to race toward Block 36; midway,
110 I met my father. He came toward me:

    "So? Did you pass?"

    "Yes. And you?"

    "Also."

emaciated
(ĭ-mā´shē-āt´id) *adj.* made extremely thin and weak.

---

[8] **Stubenälteste (shtyoō´bə-nĭl-tŭs´-tə):** a rank of Kapos; prisoners designated by the Nazis to be the leaders of their barracks, or rooms.

We were able to breathe again. My father had a present for me: a half ration of bread, bartered for something he had found at the depot, a piece of rubber that could be used to repair a shoe.

The bell. It was already time to part, to go to bed. The bell regulated everything. It gave me orders and I **executed** them blindly. I hated that bell. Whenever I happened to dream of a better world, I imagined a universe without a bell.

120

execute
(ĕk´sĭ-kyo͞ot´) *v.*
to carry out, or
accomplish.

A FEW DAYS passed. We were no longer thinking about the selection. We went to work as usual and loaded the heavy stones onto the freight cars. The rations had grown smaller; that was the only change.

We had risen at dawn, as we did every day. We had received our black coffee, our ration of bread. We were about to head to the work yard as always. The *Blockälteste* came running:

"Let's have a moment of quiet. I have here a list of numbers. I shall read them to you. All those called will not go to work this morning; they will stay in camp."

130

Softly, he read some ten numbers. We understood. These were the numbers from the selection. Dr. Mengele had not forgotten.

The *Blockälteste* turned to go to his room. The ten prisoners surrounded him, clinging to his clothes:

"Save us! You promised . . . We want to go to the depot, we are strong enough to work. We are good workers. We can . . .we want . . ."

He tried to calm them, to reassure them about their fate, to explain to them that staying in the camp did not mean much, had no tragic significance: "After all, I stay here every day . . ."

140

The argument was more than flimsy. He realized it and, without another word, locked himself in his room.

The bell had just rung.

"Form ranks!"

Now, it no longer mattered that the work was hard. All that mattered was to be far from the block, far from the crucible[9] of death, from the center of hell.

I saw my father running in my direction. Suddenly, I was afraid.

"What is happening?"

150

He was out of breath, hardly able to open his mouth.

"Me too, me too . . . They told me too to stay in the camp."

They had recorded his number without his noticing.

"What are we going to do?" I said anxiously.

But it was he who tried to reassure me:

---

[9] **crucible:** a vessel used for melting materials at high temperatures.

"It's not certain yet. There's still a chance. Today, they will do another selection . . . a **decisive** one . . ."

I said nothing.

decisive
(dĭ-sī´sĭv) *adj.* final or concluding.

He felt time was running out. He was speaking rapidly, he wanted to tell me so many things. His speech became confused, his
160   voice was choked. He knew that I had to leave in a few moments. He was going to remain alone, so alone . . .

"Here, take this knife," he said. "I won't need it anymore. You may find it useful. Also take this spoon. Don't sell it. Quickly! Go ahead, take what I'm giving you!"

My inheritance . . .

"Don't talk like that, Father." I was on the verge of breaking into sobs. "I don't want you to say such things. Keep the spoon and knife. You will need them as much as I. We'll see each other tonight, after work."
170   He looked at me with his tired eyes, veiled by despair. He insisted:

"I am asking you . . . Take it, do as I ask you, my son. Time is running out. Do as your father asks you . . ."

Our Kapo shouted the order to march.

The Kommando headed toward the camp gate. Left, right! I was biting my lips. My father had remained near the block, leaning against the wall. Then he began to run, to try to catch up with us. Perhaps he had forgotten to tell me something... But we were marching too fast . . . Left, right!
180   We were at the gate. We were being counted. Around us, the **din** of military music. Then we were outside.

din
(dĭn) *n.* loud noise.

ALL DAY, I PLODDED AROUND like a sleepwalker. Tibi and Yossi would call out to me, from time to time, trying to reassure me. As did the Kapo who had given me easier tasks that day. I felt sick at heart. How kindly they treated me. Like an orphan. I thought: Even now, my father is helping me.

I myself didn't know whether I wanted the day to go by quickly or not. I was afraid of finding myself alone that evening. How good it would be to die right here!
190   At last, we began the return journey. How I longed for an order to run! The military march. The gate. The camp. I ran toward Block 36.

Were there still miracles on this earth? He was alive. He had passed the second selection. He had still proved his usefulness . . . I gave him back his knife and spoon.

COLLABORATIVE DISCUSSION With a partner, discuss two unexpected details from Wiesel's description of life in the concentration camp. Explain why they were surprising, citing specific passages in your discussion.

Analyze Author's Purpose and Rhetoric

Purpose is an author's reason for writing a text. Authors may write to persuade, to inform, or to entertain. They may even write for more than one purpose, but their purpose is rarely stated directly. Instead, readers infer, or draw conclusions about, the purpose based on the author's **rhetoric,** or style, and other clues in the text.

To advance their purpose, authors must engage the reader with a compelling style that includes thoughtful ideas and interesting details. Elie Wiesel chose to write in the form of a **memoir**—an autobiographical account of his personal experiences and observations of a significant event. Use these questions to help you think about Wiesel's reason for writing *Night*.

- What is the historical context for this memoir? About what significant event and people is Wiesel sharing memories?
- What perspective do you understand from reading this first-person account?
- Think about other nonfiction books or articles that you have read about Wiesel's topic. How does Wiesel's first-person account differ from these?
- What insight do you gain into the effect this historical event had on people?

Analyze Impact of Word Choice on Tone

The **tone** of a work is the author's attitude toward the subject and audience. A writer's tone might be formal and serious, angry, or lighthearted. There could even be several tones reflected in a single work. Writers shape tone through **word choices.** Words with particular connotations subtly change the meaning of a sentence and help to create the tone of a passage. Look at the examples from the selection. Which words help create the tone?

Tone	Example from *Night*
Fear and dread	"One more hour. Then we would know the verdict: death or reprieve."
Despair	"He felt time was running out. He was speaking rapidly, he wanted to tell me so many things. His speech became confused, his voice was choked."
Upbeat and encouraging	"Were there still miracles on this earth? He was alive. He had passed the second selection. He had still proved his usefulness."

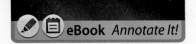
eBook *Annotate It!*

Analyzing the Text

Cite Text Evidence Support your responses with evidence from the selection.

1. **Infer** In lines 32–33, Wiesel writes, "The old men stayed in their corner, silent, motionless, hunted-down creatures. Some were praying." Which words in this quotation have strong connotations? How do these words convey the tone of Wiesel's narrative?

2. **Cite Evidence** What evidence does Wiesel provide to support the idea that though beaten down, the prisoners had creative ways of coping with their confinement and of sustaining themselves?

3. **Analyze** Look back at the scene in which Wiesel must run before the SS doctors during selection (lines 83–86). Why does Wiesel repeat his thoughts, "you are too skinny, you are too weak"? How does the repetition help readers understand his experience?

4. **Interpret** Wiesel sometimes uses punctuation and sentence structure to convey meaning. Reread the second to last paragraph in the text. Why does he use short, incomplete sentences? How does this stylistic approach affect meaning?

5. **Analyze** Wiesel includes statements and reactions from other prisoners, the head of the block, and the veterans of the camp that reveal different perspectives about life in the concentration camp. Identify examples of these different perspectives and explain what they reveal about the prisoners' ordeal.

6. **Draw Conclusions** Why do you think Wiesel chose to call his memoir *Night*? What might be the significance of that title?

PERFORMANCE TASK

Writing Activity: Analysis Elie Wiesel's account of the concentration camp is deeply personal. Think about what he wrote and what he may have wanted to achieve with his account. Then write a brief analysis in which you answer the following questions:

- Why did Wiesel write *Night*? What did he hope to accomplish? Did he succeed?
- Did his descriptions of life in the camp connect with you, the reader? How?
- Elie Wiesel's account of the Holocaust was written years after the events took place. How might *Night* be different if it had been written as a diary, a first-person account of events immediately after they happened?
- Would you recommend this memoir to others? Why?

In your writing, include evidence from the text to support your analysis and use the conventions of standard English.

Critical Vocabulary

reprieve	emaciated	execute	decisive	din

Practice and Apply Use your knowledge of the Critical Vocabulary words to respond to each question.

1. Wiesel describes one of the prisoners as **emaciated.** What did the prisoner look like?

2. When Wiesel's father passed the second **decisive** selection, Wiesel was relieved. Explain why.

3. While a prisoner, Wiesel would **execute** his orders in the camp. Did the guards likely have a complaint about his work? Explain.

4. The narrator could hear the **din** of military music in the background. What did the music sound like?

5. The prisoners at the concentration camp hoped for a **reprieve** from death. What were they hoping for?

Vocabulary Strategy: Multiple-Meaning Words

The Critical Vocabulary word *execute* means "to accomplish or carry out fully." *Execute* has another definition, "to put to death." Like *execute*, many words have **multiple meanings.** Use the strategies below to determine or clarify the meaning of multiple-meaning words.

- Use context, or the way the word is used in a sentence or paragraph, to determine meaning. This strategy requires looking at the words and sentences around the unknown word to clarify meaning. For example, look at the following sentence: *Mountain climbing was her passion, and she wanted to scale every peak.* The context tells you that *scale* refers to climbing.
- Consult general and specialized reference materials, particularly glossaries and dictionaries, to determine or clarify a word's precise meaning. Dictionary entries provide all the definitions of a word, as well as its part of speech, so select the definition that makes sense.

Practice and Apply Work in a group to locate these words in the selection: *present* (line 1), *block* (line 6), *bunks* (line 17), *reflecting* (line 96). Use context clues or reference materials to determine the precise meaning for each word.

Language and Style: Tone

An author's attitude toward a subject or an audience helps create the overall feeling that a selection conveys. Authors establish **tone** by making effective word choices for meaning and style.

Read the following sentences from the selection:

Those whose numbers had been noted were standing apart, abandoned by the whole world. Some were silently weeping.

Wiesel might have written the sentence like this:

The prisoners whose numbers had been called were standing by themselves crying.

How is the second sentence different from the first? Look again at the first sentence. Notice that Wiesel uses words with strong connotations. Words like *apart*, *abandoned, silently,* and *weeping* create strong imagery for the reader, which in turn shapes a tone of tragedy and despair. Wiesel's use of formal language also adds to the weight and seriousness of the memoir's tone. Note the difference in the use of formal versus informal language in these passages.

Formal	Informal
"Listen carefully to what I am about to tell you." For the first time, his voice quivered. "In a few moments, selection will take place. You will have to undress completely. Then you will go, one by one, before the SS doctors. I hope you will all pass."	"Listen, everyone," he said as his voice shook. "Selection's going to start soon. You'll have to take your clothes off, then walk by the SS doctors one at a time. I hope everyone passes."
"What is it now? Perhaps you think I'm lying? I'm telling you, once and for all: nothing will happen to you! Nothing! You just like to wallow in your despair, you fools!"	"What? Do you think I'm lying? Nothing's going to happen to you! You're just feeling sorry for yourselves!"

Practice and Apply Look back at the analysis you wrote in response to this selection's Performance Task. Revise it to include formal, rather than informal, language and at least two sentences that contain strong imagery. Then discuss with a partner how formal language and strong imagery improve the meaning and tone of your work.

Is Survival Selfish?

Argument by Lane Wallace

AS YOU READ Think about whether you would use the word *selfish* to describe someone who survives a disaster. Write down any questions you generate during reading.

When the ocean liner *Titanic* sank in April of 1912, one of the few men to survive the tragedy was J. Bruce Ismay, the chairman and managing director of the company that owned the ship. After the disaster, however, Ismay was savaged by the media and the general public for climbing into a lifeboat and saving himself when there were other women and children still on board. Ismay said he'd already helped many women and children into lifeboats and had only climbed in one himself when there were no other women or children in the area and the boat was ready
10 to release. But it didn't matter. His reputation was ruined. He was labeled an uncivilized coward and, a year after the disaster, he resigned his position at White Star.

The "women and children first" protocol of the *Titanic* may not be as strong a social stricture[1] as it was a century ago. But we still tend to **laud** those who risk or sacrifice themselves to save others in moments of danger or crisis and look less kindly on those who focus on saving themselves, instead.

laud
(lôd) *v.* to praise.

But is survival really selfish and uncivilized? Or is it smart? And is going in to rescue others always heroic? Or is it sometimes
20 just stupid? It's a complex question, because there are so many factors involved, and every survival situation is different.

Self-preservation is supposedly an instinct. So one would think that in life-and-death situations, we'd all be very focused on whatever was necessary to survive. But that's not always true. In July

---

[1] **social stricture:** behavioral restriction placed on society.

2007, I was having a drink with a friend in Grand Central Station[2] when an underground steam pipe exploded just outside. From where we sat, we heard a dull "boom!" and then suddenly, people were running, streaming out of the tunnels and out the doors.

My friend and I walked quickly and calmly outside, but to get any further, we had to push our way through a crowd of people who were staring, **transfixed,** at the column of smoke rising from the front of the station. Some people were crying, others were screaming, others were on their cell phones . . . but the crowd, for the most part, was *not* doing the one thing that would increase everyone's chances of survival, if in fact a terrorist bomb with god knows what inside it had just gone off—namely, moving away from the area.

We may have an instinct for survival, but it clearly doesn't always kick in the way it should. A guy who provides survival training for pilots told me once that the number one determining factor for survival is simply whether people hold it together in a crisis or fall apart. And, he said, it's impossible to predict ahead of time who's going to hold it together, and who's going to fall apart.

So what is the responsibility of those who hold it together? I remember reading the account of one woman who was in an airliner that crashed on landing. People were frozen or screaming, but nobody was moving toward the emergency exits, even as smoke began to fill the cabin. After realizing that the people around her were too paralyzed to react, she took direct action, crawling over several rows of people to get to the exit. She got out of the plane and survived. Very few others in the plane, which was soon **consumed** by smoke and fire, did. And afterward, I remember she said she battled a lot of guilt for saving herself instead of trying to save the others.

Could she really have saved the others? Probably not, and certainly not from the back of the plane. If she'd tried, she probably would have perished with them. So why do survivors **berate** themselves for not adding to the loss by attempting the impossible? Perhaps it's because we get very mixed messages about survival ethics.

On the one hand, we're told to put our own oxygen masks on first, and not to jump in the water with a drowning victim. But then the people who ignore those **edicts** and survive to tell the tale are lauded as heroes. And people who do the "smart" thing are sometimes criticized quite heavily after the fact.

In a famous mountain-climbing accident chronicled in the book and documentary *Touching the Void*, climber Simon Yates was

transfix
(trăns-fĭks´) *v.* to captivate or make motionless with awe.

consume
(kən-soom´) *v.* to completely destroy or eradicate.

berate
(bĭ-rāt´) *v.* to criticize or scold.

edict
(ē´dĭkt´) *n.* an official rule or proclamation.

---

[2] **Grand Central Station:** a large commuter-rail and subway terminal in New York City.

> # "It's impossible to predict ahead of time who's going to hold it together, and who's going to fall apart."

attempting to rope his already-injured friend Joe Simpson down a mountain in bad weather when the belay[3] went awry. Simpson
70 ended up hanging off a cliff, unable to climb up, and Yates, unable to lift him up and losing his own grip on the mountain, ended up cutting the rope to Simpson to save himself. Miraculously, Simpson survived the 100 foot fall and eventually made his way down the mountain. But Yates was criticized by some for his survival decision, even though the alternative would have almost certainly led to both of their deaths.

In Yates' case, he had time to think hard about the odds, and the possibilities he was facing, and to realize that he couldn't save anyone but himself. But what about people who have to make
80 more instantaneous decisions? If, in fact, survivors are driven by instinct not civilization, how do you explain all those who choose otherwise? Who would dive into icy waters or onto subway tracks or disobey orders to make repeat trips onto a minefield to bring wounded to safety? Are they more civilized than the rest of us? More brave? More noble?

It sounds nice, but oddly enough, most of the people who perform such impulsive rescues say that they didn't really think before acting. Which means they weren't "choosing" civilization

---

[3] **belay:** the securing of a rope to a cleat or another object.

over instinct. If survival is an instinct, it seems to me that there
must be something equally instinctive that drives us, sometimes, to
run into danger instead of away from it.

Perhaps it comes down to the ancient "fight or flight" impulse.
Animals confronted with danger will choose to attack it, or run
from it, and it's hard to say which one they'll choose, or when. Or
maybe humans are such social herd animals, dependent on the
herd for survival, that we feel a pull toward others even as we feel a
contrary pull toward our own preservation, and the two impulses
battle it out within us . . . leading to the mixed messages we send
each other on which impulse to follow.

Some people hold it together in a crisis and some people fall
apart. Some people might run away from danger one day, and
toward it the next. We pick up a thousand cues in an instant of
crisis and respond in ways that even surprise ourselves, sometimes.

But while we laud those who sacrifice themselves in an attempt
to save another, there is a fine line between brave and foolish.
There can also be a fine line between smart and selfish. And as a
friend who's served in the military for 27 years says, the truth is,
sometimes there's no line at all between the two.

COLLABORATIVE DISCUSSION With a partner, review the various stories
of survivors and discuss whether you would describe each person's
actions as *selfish*. Is being selfish always bad? Cite textual evidence as
well as your own reasoning in your discussion.

Delineate and Evaluate an Argument

In an **argument,** the author expresses a position on an issue and then attempts to support that position. A successful argument persuades readers to agree with the author's position. To **evaluate** whether an argument is successful, you must first **delineate,** or outline, its basic parts. The diagram shows a simplified outline.

- The **claim** is the author's position on the topic or issue. It is the central idea around which the argument is structured.
- **Reasons** are explanations that support the claim by answering the question *Why does the author hold that opinion?* An author's reasoning must be clear and logical to create a valid argument.
- **Evidence** includes facts, statistics, personal experiences, statements by experts, and other information. The evidence supports the reasons and, ultimately, the author's claim.

Most arguments begin by stating a claim and then present reasons and evidence for the claim. To be convincing, an argument must include evidence that is valid, relevant, and sufficient. Use this checklist to evaluate evidence presented in "Is Survival Selfish?"

Evaluating Evidence Checklist
Evidence is valid if
• it is well known or common knowledge
• the author identifies the source
• the source appears to be trustworthy
• research shows the source to be reliable
Evidence is relevant if
• it is closely related to the topic or issue
• it supports the claim
Evidence is sufficient if
• there is enough of it
• it comes from a variety of sources

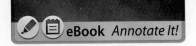
Analyzing the Text

Cite Text Evidence ▶ Support your responses with evidence from the selection.

1. **Summarize** Lane Wallace begins her argument with a series of questions to get her readers thinking about what is selfish and what is heroic. In your own words, state the claim that she expresses in lines 18–21. Take into account the information she presents in the rest of her argument, including her conclusions at the end.

2. **Analyze** Wallace writes that "the number one determining factor for survival is simply whether people hold it together in a crisis or fall apart" (lines 40–42). Is this an example of a claim, a reason, or evidence? Explain.

3. **Critique** In lines 24–37 what evidence does Wallace offer to support her idea that people are not always focused on doing "whatever [is] necessary to survive" in a crisis? Is the evidence relevant and sufficient? Explain.

4. **Evaluate** In lines 44–60, Wallace notes that survivors often suffer from feelings of guilt. Does she think these feelings are justified? Does she support her reasoning with relevant and sufficient evidence? Explain your response.

5. **Evaluate** Reread lines 86–91. As evidence for Wallace's claim, is this paragraph valid and relevant? Explain.

6. **Interpret** In the final paragraph, Wallace writes that there is "a fine line between smart and selfish," and that "sometimes there's no line at all." What does she mean by this, and how does her conclusion restate her claim?

PERFORMANCE TASK

Speaking Activity: Debate In the selection, Lane Wallace explores whether survivors are selfish for trying to save their own lives while rescuers are heroic for trying to save others. Review the author's argument before completing this activity.

1. Divide the class into two teams. One team should take the position that survivors are selfish and uncivilized and that rescuers are heroic; the other team should take the position that survivors are smart and that rescuers are foolish.

2. Work with your team to gather evidence and use it to build a well-reasoned argument.

3. Hold a debate in which members from each team take turns stating the reasons and evidence for their claim, as well as responding to the other team's argument. Use appropriate eye contact and adequate volume to emphasize ideas.

4. After the debate, write a brief evaluation of each team's argument and explain which argument was more convincing.

Critical Vocabulary

laud	transfix	consume	berate	edict

Practice and Apply Each of these word pairs contains one Critical Vocabulary word. Describe what is different and alike about the words in each pair. Use a dictionary or thesaurus as needed.

1. laud/welcome

2. transfix/stare

3. consume/fill

4. berate/battle

5. edict/tale

Vocabulary Strategy: Synonyms

Words that share the same or nearly the same meaning are called **synonyms.** Authors sometimes use synonyms to vary word choice and make their writing more interesting. For example, in line 49 of "Is Survival Selfish?" the author uses the word *paralyzed*. The synonym *transfixed* might also have worked, but the author had already used it in line 31.

   If you come across an unfamiliar word in a text, try to think of another word that would make sense in the context of the sentence. Then check a dictionary or a thesaurus to see if your word is truly a synonym for the unfamiliar word. Note any subtle differences between the synonyms and try to understand why the author chose that precise word. Ask yourself whether the context sentence has the same or a slightly different meaning with your synonym as with the author's original word.

Practice and Apply Use a print or online thesaurus to complete this activity.

1. Create a two-column chart. In the first column, write the Critical Vocabulary words. In the second column, write at least two synonyms for each word.

2. Write a sentence using each Critical Vocabulary word.

3. For each sentence you write, exchange the Critical Vocabulary word for one of its synonyms. Work together with a partner to choose the best synonym for each sentence. Discuss whether using a synonym changes the meaning of each original sentence.

Language and Style: Indefinite Pronouns

When authors want to refer to a specific person, they use personal pronouns, such as *he, she*, or *I* ("She got out of the plane and survived"). To refer to one or more people or things that are not specifically mentioned, authors use **indefinite pronouns,** such as *anyone, all,* or *some.* In "Is Survival Selfish?" Lane Wallace uses a variety of indefinite pronouns.

Read this sentence from the selection:

But Yates was criticized by <u>some</u> for his survival decision . . . .

The indefinite pronoun *some* refers to the people who criticized Yates. It would be awkward—and probably impossible—to mention by name all of those who criticized the climber, so the author's use of *some* makes sense.

This chart lists other indefinite pronouns found in "Is Survival Selfish?"

Indefinite Pronoun	Example
others	". . . sacrifice themselves to save others . . ."
one	". . . one would think that in life-and-death situations . . ."
whatever	". . . whatever was necessary to survive."
nobody	". . . nobody was moving toward the emergency exits . . ."
another	". . . in an attempt to save another . . ."

Some words that can function as indefinite pronouns can also function as adjectives. For example, read this sentence from the selection:

<u>Some</u> people hold it together in a crisis and <u>some</u> people fall apart.

Here, *some* is used as an adjective because it describes the plural noun *people.*

Indefinite pronouns are sometimes used in pairs. Consider the following examples from the selection:

. . . the mixed messages we send <u>each other</u> . . .

Very <u>few others</u> in the plane . . .

In these examples, *each other* and *few others* may be considered compound indefinite pronouns because the words in each pair act together as a pronoun.

Practice and Apply Using the topic of survival ethics, write one sentence for each of the indefinite pronouns listed in the chart above. When you are finished, discuss your sentences with a partner.

from
Deep
Survival

Science Writing by Laurence Gonzales

AS YOU READ Think about the title of the selection and consider what the term *deep survival* means to the author. Write down any questions you generate during reading.

Juliane Koepcke was flying with her mother and ninety other passengers on Christmas Eve, 1971, when lightning struck, causing an extensive structural failure of the Lockheed Electra. Juliane fell out of the broken airplane into the Peruvian jungle. She was seventeen years old, wearing her Catholic confirmation dress and white high heels. Miraculously, she suffered only cuts and a broken collarbone from the crash. Later, she reported feeling "a hefty concussion." Then she was falling toward the jungle.

As she recalled, "I remember thinking that the jungle trees below looked just like cauliflowers." To someone who knows about survival, that statement is telling. She wasn't screaming; she wasn't in a panic. She was in wonder at the world in which she found herself. She was taking it all in, touching her new reality. Checking out her environment while falling. Amazing cool.

Amazing and also characteristic of a true survivor. Bill Garleb, an American GI who survived the Bataan Death March[1] in the Philippines, found his senses increasingly sharp as he experienced a deep wonder at the birds and colors and smells of the jungle.

A dozen other passengers survived the midair **disintegration** of Juliane's plane, and their attitude, and hence their behavior and fate, were quite different from hers.

Juliane awoke alone on the floor of the jungle, still strapped into her seat. There was no sign of her mother, who'd been beside her in the plane. She spent the night trying to keep out of the rain

disintegration
(dĭs-ĭn'tĭ-grā'shən) *n.*
the process of a whole coming apart in pieces.

---

[1] **Bataan Death March:** the forced transfer of captured American and Filipino soldiers by the Japanese after the World War II Battle of Bataan. Thousands died during the ordeal in April 1942.

under her seat. The next day, she **deduced** that even the helicopters and airplanes she could hear wouldn't be able to see her through the jungle canopy.[2] She'd have to get herself out. It was another important moment: She didn't spend time bemoaning her fate. She looked to herself, took responsibility, made a plan.

Her parents were researchers who worked in the jungle, and she was familiar with that environment. But Juliane had had no survival training. She didn't know where she was or which way she ought to go, but her father had told her that if she went downhill, she'd find water. He'd said that rivers usually led to civilization. And while that strategy can just as easily lead into a swamp, at least she had a plan that she believed in. She had a task.

Meanwhile, the others who had lived through the fall decided to await rescue, which is not necessarily a bad idea either. But expecting someone else to take responsibility for your well-being can be fatal. In *Alive*, Piers Paul Read tells the story of the survivors of another airplane crash, this one in the Andes.[3] Everyone who survived the crash stayed put, assuming that they'd be rescued. Many died; the others wound up eating each other to keep from starving before someone finally walked out and found help.

Juliane had nothing except a few pieces of candy and some small cakes. She had no survival equipment, no tools, no compass or map—none of the things I'd been taught to use in survival school. But she very deliberately set up a program for herself. She set off, resting through the heat of the day and traveling during the cooler periods. She walked for eleven days through dense jungle while being literally eaten alive by leeches and strange tropical insects, which bored into her, laid their eggs, and produced worms that hatched and tunneled out through her skin.

Eventually, she came to a hut along the banks of the river she'd been following. She staggered and collapsed inside. There is always a lot of chance involved in a survival situation, both good luck and bad. It was Juliane's good fortune that three hunters turned up the next day and delivered her to a local doctor. But, as Louis Pasteur[4] said, "Luck favors the prepared mind."

Tough and clearheaded, this teenage girl, who had lost her shoes (not to mention her mother) on the first day, saved herself; the other survivors took the same eleven days to sit down and die.

The forces that put them there were beyond their control. But the course of events for those who found themselves alive on the

deduce
(dĭ-dōōs´) *v.* to know through reason or logical conclusion.

---

[2] **jungle canopy:** the dense layer formed by the leaves and branches of the tallest trees.

[3] **Andes:** a mountain range in western South America running from Venezuela to Argentina.

[4] **Louis Pasteur:** (1822–1895) French chemist and biologist.

ground were the result of deep and personal individual reactions to a new environment.

The knottiest mystery of survival is how one unequipped, ill-prepared seventeen-year-old girl gets out alive and a dozen adults in similar circumstances, better equipped, do not. But the deeper I've gone into the study of survival, the more sense such outcomes make. Making fire, building shelter, finding food, signaling, navigation— none of that mattered to Juliane's survival. Although we cannot know what the others who survived the fall were thinking and deciding, it's possible that they knew they were supposed to stay put and await rescue. They were rule followers, and it killed them.

In the World Trade Center disaster,[5] many people who were used to following the rules died because they did what they were told by authority figures. An employee of the Aon Insurance Company on the ninety-third floor of the south tower had begun his escape but returned to his office after the security guards made a general announcement that the building was safe and that people should stay inside until they were told to leave. Before he died, he spoke to his father on the phone: "Why did I listen to them—I shouldn't have." Another man, an employee of Fuji Bank, actually reached the ground-floor lobby, only to be sent back in by a security guard. A third worker called a family member and recorded a final message on the answering machine: "I can't go anywhere because they told us not to move. I have to wait for the firefighters."

In thinking for herself, Juliane wasn't even particularly brave. Survival is not about bravery and heroics. Heroes can be perfect heroes and wind up dead. By definition, survivors must live. Juliane was afraid most of the time (of everything from piranhas when she had to wade in the water to the worms that were crawling around under her skin to the real or imagined creatures of the forest). Survivors aren't fearless. They *use* fear: they turn it into anger and focus.

Conversely, searchers are always amazed to find people who have died while in possession of everything they needed to survive. John Leach writes that "Victims have been recovered from life rafts with a survival box (containing flares, rations, first-aid kit and so on) unopened and the necessary contents unused."

"Some people just give up," Ken Hill told me, referring to his search and rescue operations in Nova Scotia. "Fifteen years I've been studying this, and I can't figure out why."

What saved Juliane was an inner resource, a state of mind. She certainly didn't have any physical equipment. But she'd been

conversely
(kən-vûrs´lē) *adv.* in a way that contradicts or reverses something.

---

[5] **World Trade Center disaster:** the destruction of New York office buildings by hijacked airplanes on September 11, 2001.

prepared mentally, somehow. A lifetime of experience shapes us
to meet or be crushed by such challenges as a bad divorce, the
shattering of a career, a terrible illness or accident, a collapsing
economy, a war, prison camp, the death of a loved one, or being
stranded in the jungle. I went to survival school to try to understand
that mystery and see if I could master my own journey. . . .

We took off from Pittsfield, Massachusetts, sharing the flying
duties, and landed in Lynchburg, Virginia. As I climbed out of
the cockpit and onto the wing, I caught my first glimpse of our
instructor. Byron Kerns runs the Mountain Shepherd Survival
School. He swaggered across the fueling ramp toward us wearing
an 18-inch Panamanian machete on his belt, a big, macho-looking
guy with twelve years of military experience, including a stint with
the Marines. He had worked at the famous Air Force Survival
School in Washington State. When I saw him, I thought, We're in
for it now.

That night, Byron explained that we were going to head off into
the Virginia woods the next morning, early, and we'd be drilling for
several days on such matters as map and compass work, firecraft,
shelter, and signaling. We'd learn to find water or **distill** it from the
air. We would not think about food, because it wasn't necessary.
The Air Force plan was that you'd be found within three days.
"Your job," he said, "is to stay alive for seventy-two hours." When
he left, Jonas[6] said, "This guy's going to whip you like a redheaded
stepchild."[7]

Early the next morning, as we moved up a rocky river drainage
through the mountains, I noticed that Kerns would stop frequently
to point out something of beauty or interest. He spoke softly, as if
we were in a church. He laughed a lot. He liked to be still and just
think or smoke a cigarette. I saw no sign of the drill sergeant I'd
expected. In our first exercise, Kerns asked me and Jonas to make a
fire, and in a matter of minutes we had a roaring blaze going. Kerns
had turned away to get something from his pack. When he turned
back, the flames were leaping several feet off the ground. "Whoa,"
he said, laughing, "easy, easy. I just wanted to know if you could
start a fire. Some people can't." Then he gently separated the pile of
wood and put it out.

Byron Kerns turned out to be soft-spoken, polite, cheerfully
earnest, and gentle to a fault. He moved slowly, never hurried,
and was always carefully assessing himself and his environment.
He wasn't prone to high emotional states. He carried with him a

distill
(dĭ-stĭl′) *v.* to
transform vapor into
liquid.

---

[6] **Jonas Dovydenas:** (b. 1939) Lithuanian-born photographer.

[7] **a redheaded stepchild:** a person who is mistreated because he or she is
unwanted.

contagious air of calm. He reminded me of my father, actually.
Like so many retired pilots, my father wore soft shoes, talked softly,
and walked slowly. (As a pilot, you want to wear soft shoes so that
you can feel the rudder pedals. You don't want to make sudden,
unplanned motions in a combat aircraft cockpit, where the controls
are sensitive and lots of things can explode.) That **demeanor**, once
learned under penalty of death, is carried through the rest of your
life. Kerns also had that quiet, dark, and private humor.

Even after a lifetime in the wilderness, Kerns entered the woods
with a deep sense of respect and humility, like a man approaching
a magnificent, dangerous, and unpredictable creature. It's the same
way a good pilot approaches his aircraft.

As we worked in the wilderness, learning technical skills, Kerns
kept talking about Positive Mental Attitude. It was the number one
item on the checklist he'd given us, and that checklist was from
the Big Daddy of all checklist writers, the U.S. Air Force. Positive
Mental Attitude.

"It must be important," I told Jonas.

"Yeah, but what is it?" he asked.

"Think good thoughts and you'll be saved?"

"I'd rather have a chain saw and a cheeseburger," Jonas said. "A
cell phone and a GPS would be nice, too."

demeanor
(dĭ-mē′nər) *n.*
attitude or perceived
behavior.

As we slogged through the woods, practicing firecraft, shelter making, knots, and navigation . . . I kept asking Kerns, but he couldn't explain it. Nobody could. It meant the difference between life and death; he could tell me that. He had an adult portion of it; he assured me of that. "It's not what's in your pack," he'd say. "It's what's in here." He'd tap his chest. No wonder Tom Wolfe had called it *The Right Stuff*.[8] You couldn't exactly title a book *Positive Mental Attitude*, now, could you?

Kerns didn't always have it, though. He'd had to acquire it.
180 Early on in his Air Force days, he took a group of pilots into the mountains near Spokane for survival training maneuvers. "I was a greenhorn and just misjudged our situation," he told us. Back then, he was pretending to be the macho drill instructor I'd expected: Go, go, go, push, push, push. He was not yet cool. He was acting cool.

His class had been crossing a vast field of slushy snow, which made the going rough. The pilots began to suffer from fatigue, but Kerns kept driving them. "I now realize that was a mistake," he said. As the temperature dropped, darkness came down like a curtain. "Suddenly everybody wanted to give up. They just sat
190 down and lost all their will." Apathy is a typical reaction to any sort of disaster, and if you're exhausted in a field of snow at sundown in the mountains, you're pretty much about to witness the simple disaster of nature separating you permanently from everything you know and love in this world. That apathy can rapidly lead to complete psychological deterioration. Then you sit down and hypothermia[9] sets in, which produces more apathy, a more profound psychological deterioration, and ultimately, death.

Fatigue almost always comes as a surprise. It is as much a psychological condition as a physical one, and scientists have
200 struggled without success to understand it. It's like the difficulty of studying sand in order to understand the Sand Pile Effect. There's nothing in the muscles or nerves or even the biochemistry of the body that would seem to predict or explain fatigue. Once fatigue sets in, though, it is almost impossible to recover from it under survival conditions. It is not just a matter of being tired. It's more like a spiritual collapse, and recovery requires more than food and rest.

Following the explosive burst of activity that is sometimes required for survival, or in the panic stage when you're running
210 or climbing or swimming, you're like a woman who's just given birth to a baby. You're depleted and wide open to fatigue. It may take weeks to recover; and if you're not taking care of yourself, that

---

[8] **Tom Wolfe . . . *The Right Stuff*:** the title of Wolfe's 1979 book about the Mercury space program refers to the personal qualities required in astronauts.

[9] **hypothermia:** abnormally low body temperature.

fatigue can lead to an inability to sleep, which in turn can result in a sudden psychological collapse. The physical and psychological factors rapidly erode each other, which is why it is so important to pace yourself, rest frequently, and stay hydrated. That's why Kerns's pushing the pilots so hard had been a mistake.

A survival situation is a ticking clock: You have only so much stored energy (and water), and every time you exert yourself, you're using it up. The trick is to become extremely stingy with your scarce resources, balancing risk and reward, investing only in efforts that offer the biggest return.

In survival situations, people greatly underestimate the need for rest. While Kerns, Jonas, and I were doing map and compass exercises, he would frequently stop and look around at the woods, chatting with us. I'd be thinking: *Let's go, let's go, I know the way.* And he'd just stand there. Now I understand why. You should operate at about 60 percent of your normal level of activity, he explained, and rest and rehydrate frequently. If the weather is cool and you're sweating, you're working too hard. . . .

When Kerns at last realized how serious his situation was with his fatigued Air Force pilots, he recounted, "I fell to my knees and I prayed. Faith is a very important thing in your will to survive."

As Peter Leschak put it, "Whether a deity is actually listening or not, there is value in formally announcing your needs, desires, worries, sins, and goals in a focused, prayerful attitude. Only when you are aware can you take action." Survival psychologists have observed the same thing.

Kerns added, "All at once, it hit me that I might actually lose them. Those million-dollar pilots could die."

By chance, he found a fence and used the cedar post to start a fire. (Chance is nothing more than opportunity, and it is all around at every turn; the trick lies in recognizing it.) "It's amazing to see what fire can do. You're out in the woods, you're cold, you're lost, you're lonely. But the minute you light that fire, you're home, the lights are on, and supper's cooking. It made a world of difference going from complete darkness to light and warmth. It just turned everybody around."

Kerns learned many lessons that night. His mastery and confidence turned the pilots around even more than the fire. It showed them the way, and it made Kerns more able to save himself. That lesson was driven home again and again: Helping someone else is the best way to ensure your own survival. It takes you out of yourself. It helps you to rise above your fears. Now you're a rescuer, not a victim. And seeing how your leadership and skill buoy others up gives you more focus and energy to persevere. The cycle reinforces itself: You buoy them up, and their response buoys you

"Plan the flight and fly the plan. But don't fall in love with the plan."

up. Many people who survive alone report that they were doing it for someone else (a wife, boyfriend, mother, son) back home. When Antoine de Saint-Exupéry was lost in the Lybian Desert, it was the thought of his wife's suffering that kept him going. . . .

In the 84th-floor offices of the World Trade Center's south tower, and an hour before the collapse, Ronald DiFrancesco was one of the people who met Brian Clark, the fire warden with the flashlight who was asking people: "Up or down?" DiFrancesco went up, hoping to find air. But after ten or so floors, he encountered people who were succumbing to fatigue and smoke. The people, all of whom would die, were just giving up and falling asleep. DiFrancesco, too, was collapsing, but then he said to himself, "I've got to see my wife and kids again." And with that, he got up and bolted down the stairs to safety.

Doctors and nurses often survive better than others because they have someone to help. They have a well-defined purpose. Purpose is a big part of survival, but it must be accompanied by work. Grace without good works is not salvation. The survivor plans by setting small, manageable goals and then systematically achieving them. Hence the Air Force checklist and the notion, which my father drilled into me: Plan the flight and fly the plan. But don't fall in love with the plan. Be open to a changing world and let go of the plan when necessary so that you can make a new plan. Then, as the world and the plan both go through their book of changes, you will always be ready to do the next right thing.

People are animals with animal instincts, but they lack many of the other survival mechanisms animals possess, such as fur to keep them warm, fangs and claws, and flight or speed. Culture creates a collective survival mechanism for the species. People survive better in numbers. They survive because they use cognition to organize, say, for a hunt, and to make things, even as cognition inhibits their animalness, including strength. That's why, when
290 cognition is turned off, people are amazed by their own strength: because cognition continuously inhibits it. That is the whole secret to cognition: It is a mechanism for modulating emotional (physical) responses.

Every culture evolves survival rituals. Some, especially nontechnical ones, are devoted to not much more than survival. In Native American cultures, one ritual is the vision quest, in which a young person goes into the wild and fasts in search of a vision. It can be seen as a type of survival training, for if there is no food, no water, no way, a person has already practiced sitting still and
300 making the best of the situation. He'll have confidence in his ability to survive it.

The survival lessons that apply today are ancient. The *Tao Te Ching* is broken into two parts, "Integrity," and "The Way," which can be thought of as the two halves of surviving anything. Lao-tzu's[10] book is a handbook for a ruler, but it is also a handbook for the brain. An imbalance of the brain's functions leads us into trouble, and a triumph of balance gets us out. I've found similar lessons in Epictetus, Herodotus, Thucydides, the Bible, the Bhagavad Gītā.[11] "Is there any thing whereof it may be said, See, this is new?" says Ecclesiastes. But there are always new people who
310 haven't heard that there's nothing new under the sun. And there's always someone who doesn't get the word.

I had always wondered where our American survival rituals were. I think now that they're everywhere around us. The Boy Scouts in its original conception was a survival school. Sports are survival training in that they teach strength, agility, strategy, and the endurance of pain. But our culture is filled with survival stories as well. Cool is the ultimate American conception of the survival model. James Stockdale, a fighter pilot who was shot down over
320 Vietnam in 1965, spoke many times about how he survived seven

---

[10] *Tao Te Ching* . . . **Lao-tzu's (dao dé jīng . . . lou´dzǔ´):** a classic sixth-century B.C. Chinese text describing the way of seeing and behaving that forms the basis of the Taoist religion.

[11] **Epictetus, Herodotus, Thucydides, the Bible, the Bhagavad Gītā:** an ancient Greek philosopher, two ancient Greek historians, the Christian book of scripture, and a section of the Mahabharata, or Hindu scripture.

and a half years in prison camp. "One should include a course of familiarization with pain," he said.

Stockdale observed, "You have to practice hurting. There is no question about it. . . . You have to practice being hazed. You have to learn to take a bunch of junk and accept it with a sense of humor."

He's talking about being cool, just as he was when his F-8 fighter-bomber was hit with 57-millimeter fire. He had been on a relaxed bomb run at the time. He'd even taken off his uncomfortable oxygen mask. "I could barely keep that plane from
330 flying into the ground while I got that damned oxygen mask to my mouth so I could tell my wingman that I was about to eject. What rotten luck. And on a milk run! My mind was clear, and I said to myself, 'five years.' I knew we were making a mess of the war in Southeast Asia, but I didn't think it would last longer than that." The Spartan practice of enduring the bite of the fox is "a course of familiarization with pain." Then there are the schools like Kerns's, which attempt to teach wilderness survival by directly meeting the problem head-on with Yankee ingenuity.

Like being lost, survival is a transformation; being a leader can
340 ensure that, when you reach the final stage of that metamorphosis, it is with an attitude of commitment, not resignation. The transformation of survival is permanent. People who have had the experience often go on to become the best search and rescue professionals. They have come to understand, perhaps unconsciously, that they can only live fully by helping others through that same transformation. All the survivors I've talked to have told me how horrible the experience was. But they have also told me, often with deep puzzlement, how beautiful it was. They wouldn't trade the experience for anything in the world.
350 It gradually dawned on me that only by researching and dissecting the mysterious quality the Air Force so dully called Positive Mental Attitude would I ever understand survival.

And I thought: Wait a minute. My father was in the Army Air Corps. Maybe that's what he had that allowed him to live.[12] If so, he'd certainly never talked about it. But what pilot would? I felt as if I'd stepped to the edge of the very thing I'd been after all my life. Here, concealed in the most unimaginative phrase possible, was the deep mystery I'd been trying to unravel.

COLLABORATIVE DISCUSSION With a partner, discuss whether the title *Deep Survival* is a good fit for the selection. Cite specific evidence from the text to support your answer.

---

[12] **My father . . . allowed him to live:** During World War II, the author's father fell from a plane without a parachute and miraculously survived.

Determine Central Idea and Summarize the Text

When you **summarize** a text, you give a brief, objective account of the central idea the author presents in the work. The **central idea** is the main point that the author wants you to understand. To keep your summary **objective,** include only the author's ideas; do not include your responses or ideas about the text. Follow these steps to determine the central idea of the excerpt from *Deep Survival* and create an objective summary of the text:

1. Read the complete text without taking any notes.

2. Reread the text, focusing on the main ideas and the most important details. This time take notes, listing key words, main ideas with their supporting details, and quotations that make strong points.

3. Make an inference, or logical assumption, about the central idea of the text. Ask yourself: What do most of the ideas and details have in common? What does Gonzales want his readers to know?

4. In your own words, write a brief, objective summary of the text, focusing on the author's central idea only and omitting the supporting details.

Analyze Ideas and Events

Laurence Gonzales introduces and develops his ideas on the topic of survival through the use of **anecdotes,** or brief stories. He alternates the anecdotes with his own ideas and observations, as well as with information from experts. As you analyze the text, consider how the author utilizes particular sentences and paragraphs to communicate his ideas and how they build on one another. Consider this example:

Portion of Text	Type	Questions for Analysis
Lines 1–59	Anecdote (Juliane Koepcke's plane crash)	In lines 15–18, the author steps outside of the anecdote to present information from another survivor. How does this information clarify the point the author is making in the anecdote about Juliane?

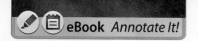

Analyzing the Text

Cite Text Evidence Support your responses with evidence from the selection.

1. **Cite Evidence** In lines 1–14, what detail does Gonzales focus on when he describes Juliane's fall from the airplane? How can you tell that he finds this detail interesting?

2. **Analyze** What comparison does Gonzales make in lines 60–76? How does this comparison support one of his main points?

3. **Connect** Reread lines 67–89. What connection does Gonzales make between the experience of passengers in the plane and the anecdote about the World Trade Center disaster?

4. **Cite Evidence** What evidence does Gonzales cite to prove the point that survival is not always a matter of luck or preparation?

5. **Interpret** Gonzales relates an anecdote about pilots who undergo survival training and get stranded in the snow (lines 179–190, 231–261). What important truths about survival are revealed by the anecdote?

6. **Connect** Gonzales provides information on survival rituals in different cultures (lines 294–312). How does this relate to Kerns's ideas about Positive Mental Attitude? How does it relate to Gonzales's statement that "Cool is the ultimate American conception of the survival model"?

7. **Draw Conclusions** What does Gonzales's analysis of survival lead him to conclude about why some people seem to have an amazing ability to survive life-threatening situations against all odds, while others seem to just give up? In other words, what is his central idea?

PERFORMANCE TASK

Writing Activity: Argument What quotation from the text best supports Laurence Gonzales's central idea—his most important message about survival? Write an argument explaining why you agree or disagree with Gonzales's ideas about survival.

1. Sum up what the author wants you to know about survival. Then, write a claim stating your position about what it takes to survive a life-threatening event.

2. Make notes about reasons that support your claim. Then, collect evidence that supports your reasons. Consider an opposing claim and list valid counterarguments.

3. Write a draft of your argument. Be sure to present your reasons and evidence in a logical order.

4. Revise your draft to eliminate unrelated or illogical evidence. Finally, check your work to make sure you have used the conventions of standard English.

Critical Vocabulary

disintegration   **deduce**   **conversely**   **distill**   **demeanor**

Practice and Apply Complete the sentences to demonstrate your comprehension of each Critical Vocabulary word.

1. The **disintegration** of an airplane in flight would cause . . .

2. Juliane **deduced** that rescue planes would not find her because . . .

3. Some people who have no survival equipment can survive life-threatening situations through wits alone; **conversely**, some people who have survival equipment . . .

4. In survival school, people learn how to **distill** water from air so that . . .

5. A calm **demeanor** is an important asset in a military pilot because . . .

Vocabulary Strategy: Context Clues

If you are uncertain of the meaning of a word, you can often figure out its meaning by using **context clues,** or information in the surrounding sentences or paragraphs. For example, the Critical Vocabulary word *disintegration* (line 19) is used in the description of a plane crash. The context includes the phrases "extensive structural failure" and "broken airplane." These clues tell you that *disintegration* means "breaking up into pieces."

Practice and Apply Find each of these words in the selection: *canopy* (line 27), *apathy* (line 190), *buoy* (line 255), *bolted* (line 271), *metamorphosis* (line 340). With a partner, discuss the context clues that can help you figure out each word's meaning. Follow these steps:

1. Determine the word's function in the sentence. For example, is it a noun that names a person, place, or thing, or is it a verb that describes an action?

2. Read the sentence in which the word appears. Does the overall meaning of the sentence allow you to guess the word's meaning?

3. If the sentence does not provide enough information, read the paragraph in which the word appears. If necessary, reread the previous paragraph and the one that follows to look for clues.

4. If you still do not have enough clues, think about the larger context of the selection. How does the word fit with what you know about the subject?

Language and Style: Colons and Semicolons

When used correctly, punctuation helps clarify meaning for readers by linking ideas and by showing places to pause. In the excerpt from *Deep Survival*, Laurence Gonzales uses both **colons** and **semicolons** to add clarity and interest to the text.

A colon is used to introduce a sentence, a quotation, or a list. A complete sentence that follows a colon usually begins with a capital letter.

Uses of Colons	
Purpose	**Example**
illustrate or provide an example of what was just stated	It was another important moment: She didn't spend time bemoaning her fate. (lines 27–28)
introduce a quotation	Before he died, he spoke to his father on the phone: "Why did I listen to them—I shouldn't have." (lines 83–85)
introduce a list	The Survival School provides training in the following skills: using maps and compasses, building and tending a fire, and signaling.

A semicolon is used to connect closely related ideas. It is stronger than a comma but less abrupt than a period. It indicates that the statement that follows will add explanation.

Uses of Semicolons	
Purpose	**Example**
separate independent clauses and add explanation	She wasn't screaming; she wasn't in a panic. (lines 11–12)
precede a conjunctive adverb that joins two clauses	Juliane had no survival training; nevertheless, she managed to survive a dangerous jungle journey without external help.
separate parallel phrases that contain commas	A survival box should contain flares, for signaling rescuers; rations, for keeping up strength; and a first-aid kit, for medical emergencies.

Practice and Apply Look back at the argument you wrote for this selection's Performance Task. Revise your argument to include at least one colon and one semicolon. Then discuss with a partner how each punctuation mark you added improved or clarified your meaning.

Louise Erdrich (b. 1954) *is best known for exploring the Native American experience in her novels, poetry, and children's books. Born in Little Falls, Minnesota, she grew up in North Dakota. Of German American and Ojibwa (Chippewa) descent, her writing reflects a fascination with the influence of family and heritage on individuals and community. She lives in Minneapolis, Minnesota, where she owns a bookstore and continues to write. Her best-known works include the novels* Love Medicine, The Beet Queen, *and* The Round House.

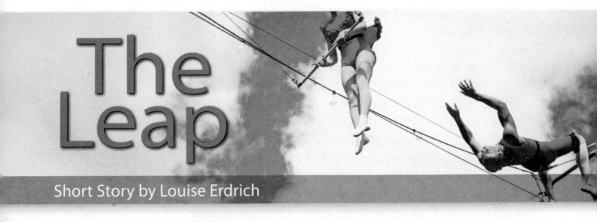

The Leap

Short Story by Louise Erdrich

AS YOU READ Pay attention to how the narrator conveys her feelings about her mother as the story unfolds. Write down any questions you generate during reading.

My mother is the surviving half of a blindfold trapeze act, not a fact I think about much even now that she is sightless, the result of **encroaching** and stubborn cataracts. She walks slowly through her house here in New Hampshire, lightly touching her way along walls and running her hands over knickknacks, books, the drift of a grown child's belongings and castoffs. She has never upset an object or as much as brushed a magazine onto the floor. She has never lost her balance or bumped into a closet door left carelessly open.

10   It has occurred to me that the catlike precision of her movements in old age might be the result of her early training, but she shows so little of the drama or flair one might expect from a performer that I tend to forget the Flying Avalons. She has kept no sequined costume, no photographs, no fliers or posters from that part of her youth. I would, in fact, tend to think that all memory of double somersaults and heartstopping catches had left her arms and legs were it not for the fact that sometimes, as I sit sewing in

encroach
(ĕn-krōch´) *v.* to gradually intrude upon or invade.

the room of the rebuilt house in which I slept as a child, I hear
the crackle, catch a whiff of smoke from the stove downstairs and
20 suddenly the room goes dark, the stitches burn beneath my fingers,
and I am sewing with a needle of hot silver, a thread of fire.

I owe her my existence three times. The first was when she
saved herself. In the town square a replica tent pole, cracked and
splintered, now stands cast in concrete. It commemorates the
disaster that put our town smack on the front page of the Boston
and New York tabloids. It is from those old newspapers, now
historical records, that I get my information. Not from my mother,
Anna of the Flying Avalons, nor from any of her in-laws, nor
certainly from the other half of her particular act, Harold Avalon,
30 her first husband. In one news account it says, "The day was mildly
overcast, but nothing in the air or temperature gave any hint of the
sudden force with which the deadly gale would strike."

I have lived in the West, where you can see the weather
coming for miles, and it is true that out here we are at something
of a disadvantage. When extremes of temperature collide, a hot
and cold front, winds generate instantaneously behind a hill and
crash upon you without warning. That, I think, was the likely
situation on that day in June. People probably commented on the
pleasant air, grateful that no hot sun beat upon the striped tent
40 that stretched over the entire center green. They bought their
tickets and surrendered them in anticipation. They sat. They ate
caramelized popcorn and roasted peanuts. There was time, before
the storm, for three acts. The White Arabians of Ali-Khazar rose on
their hind legs and waltzed. The Mysterious Bernie folded himself
into a painted cracker tin, and the Lady of the Mists made herself
appear and disappear in surprising places. As the clouds gathered
outside, unnoticed, the ringmaster cracked his whip, shouted his
introduction, and pointed to the ceiling of the tent, where the
Flying Avalons were perched.
50 They loved to drop gracefully from nowhere, like two sparkling
birds, and blow kisses as they threw off their plumed helmets and
high-collared capes. They laughed and flirted openly as they beat
their way up again on the trapeze bars. In the final vignette[1] of their
act, they actually would kiss in midair, pausing, almost hovering
as they swooped past one another. On the ground, between bows,
Harry Avalon would skip quickly to the front rows and point out
the smear of my mother's lipstick, just off the edge of his mouth.
They made a romantic pair all right, especially in the blindfold
sequence.

---

[1] **vignette:** a brief scene.

"I owe her my existence three times."

60   That afternoon, as the anticipation increased, as Mr. and Mrs.
Avalon tied sparkling strips of cloth onto each other's face and as
they puckered their lips in mock kisses, lips destined "never again
to meet," as one long breathless article put it, the wind rose, miles
off, wrapped itself into a cone, and howled. There came a rumble
of electrical energy, drowned out by the sudden roll of drums.
One detail not mentioned by the press, perhaps unknown—Anna
was pregnant at the time, seven months and hardly showing, her
stomach muscles were that strong. It seems incredible that she
would work high above the ground when any fall could be so
70   dangerous, but the explanation—I know from watching her go
blind—is that my mother lives comfortably in extreme elements.
She is one with the constant dark now, just as the air was her home,
familiar to her, safe, before the storm that afternoon.

From opposite ends of the tent they waved, blind and smiling,
to the crowd below. The ringmaster removed his hat and called
for silence, so that the two above could concentrate. They rubbed
their hands in chalky powder, then Harry launched himself and
swung once, twice, in huge calibrated[2] beats across space. He
hung from his knees and on the third swing stretched wide his

---

[2] **calibrated:** checked or determined by comparison with a standard.

80 arms, held his hand out to receive his pregnant wife as she dove
    from her shining bar.

    It was while the two were in midair, their hands about to meet,
    that lightning struck the main pole and sizzled down the guy
    wires, filling the air with a blue radiance that Harry Avalon must
    certainly have seen through the cloth of his blindfold as the tent
    buckled and the edifice toppled him forward, the swing continuing
    and not returning in its sweep, and Harry going down, down into
    the crowd with his last thought, perhaps, just a prickle of surprise at
    his empty hands.

90 My mother once said that I'd be amazed at how many things a
    person can do within the act of falling. Perhaps, at the time, she was
    teaching me to dive off a board at the town pool, for I associated the
    idea with midair somersaults. But I also think she meant that even
    in that awful doomed second one could think, for she certainly did.
    When her hands did not meet her husband's, my mother tore her
    blindfold away. As he swept past her on the wrong side, she could
    have grasped his ankle, the toe-end of his tights, and gone down
    clutching him. Instead, she changed direction. Her body twisted
    toward a heavy wire and she managed to hang on to the braided
100 metal, still hot from the lightning strike. Her palms were burned
    so terribly that once healed they bore no lines, only the blank scar
    tissue of a quieter future. She was lowered, gently, to the sawdust
    ring just underneath the dome of the canvas roof, which did not
    entirely settle but was held up on one end and jabbed through, torn,
    and still on fire in places from the giant spark, though rain and
    men's jackets soon put that out.

    Three people died, but except for her hands my mother was
    not seriously harmed until an overeager rescuer broke her arm in
    extricating her and also, in the process, collapsed a portion of the

    extricate
    (ĕk´strĭ-kāt´) *v.* to
    release or disentangle
    from.

110 tent bearing a huge buckle that knocked her unconscious. She was
    taken to the town hospital, and there she must have hemorrhaged,[3]
    for they kept her, confined to her bed, a month and a half before her
    baby was born without life.

    Harry Avalon had wanted to be buried in the circus cemetery
    next to the original Avalon, his uncle, so she sent him back with his
    brothers. The child, however, is buried around the corner, beyond
    this house and just down the highway. Sometimes I used to walk
    there just to sit. She was a girl, but I rarely thought of her as a sister
    or even as a separate person really. I suppose you could call it the
120 egocentrism[4] of a child, of all young children, but I considered her a
    less finished version of myself.

---

[3] **hemorrhaged:** bled heavily.
[4] **egocentrism:** belief in the primary or sole importance of the self.

When the snow falls, throwing shadows among the stones,
I can easily pick hers out from the road, for it is bigger than the
others and in the shape of a lamb at rest, its legs curled beneath.
The carved lamb looms larger as the years pass, though it is
probably only my eyes, the visions shifting, as what is close to me
blurs and distances sharpen. In odd moments, I think it is the edge
drawing near, the edge of everything, the unseen horizon we do
not really speak of in the eastern woods. And it also seems to me,
130   although this is probably an idle fantasy, that the statue is growing
more sharply etched, as if, instead of weathering itself into a porous
mass, it is hardening on the hillside with each snowfall, perfecting
itself.

It was during her confinement in the hospital that my mother
met my father. He was called in to look at the set of her arm, which
was complicated. He stayed, sitting at her bedside, for he was
something of an armchair traveler and had spent his war quietly,
at an air force training grounds, where he became a specialist in
arms and legs broken during parachute training exercises. Anna
140   Avalon had been to many of the places he longed to visit—Venice,
Rome, Mexico, all through France and Spain. She had no family of
her own and was taken in by the Avalons, trained to perform from
a very young age. They toured Europe before the war, then based
themselves in New York. She was illiterate.
It was in the hospital that she finally learned to read and write,
as a way of overcoming the boredom and depression of those weeks,
and it was my father who insisted on teaching her. In return for
stories of her adventures, he graded her first exercises. He bought
her her first book, and over her bold letters, which the pale guides
150   of the penmanship pads could not contain, they fell in love.
I wonder if my father calculated the exchange he offered: one
form of flight for another. For after that, and for as long as I can
remember, my mother has never been without a book. Until now,
that is, and it remains the greatest difficulty of her blindness. Since
my father's recent death, there is no one to read to her, which is why
I returned, in fact, from my failed life where the land is flat. I came
home to read to my mother, to read out loud, to read long into the
dark if I must, to read all night.
Once my father and mother married, they moved onto the old
160   farm he had inherited but didn't care much for. Though he'd been
thinking of moving to a larger city, he settled down and broadened
his practice in this valley. It still seems odd to me, when they could
have gone anywhere else, that they chose to stay in the town where
the disaster had occurred, and which my father in the first place
had found so **constricting.** It was my mother who insisted upon it,

constrict
(kən-strĭkt´) v. to limit
or impede growth.

after her child did not survive. And then, too, she loved the sagging farmhouse with its scrap of what was left of a vast acreage of woods and hidden hay fields that stretched to the game park.

I owe my existence, the second time then, to the two of them
170 and the hospital that brought them together. That is the debt we take for granted since none of us asks for life. It is only once we have it that we hang on so dearly.

I was seven the year the house caught fire, probably from standing ash. It can rekindle, and my father, forgetful around the house and perpetually exhausted from night hours on call, often emptied what he thought were ashes from cold stoves into wooden or cardboard containers. The fire could have started from a flaming box, or perhaps a buildup of creosote[5] inside the chimney was the culprit. It started right around the stove, and the heart of the house
180 was gutted. The baby-sitter, fallen asleep in my father's den on the first floor, woke to find the stairway to my upstairs room cut off by flames. She used the phone, then ran outside to stand beneath my window.

When my parents arrived, the town volunteers had drawn water from the fire pond and were spraying the outside of the

---

[5] **creosote:** a flammable, oily byproduct of burning carbon-based fuels like coal, peat, and wood.

house, preparing to go inside after me, not knowing at the time that there was only one staircase and that it was lost. On the other side of the house, the superannuated[6] extension ladder broke in half. Perhaps the clatter of it falling against the walls woke me, for I'd been asleep up to that point.

As soon as I awakened, in the small room that I now use for sewing, I smelled the smoke. I followed things by the letter then, was good at memorizing instructions, and so I did exactly what was taught in the second-grade home fire drill. I got up, I touched the back of my door before opening it. Finding it hot, I left it closed and stuffed my rolled-up rug beneath the crack. I did not hide under my bed or crawl into my closet. I put on my flannel robe, and then I sat down to wait.

Outside, my mother stood below my dark window and saw clearly that there was no rescue. Flames had pierced one side wall, and the glare of the fire lighted the massive limbs and trunk of the vigorous old elm that had probably been planted the year the house was built, a hundred years ago at least. No leaf touched the wall, and just one thin branch scraped the roof. From below, it looked as though even a squirrel would have had trouble jumping from the tree onto the house, for the breadth of that small branch was no bigger than my mother's wrist.

Standing there, beside Father, who was preparing to rush back around to the front of the house, my mother asked him to unzip her dress. When he wouldn't be bothered, she made him understand. He couldn't make his hands work, so she finally tore it off and stood there in her pearls and stockings. She directed one of the men to lean the broken half of the extension ladder up against the trunk of the tree. In surprise, he **complied**. She ascended. She vanished. Then she could be seen among the leafless branches of late November as she made her way up and, along her stomach, inched the length of a bough that curved above the branch that brushed the roof.

Once there, swaying, she stood and balanced. There were plenty of people in the crowd and many who still remember, or think they do, my mother's leap through the ice-dark air toward that thinnest extension, and how she broke the branch falling so that it cracked in her hands, cracked louder than the flames as she vaulted with it toward the edge of the roof, and how it hurtled down end over end without her, and their eyes went up, again, to see where she had flown.

I didn't see her leap through air, only heard the sudden thump and looked out my window. She was hanging by the backs of her

comply
(kəm-plī´) *v.* to obey an instruction or command.

---

[6] **superannuated:** obsolete; ready for retirement.

heels from the new gutter we had put in that year, and she was
230 smiling. I was not surprised to see her, she was so matter-of-fact.
She tapped on the window. I remember how she did it, too. It
was the friendliest tap, a bit **tentative**, as if she was afraid she had
arrived too early at a friend's house. Then she gestured at the latch,
and when I opened the window she told me to raise it wider and
prop it up with the stick so it wouldn't crush her fingers. She swung
down, caught the ledge, and crawled through the opening. Once
she was in my room, I realized she had on only underclothing, a
bra of the heavy stitched cotton women used to wear and step-in,
lace-trimmed drawers. I remember feeling light-headed, of course,
240 terribly relieved, and then embarrassed for her to be seen by the
crowd undressed.

I was still embarrassed as we flew out the window, toward
earth, me in her lap, her toes pointed as we skimmed toward the
painted target of the fire fighter's net.

I know that she's right. I knew it even then. As you fall, there
is time to think. Curled as I was, against her stomach, I was not
startled by the cries of the crowd or the looming faces. The wind
roared and beat its hot breath at our back, the flames whistled.
I slowly wondered what would happen if we missed the circle or
250 bounced out of it. Then I wrapped my hands around my mother's
hands. I felt the brush of her lips and heard the beat of her heart in
my ears, loud as thunder, long as the roll of drums.

tentative
(tĕn´tə-tĭv) *adj.* with
caution and without
confidence.

COLLABORATIVE DISCUSSION How does the narrator feel about her
mother? With a partner, discuss how the author reveals the character of
the mother through the narrator. Cite specific evidence from the text to
support your ideas.

Analyze Author's Choices:
Flashback and Tension

The ability to create **tension,** or suspense, is central to the author's craft. Tension propels a story forward and keeps the reader wondering what will happen next. One effective technique for creating tension is the **flashback**—a literary device used to manipulate time by inserting an earlier event into the present action, often by having a character recall something that happened in the past. As a flashback is introduced, the verb tense will shift from the present to the past or past perfect tense. Signal words, such as *once* (as in, *once upon a time*) and *remember* (as in, *I remember when*) might be used to alert the reader that a shift in time is about to occur. They also remind the reader that a flashback is still in effect.

The chart tracks some shifts in time and tension in "The Leap." By following the action, you can see how shifts in the story's **chronology,** or order, help to sustain or build tension. Complete your own chart as you analyze the story.

Tension Tracker		
Example	**Flashback Clues** (verb tense; signal words)	**Action Summary**
"I owe her my existence three times. The first was when…"	shift from present to past tense	narrator begins to explain her debt to her mother
"I have lived in the West…"	shift to past perfect tense	narrator provides information about her own adult life

Support Inferences About Theme

In a short story, the **theme,** or the underlying message, usually develops and emerges through **inference.** An inference is a logical conclusion based on clues in the text as well as on your own experience. To uncover the theme, begin by analyzing the story's title. Then, look for clues in the text that indicate what the title might mean. Be aware of the possibility that the title may have multiple meanings. By keeping a list of clues, you can create a summary of supporting inferences that will help you to determine the story's theme. For example, you might note that the word *leap* is in the title, and because the narrator's mother was a trapeze artist, she was probably able to make dangerous leaps. Ask yourself, what might be the figurative meaning of a *leap*? Look for these kinds of clues to determine the theme the author wants to convey.

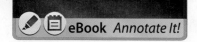

Analyzing the Text

Cite Text Evidence   Support your responses with evidence from the selection.

1. **Interpret** How do lines 15–21 act as a flashback? What clues do they give about the rest of the story? Provide specific evidence in your response.

2. **Infer** In lines 98–100, Anna decides to reach for the hot braided metal rather than for her husband as he falls. What does this reveal about her character? What inferences can you make about the story's title in this passage?

3. **Interpret** Identify the leaps in the story. Which leaps are literal? Which are figurative?

4. **Analyze** The narrator speaks of the three ways that she owes her existence to her mother. Identify the three ways and the literary techniques used to reveal them. How does each revelation affect the story's tension?

5. **Compare** What do these scenes reveal about the mother's character?

   - Anna saves herself during the trapeze accident.
   - Anna saves her daughter from the house fire.

6. **Draw Conclusions** Based upon what the narrator reveals, draw conclusions about the mother and her relationship with her daughter. Cite evidence from the text to support your response.

7. **Infer** Reread lines 227–252. What does the narrator learn? What inferences can you make about the story's theme?

PERFORMANCE TASK

Speaking Activity: Discussion Imagery about circuses occurs throughout "The Leap." Explore the author's use of circus imagery in a writing exercise and in discussion groups.

1. Reread the story, jotting down notes on specific references to the circus. Beside each reference, note whether each image contributes to character, theme, setting, or any other aspect of the story.

2. In small discussion groups, use your notes to respond to this question: In what ways does circus imagery contribute to the story? Write a brief summary of your discussion.

Critical Vocabulary

encroach   extricate   constrict   comply   tentative

Practice and Apply Answer these questions, using a dictionary or thesaurus as needed. Make sure your answers reflect your understanding of each Critical Vocabulary word's meaning.

1. Should rescue crews provide a **tentative** response to **encroaching** forest fires? Why or why not?

2. Would it feel **constricting** if one always **complied** with the wishes of others? Explain.

3. Why would you **extricate** yourself from a planned road trip upon learning of an **encroaching** blizzard?

Vocabulary Strategy: Prefixes

The Critical Vocabulary words *encroach*, *extricate*, *constrict*, and *comply* all contain **prefixes,** an affix added to the beginning of a base word. Knowing the meaning of common prefixes, such as *en-*, *ex-*, *con-*, and *com-*, will help you clarify the meaning of unknown words. Here are the meanings of some common prefixes and examples of other words that contain the prefixes:

Prefixes	Meanings	Examples
en-	to go into or onto	energy, entire
ex-	out of or away from	exchange, extend
com-, con-	together, with, jointly	comfort, contain, condition

If a base word is unfamiliar, use your knowledge of the word's prefix and how the word is used in context to clarify its meaning. If necessary, consult a dictionary to determine the precise meaning of a word.

Practice and Apply Identify a new word, either from the selection or on your own, that contains each of the prefixes in the chart. For each word you choose, follow these steps:

1. Identify the base word, the main word part. For example, the base word for *exchange* is *change*.

2. Write a definition for each word that incorporates the prefix meaning and the base word meaning. Use a dictionary to check your definition. Make changes if needed.

3. Finally, write a sample sentence for each word you chose.

Language and Style: Relative Clauses

A **clause** is a group of words that contains a subject and a predicate. **Relative clauses** describe nouns and function as adjectives. Here are the characteristics of a relative clause:

- It begins with a signal word: a relative pronoun (*that, which, who, whom, whose*) or a relative adverb (*when, where,* or *why*).
- It follows a noun or a noun phrase.
- It provides extra information about a noun or a noun phrase, or it answers the questions *What kind? How many?* or *Which one?*

Authors use relative clauses not only to convey specific meanings but also to add interest and variety to their work. Read this sentence from "The Leap":

> **It commemorates the disaster <u>that put our town smack on the front page of the Boston and New York tabloids.</u>**

The clause fulfills all the elements of a relative clause: it begins with a relative pronoun—*that*; it follows a noun—*disaster*; it answers the question *Which one?*—the disaster that put the town in the tabloids.

Erdrich could have expressed the same ideas this way:

> **It commemorates the disaster. The disaster put our town smack on the front page of the Boston and New York tabloids.**

Notice how the sentence with the relative clause is smoother and easier to read. Here are some other examples of relative clauses from the "The Leap":

Relative Clauses		
Signal Word	**Relative Clause**	**Words Modified**
which	He was called in to look at the set of her arm, <u>which was complicated.</u>	"the set of her arm"
who	. . . and it was my father <u>who insisted on teaching her.</u>	"father"
where	. . . they chose to stay in the town <u>where the disaster had occurred</u> . . .	"town"

Practice and Apply Look back at the summary you created in response to this selection's Performance Task. Revise the summary to include at least three relative clauses. With a partner, discuss your revised summaries. Then work together to identify at least five more relative clauses in "The Leap" that are not included as examples in this lesson.

Wisława Szymborska (1923–2012) *was born in western Poland and spent most of her life in Krakow, Poland. Her first two published volumes of poetry, written in post–World War II Communist-dominated Poland, were written in the style of Socialist Realism. Szymborska later disowned these works. Her disillusionment with communism was reflected in* Calling Out to Yeti, *published in 1957. Her poems, noted for their unique, ironic tone, have been translated into many languages. Szymborska was awarded the Nobel Prize in Literature in 1996.*

The End and the Beginning

Poem by Wisława Szymborska   translated by Joanna Trzeciak

AS YOU READ Think about all the aspects of daily life that are disrupted by war. Write down any questions you generate during reading.

After every war
someone has to clean up.
Things won't
straighten themselves up, after all.

5 Someone has to push the rubble
to the side of the road,
so the corpse-filled wagons
can pass.

Someone has to get mired
10 in scum and ashes,
sofa springs,
splintered glass,
and bloody rags.

Someone has to drag in a girder
15 to prop up a wall.
Someone has to glaze a window,
rehang a door.

Photogenic it's not,
and takes years.
20 All the cameras have left
for another war.

We'll need the bridges back,
and new railway stations.
Sleeves will go ragged
25 from rolling them up.

Someone, broom in hand,
still recalls the way it was.
Someone else listens
and nods with unsevered[1] head.
30 But already there are those nearby
starting to mill about[2]
who will find it dull.

From out of the bushes
sometimes someone still unearths
35 rusted-out arguments
and carries them to the garbage pile.

Those who knew
what was going on here
must make way for
40 those who know little.
And less than little.
And finally as little as nothing.

In the grass that has overgrown
causes and effects,
45 someone must be stretched out
blade of grass in his mouth
gazing at the clouds.

COLLABORATIVE DISCUSSION What part of cleaning up after a war is
the most difficult? With a partner, discuss the speaker's observations
about this. Cite specific evidence from the text to support your answer.

---

[1] **unsevered:** not cut off; not separated.
[2] **mill about:** move idly or aimlessly.

Determine Figurative Meanings and Tone

In poetry, an author's word choices, and the images that those words create, help convey the speaker's meaning and set the **tone,** or attitude toward the subject. Analyzing the precise meanings of words and phrases that a poet uses can deepen your understanding of the poem. You can analyze the significance of Wisława Szymborska's word choices in "The End and the Beginning" by looking at the elements outlined in this chart.

Imagery	Connotation	Tone
Poets often use **imagery,** or descriptive words and phrases that re-create sensory experiences for the reader. Imagery usually appeals to one or more of the five senses—sight, hearing, smell, taste, and touch—to help readers imagine exactly what is being described. For example, the striking image of "corpse-filled wagons" passing through rubble-lined roads calls to mind photographs that most readers will have seen of war-torn, bombed out cities. The image helps the reader identify with what the speaker is observing.	Poets choose words and expressions not only for their **denotative,** or dictionary, meanings, but also for their **connotative,** or subjective, meanings. Connotative meanings suggest feelings or ideas that go beyond the dictionary definitions. For example, look at these three possible word choices:	A poet's choice of language conveys his or her **tone,** or attitude. Elements to consider when evaluating tone include • words with positive or negative connotations • use of informal language such as idioms or colloquial expressions • repetition of significant words or ideas
Look for other images in the poem that engage your senses and evoke a strong emotional response.	• "someone has to clean up" • "someone has to tidy up" • "someone has to reorganize" In line 2, Szymborska chose to use *clean up*. This phrase suggests dirtiness and also casts blame on those who made the mess. The words *tidy up* and *reorganize* would not have conveyed the same precise meaning.	Szymborska repeats the word *someone* throughout this poem. The use of this indefinite pronoun adds an impersonal quality to the poem, yet the effect of war is intensely personal.

Analyzing the Text

Cite Text Evidence   Support your responses with evidence from the selection.

1. **Infer** Notice how the speaker repeats the word "someone" throughout the poem. What statement about war is she making by using an indefinite pronoun rather than referring to a specific person?

2. **Analyze** Answer these questions to explore how Szymborska creates the tone of the poem. Cite words and phrases from the poem to support your answers.

   - Does the speaker use formal or informal language? What is the effect of this choice?
   - What is the speaker's attitude toward the situation he or she is describing?
   - How does the tone of the poem change beginning with line 30?

3. **Interpret** In line 18, the speaker says the aftermath of war is not "photogenic." What images in the poem reinforce this idea about war? How does she show the dimensions of the devastation?

4. **Interpret** Reread the last stanza of the poem. What does the grass **symbolize,** or represent? What does the speaker mean when she describes someone as being "stretched out / blade of grass in his mouth / gazing at the clouds"?

5. **Draw Conclusions** Consider why Szymborska titled her poem "The End and the Beginning" rather than using the more common order "The Beginning and the End." How does the title reflect the message of the poem? Reread stanzas 5 and 10 and explain how they reflect this message.

6. **Connect** Poland experienced great political unrest and upheaval during Szymborska's lifetime: Nazi and Soviet occupations during World War II, postwar repressive Communist control, decades-long resistance of workers against the Communist regime, and, in 1989, the election of a new, non-Communist government. How does Poland's political situation inform Szymborska's choice of subject and her tone in "The End and the Beginning"?

PERFORMANCE TASK

Writing Activity: Reflection Szymborska uses vivid images that, on a literal level, describe the physical activity of recovering from a war. Think about how the images also have a figurative meaning, related to the work of rebuilding a government and a society that have been destroyed by war.

1. Select two examples of imagery from the poem and analyze the meaning of the images as they relate to rebuilding a government or a society.

2. Write a brief explanation of the figurative meaning of each image that you chose.

3. Share and discuss your findings with a partner.

To help you complete this task, use
- *Writing an Argument*
- *Writing as a Process*
- *Using Textual Evidence*

Write an Argument

Based on the evidence from at least three selections, would you say that survival requires selfishness? Synthesize your ideas by writing an argument in support of your position.

An effective argument

- makes a persuasive claim and develops it with valid reasons and relevant evidence from the texts
- anticipates counterclaims and addresses them
- establishes clear, logical relationships among claims, counterclaims, reasons, and evidence
- includes a logically structured body, including transitions
- has a satisfying conclusion that effectively summarizes the claim

Mentor Text See how this example from "Is Survival Selfish?" makes smooth transitions from one idea to the next.

> " In Yates' case, he had time to think hard about the odds, and the possibilities he was facing, and to realize that he couldn't save anyone but himself. But what about people who have to make more instantaneous decisions? "

PLAN

Analyze the Texts Reread *Night*, taking notes about survival. Is it necessary to be selfish in order to survive a selection? Then choose two other texts from the collection and make notes about survival in those texts, too.

Use the annotation tools in your eBook to find evidence from your chosen texts. Save each piece of evidence to *my*Notebook, in a folder titled *Collection 5 Performance Task A*.

ACADEMIC VOCABULARY

As you build your argument about survival, be sure to use these words.

dimension
external
statistic
sustain
utilize

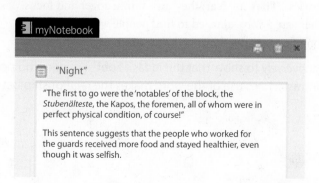

myNotebook

"Night"

"The first to go were the 'notables' of the block, the *Stubenälteste*, the Kapos, the foremen, all of whom were in perfect physical condition, of course!"

This sentence suggests that the people who worked for the guards received more food and stayed healthier, even though it was selfish.

Make a Claim

Write a claim that clearly and concisely states your position. Your claim is effective if

- it makes your position on the issue clear to readers
- you have reasons that will persuade your readers to agree
- you can support the claim with sufficient evidence from the texts

Develop Counterclaims

What might your readers say to oppose your claim? Think of at least two counterclaims that a reader might make. Decide how you would respond to each opposing claim. You may need to conduct further research. Outline the reasons and evidence for your counterclaims.

Get Organized

Organize your ideas in an outline, using the notes from your analysis. Be sure to include a clearly stated claim supported by sufficient reasons and evidence. Present claims and refute them with additional evidence.

Interactive Lessons

To help you plan your essay, complete the following lesson:
- Writing Arguments: What Is a Claim?

> PRODUCE

myWriteSmart

Write your rough draft in *my*WriteSmart. Focus on getting your ideas down, rather than perfecting your choice of language.

Draft Your Essay

Write a well-organized draft of your argument. Think about your purpose and audience as you write.

- Introduce your argument in a memorable way that will grab the attention of your readers. Clearly state your claim.
- Present your reasons, evidence, and counterarguments in logically ordered paragraphs.
- Explain how the evidence from the texts supports your ideas.
- Use transitions to connect reasons and evidence to your claim.
- Use formal language and a respectful tone.
- Write a persuasive conclusion that summarizes your position.

Interactive Lessons

To help you draft your essay, complete the following lessons in *Writing Arguments*:
- Creating a Coherent Argument
- Formal Style

Language and Style: Transition Words

Look for places in your argument where you can use transition words to link ideas, events, or reasons. Read this passage from *Deep Survival*.

> **❝** Survivors aren't fearless. They *use* fear: they turn it into anger and focus. Conversely, searchers are always amazed to find people who have died while in possession of everything they needed to survive. **❞**

Note how Gonzales uses *conversely* to show that the ideas about survivors and people who give up are being contrasted. His use of the word makes the relationship between the ideas clearer.

Improve Your Draft
Have your partner or group of peers use the questions in the chart to review your draft.

Questions	Tips	Revision Techniques
Does the introduction grab the audience's attention and include a clearly stated claim?	**Underline** the attention-grabbing text. **Highlight** the claim.	**Add** an attention-grabber. **Add** a claim or **rework** the existing one to make it clearer.
Do at least two valid reasons support the claim? Is each reason supported by relevant and sufficient evidence?	**Highlight** each reason. **Underline** each piece of evidence.	**Add** reasons or revise existing ones to make them more valid. **Insert** relevant evidence to ensure that your support is sufficient.
Do transitions connect reasons and evidence to the claim?	**Underline** each transition.	**Add** words, phrases, or clauses to connect related ideas that lack transitions.
Do I maintain a formal style throughout the argument?	**Highlight** slang and informal language.	**Reword** text to replace informal language with formal language.
Are opposing claims acknowledged and refuted with counterclaims?	**Underline** any sentence that addresses an opposing claim. **Highlight** the sentence that refutes it.	**Add** sentences that identify audience concerns, and address those opposing claims.
Does the conclusion effectively summarize the argument?	**Highlight** the summary of the argument.	**Add** sentences to restate your argument.

Have your partner or a group of peers review your draft in *my*WriteSmart. Ask your reviewers to note any reasons that do not support the claim or that lack sufficient evidence.

Interactive Lessons
To help you revise your essay, complete the following lesson:
• Writing as a Process: Revising and Editing

PRESENT

Share with a Group
Read your argument to a small group. Your classmates should listen and take notes. Do they understand your position? Have you persuaded them to agree with your argument? Be prepared to respond to any comments or questions.

PERFORMANCE TASK A RUBRIC
ARGUMENT

	Ideas and Evidence	Organization	Language
4	• The introduction is memorable and persuasive; the claim clearly states a position on a substantive topic. • Valid reasons and relevant evidence from the texts convincingly support the writer's claim. • Opposing claims are anticipated and effectively addressed with counterclaims. • The concluding section effectively summarizes the claim.	• The reasons and textual evidence are organized consistently and logically throughout the argument. • Varied transitions logically connect reasons and textual evidence to the writer's claim.	• The writing reflects a formal style and an objective, or controlled, tone. • Sentence beginnings, lengths, and structures vary and have a rhythmic flow. • Spelling, capitalization, and punctuation are correct. If handwritten, the argument is legible. • Grammar and usage are correct.
3	• The introduction could do more to capture the reader's attention; the claim states a position on an issue. • Most reasons and evidence from the texts support the writer's claim, but they could be more convincing. • Opposing claims are anticipated, but the counterclaims need to be developed more. • The concluding section restates the claim.	• The organization of reasons and textual evidence is confusing in a few places. • A few more transitions are needed to connect reasons and textual evidence to the writer's claim.	• The style is informal in a few places, and the tone is defensive at times. • Sentence beginnings, lengths, and structures vary somewhat. • Several spelling and capitalization mistakes occur, and punctuation is inconsistent. If handwritten, the argument is mostly legible. • Some grammatical and usage errors are repeated in the argument.
2	• The introduction is ordinary; the claim identifies an issue, but the writer's position is not clearly stated. • The reasons and evidence from the texts are not always logical or relevant. • Opposing claims are anticipated but not addressed logically. • The concluding section includes an incomplete summary of the claim.	• The organization of reasons and textual evidence is logical in some places, but it often doesn't follow a pattern. • Many more transitions are needed to connect reasons and textual evidence to the writer's position.	• The style becomes informal in many places, and the tone is often dismissive of other viewpoints. • Sentence structures barely vary, and some fragments or run-on sentences are present. • Spelling, capitalization, and punctuation are often incorrect but do not make comprehending the argument difficult. If handwritten, the essay may be partially illegible. • Grammar and usage are incorrect in many places, but the writer's ideas are still clear.
1	• The introduction is missing. • Significant supporting reasons and evidence from the texts are missing. • Opposing claims are neither anticipated nor addressed. • The concluding section is missing.	• An organizational strategy is not used; reasons and textual evidence are presented randomly. • Transitions are not used, making the argument difficult to understand.	• The style is inappropriate, and the tone is disrespectful. • Repetitive sentence structure, fragments, and run-on sentences make the writing monotonous and hard to follow. • Spelling and capitalization are often incorrect, and punctuation is missing. If handwritten, the argument may be partially or mostly illegible. • Many grammatical and usage errors change the meaning of the writer's ideas.

Participate in a Panel Discussion

This collection focuses on the ways people endure devastating experiences. Look back at the anchor text "The End and the Beginning" and at the other texts in the collection. How do individuals and communities adapt to radically different situations in order to survive? Synthesize your ideas by holding a panel discussion about how each selection shows people adapting for survival.

An effective participant in a panel discussion

- makes a clear, logical, and well-defended generalization about the ways people adapt for survival in one of the selections
- uses quotations and specific examples to illustrate ideas
- responds thoughtfully and politely to the ideas of the moderator and other panel members
- evaluates other panel members' contributions
- summarizes the discussion by synthesizing ideas

PLAN

Get Organized Work with your classmates to prepare for a panel discussion.

- Join a group of four classmates and select one student to be the moderator for your discussion.
- As a group, choose three texts from the collection, including "The End and the Beginning," for your group to discuss. Each student who is not the moderator will be the expert on one of these texts. Decide which student will focus on each text.
- Create a format for your discussion—a schedule that shows the order in which members of the panel will speak and for how long. It will be the moderator's job to keep the discussion on schedule.
- Set rules regarding the appropriate times for the moderator or the audience (your classmates) to ask panel members questions.

myNotebook

Use the annotation tools in your eBook to find evidence that supports your ideas about how people adapt for survival. Save each piece of evidence to your notebook.

ACADEMIC VOCABULARY

As you share what you learned from your assigned text, try to use these words.

dimension

external

statistic

sustain

utilize

Gather Evidence Analyze your assigned text. Gather evidence that you will use to discuss adaptation and survival. Note specific details, examples, and quotations. Ask yourself these questions as you take notes:

- How do the people in your text adapt to their situation in order to survive?
- What aspects of a person's character allow some people to adapt more easily to devastating situations?
- What kinds of external forces affect a person's ability to adapt to a devastating experience?
- What generalization, or broad conclusion, can you make about how people adapt to devastating events in order to survive?

During this time, the moderator should make a list of relevant questions to be asked during the panel discussion.

Interactive Lessons

To help you prepare for your discussion, complete these lessons:

- Participating in Collaborative Discussions: Preparing for Discussion
- Using Textual Evidence: Synthesizing Information

PRODUCE

Write and Practice Work individually to outline your ideas about your assigned text. Then practice with your group.

- State a clear generalization about the ways people adapt to devastating experiences.
- Write several central ideas that support your generalization. Each idea should relate your generalization to the text.
- Match each piece of evidence with the central idea it most clearly supports. Provide clear examples.
- Present your ideas to your group, using vocabulary that is specific to the domain of your assigned text. The moderator will ask questions about your ideas and examples, preparing you to "think on your feet" during the real discussion.
- If you are the moderator, use this time to decide how to introduce and conclude the discussion. Write a statement that tells the audience the topic and format. Write notes for a concluding statement. Be ready to modify your remarks if new ideas emerge from the discussion.

Write your rough draft in *my*WriteSmart. Focus on getting your ideas down, rather than perfecting your choice of language.

Interactive Lessons

To help you practice your discussion, complete the following lesson:

- Participating in Collaborative Discussions: Speaking Constructively

Reinforce Your Ideas Based on the practice session and the rubric on the following page, make changes to your outline. Consider the following questions:

- Were you able to defend your generalization? If not, revise your statement so that it better reflects your textual evidence and your central ideas.

- Were you able to answer the moderator's questions clearly and without hesitation? If not, you may need to reorganize your outline so that you can find the information you need more quickly and easily.

- Did the moderator's questions help you see your text in a new light? If so, add new evidence to your outline that you can share during the real discussion.

Have your partner or a group of peers review your outline in *my*WriteSmart. Ask your reviewers to note any evidence that does not support your generalization about how people adapt for survival.

Interactive Lessons

To help you revise your outline, complete the following lesson:
- Participating in Collaborative Discussions: Listening and Responding

PRESENT

Have the Discussion Now it's time to present your panel discussion before the rest of the class. Have your outline at hand for reference during the discussion.

- Begin by having the moderator introduce the topic, the panelists, and the basic format for the discussion. The moderator will then ask the first question and continue to facilitate the discussion in the agreed-upon format.

- Use your outline to remind you of your main points, but try to speak directly to the panel and to the audience. Don't just read from your paper. Use domain-specific vocabulary.

- Listen closely to what all speakers say so that you can respond appropriately.

- Sustain a respectful tone toward your fellow panel members, even when you disagree with their ideas.

- When all the panelists have made their statements and discussed ideas amongst themselves, the moderator should invite audience members to ask questions.

- Conclude by having the moderator summarize the discussion and thank the panelists for their participation.

Summarize Write a summary of the main points from the discussion. Then explain whether the discussion made you rethink your generalization, and why.

PERFORMANCE TASK B RUBRIC
PANEL DISCUSSION

	Ideas and Evidence	Organization	Language
4	• The panelist clearly states a valid generalization and supports it with strong, relevant ideas and well-chosen evidence from the texts. • The panel member carefully evaluates others' evidence and reasoning and responds with insightful comments and questions. • The panelist synthesizes the analysis of the texts to help listeners understand the generalization.	• The panelist's remarks are based on a well-organized outline that clearly identifies the generalization and the supporting ideas and evidence. • The panelist concludes with a statement that reinforces the generalization and includes the ideas that have emerged from the discussion.	• The panelist adapts speech to the context of the discussion, using appropriately formal English to discuss the texts and ideas. • The panelist consistently quotes accurately from the texts to support ideas. • The panelist uses domain-specific language throughout the discussion. • The panel member consistently maintains a polite and thoughtful tone throughout the discussion.
3	• The panelist states a generalization and supports it with relevant ideas and evidence from the texts. • The panel member evaluates others' evidence and reasoning and responds with appropriate comments and questions. • The panelist synthesizes some ideas and links to the generalization.	• The panelist's remarks are based on an outline that identifies the generalization, supporting ideas, and evidence. • The panelist concludes with a statement that reinforces the generalization.	• The panelist mostly uses formal English to discuss literature and ideas. • The panelist mostly quotes accurately from the texts to support ideas. • The panelist uses domain-specific language a few times during the discussion. • The panel member maintains a polite and thoughtful tone throughout most of the discussion.
2	• The panelist states a reasonably clear generalization and supports it with some ideas and evidence. • The panel member's response to others' comments shows limited evaluation of the evidence and reasoning. • The panelist does not synthesize ideas but simply repeats the generalization in a vague way.	• The panelist's remarks reflect an outline that may identify the generalization but does not organize ideas and evidence very effectively. • The panelist makes a weak concluding statement that does little to reinforce the generalization.	• The panelist uses some formal and some informal English to discuss the texts and ideas. • The panelist's quotations and examples sometimes do not accurately reflect the texts. • The panelist rarely uses domain-specific language. • The panel member occasionally forgets to maintain a polite tone when responding to others' comments and questions.
1	• The panelist's generalization is unclear; ideas and evidence are not coherent. • The panel member does not evaluate others' evidence and reasoning. • The panelist does not synthesize ideas.	• The panelist does not follow an outline that organizes ideas and evidence. • The panelist's remarks lack any kind of conclusion or summary.	• The panelist uses informal English and/or slang, resulting in a lack of clarity. • The panelist's quotations and examples do not accurately reflect the texts. • The panelist does not use domain-specific language. • The panel member does not maintain a polite tone when responding to others' comments and questions.

Heroes and Quests

"If a journey doesn't have something to teach you about yourself, then what kind of journey is it?"

Heroes and Quests

The hero's journey takes many forms, from traveling through forbidding places to exploring the mind.

Stream to Start

hmhfyi.com

Channel One News®

COLLECTION
PERFORMANCE TASK Preview

At the end of this collection, you will have the opportunity to complete a task:

• Write an analytical essay about why people undertake arduous journeys.

ACADEMIC VOCABULARY

Study the words and their definitions in the chart below. You will use these words as you discuss and write about the texts in this collection.

Word	Definition	Related Forms
motivate (mō´tə-vāt´) v.	to provide a cause for doing something	motivation, motivational
objective (əb-jĕk´tĭv) n.	an intention, purpose, or goal	objectively, subjective
pursuit (pər-sōot´) n.	the action of chasing or following something	pursue, pursuer
subsequent (sŭb´sĭ-kwĕnt´) adj.	coming after or following	subsequently, sequential
undertake (ŭn´dər-tāk´) v.	to assume responsibility for or take on a job or course of action	undertaking, undertook

The Epic

Extraordinary heroes in pursuit of hideous monsters. Brutal battles fought and perilous quests undertaken. Spectacular triumphs and crushing defeats. The epic, still very much alive in today's novels and movies, began thousands of years ago in the oral tradition of ancient Greece. There, listeners gathered around poet-storytellers to hear the daring exploits of the hero Odysseus. Across storm-tossed seas, through wild forests, amid countless dangers and subsequent narrow escapes, the hero, motivated by a singular focus on his objective, prevails against all odds. It's no wonder that Homer's **Odyssey** *remains one of the most beloved epics in Western literature. It captivates us and carries us off into a time and place quite different from—yet somehow similar to—our own.*

Characteristics of the Epic

An **epic** is a long narrative poem. It recounts the adventures of an epic hero, a larger-than-life figure who undertakes great journeys and performs deeds requiring remarkable bravery and cunning. As you begin your own journey through Homer's epic, you can expect to encounter the following elements.

Elements of the Epic	
Epic Hero • Possesses superhuman strength, craftiness, and confidence • Helped or harmed by gods or fate • Embodies qualities valued by the culture • Overcomes perilous situations	**Archetypes** Characters and situations recognizable across times and cultures • brave hero • evil temptress • sea monster • loyal servant • suitors' contest • buried treasure
Epic Plot Depicts a long, strange journey filled with such complications as • strange creatures • divine intervention • treacherous weather • large-scale events	**Epic Themes** Reflect universal concerns, such as • courage • the fate of a nation • loyalty • life and death • beauty • a homecoming
Epic Setting • Includes fantastic or exotic lands • Involves more than one nation or culture	

The Language of Homer

Since Homer's work originated as ancient Greek verse, you will read an English translation. Many translations of the *Odyssey* have appeared over the years, and each translator has interpreted it differently. Consider, for example, these two passages from Book 2. The first adopts a formal tone that is much closer to the original. The second version employs a more conversational voice.

Translation 1	Translation 2
When Primal Dawn spread on the eastern sky her fingers of pink light, Odysseus's true son stood up, drew on his tunic and mantle, slung on a sword-belt and a new-edged sword, tied his smooth feet into good rawhide sandals, and left his room, a god's brilliance upon him. —translated by Robert Fitzgerald (1961)	Dawn came, showing her rosy fingers through the early mists, and Telemachus leapt out of bed. He dressed himself, slung a sharp sword over his shoulder, strapt a stout pair of boots on his lissom feet, and came forth from his chamber like a young god. —translated by W.H.D. Rouse (1937)

The people of ancient Greece who first experienced the *Odyssey* heard it sung in a live performance. The poet, or another performer, used epic similes, epithets, and allusions to help keep the audience enthralled.

- A **simile** is a comparison between two unlike things, using the word *like* or *as*. Homer often employs the **epic simile**, a comparison developed at great length over several lines. For example, the epic simile in the following passage compares an angry Odysseus to a roasting sausage.

>   His rage
> held hard in leash, submitted to his mind,
> while he himself rocked, rolling from side to side,
> as a cook turns a sausage, big with blood
> and fat, at a scorching blaze, without a pause,
> to broil it quick: so he rolled left and right, . . .

- An **epithet** renames a person or thing with a descriptive phrase. To maintain the meter of the poem or complete a line of verse, the poet would often use an epithet containing the necessary number of syllables. For example, Homer often refers to Odysseus by such epithets as "son of Laertes" and "raider of cities."
- An **allusion** is a reference to a literary or historical person, place, event, or composition. For example, when Telemachus, Odysseus' son, beholds the palace of Menelaus, he exclaims, "This is the way the court of Zeus must be." Every listener in Greece immediately understood the allusion to Zeus, the ruler of the gods.

Reading the Epic

Any journey through the *Odyssey* offers the reader a complex experience. On one level, Homer provides an action-packed narrative that makes us eagerly anticipate each thrilling step in the adventure. On another level, readers can analyze and appreciate the poem as a work of art. The following strategies can help you navigate your own voyage.

Reading the Epic as Narrative

- Pay close attention to the changing narrators. Who is telling the story at a given point? Consider the ways in which different narrators deepen your understanding of characters and events.
- Visualize the setting and the action by observing key details in the text.
- Note major events and conflicts and try to predict their outcomes. Use a chart like the one shown to track characters, including gods and goddesses. Categorize characters as friends or foes, and explain how they help or hinder Odysseus's efforts.

Characters Who Help	Characters Who Hinder
Goddess Athena pleads with Zeus to help Odysseus escape from Calypso's island.	The god Poseidon stirs up powerful storms that cause problems for Odysseus and his crew.

Reading the Epic as Poetry

- Read the epic aloud. Listen for sound devices, such as **alliteration, meter,** and **rhyme,** and notice how they reflect and enhance meaning.
- Follow punctuation closely, and remember that the end of a line does not indicate the end of a thought.
- Consider how imagery and figurative language, including epic similes, reveal characters and events. Note allusions and epithets.

Reading the Epic within the Context of Its Time

- Look closely at how Odysseus behaves. What character traits does he display? What do these traits tell you about the values of the time?
- Draw upon your own prior knowledge of ancient Greek civilization and history. What events and customs would have influenced Homer?
- Remember that the Greeks of Homer's time believed the gods took an active interest in human affairs. (In fact, the gods themselves behaved very much like humans.) How do such religious beliefs influence the epic?

Examining the Homeric Epics

Considered the greatest masterpieces of the epic form, the *Iliad* and the *Odyssey* present high drama and intense emotions. In both books, important plot elements include the interference of gods in human affairs, the epic heroism of the central characters, and the saga of the Trojan War and its aftermath.

The Trojan War

The legendary conflict between Greece (or Achaea) and Troy began around 1200 BC. Paris, a Trojan prince, kidnapped Helen, the wife of Menelaus, king of Sparta. Menelaus recruited the armies of allied kingdoms to attack Troy and recover his wife. For ten years the Greek forces held Troy under siege, but they could not penetrate the walls of the city.

Finally, Odysseus, king of Ithaca, came up with a plan to break the stalemate. He ordered his men to build a giant wooden horse. One morning the people of Troy awoke to find that horse outside the city gates—and no Greeks in sight. Assuming the Greeks had retreated and had left the horse as a peace offering, they brought the horse inside the gates. They soon discovered, too late, that the horse was filled with Greek soldiers and that their city was doomed.

Heroism

Great heroes play key roles in Homer's epics. The *Iliad* tells the story of Achilles, the mightiest Greek warrior, and of his bitter quarrel with Agamemnon, brother of Menelaus and commander of the Greek forces at Troy. The tale climaxes in a fierce battle between Achilles and Hector, Paris's brother, and Hector's subsequent funeral.

The *Odyssey* recounts Odysseus' adventures as he struggles to make his way home from post-war Troy, along with the conflicts that arise in Ithaca just before and after his return. He prevails against gruesome monsters, enchanting women, and greedy rivals intent on preventing him from reaching his objective. Although Odysseus lacks the superhuman martial abilities of Achilles, he employs great cleverness and guile to get out of difficult situations.

The Intervention of Gods

Adding to the heroes' struggles are the residents of Mount Olympus, bickering gods who like nothing better than influencing and manipulating human affairs. For example, Athena, goddess of wisdom, supports the Greeks in the Trojan War; Aphrodite, goddess of love, sides with Troy. Further, the heroes often displease other gods who place additional obstacles in their paths. The Olympians display human shortcomings and petty jealousies, and people become pawns as the gods pursue advantages in their internal quarrels.

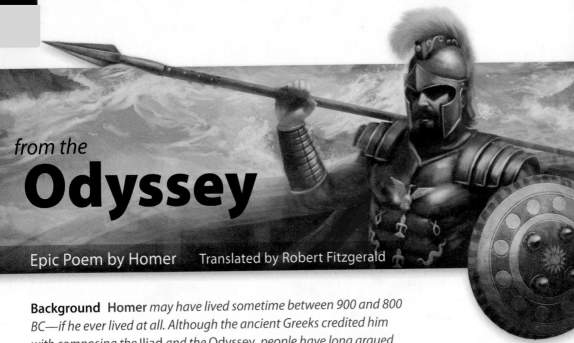

from the
Odyssey

Epic Poem by Homer   Translated by Robert Fitzgerald

Background **Homer** *may have lived sometime between 900 and 800 BC—if he ever lived at all. Although the ancient Greeks credited him with composing the* Iliad *and the* Odyssey, *people have long argued about whether or not he really existed. Many theories speculate on who Homer may have been and where he may have lived. Details in the stories suggest that he was born and lived in the eastern Aegean Sea, either on the islands of Chios or Smyrna, and that he was blind.*

Whatever position modern scholars take on the debate, most believe that one or two exceptionally talented individuals created the Homeric epics. The Iliad *and the* Odyssey *each contain 24 books of verse, but they probably predate the development of writing in Greece. The verses, which were originally sung, gradually became part of an important oral tradition. Generations of professional reciters memorized and performed the poems at festivals throughout Greece. By 300 BC, several versions of the books existed, and scholars undertook the job of standardizing the texts.*

Homer's poems profoundly influenced Greek culture and, as a result, contributed to the subsequent development of Western literature, ideas, and values. The Roman poet Virgil wrote a related poem, the Aeneid, *in Latin, and Odysseus appears in Dante's* Inferno. *Poets throughout English literature, from Geoffrey Chaucer in the Middle Ages to William Shakespeare in the Renaissance to John Keats in the Romantic era, have found inspiration in Homer. James Joyce's 1922 novel* Ulysses *(the Latin form of Odysseus' name) transforms one ordinary Dublin day into an Odyssean journey. Dozens of movies have retold the saga of the Trojan War and the long journey home, both directly and symbolically. For thousands of years people have taken the tales of a wandering Greek bard and made them their own.*

Important Characters in the *Odyssey* *(in order of mention)*

Book 1

Helios (hē′lē-ŏs′)—the sun god, who raises his cattle on the island of Thrinacia (thrĭ-nā′shə)

Zeus (zo͞os)—the ruler of the Greek gods and goddesses; father of Athena and Apollo

Telemachus (tə-lĕm′ə-kəs)—Odysseus' son

Penelope (pə-nĕl′ə-pē)—Odysseus' wife

Book 9

Alcinous (ăl-sĭn′ō-əs)—the king of the Phaeacians (fē-ā′shənz)

Circe (sûr′sē)—a goddess and enchantress who lives on the island of Aeaea (ē-ē′ə)

Cicones (sĭ-kō′nēz)—allies of the Trojans, who live at Ismarus (ĭs-măr′əs)

Lotus Eaters—inhabitants of a land Odysseus visits

Cyclopes (sī-klō′pēz)—a race of one-eyed giants; an individual member of the race is a Cyclops (sī′klŏps)

Apollo (ə-pŏl′ō)—the god of music, poetry, prophecy, and medicine

Poseidon (pō-sīd′n)—the god of the seas, earthquakes, and horses; father of the Cyclops who battles Odysseus

Athena (ə-thē′nə)—the goddess of war, wisdom, and cleverness; goddess of crafts

Book 10

Aeolus (ē′ə-ləs)—the guardian of the winds

Laestrygones (lĕs′trĭ-gō′nēz)—cannibal inhabitants of a distant land

Eurylochus (yo͝o-rĭl′ə-kəs)—a trusted officer of Odysseus

Persephone (pər-sĕf′ə-nē)—the wife of Hades, ruler of the underworld

Tiresias (tī-rē′sē-əs) of Thebes (thēbz)—a blind prophet whose spirit Odysseus visits in the underworld

Book 11

Elpenor (ĕl-pē′nôr)—one of Odysseus' crew, killed in an accident

Book 12

Sirens (sī′rənz)—creatures, part woman and part bird, whose songs lure sailors to their death

Scylla (sĭl′ə)—a six-headed sea monster who devours sailors

Charybdis (kə-rĭb′dĭs)—a dangerous whirlpool personified as a female sea monster

Book 17

Argos (är′gŏs)—Odysseus' dog

Eumaeus (yo͞o-mē′əs)—a servant in Odysseus' household

Books 21–23

Antinous (ăn-tĭn′ō-əs)—a suitor of Penelope's

Eurymachus (yo͝o-rĭm′ə-kəs)—a suitor of Penelope's

Philoetius (fĭ-lē′shəs)—a servant in Odysseus' household

Amphinomus (ăm-fĭn′ə-məs)—a suitor of Penelope's

Eurynome (yo͝o-rĭn′ə-mē)—a female servant in Odysseus' household

Eurycleia (yo͝or′ĭ-klē′ə)—an old female servant, still loyal to Odysseus

PART ONE: THE WANDERINGS OF ODYSSEUS

AS YOU READ Pay attention to details that tell how Odysseus confronts the various challenges of his journey. Write down any questions you generate during reading.

BOOK 1:

A Goddess Intervenes

Sing in me, Muse, and through me tell the story
of that man skilled in all ways of contending,
the wanderer, **harried** for years on end,
after he plundered the stronghold
5   on the proud height of Troy.

                              He saw the townlands
and learned the minds of many distant men,
and weathered many bitter nights and days
in his deep heart at sea, while he fought only
to save his life, to bring his shipmates home.
10 But not by will nor valor could he save them,
for their own recklessness destroyed them all—
children and fools, they killed and feasted on
the cattle of Lord Helios, the Sun,
and he who moves all day through heaven
15 took from their eyes the dawn of their return.

Of these adventures, Muse, daughter of Zeus,
tell us in our time, lift the great song again. . . .

*The story of Odysseus begins with the goddess Athena's appealing to
Zeus to help Odysseus, who has been wandering for ten years on the
seas, to find his way home to his family on Ithaca. While Odysseus
has been gone, his son, Telemachus, has grown to manhood and his
wife, Penelope, has been besieged by suitors wishing to marry her and
gain Odysseus' wealth. The suitors have taken up residence in her
home and are constantly feasting on the family's cattle, sheep, and
goats. They dishonor Odysseus and his family. Taking Athena's
advice, Telemachus travels to Pylos for word of his father. Meanwhile,
on Ithaca, the evil suitors plot to kill Telemachus when he returns.*

1 Muse: a daughter of Zeus, credited with divine inspiration.

harried (hăr´ēd) *adj.* tormented; harassed
harry *v.*

11–13 their own recklessness . . . the Sun: a reference to an event occurring later in the poem—an event that causes the death of Odysseus' entire crew.

BOOK 9:

New Coasts and Poseidon's Son

*For seven of the ten years Odysseus has spent wandering the
Mediterranean Sea, he has been held captive by the goddess Calypso
on her island. In Book 5, Zeus sends the god Hermes to tell Calypso
to release Odysseus; she helps him build a raft on which he can sail to
his next destination. He must sail for 20 days before landing on the
island of Scheria, where he will be helped in his effort to return home.
In Books 6–8, Odysseus is welcomed by King Alcinous, who gives a
banquet in his honor. That night the king begs Odysseus to tell who
he is and what has happened to him. In Books 9–12, Odysseus relates
to the king his adventures.*

"I AM LAERTES' SON"

"What shall I
say first? What shall I keep until the end?
The gods have tried me in a thousand ways.
But first my name: let that be known to you,
5 and if I pull away from pitiless death,
friendship will bind us, though my land lies far.

I am Laertes' son, Odysseus.

Men hold me
formidable for guile in peace and war:
this fame has gone abroad to the sky's rim.
10 My home is on the peaked sea-mark of Ithaca
under Mount Neion's wind-blown robe of leaves,
in sight of other islands—Dulichium,
Same, wooded Zacynthus—Ithaca
being most lofty in that coastal sea,
15 and northwest, while the rest lie east and south.
A rocky isle, but good for a boy's training;
I shall not see on earth a place more dear,
though I have been detained long by Calypso,
loveliest among goddesses, who held me
20 in her smooth caves, to be her heart's delight,
as Circe of Aeaea, the enchantress,
desired me, and detained me in her hall.
But in my heart I never gave consent.
Where shall a man find sweetness to surpass
25 his own home and his parents? In far lands

**7–8 hold me
formidable for guile:**
consider me impressive
for my cunning and
craftiness.

11–13 Mount Neion's
(nē´ŏnz´); **Dulichium**
(dōō-lĭk´ē-əm); **Same**
(sā´mē); **Zacynthus**
(zə-sĭn´thəs).

18–26 Odysseus
refers to two beautiful
goddesses, Calypso and
Circe, who have delayed
him on their islands.
(Details about Circe
appear in Book 10.)

he shall not, though he find a house of gold.
What of my sailing, then, from Troy?

What of those years

of rough adventure, weathered under Zeus? . . ."

*Odysseus explains that soon after leaving Troy, he and his crew land
near Ismarus, the city of the Cicones. The Cicones are allies of the
Trojans and therefore enemies of Odysseus. Odysseus and his crew
raid the Cicones, robbing and killing them, until the Ciconian army
kills 72 of Odysseus' men and drives the rest out to sea. Delayed by a
storm for two days, Odysseus and his remaining companions then
continue their journey.*

THE LOTUS EATERS

"I might have made it safely home, that time,
30   but as I came round Malea the current
took me out to sea, and from the north
a fresh gale drove me on, past Cythera.
Nine days I drifted on the teeming sea
before dangerous high winds. Upon the tenth
35   we came to the coastline of the Lotus Eaters,
who live upon that flower. We landed there
to take on water. All ships' companies
mustered alongside for the mid-day meal.
Then I sent out two picked men and a runner
40   to learn what race of men that land sustained.
They fell in, soon enough, with Lotus Eaters,
who showed no will to do us harm, only
offering the sweet Lotus to our friends—
but those who ate this honeyed plant, the Lotus,
45   never cared to report, nor to return:
they longed to stay forever, browsing on
that native bloom, forgetful of their homeland.
I drove them, all three wailing, to the ships,
tied them down under their rowing benches,
50   and called the rest: 'All hands aboard;
come, clear the beach and no one taste
the Lotus, or you lose your hope of home.'
Filing in to their places by the rowlocks
my oarsmen dipped their long oars in the surf,
55   and we moved out again on our sea faring.

30 Malea (mä-lē´ä).

32 Cythera (sĭ-thîr´ə).

38 mustered:
assembled; gathered.

THE CYCLOPS

In the next land we found were Cyclopes,
giants, louts, without a law to bless them.
In ignorance leaving the fruitage of the earth in mystery
to the immortal gods, they neither plow
60 nor sow by hand, nor till the ground, though grain—
wild wheat and barley—grows untended, and
wine-grapes, in clusters, ripen in heaven's rain.
Cyclopes have no muster and no meeting,
no consultation or old tribal ways,
65 but each one dwells in his own mountain cave
dealing out rough justice to wife and child,
indifferent to what the others do. . . ."

56 Cyclopes (sī-klō´pēz): refers to the creatures in plural; *Cyclops* is singular.

Across the bay from the land of the Cyclopes is a lush, deserted island. Odysseus and his crew land on the island in a dense fog and spend days feasting on wine and wild goats and observing the mainland, where the Cyclopes live. On the third day, Odysseus and his company of men set out to learn if the Cyclopes are friends or foes.

"When the young Dawn with finger tips of rose
came in the east, I called my men together
70 and made a speech to them:

                         'Old shipmates, friends,
the rest of you stand by; I'll make the crossing
in my own ship, with my own company,
and find out what the mainland natives are—
for they may be wild savages, and lawless,
75 or hospitable and god fearing men.'

At this I went aboard, and gave the word
to cast off by the stern. My oarsmen followed,
filing in to their benches by the rowlocks,
and all in line dipped oars in the gray sea.

77 stern: the rear end of a ship.

80 As we rowed on, and nearer to the mainland,
at one end of the bay, we saw a cavern
yawning above the water, screened with laurel,
and many rams and goats about the place
inside a sheepfold—made from slabs of stone
85 earthfast between tall trunks of pine and rugged
towering oak trees.

82 screened with laurel: partially hidden by laurel trees.

                                    A prodigious man
      slept in this cave alone, and took his flocks
      to graze afield—remote from all companions,
      knowing none but savage ways, a brute
90   so huge, he seemed no man at all of those
      who eat good wheaten bread; but he seemed rather
      a shaggy mountain reared in solitude.
      We beached there, and I told the crew
      to stand by and keep watch over the ship;
95   as for myself I took my twelve best fighters
      and went ahead. I had a goatskin full
      of that sweet liquor that Euanthes' son,
      Maron, had given me. He kept Apollo's
      holy grove at Ismarus; for kindness
100   we showed him there, and showed his wife and child,
      he gave me seven shining golden talents
      perfectly formed, a solid silver winebowl,
      and then this liquor—twelve two-handled jars
      of brandy, pure and fiery. Not a slave
105   in Maron's household knew this drink; only
      he, his wife and the storeroom mistress knew;
      and they would put one cupful—ruby-colored,
      honey-smooth—in twenty more of water,
      but still the sweet scent hovered like a fume
110   over the winebowl. No man turned away
      when cups of this came round.

97–98 Euanthes
(yo͞o-ăn´thēz); **Maron**
(mâr´ŏn´).

101 talents: bars
of gold or silver of a
specified weight, used
as money in ancient
Greece.

A wineskin full

I brought along, and victuals in a bag,
for in my bones I knew some towering brute
would be upon us soon—all outward power,
115 a wild man, ignorant of civility.

We climbed, then, briskly to the cave. But Cyclops
had gone afield, to pasture his fat sheep,
so we looked round at everything inside:
a drying rack that sagged with cheeses, pens
120 crowded with lambs and kids, each in its class:
firstlings apart from middlings, and the 'dewdrops,'
or newborn lambkins, penned apart from both.
And vessels full of whey were brimming there—
bowls of earthenware and pails for milking.
125 My men came pressing round me, pleading:

'Why not

take these cheeses, get them stowed, come back,
throw open all the pens, and make a run for it?
We'll drive the kids and lambs aboard. We say
put out again on good salt water!'

Ah,

130 how sound that was! Yet I refused. I wished
to see the caveman, what he had to offer—
no pretty sight, it turned out, for my friends.
We lit a fire, burnt an offering,
and took some cheese to eat; then sat in silence
135 around the embers, waiting. When he came
he had a load of dry boughs on his shoulder
to stoke his fire at suppertime. He dumped it
with a great crash into that hollow cave,
and we all scattered fast to the far wall.
140 Then over the broad cavern floor he ushered
the ewes he meant to milk. He left his rams
and he-goats in the yard outside, and swung
high overhead a slab of solid rock
to close the cave. Two dozen four-wheeled wagons,
145 with heaving wagon teams, could not have stirred
the tonnage of that rock from where he wedged it
over the doorsill. Next he took his seat
and milked his bleating ewes. A practiced job
he made of it, giving each ewe her suckling;
150 thickened his milk, then, into curds and whey,
sieved out the curds to drip in withy baskets,
and poured the whey to stand in bowls

112 victuals (vĭt'lz): food.

121–122 The Cyclops has separated his lambs into three age groups.

123 whey: the watery part of milk, which separates from the curds, or solid part, during the making of cheese.

129 good salt water: the open sea.

133 burnt an offering: burned a portion of the food as an offering to secure the gods' goodwill. (Such offerings were frequently performed by Greek sailors during difficult journeys.)

151 withy baskets: baskets made from twigs.

cooling until he drank it for his supper.
When all these chores were done, he poked the fire,
heaping on brushwood. In the glare he saw us.

155

'Strangers,' he said, 'who are you? And where from?
What brings you here by sea ways—a fair traffic?
Or are you wandering rogues, who cast your lives
like dice, and ravage other folk by sea?'

157 fair traffic: honest trading.

160   We felt a pressure on our hearts, in dread
of that deep rumble and that mighty man.
But all the same I spoke up in reply:

'We are from Troy, Achaeans, blown off course
by shifting gales on the Great South Sea;
165   homeward bound, but taking routes and ways
uncommon; so the will of Zeus would have it.
We served under Agamemnon, son of Atreus—
the whole world knows what city
he laid waste, what armies he destroyed.
170   It was our luck to come here; here we stand,
beholden for your help, or any gifts
you give—as custom is to honor strangers.
We would entreat you, great Sir, have a care
for the gods' courtesy; Zeus will avenge
175   the unoffending guest.'
                                          He answered this
from his brute chest, unmoved:

172–175 It was a sacred Greek custom to honor strangers with food and gifts. Odysseus is reminding the Cyclops that Zeus will punish anyone who mistreats a guest.

                                          'You are a ninny,
or else you come from the other end of nowhere,
telling me, mind the gods! We Cyclopes
care not a whistle for your thundering Zeus
180   or all the gods in bliss; we have more force by far.
I would not let you go for fear of Zeus—
you or your friends—unless I had a whim to.
Tell me, where was it, now, you left your ship—
around the point, or down the shore, I wonder?'

185   He thought he'd find out, but I saw through this,
and answered with a ready lie:

                                          'My ship?
Poseidon Lord, who sets the earth a-tremble,
broke it up on the rocks at your land's end.
A wind from seaward served him, drove us there.
190   We are survivors, these good men and I.'

Neither reply nor pity came from him,
but in one stride he clutched at my companions
and caught two in his hands like squirming puppies
to beat their brains out, spattering the floor.
195   Then he dismembered them and made his meal,
gaping and crunching like a mountain lion—
everything: innards, flesh, and marrow bones.
We cried aloud, lifting our hands to Zeus,
powerless, looking on at this, appalled;
200   but Cyclops went on filling up his belly
with manflesh and great gulps of whey,
then lay down like a mast among his sheep.
My heart beat high now at the chance of action,
and drawing the sharp sword from my hip I went
205   along his flank to stab him where the midriff
holds the liver. I had touched the spot
when sudden fear stayed me: if I killed him
we perished there as well, for we could never
move his **ponderous** doorway slab aside.
210   So we were left to groan and wait for morning.

When the young Dawn with fingertips of rose
lit up the world, the Cyclops built a fire
and milked his handsome ewes, all in due order,
putting the sucklings to the mothers. Then,
215   his chores being all dispatched, he caught
another brace of men to make his breakfast,
and whisked away his great door slab
to let his sheep go through—but he, behind,
reset the stone as one would cap a quiver.
220   There was a din of whistling as the Cyclops
rounded his flock to higher ground, then stillness.
And now I pondered how to hurt him worst,
if but Athena granted what I prayed for.
Here are the means I thought would serve my turn:

225   a club, or staff, lay there along the fold—
an olive tree, felled green and left to season
for Cyclops' hand. And it was like a mast
a lugger of twenty oars, broad in the beam—
a deep-sea-going craft—might carry:
230   so long, so big around, it seemed. Now I
chopped out a six foot section of this pole
and set it down before my men, who scraped it;
and when they had it smooth, I hewed again
to make a stake with pointed end. I held this

ponderous (pŏn′dər-əs)
adj. heavy in a clumsy
way; bulky.

216 brace: pair.

218–219 The Cyclops
reseals the cave with the
massive rock as easily
as an ordinary human
places the cap on a
container of arrows.

226 left to season: left
to dry out and harden.

228 lugger: a small,
wide sailing ship.

235   in the fire's heart and turned it, toughening it,
then hid it, well back in the cavern, under
one of the dung piles in **profusion** there.
Now came the time to toss for it: who ventured
along with me? whose hand could bear to thrust
240   and grind that spike in Cyclops' eye, when mild
sleep had mastered him? As luck would have it,
the men I would have chosen won the toss—
four strong men, and I made five as captain.

At evening came the shepherd with his flock,
245   his woolly flock. The rams as well, this time,
entered the cave: by some sheep-herding whim—
or a god's bidding—none were left outside.
He hefted his great boulder into place
and sat him down to milk the bleating ewes
250   in proper order, put the lambs to suck,
and swiftly ran through all his evening chores.
Then he caught two more men and feasted on them.
My moment was at hand, and I went forward
holding an ivy bowl of my dark drink,
255   looking up, saying:

                        'Cyclops, try some wine.
Here's liquor to wash down your scraps of men.
Taste it, and see the kind of drink we carried
under our planks. I meant it for an offering
if you would help us home. But you are mad,
260   unbearable, a bloody monster! After this,
will any other traveller come to see you?'

He seized and drained the bowl, and it went down
so fiery and smooth he called for more:

'Give me another, thank you kindly. Tell me,
265   how are you called? I'll make a gift will please you.
Even Cyclopes know the wine-grapes grow
out of grassland and loam in heaven's rain,
but here's a bit of nectar and ambrosia!'

Three bowls I brought him, and he poured them down.
270   I saw the fuddle and flush come over him,
then I sang out in cordial tones:

                           'Cyclops,
you ask my honorable name? Remember
the gift you promised me, and I shall tell you.

profusion
(prə-fyoō´zhən) *n.*
abundance.

268 nectar (nĕk´tər) **and
ambrosia** (ăm-brō´zhə):
the drink and food of the
gods.

270 fuddle and flush:
the state of confusion
and redness of the face
caused by drinking
alcohol.

My name is Nohbdy: mother, father, and friends,
275 everyone calls me Nohbdy.'

                                        And he said:
'Nohbdy's my meat, then, after I eat his friends.
Others come first. There's a noble gift, now.'

Even as he spoke, he reeled and tumbled backward,
his great head lolling to one side: and sleep
280 took him like any creature. Drunk, hiccupping,
he dribbled streams of liquor and bits of men.

Now, by the gods, I drove my big hand spike
deep in the embers, charring it again,
and cheered my men along with battle talk
285 to keep their courage up: no quitting now.
The pike of olive, green though it had been,
reddened and glowed as if about to catch.
I drew it from the coals and my four fellows
gave me a hand, lugging it near the Cyclops
290 as more than natural force nerved them; straight
forward they sprinted, lifted it, and rammed it
deep in his crater eye, and I leaned on it
turning it as a shipwright turns a drill
in planking, having men below to swing
295 the two-handled strap that spins it in the groove.
So with our brand we bored that great eye socket
while blood ran out around the red hot bar.
Eyelid and lash were seared; the pierced ball
hissed broiling, and the roots popped.

                                        In a smithy
300 one sees a white-hot axehead or an adze
plunged and wrung in a cold tub, screeching steam—
the way they make soft iron hale and hard—:
just so that eyeball hissed around the spike.
The Cyclops bellowed and the rock roared round him,
305 and we fell back in fear. Clawing his face
he tugged the bloody spike out of his eye,
threw it away, and his wild hands went groping;
then he set up a howl for Cyclopes
who lived in caves on windy peaks nearby.
310 Some heard him; and they came by divers ways
to clump around outside and call:

286 the pike: the pointed stake.

299 smithy: blacksmith's shop.

300 adze (ădz): an axlike tool with a curved blade.

310 divers: various.

          'What ails you,
Polyphemus? Why do you cry so sore
in the starry night? You will not let us sleep.
Sure no man's driving off your flock? No man

315 has tricked you, ruined you?'

             Out of the cave
the mammoth Polyphemus roared in answer:

'Nohbdy, Nohbdy's tricked me, Nohbdy's ruined me!'

To this rough shout they made a sage reply:

'Ah well, if nobody has played you foul
320 there in your lonely bed, we are no use in pain
given by great Zeus. Let it be your father,
Poseidon Lord, to whom you pray.'

            So saying
they trailed away. And I was filled with laughter
to see how like a charm the name deceived them.
325 Now Cyclops, wheezing as the pain came on him,
fumbled to wrench away the great doorstone
and squatted in the breach with arms thrown wide
for any silly beast or man who bolted—
hoping somehow I might be such a fool.
330 But I kept thinking how to win the game:
death sat there huge; how could we slip away?
I drew on all my wits, and ran through tactics,
reasoning as a man will for dear life,
until a trick came—and it pleased me well.
335 The Cyclops' rams were handsome, fat, with heavy
fleeces, a dark violet.

          Three abreast
I tied them silently together, twining
cords of willow from the ogre's bed;
then slung a man under each middle one
340 to ride there safely, shielded left and right.
So three sheep could convey each man. I took
the woolliest ram, the choicest of the flock,
and hung myself under his kinky belly,
pulled up tight, with fingers twisted deep
345 in sheepskin ringlets for an iron grip.
So, breathing hard, we waited until morning.

312 Polyphemus
(pŏl´ə-fē´məs): the name
of the Cyclops.

318 sage: wise.

319–322 Odysseus'
lie about his name has
paid off.

327 breach: opening.

When Dawn spread out her finger tips of rose
the rams began to stir, moving for pasture,
and peals of bleating echoed round the pens
350 where dams with udders full called for a milking.
Blinded, and sick with pain from his head wound,
the master stroked each ram, then let it pass,
but my men riding on the pectoral fleece
the giant's blind hands blundering never found.
355 Last of them all my ram, the leader, came,
weighted by wool and me with my meditations.
The Cyclops patted him, and then he said:

'Sweet cousin ram, why lag behind the rest
in the night cave? You never linger so,
360 but graze before them all, and go afar
to crop sweet grass, and take your stately way
leading along the streams, until at evening
you run to be the first one in the fold.
Why, now, so far behind? Can you be grieving
365 over your Master's eye? That carrion rogue
and his accurst companions burnt it out
when he had conquered all my wits with wine.
Nohbdy will not get out alive, I swear.
Oh, had you brain and voice to tell
370 where he may be now, dodging all my fury!
Bashed by this hand and bashed on this rock wall
his brains would strew the floor, and I should have
rest from the outrage Nohbdy worked upon me.'

He sent us into the open, then. Close by,
375 I dropped and rolled clear of the ram's belly,
going this way and that to untie the men.
With many glances back, we rounded up
his fat, stiff-legged sheep to take aboard,
and drove them down to where the good ship lay.
380 We saw, as we came near, our fellows' faces
shining; then we saw them turn to grief
tallying those who had not fled from death.
I hushed them, jerking head and eyebrows up,
and in a low voice told them: 'Load this herd;
385 move fast, and put the ship's head toward the breakers.'
They all pitched in at loading, then embarked
and struck their oars into the sea. Far out,
as far off shore as shouted words would carry,
I sent a few back to the **adversary**:

353 pectoral fleece: the wool covering a sheep's chest.

385 put ... the breakers: turn the ship around so that it is heading toward the open sea.

adversary (ăd´vər-sĕr´ē) *n.* an opponent; enemy.

390 'O Cyclops! Would you feast on my companions?
Puny, am I, in a Caveman's hands?
How do you like the beating that we gave you,
you damned cannibal? Eater of guests
under your roof! Zeus and the gods have paid you!'

395 The blind thing in his doubled fury broke
a hilltop in his hands and heaved it after us.
Ahead of our black prow it struck and sank
whelmed in a spuming geyser, a giant wave
that washed the ship stern foremost back to shore.
400 I got the longest boathook out and stood
fending us off, with furious nods to all
to put their backs into a racing stroke—
row, row, or perish. So the long oars bent
kicking the foam sternward, making head
405 until we drew away, and twice as far.
Now when I cupped my hands I heard the crew
in low voices protesting:

                                'Godsake, Captain!

Why bait the beast again? Let him alone!'
'That tidal wave he made on the first throw
410 all but beached us.'

390–394 Odysseus assumes that the gods are on his side.

395–403 The hilltop thrown by Polyphemus lands in front of the ship, causing a huge wave that carries the ship back to the shore. Odysseus uses a long pole to push the boat away from the land.

406 cupped my hands: put his hands on either side of his mouth in order to magnify his voice.

'All but stove us in!'

'Give him our bearing with your trumpeting,
he'll get the range and lob a boulder.'

'Aye

He'll smash our timbers and our heads together!'

I would not heed them in my glorying spirit,
415   but let my anger flare and yelled:

'Cyclops,

if ever mortal man inquire
how you were put to shame and blinded, tell him
Odysseus, raider of cities, took your eye:
Laertes' son, whose home's on Ithaca!'

420   At this he gave a mighty sob and rumbled:

'Now comes the weird upon me, spoken of old.
A wizard, grand and wondrous, lived here—Telemus,
a son of Eurymus; great length of days
he had in wizardry among the Cyclopes,
425   and these things he foretold for time to come:
my great eye lost, and at Odysseus' hands.
Always I had in mind some giant, armed
in giant force, would come against me here.
But this, but you—small, pitiful and twiggy—
430   you put me down with wine, you blinded me.
Come back, Odysseus, and I'll treat you well,
praying the god of earthquake to befriend you—
his son I am, for he by his avowal
fathered me, and, if he will, he may
435   heal me of this black wound—he and no other
of all the happy gods or mortal men.'

Few words I shouted in reply to him:
'If I could take your life I would and take
your time away, and hurl you down to hell!
440   The god of earthquake could not heal you there!'

At this he stretched his hands out in his darkness
toward the sky of stars, and prayed Poseidon:
'O hear me, lord, blue girdler of the islands,
if I am thine indeed, and thou art father:
445   grant that Odysseus, raider of cities, never
see his home: Laertes' son, I mean,

**421 Now comes . . .
of old:** Now I recall the
destiny predicted long
ago.

**421–430 Now comes
. . . you blinded me:**
Polyphemus tells of a
prophecy made long
ago by Telemus, a
prophet who predicted
that Polyphemus would
lose his eye at the hands
of Odysseus.

**432 the god of
earthquake:** Poseidon.

433 avowal: honest
admission.

who kept his hall on Ithaca. Should destiny
intend that he shall see his roof again
among his family in his father land,
450 far be that day, and dark the years between.
Let him lose all companions, and return
under strange sail to bitter days at home.'

In these words he prayed, and the god heard him.
Now he laid hands upon a bigger stone
455 and wheeled around, titanic for the cast,
to let it fly in the black-prowed vessel's track.
But it fell short, just aft the steering oar,
and whelming seas rose giant above the stone
to bear us onward toward the island.

                                        There
460 as we ran in we saw the squadron waiting,
the trim ships drawn up side by side, and all
our troubled friends who waited, looking seaward.
We beached her, grinding keel in the soft sand,
and waded in, ourselves, on the sandy beach.
465 Then we unloaded all the Cyclops' flock
to make division, share and share alike,
only my fighters voted that my ram,
the prize of all, should go to me. I slew him
by the sea side and burnt his long thighbones
470 to Zeus beyond the stormcloud, Cronus' son,
who rules the world. But Zeus disdained my offering;
destruction for my ships he had in store
and death for those who sailed them, my companions.

Now all day long until the sun went down
475 we made our feast on mutton and sweet wine,
till after sunset in the gathering dark
we went to sleep above the wash of ripples.

When the young Dawn with finger tips of rose
touched the world, I roused the men, gave orders
480 to man the ships, cast off the mooring lines;
and filing in to sit beside the rowlocks
oarsmen in line dipped oars in the gray sea.
So we moved out, sad in the vast offing,
having our precious lives, but not our friends."

455 titanic for the cast: drawing on all his enormous strength in preparing to throw.

457 aft: behind.

459 the island: the deserted island where most of Odysseus' men had stayed behind.

470 Cronus' son: Zeus' father, Cronus, was a Titan, one of an earlier race of gods.

483 offing: the part of the deep sea visible from the shore.

BOOK 10:

Circe, the Grace of the Witch

*Odysseus and his men next land on the island of Aeolus, the wind
king, and stay with him a month. To extend his hospitality, Aeolus
gives Odysseus two parting gifts: a fair west wind that will blow the
fleet of ships toward Ithaca, and a great bag holding all the
unfavorable, stormy winds. Within sight of home, and while
Odysseus is sleeping, the men open the bag, thinking it contains gold
and silver. The bad winds thus escape and blow the ships back to
Aeolus' island. The king refuses to help them again, believing now
that their voyage has been cursed by the gods.*

*The discouraged mariners next stop briefly in the land of the
Laestrygones, fierce cannibals who bombard the fleet of ships with
boulders. Only Odysseus, his ship, and its crew of 45 survive the
shower of boulders. The lone ship then sails to Aeaea, home of the
goddess Circe, who is considered by many to be a witch. There,
Odysseus divides his men into two groups. Eurylochus leads one
platoon to explore the island, while Odysseus stays behind on the ship
with the remaining crew.*

"In the wild wood they found an open glade,
around a smooth stone house—the hall of Circe—
and wolves and mountain lions lay there, mild
in her soft spell, fed on her drug of evil.
5 None would attack—oh, it was strange, I tell you—
but switching their long tails they faced our men
like hounds, who look up when their master comes
with tidbits for them—as he will—from table.
Humbly those wolves and lions with mighty paws
10 fawned on our men—who met their yellow eyes
and feared them.

            In the entrance way they stayed
to listen there: inside her quiet house
they heard the goddess Circe.

                   Low she sang
in her beguiling voice, while on her loom
15 she wove ambrosial fabric sheer and bright,
by that craft known to the goddesses of heaven.
No one would speak, until Polites—most
faithful and likable of my officers, said:

10 fawned on: showed affection for.

15 ambrosial: fit for the gods.

17 Polites (pə-lī′tēz).

'Dear friends, no need for stealth: here's a young weaver

20   singing a pretty song to set the air
a-tingle on these lawns and paven courts.
Goddess she is, or lady. Shall we greet her?'

So reassured, they all cried out together,
and she came swiftly to the shining doors

25   to call them in. All but Eurylochus—
who feared a snare—the innocents went after her.
On thrones she seated them, and lounging chairs,
while she prepared a meal of cheese and barley
and amber honey mixed with Pramnian wine,

30   adding her own vile pinch, to make them lose
desire or thought of our dear father land.
Scarce had they drunk when she flew after them
with her long stick and shut them in a pigsty—
bodies, voices, heads, and bristles, all

35   swinish now, though minds were still unchanged.
So, squealing, in they went. And Circe tossed them
acorns, mast, and cornel berries—fodder
for hogs who rut and slumber on the earth.

Down to the ship Eurylochus came running

40   to cry alarm, foul magic doomed his men!
But working with dry lips to speak a word
he could not, being so shaken; blinding tears
welled in his eyes; **foreboding** filled his heart.
When we were frantic questioning him, at last

45   we heard the tale: our friends were gone. . . ."

foreboding
(fôr-bō´dĭng) *n.* a sense
of approaching evil.

*Eurylochus tells Odysseus what has happened and begs him to sail
away from Circe's island. Against this advice, however, Odysseus
rushes to save his men from the enchantress. On the way, he meets
the god Hermes, who gives him a magical plant called moly to protect
him from Circe's power. Still, Hermes warns Odysseus that he must
make the goddess swear she will play no "witches' tricks." Armed with
the moly and Hermes' warning, Odysseus arrives at Circe's palace.*

    *Circe gives Odysseus a magic drink, but it does not affect
him and he threatens to kill her with his sword. Circe turns the pigs
back into men but puts them all into a trance. They stay for one year,
until Odysseus finally begs her to let them go home. She replies that
they must first visit the land of the dead and hear a prophecy from
the ghost of Tiresias.*

BOOK 11:

The Land of the Dead

*Odysseus and his crew set out for the land of the dead. They arrive
and find the place to which Circe has directed them.*

"Then I addressed the blurred and breathless dead,
vowing to slaughter my best heifer for them
before she calved, at home in Ithaca,
and burn the choice bits on the altar fire;
5   as for Tiresias, I swore to sacrifice
a black lamb, handsomest of all our flock.
Thus to **assuage** the nations of the dead
I pledged these rites, then slashed the lamb and ewe,
letting their black blood stream into the wellpit.
10   Now the souls gathered, stirring out of Erebus,
brides and young men, and men grown old in pain,
and tender girls whose hearts were new to grief;
many were there, too, torn by brazen lanceheads,
battle-slain, bearing still their bloody gear.
15   From every side they came and sought the pit
with rustling cries; and I grew sick with fear.
But presently I gave command to my officers
to flay those sheep the bronze cut down, and make
burnt offerings of flesh to the gods below—
20   to sovereign Death, to pale Persephone.
Meanwhile I crouched with my drawn sword to keep
the surging phantoms from the bloody pit
till I should know the presence of Tiresias.

One shade came first—Elpenor, of our company,
25   who lay unburied still on the wide earth
as we had left him—dead in Circe's hall,
untouched, unmourned, when other cares compelled us.
Now when I saw him there I wept for pity
and called out to him:

                  'How is this, Elpenor,
30   how could you journey to the western gloom
swifter afoot than I in the black lugger?'

He sighed, and answered:

                  'Son of great Laertes,
Odysseus, master mariner and soldier,
bad luck shadowed me, and no kindly power;

assuage (ə-swāj´) *v.* to calm or pacify

10 Erebus (ĕr´ə-bəs): a region of the land of the dead, also known as the underworld or Hades. Hades is also the name of the god of the underworld.

18 flay: to strip off the outer skin of.

"Do not abandon me unwept, unburied, to tempt the gods' wrath, while you sail for home."

35   ignoble death I drank with so much wine.
     I slept on Circe's roof, then could not see
     the long steep backward ladder, coming down,
     and fell that height. My neck bone, buckled under,
     snapped, and my spirit found this well of dark.
40   Now hear the grace I pray for, in the name
     of those back in the world, not here—your wife
     and father, he who gave you bread in childhood,
     and your own child, your only son, Telemachus,
     long ago left at home.

                                When you make sail
45   and put these lodgings of dim Death behind,
     you will moor ship, I know, upon Aeaea Island;
     there, O my lord, remember me, I pray,
     do not abandon me unwept, unburied,
     to tempt the gods' wrath, while you sail for home;
50   but fire my corpse, and all the gear I had,
     and build a cairn for me above the breakers—
     an unknown sailor's mark for men to come.
     Heap up the mound there, and implant upon it
     the oar I pulled in life with my companions.'

50–51 fire my corpse . . . cairn: Elpenor wants Odysseus to hold a funeral for him.

55   He ceased, and I replied:

                                   'Unhappy spirit,
   I promise you the barrow and the burial.'

   So we conversed, and grimly, at a distance,
   with my long sword between, guarding the blood,
   while the faint image of the lad spoke on.
60 Now came the soul of Anticlea, dead,
   my mother, daughter of Autolycus,
   dead now, though living still when I took ship
   for holy Troy. Seeing this ghost I grieved,
   but held her off, through pang on pang of tears,
65 till I should know the presence of Tiresias.
   Soon from the dark that prince of Thebes came forward
   bearing a golden staff; and he addressed me:

   'Son of Laertes and the gods of old,
   Odysseus, master of land ways and sea ways,
70 why leave the blazing sun, O man of woe,
   to see the cold dead and the joyless region?
   Stand clear, put up your sword;
   let me but taste of blood, I shall speak true.'

   At this I stepped aside, and in the scabbard
75 let my long sword ring home to the pommel silver,
   as he bent down to the sombre blood. Then spoke
   the prince of those with gift of speech:

                            'Great captain,
   a fair wind and the honey lights of home
   are all you seek. But anguish lies ahead;
80 the god who thunders on the land prepares it,
   not to be shaken from your track, implacable,
   in rancor for the son whose eye you blinded.
   One narrow strait may take you through his blows:
   denial of yourself, restraint of shipmates.
85 When you make landfall on Thrinacia first
   and quit the violet sea, dark on the land
   you'll find the grazing herds of Helios
   by whom all things are seen, all speech is known.
   Avoid those kine, hold fast to your intent,
90 and hard seafaring brings you all to Ithaca.
   But if you raid the beeves, I see destruction
   for ship and crew. Though you survive alone,
   bereft of all companions, lost for years,
   under strange sail shall you come home, to find

**58 with my long sword
... blood:** the ghosts are
attracted to the blood of
the sacrifice; Odysseus
must hold them at bay
with his sword.

66 prince of Thebes:
Tiresias, the blind seer,
comes from the city of
Thebes (thēbz).

89–91 kine; beeves:
two words for cattle.

95 your own house filled with trouble: insolent men
    eating your livestock as they court your lady.
    Aye, you shall make those men atone in blood!
    But after you have dealt out death—in open
    combat or by stealth—to all the suitors,
100 go overland on foot, and take an oar,
    until one day you come where men have lived
    with meat unsalted, never known the sea,
    nor seen seagoing ships, with crimson bows
    and oars that fledge light hulls for dipping flight.
105 The spot will soon be plain to you, and I
    can tell you how: some passerby will say,
    "What winnowing fan is that upon your shoulder?"
    Halt, and implant your smooth oar in the turf
    and make fair sacrifice to Lord Poseidon:
110 a ram, a bull, a great buck boar; turn back,
    and carry out pure hekatombs at home
    to all wide heaven's lords, the undying gods,
    to each in order. Then a seaborne death
    soft as this hand of mist will come upon you
115 when you are wearied out with rich old age,
    your country folk in blessed peace around you.
    And all this shall be just as I foretell.' . . ."

101–102 where men have lived with meat unsalted: refers to an inland location where men do not eat salted (preserved) meat as sailors do aboard a ship.

Odysseus speaks to the shade of his mother. She tells him that Penelope and Telemachus are still grieving for him and that his father, Laertes, has moved to the country, where he, too, mourns his son. Odysseus' mother explains that she died from a broken heart. Odysseus also speaks with the spirits of many great ladies and men who died, as well as those who were being punished for their earthly sins. Filled with horror, Odysseus and his crew set sail.

BOOK 12:

The Sirens; Scylla and Charybdis

*Odysseus and his men return to Circe's island. While the men sleep,
Circe takes Odysseus aside to hear about the underworld and to offer
advice.*

"Then said the Lady Circe:
'So: all those trials are over.

                     Listen with care
to this, now, and a god will arm your mind.
Square in your ship's path are Sirens, crying
5 beauty to bewitch men coasting by;
woe to the innocent who hears that sound!
He will not see his lady nor his children
in joy, crowding about him, home from sea;
the Sirens will sing his mind away
10 on their sweet meadow lolling. There are bones
of dead men rotting in a pile beside them
and flayed skins shrivel around the spot.

                        Steer wide;
keep well to seaward; plug your oarsmen's ears
with beeswax kneaded soft; none of the rest
15 should hear that song.

                    But if you wish to listen,
let the men tie you in the lugger, hand
and foot, back to the mast, lashed to the mast,
so you may hear those harpies' thrilling voices;
shout as you will, begging to be untied,
20 your crew must only twist more line around you
and keep their stroke up, till the singers fade.
What then? One of two courses you may take,
and you yourself must weigh them. I shall not
plan the whole action for you now, but only
25 tell you of both.

                  Ahead are beetling rocks
and dark blue glancing Amphitrite, surging,
roars around them. Prowling Rocks, or Drifters,
the gods in bliss have named them—named them well.
Not even birds can pass them by. . . .

30   A second course
lies between headlands. One is a sharp mountain
piercing the sky, with stormcloud round the peak
dissolving never, not in the brightest summer,

2–3 In Circe, Odysseus has found a valuable ally. In the next hundred lines, she describes in detail each danger that he and his men will meet on their way home.

14 kneaded (nē´dĭd): squeezed and pressed.

18 those harpies' thrilling voices: the delightful voices of those horrible female creatures.

25 beetling: jutting or overhanging.

26 glancing Amphitrite (ăm´fĭ-trī´tē): sparkling seawater. (Amphitrite is the goddess of the sea and the wife of Poseidon. Here, Circe uses the name to refer to the sea itself.)

31 headlands: points of land jutting out into the sea; promontories.

to show heaven's azure there, nor in the fall.

35 No mortal man could scale it, nor so much
as land there, not with twenty hands and feet,
so sheer the cliffs are—as of polished stone.
Midway that height, a cavern full of mist
opens toward Erebus and evening. Skirting

40 this in the lugger, great Odysseus,
your master bowman, shooting from the deck,
would come short of the cavemouth with his shaft;
but that is the den of Scylla, where she yaps
abominably, a newborn whelp's cry,

45 though she is huge and monstrous. God or man,
no one could look on her in joy. Her legs—
and there are twelve—are like great tentacles,
unjointed, and upon her serpent necks
are borne six heads like nightmares of ferocity,

50 with triple serried rows of fangs and deep
gullets of black death. Half her length, she sways
her heads in air, outside her horrid cleft,
hunting the sea around that promontory
for dolphins, dogfish, or what bigger game

55 thundering Amphitrite feeds in thousands.
And no ship's company can claim
to have passed her without loss and grief; she takes,
from every ship, one man for every gullet.

The opposite point seems more a tongue of land

60 you'd touch with a good bowshot, at the narrows.
A great wild fig, a shaggy mass of leaves,
grows on it, and Charybdis lurks below
to swallow down the dark sea tide. Three times
from dawn to dusk she spews it up

65 and sucks it down again three times, a whirling
maelstrom; if you come upon her then
the god who makes earth tremble could not save you.
No, hug the cliff of Scylla, take your ship
through on a racing stroke. Better to mourn

70 six men than lose them all, and the ship, too.'

So her advice ran; but I faced her, saying:

'Only instruct me, goddess, if you will,
how, if possible, can I pass Charybdis,
or fight off Scylla when she raids my crew?'

75 Swiftly that loveliest goddess answered me:

34 heaven's azure
(ăzh´ər): the blue sky.

abominably
(ə-bŏm´ə-nə-blē) *adv.* in a
hateful way; horribly.

66 maelstrom
(māl´strəm): a large,
violent whirlpool.

'Must you have battle in your heart forever?
The bloody toil of combat? Old contender,
will you not yield to the immortal gods?
That nightmare cannot die, being eternal
80 evil itself—horror, and pain, and chaos;
there is no fighting her, no power can fight her,
all that avails is flight.

82 all . . . flight: all you can do is flee.

Lose headway there

along that rockface while you break out arms,
and she'll swoop over you, I fear, once more,
85 taking one man again for every gullet.
No, no, put all your backs into it, row on;
invoke Blind Force, that bore this scourge of men,
to keep her from a second strike against you.

87 invoke . . . men: pray to the goddess Blind Force, who gave birth to Scylla.

Then you will coast Thrinacia, the island
90 where Helios' cattle graze, fine herds, and flocks
of goodly sheep. The herds and flocks are seven,
with fifty beasts in each.

89 coast: sail along the coast of.

No lambs are dropped,

or calves, and these fat cattle never die.
Immortal, too, their cowherds are—their shepherds—
95 Phaethusa and Lampetia, sweetly braided
nymphs that divine Neaera bore
to the overlord of high noon, Helios.
These nymphs their gentle mother bred and placed
upon Thrinacia, the distant land,
100 in care of flocks and cattle for their father.

95–96 Phaethusa (fā´ə-thōō´sə); **Lampetia** (lăm-pē´shə); **Neaera** (nē-ē´rə).

Now give those kine a wide berth, keep your thoughts
intent upon your course for home,
and hard seafaring brings you all to Ithaca.
But if you raid the beeves, I see destruction
105 for ship and crew.

101–105 Circe warns Odysseus not to steal Helios' fine cattle because Helios will take revenge.

Rough years then lie between

you and your homecoming, alone and old,
the one survivor, all companions lost.' . . ."

*At dawn, Odysseus and his men continue their journey. Odysseus
decides to tell the men only of Circe's warnings about the Sirens,
whom they will soon encounter. He is fairly sure that they can survive
this peril if he keeps their spirits up. Suddenly, the wind stops.*

"The crew were on their feet
briskly, to furl the sail, and stow it; then,

110 each in place, they poised the smooth oar blades
and sent the white foam scudding by. I carved
a massive cake of beeswax into bits
and rolled them in my hands until they softened—
no long task, for a burning heat came down
115 from Helios, lord of high noon. Going forward
I carried wax along the line, and laid it
thick on their ears. They tied me up, then, plumb
amidships, back to the mast, lashed to the mast,
and took themselves again to rowing. Soon,
120 as we came smartly within hailing distance,
the two Sirens, noting our fast ship
off their point, made ready, and they sang. . . .

The lovely voices in ardor appealing over the water
made me crave to listen, and I tried to say
125 'Untie me!' to the crew, jerking my brows;
but they bent steady to the oars. Then Perimedes
got to his feet, he and Eurylochus,
and passed more line about, to hold me still.
So all rowed on, until the Sirens
130 dropped under the sea rim, and their singing
dwindled away.

                       My faithful company

rested on their oars now, peeling off
the wax that I had laid thick on their ears;
then set me free.

                    But scarcely had that island
135 faded in blue air than I saw smoke
and white water, with sound of waves in tumult—
a sound the men heard, and it terrified them.
Oars flew from their hands; the blades went knocking
wild alongside till the ship lost way,
140 with no oarblades to drive her through the water.
Well, I walked up and down from bow to stern,
trying to put heart into them, standing over
every oarsman, saying gently,

                              'Friends,

have we never been in danger before this?
145 More fearsome, is it now, than when the Cyclops
penned us in his cave? What power he had!
Did I not keep my nerve, and use my wits
to find a way out for us?

**117–118 plumb
amidships:** exactly in
the center of the ship.

126 Perimedes
(pĕr´ĭ-mē´dēz).

134–139 The men
panic when they hear
the thundering surf.

                                                                    Now I say
    by hook or crook this peril too shall be
150 something that we remember.
                                                    Heads up, lads!
    We must obey the orders as I give them.
    Get the oarshafts in your hands, and lay back
    hard on your benches; hit these breaking seas.
    Zeus help us pull away before we founder.   **154 founder:** sink.
155 You at the tiller, listen, and take in
    all that I say—the rudders are your duty;
    keep her out of the combers and the smoke;   **157 combers:** breaking
    steer for that headland; watch the drift, or we   waves.
    fetch up in the smother, and you drown us.'   **158–159 watch . . .
                                                                    smother:** keep the ship
                                                                    on course, or it will be
160 That was all, and it brought them round to action.   crushed in the rough
    But as I sent them on toward Scylla, I   water.
    told them nothing, as they could do nothing.
    They would have dropped their oars again, in panic,
    to roll for cover under the decking. Circe's
165 bidding against arms had slipped my mind,
    so I tied on my cuirass and took up
    two heavy spears, then made my way along
    to the foredeck—thinking to see her first from there,
    the monster of the gray rock, harboring
170 torment for my friends. I strained my eyes
    upon that cliffside veiled in cloud, but nowhere
    could I catch sight of her.
                                            And all this time,
    in **travail**, sobbing, gaining on the current,   **travail** (trə-vāl´) *n.*
    we rowed into the strait—Scylla to port   painful effort.
175 and on our starboard beam Charybdis, dire
    gorge of the salt sea tide. By heaven! when she   **176 gorge:** throat;
    vomited, all the sea was like a cauldron   gullet.
    seething over intense fire, when the mixture
    suddenly heaves and rises.
                                            The shot spume   **179 shot spume:** flying
180 soared to the landside heights, and fell like rain.   foam.

    But when she swallowed the sea water down
    we saw the funnel of the maelstrom, heard
    the rock bellowing all around, and dark
    sand raged on the bottom far below.
185 My men all blanched against the gloom, our eyes   **185 blanched:** became
    were fixed upon that yawning mouth in fear   pale.
    of being devoured.

Then Scylla made her strike,
whisking six of my best men from the ship.
I happened to glance aft at ship and oarsmen

190 and caught sight of their arms and legs, dangling
high overhead. Voices came down to me
in anguish, calling my name for the last time.

A man surfcasting on a point of rock
for bass or mackerel, whipping his long rod

195 to drop the sinker and the bait far out,
will hook a fish and rip it from the surface
to dangle wriggling through the air:

so these

were borne aloft in spasms toward the cliff.

She ate them as they shrieked there, in her den,

200 in the dire grapple, reaching still for me—
and deathly pity ran me through
at that sight—far the worst I ever suffered,
questing the passes of the strange sea.

We rowed on.

The Rocks were now behind; Charybdis, too,

205 and Scylla dropped astern. . . ."

189 aft: toward the rear of the ship.

198 borne aloft in spasms: lifted high while struggling violently.

200 grapple: grasp.

Odysseus tries to persuade his men to bypass Thrinacia, the island of the sun god, Helios, but they insist on landing. Driven by hunger, they ignore Odysseus' warning not to feast on Helios' cattle. This disobedience angers the sun god, who threatens to stop shining if payment is not made for the loss of his cattle. To appease Helios, Zeus sends down a thunderbolt to sink Odysseus' ship. Odysseus alone survives. He eventually drifts to Ogygia, the home of Calypso, who keeps him on her island for seven years. With this episode, Odysseus ends the telling of his tale to King Alcinous.

COLLABORATIVE DISCUSSION In what instances does Odysseus demonstrate his greatest acts of heroism? Discuss your ideas with a partner. Cite specific textual evidence to support your ideas.

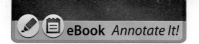
Analyze Character: Epic Hero

Odysseus is an **epic hero**—a larger-than-life character who embodies the ideals of a nation or race. Epic heroes take part in long, dangerous adventures and accomplish great deeds. They are considered **archetypes** because they can be found in many works from different cultures throughout the ages.

Although epic heroes may have superhuman abilities, they still have human flaws. These flaws make them more complex and appealing. For example, Odysseus demonstrates extraordinary strength and courage, but his overconfidence results in a tendency to dismiss warnings. His imperfections help make him more likable than a perfect character, and the audience can relate to his mistakes. These questions can help you analyze how the complex character of Odysseus develops over the course of the epic:

- What do you learn about Odysseus' character through how he faces various conflicts?
- What traits, or qualities, does Odysseus show through his interactions with other characters?
- What do Odysseus' character traits tell you about what the ancient Greeks found admirable?

Analyzing the Text

Cite Text Evidence   Support your responses with evidence from the selection.

1. **Infer** What do you learn about the character of Odysseus through the poet's introduction in Book 1 (lines 1–17)?

2. **Summarize** How does Odysseus regard the Cyclopes, based on the description in lines 56–67 of Book 9? What does this description reveal about Odysseus' values as well as the values of the ancient Greeks?

3. **Interpret** As Odysseus recalls his men's pleas to flee the Cyclops' cave, he remarks, "Ah, / how sound that was! Yet I refused. I wished / to see the caveman, what he had to offer." What qualities of an epic hero does Odysseus reveal in this comment?

4. **Analyze** What strengths does Odysseus demonstrate in his encounter with the Cyclops? Explain.

5. **Summarize** Why does Odysseus continue to taunt the Cyclops as he pulls away from the shore? What traits does he demonstrate through this behavior, and what are the consequences?

6. **Analyze** A **foil** is a character who contrasts with another character. How does the character of Eurylochus serve as a foil to Odysseus in Book 10?

7. **Infer** What does the audience learn about Odysseus from his encounters with his shipmate Elpenor and his mother Anticlea in Book 11?

Critical Vocabulary

harried	ponderous	profusion	adversary
foreboding	assuage	abominably	travail

Practice and Apply   Use the Critical Vocabulary words to answer the questions. Then, with a partner, take turns providing evidence to support your answers.

1. Which word is an antonym, or a word with the opposite meaning, of *friend*?

2. Which word most closely relates to *prediction*?

3. Which word is an antonym of *calm*?

4. Which word most closely relates to *atrociously*?

5. Which word is an antonym of *shortage*?

6. Which word most closely relates to *soothe*?

7. Which word most closely relates to *struggle*?

8. Which word most closely relates to *awkward*?

Vocabulary Strategy: Prefixes

Recognizing **prefixes** can help you understand the meanings of unfamiliar words. For example, in the Critical Vocabulary word *foreboding*, the prefix *fore-*, meaning "beforehand," combines with the verb *bode*, meaning "to give signs of something." This can help you understand the definition "a sense of impending doom." Here are some more examples.

Prefixes	Meanings	Examples
ad-, as-	to, toward, before	adversary, assuage
pro-	in place of, in favor of, forward	profusion, proceed
ab-	away from	abominably, abject
sub-	below, almost, close after	subsequent, subordinate
ob-	before, toward, inversely	objective, obligate

Practice and Apply   Consult a dictionary to determine the meaning of each example word in the chart. Then, discuss with a partner how each word's prefix relates to its meaning. Finally, identify another example word for each prefix, and use the word in a sentence.

PART TWO: THE HOMECOMING

AS YOU READ Pay attention to how the events in the epic build toward a resolution. Write down any questions you generate during reading.

BOOK 17:

The Beggar at the Manor

In Books 13–15, King Alcinous and his friends send Odysseus on his way home. Odysseus sleeps while the rowers bring him to Ithaca. When he awakens, he fails to recognize his homeland until Athena appears and tells him that he is indeed home. She disguises him as an old man, so that he can surprise the suitors, and then urges him to visit his faithful swineherd, Eumaeus. Athena goes to Telemachus and tells him to return home. She warns him of the suitors' plot to kill him and advises him to stay with the swineherd for a night. Telemachus does as she bids.

    In Book 16, Odysseus reveals his identity to Telemachus, and a tearful reunion ensues. Telemachus lets Odysseus know that they face more than 100 suitors. Odysseus tells Telemachus to return home. He will follow, and Telemachus must pretend not to know him. He must also lock away Odysseus' weapons and armor. Telemachus returns home, and Odysseus and the swineherd soon follow. Odysseus is still diguised as a beggar.

                       While he spoke
an old hound, lying near, pricked up his ears
and lifted up his muzzle. This was Argos,
trained as a puppy by Odysseus,
5 but never taken on a hunt before
his master sailed for Troy. The young men, afterward,
hunted wild goats with him, and hare, and deer,
but he had grown old in his master's absence.
Treated as rubbish now, he lay at last
10 upon a mass of dung before the gates—
manure of mules and cows, piled there until
fieldhands could spread it on the king's estate.
Abandoned there, and half destroyed with flies,
old Argos lay.

But when he knew he heard
15 Odysseus' voice nearby, he did his best
to wag his tail, nose down, with flattened ears,
having no strength to move nearer his master.
And the man looked away,
wiping a salt tear from his cheek; but he
20 hid this from Eumaeus. Then he said:

"I marvel that they leave this hound to lie
here on the dung pile;
he would have been a fine dog, from the look of him,
though I can't say as to his power and speed
25 when he was young. You find the same good build
in house dogs, table dogs landowners keep
all for style."

And you replied, Eumaeus:

"A hunter owned him—but the man is dead
in some far place. If this old hound could show
30 the form he had when Lord Odysseus left him,
going to Troy, you'd see him swift and strong.
He never shrank from any savage thing
he'd brought to bay in the deep woods; on the scent
no other dog kept up with him. Now misery
35 has him in leash. His owner died abroad,
and here the women slaves will take no care of him.
You know how servants are: without a master
they have no will to labor, or excel.
For Zeus who views the wide world takes away
40 half the manhood of a man, that day
he goes into captivity and slavery."

Eumaeus crossed the court and went straight forward
into the mégaron among the suitors;
but death and darkness in that instant closed
45 the eyes of Argos, who had seen his master,
Odysseus, after twenty years. . . .

43 mégaron: the main hall of a palace or house

*Odysseus enters his home as a beggar, and the suitors mock and
abuse him. Penelope asks to speak with the beggar, but Odysseus puts
her off until nightfall.*

BOOK 21:

The Test of the Bow

*In Books 18–20, Odysseus observes the suitors and finds that two in
particular, Antinous and Eurymachus, are rude and demanding.
Penelope asks Odysseus the beggar for news of her husband. He says
he has heard that Odysseus is on his way home. Penelope, however,
has given up hope for Odysseus' return. She proposes an archery
contest to the suitors, with marriage to her as the prize. She enters
the storeroom and takes down the heavy bow that Odysseus left
behind.*

Now the queen reached the storeroom door and halted.
Here was an oaken sill, cut long ago
and sanded clean and bedded true. Foursquare
the doorjambs and the shining doors were set
5 by the careful builder. Penelope untied the strap
around the curving handle, pushed her hook
into the slit, aimed at the bolts inside
and shot them back. Then came a rasping sound
as those bright doors the key had sprung gave way—
10 a bellow like a bull's vaunt in a meadow—
followed by her light footfall entering
over the plank floor. Herb-scented robes
lay there in chests, but the lady's milkwhite arms
went up to lift the bow down from a peg
15 in its own polished bowcase.

                    Now Penelope

sank down, holding the weapon on her knees,
and drew her husband's great bow out, and sobbed
and bit her lip and let the salt tears flow.
Then back she went to face the crowded hall,
20 tremendous bow in hand, and on her shoulder hung
the quiver spiked with coughing death. Behind her
maids bore a basket full of axeheads, bronze
and iron implements for the master's game.
Thus in her beauty she approached the suitors,
25 and near a pillar of the solid roof
she paused, her shining veil across her cheeks,
her maids on either hand and still,
then spoke to the banqueters:

15–18 Notice that
Penelope still grieves for
Odysseus, even after 20
years.

21 quiver (kwĭv´ər): a
case in which arrows are
carried.

**22–23 axeheads . . .
game:** metal heads of
axes (without handles)
that Odysseus employs
in a display of archery
skill.

"My lords, hear me:
suitors indeed, you **commandeered** this house
30   to feast and drink in, day and night, my husband
being long gone, long out of mind. You found
no justification for yourselves—none
except your lust to marry me. Stand up, then:
we now declare a contest for that prize.
35   Here is my lord Odysseus' hunting bow.
Bend and string it if you can. Who sends an arrow
through iron axe-helve sockets, twelve in line?
I join my life with his, and leave this place, my home,
my rich and beautiful bridal house, forever
40   to be remembered, though I dream it only.". . .

Despite heating and greasing the bow, the lesser suitors prove unable
to string it. The most able suitors, Antinous and Eurymachus, hold
off. While the suitors are busy with the bow, Odysseus—still disguised
as an old beggar—goes to enlist the aid of two of his trusted servants,
Eumaeus, the swineherd, and Philoetius, the cowherd.

Two men had meanwhile left the hall:
swineherd and cowherd, in companionship,
one downcast as the other. But Odysseus
followed them outdoors, outside the court,
45   and coming up said gently:

                              "You, herdsman,
and you, too, swineherd, I could say a thing to you,
or should I keep it dark?

                              No, no; speak,
my heart tells me. Would you be men enough
to stand by Odysseus if he came back?
50   Suppose he dropped out of a clear sky, as I did?
Suppose some god should bring him?
Would you bear arms for him, or for the suitors?"

The cowherd said:

                              "Ah, let the master come!
Father Zeus, grant our old wish! Some courier
55   guide him back! Then judge what stuff is in me
and how I manage arms!"

                              Likewise Eumaeus
fell to praying all heaven for his return,
so that Odysseus, sure at least of these,
told them:

commandeer
(kŏm´ən-dîr´) v. to take
control of by force.

35–37 Note that the
contest has two parts:
first the suitor must
bend the heavy bow
and string it—a task
that requires immense
strength and skill—and
then he must shoot an
arrow straight through
the holes in 12 axe
heads set up in a row.

"I am at home, for I am he.

60 I bore **adversities**, but in the twentieth year
I am ashore in my own land. I find
the two of you, alone among my people,
longed for my coming. Prayers I never heard
except your own that I might come again.

65 So now what is in store for you I'll tell you:
If Zeus brings down the suitors by my hand
I promise marriages to both, and cattle,
and houses built near mine. And you shall be
brothers-in-arms of my Telemachus.

70 Here, let me show you something else, a sign
that I am he, that you can trust me, look:
this old scar from the tusk wound that I got
boar hunting on Parnassus. . . ."

Shifting his rags

75 he bared the long gash. Both men looked, and knew,
and threw their arms around the old soldier, weeping,
kissing his head and shoulders. He as well
took each man's head and hands to kiss, then said—
to cut it short, else they might weep till dark—

80 "Break off, no more of this.
Anyone at the door could see and tell them.
Drift back in, but separately at intervals
after me.

Now listen to your orders:
when the time comes, those gentlemen, to a man,
85 will be dead against giving me bow or quiver.
Defy them. Eumaeus, bring the bow
and put it in my hands there at the door.
Tell the women to lock their own door tight.
Tell them if someone hears the shock of arms
90 or groans of men, in hall or court, not one
must show her face, but keep still at her weaving.
Philoetius, run to the outer gate and lock it.
Throw the cross bar and lash it.". . .

*Odysseus the beggar asks the suitors if he might try the bow. Worried
that the old man may show them up, they refuse, but Penelope urges
them to let Odysseus try. At Telemachus' request, Penelope leaves the
men to settle the question of the bow among themselves. Two trusted
servants lock the doors of the room, and Telemachus orders the bow
be given to Odysseus.*

adversity
(ăd-vûr´sĭ-tē) *n.* hardship;
misfortune.

73 Parnassus
(pär-năs´əs): a mountain
in central Greece.

And Odysseus took his time,
95 turning the bow, tapping it, every inch,
for borings that termites might have made
while the master of the weapon was abroad.
The suitors were now watching him, and some
jested among themselves:

"A bow lover!"

100 "Dealer in old bows!"

"Maybe he has one like it
at home!"

"Or has an itch to make one for himself."

"See how he handles it, the sly old buzzard!"

And one disdainful suitor added this:

"May his fortune grow an inch for every inch he bends it!"
105 But the man skilled in all ways of contending,
satisfied by the great bow's look and heft,
like a musician, like a harper, when
with quiet hand upon his instrument
he draws between his thumb and forefinger
110 a sweet new string upon a peg: so effortlessly
Odysseus in one motion strung the bow.
Then slid his right hand down the cord and plucked it,
so the taut gut vibrating hummed and sang
a swallow's note.
               In the hushed hall it smote the suitors
115 and all their faces changed. Then Zeus thundered
overhead, one loud crack for a sign.
And Odysseus laughed within him that the son
of crooked-minded Cronus had flung that omen down.
He picked one ready arrow from his table
120 where it lay bare: the rest were waiting still
in the quiver for the young men's turn to come.
He nocked it, let it rest across the handgrip,
and drew the string and grooved butt of the arrow,
aiming from where he sat upon the stool.
                       Now flashed
125 arrow from twanging bow clean as a whistle
through every socket ring, and grazed not one,
to thud with heavy brazen head beyond.
                    Then quietly

Odysseus said:

               "Telemachus, the stranger
you welcomed in your hall has not disgraced you.
130 I did not miss, neither did I take all day
stringing the bow. My hand and eye are sound,
not so **contemptible** as the young men say.
The hour has come to cook their lordships' mutton—
supper by daylight. Other amusements later,
135 with song and harping that adorn a feast."

He dropped his eyes and nodded, and the prince
Telemachus, true son of King Odysseus,
belted his sword on, clapped hand to his spear,
and with a clink and glitter of keen bronze
140 stood by his chair, in the forefront near his father.

106 heft: weight.

114 smote: struck; affected sharply.

115–116 The thunder, a sign from Zeus, indicates that the gods are on Odysseus' side.

118 Cronus (krō´nəs): Zeus' father.

122 nocked it: placed the arrow's feathered end against the bowstring.

127 brazen: made of brass.

contemptible (kən-tĕmp´tə-bəl) *adj.* deserving of scorn; despicable.

BOOK 22:

Death in the Great Hall

Now shrugging off his rags the wiliest fighter of the islands
leapt and stood on the broad door sill, his own bow in his hand.
He poured out at his feet a rain of arrows from the quiver
and spoke to the crowd:

"So much for that. Your clean-cut game is over.
5 Now watch me hit a target that no man has hit before,
if I can make this shot. Help me, Apollo."

He drew to his fist the cruel head of an arrow for Antinous
just as the young man leaned to lift his beautiful drinking cup,
embossed, two-handled, golden: the cup was in his fingers:
10 the wine was even at his lips: and did he dream of death?
How could he? In that **revelry** amid his throng of friends
who would imagine a single foe—though a strong foe indeed—
could dare to bring death's pain on him and darkness on his
      eyes?
Odysseus' arrow hit him under the chin
15 and punched up to the feathers through his throat.

Backward and down he went, letting the winecup fall
from his shocked hand. Like pipes his nostrils jetted
crimson runnels, a river of mortal red,
and one last kick upset his table
20 knocking the bread and meat to soak in dusty blood.

Now as they craned to see their champion where he lay
the suitors jostled in uproar down the hall,
everyone on his feet. Wildly they turned and scanned
the walls in the long room for arms; but not a shield,
25 not a good ashen spear was there for a man to take and throw.
All they could do was yell in outrage at Odysseus:

"Foul! to shoot at a man! That was your last shot!"

"Your own throat will be slit for this!"

"Our finest lad is down!

You killed the best on Ithaca."

"Buzzards will tear your eyes out!"

30 For they imagined as they wished—that it was a wild shot,
    an unintended killing—fools, not to comprehend
    they were already in the grip of death.
    But glaring under his brows Odysseus answered:

    "You yellow dogs, you thought I'd never make it
35 home from the land of Troy. You took my house to plunder,
    twisted my maids to serve your beds. You dared
    bid for my wife while I was still alive.
    Contempt was all you had for the gods who rule wide heaven,
    contempt for what men say of you hereafter.
40 Your last hour has come. You die in blood."

    As they all took this in, sickly green fear
    pulled at their entrails, and their eyes flickered   **42 entrails:** internal
    looking for some hatch or hideaway from death.   organs.
    Eurymachus alone could speak. He said:

45 "If you are Odysseus of Ithaca come back,
    all that you say these men have done is true.
    Rash actions, many here, more in the countryside.   **47 rash:** foolish;
    But here he lies, the man who caused them all.   thoughtless.
    Antinous was the ringleader; he whipped us on
50 to do these things. He cared less for a marriage
    than for the power Cronion has denied him   **51 Cronion**
    as king of Ithaca. For that   (krō′nē-ŏn′): Zeus, the
    he tried to trap your son and would have killed him.   son of Cronus.
    He is dead now and has his portion. Spare
55 your own people. As for ourselves, we'll make   **restitution**
    restitution of wine and meat consumed,   (rĕs′tĭ-tōō′shən) n. a
    and add, each one, a tithe of twenty oxen   making good for loss or
    with gifts of bronze and gold to warm your heart.   damage; repayment.
    Meanwhile we cannot blame you for your anger."
                                                                57 tithe: payment.

60 Odysseus glowered under his black brows
    and said:
                    "Not for the whole treasure of your fathers,
    all you enjoy, lands, flocks, or any gold
    put up by others, would I hold my hand.
    There will be killing till the score is paid.
65 You forced yourselves upon this house. Fight your way out,
    or run for it, if you think you'll escape death.
    I doubt one man of you skins by."   **67 skins by:** sneaks
                                                                away.

    They felt their knees fail, and their hearts—but heard
    Eurymachus for the last time rallying them.

70   "Friends," he said, "the man is **implacable**.
     Now that he's got his hands on bow and quiver
     he'll shoot from the big door stone there
     until he kills us to the last man.

                                                    Fight, I say,

     let's remember the joy of it. Swords out!
75   Hold up your tables to deflect his arrows.
     After me, everyone: rush him where he stands.
     If we can budge him from the door, if we can pass
     into the town, we'll call out men to chase him.
     This fellow with his bow will shoot no more."

80   He drew his own sword as he spoke, a broadsword of fine
             bronze,
     honed like a razor on either edge. Then crying hoarse and loud
     he hurled himself at Odysseus. But the kingly man let fly
     an arrow at that instant, and the quivering feathered butt
     sprang to the nipple of his breast as the barb stuck in his liver.
85   The bright broadsword clanged down. He lurched and fell
             aside,
     pitching across his table. His cup, his bread and meat,
     were spilt and scattered far and wide, and his head slammed
             on the ground.
     Revulsion, anguish in his heart, with both feet kicking out,
     he downed his chair, while the shrouding wave of mist closed
             on his eyes.

90   Amphinomus now came running at Odysseus,
     broadsword naked in his hand. He thought to make
     the great soldier give way at the door.
     But with a spear throw from behind Telemachus hit him
     between the shoulders, and the lancehead drove
95   clear through his chest. He left his feet and fell
     forward, thudding, forehead against the ground.

     Telemachus swerved around him, leaving the long dark spear
     planted in Amphinomus. If he paused to yank it out
     someone might jump him from behind or cut him down with
             a sword
100 at the moment he bent over. So he ran—ran from the tables
     to his father's side and halted, panting, saying:

     "Father let me bring you a shield and spear,
     a pair of spears, a helmet.
     I can arm on the run myself; I'll give
105 outfits to Eumaeus and this cowherd.
     Better to have equipment."

"Run then, while I hold them off with arrows as long as the arrows last."

Said Odysseus:

"Run then, while I hold them off with arrows
as long as the arrows last. When all are gone
if I'm alone they can dislodge me."

                                 Quick

110 upon his father's word Telemachus
ran to the room where spears and armor lay.
He caught up four light shields, four pairs of spears,
four helms of war high-plumed with flowing manes,
and ran back, loaded down, to his father's side.

115 He was the first to pull a helmet on
and slide his bare arm in a buckler strap.
The servants armed themselves, and all three took their stand
beside the master of battle.

                            While he had arrows
he aimed and shot, and every shot brought down

120 one of his huddling enemies.
But when all barbs had flown from the bowman's fist,
he leaned his bow in the bright entry way
beside the door, and armed: a four-ply shield
hard on his shoulder, and a crested helm,

125 horsetailed, nodding stormy upon his head,
then took his tough and bronze-shod spears. . . .

113 helms: helmets.

The suitors make various unsuccessful attempts to expel Odysseus from his post at the door. Athena urges Odysseus on to battle, yet holds back her fullest aid, waiting for Odysseus and Telemachus to prove themselves. Six of the suitors attempt an attack on Odysseus, but Athena deflects their arrows. Odysseus and his men seize this opportunity to launch their own attack, and the suitors begin to fall. At last Athena's presence becomes known to all, as the shape of her shield becomes visible above the hall. The suitors, recognizing the intervention of the gods on Odysseus' behalf, are frantic to escape but to no avail. Odysseus and his men are compared to falcons who show no mercy to the flocks of birds they pursue and capture. Soon the room is reeking with blood. Thus the battle with the suitors comes to an end, and Odysseus prepares himself to meet Penelope.

BOOK 23:

The Trunk of the Olive Tree

Greathearted Odysseus, home at last,
was being bathed now by Eurynome
and rubbed with golden oil, and clothed again
in a fresh tunic and a cloak. Athena
5   lent him beauty, head to foot. She made him
taller, and massive, too, with crisping hair
in curls like petals of wild hyacinth
but all red-golden. Think of gold infused
on silver by a craftsman, whose fine art
10 Hephaestus taught him, or Athena: one
whose work moves to delight: just so she lavished
beauty over Odysseus' head and shoulders.
He sat then in the same chair by the pillar,
facing his silent wife, and said:

                        "Strange woman,
15 the immortals of Olympus made you hard,
harder than any. Who else in the world
would keep aloof as you do from her husband
if he returned to her from years of trouble,
cast on his own land in the twentieth year?

20 Nurse, make up a bed for me to sleep on.
Her heart is iron in her breast."

                        Penelope
spoke to Odysseus now. She said:

                        "Strange man,
if man you are . . . This is no pride on my part
nor scorn for you—not even wonder, merely.
25 I know so well how you—how he—appeared
boarding the ship for Troy. But all the same . . .
Make up his bed for him, Eurycleia.
Place it outside the bedchamber my lord
built with his own hands. Pile the big bed
30 with fleeces, rugs, and sheets of purest linen."

With this she tried him to the breaking point,
and he turned on her in a flash raging:

"Woman, by heaven you've stung me now!
Who dared to move my bed?

2 Eurynome
(yŏo-rĭn´ə-mē): a female
servant.

10 Hephaestus
(hĭ-fĕs´təs): the god of
metalworking.

11 lavished: showered.

**15 immortals of
Olympus:** the gods, who
live on Mount Olympus.

27–30 The bed, built
from the trunk of an
olive tree still rooted in
the ground, is actually
unmovable.

35 No builder had the skill for that—unless
   a god came down to turn the trick. No mortal
   in his best days could budge it with a crowbar.
   There is our pact and pledge, our secret sign,
   built into that bed—my handiwork
40 and no one else's!

                            An old trunk of olive
   grew like a pillar on the building plot,
   and I laid out our bedroom round that tree,
   lined up the stone walls, built the walls and roof,
   gave it a doorway and smooth-fitting doors.
45 Then I lopped off the silvery leaves and branches,
   hewed and shaped that stump from the roots up
   into a bedpost, drilled it, let it serve
   as model for the rest. I planed them all,
   inlaid them all with silver, gold and ivory,
50 and stretched a bed between—a pliant web
   of oxhide thongs dyed crimson.
                                There's our sign!
   I know no more. Could someone else's hand
   have sawn that trunk and dragged the frame away?"

   Their secret! as she heard it told, her knees
55 grew **tremulous** and weak, her heart failed her.
   With eyes brimming tears she ran to him,
   throwing her arms around his neck, and kissed him,
   murmuring:

                     "Do not rage at me, Odysseus!
   No one ever matched your caution! Think
60 what difficulty the gods gave: they denied us
   life together in our prime and flowering years,
   kept us from crossing into age together.
   Forgive me, don't be angry. I could not
   welcome you with love on sight! I armed myself
65 long ago against the frauds of men,
   impostors who might come—and all those many
   whose underhanded ways bring evil on!
   Helen of Argos, daughter of Zeus and Leda,
   would she have joined the stranger, lain with him,
70 if she had known her destiny? known the Achaeans
   in arms would bring her back to her own country?
   Surely a goddess moved her to adultery,
   her blood unchilled by war and evil coming,
   the years, the **desolation**; ours, too.

50–51 a pliant web ...
crimson: a network of
ox-hide straps, dyed red,
stretched between the
sides of the bed to form
a springy base for the
bedding.

tremulous
(trĕm´yə-ləs) *adj.* marked
by trembling or shaking.

68 Argos (är´gŏs); Leda
(lē´də).

desolation
(dĕs´ə-lā´shən) *n.* lonely
grief; misery.

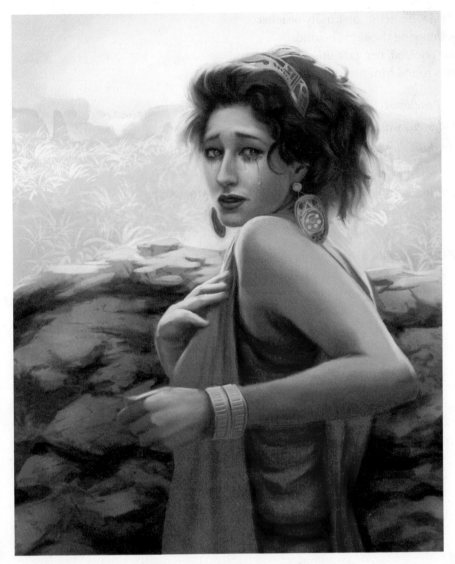

75 But here and now, what sign could be so clear
as this of our own bed?
No other man has ever laid eyes on it—
only my own slave, Actoris, that my father   **78 Actoris** (ăk-tôrˊĭs).
sent with me as a gift—she kept our door.
80 You make my stiff heart know that I am yours."

Now from his breast into his eyes the ache
of longing mounted, and he wept at last,
his dear wife, clear and faithful, in his arms,
longed for
              as the sunwarmed earth is longed for by a swimmer
85 spent in rough water where his ship went down
under Poseidon's blows, gale winds and tons of sea.
Few men can keep alive through a big surf

to crawl, clotted with brine, on kindly beaches
in joy, in joy, knowing the abyss behind:
90 and so she too rejoiced, her gaze upon her husband,
her white arms round him pressed as though forever. . . .

*Odysseus and Penelope tell each other about all that happened to
them while Odysseus was away. Then Odysseus visits his father,
Laertes, to give him the good news of his safe return. Meanwhile, the
townspeople, angry about the deaths of the young suitors, gather to
fight Odysseus. In the end, Athena steps in and makes peace among
them all.*

COLLABORATIVE DISCUSSION What are the moments of greatest
tension in Part 2? With a partner, discuss what details in the text help
build tension. Cite specific textual evidence to support your ideas.

Analyze Author's Choices: Epic Poem

In the simplest terms, an epic is a long adventure story. An **epic** plot spans many years and involves a long journey. Often, the fate of an entire nation is at stake. An epic **setting** spans great distances and foreign lands. Epic **themes** reflect timeless concerns, such as courage, honor, life, and death.

Consider these questions as you analyze how the author's choices about the structure of the *Odyssey* help create a compelling narrative:

- How are the characteristics of an epic reflected in the plot, setting, characters, and themes?
- In what ways does the *Odyssey* embody the qualities and ideals of ancient Greek culture?
- What themes are still applicable today?

Analyze Figurative Meanings

Epics are often rich with **figurative language,** or words used to symbolize ideas and evoke emotions rather than to convey literal meanings. As you analyze the figurative meanings in the *Odyssey*, consider the cumulative impact that this language has on the reader's ability to imagine the settings, characters, and events.

Figurative Language	Example
An **epic simile** (also called a Homeric simile) is a long, elaborate comparison that often continues for a number of lines.	Odysseus compares gouging out the Cyclops's eye to turning a huge drill: "I leaned on it / turning it as a shipwright turns a drill / in planking, having men below to swing / the two-handled strap that spins it in the groove. / So with our brand we bored that great eye socket. . . ."
An **epithet** is a brief phrase that reflects traits associated with a particular person or thing.	Odysseus is referred to as "son of Laertes," "raider of cities," and "that man skilled in all ways of contending".
An **allusion** is an indirect reference to a famous person, place, event, or literary work.	The poet calls upon a daughter of Zeus, often credited with inspiration: "Sing in me, Muse, and through me tell the story".
A **metaphor** directly compares two things by saying that one thing *is* another.	Odysseus comments on Penelope's aloofness: "Her heart is iron in her breast".

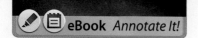
Analyzing the Text

Cite Text Evidence   Support your responses with evidence from the selection.

1. **Summarize** In what ways does the role of the gods in Part Two reflect the characteristics of an epic?

2. **Identify** What universal themes does Homer explore in the *Odyssey*? Choose two events from either Part One or Part Two, and explain how Homer conveys a **theme,** or central message, in each.

3. **Analyze** What motivates Penelope to test Odysseus' identity? What does this reveal about her character and how she has been affected by her husband's absence?

4. **Interpret** How does the order in which Odysseus reveals himself to his friends and loved ones build suspense? Explain.

5. **Compare** In what ways are Penelope's struggles similar to and different from those of Odysseus? What ideal traits do both characters possess?

6. **Analyze** The epithet "that man skilled in all ways of contending" first appears in Book 1 and subsequently in Book 21 as Odysseus strings his bow in front of the suitors. How does this epithet have greater impact and meaning in Book 21 in the epic?

7. **Interpret** Determine the meaning of the figurative language in this line: "He poured out at his feet a rain of arrows from the quiver" (Book 22, line 3). What impact does this metaphor have on the description of Odysseus as a warrior?

PERFORMANCE TASK

Writing Activity: Narrative The point of view in the *Odyssey* rarely wavers from Odysseus' perspective. Nevertheless, other characters' words and actions hint at what they are thinking. Explore the epic from another point of view through this brief writing task:

- Narrate an event from the *Odyssey* from the point of view one of the following characters: Polyphemus, Circe, Eurylochus, Tiresias, Scylla, Athena, Eumaeus, Telemachus, Eurymachus, or Penelope.

- Engage and orient the reader using techniques such as dialogue and description to set up the situation and create a smooth progression of events.
- Use precise words and phrases, telling details, and sensory language to convey a vivid picture of the events.

Critical Vocabulary

commandeer	adversity	contemptible	revelry
restitution	implacable	tremulous	desolation

Practice and Apply Use your knowledge of the Critical Vocabulary words to answer each question. Then, take turns explaining your answers to a partner.

1. Would it be effective for a person trying to **commandeer** a situation to speak in a **tremulous** voice? Why?

2. Why might people who have survived some kind of **adversity** engage in **revelry?**

3. Is it always possible to make **restitution** after doing something **contemptible?** Why?

4. How might an **implacable** assault on a city lead to **desolation?**

Vocabulary Strategy: Words from Latin

Recognizing **word roots** can help you determine the meanings of unfamiliar words. For example, the Critical Vocabulary word *desolation*, meaning "a feeling of loneliness," contains the Latin root *sol*, which means "alone." This root is found in numerous other English words. Study the Latin roots and their meanings in the chart, along with example words that contain each root.

Latin Root	Meaning	Examples
sol-	alone	soliloquy, solo
trem-	tremble	tremor, tremulous
plac-	calm	implacable, placate
vers-	turn	adversity, versatile

Practice and Apply For each Latin root in the chart, follow these steps:

1. Look online or in print resources for one additional example of a word that uses the Latin root.

2. Use your knowledge of the root's meaning to write a definition for each example word.

3. Consult a dictionary to confirm each example word's meaning.

4. Use each example word in a sentence.

Language and Style: Absolute Phrases

An **absolute phrase** consists of a noun and a participle, a verb form ending in -*ed* or -*ing* that acts as an adjective. Absolute phrases must be set off with commas and may also contain objects of the participle and any modifiers. Rather than modifying a specific word in a sentence, absolute phrases describe the main clause of a sentence. Absolute phrases are a helpful way to add information to a sentence.

Look at this example of an absolute phrase from the *Odyssey*.

**I drove them, <u>all three wailing</u>, to the ships,
tied them down under their rowing benches,
and called the rest.**

In this sentence, the absolute phrase *all three wailing* is also an example of imagery. The phrase adds information and helps evoke a sense of what it was like for Odysseus to drag his men from the land of the Lotus Eaters.

This chart shows two other examples of absolute phrases.

Absolute Phrase	What It Modifies
<u>Arrows soaring past them</u>, the suitors scanned the room looking for weapons and shields.	The noun *arrows* is modified by the participle *soaring* and the additional modifiers *past them*. The absolute phrase modifies, or describes, the rest of the sentence, *the suitors scanned the room looking for weapons and shields.*
Odysseus dreamed only of his return to Ithaca, <u>his mind focused on his reunion with Penelope.</u>	The noun *mind* is modified by the participle *focused* and the additional modifiers *his* and *on his reunion with Penelope.* The absolute phrase modifies the rest of the sentence, *Odysseus dreamed only of his return to Ithaca.*

Practice and Apply Look back at the narrative you wrote in response to this selection's Performance Task. Revise your narrative to include at least two absolute phrases. Share your revised narrative with a partner and discuss how your revisions add variety and interest.

Kira Salak (b. 1971) *wrote* The Cruelest Journey *to document her 600-mile solo kayak trip on the Niger River. The first person to ever achieve this feat, she traveled through a remote and dangerous region in Africa. Salak is an adventurer, an explorer, and a journalist. She has covered the civil war in the Democratic Republic of Congo, traveled across Papua New Guinea, and biked across Alaska. In 2005, she received a National Geographic Emerging Explorer Award, which recognizes people who are helping build world knowledge through exploration.*

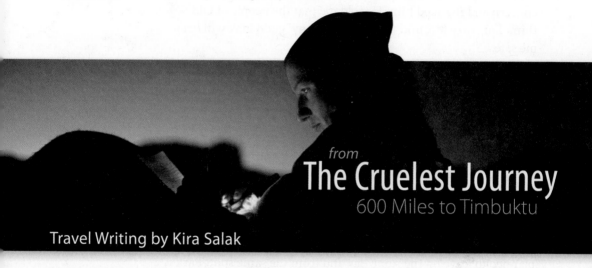

from
The Cruelest Journey
600 Miles to Timbuktu

Travel Writing by Kira Salak

AS YOU READ What does Salak think and feel about her journey? Make note of her thoughts, comments, and any telling details you notice. Write down any questions you generate during reading.

from Chapter One

In the beginning, my journeys feel at best ludicrous, at worst insane. This one is no exception. The idea is to paddle nearly 600 miles on the Niger River in a kayak, alone, from the Malian town of Old Ségou to Timbuktu. And now, at the very hour when I have decided to leave, a thunderstorm bursts open the skies, sending down apocalyptic rain, washing away the very ground beneath my feet. It is the rainy season in Mali, for which there can be no comparison in the world. Lightning pierces trees, slices across houses. Thunder racks the skies and pounds the earth like mortar
10   fire, and every living thing huddles in tenuous shelter, expecting the world to end. Which it doesn't. At least not this time. So that we all give a collective sigh to the salvation of the passing storm as it rumbles its way east, and I survey the river I'm to leave on this morning. Rain or no rain, today is the day for the journey to begin.

And no one, not even the oldest in the village, can say for certain whether I'll get to the end.

"Let's do it," I say, leaving the shelter of an adobe hut. My guide from town, Modibo, points to the north, to further storms. He says he will pray for me. It's the best he can do. To his knowledge, no man has ever completed such a trip, though a few have tried. And certainly no woman has done such a thing. This morning he took me aside and told me he thinks I'm crazy, which I understood as concern and thanked him. He told me that the people of Old Ségou think I'm crazy too, and that only uncanny[1] good luck will keep me safe.

Still, when a person tells me I can't do something, I'll want to do it all the more. It may be a failing of mine. I carry my inflatable kayak through the narrow passageways of Old Ségou, past the small adobe huts melting in the rains, past the huddling goats and smoke of cooking fires, people peering out at me from the dark entranceways. It is a labyrinth[2] of ancient homes, built and rebuilt after each storm, plastered with the very earth people walk upon. Old Ségou must look much the same as it did in Scottish explorer Mungo Park's time when, exactly 206 years ago to the day, he left on the first of his two river journeys down the Niger to Timbuktu, the first such attempt by a Westerner. It is no coincidence that I've planned to leave on the same day and from the same spot. Park is my benefactor of sorts, my guarantee. If he could travel down the Niger, then so can I. And it is all the guarantee I have for this trip— that an obsessed 19th-century adventurer did what I would like to do. Of course Park also died on this river, but I've so far managed to overlook that.

I gaze at the Niger through the adobe passageways, staring at waters that began in the mountainous rain forests of Guinea and traveled all this way to central Mali—waters that will journey northeast with me to Timbuktu before cutting a great circular swath through the Sahara and retreating south, through Niger, on to Nigeria, passing **circuitously** through mangrove swamps and jungle, resting at last in the Atlantic in the Bight of Benin.[3] But the Niger is more than a river; it is a kind of faith. Bent and plied by Saharan sands, it perseveres more than 2,600 miles from beginning to end through one of the hottest, most desolate regions of the world. And when the rains come each year, it finds new strength of purpose, surging through the sunbaked lands, giving people the boons of crops and livestock and fish, taking nothing, asking nothing. It humbles all who see it.

circuitously
(sər-kyoōˈĭ-təs-lē) *adv.*
in an indirect and lengthy manner.

---

[1] **uncanny:** mysterious or impossible to explain.
[2] **labyrinth:** a complex collection of paths, such as a maze.
[3] **Bight of Benin:** a gulf on Africa's west coast between Ghana and Nigeria.

If I were to try to explain why I'm here, why I chose Mali and the Niger for this journey—now that is a different matter. I can already feel the resistance in my gut, the familiar clutch of fear.

60 I used to avoid stripping myself down in search of motivation, scared of what I might uncover, scared of anything that might suggest a taint of the pathological.[4] And would it be enough to say that I admire Park's own trip on the river and want to try a similar challenge? That answer carries a whiff of the **disingenuous;** it sounds too easy to me. Human motivation, itself, is a complicated thing. If only it was simple enough to say, "Here is the Niger, and I want to paddle it." But I'm not that kind of traveler, and this isn't that kind of trip. If a journey doesn't have something to teach you about yourself, then what kind of journey is it? There is one

70 thing I'm already certain of: Though we may think we choose our journeys, they choose us.

Hobbled donkeys cower under a new onslaught of rain, ears back, necks craned. Little children dare each other to touch me, and I make it easy for them, stopping and holding out my arm. They stroke my white skin as if it were velvet, using only the pads of their fingers, then stare at their hands to check for wet paint.

Thunder again. More rain falls. I stop on the shore, near a centuries-old kapok tree under which I imagine Park once took shade. I open my bag, spread out my little red kayak, and start to

80 pump it up. I'm doing this trip under the sponsorship of *National Geographic Adventure,* which hopes to run a magazine story about it. This means that they need photos, lots of photos, and so a French photographer named Rémi Bénali feverishly snaps pictures of me. I don't know what I hate more—river storms or photo shoots. I value the privacy and **integrity** of my trips, and I don't want my journey turning into a circus. The magazine presented the best compromise it could: Rémi, renting a motor-driven pirogue,[5] was given instructions to find me on the river every few days to do his thing.

90 My kayak is nearly inflated. A couple of women nearby, with colorful cloth wraps called *pagnes* tied tightly about their breasts, gaze at me cryptically, as if to ask: *Who are you and what do you think you're doing?* The Niger churns and slaps the shore, in a surly mood. I don't pretend to know what I'm doing. Just one thing at a time now, kayak inflated, kayak loaded with my gear. Paddles fitted together and ready. Modibo is standing on the shore, watching me.

"I'll pray for you," he reminds me.

I balance my gear, adjust the straps, get in. And, finally, irrevocably, I paddle away. . . .

disingenuous
(dĭs´ĭn-jĕn´yoo-əs)
adj. insincere,
deceitful.

integrity
(ĭn-tĕg´rĭ-tē) *n.*
consistency and
strength of purpose.

---

[4] **taint of the pathological:** trace of mental illness.

[5] **pirogue (pĭ-rōg´):** a canoe made from a hallowed tree trunk.

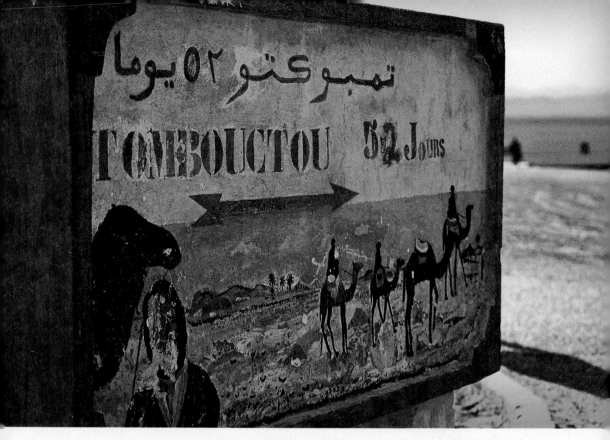

100   The storm erupts into a new overture. Torrential rains. Waves higher than my kayak, trying to capsize me. But my boat is self-bailing[6] and I stay afloat. The wind drives the current in reverse, tearing and ripping at the shores, sending spray into my face. I paddle madly, crashing and driving forward. I travel inch by inch, or so it seems, arm muscles smarting and rebelling against this journey. I crawl past New Ségou, fighting the Niger for more distance. Large river steamers rest in jumbled rows before cement docks, the town itself looking dark and deserted in the downpour. No one is out in their boats. The people know something I don't:

110 that the river dictates all travel.

    A popping feeling now and a screech of pain. My right arm lurches from a ripped muscle. But this is no time and place for such an injury, and I won't tolerate it, stuck as I am in a storm. I try to get used to the pulses of pain as I fight the river. There is only one direction to go: forward. Stopping has become anathema.[7]

I wonder what we look for when we **embark** on these kinds of trips. There is the pat answer that you tell the people you don't know: that you're interested in seeing a place, learning about its people. But then the trip begins and the hardship comes, and hardship is

embark
(ĕm-bärk´) v. to set out on a course or a journey (often aboard a boat).

---

[6] **self-bailing:** the boat has holes, or scuppers, that allow water to drain from the cockpit.

[7] **anathema:** something hated or despised.

120 more honest: it tells us that we don't have enough patience yet, nor humility, nor gratitude. And we thought that we did. Hardship brings us closer to truth, and thus is more difficult to bear, but from it alone comes compassion. And so I've told the world that it can do what it wants with me during this trip if only, by the end, I have learned something more. A bargain, then. The journey, my teacher.

And where is the river of just this morning, with its whitecaps that would have liked to drown me, with its current flowing backward against the wind? Gone to this: a river of smoothest glass, a placidity unbroken by wave or eddy, with islands of lush greenery
130 awaiting me like distant Xanadus.[8] The Niger is like a mercurial god, meting out punishment and benediction on a whim. And perhaps the god of the river sleeps now, returning matters to the mortals who ply its waters? The Bozo and Somono[9] fishermen in their pointy canoes. The long passenger pirogues, overloaded with people and merchandise, rumbling past, leaving diesel fumes in their wake. And now, inexplicably, the white woman in a little red boat, paddling through waters that flawlessly mirror the cumulus clouds above. We all belong here, in our way. It is as if I've entered a very lucid dream, continually surprised to find myself here on
140 this river—I've become a hapless actor in a mysterious play, not yet knowing what my part is, left to gape at the wonder of what I have set in motion. Somehow: I'm in a kayak, on the Niger River, paddling very slowly but very surely to Timbuktu.

As Salak continues on her journey, she encounters raging storms, dangerous hippos, and unrelenting heat. Because she is traveling in a small kayak and unable to carry many supplies, she comes ashore each night, seeking shelter and food from the locals, who live along the banks of the river. The locals are very curious about a woman undertaking such a dangerous journey alone. Some of them greet her warmly and generously; others with hostility. Finally, weak from dysentery, she approaches her final destination—Timbuktu.

from Chapter Thirteen

"This river will never end," I say out loud, over and over again, like a mantra. My map shows an obvious change to the northeast, but that turn hasn't come for hours, may never come at all. To be so close to Timbuktu, and yet so immeasurably far away. All I know is that I must keep paddling. I *have* to be close. Determined still to get

---

[8] **Xanadus (zăn´ə-dōoz´):** Xanadu, the summer palace of Kublai Khan; connotes an elaborate, ideal paradise.

[9] **Bozo and Somono:** ethnic groups native to Mali and the Niger River delta.

to Timbuktu's port of Korioumé by nightfall, I shed the protection
150 of my long-sleeved shirt, pull the kayak's thigh straps in tight, and
prepare for the hardest bout of paddling yet.

I paddle like a person possessed. I paddle the hours away, the
sun falling aside to the west but still keeping its heat on me. I keep
up a cadence in my head, keep my breaths regular and deep, in
synch with my arm movements. The shore passes by slowly, but it
passes. As the sun gets ominously low, burning a flaming orange,
the river turns almost due north and I can see a distant, square-
shaped building made of cement: the harbinger of what can only
be Korioumé. Hardly a tower of gold, hardly an El Dorado, but I'll
160 take it. I paddle straight toward it, ignoring the pains in my body,
my raging headache. *Timbuktu, Timbuktu!* Bozo fishermen ply
the river out here, and they stare at me as I pass. They don't ask for
money or cadeaux[10]—can they see the determination in my face,
sense my fatigue? All they say is, *"Ça va, madame?"*[11] with obvious
concern. One man actually stands and raises his hands in a cheer,
urging me on. I take his kindness with me into the final stretch,
rounding the river's sharp curve to the port of Korioumé.

I see Rémi's boat up ahead; he waits for me by the port, telephoto
lens in hand. It's the first time during this trip that I'm not fazed by
170 being photographed. I barely notice him. I barely notice anything
except the port ahead of me. All I can think about is stopping. Here
is the ending I've promised myself for weeks. Here I am, 600 miles of
river covered, with the port of Timbuktu straight ahead.

Something tugs at my kayak. I'm yanked back: fishnets,
caught in my rudder. To be this close, within sight of my goal, and
thwarted by yet one more thing. The universe surely has a sense of
humor. I jump into the water, fumbling at the nylon netting tangled
around the screws holding the rudder to the inflatable rubber. It's
shallow here, and my bare feet sink into river mud full of sharp
180 pieces of rock that cut instantly into my soles. I try to ignore the
pain, working fast, pulling the netting off until I free my kayak.
When I get inside, the blood from my feet mixes with gray river
water like a final offering to the Niger. I maneuver around the nets,
adjust my course for the dock of Korioumé, and paddle hard.

Just as the last rays of the sun color the Niger, I pull up beside
a great white river steamer, named, appropriately, the *Tombouctou*.
Rémi's boat is directly behind me, the flash from his camera
lighting up the throng of people gathering on shore. There is no
more paddling to be done. I've made it. I can stop now. I stare up
190 at the familiar crowd waiting in the darkness. West African pop
music blares from a party on the *Tombouctou*.

---

[10] **cadeaux (kə-dō´):** French word meaning "gifts."
[11] **Ça va, madame? (sävä, mä-däm´):** French for "How are you, madam?"

Slowly, I undo my thigh straps and get out of my kayak, hauling it from the river and dropping it onshore for the last time. A huge crowd has gathered around me, children squeezing in to stroke my kayak. People ask where I have come from and I tell them, "Old Ségou." They can't seem to believe it.

"Ségou?" one man asks. He points down the Niger. His hand waves and curves as he follows the course of the river in his mind.

"*Oui,*" I say.

200   "Ehh!" he exclaims.

"Ségou, Ségou, Ségou?" a woman asks.

I nod. She runs off to tell other people, and I can see passersby rushing over to take a look at me. What does a person look like who has come all the way from Ségou? They stare down at me in my sweat-stained tank top, my clay-smeared skirt, my sandals both held together with plastic ties.

I unload my things to the clamor of their questions, but even speaking seems to pain me now. Such a long time getting here. And was the journey worth it? Or is it blasphemy to ask that now? I can

210   barely walk, have a high fever. I haven't eaten anything for more than a day. How do you know if the journey is worth it? I would give a great deal right now for silence. For stillness.

My exhaustion and sickness begin to alter this arrival, numbing the sense of finish and self-congratulation and replacing it with only the most important of questions. I've found that illness does this to me, quiets the busy thoughts of the mind, gives me a rare clarity that I don't usually have. I see the weeks on the river, the changing tribal groups, the lush shores down by Old Ségou metamorphosing[12] slowly into the treeless, sandy spread near

220   Timbuktu. I'm wishing I could explain it to people—the subtle yet certain way the world has altered over these past few weeks. The inevitability of it. The grace of it. Grace, because in my life back home every day had appeared the same as the one before. Nothing seemed to change; nothing took on new variety. It had felt like a **stagnant** life.

I know now, with the utter conviction of my heart, that I want to avoid that stagnant life. I want the world to always be offering me the new, the grace of the unfamiliar. Which means—and I pause with the thought—a path that will only lead through my fears.

230   Where there are certainty and guarantees, I will never be able to meet that unknown world.

Night settles on the shore, and Rémi pulls his boat up alongside the cement dock. I deflate my kayak for the last time and pack it up, carrying it and my things onto the boat. Heather[13] and Rémi

stagnant
(stăg′nənt) *adj.*
unchanging;
without activity or
development.

---

[12]**metamorphosing:** completely changing into another form.

[13]**Heather:** photographer Rémi Bénali's girlfriend, who is traveling with him.

both give me a hug of congratulation, but I'm still too numb to really comprehend that I've done it yet. To celebrate, Rémi offers me my choice of their onboard selection of soft drinks. I take an Orange Fanta. Outside, barely discernible in the darkness, the crowd of onlookers continues to discuss what I've done. I can hear them exchanging the word "Ségou" and I wonder if they believe that I've paddled this far. But it doesn't matter. I lie down on one of the benches. My head feels hot, and it aches to the metronome-like beating[14] of my heart.

Rémi has gone onshore and tries valiantly to get us a taxi into Timbuktu, but the driver of the only car available at this late hour demands an exorbitant sum of more than $150 to drive 30 kilometers. It is the first time I've seen Rémi get so blustering and assertive, and he argues passionately for a lower sum. We are all hoping for what we've promised ourselves tonight—a hotel room in Timbuktu with blessed air-conditioning—but the driver won't budge his price, thinking he has us. As we're all nearly out of our magazine expense money, I suggest we camp and go to Timbuktu the next morning, when there are sure to be plenty of taxis to take us there at a reasonable price. For the first time, I see this disappointment as just another uncontrollable part of life, like the storms that arose on the Niger. Nothing personal.

I point to the opposite shore as a place to camp away from the crowds. Rémi and Heather agree, and so the great boat is started up and we speed over the Niger beneath a sky dazed with stars. We ground the boat on the opposite shore, and I go about setting up my tent. I'm too sick to fully acknowledge the end of my trip. Rémi offers me a drink to celebrate, but I know I wouldn't be able to keep it down. I do manage to swallow some antibiotics and antinausea pills, which quiet my stomach enough to allow me to eat a mango and some of the noodles Rémi's cook has made for us. As I sit to eat, I'm swaying back and forth in my mind, as if I were still careering over the waves of the Niger. I've heard that this happens to sailors, that they get so attached to being tossed by the waves that they have trouble readjusting to solid ground. For me, it is as if the Niger still keeps a part of me, as if to tell me that I finally belong to it.

COLLABORATIVE DISCUSSION Were you surprised by how Salak felt at the end of her trip? With a partner, discuss Salak's thoughts on beginning the trip and details that may have led to her feelings at the end of the trip. Cite specific evidence from the text to support your ideas.

---

[14] **metronome-like beating:** steady, rhythmic pulsing.

Analyze Ideas and Events

A **travel narrative** is a type of nonfiction that records an author's experiences exploring new places. Travel writers don't just present a series of facts; they tell a story that includes characters, a conflict to be resolved, and themes about life. In this excerpt, Kira Salak uses narrative techniques to reveal her own reflections on her journey. She doesn't just tell you what she sees, she shows you how she feels. By including vivid details and imagery to describe people, places, and events, Salak builds tension and gets readers involved in her adventure. In addition to description and imagery, Salak uses other techniques in her narrative:

- The **mood** of a work is the emotional response it creates in readers. What details does Salak include to create the mood of her narrative?
- **Pacing** refers to the passage of time in a written work. Short, choppy sentences can speed up a narrative, while longer sentences slow it down. The use of the present tense adds immediacy, giving readers the sense that events are unfolding right now. How does Salak vary the pacing in her narrative?
- Writers of nonfiction may use **dialogue** to show what people are like and to advance the action of the story. How does Salak use dialogue in her narrative?

Determine Central Idea and Cite Evidence

The author of a travel narrative aims to tell a good story full of interesting people, places, and events. In most cases, the author also wants to communicate a **central idea** about life and people. To determine the central idea, ask yourself what purpose the author has for sharing certain details—including descriptions of the journey as well as the author's reflections on what happens.

As you think about the central idea of this selection, consider how Salak feels at the beginning of her journey and what she has learned about herself by the end. Look for specific evidence in the text to support your analysis. Two methods you can use to **cite textual evidence** are quoting the text and paraphrasing the text.

Quoting	Paraphrasing
Quoting the text means using the author's exact words to support an analysis of the text. Use a quotation when the author's specific words are critical to making your point. Always use quotation marks to show that you are using the author's words rather than your own. *Kira Salak begins her narrative by writing, "In the beginning, my journeys feel at best ludicrous, at worst insane."*	**Paraphrasing** the text is restating something in your own words. Paraphrasing helps you clarify the author's meaning, because you must understand it before you can rephrase it. For example, the first sentence of the selection could be paraphrased this way: *The author says that early on, her journeys always feel foolish or crazy.*

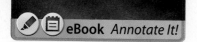

Analyzing the Text

Cite Text Evidence Support your responses with evidence from the selection.

1. **Identify Patterns** Many travel narratives follow an arc similar to the plot of a story—a conflict is introduced, intensifies, comes to a climax, and is resolved. Outline the arc of the story told in this travel narrative.

2. **Analyze** The mood at the beginning of Chapter One is ominous. What is the mood as the excerpt from Chapter Thirteen begins? What details create this mood?

3. **Interpret** Reread lines 57–71. What reasons does Salak give for making this trip? Why does she really undertake this journey? What does she expect to learn from this experience?

4. **Compare** Compare the pacing in lines 100–115 to that in lines 116–143. Which section seems to move faster, and why? How does the pacing help convey what the author is saying in each passage?

5. **Evaluate** Salak writes, "In the beginning, my journeys feel at best ludicrous, at worst insane." Do you think Salak's journey to Timbuktu was either of these things? Use quotations and paraphrases of the text to support your response.

6. **Analyze** What does the dialogue in lines 197–201 add to the narrative? How does the dialogue contribute to the central idea of the selection?

7. **Summarize** Briefly describe the author. What seems to motivate Salak to undertake these journeys? Support your description with details about her actions, words, and thoughts.

PERFORMANCE TASK

Writing Activity: Analysis At first glance, you might think this selection is about travel on the Niger River, an adventure in Mali, or a long journey. What central idea gives meaning to all the details about Salak's adventure?

- Write a brief essay that analyzes the central idea of this selection. State the central idea and then use quotations and paraphrases to support your analysis.
- Remember to follow the conventions of standard English in your writing.

- Exchange essays with a partner and give each other feedback. Did you both use quotation marks to indicate the author's words? Are your paraphrases accurate? Does your evidence support the central idea you identified?

Critical Vocabulary

circuitously   disingenuous   integrity   embark   stagnant

Practice and Apply Answer each question in a way that demonstrates your comprehension of the Critical Vocabulary word.

1. What might be the benefits of traveling **circuitously** to an unfamiliar destination?

2. Have you ever given a **disingenuous** answer? Explain.

3. When have you acted with **integrity?** Explain.

4. What would you do to get ready to **embark** on a trip around the world?

5. What would you do if you felt your life was **stagnant?**

Vocabulary Strategy: Denotation and Connotation

The **denotation,** or dictionary meaning, of the Critical Vocabulary word *embark* is "to start something." *Embark* also has certain **connotations,** or associations that are suggested by the word but that go beyond the literal meaning of the word.

embark	
Denotation	Connotation
To start something	To start something long or challenging

You wouldn't *embark* on a quick errand, but you would *embark* on a long voyage.

Practice and Apply The words in each pair have similar denotations. Write sentences that demonstrate differences in the connotations of the words in each pair.

1. *still* and *stagnant*

2. *leave* and *embark*

3. *purity* and *integrity*

4. *dishonest* and *disingenuous*

5. *indirectly* and *circuitously*

Language and Style: Sentence Length

Authors vary **sentence length** and style to keep a piece from becoming monotonous. Authors also use sentence length to achieve a specific effect. For example, long sentences tend to slow readers down, while short sentences are read more quickly. A series of short, choppy sentences can also add tension.

Read this sentence from the selection:

I gaze at the Niger through the adobe passageways, staring at waters that began in the mountainous rain forests of Guinea and traveled all this way to central Mali—waters that will journey northeast with me to Timbuktu before cutting a great circular swath through the Sahara and retreating south, through Niger, on to Nigeria, passing circuitously through mangrove swamps and jungle, resting at last in the Atlantic in the Bight of Benin.

Salak could have written the passage this way:

I gaze at the Niger through the adobe passageways. I stare at waters that began in the mountainous rain forests of Guinea and traveled all this way to central Mali. These waters will journey northeast with me to Timbuktu. Then they will cut a great circular swath through the Sahara and retreat south, through Niger, on to Nigeria. Along the way, they will pass circuitously through mangrove swamps and jungle. They will rest at last in the Atlantic in the Bight of Benin.

By using a long, winding sentence, the author mirrors the flow of the river she is describing.

Later, Salak changes her sentence style as shown in this example:

Just one thing at a time now, kayak inflated, kayak loaded with my gear. Paddles fitted together and ready.

Here, Salak uses shorter phrases and sentences to mirror the sequence of quick actions she is performing.

Authors also use breaks in sentences for effect. Consider this sentence:

Which means—and I pause with the thought—a path that will only lead through my fears.

The use of dashes to offset Salak's side comment causes readers to pause with her and think carefully about the insight she is sharing.

Practice and Apply Go back to the analysis you wrote in response to this selection's Performance Task. Find at least three places where you can enhance your essay by using different sentence lengths.

Background **Michael Griffin** *served as the administrator of the National Aeronautics and Space Administration (NASA) from 2005 to 2009. President Eisenhower founded NASA in 1958 soon after the Soviet Union launched the first artificial satellite. NASA has sent Americans into space, created the space shuttle as a reusable spacecraft, worked on the International Space Station, and landed rovers to learn about the conditions on Mars. NASA works to learn more about space, find ways to get to and explore space, and determine how our knowledge of space affects us on Earth.*

The Real Reasons We Explore Space

Argument by Michael Griffin

AS YOU READ Notice which reasons Griffin examines before he outlines the real reason he thinks we explore space. Write down any questions you generate during reading.

I am convinced that if NASA were to disappear tomorrow, if we never put up another Hubble Space Telescope, never put another human being in space, people in this country would be profoundly distraught. Americans would feel that we had lost something that matters, that our best days were behind us, and they would feel themselves somehow diminished. Yet I think most would be unable to say why.

There are many good reasons to continue to explore space, which most Americans have undoubtedly heard. Some have been
10 debated in public policy circles and evaluated on the basis of financial investment. . . .

But these are not reasons that would make Americans miss our space program. They are merely the reasons we are most comfortable discussing. I think of them as "acceptable reasons" because they can be logically defended. When we **contemplate** committing large sums of money to a project, we tend to dismiss reasons that are emotional or value-driven or can't be captured on a

contemplate
(kŏn′təm-plāt′) *v.*
think carefully about.

spreadsheet.[1] But in space exploration those are the reasons—what I think of as "real reasons"—that are the most important.

When Charles Lindbergh[2] was asked why he crossed the Atlantic, he never once answered that he wanted to win the $25,000 that New York City hotel owner Raymond Orteig offered for the first nonstop aircraft flight between New York and Paris. Burt Rutan and his backer, Paul Allen, certainly didn't develop a private spacecraft to win the Ansari X-Prize for the $10 million in prize money. They spent twice as much as they made. Sergei Korolev and the team that launched Sputnik[3] were not tasked by their government to be the first to launch an artificial satellite; they had to fight for the honor and the resources to do it.

I think we all know why people strive to accomplish such things. They do so for reasons that are **intuitive** and compelling to all of us but that are not necessarily logical. They're exactly the opposite of acceptable reasons, which are eminently logical but neither intuitive nor emotionally compelling.

First, most of us want to be, both as individuals and as societies, the first or the best in some activity. We want to stand out. This behavior is rooted in our genes. We are today the descendants of people who survived by outperforming others. Without question that drive can be carried to an unhealthy extreme; we've all seen more wars than we like. But just because the trait can be taken too far doesn't mean that we can do without it completely.

A second reason is curiosity. Who among us has not had the urge to know what's over the next hill? What child has not been drawn to explore beyond the familiar streets of the neighborhood?

Finally, we humans have, since the earliest civilizations, built monuments. We want to leave something behind to show the next generation, or the generations after that, what we did with our time here. This is the impulse behind cathedrals and pyramids, art galleries and museums.

Cathedral builders would understand what I mean by real reasons. The monuments they erected to the awe and mystery of their God required a far greater percentage of their gross domestic product[4] than we will ever put into the space business, but we look back across 600 or 800 years of time, and we are still awed by what

intuitive
(ĭn-tōō′ĭ-tĭv) *adj.* known or understood without reasoning; instinctive.

---

[1] **spreadsheet:** a computer program, often used in accounting, that calculates data entered into its rows and columns.

[2] **Charles Lindbergh:** (1902–1974) an American pilot who in 1927 became the first person to successfully fly alone across the Atlantic.

[3] **Sergei Korolev . . . Sputnik (sûr′gā kô-rô′lĕv . . . spŏŏt′nĭk):** Korolev (1907–1966), a Russian engineer, designed the rocket that carried the first satellite (*Sputnik*) into space in 1957.

[4] **gross domestic product:** the monetary value of all the goods and services that a country produces during a certain time period.

the builders accomplished. Those buildings, therefore, also stand as monuments to the builders.

The return the cathedral builders made on their investment could not have been summarized in a cost/benefit analysis. They began to develop civil engineering, the core discipline for any society if it wishes to have anything more than thatched huts. They gained societal advantages that were probably even more important than learning how to build walls and roofs. For example, they learned to embrace deferred gratification, not just on an individual level, where it is a crucial element of maturity, but on a societal level, where it is equally vital. The people who started the cathedrals didn't live to finish them. The society as a whole had to be dedicated to the completion of those projects. We owe Western civilization as we know it today to that kind of thinking: the ability to have a constancy of purpose across years and decades.

It is my **contention** that the products of our space program are today's cathedrals. The space program satisfies the desire to compete, but in a safe and productive manner, rather than in a harmful one. It speaks abundantly to our sense of human curiosity, of wonder and awe at the unknown. Who can watch people assembling the greatest engineering project in the history of mankind—the International Space Station—and not wonder at the ability of people to conceive and to execute the project? And it also addresses our need for leaving something for future generations.

Of course the space program also addresses the acceptable reasons, and in the end this is **imperative**. Societies will not succeed in the long run if they place their resources and their efforts in enterprises that, for whatever reason, don't provide concrete value. But I believe that projects done for the real reasons that motivate humans also serve the acceptable reasons. In that sense, the value of space exploration really is in its spinoffs, as many have argued. But it's not in spinoffs like Teflon and Tang and Velcro, as the public is so often told—and which in fact did not come from the space program. And it's not in spinoffs in the form of better heart monitors or cheaper prices for liquid oxygen for hospitals, although the space program's huge demand for liquid oxygen spurred fundamental improvements in the production and handling of this volatile substance. The real spinoffs are, just as they were for cathedral builders, more fundamental.

Anyone who wants to build spacecraft, who wants to be a subcontractor, or who even wants to supply bolts and screws to the space industry must work to a higher level of precision than human beings had to do before the space industry came along. And that standard has influenced our entire industrial base, and therefore our economy.

contention
(kən-tĕn′shən) *n.*
argued assertion.

imperative
(ĭm-pĕr′ə-tĭv) *adj.*
crucial, necessary.

100   As for national security, what is the value to the United States of being involved in enterprises which lift up human hearts everywhere? What is the value to the United States of being a leader in such efforts, in projects in which every technologically capable nation wants to take part? The greatest strategy for national security, more effective than having better guns and bombs than everyone else, is being a nation that does the kinds of things that make others want to do them with us.

What do you have to do, how do you have to behave, to do space projects? You have to value hard work. You have to live
110   by excellence, or die from the lack of it. You have to understand and practice both leadership and followership. You have to build partnerships; leaders need partners and allies, as well as followers.

You have to accept the challenge of the unknown, knowing that you might fail, and to do so not without fear but with mastery of fear and a determination to go anyway. You have to defer gratification because we work on things that not all of us will live to see—and we know it.

We now believe that 95 percent of the universe consists of dark energy or dark matter, terms for things that we as yet know nothing
120   about. Is it even conceivable that one day we won't learn to harness them? As cavemen learned to harness fire, as people two centuries ago learned to harness electricity, we will learn to harness these new things. It was just a few years ago that we confirmed the existence of dark matter, and we would not have done so without the space program. What is the value of knowledge like that? I cannot begin to guess. A thousand years from now there will be human beings who don't have to guess; they will know, and they will know we gave this to them.

COLLABORATIVE DISCUSSION With a partner, discuss the various reasons Griffin cites for exploring space. Are they good reasons? Cite specific textual evidence to support your ideas.

Delineate and Evaluate an Argument

To **delineate,** or outline, an **argument,** first identify the author's claim. Look at the introduction, where the author often states the claim, and at the conclusion, where the author often restates the claim, sums up key points, or suggests actions based on conclusions. Then identify the specific reasons and evidence the author uses to support that position.

Consider whether the tone of the argument is objective or biased. Is the author supporting the claim with evidence including facts, statistics, personal experiences, statements by experts, and other information? Can the facts be verified? Are the author's sources reliable? Then assess whether the author's reasoning is valid. Look for false statements and fallacious reasoning, such as the examples in the chart.

Technique	Example	Explanation
False Cause and Effect	I ate shrimp last night and feel sick today. The shrimp must have been bad.	A connection between two ideas doesn't always mean that one causes the other.
Circular Reasoning	Ms. Vasquez is a great teacher because she does a great job teaching.	Circular reasoning restates the argument as a reason to support it.
Overgeneralization	I saw three shooting stars this past winter. Shooting stars appear in winter.	Generalizations based on limited data may not be accurate. Stereotypes are a form of generalization.

Evaluate whether the author plays on readers' emotions with words and phrases. While authors often appeal to emotions, they should also offer evidence and logical thinking. As a reader, be aware of ways authors may try to manipulate your emotions:

- **Bandwagon** (everyone is doing it)
- **Personal attack** (discrediting an idea by attacking the person who expressed it)
- **Transfer** (connecting feelings about one thing to something else)
- **Loaded language** (choosing words that elicit strong feelings)

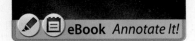

Analyzing the Text

Cite Text Evidence   Support your responses with evidence from the selection.

1. **Summarize** Identify Griffin's claim, or central idea, and delineate the key ideas of his argument.

2. **Evaluate** Griffin makes a distinction between "acceptable" reasons and "real" reasons for exploring space. Explain what he means by each type of reason. Which type of reason does he use to support his claim?

3. **Analyze** Does Griffin appeal to logic, emotion, or both in this piece? Cite examples that support your response.

4. **Interpret** In what part of the argument does Griffin make use of a bandwagon approach to convince readers of the validity of his claim? Explain.

5. **Analyze** Why does Griffin include Charles Lindbergh, Burt Rutan and Paul Allen, and Sergei Korolev in this selection? How does their motivation provide supporting evidence for Griffin's claim?

6. **Interpret** How does the analogy in Griffin's statement, "It is my contention that the products of our space program are today's cathedrals," connect to his claim?

7. **Evaluate** What purpose might Griffin have had for writing this piece? Given that purpose, how effective is Griffin's argument? Why?

PERFORMANCE TASK

Writing Activity: Editorial Michael Griffin argues that exploring space is important and provides both "acceptable" and "real" value. However, space exploration comes with a large price tag. Is that price tag worth it? Should exploring space be part of our national budget?

Write an editorial for or against continuing the space program. In your editorial,

- state a clear claim for your argument and present at least three supporting reasons
- use evidence consisting of examples, questions, and facts

- avoid faulty logic
- include a conclusion restating your claim
- use the conventions of standard English

Critical Vocabulary

contemplate   intuitive   contention   imperative

Practice and Apply Choose which of the two situations best fits each vocabulary word's meaning.

1. **Contemplate**
   a. You carefully consider the options before making a decision.
   b. You choose carelessly without considering the consequences.

2. **Intuitive**
   a. You weigh the advantages and disadvantages of a situation.
   b. You follow your instincts when making an important decision.

3. **Contention**
   a. You come to a decision after evaluating evidence.
   b. You assert an opinion about a specific issue.

4. **Imperative**
   a. You take a class that is required for graduation.
   b. You fill your schedule with electives.

Vocabulary Strategy: Synonyms and Antonyms

Synonyms are words that have the same or similar meanings. **Antonyms** are words with opposite meanings. As a reader, recognizing synonyms and antonyms can help you understand new vocabulary words. For example, the word *necessary* is a synonym for the Critical Vocabulary word *imperative*, while *optional* is an antonym. You can use an online or print thesaurus to find synonyms and antonyms.

Practice and Apply Use a thesaurus to find a synonym and antonym for the remaining Critical Vocabulary words. Then write sentences using the synonym and the antonym as shown in this example:

imperative
synonym: *necessary*
Eating well is <u>necessary</u> to good health, but it is <u>imperative</u> that you exercise, too.
antonym: *optional*
Many people think that space exploration is <u>optional</u>, but I argue it is <u>imperative</u>.

Language and Style: Transitions

Transitions are words or phrases that help connect ideas in a piece of writing. Read the following sentence from the selection:

> <u>But</u> these are not reasons that would make Americans miss our space program.

The word *but* lets the reader know that the author is shifting ideas. This statement as a whole leads the reader from the reasons Americans have heard to what the author thinks are the real reasons to explore space.

Later, the author identifies three reasons people strive to accomplish things. In the paragraphs that follow, he begins with these words and phrases: *First, A second reason*, and *Finally*. These transitions make it clear that the author is moving from one idea to another and then another. They also show that these three ideas are examples of the intuitive reasons the author wants to explain.

Given these examples, you can see that transitions are able to create a contrast between ideas, or they can link ideas. However, transitions can also

- introduce a sequence
- help orient readers in time or space
- identify examples, causes, or effects
- indicate conclusions

The chart below contains examples of transitional words and phrases related to a specific purpose.

Common Transitional Words and Phrases	
Purpose	**Examples**
Contrast ideas	but, however, although, on the other hand, while
Connect ideas	also, in addition, furthermore, too, first, second, finally
Introduce sequence	first, second, finally, initially, next, then, later
Orient readers in time or space	while, before, after, then, so far, meanwhile, here, nearby, above, below, next to
Identify examples, causes, or effects	for example, for instance, as a result, therefore, consequently
Indicate a conclusion	in conclusion, in summary

Practice and Apply Look back at the editorial you wrote in response to this selection's Performance Task. Identify the transitions that you used and revise your essay to add appropriate or stronger transitions. Then discuss with a partner how these transitions affect the flow of your essay and the connections between ideas.

The Journey

Poem by Mary Oliver

Mary Oliver (b.1935) *is known for observing the natural world in a way that is both romantic and unflinchingly honest. Oliver's poems often draw attention to small details—a bird calling, a still pond, a grasshopper. Her vivid imagery of the natural world opens a window for her to explore larger issues, such as love, loss, wonder, and grief.*

Oliver published her first book of poetry, No Voyage and Other Poems, *in 1963. She has published numerous other collections, including* American Primitive, *which won the Pulitzer Prize for Poetry in 1984. She has also won the National Book Award. But Oliver is not just an award-winning poet; she is also a popular poet whose work appeals to many readers.*

Besides writing poetry, Oliver has taught at colleges and universities including Bennington College in Vermont. She has also written many essays, as well as two books about the craft of writing poetry. Her former residence in Provincetown, Massachusetts, has inspired much of her writing with its natural beauty.

AS YOU READ Pay attention to details that describe barriers to the journey in the poem. Write down any questions you generate during reading.

The Journey

One day you finally knew
what you had to do, and began,
though the voices around you
kept shouting
5   their bad advice—
though the whole house
began to tremble
and you felt the old tug
at your ankles.
10   "Mend my life!"
each voice cried.
But you didn't stop.
You knew what you had to do,
though the wind pried
15   with its stiff fingers
at the very foundations—
though their melancholy
was terrible.
It was already late
20   enough, and a wild night,
and the road full of fallen
branches and stones.
But little by little,
as you left their voices behind,
25   the stars began to burn
through the sheets of clouds,
and there was a new voice,
which was slowly
recognized as your own,
30   that kept you company
as you strode deeper and deeper
into the world,
determined to do
the only thing you could do—
35   determined to save
the only life you could save.

COLLABORATIVE DISCUSSION What kind of journey do *you* take in this poem? With a partner, discuss what obstacles need to be overcome to complete this journey. Is the journey worth the effort? Cite specific textual evidence to support your ideas.

Interpret Figurative Language

Figurative language is language that communicates meanings beyond the literal meanings of words. In figurative language, words are often used to represent ideas and concepts they would not otherwise be associated with. Poets use figurative language to make interesting comparisons and to help readers see subjects in a new light.

In "The Journey," Mary Oliver uses two types of figurative language—personification and metaphor.

Personification	Metaphor
Authors use **personification** to give human qualities to an object, animal, or idea. For example, an author might describe what a beach looks like during a storm by giving the sea human qualities: *"The angry sea took hungry bites from the shore."*	Authors use **metaphors** to compare two things that are basically unlike but have something in common. Unlike similes, metaphors do not use the words *like* or *as*. The author describing the storm might instead use a metaphor: *"The sea was a wild animal attacking the shore."* An **extended metaphor** is a longer metaphor that continues the comparison at length, even throughout an entire poem or literary work.

You probably noticed some examples of figurative language and imagery during your first reading of "The Journey." In subsequent readings, analyze Oliver's use of these devices more closely. Ask yourself how the devices make her poem more vivid and powerful.

Analyzing the Text

Cite Text Evidence   Support your responses with evidence from the selection.

1. **Interpret** In line 3, who are "the voices around you"? What might the voices represent?

2. **Analyze** How does Oliver personify the wind? What is the figurative meaning of this strong wind outside the home of a person who is undertaking a journey?

3. **Interpret** Notice that the poem is written in one long stanza, not broken into smaller stanzas. How does Oliver use this structure to develop an extended metaphor?

4. **Analyze** Trace the nature images that occur throughout the poem. How does Oliver use each image to develop the extended metaphor in the poem?

5. **Interpret** What do the branches and stones on the road **symbolize,** or represent?

6. **Infer** What is the **theme,** or underlying message, of the poem? How do the title and structure of the poem help convey the theme?

PERFORMANCE TASK

Speaking Activity: Response to Literature Think about the journey portrayed in this poem and the journey Kira Salak undertakes in *The Cruelest Journey: 600 Miles to Timbuktu* (also in this collection). What similarities and differences are there between the journeys?

- Review both selections and consider how you might answer the question. Cite text evidence from both selections that support your ideas.
- Think about how you can best present your ideas in a clear, concise way. You might discuss the poem first, and then the travel writing. Alternately, you might discuss one similarity or difference between the journeys at a time.

- Write a summary of the similarities and differences between the two journeys to present to the class.
- Note on your summary where you might adjust the volume or make eye contact to emphasize important points. Then deliver your presentation to the class.

COLLECTION 6
PERFORMANCE TASK

To help you complete this task, use
• *Conducting Research*
• *Writing Informative Texts*
• *Writing as a Process*

Research and Write an Analytical Essay

Review the journeys taken in three texts in this collection, including the *Odyssey*. What compels characters or real people to set off on a journey—physical, mental, or spiritual—and what do they learn? Synthesize your ideas in an analytical essay. Use evidence from the texts and from additional sources to support your conclusions.

An effective analytical essay

- includes a clear thesis statement about how and why people gain insights from their travel or their mental/spiritual journeys
- engages the reader in the introduction with an interesting observation, quotation, or detail from one of the selections
- organizes central ideas in a logically structured body
- smoothly integrates source information that avoids plagiarism, with correctly cited sources
- uses transitions to show how ideas are related
- includes quotations or examples to illustrate central ideas
- has a concluding section that sums up the central ideas

Visit hmhfyi.com to explore your topic and enhance your research.

PLAN ⟩

Analyze the Texts
Review and take notes on the *Odyssey* and two other texts. Note details, examples, and relevant quotations from all three texts that support your central idea about journeys.

Use the annotation tools in your eBook to find evidence from your chosen texts. Save each piece of evidence to *my*Notebook, in a folder titled *Collection 6 Performance Task*.

ACADEMIC VOCABULARY

As you share your ideas about journeys, be sure to use these words.

motivate
objective
pursuit
subsequent
undertake

Conduct Further Research Search for additional evidence in print and digital sources to support your thesis statement. Be sure to include source information so that you can accurately cite your sources.

Interactive Lessons
To help you research your essay, complete the following lesson:
· Conducting Research: Taking Notes

Get Organized Prioritize your ideas in a graphic organizer.

- Write a thesis statement about the journeys people take and subsequent effects on the traveler.

- Decide what organizational pattern you will use to develop your essay. Will you begin your essay with your strongest reason or save it for last?

- Use a graphic organizer to prioritize your reasons and evidence.

- Write down some ideas for your conclusion.

Interactive Lessons
To help you plan your essay, complete the following lesson:
· Writing Informative Texts: Organizing Ideas

PRODUCE

Draft Your Essay Write a draft of your essay. Consider your purpose and audience and remember that essay writing requires formal language and a respectful tone. Essays that analyze texts are expected to be appropriate for an academic context.

WriteSmart
Write your rough draft in *my*WriteSmart. Focus on getting your ideas down, rather than perfecting your choice of language.

- Introduce a clear and concise thesis statement.

- Present your details, quotations, and examples from the selections and additional sources in logically ordered paragraphs.

- Each paragraph should have a central idea related to your thesis statement with evidence to support it. Explain how each piece of evidence supports the central idea.

- Use transitions to connect the main sections of your essay and to clarify the relationships among your ideas.

- Write a conclusion that summarizes your analysis and presents a final synthesis of your central ideas.

Language and Style: Cite Sources

When you use text, ideas, or information from a source, avoid plagiarism by giving credit to that source. One way to cite a source is to use a parenthetical citation in which you give the author's name and a page number in parentheses at the end of the sentence where the idea is found. See the following example.

> " As Kira Salak says in *The Cruelest Journey: 600 Miles to Timbuktu*, 'There is one thing I'm already certain of: Though we may think we choose our journeys, they choose us.' (Salak, quoted in *Collections* 423) "

Use footnotes or endnotes when you quote or paraphrase a text, to direct your readers to the sources you used to develop your essay. Both are linked to sources through a superscript number. Your teacher will guide you to follow a standard format for citation, such as *The Chicago Manual of Style*.

Improve Your Draft
Have your partner or group of peers use the questions in the chart to review your draft.

Questions	Tips	Revision Techniques
Does the introduction include a clear thesis statement?	**Underline** the thesis statement.	**Add** a thesis statement that states the topic and main idea.
Are paragraphs organized logically, with clear central ideas?	**Highlight** the central idea of each paragraph.	**Add** central ideas to paragraphs. **Reorder** paragraphs so that the sequence makes sense.
Do details, quotations, and examples support each central idea?	**Underline** each piece of evidence that supports a central idea.	**Insert** details, quotations, and examples to support central ideas. **Delete** any that do not support an idea.
Are all sources cited correctly?	**Highlight** any quotations or ideas that came from sources.	**Add** source citations for any text, ideas, and information.
Do appropriate and varied transitions connect ideas?	**Underline** each transitional word or phrase.	**Add** transitions to clarify the relationships between ideas.
Does the conclusion synthesize the central ideas of the essay?	**Highlight** the phrases that synthesize the central ideas.	**Add** a synthesis that connects the central ideas.

Have your partner or a group of peers review your draft in *my*WriteSmart. Ask your reviewers to note any ideas or evidence that does not support your thesis statement.

Interactive Lessons
To help you revise your essay, complete the following lesson:
• Writing as a Process: Revising and Editing

Share Your Essay
When your final draft is completed, read your essay aloud to a small group. Your audience should listen, take notes, and be prepared to comment or ask questions.

Publish Online
Create a class blog about journeys. Upload your essays to allow your classmates and other readers to comment on the ideas expressed in your analyses. You may also want to share your own travel experiences and what you learned about yourself.

PERFORMANCE TASK RUBRIC
ANALYTICAL ESSAY

	Ideas and Evidence	Organization	Language
4	• An eloquent introduction includes the titles and authors of the selections; the thesis statement describes the view of journeys presented in the selections. • Specific, relevant details support the central ideas. • A satisfying concluding section synthesizes the ideas and summarizes the analysis.	• Central ideas and supporting evidence are organized logically throughout the essay. • Varied transitions show the relationships between ideas. • Sources for all details, ideas, and evidence are credited.	• The analysis has an appropriately formal style and a knowledgeable, objective tone. • Language is precise and captures the writer's thoughts with originality. • Sentence beginnings, lengths, and structures vary and have a rhythmic flow. • Spelling, capitalization, and punctuation are correct. If handwritten, the analysis is legible. • Grammar and usage are correct.
3	• The introduction identifies the titles and authors of the selections but could be more engaging; the thesis statement encompasses the view of journeys in at least two selections. • One or two central ideas need more support. • The concluding section synthesizes most of the ideas and summarizes most of the analysis.	• The organization of central ideas and supporting evidence is confusing in a few places. • A few more transitions are needed to clarify the relationships between ideas. • One or two details or ideas from sources are not credited.	• The style becomes informal in a few places, and the tone does not always communicate confidence. • Most language is precise. • Sentence beginnings, lengths, and structures vary somewhat. • Several spelling, capitalization, and punctuation mistakes occur. If handwritten, the analysis is mostly legible. • Some grammatical and usage errors are repeated in the essay.
2	• The introduction identifies the titles and the authors of the selections; the thesis statement only hints at the main idea of the analysis. • Details support some central ideas but are often too general. • The concluding section gives an incomplete summary of the analysis and merely restates the thesis.	• Most central ideas are organized logically, but many supporting details are out of place. • More transitions are needed throughout the essay to connect ideas. • Most details and ideas from sources are not clearly credited.	• The style is informal in many places, and the tone reflects a superficial understanding of the selections. • Language is repetitive or vague at times. • Sentence structures barely vary, and some fragments or run-on sentences are present. • Spelling, capitalization, and punctuation are often incorrect but do not make comprehending the essay difficult. If handwritten, the analysis may be partially illegible. • Grammar and usage are incorrect in many places, but the writer's ideas are still clear.
1	• The appropriate elements of an introduction are missing. • Details and evidence are irrelevant or missing. • The analysis lacks a concluding section.	• A logical organization is not used; ideas are presented randomly. • Transitions are not used, making the essay difficult to understand. • Credit for sources is missing.	• The style and tone are inappropriate. • Language is inaccurate, repetitive, and vague. • Repetitive sentence structure, fragments, and run-on sentences make the writing monotonous and difficult to follow. • Spelling, capitalization, and punctuation are incorrect throughout. If handwritten, the analysis may be partially or mostly illegible. • Many grammatical and usage errors change the meaning of the writer's ideas.

Performance Task Reference Guide — R2

Writing Arguments — R2

Writing Informative Essays — R4

Writing Narratives — R6

Conducting Research — R8

Participating in a Collaborative Discussion — R12

Debating an Issue — R14

Reading Arguments — R16

Analyzing an Argument — R16

Recognizing Persuasive Techniques — R17

Analyzing Logic and Reasoning — R17

Identifying Faulty Reasoning — R19

Evaluating Arguments — R20

Grammar — R22

Quick Reference:

Parts of Speech — R22

The Sentence and Its Parts — R24

Punctuation — R25

Capitalization — R27

Grammar Handbook:

1 Nouns — R29

2 Pronouns — R29

3 Verbs — R32

4 Modifiers — R34

5 The Sentence and Its Parts — R37

6 Phrases — R38

7 Verbals and Verbal Phrases — R39

8 Clauses — R41

9 The Structure of Sentences — R43

10 Writing Complete Sentences — R44

11 Subject-Verb Agreement — R45

Vocabulary and Spelling — R48

1 Using Context Clues — R48

2 Analyzing Word Structure — R49

3 Understanding Word Origins — R50

4 Synonyms and Antonyms — R51

5 Denotation and Connotation — R51

6 Analogies — R51

7 Homonyms and Homophones — R51

8 Words with Multiple Meanings — R52

9 Specialized Vocabulary — R52

10 Using Reference Sources — R52

11 Spelling Rules — R53

12 Commonly Confused Words — R55

Glossary of Literary and Informational Terms — R57

Pronunciation Key — R76

Glossary of Academic Vocabulary — R77

Glossary of Critical Vocabulary — R78

Index of Skills — R81

Index of Titles and Authors — R92

Acknowledgments — R93

Writing Arguments

Many of the Performance Tasks in this book ask you to craft an argument in which you support your ideas with text evidence. Any argument you write should include the following sections and characteristics.

Introduce Your Claim

Clearly state your **claim**—the point your argument makes. As needed, provide context or background information to help readers understand your position. Note the most common opposing views as a way to distinguish and clarify your ideas. From the very beginning, make it clear for readers why your claim is strong; consider providing an overview of your reasons or a quotation that emphasizes your view in your introduction.

EXAMPLES

Vague claim: We need more recreational facilities.	**Precise claim:** The city should build a new skate park downtown.
Not distinguished from opposing view: There are plenty of people who consider skate parks unsafe.	**Distinguished from opposing view:** While some people consider skate parks unsafe, the facts say differently.
Confusing relationship of ideas: Teens need more to do. Skate parks are enjoyed by people of all ages.	**Clear relationship of ideas:** By providing a safe activity not only for teens but for people of all ages, a skate park would benefit the entire community.

Develop Your Claim

The body of your argument must provide strong, logical reasons for your claim and must support those reasons with relevant evidence. A **reason** tells why your claim is valid; **evidence** provides specific examples that illustrate a reason. In the process of developing your claim, you should also refute **counterclaims,** or opposing views, with equally strong reasons and evidence. To demonstrate that you have thoroughly considered your view, provide a well-rounded look at both the strengths and limitations of your claim and opposing claims. The goal is not to undercut your argument but rather to answer your readers' potential objections to it. Be sure, too, to consider how much your audience may already know about your topic in order to avoid boring or confusing your readers.

EXAMPLES

Claim lacking reasons: A skate park would be a good thing.	**Claim developed by reasons:** Among the benefits of a skate park are a potential reduction in petty crimes committed by bored teens and improved physical fitness across the community.
Omission of limitations: The people opposed to this idea wouldn't use a skate park.	**Fair discussion of limitations:** We should not dismiss safety concerns. Planning for the park should include safe ramp designs, first aid facilities, and ongoing maintenance.
Inattention to audience's knowledge: A kick-flip ollie can be executed just about anywhere, but with a half-pipe more advanced tricks are possible.	**Awareness of audience's knowledge:** Readers unfamiliar with skateboarding may be surprised to learn that most injuries happen to beginners in their driveways, not in well-planned skate parks.

Link Ideas

Even the strongest reasons and evidence will fail to sway readers if it is unclear how the reasons relate to the central claim of an argument. Make the connections clear for your readers, using not only transitional words and phrases, but also clauses and even entire sentences as bridges between ideas you have already discussed and ideas you are introducing.

EXAMPLES

Transitional word linking claim and reason: The entire community will benefit from a skate park downtown. First, health care and law enforcement costs may be reduced if bored or sedentary teens spend their free time there instead of in less productive activities.

Transitional phrase linking reason and evidence: Skating in a planned park would actually reduce injuries. In fact, the American Academy of Pediatrics states that "communities should be encouraged to develop safe skateboarding areas away from pedestrian and motor vehicle traffic."

Transitional clause linking claim and counterclaim: The health benefits of the park are clear. Those opposed to the park plan, though, would say otherwise: They feel that there is too much potential for injuries from falls.

Use Appropriate Style and Tone

An effective argument is most often written in a direct and formal style. The style and tone you choose in an argument should not be an afterthought—the way you express your argument can either drive home your ideas or detract from them. Even as you argue in favor of your viewpoint, take care to remain objective in tone—avoid using loaded language when discussing opposing claims.

EXAMPLES

Informal style: The park will help out the whole city, so they should be the ones to fork out for it.	**Formal style:** Because the benefits of the park include everyone in the city, it is logical for the city to provide the funding for the project.

continued

Biased tone: It doesn't make any sense to be against this plan.	**Objective tone:** Arguments opposing this plan have been refuted by statistics from many sources.
Inattention to conventions: We need to make this dream a reality!	**Attention to conventions:** This proposal, which will greatly benefit the community at little cost, deserves City Council attention.

Conclude Your Argument

Your conclusion may range from a sentence to a full paragraph, but it must wrap up your argument in a satisfying way; a conclusion that sounds tacked-on helps your argument no more than providing no conclusion at all. A strong conclusion is a logical extension of the argument you have presented. It carries forth your ideas through an inference, question, quotation, or challenge.

EXAMPLES

Inference: Support for a safe and enjoyable city begins with our youth.

Question: Who doesn't want to live in an active city with engaged young people?

Quotation: As the First Lady's Let's Move campaign points out, "community leaders can promote physical fitness by . . . revitalizing parks, playgrounds, and community centers; and by providing fun and affordable sports and fitness programs."

Challenge: Facilities of this type make the difference between an average city and a truly great one.

Writing
Informative Essays

Most of the Performance Tasks in this book ask you to write informational or explanatory essays in which you present a topic and examine it thoughtfully, through a well-organized analysis of relevant content. Any informative or explanatory essay that you create should include the following parts and features.

Introduce Your Topic

Develop a strong **thesis statement**. That is, clearly state your **topic** and the **organizational framework** through which you will connect or distinguish elements of your topic. For example, you might state that your essay will compare ideas, examine causes and effects, or explore a problem and its solutions.

EXAMPLES

Topic: animal shelters
Sample Thesis Statements
Compare-contrast: To decide whether to adopt a pet from a shelter or buy one from a breeder, consider the costs and then benefits of each source.
Cause-effect: While the causes of overcrowding in community animal shelters aren't difficult to guess at, the results are often hidden from the public eye.
Problem-solution: Our town's animal shelter faces a growing problem with overcrowding, but through community action we can manage the issue.

Clarifying the organizational framework up front will help you organize the body of your essay, suggest **headers** you can use to guide your readers, and help you identify **graphics** that you may need to clarify information. For example, if you compare and contrast the costs and benefits of adopting versus buying a pet, you might create a chart like the one shown to guide your writing. You could include the same chart in your essay as a graphic for readers. The row or column headings serve as natural paragraph headings.

	Animal Shelter	Reputable Breeding Facility
Costs	Minimal fee to cover spay/neuter and immunization costs	Usually several hundred dollars
Benefits	Knowledge that you have rescued a pet from a crowded kennel and probably euthanasia	Getting a specific pedigree with predictable traits

Develop Your Topic

In the body of your essay, flesh out the organizational framework you established in your introduction with strong supporting paragraphs. Include only support directly relevant to your topic. Don't rely on a single source, and make sure the sources you do use are reputable and current. The following table illustrates types of support you might use to develop aspects of your topic. It also shows how transitions link text sections, create cohesion, and clarify the relationships among ideas.

Types of Support in Informative Essays	Uses of Transitions in Informative Essays
Facts and examples: <u>One cause</u> of overcrowding is economic hardship; <u>for example,</u> when home foreclosures increase, the population of animal shelters also rises.	*One cause* signals the shift from the introduction to the body text in a cause-and-effect essay. *For example* introduces the support for the cause being cited.

continued

Types of Support in Explanatory/ Informative Essays	Uses of Transitions in Explanatory/ Informative Essays
Concrete details: On the other hand, if you want to choose from among a wide variety of dogs, visit your local shelter. Our shelter currently lists German shepherds, a labradoodle, a Pomeranian, and dozens more on its Website.	*On the other hand* transitions the reader from one point of comparison to another in a compare-contrast essay.
Statistics: Turn to the Humane Society of the United States if you doubt the scope of the problem. The HSUS estimates that shelters euthanize 3 to 4 million cats and dogs annually.	The entire transitional sentence introduces the part of a problem-solution essay that demonstrates the existence of a problem.

You can't always include all of the information you'd like to in a short essay, but you can plan to point readers directly to useful **multimedia links** either in the body of or at the end of your essay.

Use Appropriate Style and Tone

Use **formal English** to establish your credibility as a source of information. To project authority, use the language of the domain, or field, that you are writing about. However, be sure to define unfamiliar terms to avoid using jargon your audience may not know. Provide extended definitions when your audience is likely to have limited knowledge of the topic. Using quotations from reputable sources can also give your text authority; be sure to credit the source of quoted material. In general, keep the tone objective, avoiding using slang or biased expressions.

Informal, jargon-filled, biased language: Puppy mill owners should be forced to live as horribly as the animals they raise. They have no feelings for the pooches they proliferate except maybe greed for the coin these cash cows create.

Extended definition in formal style and objective tone: A "puppy mill" refers to a large-scale dog breeding operation that places profit before the well-being of its dogs, often housing them in tight quarters, forcing them to breed continuously, and neglecting their emotional, physical, and genetic health. According to Melanie Kahn, an HSUS spokesperson, "Many people don't realize that when they buy a puppy from a pet store or online they are likely supporting a puppy mill."

Conclusion

Wrap up your essay with a concluding statement or section that sums up or extends the information in your essay.

EXAMPLES

Articulate implications: Twenty-five percent of dogs in shelters are purebred. If we can encourage people who would normally seek a purebred dog from a breeder to adopt a shelter pet instead, we can significantly reduce the number of animals euthanized each year.

Emphasize significance: The number of pets languishing in shelters each year is small compared to the number of pets owned by U.S. households; a fractional increase in household pet ownership could save these animals from euthanasia.

Writing Narratives

When you are writing a fictional tale, an autobiographical incident, or a firsthand biography, you write in the narrative mode. That means telling a story with a beginning, a climax, and a conclusion. Though there are important differences between fictional and nonfiction narratives, you use similar processes to develop them.

Identify a Problem, Situation, or Observation

For a nonfiction **narrative,** dig into your memory bank for a problem you dealt with or an observation you've made about your life. For fiction, try to invent a problem or situation that can unfold in interesting ways.

EXAMPLES

Problem (nonfiction)	Last year I wanted to raise money to participate in a class trip to Washington, D.C.
Situation (fiction)	A social media website user periodically notices mysterious changes to his "status."

Establish a Point of View

Decide who will tell your story. If you are writing a reflective essay about an important experience or person in your own life, you will be the **narrator** of the events you relate. If you are writing a work of fiction, you can choose to create a first person narrator or tell the story from the third-person point of view. In that case, the narrator can focus on one character or reveal the thoughts and feelings of all the characters. These examples show the differences between a first- and third-person narrator.

EXAMPLES

First-person narrator (nonfiction)	Seven hundred fifty dollars: That's what it would cost me to go on the class trip to Washington D.C., but it might as well have been a million dollars.
Third-person narrator (fiction)	Peter's fingers froze over the "What's new with you" prompt of his status page. The box was already filled out, waiting for him to press the Update key. "My mom found a new job!" said the box. Peter hadn't written those words. And, as far as he knew, his mother had stopped looking for work months ago.

Gather Details

To make real or imaginary experiences come alive on the page, you will need to use **narrative techniques** like description and dialogue. Use the questions in the left column of the following chart to help you search your memory or imagination for the details that will form the basis of your narrative. You don't have to respond in full sentences, but try to capture the sights, sounds, and feelings that bring your narrative to life.

Who, What, When, Where?	Narrative Techniques
People: Who are the people or characters involved in the experience? What did they look like? What did they do? What did they say?	**Description:** Mr. Maguire, social studies teacher. Wears funny ties and cracks jokes but doesn't get to know students personally, in my opinion. **Dialogue:** He once said, "The families in this town are completely removed from the problems of two-thirds of the world." I said under my breath, "You don't know my family."

continued

Who, What, When, Where?	Narrative Techniques
Experience: What led up to or caused the event? What is the main event in the experience? What happened as a result of the event?	**Description:** A big deposit for the class trip—$200—would be due by Thanksgiving; I knew my family didn't have the cash. I would have to figure out a way to raise it myself. When schools were closed after a blizzard, I got my chance. After stoking up the courage to knock on doors, I shoveled until my blistered hands were numb, my back ached, and my clothes were wet with freezing perspiration.
Places: When and where did the events take place? What were the sights, sounds, and smells of this place?	**Description:** Fall of eighth grade—it was the last year of middle school and we felt special—top of the heap. The smell of autumn filled the air—decaying leaves, wood-burning stoves. Local farmers were predicting an early and rough winter.

Sequence Events

Before you begin writing, list the key events of the experience or story in **chronological,** or time, order. Place a star next to the point of highest tension—for example, the point at which a key decision determines the outcome of events. In fiction, this point is called the **climax,** but a gripping nonfiction narrative will also have a climactic event.

To build **suspense**—the uncertainty a reader feels about what will happen next—you'll want to think about the **pacing** or rhythm of your narrative. Consider disrupting the chronological order of events by beginning at the end and then starting over. Or interrupt the forward progression or flow of events with a **flashback,** which takes the reader to an earlier point in the narrative.

Another way to build suspense is with **multiple plot lines.** For example, the personal narrative about the class trip involves a second plot line in which a snowstorm is bearing down on the narrator's hometown. Both plot lines intersect when the narrator shovels snow for a week and as a result raises money for the class trip.

First Draft	Revision
My father, who is an incurable optimist, said the storm could be the break I needed.	Wiggling his eyebrows, my father said, "When life gives you a snowstorm, invest in a snow shovel!" [telling details]
Piles of snow were everywhere, and people couldn't get out of their driveways.	Snow banks three feet high lined the streets, and neighbors batted kitchen brooms at the snow around their cars. [precise words and phrases]
Peter felt weirded out by the mysterious post on his "What's new with you" page.	As Peter read the mysterious post, the tiny hairs at the base of his scalp rose and his palms sweated. [sensory details]

Conclude Your Narrative

At the conclusion of the narrative, you or your narrator will reflect on the meaning of the events. The conclusion should follow logically from the climactic moment of the narrative. The narrator of a personal narrative usually reflects on the significance of the experience—the lessons learned or the legacy left.

EXAMPLE

The school steps were piled with luggage that balmy Friday as excited students waited to board the buses. I stood by, remembering the tingle of frostbite in my fingertips and the ache in my back from that marathon week of shoveling snow. This scene, the one before me now, is what had kept me going. Straightening my back and flexing my fingers, I reached down and picked up my bag. With a satisfied smile, I joined my friends on the bus.

Conducting Research

The Performance Tasks in this book will require you to complete research projects related to the texts you've read in the collections. Whether the topic is stated in a Performance Task or is one you generate, the following information will guide you through your research project.

Focus Your Research and Formulate a Question

Some topics for a research project can be effectively covered in three pages; others require an entire book for a thorough treatment. Begin by developing a topic that is neither too narrow nor too broad for the time frame of the assignment. Also check your school and local libraries and databases to help you determine how to choose your topic. If there's too little information, you'll need to broaden your focus; if there's too much, you'll need to limit it.

With a topic in hand, formulate a **research question;** it will keep you on track as you conduct your research. A good research question cannot be answered in a single word and should be open-ended. It should require investigation. You can also develop related research questions to explore your topic in more depth.

EXAMPLES

Possible topics for the *Odyssey*	The hero Odysseus—too broad
	The monster the Cyclops—too narrow
	Settings and events—fact or fiction?
Possible research question	To what degree are settings and events in the *Odyssey* based on fact?
Related questions	If any of the events are real, where did they take place?
	To what extent do historians agree or disagree on which aspects of the *Odyssey* are real?

Locate and Evaluate Sources

To find answers to your research question, you'll need to investigate primary and secondary sources, whether in print or digital formats. **Primary sources** contain original, firsthand information, such as diaries, autobiographies, interviews, speeches, and eyewitness accounts. **Secondary sources** provide other people's versions of primary sources in encyclopedias, newspaper and magazine articles, biographies, and documentaries.

Your search for sources begins at the library and on the Internet. Use advanced search features to help you find things quickly. Add a minus sign (-) before a word that should not appear in your results. Use an asterisk (*) in place of unknown words. List the name of and location of each possible source, adding comments about its potential usefulness. Assessing, or evaluating, your sources is an important step in the research process. Your goal is to use sources that are **credible,** or reliable and trustworthy.

Criteria for Assessing Sources	
Relevance: It covers the target aspect of my topic.	• How will the source be useful in answering my research question?
Accuracy: It includes information that can be verified by more than one authoritative source.	• Is the information up-to-date? Are the facts accurate? How can I verify them? • What qualifies the author to write about this topic? Is he or she an authority?
Objectivity: It presents multiple viewpoints on the topic.	• What, if any, biases can I detect? Does the writer favor one view of the topic?

Incorporate and Cite Sources

When you draft your research project, you'll need to include material from your sources. This material can be **direct quotations, summaries,** or **paraphrases** of the original source material. Two well-known **style manuals** provide information on how to cite a range of print and digital sources: the *MLA Handbook for Writers of Research Papers* (published by the Modern Language Association) and Kate L. Turabian's *A Manual for Writers of Research Papers, Theses, and Dissertations* (published by The University of Chicago Press). Both style manuals provide a wealth of information about conducting, formatting, drafting, and presenting your research, including guidelines for citing sources within the text (called parenthetical citations) and preparing the list of Works Cited, as well as correct use of the mechanics of writing. Your teacher will indicate which style manual you should use. The following examples use the format in the *MLA Handbook*.

Any material from sources must be completely documented, or you will commit **plagiarism,** the unauthorized use of someone else's words or ideas. Plagiarism is not honest. As you take notes for your research project, be sure to keep complete information about your sources so that you can cite them correctly in the body of your paper. This applies to all sources, whether print or digital. Having complete information will also enable you to prepare the list of Works Cited. The list of Works Cited, which concludes your research project, provides author, title, and publication information for both print and digital sources. The following pages show the *MLA Handbook's* Works Cited citation formats for a variety of sources.

EXAMPLES

Direct quotation [The writer is citing the poet Homer's word in the *Odyssey*, page 74.]	In Book Four of the *Odyssey,* Menelaus describes the island of Pharos as "as far out as the distance a hollow ship can make in a whole day's sailing" (Homer 74).
Summary [The writer is summarizing the conclusion of Tim Severin on page 75 of *The Ulysses Voyage: Sea Search for the Odyssey*.]	Severin was unable to trace Odysseus' journey exactly and found many parts of Homer's tale puzzling. He concluded that the geographies of folklore and navigation overlapped (245).
Paraphrase [The writer is paraphrasing, or stating in her own words, material from page 25 of Bernard Knox's book and from the *Brittanica Student Encyclopedia* on the Homeric Legend.]	The third-century-B.C. geographer Eratosthenes, for example, thought that Homer's story was completely imaginary (Knox 25; "Homeric Legend").

MLA Citation Guidelines

Today, you can find free websites that generate ready-made citations for research papers, using the information you provide. Such sites have some time-saving advantages when you're developing a Works Cited list. However, you should always check your citations carefully before you turn in your final paper. If you are following MLA style, use these guidelines to evaluate and finalize your work.

Books

One author

Severin, Tim. *The Ulysses Voyage: Sea Search for the Odyssey.* London: Hutchinson, 1987. Print.

Two authors or editors

Steiner, George, and Robert Fagles, eds. *Homer: A Collection of Critical Essays.* Englewood Cliffs: Prentice, 1962. Print.

Three authors

Heubeck, Alfred, Stephanie West, and J. B. Hainsworth. *A Commentary on Homer's Odyssey.* New York: Oxford UP, 1988. Print.

Four or more authors

The abbreviation et al. means "and others." Use et al. instead of listing all the authors.

Melick, Peter, et al. *The Odyssey Explained.* New York: Garden UP, 1997. Print.

No author given

Greek Literature: An Overview. New York: Sunrise, 1993. Print.

An author and a translator

Homer. *The Odyssey of Homer: A Modern Translation.* Trans. Richmond Lattimore. New York: Harper, 1967. Print.

An author, a translator, and an editor

La Fontaine, Jean de. *Selected Fables.* Trans. Christopher Wood. Ed. Maya Slater. New York: Oxford UP, 1995. Print.

Parts of Books

An introduction, a preface, a foreword, or an afterword written by someone other than the author(s) of a work

Knox, Bernard. Introduction. *The Odyssey of Homer.* Trans. Robert Fagles. New York: Penguin, 1996. 3–64. Print.

A poem, a short story, an essay, or a chapter in a collection of works by one author

Sappho. "He Is More Than a Hero." *The Works of Sappho.* Trans. Edward Osmond. New York: Garden UP, 1990. 53. Print.

A poem, a short story, an essay, or a chapter in an anthology of works by several authors

Solonos, Costa. "Journeys." Trans. Carl Foreman. *Greek Voices.* Ed. Katharine Greene and Gerald Spencer. London: Greenwood, 1985. 83–85. Print.

A novel or a play in a collection

Sophocles. *Antigone. The Three Theban Plays.* Trans. Robert Fagles. New York: Penguin, 1984. Print.

Magazines, Newspapers, and Encyclopedias

An article in a newspaper

Wilford, John Noble. "Was Troy a Metropolis? Homer Isn't Talking." *New York Times* 22 Oct. 2002: D1+. Print.

An article in a magazine

Severin, Tim. "The Quest for Ulysses." *National Geographic* Aug. 1986: 194–225. Print.

An article in an encyclopedia

"Homer." *The World Book Encyclopedia.* 2000 ed. Print.

Miscellaneous Nonprint Sources

An interview

Baldwin, Richard. Personal interview. 13 Mar. 2011.

A video recording

The Odyssey of Troy. A&E Home Video, 1994. DVD.

Electronic Publications

A CD-ROM

"Homeric Legend." *Britannica Student Encyclopedia.* 2004 ed. Chicago: Encyclopaedia Britannica, 2004. CD-ROM.

A document from an Internet site

Entries for online sources should contain as much of the information shown as available.

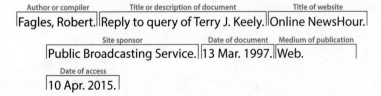

Struck, Peter. "Map of Odysseus' Journey." Mythology. Course pages. Dept. of Classical Studies, U of Pennsylvania. 2004. Web. 9 Mar. 2011.

Participating in a Collaborative Discussion

Often, class activities, including the Performance Tasks in this book, will require you to work collaboratively with classmates. Whether your group will analyze a work of literature or try to solve a community problem, use the following guidelines to ensure a productive discussion.

Prepare for the Discussion

A productive discussion is one in which all the participants bring useful information and ideas to share. If your group will discuss a short story the class read, first re-read and annotate a copy of the story. Your annotations will help you quickly locate evidence to support your points.

Participants in a discussion about an important issue should first research the issue and bring notes or information sources that will help guide the group. If you disagree with a point made by another group member, your case will be stronger if you back it up with specific evidence from your sources.

EXAMPLES

Disagreeing without evidence: It doesn't make sense to be concerned about the school's environmental footprint.

Providing evidence for disagreement: I disagree about the relevance of environmental concerns to our school community. Several national environmental organizations point out that schools can play an important role in reducing the community's environmental footprint.

Set Ground Rules

The rules your group needs will depend on what your group is expected to accomplish. A discussion of themes in a poem will be unlikely to produce a single consensus; however, a discussion aimed at developing a solution to a problem should result in one strong proposal that all group members support. Answer the following questions to set ground rules that fit your group's purpose:

- What will this group produce? A range of ideas, a single decision, a plan of action, or something else?
- How much time is available? How much of that time should be allotted to each part of our discussion (presenting ideas, summarizing or voting on final ideas, creating a product such as a written analysis or a speech)?
- What roles need to be assigned within the group? Do we need a leader, a note-taker, a timekeeper, or other specific roles?
- What is the best way to synthesize our group's ideas? Should we take a vote, list group members as "for" or "against" in a chart, or use some other method to reach consensus or sum up the results of the discussion?

Move the Discussion Forward

Everyone in the group should be actively involved in synthesizing ideas. To make sure this happens, ask questions that draw out ideas, especially from less-talkative members of the group. If an idea or statement is confusing, try to paraphrase it or ask the speaker to explain more about it. If you disagree with a statement, say so politely and explain in detail why you disagree.

SAMPLE DISCUSSION

EFFECTIVE BEHAVIOR	WHAT IT LOOKS LIKE
Support others' contributions. In this example, Raul realizes that Kenisha's views are different from his. Instead of interrupting, he listens carefully to make sure he understands her evidence and what she thinks it means.	Raul listens to Kenisha while she presents her research and views on how to calculate their school's environmental footprint. "I read that article, too," Raul thinks to himself. "Then I read a more recent article that included a much longer list of considerations than those that were in the first article. I'll make a note about it and let Kenisha finish."
State your own views thoughtfully. As the discussion continues, Raul explains how his research turned up different results. He shows that he has used a reliable source.	"I read the same article Kenisha did," Raul begins, "but I found a more recent and I think more useful article on sustainable building in the journal *Architectural Engineering and Construction*. It describes how one high school calculated its environmental footprint before building a new addition."

Respond to Ideas

In a diverse group, everyone may have a different perspective on the topic of discussion, and that's a good thing. Consider what everyone has to say, and don't resist changing your view if other group members provide convincing evidence for theirs. If, instead, you feel more strongly than ever about your view, don't hesitate to say so and provide reasons related to what those with opposing views have said. Before wrapping up the discussion, try to sum up the points on which your group agrees and disagrees.

SAMPLE DISCUSSION

EFFECTIVE BEHAVIOR	WHAT IT LOOKS LIKE
Summarize agreements and disagreements. Cecilia compares the key points. She notices that Raul and Kenisha agree except for one point.	Cecilia is going to speak next, but rather than silently rehearsing her views, she compares Raul's views with Kenisha's. "Raul listed the same five considerations that Kenisha did. The only difference between them is how water consumption is calculated."
Justify your views or consider new ones. Considering Cecilia's comments, Raul sees that he and Kenisha differ on one point. He can justify his view but is willing to combine his approach with Kenisha's and Cecilia's.	Cecilia points out that Kenisha's and Raul's views differ in only one important respect. As Raul listens to Cecilia's summary, he thinks, "Cecilia is right. Kenisha's view and mine are almost the same except for one issue." He makes a mental note of this and continues to listen to Cecilia for more information and insight.

Debating an Issue

The selection and collection Performance Tasks in this text will direct you to engage in debates about issues relating to the selections you've read. Use the guidelines that follow to have a productive and balanced argument about both sides of an issue.

The Structure of a Formal Debate

In a debate, two teams compete to win the support of the audience about an issue. In a **formal debate,** two teams, each with three members, present their arguments on a given **proposition** or **policy statement.** One team argues for the proposition or statement and the other team argues against it. Each debater must consider the proposition closely and must research both sides of it. To argue convincingly either for or against a proposition, a debater must be familiar with both sides of the issue.

Plan the Debate

The purpose of a debate is to allow participants and audience members to consider both sides of an issue. Use these planning suggestions to hold a balanced and productive debate:

- **Identify Debate Teams** Form groups of six members based on the issue presented in the Performance Task. Three members of the team will argue for the **affirmative side** of the issue—that is, they support the issue. The other three members will argue for the **negative side** of the issue—that is, they do not support the issue.
- **Appoint a Moderator** The moderator will present the topic and goals of the debate, keep track of the time, and introduce and thank the participants.
- **Research and Prepare Notes** Search the texts you've read as well as print and online sources for **valid reasons** and **evidence** to support your team's claim. As with argument, be sure to anticipate possible opposing claims and compile evidence to counter those claims. You will use notes from your research during the debate.

- **Assign Debate Roles** One team member will introduce the team's **claim** and supporting evidence. Another team member will respond to questions and **opposing claims** in an exchange with a member of the opposing team. The last member will present a strong closing argument.

Hold the Debate

A formal debate is not a shouting match—rather, a well-run debate is an excellent forum for participants to express their viewpoints, build on others' ideas, and have a thoughtful, well-reasoned exchange of ideas. The moderator will begin by stating the topic or issue and introducing the participants. Participants should follow the moderator's instructions concerning whose turn it is to speak and how much time each speaker has.

FORMAL DEBATE FORMAT

SPEAKER	ROLE	TIME
Affirmative Speaker 1	Present the claim and supporting evidence for the affirmative ("pro") side of the argument.	5 minutes
Negative Speaker 1	Ask probing questions that will prompt the other team to address flaws in the argument.	3 minutes
Affirmative Speaker 2	Respond to the questions posed by the opposing team and counter any concerns.	3 minutes

continued

SPEAKER	ROLE	TIME
Negative Speaker 2	Respond to any questions posed by the opposing team, and counter any concerns.	5 minutes
Affirmative Speaker 3	Summarize the claim and evidence for the affirmative side, and explain why your reasoning is more valid.	3 minutes
Negative Speaker 3	Summarize the claim and evidence for the negative side, and explain why your reasoning is more valid.	3 minutes

Evaluate the Debate

Use the following guidelines to evaluate a team in a debate:

- Did the team prove that the issue is significant? How thorough was the analysis?
- How did the team effectively argue that you should support their affirmative or negative side of the proposition or issue?
- How effectively did the team present reasons and evidence, including evidence from the texts, to support the proposition?
- How effectively did the team rebut, or respond to, arguments made by the opposing team?
- Did the speakers maintain eye contact and speak at an appropriate rate and volume?
- Did the speakers observe proper debate etiquette—that is, did they follow the moderator's instructions, stay within their allotted time limits, and treat their opponents respectfully?

Reading Arguments

An **argument** expresses a position on an issue or problem and supports it with reasons and evidence. Being able to analyze and evaluate arguments will help you distinguish between claims you should accept and those you should not.

Analyzing an Argument

A sound argument should appeal strictly to reason. An argument includes the following elements:

- A **claim** (or **thesis** or **controlling idea**) is the writer's position on an issue or problem.
- **Support** is any material that serves to prove a claim. In an argument, support usually consists of reasons and evidence.
- **Reasons** are declarations made to justify an action, decision, or belief.
- **Evidence** is the specific references, quotations, facts, examples, and opinions that support a claim. Evidence may also consist of statistics, reports of personal experience, or the views of experts.
- **Counterarguments** and **counterclaims** are arguments made to oppose other arguments. A good argument anticipates opposing counterclaims by providing counterarguments to answer them.

Claim	My curfew should be extended from 11 P.M. to midnight on Saturday night.

Reason	I don't have enough time to spend with my friends on weekdays because of homework and my job.

Evidence	On weekends I spend four hours doing homework and four hours at my job.

Counter-argument	I know that it's difficult for you to sleep when I'm out late, but you need to trust that I'll be home by midnight and give me a chance to prove it.

On the second Monday in October, Americans celebrate Columbus Day. We honor the Italian explorer who has been credited with discovering the Americas in 1492. Some people, however, think that we need to look more closely at what Christopher Columbus actually did and at his place in our history. I am one of those people.

First of all, although we honor Columbus as the first European to set foot in the Americas, he may not have been the first. Archaeologists have found Norse ruins in Greenland and what is now Newfoundland, dating from around AD 1000. This evidence seems to prove that Vikings actually reached the North American continent nearly 500 years before Columbus ever left the shores of Spain.

Second, although Columbus did reach the Americas, he did not discover them. Millions of people were already living here when he arrived.

Defenders of Columbus argue that, in a way, he did discover the Americas. Even if he wasn't the first European to set foot on the land, his voyages made the rest of the world aware of the Americas. In the years following Columbus' voyages, Europeans came to establish colonies and to explore the land.

I argue that this spread of culture brought great harm as well as great good to the Americas. The Europeans who came to the Americas brought deadly diseases with them. The native people had no immunity to such diseases as mumps, measles, smallpox, and typhus. As a result, hundreds of thousands of people died.

In conclusion, I don't suggest that people should boycott their local Columbus Day parades. I do think, though, that we should create a more balanced picture of the man we're honoring.

Recognizing Persuasive Techniques

Argumentative texts typically rely on more than just the logical appeal of an argument to be convincing. They also rely on **persuasive techniques**—devices that can sway you to adopt a position or take an action. Persuasive techniques are used in advertising, political speeches, films, and fundraisers. The chart shown here explains several ways a writer may attempt to sway you to adopt his or her position. Learn to recognize these techniques, and you will be less likely to be influenced by them.

Persuasive Technique	Example
Appeals by Association	
Bandwagon appeal Uses the argument that a person should believe or do something because "everyone else" does	More and more people are making the switch to Discountline long-distance service.
Testimonial Relies on endorsements from well-known people or satisfied customers	Pierre DuPont, world-class rock climber, would be left hanging without DuraTwine rope.
Snob appeal Taps into people's desire to be special or part of an elite group	Treat yourself to Tropical Paradise because, after all, you deserve the best under the sun.
Transfer Connects a product, candidate, or cause with a positive emotion or idea	Freedom . . . you can feel it the instant you put your hands on the wheel of a Farnsworth 4 × 4 SL.
Appeal to loyalty Relies on people's affiliation with a particular group	This car is made in America by Americans.
Emotional Appeals	
Appeals to pity, fear, or vanity Use strong feelings, rather than facts, to persuade	Without more police, we'll be at the mercy of thieves.

Word Choice

Glittering generality Makes a generalization that includes a word or phrase with positive connotations, such as freedom and honor, to promote a product or idea.	A vote for Evan Smith is a vote for democracy.

Practice and Apply

Identify the persuasive techniques used in the model.

Indiana and Issun Boshi— Building Another Great Team

Indiana is basketball country. Names like Bobby Knight, Larry Bird, and Isaiah Thomas have added greatness to the game for over a quarter century.

That's why Issun Boshi, Japan's leading automobile company, chose Indiana as its U.S. teammate. The new plant will produce 150,000 new vehicles a year, built by 25,000 hard-working Hoosiers just like you. In addition, many of those workers will be driving the cars they make at a special discount—that's only fair; that's the American way. It's how we play the game.

Just ask Indiana sportscaster Wally Elliot, who says, "Issun Boshi and Hoosier pride— now that's what I call an expansion team."

Analyzing Logic and Reasoning

When you evaluate an argument, you need to look closely at the writer's logic and reasoning. To do this, it is helpful to identify the type of reasoning the writer is using.

The Inductive Mode of Reasoning

When a writer leads from specific evidence to a general principle or generalization, that writer is using **inductive reasoning.** Here is an example of inductive reasoning.

Specific Facts

Fact 1 The American Society of Composers, Authors, and Publishers (ASCAP) was formed on Friday, February 13, 1914, to collect royalties on copyrighted music.

continued

Specific Facts

Fact 2 The licensing of the first female flight instructor took place on Friday, October 13, 1939.

Fact 3 On Friday, February 13, 1948, Orville Wright announced that he was giving the famous flying machine *Kitty Hawk* to the Smithsonian Institution.

Generalization

Good things can happen on Friday the 13th.

Strategies for Evaluating Inductive Arguments

Ask yourself the following questions to evaluate an inductive argument:

- **Is the evidence valid and sufficient support for the conclusion?** Inaccurate facts lead to inaccurate conclusions.
- **Does the conclusion follow logically from the evidence?** From the facts listed in the previous example, the conclusion that good things happen only on Friday the 13th would be too broad a generalization.
- **Is the evidence drawn from a large enough sample?** Even though there are only three facts listed above, the sample is large enough to support the claim. If you wanted to support the conclusion that only good things happen on Friday the 13th, the sample is not large enough.

The Deductive Mode of Reasoning

When a writer arrives at a conclusion by applying a general principle to a specific situation, the writer is using **deductive reasoning.** Here's an example.

Journalism that stretches the truth is deceptive.	General principle or premise
Hollywood Snoop Magazine stretches the truth.	Specific situation
Hollywood Snoop Magazine practices deceptive journalism.	Specific conclusion

Strategies for Evaluating Deductive Arguments

Ask yourself the following questions to evaluate a deductive argument:

- **Is the general principle actually stated, or is it implied?** Note that writers often use deductive reasoning in an argument without stating the general principle. They just assume that readers will recognize and agree with the principle. So you may want to identify the general principle for yourself.
- **Is the general principle sound?** Don't just assume the general principle is sound. Ask yourself whether it is really true.
- **Is the conclusion valid?** To be valid, a conclusion in a deductive argument must follow logically from the general principle and the specific situation.

The following chart shows two conclusions drawn from the same general principle.

All team members wore school colors on Friday.	
Accurate Deduction	**Inaccurate Deduction**
Mara is on the volleyball team; therefore, Mara wore school colors on Friday.	Jaime wore school colors on Friday; therefore, Jaime is on a school team.

Jaime could have worn school colors in support of a team without being a member.

Practice and Apply

Identify the mode of reasoning used in the following paragraph.

Preteens and teenagers have access to a range of technology that their parents didn't have. Information that was once hard to find can now be obtained easily on the Internet. Smart phones provide many ways to communicate—text messages, social media sites, and decreasingly, old-fashioned phone calls. The effect is a childhood different than that experienced in the past.

Identifying Faulty Reasoning

Sometimes an argument at first appears to make sense but isn't valid because it is based on a fallacy. A fallacy is an error in logic. Learn to recognize these common **rhetorical** and **logical fallacies.**

Type of Fallacy	Definition	Example
Circular reasoning	Supporting a statement by simply repeating it in different words	Teenagers should avoid fad diets, because it is important for **adolescents to stay away from popular weight-loss plans.**
Either/or fallacy	A statement that suggests that there are only two choices available in a situation that really offers more than two options	**Either** students should be allowed to leave school to have lunch at nearby fast-food restaurants, **or** they should be allowed to choose the cafeteria menu.
Oversimplification	An explanation of a complex situation or problem as if it were much simpler than it is	Making the team depends on **whether the coach likes you.**
Overgeneralization	A generalization that is too broad. You can often recognize overgeneralizations by the use of words such as *all, everyone, every time, anything, no one,* and *none.*	**No one** cares that there is not enough parking downtown.
Stereotyping	A dangerous type of overgeneralization. Stereotypes are broad statements about people on the basis of their gender, ethnicity, race, or political, social, professional, or religious group.	The only thing **the members of that political party** care about is big business.
Attacking the person or name-calling	An attempt to discredit an idea by attacking the person or group associated with it. Candidates often engage in name-calling during political campaigns.	**My opponent is not smart enough** to be mayor.
Evading the issue	Refuting an objection with arguments and evidence that do not address its central point	Yes, I broke my campaign promise not to raise taxes, **but higher taxes have led to increases in police patrols, paved highways, and smaller class size in schools.**
Non sequitur	A statement that uses irrelevant "proof" to support a claim. A non sequitur is sometimes used to win an argument by diverting the reader's attention to proof that can't be challenged.	I know I'll pass math. **Mr. Gray is my math teacher and my football coach.**
False cause	The mistake of assuming that because one event occurred after another event in time, the first event caused the second one to occur	The mayor declared a get-tough crime policy, and sure enough, **crime rates dropped.**

Type of Fallacy	Definition	Example
False analogy	A comparison that doesn't hold up because of a critical difference between the two subjects	She walks to the store and back every day, **so surely she can walk in the 10K race.**
Hasty generalization	A conclusion drawn from too little evidence or from evidence that is biased	That corner must be dangerous. **There were two car accidents there last week.**

Practice and Apply

Look for examples of logical fallacies in the following argument. Identify each one and explain why you identified it as such.

Watching television causes a child's grades to drop. What other conclusion can be drawn? Money-hungry media moguls produce horrible programming just to sell advertising time. These programs interfere with children's thinking. If you say television isn't bad for children, you would probably say the earth is flat. Parents who care should at least limit their children's viewing. The most responsible parents should turn off the TV—permanently. They can either unplug the TV or expect their children to become uneducated slugs.

Evaluating Arguments

Learning how to evaluate a text's arguments and identify bias will help you become more selective when doing research and also help you improve your own reasoning and arguing skills. **Bias** is an inclination for or against a particular opinion or viewpoint. A writer may reveal a strongly positive or negative opinion on an issue by presenting only one way of looking at it or by heavily weighting the evidence on one side of the argument. Additionally, the presence of either of the following is often a sign that a writer is biased:

Loaded language consists of words with strongly positive or negative connotations that are intended to influence a reader's attitude.

EXAMPLE

The safety of our children depends on our driving the savage criminals out of this horrible neighborhood. (*Savage* and *horrible* have very negative connotations.)

Propaganda is any form of communication that is so distorted that it conveys false or misleading information. Some politicians create and distribute propaganda. Logical fallacies are often used in propaganda. For instance, the following example shows an oversimplification. The writer uses one fact to support a particular point of view but does not reveal another fact that does not support that viewpoint.

EXAMPLE

Since the new park opened, vandalism in the area has increased by 10 percent. Clearly, the park has had a negative impact on the area. (The writer does not include the fact that the vandalism was caused by people who were not drawn into the area by the park.)

Strategies for Evaluating Evidence

It is important to have a set of standards by which you can evaluate arguments. Use the questions below to help you critically assess an argument.

- **Are the facts presented credible and thus verifiable?** Facts can be proved by eyewitness accounts, authoritative sources such as encyclopedias and almanacs, experts, or research.

- **Are the opinions presented well substantiated?** Any opinions offered should be supported by facts, be based on research or eyewitness accounts, or be the opinions of experts on the topic.

- **Is the evidence relevant and sufficient?** Relevant evidence applies to the conclusion, and sufficient evidence leaves no reasonable questions unanswered. If a choice is offered, background for making the choice should be provided. If taking a side is called for, all sides of the issue should be presented.

- **Is the evidence biased?** Be alert to evidence that contains loaded language or other signs of bias.
- **Is the evidence authoritative?** The people, groups, or organizations that provided the evidence should have credentials that support their authority.
- **Is it important that the evidence be current?** Where timeliness is crucial, as in the areas of medicine and technology, the evidence should reflect the latest developments in the areas.

Practice and Apply

Read the argument below. Identify the facts, opinion, and elements of bias.

Why are students who show up late for tests, fill in answers randomly, and then snooze for the rest of the period allowed to jeopardize school test scores and reduce the quality of instruction for motivated kids? The answer is simple—compulsory attendance laws. These laws say that kids must be in school. But a study by economists William Landes and Lewis Solomon found little evidence that such laws increase attendance rates at all. Why not tell poor attenders, who are almost always failing too, "You're done. You don't belong here." Private schools do it, and the ability to expel students contributes to a positive climate.

Strategies for Determining a Strong Argument

Make sure that all or most of the following statements are true:

- The argument presents a claim or controlling idea.
- The claim is connected to its support by a general principle that most readers would readily agree with. Valid general principle: *It is the job of a school to provide a well-rounded physical education program.* Invalid general principle: *It is the job of a school to produce healthy, physically fit people.*
- The reasons make sense.
- The reasons are presented in a logical and effective order.
- The claim and all reasons are adequately supported by sound evidence.
- The evidence is sufficient, credible, and relevant.

- The logic is sound. There are no instances of faulty reasoning.
- The argument adequately anticipates and addresses reader concerns and counterclaims with counterarguments.

Practice and Apply

Use the preceding criteria to evaluate the strength of the following editorial.

According to veterinarian and animal-rights advocate Dr. Michael W. Fox, more than 100 million animals are used each year in laboratory tests. These animals are used to study such things as the causes and effects of illnesses and to test drugs. This unnecessary and cruel animal testing must be stopped.

The most important reason to stop this testing is that it's wrong to make living creatures suffer. Even though they can't talk or use tools as people do, animals have feelings. Zoologist Ann Speirs says that animals may suffer even more than people do, because they can't understand what's happening to them.

People who favor animal research argue that the medical advances gained justify animal experimentation. They also say that the suffering experienced by the animals is minor. People like that are dumber than any guinea pig or rat.

Another important reason to stop this testing is that everybody knows it isn't reliable. Many drugs that help animals are harmful to people. One example is the drug thalidomide. After it was tested in animals in the 1950s and early 1960s, it was given to pregnant women. More than 10,000 of these women gave birth to handicapped babies. The process works the other way, too. Many drugs that help people kill animals. Two common examples are penicillin and aspirin.

Animal testing also affects the environment. The Animal Protection Service says that a quarter of a million chimpanzees, monkeys, and baboons are taken from their natural homes and used in laboratory experiments every year. Those animals will never be able to reproduce, and whole species may become extinct.

A final reason for not using animals in experiments is that there are other research methods available. Two examples are using bits of animal tissue and cells and using computer models.

In conclusion, animal testing has to stop because it just can't go on.

Grammar

Writing that is full of mistakes can confuse or even annoy a reader. A business letter with a punctuation error might lead to a miscommunication and delay a reply. Or a sentence fragment might lower your grade on an essay. Paying attention to grammar, punctuation, and capitalization rules can make your writing clearer and easier to read.

Quick Reference: Parts of Speech

Part of Speech	Function	Examples
Noun	names a person, a place, a thing, an idea, a quality, or an action	
Common	serves as a general name, or a name common to an entire group	poet, novel, love, journey
Proper	names a specific, one-of-a-kind person, place, or thing	Lewis, Jackson, Pleasant Street, Stanley Cup
Singular	refers to a single person, place, thing, or idea	child, park, flower, truth
Plural	refers to more than one person, place, thing, or idea	children, parks, flowers, truths
Concrete	names something that can be perceived by the senses	roof, flash, Dublin, battle
Abstract	names something that cannot be perceived by the senses	intelligence, fear, joy, loneliness
Compound	expresses a single idea through a combination of two or more words	haircut, father-in-law, Christmas Eve
Collective	refers to a group of people or things	army, flock, class, species
Possessive	shows who or what owns something	Strafford's, Bess's, children's, witnesses'
Pronoun	takes the place of a noun or another pronoun	
Personal	refers to the person making a statement, the person(s) being addressed, or the person(s) or thing(s) the statement is about	I, me, my, mine, we, us, our, ours, you, your, yours, she, he, it, her, him, hers, his, its, they, them, their, theirs
Reflexive	follows a verb or preposition and refers to a preceding noun or pronoun	myself, yourself, herself, himself, itself, ourselves, yourselves, themselves
Intensive	emphasizes a noun or another pronoun	(same as reflexives)
Demonstrative	points to one or more specific persons or things	this, that, these, those

continued

Part of Speech	Function	Examples
Interrogative	signals a question	who, whom, whose, which, what
Indefinite	refers to one or more persons or things not specifically mentioned	both, all, most, many, anyone, everybody, several, none, some
Relative	introduces an adjective clause by relating it to a word in the clause	who, whom, whose, which, that
Reciprocal	refers to individual parts of a plural antecedent	each other, one another
Verb	expresses an action, a condition, or a state of being	
Action	tells what the subject does or did, physically or mentally	run, reaches, listened, consider, decides, dreamed
Linking	connects the subject to something that identifies or describes it	am, is, are, was, were, sound, taste, appear, feel, become, remain, seem
Auxiliary	precedes the main verb in a verb phrase	be, have, do, can, could, will, would, may, might
Transitive	directs the action toward someone or something; always has an object	The storm **sank** the ship.
Intransitive	does not direct the action toward someone or something; does not have an object	The ship **sank**.
Adjective	modifies a noun or pronoun	**strong** women, **two** epics, **enough** time
Adverb	modifies a verb, an adjective, or another adverb	walked **out**, **really** funny, **far** away
Preposition	relates one word to another word	at, by, for, from, in, of, on, to, with
Conjunction	joins words or word groups	
Coordinating	joins words or word groups used the same way	and, but, or, for, so, yet, nor
Correlative	used as a pair to join words or word groups used the same way	both . . . and, either . . . or, neither . . . nor
Subordinating	introduces a clause that cannot stand by itself as a complete sentence	although, after, as, before, because, when, if, unless
Interjection	expresses emotion	wow, ouch, hurrah

Quick Reference: The Sentence and Its Parts

The diagrams that follow will give you a brief review of the essentials of a sentence and some of its parts.

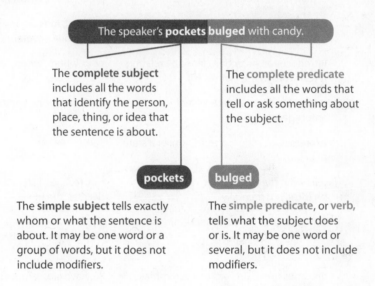

The speaker's **pockets bulged** with candy.

The **complete subject** includes all the words that identify the person, place, thing, or idea that the sentence is about.

The **complete predicate** includes all the words that tell or ask something about the subject.

pockets

bulged

The **simple subject** tells exactly whom or what the sentence is about. It may be one word or a group of words, but it does not include modifiers.

The **simple predicate**, or **verb**, tells what the subject does or is. It may be one word or several, but it does not include modifiers.

Every word in a sentence is part of a complete subject or a complete predicate.

At the **drugstore,** an understanding clerk **had given** the speaker a chocolate bar.

A **prepositional phrase** consists of a preposition, its object, and any modifiers of the object. In this phrase, *at* is the preposition and *drugstore* is its object.

subject

A **direct object** is a word or group of words that tells who or what receives the action of the verb.

An **indirect object** is a word or group of words that tells to whom or for whom or to what or for what the verb's action is performed. A sentence can have an indirect object only if it has a direct object. The indirect object always comes before the direct object.

Verbs often have more than one part. A verb may be made up of a **main verb,** like *given,* and one or more **auxiliary,** or **helping, verbs,** like *had.*

Quick Reference: Punctuation

Mark	Function	Examples
End Marks period, question mark, exclamation point	ends a sentence	We can start now. When would you like to leave? What a fantastic hit!
period	follows an initial or abbreviation **Exception:** postal abbreviations of states	Mrs. Dorothy Parker, C. P. Cavafy, p.m., lb., oz., Blvd., Dr., NE (Nebraska), NV (Nevada)

period	follows a number or letter in an outline	I. Volcanoes
		  A. Central-vent
		    1. Shield

Comma	separates part of a compound sentence	I had never liked poetry, but now I really love it.
	separates items in a series	She is brave, loyal, and kind.
	separates adjectives of equal rank that modify the same noun	The slow, easy route is best.
	sets off a term of address	Maria, how can I help you? You must do something, soldier.
	sets off a parenthetical expression	Hard workers, as you know, don't quit. I'm not a quitter, believe me.
	sets off an introductory word, phrase, or dependent clause	Yes, I forgot my key. At the beginning of the day, I feel fresh. While she was out, I was here. Having finished my chores, I went out.
	sets off a nonrestrictive, or nonessential, phrase or clause	Ed Pawn, the captain of the chess team, won. Ed Pawn, who is the captain, won. The two leading runners, sprinting toward the finish line, finished in a tie.
	sets off parts of dates and addresses	Mail it by May 14, 2015, to the Hauptman Company, 321 Market Street, Memphis, Tennessee.
	follows the salutation and closing of a letter	Dear Jim, Sincerely yours,
	separates words to avoid confusion	By noon, time had run out. What the minister does, does matter. While cooking, Jim burned his hand.

continued

Mark	Function	Examples
Semicolon	separates items that contain commas in a series	We spent the first week of summer vacation in Chicago, Illinois; the second week in St. Louis, Missouri; and the third week in Albany, New York.
	separates parts of a compound sentence that are not joined by a coordinating conjunction	The last shall be first; the first shall be last. I read the Bible; however, I have not memorized it.
	separates parts of a compound sentence when the parts contain commas	After I ran out of money, I called my parents; but only my sister was home, unfortunately.
Colon	introduces a list	Those we wrote were the following: Dana, John, and Will.
	introduces a long quotation	Abraham Lincoln wrote: "Four score and seven years ago, our fathers brought forth on this continent a new nation. . . ."
	follows the salutation of a business letter	To Whom It May Concern: Dear Leonard Atole:
	separates certain numbers	1:28 p.m., Genesis 2:5
Dash	emphasizes parenthetical information or indicates an abrupt break in thought	I was thinking of my mother—who is arriving tomorrow—just as you walked in.
Parentheses	enclose less-important material	It was so unlike him (John is always on time) that I began to worry. The last World Series game (did you see it?) was fun.
Hyphen	joins parts of a compound adjective before a noun	The not-so-rich taxpayer won't stand for this!
	joins part of a compound with *all-, ex-, self-,* or *-elect*	The ex-firefighter helped rescue him. Our president-elect is self-conscious.
	joins part of a compound number (to ninety-nine)	Today, I turned twenty-one.
	joins part of a fraction	My cup is one-third full.
	joins a prefix to a word beginning with a capital letter	Which Pre-Raphaelite painter do you like best? It snowed in mid-October.
	indicates that a word is divided at the end of a line	How could you have any reason-able expectations of getting a new computer?
Apostrophe	used with *s* to form the possessive of a noun or an indefinite pronoun	my friend's book, my friends' books, anyone's guess, somebody else's problem

continued

Mark	Function	Examples
	replaces one or more omitted letters in a contraction or numbers in a date	don't (omitted *o*), he'd (omitted *woul*), the class of '99 (omitted *19*)
	used with *s* to form the plural of a letter	I had two A's on my report card.
Quotation Marks	set off a speaker's exact words	Sara said, "I'm finally ready." "I'm ready," Sara said, "finally." Did Sara say, "I'm ready"? Sara said, "I'm ready!"
	set off the title of a story, article, short poem, essay, song, or chapter	I liked McLean's "Marine Corps Issue" and Oliver's "The Journey." I like Joplin's "Me and Bobby McGee."
	indicate sarcasm or irony	Chris is a real "friend." He always shows up when he needs help but never when I do.
Ellipses	replace material omitted from a quotation	"When in the course of human events . . . and to assume among the powers of the earth. . . ."
Italics	indicate the title of a book, play, magazine, long poem, opera, film or TV series, or the name of a ship	*The Hunger Games, Hamlet, People,* the *Odyssey, Madama Butterfly, Gone with the Wind, The Big Bang Theory,* USS Constitution

Quick Reference: Capitalization

Category	Examples
People and Titles	
Names and initials of people	Amy Tan, W. H. Auden
Titles used before names	Professor Holmes, Senator Long
Deities and members of religious groups	Jesus, Allah, Buddha, Zeus, Baptists, Roman Catholics
Names of ethnic and national groups	Hispanics, Jews, African Americans
Geographical Names	
Cities, states, countries, continents	Philadelphia, Kansas, Japan, Europe
Regions, bodies of water, mountains	the South, Lake Baikal, Mount Everest
Geographic features, parks	Great Basin, Yellowstone National Park
Streets and roads, planets	318 East Sutton Drive, Charles Court, Jupiter, Pluto
Organizations, Events, Etc.	
Companies, organizations, teams	Ford Motor Company, Boy Scouts of America, St. Louis Cardinals

continued

Category	Examples
Buildings, bridges, monuments	Empire State Building, Eads Bridge, Washington Monument
Documents, awards	Declaration of Independence, Stanley Cup
Special named events	Mardi Gras, World Series
Government bodies, historical periods and events	U.S. Senate, House of Representatives, Middle Ages, Vietnam War
Days and months, holidays	Thursday, March, Thanksgiving, Labor Day
Specific cars, boats, trains, planes	Porsche, *Mississippi Queen*, *Stourbridge Lion*, *Concorde*
Proper Adjectives	
Adjectives formed from proper nouns	French cooking, Freudian psychology, Edwardian age, Midwestern university
First Words and the Pronoun *I*	
First word in a sentence or quotation	This is it. He said, "Let's go."
First word of sentence in parentheses that is not within another sentence	The spelling rules are covered in another section. (Consult that section for more information.)
First words in the salutation and closing of a letter	Dear Madam, Very truly yours,
First word in each line of most poetry Personal pronoun *I*	Then am I A happy fly If I live Or if I die.
First word, last word, and certain parts of speech in a title	*A Tale of Two Cities*, "The World Is Too Much with Us"

Grammar Handbook

1 Nouns

A **noun** is a word used to name a person, a place, a thing, an idea, a quality, or an action. Nouns can be classified in several ways.

1.1 COMMON NOUNS

Common nouns are general names, common to entire groups.

1.2 PROPER NOUNS

Proper nouns name specific, one-of-a-kind people, places, and things.

Common	Proper
guitarist, museum, lake, month	B.B. King, Rock and Roll Hall of Fame, Lake Pontchartrain, February

1.3 SINGULAR AND PLURAL NOUNS

A noun may take a **singular form** (*city, foot*) or a **plural form** (*cities, feet*), depending on whether it names a single person, place, thing, or idea or more than one. Be sure to spell plural forms correctly.

For more information, see **Forming Plural Nouns**, page R54.

1.4 POSSESSIVE NOUNS

A **possessive noun** shows who or what owns something.

2 Pronouns

A **pronoun** is a word that is used in place of a noun or another pronoun. The word or word group to which the pronoun refers is called its **antecedent.**

2.1 PERSONAL PRONOUNS

Personal pronouns change their form to express person, number, gender, and case. The forms of these pronouns are shown in the following chart.

	Nominative	Objective	Possessive
Singular			
First person	I	me	my, mine
Second person	you	you	your, yours
Third person	she, he, it	her, him, it	her, hers, his, its
Plural			
First person	we	us	our, ours
Second person	you	you	your, yours
Third person	they	them	their, theirs

2.2 AGREEMENT WITH ANTECEDENT

Pronouns should agree with their antecedents in number, gender, and person.

If an antecedent is singular, use a singular pronoun.

> EXAMPLE: *I lost my new **cell phone**. I may have left it on the bus.*

If an antecedent is plural, use a plural pronoun.

> EXAMPLES: *Take the **snacks** out of the grocery bag, and put them in the pantry. **Delores and Arnetta** rode their bikes to the park.*

The gender of a pronoun must be the same as the gender of its antecedent.

> EXAMPLE: *The **man** thought he left his hat in the **room**. He ran back to it to look for the hat.*

The person (first, etc.) of the pronoun must be the same as the person of its antecedent.

> EXAMPLE: *You folks will have to go to the stadium to buy your tickets for the concert.*

Rewrite each sentence so that the underlined pronoun agrees with its antecedent.

1. The story "A Sound of Thunder" tells about a man who travels back in time and _its_ adventures.
2. Eckels panics at the size of the dinosaur and _his_ enormous teeth.
3. Travis looks at Eckels's shoes and notices dirt on _it_.
4. Travis feels _they_ has to kill Eckels, so he shoots him.

Replace the underlined words with an appropriate pronoun, and identify the pronoun's case.

1. In "The Necklace," _Mme. Loisel_ was not happy about her life.
2. Mme. Loisel married a clerk but wished _the couple_ could be wealthy.
3. She hated _the apartment's_ dirty walls.
4. One evening _Mme. Loisel's_ husband said, "I have something for you."
5. Mme. Loisel's reaction to the party invitation was puzzling to _M. Loisel_.

2.3 PRONOUN CASE

Personal pronouns change form to show how they function in sentences. Different functions are shown by different **cases: nominative, objective,** and **possessive.** For examples, see Section 2.1.

A **nominative pronoun** is used as a subject or a predicate nominative in a sentence.

An **objective pronoun** is used as a direct object, an indirect object, or the object of a preposition.

SUBJECT   OBJECT   OBJECT OF PREPOSITION

He will lead them to us.

A **possessive pronoun** shows ownership. The pronouns _mine, yours, hers, his, its, ours,_ and _theirs_ can be used in place of nouns.

EXAMPLE: _This horse is mine._

The pronouns _my, your, her, his, its, our,_ and _their_ are used before nouns.

EXAMPLE: _This is my horse._

WATCH OUT! Many spelling errors can be avoided if you watch out for _its_ and _their._ Don't confuse the possessive pronouns _its_ and _their_ with the contractions _it's_ and _they're._

TIP To decide which pronoun to use in a comparison, such as "She works harder than (I or me)," fill in the missing word(s): _She works harder than I work._

2.4 REFLEXIVE AND INTENSIVE PRONOUNS

These pronouns are formed by adding _-self_ or _-selves_ to certain personal pronouns. Their forms are the same, and they differ only in how they are used.

A **reflexive pronoun** follows a verb or preposition and reflects back on an earlier noun or pronoun.

EXAMPLES: _He likes himself too much. She is now herself again._

Intensive pronouns intensify or emphasize the nouns or pronouns to which they refer.

EXAMPLES: _They themselves will educate their children. You did it yourself._

WATCH OUT! Avoid using _hisself_ or _theirselves._ Standard English does not include these forms.

NONSTANDARD: _The sniper kept hisself hidden behind a chimney._

STANDARD: _The sniper kept himself hidden behind a chimney._

2.5 RECIPROCAL PRONOUNS

The **reciprocal pronouns** _each other_ and _one another_ refer to the individual members of a plural antecedent. These pronouns express mutual actions or relationships between the members they represent. Reciprocal pronouns can also take the possessive forms _each other's_ and _one another's._

EXAMPLES: *The ducks on the pond quacked at one another.*
John and Pedro borrowed each other's favorite book.

TIP Some authorities hold that *each other* should be used in reference to two things or people and that *one another* should be used in reference to more than two. Following traditional usage guidelines such as this can give your writing a more formal tone.

2.6 DEMONSTRATIVE PRONOUNS

Demonstrative pronouns point out things and persons near and far.

	Singular	Plural
Near	this	these
Far	that	those

2.7 INDEFINITE PRONOUNS

Indefinite pronouns do not refer to specific persons or things and usually have no antecedents. The chart shows some commonly used indefinite pronouns.

Singular	Plural	Singular or Plural	
another	both	all	most
anybody	few	any	none
no one	many	more	some
neither	several		

TIP Indefinite pronouns that end in *one*, *body*, or *thing* are always singular.

INCORRECT: *Did everybody play their part well?*

CORRECT: *Did everybody play his or her part well?*

If the indefinite pronoun might denote either a male or a female, *his or her* may be used to refer to it, or the sentence may be recast.

EXAMPLES: *Did everybody play his or her part well?*
Did all the students play their parts well?

2.8 INTERROGATIVE PRONOUNS

An **interrogative pronoun** tells a reader or listener that a question is coming. The interrogative pronouns are *who, whom, whose, which,* and *what.*

EXAMPLES: *Who is going to rehearse with you?*
From whom did you receive the script?

TIP *Who* is used as a subject; *whom,* as an object. To find out which pronoun you need to use in a question, change the question to a statement.

QUESTION: *(Who/Whom) did you meet there?*

STATEMENT: *You met (?) there.*

Since the verb has a subject (you), the needed word must be the object form, whom.

EXAMPLE: *Whom did you meet there?*

WATCH OUT! A special problem arises when you use an interrupter, such as *do you think,* within a question.

EXAMPLE: *(Who/Whom) do you think will win?*

If you eliminate the interrupter, it is clear that the word you need is *who.*

2.9 RELATIVE PRONOUNS

Relative pronouns relate, or connect, adjective clauses to the words they modify in sentences. The noun or pronoun that a relative clause modifies is the antecedent of the relative pronoun. Here are the relative pronouns and their uses.

	Subject	Object	Possessive
Person	who	whom	whose
Thing	which	which	whose
Thing/Person	that	that	whose

Often short sentences with related ideas can be combined by using a relative pronoun to create a more effective sentence.

SHORT SENTENCE: *Poe wrote "The Raven."*

RELATED SENTENCE: *"The Raven" is one of the most famous poems in American literature.*

COMBINED SENTENCE: *Poe wrote "The Raven," which is one of the most famous poems in American literature.*

Write the correct form of each incorrect pronoun.

1. Whom has read "The Gift of the Magi"?
2. Jim needs money for a present for Della, so he takes his watch to the pawnshop hisself.
3. Would anybody else sell their watch to buy a Christmas present?
4. He chooses a beautiful pair of them jeweled combs for Della's hair.
5. Della sells her long hair to buy a watch chain for himself.

2.10 PRONOUN REFERENCE PROBLEMS

The referent of a pronoun should always be clear. Avoid problems by rewriting sentences.

An **indefinite reference** occurs when the pronoun *it, you,* or *they* does not clearly refer to a specific antecedent.

UNCLEAR: *In the new production of Romeo and Juliet, you have more experienced actors.*

CLEAR: *The new production of Romeo and Juliet has more experienced actors.*

A **general reference** occurs when the pronoun *it, this, that, which,* or *such* is used to refer to a general idea rather than a specific antecedent.

UNCLEAR: *Jenna takes acting lessons. This has improved her chances of getting a part in the school play.*

CLEAR: *Jenna takes acting lessons. The lessons have improved her chances of getting a part in the school play.*

Ambiguous means "having more than one possible meaning." An **ambiguous reference** occurs when a pronoun could refer to two or more antecedents.

UNCLEAR: *Odysseus escaped from Cyclops, and he blinded him.*

CLEAR: *Odysseus escaped from Cyclops, and he blinded Cyclops.*

Rewrite the following sentences to correct indefinite, ambiguous, and general pronoun references.

1. In Miss Lottie's yard you don't have any grass.
2. Miss Lottie plants marigolds. This makes her barren yard look strange.
3. Lizabeth and her brother throw stones at the marigolds, which ends Miss Lottie's planting.
4. Miss Lottie stares at Lizabeth as if she is strange.

3 Verbs

A **verb** is a word that expresses an action, a condition, or a state of being.

3.1 ACTION VERBS

Action verbs express mental or physical activity.

EXAMPLE: *Mr. Cho slept with the window open.*

3.2 LINKING VERBS

Linking verbs join subjects with words or phrases that rename or describe them.

EXAMPLE: *When he awoke the next morning, his bed was wet from the rain.*

3.3 PRINCIPAL PARTS

Action and linking verbs typically have four principal parts, which are used to form verb tenses. The principal parts are the **present,** the **present participle,** the **past,** and the **past participle.**

Action verbs and some linking verbs also fall into two categories: regular and irregular. A **regular verb** is a verb that forms its past and past participle by adding *-ed* or *-d* to the present form.

Present	Present Participle	Past	Past Participle
risk	(is) risking	risked	(has) risked
solve	(is) solving	solved	(has) solved
drop	(is) dropping	dropped	(has) dropped
carry	(is) carrying	carried	(has) carried

An **irregular verb** is a verb that forms its past and past participle in some other way than by adding -*ed* or -*d* to the present form.

Present	Present Participle	Past	Past Participle
begin	(is) beginning	began	(has) begun
break	(is) breaking	broke	(has) broken
go	(is) going	went	(has) gone

3.4 VERB TENSE

The **tense** of a verb indicates the time of the action or state of being. An action or state of being can occur in the present, the past, or the future. There are six tenses, each expressing a different range of time.

The **present tense** expresses an action or state that is happening at the present time, occurs regularly, or is constant or generally true. Use the present part.

NOW: *That snow looks deep.*

REGULAR: *It snows every day.*

GENERAL: *Snow falls.*

The **past tense** expresses an action that began and ended in the past. Use the past part.

EXAMPLE: *The storyteller finished his tale.*

The **future tense** expresses an action or state that will occur. Use *shall* or *will* with the present part.

EXAMPLE: *They will attend the next festival.*

The **present perfect tense** expresses an action or state that (1) was completed at an indefinite time in the past or (2) began in the past and continues into the present. Use *have* or *has* with the past participle.

EXAMPLE: *Poetry has inspired many readers.*

The **past perfect tense** expresses an action in the past that came before another action in the past. Use *had* with the past participle.

EXAMPLE: *He had built a fire before the dog ran away.*

The **future perfect tense** expresses an action in the future that will be completed before another action in the future. Use *shall have* or *will have* with the past participle.

EXAMPLE: *They will have read the novel before they see the movie version of the tale.*

An auxiliary verb is not used with a past-tense irregular verb, but it is always used with a past-participle irregular verb.

INCORRECT: *I have saw her before.* (*Saw* is the past tense form and shouldn't be used with *have*.)

CORRECT: *I have seen her somewhere before.*

INCORRECT: *I seen her before.* (*Seen* is the past participle form of an irregular verb and shouldn't be used without an auxiliary verb.)

3.5 PROGRESSIVE FORMS

The progressive forms of the six tenses show ongoing actions. Use forms of *be* with the present participles of verbs.

PRESENT PROGRESSIVE: *She is rehearsing her lines.*

PAST PROGRESSIVE: *She was rehearsing her lines.*

FUTURE PROGRESSIVE: *She will be rehearsing her lines.*

PRESENT PERFECT PROGRESSIVE: *She has been rehearsing her lines.*

PAST PERFECT PROGRESSIVE: *She had been rehearsing her lines.*

FUTURE PERFECT PROGRESSIVE: *She will have been rehearsing her lines.*

WATCH OUT! Do not shift from tense to tense needlessly. Watch out for these special cases.

- In most compound sentences and in sentences with compound predicates, keep the tenses the same.

  INCORRECT: *His boots freeze, and he shook with cold.*

  CORRECT: *His boots freeze, and he shakes with cold.*

- If one past action happens before another, do shift tenses.

  INCORRECT: *They wished they started earlier.*

  CORRECT: *They wished they had started earlier.*

Practice and Apply

Rewrite each sentence, using a form of the verb in parentheses. Identify each form that you use.

1. Many people (benefit) from the civil rights movement.
2. Martin Luther King Jr. (remain) a towering figure in the history of nonviolent protest.
3. King (become) the leader of the Montgomery bus boycott.
4. When he (speak) to the crowds in Washington, D.C., more than 200,000 people heard his words.
5. Our class (read) his speech "I Have a Dream."

Rewrite each sentence to correct an error in tense.

6. It is a chilly morning as Rosa Parks went to work.
7. She leaves her job early and was preparing to go out of town.
8. She boarded the bus and is taking a seat in the "colored" section.
9. After several more stops, there are no more seats in the front of the bus.
10. Rosa Parks refused to give up her seat and is arrested.

3.6 ACTIVE AND PASSIVE VOICE

The voice of a verb tells whether its subject performs or receives the action expressed by the verb. When the subject performs the action, the verb is in the **active voice.** When the subject is the receiver of the action, the verb is in the **passive voice.**

Compare these two sentences:

ACTIVE: *Richard Wilbur wrote "The Writer."*

PASSIVE: *"The Writer" was written by Richard Wilbur.*

To form the passive voice, use a form of *be* with the past participle of the verb.

WATCH OUT! Use the passive voice sparingly. It can make writing awkward and less direct.

AWKWARD: *"The Writer" is a poem that was written by Richard Wilbur.*

BETTER: *Richard Wilbur wrote the poem "The Writer."*

There are occasions when you will choose to use the passive voice because

- you want to emphasize the receiver: *The king was shot.*
- the doer is unknown: *My books were stolen.*
- the doer is unimportant: *French is spoken here.*

4 Modifiers

Modifiers are words or groups of words that change or limit the meanings of other words. Adjectives and adverbs are common modifiers.

4.1 ADJECTIVES

Adjectives modify nouns and pronouns by telling which one, what kind, how many, or how much.

WHICH ONE: *this, that, these, those*

EXAMPLE: *That bird is a scarlet ibis.*

WHAT KIND: *small, sick, courageous, black*

EXAMPLE: *The sick bird sways on the branch.*

HOW MANY: *some, few, ten, none, both, each*

EXAMPLE: *Both brothers stared at the bird.*

HOW MUCH: *more, less, enough, fast*

EXAMPLE: *The bird did not have enough strength to remain perched.*

4.2 PREDICATE ADJECTIVES

Most adjectives come before the nouns they modify, as in the examples above. A **predicate adjective,** however, follows a linking verb and describes the subject.

EXAMPLE: *My friends are very intelligent.*

Be especially careful to use adjectives (not adverbs) after such linking verbs as *look, feel, grow, taste,* and *smell.*

EXAMPLE: *The bread smells wonderful.*

4.3 ADVERBS

Adverbs modify verbs, adjectives, and other adverbs by telling where, when, how, or to what extent.

WHERE: *The children played outside.*

WHEN: *The author spoke yesterday.*

HOW: *We walked slowly behind the leader.*

TO WHAT EXTENT: *He worked very hard.*

Adverbs may occur in many places in sentences, both before and after the words they modify.

EXAMPLES: *Suddenly the wind shifted.*

The wind suddenly shifted.

The wind shifted suddenly.

4.4 ADJECTIVE OR ADVERB?

Many adverbs are formed by adding *-ly* to adjectives.

EXAMPLES: *sweet, sweetly; gentle, gently*

However, *-ly* added to a noun will usually yield an adjective.

EXAMPLES: *friend, friendly; woman, womanly*

4.5 COMPARISON OF MODIFIERS

Modifiers can be used to compare two or more things. The form of a modifier shows the degree of comparison. Both adjectives

and adverbs have **comparative** and **superlative** forms.

The **comparative form** is used to compare two things, groups, or actions.

EXAMPLES: *His father's hands were stronger than his own.*

His father was more courageous than the other man.

The **superlative form** is used to compare more than two things, groups, or actions.

EXAMPLES: *His father's hands were the strongest in the family.*

His father was the most courageous of them all.

4.6 REGULAR COMPARISONS

Most one-syllable and some two-syllable adjectives and adverbs have comparatives and superlatives formed by adding *-er* and *-est.* All three-syllable and most two-syllable modifiers have comparatives and superlatives formed with *more* or *most.*

Modifier	Comparative	Superlative
small	smaller	smallest
thin	thinner	thinnest
sleepy	sleepier	sleepiest
useless	more useless	most useless
precisely	more precisely	most precisely

WATCH OUT! Note that spelling changes must sometimes be made to form the comparatives and superlatives of modifiers.

EXAMPLES: *friendly, friendlier* (Change *y* to *i,* and add the ending.)

sad, sadder (Double the final consonant, and add the ending.)

4.7 IRREGULAR COMPARISONS

Some commonly used modifiers have irregular comparative and superlative forms. They are listed in the following chart. You may wish to memorize them.

Modifier	Comparative	Superlative
good	better	best
bad	worse	worst
far	farther *or* further	farthest *or* furthest
little	less *or* lesser	least
many	more	most
well	better	best
much	more	most

4.8 PROBLEMS WITH MODIFIERS

Study the tips that follow to avoid common mistakes:

Farther and Further Use *farther* for distances; use *further* for everything else.

Double Comparisons Make a comparison by using -*er*/-*est* or by using *more/most*. Using -*er* with *more* or using -*est* with *most* is incorrect.

> INCORRECT: *I like her more better than she likes me.*

> CORRECT: *I like her better than she likes me.*

Illogical Comparisons An illogical or confusing comparison results when two unrelated things are compared or when something is compared with itself. The word *other* or the word *else* should be used when comparing an individual member to the rest of a group.

> ILLOGICAL: *The narrator was more curious about the war than any student in his class.* (implies that the narrator isn't a student in the class)

> LOGICAL: *The narrator was more curious about the war than any other student in his class.* (identifies that the narrator is a student)

Bad vs. Badly *Bad*, as an adjective, is used before a noun or after a linking verb. *Badly*, always an adverb, never modifies a noun. Be sure to use the right form after a linking verb.

> INCORRECT: *Ed felt badly after his team lost.*

> CORRECT: *Ed felt bad after his team lost.*

Good vs. Well *Good*, as an adjective, is used before a noun or after a linking verb. *Well* is often an adverb meaning "expertly" or "properly." *Well* can also be used as an adjective after a linking verb when it means "in good health."

> INCORRECT: *Helen writes very good.*

> CORRECT: *Helen writes very well.*

> CORRECT: *Yesterday I felt bad; today I feel well.*

Double Negatives If you add a negative word to a sentence that is already negative, the result will be an error known as a double negative. When using *not* or -*n't* with a verb, use *any-* words, such as *anybody* or *anything*, rather than *no-* words, such as *nobody* or *nothing*, later in the sentence.

> INCORRECT: *We haven't seen nobody.*

> CORRECT: *We haven't seen anybody.*

Using *hardly, barely,* or *scarcely* after a negative word is also incorrect.

> INCORRECT: *They couldn't barely see two feet ahead.*

> CORRECT: *They could barely see two feet ahead.*

Misplaced Modifiers Sometimes a modifier is placed so far away from the word it modifies that the intended meaning of the sentence is unclear. Place modifiers as close as possible to the words they modify.

> MISPLACED: *We found the child in the park who was missing.* (The child was missing, not the park.)

> CLEARER: *We found the missing child in the park.*

Dangling Modifiers Sometimes a modifier doesn't appear to modify any word in a sentence. Most dangling modifiers are participial phrases or infinitive phrases.

> DANGLING: *Looking out the window, his brother was seen driving by.*

> CLEARER: *Looking out the window, Josh saw his brother driving by.*

continued

Type	Definition	Example
Interrogative	asks a question	Did you read "Pancakes"?
Imperative	gives a command or direction	Read the story.
Exclamatory	expresses strong feeling or excitement	The story is funny!

Practice and Apply

Choose the correct word or words from each pair in parentheses.

1. *The House on Mango Street* gives (better, more better) insight into Mexican-American culture than any other book I've read.
2. Sandra Cisneros's family moved so often that she hardly had (any, no) friends.
3. She felt (bad, badly) that she didn't live in a perfect house like the ones she saw on TV.
4. At one time Cisneros didn't think (nothing, anything) was positive about belonging to a different culture.

Practice and Apply

Rewrite each sentence that contains a misplaced or dangling modifier. Write "correct" if the sentence is written correctly.

1. The house on Loomis Street belongs to Esperanza's family with the broken water pipes.
2. Esperanza has to carry water from the house in empty milk jugs.
3. A nun asks Esperanza from the convent where she lives.
4. Feeling bad about the nun's reaction, the house is no longer good enough for Esperanza.

5 The Sentence and Its Parts

A **sentence** is a group of words used to express a complete thought. A complete sentence has a subject and a predicate.

5.1 KINDS OF SENTENCES

There are four basic types of sentences.

Type	Definition	Example
Declarative	states a fact, a wish, an intent, or a feeling	Joan Bauer understands youths.

5.2 COMPOUND SUBJECTS AND PREDICATES

A compound subject consists of two or more subjects that share the same verb. They are typically joined by the coordinating conjunction *and* or *or*.

> EXAMPLE: *A short story or novel will keep you engaged.*

A compound predicate consists of two or more predicates that share the same subject. They too are typically joined by a coordinating conjunction, usually *and, but,* or *or*.

> EXAMPLE: *The class finished all the poetry but did not read the short stories.*

5.3 COMPLEMENTS

A **complement** is a word or group of words that completes the meaning of the sentence. Some sentences contain only a subject and a verb. Most sentences, however, require additional words placed after the verb to complete the meaning of the sentence. There are three kinds of complements: direct objects, indirect objects, and subject complements.

Direct objects are words or word groups that receive the action of action verbs. A direct object answers the question *what* or *whom*.

> EXAMPLES: *The students asked many questions.* (Asked what?)
>
> *The teacher quickly answered the students.* (Answered whom?)

Indirect objects tell to whom or what or for whom or what the actions of verbs are performed. Indirect objects come before direct objects. In the examples that follow, the indirect objects are highlighted.

> EXAMPLES: *My sister usually gave her friends good advice.* (Gave to whom?)
>
> *Her brother sent the store a heavy package.* (Sent to what?)

Subject complements come after linking verbs and identify or describe the subjects. A subject complement that names or identifies a subject is called a **predicate nominative.** Predicate nominatives include **predicate nouns** and **predicate pronouns.**

> EXAMPLES: *My friends are very hard workers.*
>
> *The best writer in the class is she.*

A subject complement that describes a subject is called a predicate adjective.

> EXAMPLE: *The pianist appeared very energetic.*

6 | Phrases

A **phrase** is a group of related words that does not contain a subject and a predicate but functions in a sentence as a single part of speech.

6.1 NOUN PHRASES

A **noun phrase** includes a noun and the modifiers that distinguish it. Modifiers might come before or after the noun.

> EXAMPLES: *The record-breaking quarterback led his team to the state championship game.*
>
> *The quarterback who threw four interceptions in one game was traded to another team.*

In these examples, the noun *quarterback* is modified by *record-breaking* and *who threw four interceptions in one game.* The noun and its modifiers form the noun phrase.

Practice and Apply

Add a modifier to at least one noun in each of the following sentences to create a noun phrase.

1. The man hit another car on his drive to work.
2. The gumbo set my mouth on fire.
3. A noise awakened her in the middle of the night.
4. My cousin borrowed my aunt's car without asking for permission to use it.
5. Before he left for Europe, my friend called me from the airport.

6.2 VERB PHRASES

A **verb phrase** consists of at least one main verb and one or more helping verbs. A helping verb (also called an auxiliary verb) helps the main verb express action or state of being.

Besides all forms of the verb *be,* some common helping verbs are *can, could, did, do, does, had, have, may, might, must, shall, should, will,* and *would.*

> EXAMPLE: *She should think about her future.*

Sometimes the parts of a verb phrase are interrupted by other parts of speech.

> EXAMPLE: *She had always been thinking about her future.*

In this example, the adverb *always* interrupts the verb phrase *had been thinking.*

The word *not* is an adverb. It is never part of a verb phrase, even when it is joined to a verb as the contraction *–n't.*

> EXAMPLES: *She should not have lifted that rock.*
>
> *She shouldn't have lifted that rock.*

continued

Practice and Apply

Rewrite each sentence to include a helping verb.

1. His physical therapist designed an exercise program for him.
2. Before exercising he spends at least five minutes warming up.
3. When lifting heavy objects, he wears a back brace.
4. The doctor reminds him of proper lifting techniques at every check-up.
5. Without physical therapy, healing is often difficult.

6.3 PREPOSITIONAL PHRASES

A **prepositional phrase** is a phrase that consists of a preposition, its object, and any modifiers of the object. Prepositional phrases that modify nouns or pronouns are called **adjective phrases.** Prepositional phrases that modify verbs, adjectives, or adverbs are **adverb phrases.**

> ADJECTIVE PHRASE: *The central character of the story is a villain.*

> ADVERB PHRASE: *He reveals his nature in the first scene.*

Remember that adjectives modify nouns by telling which one, what kind, how much, or how many. Adverbs modify verbs, adjectives, and other adverbs by telling where, when, how, or to what extent. The same is true of prepositional phrases that act as adjective phrases or adverb phrases.

Practice and Apply

Identify the prepositional phrases and the words they modify in the following sentences. State whether the prepositional phrase is an adjective phrase or an adverb phrase.

1. A daily newspaper has something for almost everyone.
2. Our entire family reads the newspaper in the morning.
3. Dad always begins with the sports page; Mom prefers the national news.

Practice and Apply

4. My sister's favorite part of the newspaper is the lifestyle section.
5. She enjoys features like "How-to Hints."

6.4 APPOSITIVES AND APPOSITIVE PHRASES

An **appositive** is a noun or pronoun that identifies or renames another noun or pronoun. An **appositive phrase** includes an appositive and modifiers of it.

An appositive can be either **essential** or **nonessential.** An **essential appositive** provides information that is needed to identify what is referred to by the preceding noun or pronoun.

> EXAMPLE: *The book is about the author Richard Wright.*

A **nonessential appositive** adds extra information about a noun or pronoun whose meaning is already clear. Nonessential appositives and appositive phrases are set off with commas.

> EXAMPLE: *The book, an autobiography, tells how he began writing.*

7 Verbals and Verbal Phrases

A **verbal** is a verb form that is used as a noun, an adjective, or an adverb. A **verbal phrase** consists of a verbal along with its modifiers and complements. There are three kinds of verbals: **infinitives, participles,** and **gerunds.**

7.1 INFINITIVES AND INFINITIVE PHRASES

An **infinitive** is a verb form that usually begins with *to* and functions as a noun, an adjective, or an adverb. An **infinitive phrase** consists of an infinitive plus its modifiers and complements. The examples that follow show several uses of infinitive phrases.

> NOUN: *To know her is my only desire.* (subject)

> I'm *planning to walk with you.* (direct object)

ADJECTIVE: *We saw his need to be loved.* (adjective modifying need)

ADVERB: *She wrote to voice her opinions.* (adverb modifying wrote)

Because *to,* the sign of the infinitive, precedes infinitives, it is usually easy to recognize them. However, sometimes *to* may be omitted.

EXAMPLE: *Let no one dare [to] enter this shrine.*

7.2 PARTICIPLES AND PARTICIPIAL PHRASES

A **participle** is a verb form that functions as an adjective. Like adjectives, participles modify nouns and pronouns. Most participles are present-participle forms, ending in *-ing,* or past-participle forms ending in *-ed* or *-en.* In the examples below, the participles are highlighted.

MODIFYING A NOUN: *The dying man had a smile on his face.*

MODIFYING A PRONOUN: *Frustrated, everyone abandoned the cause.*

Participial phrases are participles with all their modifiers and complements.

MODIFYING A NOUN: *The dogs searching for survivors are well trained.*

MODIFYING A PRONOUN: *Having approved your proposal, we are ready to act.*

Practice and Apply

Identify the participial phrases in the following sentences, and indicate which word each phrase modifies.

1. How are skyscrapers created, and what keeps them standing tall?
2. From this foundation rises a steel skeleton, supporting the walls and floors.
3. Chicago, nearly destroyed by fire in 1871, was later rebuilt with innovative designs.
4. The first skyscraper constructed on a metal frame was built there during this period.
5. Architects, using the latest materials, were glad to design in new ways.

7.3 DANGLING AND MISPLACED PARTICIPLES

A participle or participial phrase should be placed as close as possible to the word that it modifies. Otherwise the meaning of the sentence may not be clear.

MISPLACED: *The boys were looking for squirrels searching the trees.*

CLEARER: *The boys searching the trees were looking for squirrels.*

A participle or participial phrase that does not clearly modify anything in a sentence is called a dangling participle. A **dangling participle** causes confusion because it appears to modify a word that it cannot sensibly modify. Correct a dangling participle by providing a word for the participle to modify.

DANGLING: *Running like the wind, my hat fell off.* (The hat wasn't running.)

CLEARER: *Running like the wind, I lost my hat.*

7.4 GERUNDS AND GERUND PHRASES

A gerund is a verb form ending in *-ing* that functions as a noun. Gerunds may perform any function nouns perform.

SUBJECT: *Running is my favorite pastime.*

DIRECT OBJECT: *I truly love running.*

INDIRECT OBJECT: *You should give running a try.*

SUBJECT COMPLEMENT: *My deepest passion is running.*

OBJECT OF PREPOSITION: *Her love of running keeps her strong.*

Gerund phrases are gerunds with all their modifiers and complements.

SUBJECT: *Wishing on a star never got me far.*

OBJECT OF PREPOSITION: *I will finish before leaving the office.*

APPOSITIVE: *Her avocation, flying airplanes, finally led to full-time employment.*

Rewrite each sentence, adding the phrase shown in parentheses.

1. "Daughter of Invention" was written by Julia Alvarez. (a short story)
2. The narrator loves writing. (to record her experiences)
3. She will appear at an assembly. (to give a speech)
4. She finally finishes her speech. (working feverishly for hours)
5. She reads her speech to her parents. (feeling proud)

7.5 ABSOLUTE PHRASES

An **absolute phrase** is a noun or pronoun, its participle, and any modifiers. It modifies an entire sentence, or independent clause, rather than just one word.

> EXAMPLE: *The theater buzzing with excitement, the crowd waited for the band to take the stage.*

In this example, *The theater buzzing with excitement* is an absolute phrase that modifies the sentence *the crowd waited for the band to take the stage.* The noun *theater* is modified by the participle *buzzing* and by the prepositional phrase *with excitement.* Notice that a comma separates the absolute phrase from the sentence, or independent clause.

Add an absolute phrase to modify each sentence. With a partner, discuss how the additions improve the original sentences.

1. The kids ate the entire bowl of oranges.
2. The sun set beyond the sparkling lake.
3. The board of directors rejected her proposal.
4. He decided to join the drama club.
5. We ran through the field of tall grass.

8 Clauses

A **clause** is a group of words that contains a subject and a predicate. There are two kinds of clauses: independent clauses and subordinate clauses.

8.1 INDEPENDENT AND SUBORDINATE CLAUSES

An **independent clause** can stand alone as a sentence, as the word *independent* suggests.

> INDEPENDENT CLAUSE: *Taos is famous for its Great Bank Robbery.*

A sentence may contain more than one independent clause.

> EXAMPLE: *Many people remember the robbery, and they will tell you all about it.*

In the preceding example, the coordinating conjunction *and* joins two independent clauses.

Two independent clauses can also be joined with a **conjunctive adverb,** such as *consequently, finally, furthermore, however, moreover,* or *nevertheless.* To separate the two independent clauses, a semicolon is used before the conjunctive adverb.

> EXAMPLE: *The painter decided to take up sculpture; however, his studio was not big enough for large projects using granite.*

A **subordinate clause,** or dependent clause, cannot stand alone as a sentence. It is subordinate to, or dependent on, an independent clause.

> EXAMPLE: *Although the two men needed cash, they didn't get it from the bank.*

The highlighted clause cannot stand by itself.

Identify each italicized clause in the following sentences as independent or subordinate (dependent). Then explain your answers.

1. The fire started *because someone did not smother a campfire.*
2. *The family that bought our house* is moving next week.
3. *Since she had practiced diligently,* she won the golf match.
4. Wherever Maggie goes, *her golden retriever Hopper follows her.*
5. According to our math teacher, *the binary system is important to know.*

8.2 ADJECTIVE CLAUSES

An **adjective clause,** or relative clause, is a subordinate clause used as an adjective. It usually follows the noun or pronoun it modifies.

EXAMPLE: *Tony Hillerman is someone whom millions know as a mystery writer.*

Adjective clauses are typically introduced by the relative pronoun *who, whom, whose, which,* or *that.*

For more information, see **Relative Pronouns**, page R31.

EXAMPLES: *A person who needs money should get a job.*

The robbers, whose names were Gomez and Smith, entered the bank.

An adjective clause can be either essential or nonessential. An **essential adjective clause** provides information that is necessary to identify the preceding noun or pronoun.

EXAMPLE: *One robber wore a disguise that was meant to fool Taos's residents.*

A **nonessential adjective clause** adds additional information about a noun or pronoun whose meaning is already clear. Nonessential clauses are set off with commas.

EXAMPLE: *The suspects, who drove away in a pickup truck, sideswiped a car driven by a minister.*

TIP The relative pronouns *whom, which,* and *that* may sometimes be omitted when they are objects in adjective clauses.

EXAMPLE: *Hillerman is a writer [whom] millions enjoy.*

Practice and Apply

Revise the following sentences by substituting an adjective clause (relative clause) for each italicized adjective. Add specific details to make the sentences more interesting.

1. As I entered the building, a *colorful* painting caught my eye.
2. The *patient* photographer sat on a small ledge all day.

continued

Practice and Apply

3. The two attorneys argued over the *important* contract.
4. At the assembly, Ms. Bailey made two *surprising* announcements.
5. Saburo and his friends cautiously entered the *dark* cave.

8.3 ADVERB CLAUSES

An **adverb clause** is a subordinate clause that is used to modify a verb, an adjective, or an adverb. It is introduced by a subordinating conjunction.

Adverb clauses typically occur at the beginning or end of sentences.

MODIFYING A VERB: *When we need you, we will call.*

MODIFYING AN ADVERB: *I'll stay here where there is shelter from the rain.*

MODIFYING AN ADJECTIVE: *Roman felt as good as he had ever felt.*

Practice and Apply

Identify each adverb clause in the following sentences. Then write what the clause tells: *when, where, why, how, to what extent,* or *under what condition.*

1. If you look through the newspapers from the first half of the twentieth century, you will see many pictures of Mohandas K. Gandhi.
2. This man led India to independence from Britain, and he took his spinning wheel wherever he went.
3. He did so because he viewed spinning as a symbol of the peaceful, traditional Indian lifestyle.
4. He also hoped to encourage the Indian people to make their own clothes so that they would not have to depend on British industries.
5. As a form of protest, Gandhi led marches or fasted until the government met his demands.

8.4 NOUN CLAUSES

A **noun clause** is a subordinate clause that is used as a noun. A noun clause may be used as a subject, a direct object, an indirect object, a predicate nominative, or the object of a preposition. Noun clauses are introduced either by pronouns, such as *that, what, who, whoever, which,* and *whose,* or by subordinating conjunctions, such as *how, when, where, why,* and *whether.*

TIP Because the same words may introduce adjective and noun clauses, you need to consider how a clause functions within its sentence. To determine if a clause is a noun clause, try substituting *something* or *someone* for the clause. If you can do it, it is probably a noun clause.

> EXAMPLE: *I know whose woods these are.* ("I know *something.*" The clause is a noun clause, direct object of the verb *know.*)

Practice and Apply

Identify the noun clause in each sentence. Then tell how the clause is used: as a subject, a predicate nominative, a direct object, an indirect object, or an object of a preposition.

1. We moved to Massachusetts and did not know what we would find there.
2. What surprised me first were the yellowish green fire engines.
3. Our neighbors explained that this color keeps the fire engines from being confused with other large red trucks.
4. Write your research paper about whomever you admire most.
5. The small grapefruit-sized bowling balls with no finger holes were not what she usually used.

Practice and Apply

Add descriptive details to each sentence by writing the type of clause indicated in parentheses.

1. My aunt has an interesting hobby. (adjective clause)
2. She works on her craft at night. (adverb clause)

continued

Practice and Apply

3. She writes. (noun clause)
4. She has written several books. (adjective clause)
5. I asked her to write a story about me. (adverb clause)

9 The Structure of Sentences

When classified by their structure, there are four kinds of sentences: simple, compound, complex, and compound-complex.

9.1 SIMPLE SENTENCES

A **simple sentence** is a sentence that has one independent clause and no subordinate clauses. The fact that such a sentence is called simple does not mean that it is uncomplicated. Various parts of simple sentences may be compound, and simple sentences may contain grammatical structures such as appositive and verbal phrases.

> EXAMPLES: *Ray Bradbury, a science fiction writer, has written short stories and novels.* (appositive and compound direct object)
>
> *The narrator, recalling the years of his childhood, tells his story.* (participial phrase)

9.2 COMPOUND SENTENCES

A **compound sentence** consists of two or more independent clauses. The clauses in compound sentences are joined with commas and coordinating conjunctions *(and, but, or, nor, yet, for, so)* or with semicolons. Like simple sentences, compound sentences do not contain any subordinate clauses.

> EXAMPLES: *I enjoyed Bradbury's story "The Utterly Perfect Murder," and I want to read more of his stories.*
>
> *The narrator has lived a normal, complete life; however, he decides to kill his childhood playmate.*

WATCH OUT! Do not confuse compound sentences with simple sentences that have compound parts.

> EXAMPLE: *A subcommittee drafted a document and immediately presented it to the entire group.* (Here *and* joins parts of a compound predicate, not a compound sentence.)

9.3 COMPLEX SENTENCES

A **complex sentence** consists of one independent clause and one or more subordinate clauses. Each subordinate clause can be used as a noun or as a modifier. If it is used as a modifier, a subordinate clause usually modifies a word in the independent clause, and the independent clause can stand alone. However, when a subordinate clause is a noun clause, it is a part of the independent clause; the two cannot be separated.

> MODIFIER: *One should not complain unless one has a better solution.*

> NOUN CLAUSE: *We sketched pictures of whomever we wished.* (The noun clause is the object of the preposition *of* and cannot be separated from the rest of the sentence.)

9.4 COMPOUND-COMPLEX SENTENCES

A **compound-complex sentence** contains two or more independent clauses and one or more subordinate clauses. Compound-complex sentences are, simply, both compound and complex. If you start with a compound sentence, all you need to do to form a compound-complex sentence is add a subordinate clause.

> COMPOUND: *All the students knew the answer, yet they were too shy to volunteer.*

> COMPOUND-COMPLEX: *All the students knew the answer that their teacher expected, yet they were too shy to volunteer.*

9.5 PARALLEL STRUCTURE

When you write sentences, make sure that coordinate parts are equivalent, or **parallel,** in structure.

> NOT PARALLEL: *Erin loved basketball and to play hockey.* (*Basketball* is a noun; *to play hockey* is a phrase.)

> PARALLEL: *Erin loved basketball and hockey.* (*Basketball* and *hockey* are both nouns.)

> NOT PARALLEL: *He wanted to rent an apartment, a new car, and traveling around the country.* (*To rent* is an infinitive, *car* is a noun, and *traveling* is a gerund.)

> PARALLEL: *He wanted to rent an apartment, to drive a new car, and to travel around the country.* (*To rent, to drive,* and *to travel* are all infinitives.)

10 Writing Complete Sentences

Remember, a sentence is a group of words that expresses a complete thought. In writing that you wish to share with a reader, try to avoid both sentence fragments and run-on sentences.

10.1 CORRECTING FRAGMENTS

A **sentence fragment** is a group of words that is only part of a sentence. It does not express a complete thought and may be confusing to a reader or listener. A sentence fragment may be lacking a subject, a predicate, or both.

> FRAGMENT: *Waited for the boat to arrive.* (no subject)

> CORRECTED: *We waited for the boat to arrive.*

> FRAGMENT: *People of various races, ages, and creeds.* (no predicate)

> CORRECTED: *People of various races, ages, and creeds gathered together.*

> FRAGMENT: *Near the old cottage.* (neither subject nor predicate)

> CORRECTED: *The burial ground is near the old cottage.*

In your writing, fragments may be a result of haste or incorrect punctuation. Sometimes fixing a fragment will be a matter of attaching it to a preceding or following sentence.

FRAGMENT: *We saw the two girls. Waiting for the bus to arrive.*

CORRECTED: *We saw the two girls waiting for the bus to arrive.*

10.2 CORRECTING RUN-ON SENTENCES

A **run-on sentence** is made up of two or more sentences written as though they were one. Some run-ons have no punctuation within them. Others may have only commas where conjunctions or stronger punctuation marks are necessary. Use your judgment in correcting run-on sentences, as you have choices. You can make a run-on two sentences if the thoughts are not closely connected. If the thoughts are closely related, you can keep the run-on as one sentence by adding a semicolon or a conjunction.

RUN-ON: *We found a place for the picnic by a small pond it was three miles from the village.*

MAKE TWO SENTENCES: *We found a place for the picnic by a small pond. It was three miles from the village.*

RUN-ON: *We found a place for the picnic by a small pond it was perfect.*

USE A SEMICOLON: *We found a place for the picnic by a small pond; it was perfect.*

ADD A CONJUNCTION: *We found a place for the picnic by a small pond, and it was perfect.*

WATCH OUT! When you form compound sentences, make sure you use appropriate punctuation: a comma before a coordinating conjunction, a semicolon when there is no coordinating conjunction. A very common mistake is to use a comma alone instead of a comma and a conjunction. This error is called a **comma splice.**

INCORRECT: *He finished the apprenticeship, he left the village.*

CORRECT: *He finished the apprenticeship, and he left the village.*

11 Subject-Verb Agreement

The subject and verb in a clause must agree in number. Agreement means that if the subject is singular, the verb is also singular, and if the subject is plural, the verb is also plural.

11.1 BASIC AGREEMENT

Fortunately, agreement between subjects and verbs in English is simple. Most verbs show the difference between singular and plural only in the third person of the present tense. In the present tense, the third-person singular form ends in *-s.*

Present-Tense Verb Forms	
Singular	**Plural**
I sleep	we sleep
you sleep	you sleep
she, he, it sleeps	they sleep

11.2 AGREEMENT WITH *BE*

The verb *be* presents special problems in agreement, because this verb does not follow the usual verb patterns.

Forms of *Be*			
Present Tense		**Past Tense**	
Singular	**Plural**	**Singular**	**Plural**
I am	we are	I was	we were
you are	you are	you were	you were
she, he, it is	they are	she, he, it was	they were

11.3 WORDS BETWEEN SUBJECT AND VERB

A verb agrees only with its subject. When words come between a subject and a verb, ignore them when considering proper agreement. Identify the subject, and make sure the verb agrees with it.

EXAMPLES: *A story in the newspapers tells about the 1890s.*

Dad as well as Mom reads the paper daily.

11.4 AGREEMENT WITH COMPOUND SUBJECTS

Use plural verbs with most compound subjects joined by the word *and*.

> **EXAMPLE:** *My father and his friends read the paper daily.*

To confirm that you need a plural verb, you could substitute the plural pronoun *they* for *my father and his friends.*

If a compound subject is thought of as a unit, use a singular verb. Test this by substituting the singular pronoun *it.*

> **EXAMPLE:** *Peanut butter and jelly [it] is my brother's favorite sandwich.*

Use a singular verb with a compound subject that is preceded by *each, every,* or *many a.*

> **EXAMPLE:** *Each novel and short story seems grounded in personal experience.*

When the parts of a compound subject are joined by *or, nor,* or the correlative conjunctions *either ... or* or *neither ... nor,* make the verb agree with the noun or pronoun nearest the verb.

> **EXAMPLES:** *Cookies or ice cream is my favorite dessert.*
>
> *Either Cheryl or her friends are being invited. Neither ice storms nor snow is predicted today.*

11.5 PERSONAL PRONOUNS AS SUBJECTS

When using a personal pronoun as a subject, make sure to match it with the correct form of the verb **be**. (See the chart in Section 11.2.) Note especially that the pronoun *you* takes the forms *are* and *were,* regardless of whether it is singular or plural.

> **WATCH OUT!** *You is* and *you was* are nonstandard forms and should be avoided in writing and speaking. *We was* and *they was* are also forms to be avoided.
>
> INCORRECT: *You was a good student.*
>
> CORRECT: *You were a good student.*
>
> INCORRECT: *They was starting a new school.*
>
> CORRECT: *They were starting a new school.*

11.6 INDEFINITE PRONOUNS AS SUBJECTS

Some indefinite pronouns are always singular; some are always plural.

Singular Indefinite Pronouns			
another	either	neither	one
anybody	everbody	nobody	some-body
anyone	everyone	no one	some-one
anything	every-thing	nothing	some-thing
each	much		

> **EXAMPLES:** *Each of the writers was given an award. Somebody in the room upstairs is sleeping.*

Plural Indefinite Pronouns			
both	few	many	several

> **EXAMPLES:** *Many of the books in our library are not in circulation.*
>
> *Few have been returned recently.*

Still other indefinite pronouns may be either singular or plural.

Singular or Plural Indefinite Pronouns		
all	more	none
any	most	some

The number of the indefinite pronoun *any* or *none* often depends on the intended meaning.

> **EXAMPLES:** *Any of these topics has potential for a good article.* (any one topic)
>
> *Any of these topics have potential for good articles.* (all of the many topics)

The indefinite pronouns *all, some, more, most,* and *none* are singular when they refer to quantities or parts of things. They are plural when they refer to numbers of individual things. Context will usually give a clue.

> **EXAMPLES:** *All of the flour is gone.* (referring to a quantity)
>
> *All of the flowers are gone.* (referring to individual items)

11.7 INVERTED SENTENCES

Problems in agreement often occur in inverted sentences beginning with *here* or *there;* in questions beginning with *how, when, why, where,* or *what;* and in inverted sentences beginning with phrases. Identify the subject—wherever it is—before deciding on the verb.

EXAMPLES: *There clearly are far too many cooks in this kitchen.*

Far from the embroiled cooks stands the master chef.

Practice and Apply

Locate the subject of each verb in parentheses in the sentences below. Then choose the correct verb form.

1. Many Greeks sail home from Troy, but few (struggles, struggle) as hard as Odysseus to get there.
2. Neither Odysseus nor his men (know, knows) what dangers lie ahead.
3. There (is, are) more dangers awaiting him than there (is, are) gods to save him.
4. Everybody who has read about Odysseus' trials (knows, know) what he endured.
5. There (is, are) few friends who can help him during his ten-year odyssey.

11.8 SENTENCES WITH PREDICATE NOMINATIVES

When a predicate nominative serves as a complement in a sentence, use a verb that agrees with the subject, not the complement.

EXAMPLES: *The speeches of Martin Luther King Jr. are a landmark in American civil rights history.* (*Speeches* is the subject and it takes the plural verb *are.*)

One landmark in American civil rights history is the speeches of Martin Luther King Jr. (The subject is *landmark* and it takes the singular verb *is.*)

11.9 *DON'T* AND *DOESN'T* AS AUXILIARY VERBS

The auxiliary verb *doesn't* is used with singular subjects and with the personal pronouns *she, he,* and *it.* The auxiliary verb *don't* is used with plural subjects and with the personal pronouns *I, we, you,* and *they.*

SINGULAR: *She doesn't know Martin Luther King's famous "I Have a Dream" speech.*

Doesn't the young woman read very much?

PLURAL: *We don't have the speech memorized. Don't speakers usually memorize their speeches?*

11.10 COLLECTIVE NOUNS AS SUBJECTS

Collective nouns are singular nouns that name groups of persons or things. *Team,* for example, is the collective name of a group of individuals. A collective noun takes a singular verb when the group acts as a single unit. It takes a plural verb when the members of the group act separately.

EXAMPLES: *Our team usually wins.* (The team as a whole wins.)

Our team vote differently on most issues. (The individual members vote.)

11.11 RELATIVE PRONOUNS AS SUBJECTS

When the relative pronoun *who, which,* or *that* is used as a subject in an adjective clause, the verb in the clause must agree in number with the antecedent of the pronoun.

SINGULAR: *I didn't read the **poem** about fireworks that was assigned.*

The antecedent of the relative pronoun *that* is the singular **poem;** therefore, *that* is singular and must take the singular verb *was.*

PLURAL: ***William Blake and Amy Lowell,** who are very different from each other, are both outstanding poets.*

The antecedent of the relative pronoun *who* is the plural compound subject *William Blake and Amy Lowell.* Therefore *who* is plural, and it takes the plural verb *are.*

Vocabulary and Spelling

The key to becoming an independent reader is to develop a toolkit of vocabulary strategies. By learning and practicing the strategies, you'll know what to do when you encounter unfamiliar words while reading. You'll also know how to refine the words you use for different situations—personal, school, and work.

Being a good speller is important when communicating your ideas in writing. Learning basic spelling rules and checking your spelling in a dictionary will help you spell words that you may not use frequently.

1 Using Context Clues

The context of a word is made up of the punctuation marks, words, sentences, and paragraphs that surround it. A word's context can give you important clues about its meaning, including both its denotation and connotation.

1.1 GENERAL CONTEXT

Sometimes you need to infer the meaning of a word by reading all the information in a passage.

After twelve hours without food, I was so ravenous that I ate seven slices of pizza.

You can figure out from the context that *ravenous* means "extremely hungry."

1.2 SPECIFIC CONTEXT CLUES

Sometimes writers help you understand the meanings of words by providing specific clues such as those shown in the chart.

Specific Context Clues		
Type of Clue	**Key Words/Phrases**	**Example**
Definition or restatement of the meaning of the word	or, which is, that is, in other words, also known as, also called	His first conjecture, **or guess,** was correct.
Example following an unfamiliar word	such as, like, as if, for example, especially, including	She loved macabre stories, **such as those by Edgar Allan Poe and Stephen King.**
Comparison with a more familiar word or concept	as, like, also, similar to, in the same way, likewise	Despite his physical suffering, his mind was as **lucid** as any **rational** person's.
Contrast with a familiar word or experience	unlike, but, however, although, on the other hand, on the contrary	Unlike her **clumsy** partner, she was an **agile** dancer.
Cause-and-effect relationship in which one term is familiar	because, since, when, consequently, as a result, therefore	Because this perfume has such a **sharp** scent, I will buy the one with a **subtle** fragrance.

1.3 IDIOMS, SLANG, AND FIGURATIVE LANGUAGE

An **idiom** is an expression whose overall meaning is different from the meaning of the individual words. **Slang** is informal language in which made-up words and ordinary words are used to mean something different from their meanings in formal English. **Figurative language** is language that communicates meaning beyond the literal meaning of the words. Use context clues to figure out the meanings of idioms, slang, and figurative language.

> The mosquitoes drove us crazy on our hike through the woods. (idiom; means "bothered")
> That's a really cool backpack that you're wearing. (slang; means "excellent" or "first-rate")
> I was angry. Heat rose under my skin until I felt as if searing flames were threatening to engulf my whole body. (figurative language; hot skin and flames symbolize anger)

2 Analyzing Word Structure

Many words can be broken into smaller parts. These word parts include base words, roots, prefixes, and suffixes.

2.1 BASE WORDS

A **base word** is a word part that by itself is also a word. Other words or word parts can be added to base words to form new words.

2.2 ROOTS

A **root** is a word part that contains the core meaning of the word. Many English words contain roots that come from older languages such as Greek, Latin, Old English (Anglo-Saxon), and Norse. Knowing the meaning of the word's root can help you determine the word's meaning.

Root	Meaning	Examples
bi (Greek)	life	biography
gramm (Greek)	letter, something written	grammar
grad (Latin)	step, degree	graduate
man (Latin)	hand	manual
hēadfod (Old English)	head, top	headfirst

2.3 PREFIXES

A **prefix** is a word part attached to the beginning of a word. Most prefixes come from Greek, Latin, or Old English.

Prefix	Meaning	Examples
pre-	before	preschool
ex-	out, from	extend
re-	again, back	return

2.4 SUFFIXES

A **suffix** is a word part that appears at the end of a root or base word to form a new word. Some suffixes do not change word meaning. These suffixes are

- added to nouns to change the number of persons or objects
- added to verbs to change the tense
- added to modifiers to change the degree of comparison

Suffix	Meaning	Examples
-s, -es	to change the number of a noun	snack + s = snacks
-d, -ed, -ing	to change verb tense	walk + ed = walked
-er, -est	to change the degree of comparison in modifiers	wild + er = wilder fast + est = fastest

Other suffixes can be added to a root or base to change the word's meaning. These suffixes can also determine a word's part of speech.

Suffix	Meaning	Examples
-age	action or process	pilgrimage
-able	ability	enjoyable
-ize	to make	criticize

Strategies for Understanding Unfamiliar Words

- Look for any prefixes or suffixes. Remove them to isolate the base word or the root.
- See if you recognize any elements— prefix, suffix, root, or base—of the word. You may be able to guess its meaning by analyzing one or two elements.
- Consider the way the word is used in the sentence. Use the context and the word parts to make a logical guess about the word's meaning.
- Consult a dictionary to see whether you are correct.

3 Understanding Word Origins

3.1 ETYMOLOGIES

Etymologies show the origin and historical development of a word. When you study a word's history and origin, you can find out when, where, and how the word came to be.

dra·ma (drä′mə) *n.* **1.** A work that is meant to be performed by actors. **2.** Theatrical works of a certain type or period in history. [Late Latin *drāma, drāmat-*, from Greek *drān*, to do or perform.]

for·mi·car·y (fôr′mĭ-kĕr′ē) *n., pl.* **-ies** A nest of ants; an anthill. [Medieval Latin *formīcārium*, from Latin *formīca*, ant.]

lock² (lŏk) *n.* **1a.** A length or curl of hair; a tress. **b.** The hair of the head. Often

used in the plural. **2.** A small wisp or tuft, as of wool or cotton. [Middle English *lok* from Old English *loc, locc*.]

3.2 WORD FAMILIES

Words that have the same root make up a word family and have related meanings. The chart shows a common Greek and a common Latin root. Notice how the meanings of the example words are related to the meanings of their roots.

Latin Root	*vid, vis:* "see"
English	**vision** eyesight **video** visual portion of a televised broadcast **visible** possible to see
Greek Root	*phonē:* "sound"
English	**homophone** word that sounds like another word **phonetics** the study of speech sounds **telephone** a device that converts voice into a form that can be transmitted as sound waves

3.3 WORDS FROM CLASSICAL MYTHOLOGY

The English language includes many words from classical mythology. You can use your knowledge of Greek, Roman, and Norse myths to understand the origins and meanings of these words. For example, *herculean task* refers to the strongman Hercules. Thus *herculean task* probably means "a job that is large or difficult." The chart shows a few common words from mythology.

Greek	Roman	Norse
Achilles' heel	cereal	Thursday
aegis	volcano	berserk
muse	cupid	rune
Midas touch	floral	valkyrie

3.4 FOREIGN WORDS

The English language has grown to include words from diverse languages such as French, Dutch, Spanish, Italian, Portuguese, and Chinese. Many of these words stayed the way they were in their original languages.

French	Dutch	Spanish	Italian
ballet	boss	canyon	diva
beret	caboose	rodeo	carnival
mirage	dock	salsa	spaghetti

4 Synonyms and Antonyms

4.1 SYNONYMS

A **synonym** is a word with a meaning similar to that of another word. You can find synonyms in a thesaurus or a dictionary. In a dictionary, synonyms are often given as part of the definition of the word. The following word pairs are synonyms:

happy/joyful   sad/unhappy

angry/mad   beautiful/lovely

4.2 ANTONYMS

An **antonym** is a word with a meaning opposite that of another word. The following word pairs are antonyms:

best/worst   well/ill

light/dark   happy/sad

5 Denotation and Connotation

5.1 DENOTATION

A word's dictionary meaning is called its **denotation.** For example, the denotation of the word *rascal* is "an unethical, dishonest person."

5.2 CONNOTATION

The images or feelings you connect to a word add a finer shade of meaning, called **connotation.** The connotation of a word goes beyond its basic dictionary definition. Writers use connotations of words to communicate positive or negative feelings.

Positive	Neutral	Negative
gaze	look	glare
slender	thin	scrawny
playful	active	rowdy

Make sure you understand the denotation and connotation of a word when you read it or use it in your writing.

6 Analogies

An analogy is a comparison between two things that are similar in some way. Analogies are sometimes used in writing when unfamiliar objects or ideas are described or explained in terms of familiar ones. Analogies often appear on tests as well, usually in a format like this:

bird : fly ::   A) boat : water

B) bear : cave

C) fish : scales

D) fish : swim

E) sparrow : wings

Follow these steps to determine the correct answer:

- Read the first half of the analogy as "*bird* is to *fly* as. . . ."
- Read the answer choices as "*boat* is to *water*," "*bear* is to *cave*," and so on.
- Ask yourself how the words *bird* and *fly* are related. (A bird can fly.)
- Ask yourself which of the choices shows the same relationship. (A boat can't water and a bear can't cave, but a fish can swim. Therefore, the answer is D.)

7 Homonyms and Homophones

7.1 HOMONYMS

Homonyms are words that have the same spelling and sound but have different meanings.

The girl had to stoop to find her ball under the stoop.

Stoop can mean "a small porch," but an identically spelled word means "to bend down." Because the words have different meanings, each word has its own dictionary entry.

The lawyer argued the case of the missing jewelry case.

Case can mean "evidence in support of a claim." However, another identically spelled word means "container." Each word has a different meaning and its own dictionary entry.

Sometimes only one of the meanings of a homonym may be familiar to you. Use context clues to help you figure out the meaning of an unfamiliar word.

7.2 HOMOPHONES

Homophones are words that sound alike but have different meanings and spellings. The following homophones are frequently misused:

it's/its   they're/their/there

to/too/two   stationary/stationery

Many misused homophones are pronouns and contractions. Whenever you are unsure whether to write *your* or *you're* and *who's* or *whose*, ask yourself if you mean *you are* or *who is/has*. If you do, write the contraction. For other homophones, such as *fair* and *fare*, use the meaning of the word to help you decide which one to use.

8 Words with Multiple Meanings

Some words have acquired additional meanings over time that are based on the original meaning.

Thinking of the horror movie made my skin creep. I saw my little brother creep around the corner.

These two uses of *creep* have different meanings, but both of them have the same origin. You will find all the meanings of *creep* listed in one entry in the dictionary.

9 Specialized Vocabulary

Specialized vocabulary is special terms suited to a particular field, or domain, of study or work. For example, science, mathematics, and history all have their own domain-specific technical or specialized vocabularies. To figure out specialized terms, you can use context clues; your knowledge of Latin, Greek, and Old English roots and affixes; and reference sources, such as dictionaries on specific subjects, atlases, or manuals.

10 Using Reference Sources

10.1 DICTIONARIES

A **general dictionary** will tell you not only a word's definitions but also its pronunciation, parts of speech, and history and origin. A **specialized dictionary** focuses on terms related to a particular field of study or work. Use a dictionary to check the spelling of any word you are unsure of in your English class and for other subjects as well.

10.2 THESAURI

A **thesaurus** (plural, thesauri) is a dictionary of synonyms. A thesaurus can be especially helpful when you find yourself using the same modifiers over and over again.

10.3 SYNONYM FINDERS

A **synonym finder** is often included in word processing software. It enables you to highlight a word and be shown a display of its synonyms.

10.4 GLOSSARIES

A **glossary** is a list of specialized terms and their definitions. It is often found in the back of a book and sometimes includes pronunciations. Many textbooks contain glossaries. In fact, this textbook has three glossaries: the **Glossary of Literary and Informational Terms**, the **Glossary of Academic Vocabulary** and the **Glossary of Critical Vocabulary**. Use these glossaries to help you understand how terms are used in this textbook.

11 Spelling Rules

11.1 WORDS ENDING IN A SILENT *E*

Before adding a suffix beginning with a vowel or *y* to a word ending in a silent *e*, drop the *e* (with some exceptions).

> amaze + -ing = amazing
>
> love + -able = lovable
>
> create + -ed = created
>
> nerve + -ous = nervous

Exceptions: *change + -able = changeable; courage + -ous = courageous*

When adding a suffix beginning with a consonant to a word ending in a silent *e*, keep the *e* (with some exceptions).

> late + -ly = lately
>
> spite + -ful = spiteful
>
> noise + -less = noiseless
>
> state + -ment = statement

Exceptions: *truly, argument, ninth, wholly, awful,* and others.

When a suffix beginning with *a* or *o* is added to a word with a final silent *e*, the final *e* is usually retained if it is preceded by a soft *c* or a soft *g*.

> bridge + -able = bridgeable
>
> peace + -able = peaceable
>
> outrage + -ous = outrageous
>
> advantage + -ous = advantageous

When a suffix beginning with a vowel is added to words ending in *ee* or *oe*, the final silent *e* is retained.

> agree + -ing = agreeing   free + -ing = freeing
>
> hoe + -ing = hoeing   see + -ing = seeing

11.2 WORDS ENDING IN *Y*

Before adding most suffixes to a word that ends in *y* preceded by a consonant, change the *y* to *i*.

> easy + -est = easiest
>
> crazy + -est = craziest
>
> silly + -ness = silliness
>
> marry + -age = marriage

Exceptions: *dryness, shyness,* and *slyness.*

However, when you add *-ing,* the *y* does not change.

> empty + -ed = emptied but
>
> empty + -ing = emptying

When adding a suffix to a word that ends in *y* preceded by a vowel, the *y* usually does not change.

> play + -er = player
>
> employ + -ed = employed
>
> coy + -ness = coyness
>
> pay + -able = payable

11.3 WORDS ENDING IN A CONSONANT

In one-syllable words that end in one consonant preceded by one short vowel, double the final consonant before adding a suffix beginning with a vowel, such as *-ed* or *-ing.* These are sometimes called 1+1+1 words.

> dip + -ed = dipped   set + -ing = setting
>
> slim + -est = slimmest   fit + -er = fitter

The rule does not apply to words of one syllable that end in a consonant preceded by two vowels.

> feel + -ing = feeling   peel + -ed = peeled
>
> reap + -ed = reaped   loot + -ed = looted

In words of more than one syllable, double the final consonant when (1) the word ends with one consonant preceded by one vowel and (2) the word is accented on the last syllable.

> be·gin´   per·mit´   re·fer´

In the following examples, note that in the new words formed with suffixes, the accent remains on the same syllable:

> be·gin´ + -ing = be·gin´ning = beginning
>
> per·mit´ + -ed = per·mit´ted = permitted

In some words with more than one syllable, though the accent remains on the same syllable when a suffix is added, the final consonant is nevertheless not doubled, as in the following examples:

> tra´vel + er = tra´vel·er = traveler
>
> mar´ket + er = mar´ket·er = marketer

In the following examples, the accent does not remain on the same syllable; thus, the final consonant is not doubled:

re•fer´ + -ence = ref´er•ence = reference

con•fer´ + -ence = con´fer•ence = conference

11.4 PREFIXES AND SUFFIXES

When adding a prefix to a word, do not change the spelling of the base word. When a prefix creates a double letter, keep both letters.

dis- + approve = disapprove

re- + build = rebuild

ir- + regular = irregular

mis- + spell = misspell

anti- + trust = antitrust

il- + logical = illogical

When adding -ly to a word ending in l, keep both l's. When adding -ness to a word ending in n, keep both n's.

careful + -ly = carefully

sudden + -ness = suddenness

final + -ly = finally

thin + -ness = thinness

11.5 FORMING PLURAL NOUNS

To form the plural of most nouns, just add -s.

prizes   dreams   circles   stations

For most singular nouns ending in o, add -s.

solos   halos   studios   photos   pianos

For a few nouns ending in o, add -es.

heroes   tomatoes   potatoes   echoes

When the singular noun ends in s, sh, ch, x, or z, add -es.

waitresses   brushes   ditches

axes   buzzes

When a singular noun ends in y with a consonant before it, change the y to i and add -es.

army—armies   candy—candies

baby—babies   diary—diaries

ferry—ferries   conspiracy—conspiracies

When a vowel (a, e, i, o, u) comes before the y, just add -s.

boy—boys   way—ways

array—arrays   alloy—alloys

weekday—weekdays   jockey—jockeys

For most nouns ending in f or fe, change the f to v and add -es or -s.

life—lives   calf—calves   knife—knives

thief—thieves shelf—shelves loaf—loaves

For some nouns ending in f, add -s to make the plural.

roofs   chiefs   reefs   beliefs

Some nouns have the same form for both singular and plural.

deer   sheep   moose   salmon   trout

For some nouns, the plural is formed in a special way.

man—men   goose—geese

ox—oxen   woman—women

mouse—mice   child—children

For a compound noun written as one word, form the plural by changing the last word in the compound to its plural form.

stepchild—stepchildren   firefly—fireflies

If a compound noun is written as a hyphenated word or as two separate words, change the most important word to the plural form.

brother-in-law—brothers-in-law

life jacket—life jackets

11.6 FORMING POSSESSIVES

If a noun is singular, add 's.

mother—my mother's car Ross—Ross's desk

Exception: The s after the apostrophe is dropped after *Jesus', Moses',* and certain names in classical mythology (*Zeus'*). These possessive forms can thus be pronounced easily.

If a noun is plural and ends with s, just add an apostrophe.

parents—my parents' car

the Santinis—the Santinis' house

If a noun is plural but does not end in s, add 's.

people—the people's choice

women—the women's coats

11.7 SPECIAL SPELLING PROBLEMS

Only one English word ends in -sede: supersede. Three words end in -ceed: exceed, proceed, and succeed. All other verbs ending in the sound "seed" (except for the verb seed) are spelled with -cede.

concede   precede   recede   secede

In words with ie or ei, when the sound is long e (as in she), the word is spelled ie except after c (with some exceptions).

i before *e*	thief	relieve	field
	piece	grieve	pier
except after *c*	conceit	perceive	ceiling
	receive	receipt	
Exceptions:	either	neither	weird
	leisure	seize	

12 Commonly Confused Words

words	definitions	examples
accept/except	The verb *accept* means "to receive or believe"; *except* is usually a preposition meaning "excluding."	**Except** for some of the more extraordinary events, I can **accept** that the *Odyssey* recounts a real journey.
advice/advise	*Advise* is a verb; *advice* is a noun naming that which an *adviser* gives.	I **advise** you to take that job. Whom should I ask for **advice**?
affect/effect	As a verb, *affect* means "to influence." *Effect* as a verb means "to cause." If you want a noun, you will almost always want *effect*.	Did Circe's wine **affect** Odysseus' mind? It did **effect** a change in Odysseus' men. In fact, it had an **effect** on everyone else who drank it.
all ready/already	*All ready* is an adjective meaning "fully ready." *Already* is an adverb meaning "before or by this time."	He was **all ready** to go at noon. I have **already** seen that movie.
allusion/illusion	An *allusion* is an indirect reference to something. An *illusion* is a false picture or idea.	There are many **allusions** to the works of Homer in English literature. The world's apparent flatness is an **illusion**.
among/between	*Between* is used when you are speaking of only two things. *Among* is used for three or more.	**Between** *Hamlet* and *King Lear*, I prefer the latter. Emily Dickinson is **among** my favorite poets.
bring/take	*Bring* is used to denote motion toward a speaker or place. *Take* is used to denote motion away from such a person or place.	**Bring** the books over here, and I will **take** them to the library.

words	definitions	examples
fewer/less	*Fewer* refers to the number of separate, countable units. *Less* refers to bulk quantity.	We have **less** literature and **fewer** selections in this year's curriculum.
leave/let	*Leave* means "to allow something to remain behind." *Let* means "to permit."	The librarian will **leave** some books on display but will not **let** us borrow any.
lie/lay	To *lie* is "to rest or recline." It does not take an object. *Lay* always takes an object.	Rover loves to **lie** in the sun. We always **lay** some bones next to him.
loose/lose	*Loose* (lo͞os) means "free, not restrained"; *lose* (lo͞oz) means "to misplace or fail to find."	Who turned the horses **loose**? I hope we won't **lose** any of them.
precede/proceed	*Precede* means "to go or come before." Use *proceed* for other meanings.	Emily Dickinson's poetry **precedes** that of Alice Walker. You may **proceed** to the next section of the test.
than/then	Use *than* in making comparisons; use *then* on all other occasions.	Who can say whether Amy Lowell is a better poet **than** Denise Levertov? I will read Lowell first, and **then** I will read Levertov.
their/there/they're	*Their* means "belonging to them." *There* means "in that place." *They're* is the contraction for "they are."	**There** is a movie playing at 9 p.m. **They're** going to see it with me. Sakara and Erin drove away in **their** car after the movie.
two/too/to	*Two* is the number. *Too* is an adverb meaning "also" or "very." Use *to* before a verb or as a preposition.	Meg had **to** go **to** town, **too**. We had **too** much reading **to** do. **Two** chapters is **too** many.

Glossary of Literary and Informational Terms

Act An act is a major division within a play, similar to a chapter in a book. Each act may be further divided into smaller sections, called scenes. Plays can have as many as five acts, or as few as one.

Allegory An allegory is a work with two levels of meaning—a literal one and a symbolic one. In such a work, most of the characters, objects, settings, and events represent abstract qualities. Personification is often used in traditional allegories. As in a fable or a parable, the purpose of an allegory may be to convey truths about life, to teach religious or moral lessons, or to criticize social institutions.

Alliteration Alliteration is the repetition of consonant sounds at the beginning of words. Note the repetition of the *d* sound in these lines: The dare devil dove into the deep sea.

See also Consonance.

Allusion An allusion is an indirect reference to a famous person, place, event, or literary work.

Almanac *See* Reference Works.

Analogy An analogy is a point-by-point comparison between two things that are alike in some respect. Often, writers use analogies in nonfiction to explain unfamiliar subjects or ideas in terms of familiar ones.

See also Extended Metaphor; Metaphor; Simile.

Antagonist An antagonist is a principal character or force in opposition to a **protagonist,** or main character. The antagonist is usually another character but sometimes can be a force of nature, a set of circumstances, some aspect of society, or a force within the protagonist.

Archetype An archetype is a pattern in literature that is found in a variety of works from different cultures throughout the ages. An archetype can be a plot, a character, an image, or a setting. For example, the association of death and rebirth with winter and spring is an archetype common to many cultures.

Argument An argument is speech or writing that presents a claim about an issue or problem and supports it with reasons and evidence. An argument often takes into account other points of view, anticipating and answering objections that opponents of the position might raise.

See also Claim; Counterargument; Evidence.

Argumentative Essay *See* Essay.

Aside In drama, an aside is a short speech directed to the audience, or another character, that is not heard by the other characters on stage.

See also Soliloquy.

Assonance Assonance is the repetition of vowel sounds within nonrhyming words. An example of assonance is the repetition of the *u* sound in the following line: I made my usual maneuver on my snowboard.

Assumption An assumption is an opinion or belief that is taken for granted. It can be about a specific situation, a person, or the world in general. Assumptions are often unstated.

Author's Message An author's message is the main idea or theme of a particular work.

See also Main Idea; Theme.

Author's Perspective An author's perspective, or point of view, is a unique combination of ideas, values, feelings, and beliefs that influences the way the writer looks at a topic. **Tone,** or attitude, often reveals an author's perspective.

See also Author's Purpose; Tone.

Author's Position An author's position is his or her opinion on an issue or topic.

See also Claim.

Author's Purpose A writer usually writes for one or more of these purposes: to express thoughts or feelings, to inform or explain, to persuade, to entertain.

See also Author's Perspective.

Autobiography An autobiography is a writer's account of his or her own life. In almost every case, it is told from the first-person point of view. Generally, an autobiography focuses on the most significant events and people in the writer's life over a period of time. Shorter autobiographical narratives include **journals, diaries,** and **letters.** An **autobiographical essay,** another type of short autobiographical work, focuses on a single person or event in the writer's life.

See also Memoir.

Ballad A ballad is a type of narrative poem that tells a story and was originally meant to be sung or recited. Because it tells a story, a ballad has a setting, a plot, and characters. **Traditional ballads** are written in four-line stanzas with regular rhythm and rhyme. **Folk ballads** were composed orally and handed down by word of mouth. These ballads usually tell about ordinary people who have unusual adventures or perform daring deeds. A **literary ballad** is a poem written by a poet in imitation of the form and content of a folk ballad.

Bias Bias is an inclination toward a particular judgment on a topic or issue. A writer often reveals a strongly positive or strongly negative opinion by presenting only one way of looking at an issue or by heavily weighting the evidence. Words with intensely positive or negative connotations are often a signal of a writer's bias.

Bibliography A bibliography is a list of books and other materials related to the topic of a text. Bibliographies can be good sources of works for further study on a subject.

See also Works Consulted.

Biography A biography is the true account of a person's life, written by another person. As such, a biography is usually told from a third-person point of view. The writer of a biography usually researches his or her subject in order to present accurate information. The best biographers strive for honesty and balance in their accounts of their subjects' lives.

Blank Verse Blank verse is unrhymed poetry written in **iambic pentameter.** That is, each line of blank verse has five pairs of syllables. In most pairs, an unstressed syllable is followed by a stressed syllable. The most versatile of poetic forms, blank verse imitates the natural rhythms of English speech. Much of Shakespeare's drama is in blank verse.

See also Iambic Pentameter.

Business Correspondence Business correspondence includes all written business communications, such as business letters, e-mails, and memos. In general, business correspondence is brief, to the point, clear, courteous, and professional.

Cast of Characters In the script of a play, a cast of characters is a list of all the characters in the play, usually in order of appearance. It may include a brief description of each character.

Cause and Effect A **cause** is an event or action that directly results in another event or action. An **effect** is the direct or logical outcome of an event or action. Basic **cause-and-effect relationships** include a single cause with a single effect, one cause with multiple effects, multiple causes with a single effect, and a chain of causes and effects. The concept of cause and effect also provides a way of organizing a piece of writing. It helps a writer show the relationships between events or ideas.

Central Idea *See* Main Idea; Theme.

Character Characters are the individuals who participate in the action of a literary work. Like real people, characters display certain qualities, or **character traits;** they develop and change over time; and they usually have **motivations,** or reasons, for their behaviors. Complex characters can have multiple or conflicting motivations.

> **Main characters:** Main characters are the most important characters in literary works. Generally, the plot of a short story focuses on one main character, but a novel may have several main characters.

> **Minor characters:** The less prominent characters in a literary work are known as minor characters. Minor characters support the plot. The story is not centered on them, but they help carry out the action of the story and help the reader learn more about the main character.

> **Dynamic character:** A dynamic character is one who undergoes important changes as a plot unfolds. The changes occur because of his or her actions and experiences in the story. The change is usually internal and may be good or bad. Main characters are usually, though not always, dynamic.

Static character: A static character is one who remains the same throughout a story. The character may experience events and have interactions with other characters, but he or she is not changed because of them.

Round character: A round character is one who is complex and highly developed, having a variety of traits and different sides to his or her personality. Some of the traits may create conflict in the character. Round characters tend to display strengths, weaknesses, and a full range of emotions. The writer provides enough detail for the reader to understand their feelings and emotions.

Flat character: A flat character is one who is not highly developed. A flat character is one-sided: he or she usually has one outstanding trait, characteristic, or role. Flat characters exist mainly to advance the plot, and they display only the traits needed for their limited roles. Minor characters are usually flat characters.

See also Characterization.

Characterization The way a writer creates and develops characters' personalities is known as characterization. There are four basic methods of characterization:

- The writer may make direct comments about a character's personality or nature through the voice of the narrator.
- The writer may describe the character's physical appearance.
- The writer may present the character's own thoughts, speech, and actions.
- The writer may present thoughts, speech, and actions of other characters in response to a character.

See also Character.

Chorus In early Greek tragedy, the chorus commented on the actions of the characters in a drama. In some Elizabethan plays, such as Shakespeare's *Romeo and Juliet,* the role of the chorus is taken by a single actor who serves as a narrator and speaks the lines in the **prologue** (and sometimes in an **epilogue**). The chorus serves to foreshadow or summarize events.

Chronological Order Chronological order is the arrangement of events in their order of occurrence. This type of organization is used in both fictional narratives and in historical writing, biography, and autobiography.

Claim In an argument, a claim is the writer's position on an issue or problem. Although an argument focuses on supporting one claim, a writer may make more than one claim in a work.

See also Argument; Thesis Statement.

Clarify Clarifying is a reading strategy that helps a reader to understand or make clear what he or she is reading. Readers usually clarify by rereading, reading aloud, or discussing.

Classification Classification is a pattern of organization in which objects, ideas, or information is presented in groups, or classes, based on common characteristics.

Cliché A cliché is an overused expression. "Better late than never" and "hard as nails" are common examples. Good writers generally avoid clichés unless they are using them in dialogue to indicate something about characters' personalities.

Climax In a plot, the climax is the point of maximum interest or tension. Usually the climax is a turning point in the story, which occurs after the reader has understood the **conflict** and become emotionally involved with the characters. The climax sometimes, but not always, points to the **resolution** of the conflict.

See also Plot.

Comedy A comedy is a dramatic work that is light and often humorous in tone, usually ending happily with a peaceful resolution of the main conflict. A comedy differs from a farce by having a more believable plot, more realistic characters, and less boisterous behavior.

Comic Relief Comic relief consists of humorous scenes, incidents, or speeches that are included in a serious drama to provide a reduction in emotional intensity. Because comic relief breaks the tension, it allows an audience to prepare emotionally for events to come. Shakespeare often uses this device in his tragedies.

Compare and Contrast To compare and contrast is to identify similarities and differences in two or more subjects. Compare-and-contrast organization can be used to structure a piece of writing, serving as a framework for analyzing the similarities and differences in two or more subjects.

Complex Character *See* Character.

Complication A complication is an additional factor or problem introduced into the rising action of a story to make the conflict more difficult. Often, a plot complication makes it seem as though the main character is getting farther away from the thing he or she wants.

Conclusion A conclusion is a statement of belief based on evidence, experience, and reasoning. A **valid conclusion** is a conclusion that logically follows from the facts or statements upon which it is based. A **deductive conclusion** is one that follows from a particular generalization or premise. An **inductive conclusion** is a broad conclusion or generalization that is reached by arguing from specific facts and examples.

Conflict A conflict is a struggle between opposing forces. Almost every story has a main conflict—a conflict that is the story's focus. An **external conflict** involves a character pitted against an outside force, such as nature, a physical obstacle, or another character. An **internal conflict** is one that occurs within a character.

See also Plot.

Connect Connecting is a reader's process of relating the content of a text to his or her own knowledge and experience.

Connotation A connotation is an attitude or a feeling associated with a word, in contrast to the word's **denotation,** which is its literal, or dictionary, meaning. The connotations of a word may be positive or negative. For example, *enthusiastic* has positive associations, while *rowdy* has negative ones. Connotations of words can have an important influence on style and meaning and are particularly important in poetry.

Consonance Consonance is the repetition of consonant sounds within and at the end of words, as in "lonely afternoon." Consonance is unlike rhyme in that the vowel sounds preceding or following the repeated consonant sounds differ. Consonance is often used together with **alliteration, assonance,** and **rhyme** to create a musical quality, to emphasize certain words, or to unify a poem.

See also Alliteration.

Consumer Documents Consumer documents are printed materials that accompany products and services. They are intended for the buyers or users of the products or services and usually provide information about use, care, operation, or assembly. Some common consumer documents are applications, contracts, warranties, manuals, instructions, package inserts, labels, brochures, and schedules.

Context Clues When you encounter an unfamiliar word, you can often use context clues as aids for understanding. Context clues are the words and phrases surrounding the word that provide hints about the word's meaning.

Controlling Idea *See* Main Idea.

Counterargument A counterargument is an argument made to answer an opposing argument, or **counterclaim.** A good argument anticipates opposing viewpoints and provides counterarguments to refute (disprove) or answer them.

Counterclaim *See* Counterargument.

Couplet A couplet is a rhymed pair of lines. A couplet may be written in any rhythmic pattern, for example:

> Follow your heart's desire
> And good things may transpire.

See also Stanza.

Credibility Credibility refers to the believability or trustworthiness of a source and the information it contains.

Critical Essay *See* Essay.

Critical Review A critical review is an evaluation or critique by a reviewer or critic. Different types of reviews include film reviews, book reviews, music reviews, and art show reviews.

Critique *See* Critical Review.

Database A database is a collection of information that can be quickly and easily accessed and searched and from which information can be easily retrieved. It is frequently presented in an electronic format.

Debate A debate is basically an argument—but a very structured one that requires a good deal of preparation. In academic settings, debate usually refers to a formal argumentation contest in which two opposing teams defend and attack a proposition.

See also Argument.

Deductive Reasoning Deductive reasoning is a way of thinking that begins with a generalization, presents a specific situation, and then advances with facts and evidence to a logical conclusion. The following passage has a deductive argument embedded in it: "All students in the drama class must attend the play on Thursday. Since Ava is in the class, she had better show up." This deductive argument can be broken down as follows: generalization—all students in the drama class must attend the play on Thursday; specific situation—Ava is a student in the drama class; conclusion—Ava must attend the play.

Denotation *See* Connotation.

Dénouement *See* Falling Action.

Dialect A dialect is a form of language that is spoken in a particular geographic area or by a particular social or ethnic group. A group's dialect is reflected in its pronunciations, vocabulary, expressions, and grammatical structures. Writers use dialects to capture the flavors of locales and to bring characters to life, re-creating the way they actually speak.

Dialogue Dialogue is written conversation between two or more characters. Writers use dialogue to bring characters to life and to give readers insights into the characters' qualities, traits, and reactions to other characters. Realistic, well-paced dialogue also advances the plot of a narrative. In fiction, dialogue is usually set off with quotation marks. In drama, stories are told primarily through dialogue. Playwrights use stage directions to indicate how they intend the dialogue to be interpreted by actors.

Diary A diary is a daily record of a writer's thoughts, experiences, and feelings. As such, it is a type of autobiographical writing. The terms *diary* and *journal* are often used synonymously.

Diction A writer's or speaker's choice of words and way of arranging the words in sentences is called diction. Diction can be broadly characterized as formal or informal. It can also be described as technical or common, abstract or concrete, and literal or figurative. A writer for a science journal would use a more formal, more technical, and possibly more abstract diction than would a writer for the science section of a local newspaper.

See also Style.

Dictionary *See* Reference Works.

Drama Drama is literature in which plots and characters are developed through dialogue and action; in other words, it is literature in play form. Drama is meant to be performed. Stage plays, radio plays, movies, and television programs are types of drama. Most plays are divided into acts, with each act having an emotional peak, or climax. Certain modern plays have only one act. Most plays contain stage directions, which describe settings, lighting, sound effects, the movements and emotions of actors, and the ways in which dialogue should be spoken.

Dramatic Irony *See* Irony.

Dramatic Monologue A dramatic monologue is a lyric poem in which a speaker addresses a silent or absent listener in a moment of high intensity or deep emotion, as if engaged in private conversation. The speaker proceeds without interruption or argument, and the effect on the reader is that of hearing just one side of a conversation. This technique allows the poet to focus on the feelings, personality, and motivations of the speaker.

See also Lyric Poetry; Soliloquy.

Draw Conclusions To draw a conclusion is to make a judgment or arrive at a belief based on evidence, experience, and reasoning.

Dynamic Character *See* Character.

Editorial An editorial is an opinion piece that usually appears on the editorial page of a newspaper or as part of a news broadcast. The editorial section of a newspaper presents opinions rather than objective news reports.

See also Op-Ed Piece.

Either/Or Fallacy An either/or fallacy is a statement that suggests that there are only two possible ways to view a situation or only two options to choose from. In other words, it is a statement that falsely frames a dilemma, giving the impression that no options exist but the two presented —for example, "Either we stop the construction of a new airport, or the surrounding suburbs will become ghost towns."

Elegy An elegy is an extended meditative poem in which the speaker reflects on death— often in tribute to a person who has died recently—or on an equally serious subject. Most elegies are written in formal, dignified language and are serious in tone.

Emotional Appeals Emotional appeals are messages that evoke strong feelings—such as fear, pity, or vanity—in order to persuade instead of using facts and evidence to make a point. An **appeal to fear** is a message that taps into people's fear of losing their safety or security. An **appeal to pity** is a message that taps into people's sympathy and compassion for others to build support for an idea, a cause, or a proposed action. An **appeal to vanity** is a message that attempts to persuade by tapping into people's desire to feel good about themselves.

Encyclopedia *See* Reference Works.

Epic An epic is a long narrative poem on a serious subject, presented in an elevated or formal style. It traces the adventures of a great hero whose actions reflect the ideals and values of a nation or race. Epics address universal concerns, such as good and evil, life and death, and sin and redemption. The *Odyssey* is an epic.

Epic Hero An epic hero is a larger-than-life figure who embodies the ideals of a nation or race. Epic heroes take part in dangerous adventures and accomplish great deeds. Many undertake long, difficult journeys and display great courage and superhuman strength.

Epic Simile An epic simile (also called a Homeric simile) is a long, elaborate comparison that often continues for a number of lines. Homer uses epic similes in the *Odyssey*.

See also Simile.

Epilogue An epilogue is a short addition at the end of a literary work, often dealing with the future of the characters. The concluding speech by Prince Escalus in *Romeo and Juliet* serves as an epilogue.

Epithet An epithet is a brief phrase that points out traits associated with a particular person or thing. In the *Odyssey*, Odysseus is often called "the master strategist."

Essay An essay is a short work of nonfiction that deals with a single subject. Some essays are **formal**—that is, tightly structured and written in an impersonal style. Others are **informal,** with a looser structure and a more personal style. Generally, an **informative** or **expository essay** presents or explains information and ideas. A **personal essay** is typically an informal essay in which the writer expresses his or her thoughts and feelings about a subject, focusing on the meaning of events and issues in his or her own life. In a **reflective essay,** the author makes a connection between a personal observation or experience and a universal idea, such as love, courage, or freedom. A **critical essay** evaluates a situation, a course of action, or a work of art. In an **argumentative** or **persuasive essay,** the author attempts to convince readers to adopt a certain viewpoint or to take a particular stand.

Evaluate To evaluate is to examine something carefully and judge its value or worth. Evaluating is an important skill for gaining insight into what you read. A reader can evaluate the actions of a particular character, for example, or can form an opinion about the value of an entire work.

Evidence Evidence is the specific pieces of information that support a claim. Evidence can take the form of facts, quotations, examples, statistics, or personal experiences, among others.

Exposition Exposition is the first stage of a plot in a typical story. The exposition provides important background information and introduces the setting and the important characters. The conflict the characters face may also be introduced in the exposition, or it may be introduced later, in the rising action.

See also Plot.

Expository Essay *See* Essay.

Extended Metaphor An extended metaphor is a figure of speech that compares two essentially unlike things at some length and in several ways. It does not contain the words *like* or *as*.

See also Metaphor.

External Conflict *See* Conflict.

Fable A fable is a brief tale told to illustrate a moral or teach a lesson. Often the moral of a fable appears in a distinct and memorable statement near the tale's beginning or end.

See also Moral.

Fact versus Opinion A fact is a statement that can be proved or verified. An opinion, on the other hand, is a statement that cannot be proved because it expresses a person's beliefs, feelings, or thoughts.

See also Inference; Generalization.

Fallacy A fallacy is an error in reasoning. Typically, a fallacy is based on an incorrect inference or a misuse of evidence. Some common logical fallacies are **circular reasoning, either/or fallacy, oversimplification, overgeneralization,** and **stereotyping.**

See also Either/Or Fallacy, Logical Appeal, Overgeneralization.

Falling Action In a plot, the falling action follows the climax and shows the results of the important action that happened at the climax. Tension eases as the falling action begins; however, the final outcome of the story is not yet fully worked out at this stage. Events in the falling action lead to the **resolution,** or **dénouement,** of the plot.

See also Climax; Plot.

Fantasy Fantasy is a type of fiction that is highly imaginative and portrays events, settings, or characters that are unrealistic. The setting might be a nonexistent world, the plot might involve magic or the supernatural, and the characters might employ superhuman powers.

Farce Farce is a type of exaggerated comedy that features an absurd plot, ridiculous situations, and humorous dialogue. The main purpose of a farce is to keep an audience laughing. The characters are usually stereotypes, or simplified examples of individual traits or qualities. Comic devices typically used in farces include mistaken identity, deception, physical comedy, wordplay—such as puns and double meanings—and exaggeration.

Faulty Reasoning *See* Fallacy.

Feature Article A feature article is a main article in a newspaper or a cover story in a magazine. A feature article is focused more on entertaining than informing. Features are lighter or more general than hard news and tend to be about human interest or lifestyles.

Fiction Fiction is prose writing that consists of imaginary elements. Although fiction can be inspired by actual events and real people, it usually springs from writers' imaginations. The basic elements of fiction are plot, character, setting, and theme. The novel and short story are forms of fiction.

See also Character; Novel; Plot; Setting; Short Story; Theme.

Figurative Language Figurative language is language that communicates meanings beyond the literal meanings of words. In figurative language, words are often used to symbolize ideas and concepts they would not otherwise be associated with. Writers use figurative language to create effects, to emphasize ideas, and to evoke emotions. Simile, metaphor, extended metaphor, hyperbole, and personification are examples of figurative language.

See also Hyperbole; Metaphor; Personification; Simile.

Figure of Speech *See* Figurative Language; Hyperbole; Metaphor; Personification; Simile; Understatement.

First-Person Point of View *See* Point of View.

Flashback A flashback is an account of a conversation, an episode, or an event that happened before the beginning of a story. Often, a flashback interrupts the chronological flow of a story to give the reader information needed to understand a character's present situation. Flashbacks also help create such effects as mystery, tension, or surprise.

Foil A foil is a character who provides a striking contrast to another character. By using a foil, a writer can call attention to certain traits possessed by a main character or simply enhance a character by contrast. In Shakespeare's *Romeo and Juliet,* Mercutio serves as a foil to Romeo.

Foreshadowing Foreshadowing is a writer's use of hints or clues to suggest events that will occur later in a story. The hints and clues might be included in a character's dialogue or behavior, or they might be included in details of description. Foreshadowing creates suspense, mystery, and surprise, and makes readers eager to find out what will happen.

Form Form refers to the principles of arrangement in a poem—the ways in which lines are organized. Form in poetry includes the following elements: the length of lines, the placement of lines, and the grouping of lines into stanzas.

See also Stanza.

Frame Story A frame story exists when a story is told within a narrative setting, or "frame"; it creates a story within a story. This storytelling technique has been used for over one thousand years and was employed in famous works such as *One Thousand and One Arabian Nights* and Geoffrey Chaucer's *The Canterbury Tales.*

Free Verse Free verse is poetry that does not contain regular patterns of rhythm or rhyme. The lines in free verse often flow more naturally than do rhymed, metrical lines and thus achieve a rhythm more like that of everyday speech.

Although free verse lacks conventional meter, it may contain various rhythmic and sound effects, such as repetitions of syllables or words. Free verse can be used for a variety of subjects.

See also Meter; Rhyme.

Functional Documents *See* Consumer Documents; Public Documents; Workplace Documents.

Generalization A generalization is a broad statement about a class or category of people, ideas, or things, based on a study of only some of its members.

See also Overgeneralization.

Genre The term *genre* refers to a category in which a work of literature is classified. The major genres in literature are fiction, nonfiction, poetry, and drama.

Government Publications Government publications are documents produced by government organizations. Pamphlets, brochures, and reports are just some of the many forms these publications may take. Government publications can be reliable resources for a wide variety of topics.

Graphic Aid A graphic aid is a visual tool that is printed, handwritten, or drawn. Text features such as charts, diagrams, graphs, photographs, and maps can all be graphic aids. Sometimes captions are included with a graphic aid to convey information.

Graphic Organizer A graphic organizer is a "word picture"—that is, a visual illustration of a verbal statement—that helps a reader understand a text. Charts, tables, webs, and diagrams can all be graphic organizers. Graphic organizers and graphic aids can look the same. For example, a table in a science article will not be constructed differently from a table that is a graphic organizer. However, graphic organizers and graphic aids do differ in how they are used. Graphic aids are the visual representations that people encounter when they read informational texts. Graphic organizers are visuals that people construct to help them understand texts or organize information.

Haiku Haiku is a form of Japanese poetry in which 17 syllables are arranged in three lines of 5, 7, and 5 syllables each. The rules of haiku are strict. In addition to the syllabic count, the poet must create a clear picture that will evoke a strong emotional response in the reader. Nature is a particularly important source of inspiration for Japanese haiku poets, and details from nature are often the subjects of their poems.

Hero A hero is a main character or protagonist in a story. In older literary works, heroes tend to be better than ordinary humans. They are typically courageous, strong, honorable, and intelligent. They are protectors of society who hold back the forces of evil and fight to make the world a better place. In modern literature, a hero may simply be the most important character in a story. Such a hero is often an ordinary person with ordinary problems.

Historical Documents Historical documents are writings that have played a significant role in human events or are themselves records of such events. The Declaration of Independence, for example, is a historical document.

Historical Fiction A short story or novel can be classified as historical fiction when the settings and details of the plot include real places and real events of historical importance. Historical figures may appear as major or minor characters. In historical fiction, the setting generally influences the plot in important ways.

Horror Fiction Horror fiction contains strange, mysterious, violent, and often supernatural events that create suspense and terror in the reader. Edgar Allan Poe and Stephen King are famous authors of horror fiction.

How-To Writing A how-to book or article explains how to do something—usually an activity, a sport, or a household project.

Humor In literature, there are three basic types of humor, all of which may involve exaggeration or irony. **Humor of situation** arises out of the plot of a work. It usually involves exaggerated events or **situational irony,** which arises when something happens that is different from what was expected. **Humor of character** is often based on exaggerated personalities or on characters' failure to recognize their own flaws, a form of dramatic irony. **Humor of language** may include sarcasm, exaggeration, puns, or verbal irony, in which what is said is not what is meant.
See also Irony.

Hyperbole Hyperbole is a figure of speech in which the truth is exaggerated for emphasis or humorous effect.

Iambic Pentameter Iambic pentameter is a metrical pattern of five feet, or units, each of which is made up of two syllables, the first unstressed and the second stressed. Iambic pentameter is the most common meter used in English poetry; it is the meter used in blank verse and in the sonnet. Shakespeare used iambic pentameter in his plays.
See also Blank Verse; Sonnet.

Idiom An idiom is a common figure of speech whose meaning is different from the literal meaning of its words. For example, the phrase "raining cats and dogs" does not literally mean that cats and dogs are falling from the sky; the expression means "raining heavily."

Imagery Imagery consists of descriptive words and phrases that re-create sensory experiences for the reader. Imagery usually appeals to one or more of the five senses— sight, hearing, smell, taste, and touch—to help the reader imagine exactly what is being described.

Implied Controlling Idea An implied controlling idea is one that is suggested by details rather than stated explicitly.
See also Main Idea.

Implied Main Idea *See* Main Idea.

Index The index of a book is an alphabetized list of important topics and details covered in the book and the page numbers on which they can be found. An index can be used to quickly find specific information about a topic.

Inductive Reasoning Inductive reasoning is the process of logically reasoning from specific observations, examples, and facts to arrive at a general conclusion or principle.

Inference An inference is a logical assumption that is based on observed facts and one's own knowledge and experience.

Informational Nonfiction Informational nonfiction is writing that provides factual information. It often explains ideas or teaches processes. Examples include news reports, science textbooks, software instructions, and lab reports.

Informative Essay *See* Essay.

Internal Conflict *See* Conflict.

Internet The Internet is a global, interconnected system of computer networks that allows for communication through e-mail, listserves, and the World Wide Web. The Internet connects computers and computer users throughout the world.

Interview An interview is a conversation conducted by a writer or reporter, in which facts or statements are elicited from another person, recorded, and then broadcast or published.

Irony Irony is a special kind of contrast between appearance and reality—usually one in which reality is the opposite of what it seems. One type of irony is **situational irony,** a contrast between what a reader or character expects and what actually exists or happens. Another type of irony is **dramatic irony,** in which the reader or viewer knows something that a character does not know. **Verbal irony** exists when someone knowingly exaggerates or says one thing and means another.

Journal A journal is a periodical publication issued by a legal, medical, or other professional organization. Alternatively, the term may be used to refer to a diary or daily record.

See also Diary.

Legend A legend is a story handed down from the past, especially one that is popularly believed to be based on historical events. Though legends often incorporate supernatural or magical elements, they claim to be the story of a real human being and are often set in a particular time and place. These characteristics separate a legend from a myth.

See also Myth.

Limited Point of View *See* Point of View.

Line The line is the core unit of a poem. In poetry, line length is an essential element of the poem's meaning and rhythm. **Line breaks,** where a line of poetry ends, may coincide with grammatical units. However, a line break may also occur in the middle of a grammatical or syntactical unit, creating a meaningful pause or emphasis. Poets use a variety of line breaks to manipulate sense, grammar, and syntax and thereby create a wide range of effects.

Literary Criticism *See* Text Criticism.

Literary Nonfiction Literary nonfiction is nonfiction that is recognized as being of artistic value or that is about literature. Autobiographies, biographies, essays, and eloquent speeches typically fall into this category.

Loaded Language Loaded language consists of words with strongly positive or negative connotations intended to influence a reader's or listener's attitude.

Logical Appeal A logical appeal relies on logic and facts, appealing to people's reasoning or intellect rather than to their values or emotions. Flawed logical appeals—that is, errors in reasoning—are considered logical fallacies.

See also Fallacy.

Logical Argument A logical argument is an argument in which the logical relationship between the support and the claim is sound.

Lyric Poetry A lyric poem is a short poem in which a single speaker expresses personal thoughts and feelings. Most poems other than dramatic and narrative poems are lyric poems. In ancient Greece, lyric poetry was meant to be sung. Modern lyrics are usually not intended for singing, but they are characterized by strong melodic rhythms. Lyric poetry has a variety of forms and covers many subjects, from love and death to everyday experiences.

Magical Realism Magical realism is a literary genre that combines fantastic or magical events with realistic occurrences in a matter-of-fact way to delight or surprise the reader. A famous example of magical realism is Gabriel García Márquez's novel *One Hundred Years of Solitude.*

Main Idea A main idea, or controlling idea, is the most important idea or impression about a topic that a writer or speaker conveys. It can be the central idea of an entire work or of just a paragraph. Often, the main idea of a paragraph is expressed in a topic sentence. However, a main idea may just be implied, or suggested, by details. A main idea and supporting details can serve as a basic pattern of organization in a piece of writing, with the central idea about a topic being supported by details.

Make Inferences *See* Inference.

Memoir A memoir is a form of autobiographical writing in which a writer shares his or her personal experiences and observations of significant events or people. Often informal or even intimate in tone, memoirs usually give readers insight into the impact of historical events on people's lives.

See also Autobiography.

Metaphor A metaphor is a figure of speech that makes a comparison between two things that are basically unlike but have something in common. Unlike similes, metaphors do not contain the word *like* or *as*.

See also Extended Metaphor; Figurative Language; Simile.

Meter Meter is a regular pattern of stressed and unstressed syllables in a poem. The meter of a poem emphasizes the musical quality of the language. Each unit of meter, known as a **foot,** consists of one stressed syllable and one or two unstressed syllables. In representations of meter, a stressed syllable is indicated by the symbol ´; an unstressed syllable, by the symbol ˘. The four basic types of metrical feet are the **iamb,** an unstressed syllable followed by a stressed syllable (˘ ´); the **trochee,** a stressed syllable followed by an unstressed syllable (´ ˘); the **anapest,** two unstressed syllables followed by a stressed syllable (˘ ˘ ´); and the **dactyl,** a stressed syllable followed by two unstressed syllables (´ ˘ ˘).

See also Rhythm.

Mise en Scène *Mise en scène* is a term from the French that refers to the various physical aspects of a dramatic presentation, such as lighting, costumes, scenery, makeup, and props.

Monitor Monitoring is the strategy of checking your comprehension as you are reading and

modifying the strategies you are using to suit your needs. Monitoring may include some or all of the following strategies: questioning, clarifying, visualizing, predicting, connecting, and rereading.

Mood In a literary work, mood is the feeling or atmosphere that a writer creates for the reader. Descriptive words, imagery, and figurative language contribute to the mood of a work, as do the sound and rhythm of the language used.

See also Tone.

Moral A moral is a lesson taught in a literary work, such as a fable. For example, the moral "Do not count your chickens before they are hatched" teaches that one should not count on one's fortunes or blessings until they appear.

See also Fable.

Motivation *See* Character.

Myth A myth is a traditional story, usually concerning some superhuman being or unlikely event, that was once widely believed to be true. Frequently, myths were attempts to explain natural phenomena, such as solar and lunar eclipses or the cycle of the seasons. For some peoples, myths were both a kind of science and a religion. In addition, myths served as literature and entertainment, just as they do for modern-day audiences.

Greek mythology forms much of the background in Homer's *Odyssey*. For example, the myth of the judgment of Paris describes events that led to the Trojan War. The goddesses Athena, Hera, and Aphrodite asked a mortal—Paris—to decide which of them was the most beautiful. Paris chose Aphrodite and was rewarded by her with Helen, wife of the Greek king Menelaus.

Narrative Nonfiction Narrative nonfiction is writing that reads much like fiction, except that the characters, setting, and plot are real rather than imaginary. Its purpose is usually to entertain or to express opinions or feelings. Narrative nonfiction includes, but is not limited to, autobiographies, biographies, memoirs, diaries, and journals.

Narrative Poetry Narrative poetry tells a story or recounts events. Like a short story or a novel, a narrative poem has the following elements: plot, characters, setting, and theme.

Narrator The narrator of a story is the character or voice that relates the story's events to the reader.

See also Persona; Point of View.

News Article A news article is a piece of writing that reports on a recent event. In newspapers, news articles are usually written concisely and report the latest news, presenting the most important facts first and then more detailed information. In magazines, news articles are usually more elaborate than those in newspapers because they are written to provide both information and analysis. Also, news articles in magazines do not necessarily present the most important facts first.

Nonfiction Nonfiction is writing that tells about real people, places, and events. Unlike fiction, nonfiction is mainly written to convey factual information, although writers of nonfiction shape information in accordance with their own purposes and attitudes. Nonfiction can be a good source of information, but readers frequently have to examine it carefully in order to detect biases, notice gaps in the information provided, and identify errors in logic. Nonfiction includes a diverse range of writing—newspaper articles, letters, essays, biographies, movie reviews, speeches, true-life adventure stories, advertising, and more.

Novel A novel is an extended work of fiction. Like a short story, a novel is essentially the product of a writer's imagination. Because a novel is considerably longer than a short story, a novelist can develop a wider range of characters and a more complex plot.

Novella A novella is a work of fiction that is longer than a short story but shorter than a novel. A novella differs from a novel in that it concentrates on a limited cast of characters, a relatively short time span, and a single chain of events. The novella is an attempt to combine the compression of the short story with the development of the novel.

Ode An ode is a complex lyric poem that develops a serious and dignified theme. Odes appeal to both the imagination and the intellect, and many commemorate events or praise people or elements of nature.

Omniscient Point of View *See* Point of View.

Onomatopoeia Onomatopoeia is the use of words whose sounds echo their meanings, such as *buzz, whisper, gargle,* and *murmur.* Onomatopoeia as a literary technique goes beyond the use of simple echoic words, however. Skilled writers, especially poets, choose words whose sounds intensify images and suggest meanings.

Op-Ed Piece An op-ed piece is an opinion piece that usually appears opposite ("op") the editorial page of a newspaper. Unlike editorials, op-ed pieces are written and submitted by named writers.

Organization *See* Pattern of Organization.

Overgeneralization An overgeneralization is a generalization that is too broad. You can often recognize overgeneralizations by the appearance of words and phrases such as *all, everyone, every time, any, anything, no one,* and *none.* Consider, for example, this statement: "None of the sanitation workers in our city really care about keeping the environment clean." In all probability, there are many exceptions; the writer can't possibly know the feelings of every sanitation worker in the city.

Overview An overview is a short summary of a story, a speech, or an essay. It orients the reader by providing a preview of the text to come.

Oxymoron An oxymoron is a special kind of concise paradox that brings together two contradictory terms. "Deafening silence" and "original copy" are examples of oxymorons.

Paradox A paradox is a seemingly contradictory or absurd statement that may nonetheless suggest an important truth.

Parallelism Parallelism is the use of similar grammatical constructions to express ideas that are related or equal in importance. Martin Luther King Jr. uses parallelism in his "I Have a Dream" speech.

Parallel Plot A parallel plot is a particular type of plot in which two stories of equal importance are told simultaneously. The story moves back and forth between the two plots.

Paraphrase Paraphrasing is the restating of information in one's own words.

See also Summarize.

Parody A parody is an imitation of another work, a type of literature, or a writer's style, usually for the purpose of poking fun. It may serve as an element of a larger work or be a complete work in itself. The purpose of parody may be to ridicule through broad humor, deploying such techniques as exaggeration or the use of inappropriate subject matter. Such techniques may even provide insights into the original work.

Pastoral A pastoral is a poem presenting shepherds in rural settings, usually in an idealized manner. The language and form of a pastoral tends to be formal. English Renaissance poets were drawn to the pastoral as a means of conveying their own emotions and ideas, particularly about love.

Pattern of Organization A pattern of organization is a particular arrangement of ideas and information. Such a pattern may be used to organize an entire composition or a single paragraph within a longer work. The following are the most common patterns of organization: cause-and- effect, chronological order, compare-and-contrast, classification, deductive, inductive, order of importance, problem-solution, sequential, and spatial.

See also Cause and Effect; Chronological Order; Classification; Compare and Contrast; Problem-Solution Order; Sequential Order.

Periodical A periodical is a publication that is issued at regular intervals of more than one day. For example, a periodical may be a weekly, monthly, or quarterly journal or magazine. Newspapers and other daily publications generally are not classified as periodicals.

Persona A persona is a voice that a writer assumes in a particular work. A persona is like a mask worn by the writer, separating his or her identity from that of the speaker or the narrator. It is the persona's voice—not the writer's voice—that narrates a story or speaks in a poem.

See also Narrator; Speaker.

Personal Essay *See* Essay.

Personification Personification is a figure of speech in which human qualities are given to an object, animal, or idea, for example: The night wind sings an eerie song.

See also Figurative Language.

Persuasion Persuasion is the art of swaying others' feelings, beliefs, or actions. Persuasion normally appeals to both the intellect and the emotions of readers. **Persuasive techniques** are the methods used to influence others to adopt certain opinions or beliefs or to act in certain ways. Types of persuasive techniques include emotional appeals, logical appeals, and loaded language. When used properly, persuasive techniques can add depth to writing that's meant to persuade. Persuasive techniques can, however, be misused to cloud factual information, disguise poor reasoning, or unfairly exploit people's emotions in order to shape their opinions.

See also Emotional Appeals; Loaded Language; Logical Appeal.

Persuasive Essay *See* Essay.

Play *See* Drama.

Plot The sequence of events in a story is called the plot. A plot focuses on a central **conflict** or problem faced by the main character. The actions that the characters take to resolve the conflict build toward a climax. In general, it is not long after this point that the conflict is resolved and the story ends. A plot typically develops in five stages: exposition, rising action, climax, falling action, and resolution.

See also Climax; Exposition; Falling Action; Rising Action.

Poetry Poetry is a type of literature in which words are carefully chosen and arranged to create certain effects. Poets use a variety of sound devices, imagery, and figurative language to express emotions and ideas.

See also Alliteration; Assonance; Ballad; Free Verse; Imagery; Meter; Rhyme; Rhythm; Stanza.

Point of View Point of view refers to the method of narration used in a short story, novel, narrative poem, or work of nonfiction. In a work told from a **first-person** point of view, the narrator is a character in the story. In a work told from a **third-person** point of view, the narrative voice is outside the action, not one of the characters. If a story is told from a **third-person omniscient,** or all-knowing, point of view, the narrator sees into the minds of all the characters. If events are related from a **third-person limited** point of view, the narrator tells what only one character thinks, feels, and observes.

See also Narrator.

Predict Predicting is a reading strategy that involves using text clues to make a reasonable guess about what will happen next in a story.

Primary Source *See* Sources.

Prior Knowledge Prior knowledge is the knowledge a reader already possesses about a topic. This information might come from personal experiences, expert accounts, books, films, or other sources.

Problem-Solution Order Problem-solution order is a pattern of organization in which a problem is stated and analyzed and then one or more solutions are proposed and examined. Writers use words and phrases such as *propose, conclude, reason for, problem, answer,* and *solution* to connect ideas and details when writing about problems and solutions.

Procedural Texts Procedural texts are functional texts that were created to communicate instructions, rules, processes, or other detailed, step-by-step information.

See also Consumer Documents; Public Documents; Workplace Documents.

Prologue A prologue is an introductory scene in a drama. Some Elizabethan plays include prologues that comment on the theme or moral point that will be revealed in the play. The prologue is a feature of all Greek drama.

Prop The word *prop,* originally an abbreviation of the word *property,* refers to any physical object that is used in a drama.

Propaganda Propaganda is a form of communication that may use distorted, false,

or misleading information. It usually refers to manipulative political discourse.

Prose Generally, prose refers to all forms of written or spoken expression that are not in verse. The term, therefore, may be used to describe very different forms of writing— short stories as well as essays, for example.

Protagonist A protagonist is the main character in a work of literature—the character who is involved in the central conflict of the story. Usually, the protagonist changes after the central conflict reaches a climax. He or she may be a hero and is usually the one with whom the audience tends to identify.

Public Documents Public documents are documents that were written for the public to provide information that is of public interest or concern. They include government documents, speeches, signs, and rules and regulations.

See also Government Publications.

Pun A pun is a joke that comes from a play on words. It can make use of a word's multiple meanings or of a word's sound.

Quatrain A quatrain is a four-line stanza, or group of lines, in poetry. The most common stanza in English poetry, the quatrain can have a variety of meters and rhyme schemes.

Realistic Fiction Realistic fiction is fiction that is a truthful imitation of ordinary life.

Recurring Theme *See* Theme.

Reference Works General reference works are sources that contain facts and background information on a wide range of subjects. More specific reference works contain in-depth information on a single subject. Most reference works are good sources of reliable information because they have been reviewed by experts. The following are some common reference works: encyclopedias, dictionaries, thesauri, almanacs, atlases, chronologies, biographical dictionaries, and directories.

Reflective Essay *See* Essay.

Refrain A refrain is one or more lines repeated in each stanza of a poem.

See also Stanza.

Repetition Repetition is a technique in which a sound, word, phrase, or line is repeated for emphasis or unity. Repetition often helps to reinforce meaning and create an appealing rhythm. The term includes specific devices associated with both prose and poetry, such as alliteration and parallelism.

See also Alliteration; Parallelism; Sound Devices.

Resolution *See* Falling Action.

Review *See* Critical Review.

Rhetorical Devices Rhetorical devices are techniques writers use to enhance their arguments and communicate more effectively. Rhetorical devices include analogy, parallelism, rhetorical questions, and repetition.

See also Analogy; Repetition; Rhetorical Questions.

Rhetorical Questions Rhetorical questions are those that do not require a reply. Writers use them to suggest that their arguments make the answer obvious or self-evident.

Rhyme Rhyme is the occurrence of similar or identical sounds at the end of two or more words, such as *suite, heat,* and *complete.* Rhyme that occurs within a single line of poetry is **internal rhyme.** Rhyme that occurs at the ends of lines of poetry is called **end rhyme.** End rhyme that is not exact but approximate is called **slant rhyme,** or **off rhyme.** Notice the following example of slant rhyme involving the words *care* and *dear:*

> You act like you don't care,
> But I know you do, my dear.

Rhyme Scheme A rhyme scheme is a pattern of end rhymes in a poem. A rhyme scheme is noted by assigning a letter of the alphabet, beginning with *a,* to each line. Lines that rhyme are given the same letter.

Rhythm Rhythm is a pattern of stressed and unstressed syllables in a line of poetry. Poets use rhythm to bring out the musical quality of language, to emphasize ideas, to create moods, and to heighten emotional responses. Devices such as alliteration, rhyme, assonance, consonance, and parallelism create rhythm.

See also Meter.

Rising Action Rising action is the stage in a plot in which the conflict develops and story events build toward a climax. During this stage, complications arise that make the conflict more intense. Tension grows as the characters struggle to resolve the conflict.

See also Plot.

Romance A romance refers to any imaginative story concerned with noble heroes, chivalric codes of honor, passionate love, daring deeds, and supernatural events. Writers of romances tend to idealize their heroes as well as the eras in which the heroes live. Medieval romances include stories of kings, knights, and ladies who are motivated by love, religious faith, or simply a desire for adventure.

Sarcasm Sarcasm is a kind of particularly cutting irony. Generally, sarcasm is the taunting use of praise to mean its opposite—that is, to insult someone or something.

Satire Satire is a literary technique in which ideas, customs, behaviors, or institutions are ridiculed for the purpose of improving society. Satire may be gently witty, mildly abrasive, or bitterly critical, and it often involves the use of irony and exaggeration to force readers to see something in a critical light.

Scanning Scanning is the process of searching through writing for a particular fact or piece of information. When you scan, your eyes sweep across a page, looking for key words that may lead you to the information you want.

Scansion Scansion is the notation of stressed and unstressed syllables in poetry. A stressed syllable is indicated by the symbol ´; an unstressed syllable, by the symbol ˘. Using scansion can help you determine the rhythm and meter of a poem.

See also Meter.

Scene In drama, the action is often divided into acts and scenes. Each scene presents an episode of the play's plot and typically occurs at a single place and time.

See also Act.

Scenery Scenery is a painted backdrop or other structures used to create the setting for a play.

Science Fiction Science fiction is fiction in which a writer explores unexpected possibilities of the past or the future, using known scientific data and theories as well as his or her creative imagination. Most science fiction writers create believable worlds, although some create fantasy worlds that have familiar elements.

See also Fantasy.

Screenplay A screenplay is a play written for film.

See also Teleplay.

Script The text of a play, film, or broadcast is called a script.

Secondary Source *See* Sources.

Sensory Details Sensory details are words and phrases that appeal to the reader's senses of sight, hearing, touch, smell, and taste. For example, the sensory detail "a fine film of rain" appeals to the senses of sight and touch. Sensory details stimulate the reader to create images in his or her mind.

See also Imagery.

Sequential Order A pattern of organization that shows the order in which events or actions occur is called sequential order. Writers typically use this pattern of organization to explain steps or stages in a process.

Setting Setting is the time and place of the action of a story.

See also Fiction.

Setting a Purpose The process of establishing specific reasons for reading a text is called setting a purpose.

Short Story A short story is a work of fiction that centers on a single idea and can be read in one sitting. Generally, a short story has one main conflict that involves the characters, keeps the story moving, and stimulates readers' interest.

See also Fiction.

Sidebar A sidebar is additional information set in a box alongside or within a news or feature article. Popular magazines often make use of sidebar information.

Signal Words Signal words are words and phrases that indicate what is to come in a text.

Readers can use signal words to discover a text's pattern of organization and to analyze the relationships among the ideas in the text.

Simile A simile is a figure of speech that makes a comparison between two unlike things, using the word *like* or *as,* for example: Her blue-eyed stare was like ice.

See also Epic Simile; Figurative Language; Metaphor.

Situational Irony *See* Irony.

Soliloquy In drama, a soliloquy is a speech in which a character speaks his or her thoughts aloud. Generally, the character is on the stage alone, not speaking to other characters and perhaps not even consciously addressing an audience. At the beginning of Act Two, Scene 3, of *Romeo and Juliet,* Friar Laurence has a long soliloquy. Shakespeare makes use of soliloquies in many of his plays.

See also Aside; Dramatic Monologue.

Sonnet A sonnet is a lyric poem of 14 lines, commonly written in **iambic pentameter.** Sonnets are often classified as Petrarchan or Shakespearean. The Shakespearean, or Elizabethan, sonnet consists of three quatrains, or four-line units, and a final couplet. The typical rhyme scheme is *abab cdcd efef gg.*

See also Iambic Pentameter; Rhyme Scheme.

Sound Devices Sound devices, or uses of words for their auditory effect, can convey meaning and mood or unify a work. Some common sound devices are alliteration, assonance, consonance, meter, onomatopoeia, repetition, rhyme, and rhythm.

See also Alliteration; Assonance; Consonance; Meter; Onomatopoeia; Repetition; Rhyme; Rhythm.

Sources A source is anything that supplies information. **Primary sources** are materials written by people who were present at events, either as participants or as observers. Letters, diaries, autobiographies, speeches, and photographs are primary sources. **Secondary sources** are records of events that were created sometime after the events occurred; the writers were not directly involved or were not present when the events took place. Encyclopedias, textbooks, biographies, most newspaper and magazine articles, and books and articles that interpret or review research are secondary sources.

Spatial Order Spatial order is a pattern of organization that highlights the physical positions or relationships of details or objects. This pattern of organization is typically found in descriptive writing. Writers use words and phrases such as *on the left, to the right, here, over there, above, below, beyond, nearby,* and *in the distance* to indicate the arrangement of details.

Speaker In poetry the speaker is the voice that "talks" to the reader, similar to the narrator in fiction. The speaker is not necessarily the poet.

See also Persona.

Speech A speech is a talk or public address. The purpose of a speech may be to entertain, to explain, to present a claim, to inspire, or any combination of these aims. "I Have a Dream" by Martin Luther King Jr. was written and delivered in order to inspire an audience.

Stage Directions A play typically includes instructions called stage directions, which are usually printed in italic type. They serve as a guide to directors, set and lighting designers, performers, and readers. When stage directions appear within passages of dialogue, parentheses are usually used to set them off from the words spoken by characters.

Stanza A stanza is a group of two or more lines that form a unit in a poem. A stanza is comparable to a paragraph in prose. Each stanza may have the same number of lines, or the number of lines may vary.

See also Couplet; Form; Poetry; Quatrain.

Static Character *See* Character.

Stereotype In literature, a simplified or stock character who conforms to a fixed pattern or is defined by a single trait is known as a stereotype. Such a character does not usually demonstrate the complexity of a real person. Familiar stereotypes in popular literature include the absentminded professor and the busybody.

Stereotyping Stereotyping is a type of overgeneralization. Stereotypes are broad statements made about people on the basis of their gender, ethnicity, race, or political, social, professional, or religious group.

Stream of Consciousness Stream of consciousness is a literary technique developed by modern writers, in which thoughts, feelings, moods, perceptions, and memories are presented as they randomly flow through a character's mind.

Structure Structure is the way in which the parts of a work of literature are put together. In poetry, structure involves the arrangement of words and lines to produce a desired effect. A common structural unit in poetry is the stanza, of which there are numerous types. In prose, structure is the arrangement of larger units or parts of a work. Paragraphs, for example, are basic units in prose, as are chapters in novels and acts in plays. The structure of a poem, short story, novel, play, or nonfictional work usually emphasizes certain important aspects of content.

See also Act; Stanza.

Style Style is the particular way in which a work of literature is written—not *what* is said but *how* it is said. It is the writer's unique way of communicating ideas. Many elements contribute to style, including word choice, sentence structure and length, tone, figurative language, and point of view. A literary style may be described in a variety of ways, such as formal, informal, journalistic, conversational, wordy, ornate, poetic, or dynamic.

Summarize To summarize is to briefly retell, or encapsulate, the main ideas of a piece of writing in one's own words.

See also Paraphrase.

Support Support is any material that serves to prove a claim. In an argument, support typically consists of reasons and evidence. In persuasive texts and speeches, however, support may include appeals to the needs and values of the audience.

Supporting Detail *See* Main Idea.

Surprise Ending A surprise ending is an unexpected plot twist at the end of a story. The surprise may be a sudden turn in the action or a piece of information that gives a different perspective to the entire story.

Suspense Suspense is the excitement or tension that readers feel as they wait to find out how a story ends or a conflict is resolved. Writers create suspense by raising questions in readers' minds about what might happen next. The use of **foreshadowing** and **flashback** are two ways in which writers create suspense.

See also Foreshadowing; Flashback.

Symbol A symbol is a person, a place, an object, or an activity that stands for something beyond itself. For example, a flag is a colored piece of cloth that stands for a country. A white dove is a bird that represents peace.

Synthesize To synthesize information is to take individual pieces of information and combine them with other pieces of information and with prior knowledge or experience to gain a better understanding of a subject or to create a new product or idea.

Tall Tale A tall tale is a humorously exaggerated story about impossible events, often involving the supernatural abilities of the main character. Stories about folk heroes such as Pecos Bill and Paul Bunyan are typical tall tales.

Teleplay A teleplay is a play written for television. In a teleplay, scenes can change quickly and dramatically. The camera can focus the viewer's attention on specific actions. The camera directions in teleplays are much like the stage directions in stage plays.

Text Criticism Text criticism is writing in which literary works, including their various elements, are analyzed, interpreted, evaluated, or compared.

Text Features Text features are design elements that indicate the organizational structure of a text and help make the key ideas and supporting information understandable. Text features include headers, boldface type, italic type, bulleted or numbered lists, sidebars, captions, and graphic aids such as charts, tables, timelines, illustrations, and photographs.

Theme A theme, or central idea, is an underlying message about life or human nature that a writer wants the reader to understand.

It is a perception about life or human nature that the writer shares with the reader. In most cases, themes are not stated directly but must be inferred. A theme may imply how a person should live but should not be confused with a **moral.**

Recurring themes are themes found in a variety of works. For example, authors from varying backgrounds might convey similar themes having to do with the importance of family values. **Universal themes** are themes that are found throughout the literature of all time periods. For example, the *Odyssey* contains a universal theme relating to the hero's search for truth, goodness, and honor.

See also Moral.

Thesaurus *See* Reference Works.

Thesis Statement In an argument, a thesis statement is an expression of the claim that the writer or speaker is trying to support. In an essay, a thesis statement is an expression, in one or two sentences, of the main idea or purpose of the piece of writing.

See also Claim.

Third-Person Point of View *See* Point of View.

Tone Tone is the attitude a writer takes takes toward a subject. Unlike mood, which is intended to shape the reader's emotional response, tone reflects the feelings of the writer. A writer communicates tone through choice of words and details. Tone may often be described by a single word, such as *serious, humorous, formal, informal, somber, sarcastic, playful, ironic, bitter,* or *objective.*

See also Author's Perspective; Mood.

Topic Sentence The topic sentence of a paragraph states the paragraph's central idea. All other sentences in the paragraph provide supporting details.

Tragedy A tragedy is a dramatic work that presents the downfall of a dignified character (**tragic hero**) or characters who are involved in historically or socially significant events. The events in a tragic plot are set in motion by a decision that is often an error in judgment (**tragic flaw**) on the part of the hero. Succeeding events are linked in a cause-and-effect relationship and lead inevitably to a disastrous conclusion, usually death. Shakespeare's *Romeo and Juliet* is a tragedy.

Tragic Flaw *See* Tragedy.

Tragic Hero *See* Tragedy.

Traits *See* Character.

Turning Point *See* Climax.

Understatement Understatement is a technique of creating emphasis by saying less than is actually or literally true. It is the opposite of **hyperbole,** or exaggeration. One of the primary devices of irony, understatement can be used to develop a humorous effect, to create satire, or to achieve a restrained tone.

See also Hyperbole; Irony.

Universal Theme *See* Theme.

Verbal Irony *See* Irony.

Visualize Visualizing is the process of forming a mental picture based on written or spoken information.

Voice Voice is a writer's unique use of language that allows a reader to "hear" a human personality in the writer's work. Elements of style that contribute to a writer's voice include sentence structure, diction, and tone. Voice can reveal much about the author's personality, beliefs, and attitudes.

Website A website is a collection of "pages" on the World Wide Web that is usually devoted to one specific subject. Pages are linked together and are accessed by clicking hyperlinks or menus, which send the user from page to page within the site. Web sites are created by companies, organizations, educational institutions, branches of the government, the military, and individuals.

Word Choice *See* Diction.

Workplace Documents Workplace documents are materials that are produced or used within a work setting, usually to aid in the functioning of the workplace. They include job applications, office memos, training manuals, job descriptions, and sales reports. Workplace documents often include text features, such as captions, graphics, and headers, that make key ideas and supporting information understandable.

Works Cited A list of works cited lists names of all the works a writer has referred to in his or her text. This list often includes not only books and articles but also nonprint sources.

Works Consulted A list of works consulted names all the works a writer consulted in order to create his or her text. It is not limited just to those works cited in the text.

See also Bibliography.

Using the Glossaries

The following glossaries list the Academic Vocabulary and Critical Vocabulary words found in this book in alphabetical order. Use these glossaries just as you would a dictionary—to determine the meanings, parts of speech, pronunciation, and syllabication of words. (Some technical, foreign, and more obscure words in this book are not listed here but are defined for you in the footnotes that accompany many of the selections.)

Many words in the English language have more than one meaning. These glossaries give the meanings that apply to the words as they are used in the selections in this book. Words closely related in form and meaning are listed together in one entry (for instance,

consumption and **consume**), and the definition is given for the first form.

The following abbreviations are used to identify parts of speech of words:

adj. adjective   *adv.* adverb   *n.* noun   *v.* verb

Each word's pronunciation is given in parentheses. A guide to the pronunciation symbols appears in the Pronunciation Key below. The stress marks in the Pronunciation Key are used to indicate the force given to each syllable in a word. They can also help you determine where words are divided into syllables.

For more information about the words in these glossaries or for information about words not listed here, consult a dictionary.

Pronunciation Key

Symbol	Examples
ă	pat
ā	pay
ä	father
âr	care
b	bib
ch	church
d	deed, milled
ĕ	pet
ē	bee
f	fife, phase, rough
g	gag
h	hat
hw	which
ĭ	pit
ī	pie, by
îr	pier
j	judge
k	kick, cat, pique
l	lid, needle* (nēd'l)

Symbol	Examples
m	mum
n	no, sudden* (sud'n)
ng	thing
ŏ	pot
ō	toe
ô	caught, paw
ôr	core
oi	noise
ŏŏ	took
oor	lure
ōō	boot
ou	out
p	pop
r	roar
s	sauce
sh	ship, dish
t	tight, stopped
th	thin
th	this
ŭ	cut

Symbol	Examples
ûr	urge, term, firm, word, heard

Symbol	Examples
v	valve
w	with
y	yes
z	zebra, xylem
zh	vision, pleasure, garage
ə	about, item, edible, gallop, circus
ər	butter

Sounds in Foreign Words

Symbol	Examples
KH	*German* ich, ach; *Scottish* loch
N (bôn)	*French,* bon, fin
œ	*French* feu, oeuf; *German* schön
ü	*French* tu; *German* über

* In English the consonants *l* and *n* often constitute complete syllables by themselves.

Stress Marks

The relevant emphasis with which the syllables of a word or phrase are spoken, called stress, is indicated in three different ways. The strongest, or primary, stress is marked with a bold mark (´). An intermediate, or secondary, level of stress is marked with a similar but lighter mark (´). The weakest stress is unmarked. Words of one syllable show no stress mark.

Glossary of Academic Vocabulary

attribute (ăt′rə-byōōt′) *n.* a characteristic, quality, or trait.

capacity (kə-păs′ĭ-tē) *n.* the ability to contain, hold, produce, or understand.

commit (kə-mĭt′) *v.* to carry out, engage in, or perform.

confer (kən-fûr′) *v.* to grant or give to.

decline (dĭ-klīn′) *v.* to fall apart or deteriorate slowly.

dimension (dĭ-mĕn′shən) *n.* a feature, scale, or measurement of something.

emerge (ĭ-mûrj′) *v.* to come forth, out of, or away from.

enable (ĕ-nā′bəl) *v.* to give the means or opportunity.

enforce (ĕn-fôrs′) *v.* to compel observance of or obedience to.

entity (ĕn′tĭ-tē) *n.* a thing that exists as a unit.

expose (ĭk-spōz′) *v.* to make visible or reveal.

external (ĭk-stûr′nəl) *adj.* related to, part of, or from the outside.

generate (jĕn′ə-rāt′) *v.* to produce or cause something to happen or exist.

impose (ĭm-pōz′) *v.* to bring about by force.

initiate (ĭ-nĭsh′ē-āt′) *v.* to start or cause to begin.

integrate (ĭn′tĭ-grāt′) *v.* to pull together into a whole; unify.

internal (ĭn-tûr′nəl) *adj.* inner; located within something or someone.

motivate (mō′tə-vāt′) *v.* to provide a cause for doing something.

objective (əb-jĕk′tĭv) *n.* an intention, purpose, or goal.

presume (prĭ-zōōm′) *v.* to take for granted as being true; to assume something is true.

pursuit (pər-sōōt′) *n.* the action of chasing or following something.

resolve (rĭ-zŏlv′) *v.* to decide or become determined.

reveal (rĭ-vēl′) *v.* to show or make known.

statistic (stə-tĭs′tĭk) *n.* a piece of numerical data.

subsequent (sŭb′sĭ-kwĕnt′) *adj.* coming after or following.

sustain (sə-stān′) *v.* to support or cause to continue.

trace (trās) *v.* to discover or determine the origins or developmental stages of something.

underlie (ŭn′dər-lī′) *v.* to be the cause or support of.

undertake (ŭn′dər-tāk′) *v.* to assume responsibility for or take on a job or course of action

utilize (yōōt′l-īz) *v.* to make use of.

Glossary of Critical Vocabulary

abominably (ə-bŏm´ə-nə-blē) *adv.* in a hateful way; horribly.

adversary (ăd´vər-sĕr´ē) *n.* an opponent; enemy.

adversity (ăd-vûr´sĭ-tē) *n.* hardship; misfortune.

afflict (ə-flĭkt´) *v.* to cause pain to; to trouble.

allocate (ăl´ə-kāt´) *v.* to assign or designate for.

assail (ə-sāl´) *v.* attack, disturb.

assess (ə-sĕs´) *v.* to evaluate.

assuage (ə-swāj´) *v.* to calm or pacify.

audacious (ô-dā´shəs) *n.* bold, rebellious.

autonomy (ô-tŏn´ə-mē) *n.* independent self-governance.

berate (bĭ-rāt´) *v.* to criticize or scold.

bereaved (bĭ-rēvd´) *adj.* having suffered the loss of a loved one; grieving.

cadence (kād´ns) *n.* lyrical rhythm.

circuitously (sər-kyōō´ĭ-təs-lē) *adv.* in an indirect and lengthy manner.

civic (sĭv´ĭk) *adj.* related to community and citizenship.

cognition (kŏg-nĭsh´ən) *n.* the process or pattern of gaining knowledge.

commandeer (kŏm´ən-dir´) *v.* to take control of by force.

commemorate (kŏ-mĕm´ə-rāt´) *v.* to celebrate or honor.

compatriot (kəm-pā´trē-ət) *n.* a fellow citizen or person from same country.

comply (kəm-plī´) *v.* to obey an instruction or command.

concede (kən-sēd´) *v.* to surrender or acknowledge defeat.

conceive (kən-sēv´) *v.* to form or develop in the mind; devise.

constitute (kŏn´stĭ-tōōt´) *v.* to form or comprise.

constrict (kən-strĭkt´) *v.* to limit or impede growth.

consume (kən-sōōm´) *v.* to completely destroy or eradicate.

contagion (kən-tā´jən) *n.* the spreading from one to another.

contemplate (kŏn´təm-plāt´) *v.* think carefully about.

contemptible (kən-tĕmp´tə-bəl) *adj.* deserving of scorn; despicable.

contention (kən-tĕn´shən) *n.* argued assertion.

conversely (kən-vûrs´lē) *adv.* in a way that contradicts or reverses something.

convert (kən-vûrt´) *v.* to change one's system of beliefs.

decisive (dĭ-sī´sĭv) *adj.* final or concluding.

deduce (dĭ-dōōs´) *v.* to know through reason or logical conclusion.

default (dĭ-fôlt´) *v.* to fail to keep a promise to repay a loan.

degenerate (dĭ-jĕn´ər-āt´) *v.* to decline morally.

delude (dĭ-lōōd´) *v.* to deceive or instill a false belief in.

demeanor (dĭ-mē´nər) *n.* attitude or perceived behavior.

derive (dĭ-rīv´) *v.* to obtain or extract from.

desolate (dĕs´ə-lĭt) *adj.* unhappy; lonely.

desolation (dĕs´ə-la´shən) *n.* lonely grief; misery.

detract (dĭ-trăkt´) *v.* to take away from.

din (dĭn) *n.* loud noise.

discernible (dĭ-sûr´nə-bəl) *adj.* recognizable or noticeable.

discordant (dĭ-skôr´dnt) *adj.* conflicting or not harmonious.

disingenuous (dĭs´ĭn-jĕn´yōō-əs) *adj.* insincere, deceitful.

disintegration (dĭs-ĭn'tĭ-grā'shən) *n.* the process of a whole coming apart in pieces.

distend (dĭ-stĕnd') *v.* to bulge or expand.

distill (dĭ-stĭl') *v.* to transform vapor into liquid.

diversity (dĭ-vûr'sĭ-tē) *n.* having varied social and/or ethnic backgrounds.

edict (ē'dĭkt') *n.* an official rule or proclamation.

emaciated (ĭ-mā'shē-āt'ĭd) *adj.* made extremely thin and weak.

emanate (ĕm'ə-nāt') *v.* to emit or radiate from.

embark (ĕm-bärk') *v.* to set out on a course or a journey (often aboard a boat).

empathy (ĕm'pə-thē) *n.* the ability to understand and identify with another's feelings.

encroach (ĕn-krōch') *v.* to gradually intrude upon or invade.

execute (ĕk'sĭ-kyōōt') *v.* to carry out or accomplish.

exhort (ĭg-zôrt') *v.* to strongly urge or encourage.

expanse (ĭk-spăns') *n.* a large area.

extricate (ĕk'strĭ-kāt') *v.* to release or disentangle from.

foremost (fôr'mōst') *adv.* most importantly.

foreboding (fôr-bō'dĭng) *n.* a sense of approaching evil.

gradation (gră-dā'shən) *n.* a slight, successive change in color, degree, or tone.

guise (gīz) *n.* form or outward appearance; outfit.

harried (hăr'ēd) *adj.* tormented; harassed.

immerse (ĭ-mûrs') *v.* to absorb or involve deeply.

impeccably (ĭm-pĕk'ə-blē) *adv.* perfectly.

imperative (ĭm-pĕr'ə-tĭv) *adj.* crucial, necessary.

imperceptible (ĭm'pər-sĕp'tə-bəl) *adj.* unnoticeable.

implacable (ĭm'plăk'ə-bəl) *adj.* impossible to soothe; unforgiving.

implication (ĭm'plĭ-kā'shən) *n.* consequence or effect.

increment (ĭn'krə-mənt) *n.* an addition or increase by a standard measure of growth.

inextricably (ĭn-ĕk'strĭ-kə-blē) *adv.* in a way impossible to untangle.

innate (ĭ-nāt') *adj.* inborn; existing at birth.

intangible (ĭn-tăn'jə-bəl) *n.* something that is difficult to grasp or explain.

integrity (ĭn-tĕg'rĭ-tē) *n.* consistency and strength of purpose.

intention (ĭn-tĕn'shən) *n.* purpose or plan.

intermittent (ĭn'tər-mĭt'nt) *adj.* occurring at erratic or irregular intervals.

interwoven (ĭn'tər-wō'vən) *adj.* blended or laced together.

intrusion (ĭn-trōō'zhən) *n.* act of trespass or invasion.

intuitive (ĭn-tōō'ĭ-tĭv) *adj.* known or understood without reasoning; instinctive.

invocation (ĭn'və-kā'shən) *n.* a formal appeal, often used in prayer.

invoke (ĭn-vōk') *v.* to refer or call attention to.

irrelevant (ĭ-rĕl'ə-vənt) *adj.* insignificant, unimportant.

laud (lôd) *v.* to praise.

loiter (loi'tər) *v.* to stand or wait idly.

lozenge (lŏz'ĭnj) *n.* a diamond-shaped object.

momentous (mō-mĕn'təs) *adj.* very important; fateful.

negligence (nĕg'lĭ-jəns) *n.* carelessness or failure to take normal precautions.

nullify (nŭl'ə-fī') *v.* to make of no value or consequence.

opaque (ō-pāk') *adj.* clouded; difficult to see through.

parallel (păr'ə-lĕl') *adj.* related; corresponding.

perish (pĕr´ĭsh) v. to die or come to an end.

pluralistic (plŏŏr´ə-lĭs´tĭc) adj. consisting of many ethnic and cultural groups.

ponderous (pŏn´dər-əs) adj. heavy in a clumsy way; bulky.

prism (prĭz´əm) n. a transparent, light-refracting object which figuratively refers to an individual's viewpoint.

profusion (prə-fyŏŏ´zhən) n. abundance.

reclaim (rĭ-klām´) v. to retake possession; reform.

redemptive (rĭ-dĕmp´tiv) adj. causing freedom or salvation.

reiteration (rē-ĭt´ə-rā´shən) n. restatement or repetition.

reprieve (rĭ-prēv´) n. the cancellation or postponement of punishment.

repulsed (rĭ-pŭlsd´) adj. disgusted.

resolve (rĭ-zŏlv´) v. to decide or become determined.

restitution (rĕs´tĭ-tŏŏ´shən) n. a making good for loss or damage; repayment.

revelry (rĕv´əl-rē) n. noisy merrymaking; festivity.

revile (rĭ-vīl´) v. to condemn or insult.

segregate (sĕg´rĭ-gāt´) v. to cause people to be separated based on gender, race, or other factors.

serrate (sĕr´āt´) adj. having a jagged, saw-toothed edge.

sheepish (shē´pĭsh) adj. showing embarrassment.

stagnant (stăg´nənt) adj. unchanging; without activity or development.

staidness (stād´nĭs) n. the quality of being steady, calm, and serious.

subversive (səb-vûr´sĭv) adj. intended to undermine or overthrow those in power.

succession (sək-sĕsh´ən) n. sequence; ordered arrangement.

succumb (sə-kŭm´) v. to surrender or fall victim to.

supple (sŭp´əl) adj. flexible or easily adaptable.

synchronization (sĭng´krə-nĭ-zā´shən) n. coordinated, simultaneous action.

tangible (tăn´jə-bəl) n. something that can be touched.

tentative (tĕn´tə-tĭv) adj. with caution and without confidence.

transfix (trăns-fĭks´) v. to captivate or make motionless with awe.

travail (trə-vāl´) n. painful effort.

tremulous (trĕm´yə-ləs) adj. marked by trembling or shaking.

validate (văl´ĭ-dāt´) v. to establish the value, truth, or legitimacy of.

Index of Skills

A

abbreviations, 137

absolute phrases, 420, R41

abstract nouns, R22

Academic Vocabulary, 2, 37, 41, 46, 97, 102, 153, 157, 162, 301, 306, 355, 359, 364, 445. *See also* Glossary of Academic Vocabulary

accept/except, R55

accounts, first-person, 72

action verbs, R23, R32

active voice, R34

activities

  media activity, 36, 86, 152, 176

  research activity, 78

  speaking activity, 18, 25, 30, 130, 144, 150, 170, 206, 227, 265, 322, 348, 444

  writing activity, 8, 53, 72, 94, 120, 138, 252, 265, 280, 288, 298, 314, 336, 354, 418, 430, 438

actors, in Elizabethan theater, 180

acts in drama, R57

add details, 155

adjective clauses, R42

adjective form, 145

adjective phrases, 146, R39

adjectives, R23, R34–R35

  vs. adverbs, R35

  comparatives, R35–R36

  indefinite pronouns as, 324

  predicate, R35

  proper, R28

  superlatives, R35–R36

adverb clauses, 122, R42

adverb phrases, 146, R39

adverbs, 122, R23, R35

  vs. adjectives, R35

  comparatives, R35–R36

  conjunctive, R41

  superlatives, R35–R36

advice/advise, R55

A&E® (Arts and Entertainment), 181

affect/effect, R55

affirmative side, in debates, R14

allegory, R57

alliteration, 367, R57

all ready/already, R55

allusion

  definition of, 53, 417, R57

  in epics, 366

  to Shakespeare, 176

  in Shakespearean drama, 178

allusion/illusion, R55

ambiguous references, R32

among/between, R55

analogies, R51, R57. *See also* metaphors; similes

  false, R20

analysis, writing activity, 53, 314, 430

analytical essays

  body of, 445

  conclusion, 42

  draft of, 42, 302, 446

  elements of effective, 41, 301, 445

  introduction, 42, 302, 445

  Performance Task Rubric, 44, 304, 448

  planning, 41–42, 301–302, 445–446

  presenting, 43, 303, 447

  researching, 445–448

  revising, 43, 303, 447

  writing, 41–44, 301–304, 445–448

analyzing

  accounts in different mediums, 72, 85

  arguments, R16–R21

  author's choices, 17, 93, 279, 347, 417

  author's claim, 7, 129, 321, 437

  characters, 119, 279, 399

  complex characters, 279

  development of ideas, 152

  figurative meanings, 417

  ideas and events, 69, 77, 144, 169, 335, 429

  impact of word choice on tone, 77, 137, 313

  media, 36, 72, 86, 152

  point of view, 93, 137

  purpose, 29, 152, 313

  representations in different mediums, 36

  rhetoric to advance author's point of view, 29, 52, 313

  seminal U.S. documents, 29, 52

  source material, 176, 288, 297

  text and media, 36, 72, 86

  theme, 17, 119, 206, 280, 354

  tone, 130, 144, 169, 313

Analyzing Text and Media, 36, 72, 86

Analyzing Text and Video, 176

Analyzing the Media, 152

Analyzing the Text, 8, 18, 25, 30, 37, 41, 53, 69, 78, 94, 97, 120, 130, 138, 144, 150, 157, 170, 176, 206, 227, 252, 265, 280, 288, 298, 301, 314, 322, 336, 348, 354, 355, 399, 418, 430, 438, 444, 445

anapest, R67

ancient Greece, 366

anecdotes, 335

Annotate It!, 8, 18, 25, 30, 36, 53, 69, 72, 78, 86, 94, 120, 130, 138, 144, 150, 170, 176, 206, 227, 252, 265, 280, 288, 298, 314, 322, 336, 348, 354, 399, 418, 430, 438, 444

antagonists, 177, R57

antecedent, R29–R30

antonyms, 439, R51

apostrophe, R26–R27

appeals

  by association, R17

  bandwagon, 437, R17

  emotional, R17, R62

  logical, R66

  to loyalty, R17

  to pity, fear, or vanity, R17, R62

appositive phrases, R39

appositives, R39

archetypes, 365, 399, R57

argumentative essays, 97–100, 355–358, R62. *See also* arguments

arguments, R16–R21, R57

  analyzing, 438, R16–R21

  assessing validity, 321, 437, R21

  building, 97–98

  claims, 7, 53, 97, 321, R2

  conclusions to, 97, 356, R3

  counterarguments, 7, 356, R2, R16

  deductive, R18

  definition, 7, 321

  delineate and evaluate, 7, 321, 437

  drafting, 98, 356

  elements of, 7, 97, 355

  evaluating, 321, 437, R20–R21

  evidence, 7, 97–98, 321, 355

  examples, 3–6, 317–320, 433–436

  fallacious reasoning, 437, R19–R20

  identifying false statements, 437, R20

  inductive, R17–R18

  linking ideas in, R3

  logical, 7, 321, R66

  logic and reasoning in, R17–R18

  Performance Task Rubric, 100, 358

  planning, 97–98, 355–356

  presenting, 357

  reading, R16–R21

  reasons, 7, 321, 437

  recognizing persuasive techniques, 152, 437, R17

  revising, 99, 357

  speaking activity, 130

  strategies for determining strong, 7, 321, R21

  style and tone for, R3

  tone of, 437

  writing, 97–100, 355–358, R2–R3

  writing activity, 8, 336

articles, citing, R11

artistic mediums, 36, 72, 85

asides, 177, R57

assonance, R57
assumption, R57
As You Read, 3, 11, 21, 27, 48, 55, 73, 81, 89, 103, 123, 133, 141, 147, 163, 183, 207, 228, 253, 266, 283, 289, 307, 317, 325, 339, 351, 371, 401, 421, 433, 441
As You View, 71, 151
As You View and Read, 33, 173
attacking the person (faulty reasoning), R19
audience, for Elizabethan theater, 180
author's choices
  analyzing, 17, 93, 279, 347, 417
  point of view, 85, 297
author's claim, R16
  analyzing and evaluating, 7, 129, 321, 322, 438
  identifying, 437
author's cultural background, 11, 73, 81, 89, 133
author's message, 25, 53, 335, 429, R57. *See also* central idea
author's perspective, R57
author's purpose, R57. *See also* author's perspective
  analyzing, 29, 152, 313
  definition of, 29
  determining, 429
autobiographical narratives, 77
autobiography, R57–R58
auxiliary verbs, R23, R24, R47

B

bad vs. *badly*, R36
ballads, R58
bandwagon appeals, 437, R17
base words, R49
between/among, R55
bias, R20, R58
biased tone, R3, R5
bibliography, R58. *See also* works cited
biography, R58
blank verse, 178, R58
blogs, 447
body, of essay, 42
book parts, citing, R10
books, citing, R10
brainstorming, 154
bring/take, R55
business correspondence, R58

C

calls to action, 152
capitalization
  first words, R28
  geographical names, R27
  I, R28
  organizations and events, R27–R28
  people and titles, R27

proper adjectives, R28
quick reference, R27–R28
cases
  nominative, R30
  objective, R30
  possessive, R30
cast of characters, R58
cause and effect, R48, R58
cause-and-effect relationships, 179, R4, R58
CD-ROMs, citing, R11
central idea, 335. *See also* main idea; theme
  determining, 25, 53, 335, 429
  supporting, 69
characterization, R59
characters, R58
  analyzing, 119, 279, 399
  antagonist, 177, R57
  asides by, 177
  complex, 279
  development of, 119
  dynamic, R58
  epic hero, 365, 368, 399, R62
  flat, R59
  foil, 177, 206, 399, R64
  main, R58
  minor, R58
  motivations of, 279, R58
  protagonist, R70
  round, R59
  Shakespearean, 177
  soliloquies by, 177
  static, R59
  tragic hero, 177, R74
character traits, R58
chorus, R59
chronological order, 77, R7, R59
chronology, 347
circular reasoning, 437, R19
citations, 446, R9–R11
Cite Text Evidence, 8, 18, 25, 30, 36, 53, 69, 72, 78, 86, 94, 120, 130, 138, 144, 150, 152, 170, 176, 206, 227, 252, 265, 280, 288, 298, 314, 322, 336, 348, 354, 399, 418, 429, 430, 438, 444
claims. *See also* arguments; thesis statement
  analyzing, 7, 438
  author's, 129, 321, 437, R16
  counterclaims, 97, 356, R2, R16
  debating, R14–R15
  definition of, 53, 129, R59
  developing, 97–98, 356, R2
  evaluating, 7, 438
  identifying, 7, 437
  introducing, 356, R2
  linking ideas to, 356, R3
  making, 38, 97, 356
  summarizing, 8

  supporting, 7, 321, R14, R16, R73
  vague, R2
  writing activity, 8
clarify, reading strategy to, R59
classical mythology, words from, R50
classification, organizational pattern, R59
classroom discussions, R12–R13
clauses
  adjective, R42
  adverbial, 122, R42
  definition of, 300, 350, R41
  dependent, 300
  essential adjective, R42
  independent, 132, 300, 338, R41
  nonessential adjective, R42
  noun, 10, R43
  relative, 350
  subordinate, 10, 122, R41, R42
  transitional, R3
cliché, R59
climax, R7, R59
collaboration, group, 157
Collaborative Discussion, 6, 16, 24, 28, 35, 51, 68, 71, 76, 84, 92, 118, 128, 136, 143, 148, 151, 168, 175, 205, 226, 251, 264, 278, 287, 296, 312, 320, 334, 346, 352, 398, 416, 428, 436, 442
collaborative discussions, 359–362, R12–R13. *See also* panel discussions
  ground rules and goals for, 359, R12
  moving forward in, 360, R13
  posing and responding to questions in, 360–361
  preparing for, 359–360, R12
  responding to ideas in, 361, R13
collective nouns, R22, R47
colloquialisms, 137
colons, 96, 132, 338, R26
combine ideas, 42
comedy, R59
comic relief, 177, R59
commas, R25
comma splices, R45
commonly confused words, R55–R56
common nouns, R22, R29
comparative form, R35–R36
compare and contrast, R4, R60
Compare Text and Media, 36, 47, 72, 81, 85
comparisons
  as context clues, R49
  double, R36
  illogical, R36
  irregular, R35–R36
  regular, R35
complements, R37–R38

complete predicate, R24
complete subject, R24
complex characters, 279
complex sentences, R44
complication, R60
compound-complex sentences, R44
compound nouns, R22
compound predicates, R37
compound sentences, R43–R44
compound subjects, R37, R46
conclusions, R60
    to arguments, 97, 356, R3
    of essays, 42, 445, R5
    of narratives, 154, R7
conclusions, drawing, 18, 30, 36, 120,
        130, 138, 150, 152, 314, 336, 348,
        354, R61
    deductive, R60
    inductive, R60
    valid, R60
concrete nouns, R22
conflict, R59, R60
conjunctions, R23
    coordinating, R23
    correlative, R23
    subordinating, R23
conjunctive adverbs, R41
connect, as reading process, R60
connotations, 26, 77, 87, 169, 353, 431,
        R51, R60
consonance, R60
consumer documents, R60
context
    historical, 52, 367
    of words, 31, 129, 139, 171, 299, 337
context clues, 31, 129, 139, 171, 299,
        337, R48–R49, R60
contractions, 137
contrast, as context clue, 139, R48
controlling idea, R16. *See also* main
    idea
coordinating conjunctions, R23
correlative conjunctions, R23
costumes, in Elizabethan theater, 180
counterarguments, 7, 356, R16, R60
counterclaims, 97, R2, R16, R60
couplet, R60
credibility, R5, R60
credible sources, R8
criteria. *See also* Performance Task
    Rubric
    for analytical essays, 41, 301, 445
    for arguments, 97, 355
    for fictional narratives, 153
    for multimedia presentations, 157
    for speeches, 37
critical essays, R60
critical review, R60–R61
Critical Vocabulary, 9, 19, 26, 31, 54,
        70, 79, 87, 95, 121, 131, 139, 145,
        171, 299, 315, 323, 337, 349, 400,

419, 431, 439. *See also* Glossary of
    Critical Vocabulary
critique of text, 86, 322
cultural experience, analyzing, 18,
        86, 93, 137, 138

D
dactyl, R67
dangling participles, R40
dashes, 432, R26
debate activity, 227, 322
debates, R14–R15, R61
    affirmative side in, R14
    evaluating, R15
    format, R14–R15
    holding, R14
    moderators, R14
    negative side in, R14
    planning, R14
    policy statements in, R14
    propositions in, R14
    structure of formal, R14
declarative sentences, R37
deductive conclusion, R60
deductive reasoning, R18, R61
definition, as context clue, 139, R48
delineate, an argument, 7, 321, 437
demonstrative pronouns, R22, R31
denotations, 26, 87, 353, 431, R51, R60
dénouement. *See* falling action
dependent clauses, 300
description, R6–R7
details, gathering, R6–R7
determining
    author's point of view, 85
    central idea, 25, 335, 429
    figurative meanings, 353
    technical meanings, 129
    tone, 353
dialect, R61
dialogue, 429, R6–R7, R61
diary
    definition of, 77, R61
    examples, 73–76
diction, R61
dictionaries, R52
direct objects, 10, R24, R37
direct quotations, R9
discussion
    activity, 170, 206, 348
    Collaborative Discussion, 6, 16,
        24, 28, 35, 51, 68, 71, 76, 84,
        92, 118, 128, 136, 143, 148, 151,
        168, 175, 205, 226, 251, 264,
        278, 287, 296, 312, 320, 334,
        346, 352, 398, 416, 428, 436,
        442
discussions, collaborative, 359–362,
        R12–R13. *See also* panel
    discussions

ground rules and goals for, 359,
        R12
    moving forward in, 360, R13
    posing and responding to questions
        in, 360–361
    preparing for, 359–360, R12
    responding to ideas in, 361, R13
documents
    seminal, 29, 52
    workplace, R75
doesn't, R47
domain-specific vocabulary, 360
don't, R47
double comparison, R36
double negatives, R36
drafts
    analytical essays, 42, 302
    arguments, 98, 356
    essays, 42, 98, 356, 446
    fictional narrative, 154
    revising, 39, 43, 99, 155, 303, 447
    writing, 42, 98, 154, 302, 356, 446
drama, R61
    aside, 177, R57
    character types in, 177
    dramatic conventions, 177
    parallel plots in, 279
    reading, 179
    scenes, R71
    Shakespearean, 177–282
    soliloquy, 177, R72
    tragedy, 177, R74–R75
dramatic irony, 177, 265, R66
dramatic monologue, R61
dramatic readings, 265
drawing conclusions, 18, 30, 36, 120,
        130, 138, 150, 152, 314, 336, 348,
        354, R61
dynamic characters, R58

E
eBook, 8, 18, 25, 30, 36, 53, 69, 72, 78,
        86, 94, 120, 130, 138, 144, 150,
        170, 176, 206, 227, 252, 265, 280,
        288, 298, 314, 322, 336, 348, 354,
        399, 418, 430, 438, 444
editorials, 438, R62
effect, R58. *See also* cause and effect
either/or fallacy, R19, R62
electronic publications, citing, R11
elegy, R62
Elizabethan theater, 180
Elizabethan words, 178
ellipses, R27
emotional appeals, 152, R17, R62
empathy, 129
encyclopedia articles, citing, R11
end rhyme, R71
epics, 365–420, R62
    allusions in, 366, 417
    analyzing, 417

archetypes in, 365
characteristics of, 365
elements of, 365
epithets in, 366, 417
examining Homeric, 368
figurative language in, 367, 417
gods in, 368
heroes in, 365, 368, 399, R62
in historical context, 367
language of Homer, 366
metaphors in, 417
as narrative, 367
plot, 365, 417
as poems, 367
reading, 367
setting, 365, 417
themes, 365, 417
epic simile, 366, 417, R62
epilogue, R59, R62
epithets, 366, 417, R62
essays, R62
analytical, 41–44, 301–304,
445–448
argumentative, 97–100, 355–358,
R62. *See also* arguments
body of, 42, 97, 445
citing, R10
conclusion, 42, 97, 356, 445, R5
critical, R62
draft of, 42, 98, 302, 356, 446
editorial, 438, R62
examples, 21–24, 163–168
exchanging with partner, 43, 99,
303, 447
explanatory, 41–44, 301–304,
445–448
expository, 41–44, 301–304,
445–448, R62
formal, R62
informal, R62
informative, 41–44, 301–304,
445–448, R4–R5, R62
introduction, 42, 98, 302, 356, 445
personal, R62
persuasive, R62
photo essay, 33
presenting, 43, 303, 447
publishing online, 447
reflective, R62
revising, 43, 99, 303, 357, 447
thesis statement of, 41, 446
writing activity, 288
essential adjective clauses, R42
essential appositives, R39
etymologies, 19, 70, R50
eulogy, 280
evading the issue, R19
evaluating, R62
arguments, 7, 8, 321, 437, R16–R21
author's claim, 7, 129, 322, 438
debates, R15

evidence, 321, R20–R21
speeches, 53, 54
text, 18, 69, 72, 170, 252, 430
video, 72
events
analyzing, 69, 77, 335, 429
sequencing, in writing narratives,
154, R7
evidence, R62
evaluating, 321, R20–R21
gathering, 37, 42, 97–98, 157, 301,
355, 360, 445–446
to support claims, 7, 38, 98, 129,
321, 355, R2, R14, R16
from text, 8, 18, 25, 30, 53, 69, 72,
78, 86, 94, 119, 120, 130, 144,
150, 152, 170, 176, 206, 227,
252, 265, 280, 288, 298, 314,
322, 336, 348, 354, 399, 418,
429, 430, 438, 444
examples, as context clues, 139, R48
except/accept, R55
exclamation point, R25
exclamatory sentences, R37
explanatory essays, 41–44, 301–304,
445–448. *See also* analytical
essays
exposition, R63
expository essays, 41–44, 301–304,
445–448, R62
extended metaphors, 25, 52, 53, 443,
R63
external conflict, R60

F

fables, R63
fact versus opinion, 437, R63
fairy tales
elements of, 17
speaking activity, 18
fallacies, R19–R20, R63
fallacious reasoning, 437
falling action, R63
false analogy, R20
false cause, 437, R19
false statements, 437
fantasy, R63
farce, R63
farther/further, R36
faulty reasoning, 437, R19–R20. *See
also* fallacies
fear, appeals to, R17, R62
feature article, R63
fewer/less, R56
fiction, R63. *See also* drama; epics;
fictional narratives
fairy tales, 17, 18
fantasy, R63
historical, R65
novellas, R68
novels, R68

realistic, R70
romance, R71
science, R72
fictional narratives
building suspense, R7
conclusions of, R7
details for, 154, R6–R7
drafting, 154
elements of effective, 153
pacing, 93, 94, R7
Performance Task Rubric, 156
planning, 153–154
point of view for, 154, R6
presenting, 155
revising, 155
sequencing of events in, 154, R7
writing, 153–156, R6–R7
figurative language, R48, R63
analyzing, 417
in epics, 367, 417
interpreting, 149, 353, 418, 443
metaphors, 417, 443
personification, 169, 443, R69
similes, 36, 366, 417
uses of, 169
figurative meanings, 353
first-person accounts, 72
first-person narrator, 297, R6
first-person point of view, 297, R70
flashbacks, 347, R7, R64
flat characters, R59
flowcharts, 179
foils, 177, 206, 399, R64
folk ballads, R58
foreign words, R51
foreshadowing, 93, 206, R64
form, R64
formal debates, R14–R15
formal essay, R62
formal language, 316
formal tone, 137, 138, 316, R3
fragments, sentence, R44–R45
frame story, R64
free verse, R64
further/farther, R36
future perfect progressive tense, R34
future perfect tense, R33
future progressive tense, R33
future tense, R33
fyi, 2, 46, 102, 162, 306, 364

G

general dictionary, R52
generalization, R17, R64
hasty, R20
overgeneralization, R19, R68
general references, R32
genre, R64
gerund phrases, R40
gerunds, R40
glittering generalities, R17

Globe Theater, 180, 181
glossaries, R52–R53
Glossary of Academic Vocabulary,
    R76–R77
Glossary of Critical Vocabulary,
    R78–R80
Glossary of Literary and
    Informational Terms, R57–R75
gods, in Homeric epics, 368
good vs. *well*, R36
grammar
    capitalization, R27–R28
    handbook, R29–R47
    parts of speech, R22–R23
    punctuation, 96, 132, 338, R25–R27
    sentence parts, R24
    sentences, R24
graphic aid, R64
graphic novels, 84, 85, 86
graphic organizers, 29, 80, R64
    for brainstorming, 154
    charts, 297, 367
    diagrams, 321
    flowcharts, 179
    semantic maps, 95, 171
graphics, R4
Greek words, 70, 131, R50
group discussions, 154, 359–362,
    R12–R13
group multimedia presentations,
    157–160

H
haiku, R64–R65
hasty generalization, R20
headers, R4
helping verbs, 140, R24
heroes, R65
    epic, 365, 368, 399, R62
    tragic, 177, R74, R75
heroism, 368
historical context, 52, 367
historical documents, R65
historical events, information
        about, 72
historical fiction, R65
HISTORY®, 27, 33, 47, 71, 307, 369, 433
history writing, 55–68
homonyms, R51–R52
homophones, R52
horror fiction, R65
how-to writing, R65
humor, R65
    of character, R65
    of language, R65
    in Shakespearean tragedy, 206, 265
    of situation, R65
hyperbole, R65, R75
hyphens, R26

I
iamb, R67
iambic pentameter, 178, R58, R65
ideas
    analyzing, 69, 77, 169, 335, 429
    central, 25, 69, 335, 429
    controlling idea, R16
    development of, 152
    implied controlling, R65
    linking, in arguments, R3
    main, R66–R67
    reinforcing your, 361
    using graphic organizers for, 80
identifying
    bias, 437, R20
    details, 298
    dramatic irony, 265
    narrative techniques, 153
    patterns, 18, 25, 30, 430
    themes, 418
idioms, 94, R49, R65
illogical comparisons, R36
illusion/allusion, R55
imagery, 149, 353, 367, 420, R65
imperative sentences, R37
implied controlling idea, R65
indefinite pronouns, 324, R23, R31,
    R46
indefinite references, R32
independent clauses, 132, 300, 338,
    R41
index, R65
indirect objects, R24, R38
inductive conclusion, R60
inductive reasoning, R17–R18, R65
inferences, R65
    about central idea, 25, 53
    about poems, 150, 176, 354, 399
    about Shakespearean drama, 206,
        227, 280, 298
    text, 18, 30, 69, 78, 94, 120, 130,
        170, 314, 348
    about theme, 17, 18, 30, 119, 138,
        347, 444
    about tone, 144
infinitive phrases, R39–R40
infinitives, R39–R40
informal essay, R62
informal language, 316
informal tone, 137, 138, 316, R3
informational texts, 123–128,
    141–143, 325–334, R65–R66
informative essays, 41–44, 301–304,
    445–448, R4–R5, R62. *See also*
    analytical essays
informative oral report, 78
informative presentation, 30, 170
informative speeches, 37–40
intensive pronouns, R22, R30
Interactive Lessons, 37, 38, 39, 41, 42,
    43, 97, 98, 99, 153, 154, 157, 158,

159, 301, 302, 303, 355, 356, 357,
    359, 360, 361, 445, 446, 447
interjections, R23
internal conflict, R60
internal rhyme, R71
Internet, R66
Internet documents, citing, R11
interpretations, of Shakespeare, 176,
    297
interpreting
    figurative language, 149, 418, 443
    text, 25, 53, 78, 86, 94, 120, 130,
        138, 150, 170, 227, 252, 265,
        280, 298, 314, 322, 336, 348,
        354, 399, 418, 430, 438, 444
interrogative pronouns, R23, R31
interrogative sentences, R37
interviews, R66
    citing, R11
intransitive verbs, R23
introductions
    of analytical essays, 42, 301, 445
inverted sentences, R47
irony, 93, R66
    dramatic, 177, 265, R66
    sarcasm, R71
    situational, 93, R65, R66
    verbal, 93, R66
irregular verbs, R33
italics, R27

J
jargon, R5
journal entries, writing activity, 138,
    252, 298
journals, R66

L
language
    biased, R5, R20
    figurative, 169, 353, 367, 417, 443,
        R49, R63
    formal, 316
    of Homer, 366
    humor of, R65
    informal, 316
    jargon, R5
    loaded, 437, R20, R66
    propaganda, R20, R70
    of Shakespeare, 178, 179
Language and Style
    absolute phrases, 420
    add details, 155
    adjective and adverb phrases, 146
    adverbial clauses, 122
    colons, 96, 132, 338
    combine ideas, 42
    dependent clauses, 300
    indefinite pronouns, 324
    independent clauses, 300
    noun clauses, 10

noun phrases, 80
parallel structure, 32, 282
paraphrase or summarize, 99
participial phrases, 172
precise language, 302
prepositional phrases, 20
relative clauses, 350
repetition and parallelism, 54
rhetorical questions, 88
semicolons, 96, 338
sentence length, 432
tone, 316
transitions, 356, 440
understand cohesion, 39
verb phrases, 140
language conventions, R22–R47,
    R55–R56. *See also* Language
    and Style
Latin words, 19, 70, 419
lay/lie, R56
leave/let, R56
legend, R66. *See also* myths
less/fewer, R56
letters, writing activity, 94, 120, 138
lie/lay, R56
line, R66
line breaks, R66
linking verbs, R23, R32
lists, colons before, 96, 132, 338, R26
literary ballads, R58
literary nonfiction, R66
    examples, 3–6, 73–76, 81–84,
        141–143, 307–312, 421–428
literary techniques
    alliteration, 367, R57
    allusion, 53, 176, 178, 366, 417, R57
    assonance, R57
    to create tension, 93, 94, 347
    dramatic irony, 265
    foreshadowing, 93, 206, R64
    flashback, 347, 348
    hyperbole, R65, R75
    idioms, 94, R49, R65
    imagery, 149, 353, 367, 420, R65
    irony, 93, 177, 265, R66
    metaphors, 417, 443, R67
    onomatopoeia, R68
    oxymoron, R68
    paradox, R68
    personification, 169, 443, R69
    puns, 178, 281, R70
    rhetorical questions, 88, R71
    sarcasm, R71
    satire, R71
    similes, 36, 366, R72
    symbols, 17, 86, 120, 354, R74
literary text, 11–16, 34–35, 89–92,
    103–118, 133–136, 148, 174–175,
    183–278, 283–287, 289–296,
    339–346, 351–352, 371–416, 442
loaded language, 437, R20, R66

logic, analyzing, in arguments, 7, 321,
    437, R17–R18
logical appeals, R66
logical arguments, R66
logical fallacies, 437, R19–R20, R63
loose/lose, R56
loyalty, appeals to, R17
lyric poetry, R66

M
magazine articles, citing, R11
magical realism, R66
main characters, R58
main idea, R66–R67. *See also* central
    idea; theme
main verb, R24
*A Manual for Writers of Research
    Papers, Theses, and Dissertations*
    (Turabian), R9
media, 33, 71, 151, 173
    analyzing, 36, 72, 86, 152, 176
    compare text and, 36, 72, 81, 85
media activity, 36, 86, 152, 176
media analysis, 36, 72, 152, 176
mediums, analyzing different, 36,
    72, 85
memoirs, 81–83, 307–312, 313, R67
Mentor Text, 41, 97, 153, 355
metaphors, 417, 443, R67
    extended, 25, 52, 53, 443, R63
meter, 178, 367, R67
    iambic pentameter, 178
minor characters, R58
mise en scène, R67
MLA citation guidelines, R10–R11
*MLA Handbook for Writers of
    Research Papers* (MLA), R9
moderators, debate, R14
Modern Language Association
    (MLA), R9
modifiers, 80, R34
    adjectives, R34–R35
    adverbs, R35
    comparisons, R35–R36
    dangling, R36–R37
    misplaced, R36
    problems with, R36–R37
monitor as reading strategy, R67
mood, 149, 429, R67
moral, R67, R74
motif, 227
motivations, 279, R58
multimedia links, R5
multimedia presentations
    creating group, 157–160
    elements of effective, 157
    Performance Task Rubric, 160
    practicing delivery of, 159
    presenting, 159
    producing, 158
    revising, 159

storyboarding, 158
multiple-meaning words, 9, 31, 315, R52
multiple plot lines, R7
*my*Notebook, 3, 37, 41, 48, 97, 103,
    153, 157, 163, 301, 307, 355, 359,
    371, 445
myths, 283–287, R67
*my*WordList, 3, 48, 103, 163, 307, 371
*my*WriteSmart, 8, 18, 25, 30, 36, 38,
    39, 42, 43, 53, 72, 78, 86, 94, 98,
    99, 120, 130, 138, 144, 150, 154,
    155, 158, 159, 170, 176, 206, 227,
    252, 265, 280, 288, 298, 302, 303,
    314, 322, 336, 348, 354, 356, 357,
    360, 361, 418, 430, 438, 444, 446,
    447

N
name-calling, as persuasive device,
    R19
narrative nonfiction, 73–76, 82–84,
    307–312, 421–428, R67
narrative poems, 283–288, 365, R67.
    See also epics
narratives
    autobiographical, 77
    conclusions of, 154, R7
    epics as, 367
    fictional, 153–156, R6–R7
    Performance Task Rubric, 156
    techniques, identifying, 153
    travel, 429
    writing, 418, R6–R7
narrative techniques, R6–R7
narrators, 367, R6, R68
negatives, double, R36
negative side, in debates, R14
newspaper articles, R68
    citing, R11
nominative pronouns, R30
nonessential adjective clauses, R42
nonessential appositives, R39
nonfiction, R68
    literary, R66
    narrative, R67
non sequitur, R19
noun clauses, 10, R43
noun form, 145
noun modifiers, 80
noun phrases, 80, R38
nouns, R22, R29
    abstract, R22
    collective, R22, R47
    common, R22, R29
    compound, R22
    concrete, R22
    plural, R22, R29, R54
    possessive, R22, R29, R54
    predicate, R38
    proper, R22, R29
    singular, R22, R29

suffixes that form, 95
novellas, R68
novels, R68

O
objective, 335, 437
objective pronouns, R30
objective tone, R3, R5
object of preposition
    noun clause as, 10
    in prepositional phrase, 20
objects
    direct, R24, R37
    indirect, R24, R38
observations, identifying, in writing
        narratives, R6
ode, R68
off rhyme, R71
online sources, citing, R11
onomatopoeia, R68
op-ed pieces, R68
organization
    for group multimedia presentation,
        158, 160
    for panel discussions, 359
    pattern of, R69, R73
    for writing analytical essay, 42, 304
    for writing arguments, 356
    for writing essays, 302
    for writing narratives, 154, 156
organizational framework, R4
overgeneralization, 437, R19, R68
oversimplification, R19
overview, R68
oxymoron, R68

P
pacing, 93, 429, R7
panel discussions, 359–362. *See also*
        collaborative discussions
    effective participation in, 359
    Performance Task Rubric, 362
    planning, 359–360
    presenting, 361
    revising, 361
    summarize, 361
    write and practice, 360
paradox, R68
paragraphs, supporting, R4–R5
parallelism, 8, 29, 32, 52, 54, 282, R68
parallel plots, 279, R68
parallel structure, 32, 282, R44
paraphrasing, 99, 429, R9, R69
parentheses, R26
parenthetical citations, R9
parody, R69
participants, in panel discussions,
        359–362
participial phrases, 172, R40
participles, 172, 420, R40
    dangling, R40

misplaced, R40
    past, 172, R32–R33
parts of speech
    quick reference, R22–R23
    word changes and, 9
passive voice, R34
pastoral, R69
past participles, 172, R32–R33
past perfect progressive tense, R33
past perfect tense, R33
past principal part, R32–R33
past progressive tense, R33
past tense, R33
patterns
    identifying, 18, 25, 30, 430
    of organization, R69, R73
    word, 9, 95, 121, 145
peer editing, 43, 99, 303, 357, 447
Performance Task, end of collection
    creating a group multimedia
        presentation, 157–160
    participating in panel discussion,
        359–362
    Plan, Produce, Revise, Present,
        37–39, 41–43, 97–99, 153–155,
        157–159, 301–303, 355–357,
        359–361, 445–447
    presenting a speech, 37–40
    researching and writing an
        analytical essay, 445–448
    writing a fictional narrative,
        153–156
    writing an analytical essay, 41–44,
        301–304
    writing an argument, 97–100,
        355–358
Performance Task, selection
    media activity, 36, 86, 152, 176
    research activity, 78
    speaking activity, 18, 25, 30, 130,
        144, 150, 170, 206, 227, 265,
        322, 348, 444
    writing activity, 8, 53, 72, 94, 120,
        138, 252, 265, 280, 288, 298,
        314, 336, 354, 418, 430, 438
Performance Task Rubric, 40, 44,
        100, 156, 160, 304, 358, 362, 448
period, R25
periodicals, R69
persona, R69
personal attacks, 437
personal essays, R62
personal pronouns, 324, R22, R29,
        R46
personification, 169, 443, R69
perspective, 85
persuasion, R69
persuasive essays, R62
persuasive techniques, R17, R69
persuasive texts. *See also* arguments
    analyzing, R16–R17

evaluating, R20–R21
    reading, R16–R21
photo essays, 33
phrases, R38
    absolute, 420, R41
    adjective, 146, R39
    adverb, 146, R39
    appositives, R39
    gerund, R40
    infinitive, R39–R40
    noun, 80, R38
    participial, 172, R40
    prepositional, 146, R24, R39
    transitional, 440
    verbal, R39–R41
pity, appeals to, R17, R62
plagiarism, R9
Plan, Produce, Revise, Present. *See*
        under Performance Task, end of
        collection
plays, citing, R11
plots, R69
    epic, 365, 417
    falling action, R63
    multiple plot lines, R7
    parallel, 279, R68
    rising action, R71
plural nouns, R22, R29, R54
poems/poetry, R69
    citing, R10
    epic, 367
    examples, 34–35, 147–148, 174–175,
        351–352, 442
    figurative language in, 149, 443
    haiku, R64–R65
    imagery in, 149, 353
    lines, R66
    lyric, R66
    mood, 149
    narrative, 283–288, 365, R67
    pastoral, R69
    quatrain, R70
    reading aloud, 150
    refrain, R70
    rhyme, R71
    rhythm, R71
    scansion, R71
    sonnet, R72
    speaker, R73
    stanza, R73
    tone, 149
point of view, R69–R70
    analyzing, 93, 137
    author's choice of, 297
    determining author's, 85
    effect of, 297
    establishing, R6
    first-person, R70
    in narratives, 418
    third-person, R70
policy statements, R14

possessive nouns, R22, R29, R54
possessive pronouns, R30
practicing, speech delivery, 39
precede/proceed, R56
precise language, 302
predicate
    adjectives, R35
    complete, R24
    compound, R37
    nominatives, 10, R38, R47
    nouns, R38
    pronouns, R38
predict, R70
prefixes, 349, 400, R49, R54
prepositional phrases, 20, 146, R24,
    R39
prepositions, R23
    common, 20
    object of, 10, 20
presentations
    group multimedia presentation,
        157–160
    informative, 30, 170
    informative oral reports, 78
    informative speech, 37–40
    planning, 38
present participles, 172, R32–R33
present perfect progressive tense, R33
present perfect tense, R33
present principal part, R32–R33
present progressive tense, R33
present tense, R33
primary sources, R8, R72
prior knowledge, R70
problems, identifying, in writing
    narratives, R6
problem-solution order, R4, R70
procedural texts, R70
prologue, R59, R70
pronouns, R22, R29
    antecedent agreement, R29–R30
    cases, R30
    demonstrative, R22, R31
    indefinite, 324, R23, R31, R46–R47
    intensive, R22, R30
    interrogative, R23, R31
    nominative, R30
    objective, R30
    personal, 324, R22, R29, R46
    possessive, R30
    predicate, R38
    reciprocal, R23, R30–R31
    reference problems, R32
    reflexive, R22, R30
    relative, R23, R31–R32, R42, R47
pronunciation key, R76
propaganda, R20, R70
proper adjectives, R28
proper nouns, R22, R29
propositions, R14
props in drama, R70

prose, R70
protagonists, 177, R70
public documents, R70
public service announcement (PSA),
    151, 152
publishing online, 447
punctuation, 96
    apostrophe, R26–R27
    colons, 96, 132, 338, R26
    commas, R25
    dashes, 432, R26
    ellipses, R27
    in epics, 367
    exclamation point, R25
    hyphens, R26
    meaning making and, 96
    parentheses, R26
    period, R25
    question mark, R25
    quick reference, R25–R27
    quotation marks, R27
    semicolons, 96, 338, R26
puns, 178, 281, R70
purpose, analyzing, 29, 152, 313

Q

quatrain, R70
question mark, R25
questions
    research, R8
    rhetorical, 88, R71
quotation marks, R27
quotations
    colons before, 96, 132, 338, R26
    direct, R9
quoting, 429

R

reading
    arguments, R16–R21
    drama, 179
    epics, 367
    Shakespearean tragedy, 179
    Shakespeare's language, 179
realistic fiction, R70
reasoning
    circular, 437, R19
    deductive, R18, R61
    faulty, 437, R19–R20
    inductive, R17–R18, R65
reasons, to support claims, 7, 129,
    321, R2
reciprocal pronouns, R23, R30–R31
recurring themes, R74
reference sources, 79
    bibliography, R58
    dictionaries, R52
    glossaries, R52–R53
    synonym finders, R52
    thesaurus, R52
    using, R52–R53

reference works, R70
reflection activity, 176, 354
reflective essays, R62
reflexive pronouns, R22, R30
refrain, R70
regular verbs, R32–R33
relative clauses, 350
relative pronouns, R23, R31–R32,
    R42, R47
repetition, 8, 25, 29, 32, 52, 54, R71
reread, 8, 30, 97, 144, 153, 157, 172,
    280, 288, 314, 322, 335, 336, 348,
    354, 355
research
    activity, 78
    for analytical essay, 446
    conducting, R8–R9
    focus of, R8
    formulating question for, R8
resolution, R59, R63. *See also* falling
    action
response to literature, 25, 144, 444
restatement, as context clues, R48
rhetoric
    analyzing, 29, 52, 313
    point of view and, 85
rhetorical devices, 52, 53, 54, R71
rhetorical questions, 88, R71
rhyme, 367, R71
rhyme scheme, R71
rhythm, R71
rising action, R71
romance, R71
roots, 70, 131, 419, R49
rough drafts. *See* drafts
round characters, R59
rubric. *See* Performance Task Rubric
run-on sentences, R45

S

sarcasm, R71
satire, R71
scanning, R71
scansion, R71
scene, R71
scenery, R71
science fiction, R72
science writing, 123–128, 325–334
screenplay, R72
script, R72
secondary sources, R8, R72–R73
semantic maps, 95, 171
semicolons, 96, 338, R26
seminal documents, analyzing, 29, 52
sensory details, R72
sentence fragments, R44–R45
sentences, R37
    complements, R37–R38
    complete, writing, R44–R45
    complex, R44
    compound, R43–R44

compound-complex, R44
compound subjects and
   predicates, R37
declarative, R37
exclamatory, R37
imperative, R37
interrogative, R37
inverted, R47
length of, 432
parallel structure, R44
parts of, R24, R37–R38
with predicate nominatives, R47
run-on, R45
simple, R43
structure of, 137, R43–R44
topic, R74
types of, R37
sequential order, R72
setting, R72
setting a purpose, R72
setting, epic, 365, 417
Shakespearean drama, 177–282
   allusions in, 178
   asides in, 177
   characteristics of, 177
   character types in, 177
   dramatic conventions, 177
   dramatic irony in, 177, 265
   and Elizabethan theater, 180
   foreshadowing in, 206
   humor in, 177, 206, 265
   interpretations of, 176, 297
   language in, 178, 179
   motifs in, 227
   parallel plots in, 279
   parallel structure in, 282
   puns in, 178
   reading, 179, 265
   soliloquy in, 177
   Tragedy of Romeo and Juliet,
      181–205, 207–226, 228–251,
      253–264, 266–278
   word play in, 281
short stories, R72
   citing, R10
   examples, 11–16, 89–92, 103–118,
      133–136, 289–296, 339–346
sidebar, R72
signal words, 347, 350, R72
similes, 36, 366, R72
   epic, 366, 417, R62
simple sentences, R43
singular nouns, R22, R29
situational humor, R65
situational irony, 93, R65, R66
situations, identifying, in writing
   narratives, R6
slang, R49
slant rhyme, R71
snob appeal, as a persuasive device,
   R17

soliloquy, 177, R72
sonnet, R72
sound devices, R72
source material
   analyzing, 176, 288, 297
   incorporating into research
      paper, R9
sources, R72–R73
   citing, R9, R10–R11
   credible, R8
   evaluating, R8
   locating, R8
   MLA citation guidelines, R10–R11
   online, R11
   primary, R8, R72
   reference, 79
   secondary, R8, R72–R73
spatial order, R73
speaker, R73
   in poetry, 150, 354
speaking activity
   argument, 130
   debate, 227, 322
   discussion, 25, 144, 170, 206, 348,
      444
   dramatic reading, 265
   fairy tale, 18
   informative presentation, 30, 130
   poetry reading, 150
   response to literature, 25, 144, 444
   using multiple sources of media,
      157–160
specialized dictionary, R52
specialized vocabulary, R52
speeches, R73
   elements of effective, 37
   examples, 27–28, 48–51
   historical context of, 52
   informative, 37–40
   Performance Task Rubric, 40
   planning, 37–38
   practicing delivery of, 39
   presenting, 30, 37–40
   revising, 39
   writing, 38
spelling, R48
spelling rules
   plural nouns, forming, R54
   possessives, forming, R54
   prefixes, R54
   special spelling problems, R55
   suffixes, R54
   words ending in a consonant,
      R53–R54
   words ending in silent *e*, R53
   words ending in *y*, R53
stage directions, R73
staging, in Elizabethan theater, 180
stanza, R73
static characters, R59
stereotyping, R19, R73

storyboards, 158
story structure, 17, 93
stream of consciousness, R73
Stream to Start 2, 46, 102, 162, 306,
   364
structure, R73
   parallel, 8, 29, 32, 52, 54, 282
   parallel plots, 279
   sentence, 137, R43–R44
   story, 17, 93
   text, 17, 18, 69, 348, 335
style, 88, 316, 432, R73
   for arguments, R3
   for informative essay, R5
style manuals, R9
subject complements, R38
subjects
   collective nouns as, R47
   complete, R24
   compound, R37, R46
   indefinite pronouns as, R46
   noun clause as, 10
   personal pronouns as, R46
   relative pronouns as, R47
subject-verb agreement
   basic, R45
   with *be*, R45
   with collective nouns, R47
   with compound subjects, R46
   don't and *doesn't* as auxiliary verbs,
      R47
   with indefinite pronouns, R46
   inverted sentences, R47
   with personal pronouns, R46
   with predicate nominatives, R47
   with relative pronouns, R47
   with words between subject and
      verb, R45
subordinate clauses, 10, 122, R41, R42
subordinating conjunction, R23
suffixes, 95, R49–R50, R54
summaries, R9
summarizing, 99, R73. *See also*
   paraphrasing
   claims, 8, 322
   panel discussions, 361
   text, 335, 399, 418, 430, 438
superlative form, R35–R36
support
   for claims, 7, 129, 321, R16,
      R73
   inferences about themes, 17, 119,
      347
surprise ending, R73–R74
suspense, 93, 347, R7, R74
symbols, 17, 86, 120, 354, R74
synchronization, 129
synonym finders, R52
synonyms, 139, 171, 323, 439, R51
synthesize, R74

T

take/bring, R55
tall tale, R74
technical vocabulary, 129
teleplay, R74
tense, verb, R33
tension, as a literary technique 93, 347
testimonials, R17
text
  analyzing, 8, 18, 25, 30, 41, 69, 78, 86, 94, 97, 120, 130, 138, 150, 157, 170, 176, 206, 227, 252, 265, 280, 288, 298, 301, 314, 322, 336, 348, 354, 355, 399, 418, 430, 438, 444, 445
  comparing media and, 36, 47, 72, 81, 85
  evaluating, 18, 69, 72
  evidence from, 8, 18, 25, 30, 53, 69, 72, 78, 86, 94, 119, 120, 130, 144, 150, 152, 170, 176, 206, 227, 252, 265, 280, 288, 298, 314, 322, 336, 348, 354, 399, 418, 430, 438, 444
  inferences, 18, 30, 69, 78, 94, 120, 130, 170, 314, 348
  informational, 79, 123–129, 141–144, 325–334
  paraphrasing, 429
  procedural, R70
  quoting, 429
  reading arguments, R16–R21
  summarizing, 335, 399, 418, 430, 438
text criticism, R74
text features, R74
text structure, 17, 18, 69, 347, 348
than/then, R56
theater, Elizabethan, 180
their/there/they're, R56
theme, R74. *See also* central idea; main idea
  analyzing, 119
  connecting common, 288
  definition, 17, 119
  developing, 17
  epic, 365, 417
  identifying, 418
  interpreting, 206
  making inferences about, 17, 18, 30, 119, 138, 347, 444
  recurring, R74
  universal, R74
thesaurus, R52
thesis statement, 38, 41, R4, R16, R74
third-person limited, R70
third-person narrator, R6
third-person omniscient, R70
third-person point of view, R70
tone, R74

analyzing, 130, 144, 169, 313
of argument, 437, R3
biased, R3, R5
definition of, 77, 137, 149
determining, 353
formal, 137, 138, 316, R3
informal, 137, 138, 316, R3
for informative essay, R5
objective, R3, R5
poems, 149
punctuation and, 96
word choice and, 77, 130, 137, 169, 313, 316, 353
topic
  developing, R4–R5
  introducing, R4
  research, R8
topic sentence, R74
traditional ballads, R58
tragedy, R74–R75
  characteristics of Shakespearean, 177
  definition, 177
  reading, 179
tragic flaw, 177, R75
tragic heroes, 177, R74–R75
transfer technique, 437, R17
transitions, 302, 440, R3, R4, R5
transitive verbs, R23
travel narratives, 429
trochee, R67
Turabian, Kate L., R9
two/too/to, R56

U

understand cohesion, 42
understatement, R75
universal themes, R74

V

valid conclusion, R60
valid reasons, to support claims, R14
vanity, appeals to, R17, R62
verbal irony, 93, R66
verbal phrases, R39–R40
verbals, R39–R40
verb form, 145
verb phrases, R38–R39, 140
verbs, R23, R32
  action, R23, R32
  active voice, R34
  auxiliary, R23, R24, R47
  gerunds, R40
  helping, 140, R24
  intransitive, R23
  irregular, R33
  linking, R23, R32
  main, R24
  participles, 172, 420, R40
  passive voice, R34

principal parts, R32–R33
progressive forms, R33–R34
regular, R32–R33
subject-verb agreement, R45–R47
tenses, R33–R34
transitive, R23
video, 71, 72, 176, 433
video recordings, citing, R11
visualizing, R75
vocabulary
  Academic Vocabulary, 2, 37, 41, 46, 97, 102, 153, 157, 162, 301, 306, 355, 359, 364, 445
  commonly confused words, R55–R56
  Critical Vocabulary, 9, 19, 26, 31, 54, 70, 79, 87, 95, 121, 131, 139, 145, 171, 299, 315, 323, 337, 349, 400, 419, 431, 439
  specialized, R52
  strategies for understanding, R48–R53
  technical, 129
Vocabulary Strategy
  antonyms, 439
  context clues, 139, 299, 337, R48–R49
  denotations and connotations, 26, 87, 431
  domain-specific vocabulary, 360
  Greek words, 70, 131
  Latin words, 19, 70
  multiple-meaning words, 31, 315
  patterns of word changes, 9, 121, 145
  prefixes, 349, 400
  puns, 281
  reference sources, 79
  suffixes that form nouns, 95
  synonyms, 171, 323, 439
  words from Latin, 419
voice, R75

W

website, R75
well vs. *good*, R36
word changes, patterns of, 9, 95, 121, 145
word choice, 77, 130, 137, 149, 169, 313, 316, 353
word families, R50
word meanings
  determining, 129, 169, 171, 299, 337, 400, 419, 439
  figurative, 353
  and prefixes, 349
  and puns, 178, 281
word origins, R50–R51
word play, in Shakespearean drama, 178, 281
workplace documents, R75

works cited, R9, R10, R75
works consulted, R75
writing
  analytical essays, 41–44, 301–304,
     445–448
  arguments, 8, 97–100, 355–358,
     R2–R3
  complete sentences, R44–R45
  draft, 42, 98, 154, 302, 356, 446
  explanatory essays, 41–44,
     301–304, 445–448
  fictional narratives, 153–156
  informative essays, 41–44, 301–304,
     445–448, R4–R5
  narratives, 418, R6–R7
  speeches, 38
  for task, purpose, and audience, 42,
     99, 155, 303, 357, 447, R2–R7
  using technology, 41–44, 97–100,
     301–304, 355–358, 445–448
writing activity
  account, 72
  analysis, 53, 314, 430
  argument, 8
  editorial, 438
  essay, 288
  eulogy, 280
  journal entries, 138, 252, 298
  letters, 94, 120, 138, 265
  narrative, 418
  reflection, 354

Index of Titles & Authors

A

Ackerman, Diane, 163
AMERICA The Story of Us: March on
 Washington, 71
At Dusk, 147

B

Berkman, Pamela Rafael, 289
Blaeser, Kimberly M., 21

C

Cairo: My City, Our Revolution
 (excerpt), 73
Censors, The, 89
Count on Us, 151
Cruelest Journey: 600 Miles to
 Timbuktu, The (excerpt), 421

D

Deep Survival (excerpt), 325
de Waal, Frans, 123
Duty, 289

E

End and the Beginning, The, 351
Erdrich, Louise, 339
Euchner, Charles, 55

G

Gettysburg Address, The, 27
Gonzales, Laurence, 325
Gordimer, Nadine, 11
Grasshopper and the Bell Cricket,
 The, 133
Griffin, Michael, 433

H

Homer, 369

I

I Have a Dream, 47
Is Survival Selfish? 317

J

Journey, The, 441

K

Kawabata, Yasunari, 133
King, Martin Luther, Jr., 47

L

Lahiri, Jhumpa, 103
Leap, The, 339
Lincoln, Abraham, 27
Love's Vocabulary (excerpt from *A*
 Natural History of Love), 163

M

Monkey See, Monkey Do, Monkey
 Connect, 123
My Shakespeare, 173

N

Nafisi, Azar, 81
Night (excerpt), 307
Nobody Turn Me Around: A People's
 History of the 1963 March on
 Washington (excerpt), 55

O

Odyssey, the (excerpt), 369
Oliver, Mary, 441
Once Upon a Time, 11
Ovid, 283

P

Persepolis 2: The Story of a Return
 (excerpt), 84
Pyramus and Thisbe (excerpt from
 the *Metamorphoses*), 283

Q

Quilt of a Country, A, 3
Quindlen, Anna, 3

R

Reading Lolita in Tehran (excerpt), 81
Real Reasons We Explore Space, The,
 433
Ríos, Alberto, 34
Rituals of Memory (excerpt), 21
Rowe, Dorothy, 141

S

Salak, Kira, 421
Satrapi, Marjane, 82
Shakespeare, William, 181
Soueif, Ahdaf, 73
Szymborska, Wisława, 351

T

Tempest, Kate, 173
Tragedy of Romeo and Juliet, The, 181
Trethewey, Natasha, 147

V

Valenzuela, Luisa, 89
Vietnam Wall, The, 34
Views of the Wall, 33

W

Wallace, Lane, 317
Wiesel, Elie, 307
When Mr. Pirzada Came to Dine, 103
With Friends Like These. . ., 141

Acknowledgments

Excerpt from *The Age of Empathy* by Frans de Waal. Text copyright © 2009 by Frans de Waal. Reprinted by permission of Harmony Books, a division of Random House, Inc. Any third party use of this material, outside of this publication, is prohibited. Interested parties must apply directly to Random House, Inc. for permission.

Excerpt from *The American Heritage Dictionary of the English Language, Fifth Edition.* Text copyright © 2011 by Houghton Mifflin Harcourt. Adapted and reprinted by permission of Houghton Mifflin Harcourt Publishing Company.

"At Dusk" from *Native Guard* by Natasha Trethewey. Text copyright © 2006 by Natasha Trethewey. Reprinted by permission of Houghton Mifflin Harcourt Publishing Company.

Excerpt from *Cairo: My City, Our Revolution* by Ahdaf Soueif. Text copyright © 2012 by Ahdaf Soueif. Reprinted by permission of Bloomsbury Publishing and Wylie Agency Inc.

"The Censors" by Luisa Valenzuela, translated by David Unger from *Short Shorts: An Anthology of the Shortest Stories* edited by Irving Howe. Text copyright © by Luisa Valenzuela. English translation copyright © 1982 by David Unger. First published in *Short Shorts* edited by David Godine Howe. Reprinted by permission of David Unger and Luisa Valenzuela.

Excerpt from *The Cruelest Journey: 600 Miles to Timbuktu* by Kira Salak. Text copyright © 2005 by Kira Salak. Adapted and reprinted by permission of the National Geographic Society and Kira Salak.

Excerpt from *Deep Survival: Who Lives, Who Dies, and Why* by Laurence Gonzales. Text copyright © 2003 by Laurence Gonzales. Reprinted by permission of W. W. Norton & Company, Inc.

"Duty" from *Her Infinite Variety: Stories of Shakespeare and the Women He Loved* by Pamela Rafael Berkman. Text copyright © 2001 by Pamela Rafael Berkman. Adapted and reprinted by permission of Simon & Schuster, Inc. and Harvey Klinger, Inc. on behalf of Pamela Rafael. All rights reserved.

"The End and the Beginning" from *Miracle Fair: Selected Poems of Wisława Szymborska,* translated by Joanne Trzeciak. Text copyright © 2001 by Joanna Trzeciak. Reprinted by permission of W. W. Norton & Company, Inc.

"The Grasshopper and the Bell Cricket" from *Palm in the Hand and Other Stories* by Yasunari Kawabata, translated by Lane Dunlop and J. Martin Holman. Translation copyright © 1988 by Lane Dunlop and J. Martin Holman. Reprinted by permission of North Point Press, a division of Farrar, Straus and Giroux, LLC.

"I Have a Dream" speech by Martin Luther King, Jr. Text copyright © 1963 by Martin Luther King, Jr. Text copyright renewed © 1991 by Coretta Scott King. Reprinted by permission of Writers House LLC on behalf of the Heirs of the Estate of Martin Luther King, Jr.

Excerpts from "I Have a Dream" by Martin Luther King, Jr., from *Nobody Turn Me Around: A People's History of the 1963 March on Washington* by Charles Euchner. Text copyright © 1963 by Martin Luther King, Jr. Text copyright renewed © 1991 by Coretta Scott King. Reprinted by permission of Writers House LLC on behalf of the Heirs of the Estate of Martin Luther King, Jr.

Excerpt from "Introduction: Love's Vocabulary" from *A Natural History of Love* by Diane Ackerman. Text copyright © 1994 by Diane Ackerman. Reprinted by permission of Random House, Inc. and Diane Ackerman care of Janklow & Nesbit Associates. Any third party use of this material, outside of this publication, is prohibited. Interested parties must apply directly to Random House, Inc. for permission.

"Is Survival Selfish?" by Lane Wallace from *The Atlantic,* www.theatlantic.com, January 29, 2010. Text copyright © 2010 by Lane Wallace (LaneWallace.com). Reprinted by permission of Lane Wallace.

"The Journey" from *Dream Work* by Mary Oliver. Text copyright © 1986 by Mary Oliver. Reprinted by permission of Grove/Atlantic Inc. and Charlotte Sheedy Literary Agency.

"The Leap" by Louise Erdrich from *Harper's Magazine,* March 1990. Text copyright © 1990 by Harper's Magazine. Reprinted by permission of Harper's Magazine. All rights reserved.

"My Shakespeare" by Kate Tempest. Text copyright © 2012 by Kate Tempest. Reprinted by permission of William Morris Endeavor Entertainment, LLC on behalf of Kate Tempest.

Excerpt from *Night* by Elie Wiesel, translated by Marion Wiesel. Text copyright © 2006 by Elie Wiesel, translation copyright © 2006 by Marion Wiesel. Reprinted by permission of Hill and Wang, a division of Farrar, Straus and Giroux, LLC, Recorded Books and George Borchardt, Inc.

Excerpt from *Nobody Turn Me Around: A People's History of the 1963 March on Washington* by Charles Euchner. Text copyright © 2010 by Charles Euchner. Reprinted by permission of Beacon Press and Trident Media, LLC. on behalf of Charles Euchner.

Excerpts from *The Odyssey* by Homer, translated by Robert Fitzgerald. Text copyright © 1961. Text copyright renewed ©1989 by Benedict R.C. Fitzgerald on behalf of the Fitzgerald children. Reprinted by permission of Farrar, Straus and Giroux, LLC and Benedict Fitzgerald.

"Once Upon a Time" from *Jump and Other Stories* by Nadine Gordimer. Text copyright © 1991 by Felix Licensing B.V. Adapted and reprinted by permission of Penguin Group (Canada), a Division of Pearson Canada, Inc., Farrar, Straus and Giroux, LLC, A.P. Watt at United Agents on behalf of Felix Licensing, B.V., and Russell & Volkening as agents of the author.

Excerpt from *Persepolis 2* by Marjane Satrapi. Text and translation copyright © 2004 by Anjali Singh. Published